Antitrust and Global Capitalism, 1930–2004

The international spread of antitrust suggested the historical process shaping global capitalism. By the 1930s, Americans feared that big business exceeded the government's capacity to impose accountability, engendering the most aggressive antitrust campaign in history. Meanwhile, big business had emerged to varying degrees in liberal Britain, Australia, and France; Nazi Germany; and militarist Japan. These same nations nonetheless expressly rejected American-style antitrust as unsuited to their cultures and institutions. After World War II, however, governments in these nations – as well as the European Community – adopted workable antitrust regimes. By the millennium antitrust was instrumental to the clash between state sovereignty and globalization. What ideological and institutional factors explain the global change from opposing to supporting antitrust? Addressing this question, this book throws new light on the struggle over liberal capitalism during the Great Depression and World War II, the postwar Allied occupations of Japan and Germany, the reaction against American big business hegemony during the cold war, and the clash over globalization and the WTO.

Tony A. Freyer is University Research Professor of History & Law at the University of Alabama. He is the author of many articles and books, including *Regulating Big Business: Antitrust in Great Britain and America, 1880–1990* (Cambridge University Press, 1992).

Cambridge Historical Studies in American Law and Society

SERIES EDITOR

Christopher Tomlins, *American Bar Foundation*

PREVIOUSLY PUBLISHED IN THE SERIES:

Davison Douglas, *Jim Crow Moves North: The Battle over Northern School Segregation*

Andrew Wender Cohen, *The Racketeer's Progress: Chicago and the Struggle for the Modern American Economy, 1900–1940*

Michael Willrich, *City of Courts: Socializing Justice in Progressive Era Chicago*

Barbara Young Welke, *Recasting American Liberty: Gender, Race, Law, and the Railroad Revolution, 1865–1920*

Michael Vorenberg, *Final Freedom: The Civil War, The Abolition of Slavery, and the Thirteenth Amendment*

Robert J. Steinfeld, *Coercion, Contract, and Free Labor in the Nineteenth Century*

David M. Rabban, *Free Speech in Its Forgotten Years, 1870–1920*

Jenny Wahl, *The Bondsman's Burden: An Economic Analysis of the Common Law of Southern Slavery*

Michael Grossberg, *A Judgment for Solomon: The d'Hauteville Case and Legal Experience in Antebellum America*

Antitrust and Global Capitalism, 1930–2004

TONY A. FREYER

University of Alabama

CAMBRIDGE
UNIVERSITY PRESS

CAMBRIDGE UNIVERSITY PRESS

Cambridge, New York, Melbourne, Madrid, Cape Town, Singapore, São Paulo

Cambridge University Press

32 Avenue of the Americas, New York, NY 10013-2473, USA

www.cambridge.org

Information on this title: www.cambridge.org/9780521817882

First published 2006

Printed in the United States of America

A catalog record for this publication is available from the British Library.

Library of Congress Cataloging in Publication Data

Freyer, Tony Allan.
Antitrust and global capitalism, 1930–2004 / By Tony A. Freyer.
p. cm. – (Cambridge historical studies in American law and society)
ISBN 0-521-81788-9
1. Antitrust law – History. 2. Antitrust law – United States – History.
3. Antitrust law – Japan – History. 4. Antitrust law – Europe – History.
5. Antitrust law – Australia – History. 6. Capitalism – Moral and ethical aspects.
7. Free enterprise – Moral and ethical aspects. I. Title. II. Series.
K3850.F74 2007
343′.07210904–dc22
2006006972

ISBN-13 978-0-521-81788-2 hardback
ISBN-10 0-521-81788-9 hardback

To my father, Robert A. Freyer,
and the memory of my
father-in-law, Harold E. Faller

The thing that hath been, it is that which shall be; and that which is done is that which shall be done: and there is no new thing under the sun.

Ecclesiastes 1:9

One thing that is new is the prevalence of newness, the changing scale and scope of change itself, so that the world alters as we walk in it. . . .The techniques, among which and by which we live, multiply and ramify, so that the whole world is bound together by communication, blocked here and there by the immense synapses of political tyranny. What is new in the world is the massive character of the dissolution and corruption of authority, in belief, in ritual, and in temporal order. Yet this is the world we have come to live in. To assail the changes that have unmoored us from the past is futile, and in a deep sense I think wicked. We need to recognize the change, and learn what resources we have.

J. Robert Oppenheimer, from a speech at Columbia University, 1954

Contents

Acknowledgments   *page xi*

Introduction   1

1. Reconstituting American Antitrust, 1937–1945   8

2. Protectionism over Competition: Europe, Australia,
    and Japan, 1930–1945   60

3. American Antitrust since 1945   102

4. Japanese Antitrust since 1945   160

5. Antitrust in Postwar European Social Welfare Capitalism   245

6. Antitrust Resurgence and Social Welfare Capitalism in
    Postwar Australia   315

Conclusion   393

Index   407

Acknowledgments

I am grateful to the following for assistance and support: Mr. Charles S. Stark and Mr. Stuart M. Chemtob; Mr. Akinori Uesugi; Professor Hidekatsu Hirabayashi; Professor Shoji Ishii; Professor Mitsuo Matsushita; Ms. Toshi Morikawa; Mr. Tadaharu Wakabayashi; Professor T. Nogimura; Professor Scott P. O'Bryan; Professor John Braithwaite; Professor Allan Fels; Professor David Merrett; Professor Christine Parker; Professor David J. Gerber; Professor Leslie Hannah; Dr. Terry Gourvish; Professor Steven Tolliday; Dr. Anna Fornalczyk; Dr. Clifford A. Jones; Professor Eleanor M. Fox; Professor Frank K. Upham; Professor Chalmers Johnson; Professor Hans Baade; Mrs. Helene Kime Lewis; Mr. Stanley R. Lewis; Karen Ferguson; and Sidney H. Willner. Also, for many interviews I thank these and others cited in the notes.

Throughout the notes I cite the archives and libraries which provided the basic primary and secondary sources for this study. At these places the staffs were invaluable, but I should recognize in particular David Wigdor, David Warrington, and the International House of Japan Library. For essential continuing assistance at the University of Alabama School of Law Library I thank Penny Gibson, Creighton Miller, Paul M. Pruitt, David Durham, and Diana May. At the University's Gorgas Library I also thank Janice M. Simpson and Dr. Marilyn B. Emplaincourt of the Japan Program.

The University of Alabama School of Law Dean, Kenneth C. Randall, has supported this work over many years. I am grateful to Christopher Tomlins and Frank Smith at Cambridge University Press for patience, and for the critique of two external readers. I am most indebted to Forrest and Ellen McDonald, without whom the work would never have been published.

The research could not have been accomplished without external funding from: Abe Fellowship, 1994–96 Japan Center for Global Partnership and Social Science Research Council; Senior Fulbright Award Australia (Summer 1993); Fulbright Distinguished Chair in American Studies, Warsaw University, Poland (2000); and Earhart Foundation Research Fellowship 2002–03. I am grateful for continuing support, too, from: The University of Alabama School of Law Foundation and the Edward Brett

Randolph Fund, the History Department and College of Arts and Sciences, Sabbatical 2002–03, and the Office of Academic Affairs, University Research Professor which I hold. Of course, I am alone responsible for what follows.

Tony A. Freyer
Tuscaloosa
August 2005

Antitrust and Global Capitalism, 1930–2004

Introduction

The international spread of antitrust since World War II suggested the historical process shaping global capitalism. During the closing decades of the nineteenth century, the growing separation between owners and operators resulted in managers becoming the primary decision makers. This transformation of capitalism constituted what historian Alfred Chandler called the managerial revolution in American business. Managerial capitalism nonetheless spawned popular anxiety that big business had exceeded the government's capacity to impose accountability, engendering the creation of a regulatory regime known as antitrust. By the 1930s managerial capitalism had appeared in varying degrees in the industrial nations of Europe and in some European settler societies such as Australia, and Japan. Generally, however, these nations expressly rejected American-style antitrust as unsuited to their cultures. The perception of antitrust as a distinctly American response to big business changed after World War II. Governments increasingly adopted workable antitrust regimes; by the turn of the millennium, antitrust was instrumental to the clash between state sovereignty and globalization associated with the World Trade Organization (WTO).

The internationalization of antitrust occurred within a contested cross-cultural public discourse that recognized Americanization as an active element primarily in relation to indigenous factors already constituting capitalist systems. Given this interaction, what foreign and indigenous elements explain the global change from opposing antitrust to supporting it? The Allied occupations of Germany and Japan following World War II suggest the difficulties in answering this question. By 1970 the prevailing view was that American pressure resulted in establishing an effective antitrust regime in Germany but not Japan. Reconsidering the U.S. policy toward instituting antitrust in Germany, this book presents evidence of contemporary public opinion prior to 1950 showing that Americans and Germans alike concluded that the U.S. effort had *failed*. In Japan, by contrast, similar evidence reveals that in response to the occupation's order requiring the installation of an antitrust regime, the Japanese quickly learned enough about U.S. antitrust policy and history to seize and maintain the

initiative over the Americans during the drafting of the Antimonopoly Law
of 1947 and its subsequent enforcement until the occupation ended in 1952.

The internationalization of antitrust raises further challenging questions.
The prevailing view holds that Franklin Roosevelt's Antimonopoly message
of 1938 and antitrust critic-turned-activist Thurman Arnold's efforts to
enforce it by 1943 had at best a modest impact on the powerful postwar
expansion of American big business. If so, how do we account for the
contemporary official and business opinion that stated during and after
World War II that the implementation of Arnold's policies by his successors
made exceptional involvement of American big business in international
cartels that had been commonplace before 1941, while these same officials
also compelled technology transfers aiding postwar America's foreign
competitors, including Japanese and German enterprise? In light
of repeated assertions by foreign officials, businessmen, and experts that
Japanese antitrust was of marginal significance, why did Japanese
bureaucrats, big businesses, and political officials repeatedly attempt but
fail to do away with it during the postwar economic growth "miracle";
once the miracle ended in the 1990s, why did those same groups switch to
supporting the most vigorous antitrust enforcement since the occupation?
Despite the heritage of condemning U.S. style antitrust, why did postwar
European authorities install their own version of antitrust in order to
pursue economic integration capable of enforcing equal opportunity
throughout the common market? And why, after abandoning an antitrust
law before World War I, did Australia not only enact new legislation during
the 1960s and 1970s, but by the 1990s also implement one of the world's
most active and innovative antitrust regimes?

Offering answers to these and related questions, this book suggests a new
perspective on antitrust. It locates the particular doctrines and rules constituting antitrust within changing historical and comparative contexts
since the 1930s; it then considers how within these distinct institutional and
cultural contexts formal legalities have shaped business' two principal
organizational approaches to risk, the large-scale corporation defined as
managerial capitalism and popularly known as big business, and looser
anticompetitive arrangements identified with cartel practices. During the
Great Depression in the United States, antitrust had acquired a metapho-
rical meaning that Thurman Arnold identified with the folklore of American
capitalism. This reimagining of antitrust's relation to capitalism expressed
ambivalent public values: Americans embraced the consumer benefits that
big corporations made possible, but feared that large concentrations of
economic power threatened individual opportunity and democratic government. Antitrust thus embodied an American ideal that big business
should be held accountable to power outside itself. Prior to World War II,
other nations rejected this ideal. Indeed, in authoritarian states and
liberal democracies alike government officials and business people, as well

as political party leaders and legal–economic professionals, assumed that anticompetitive collaboration through cartels among business, government, and producers was necessary to preserve social order at home and competitive advantage abroad.

During the 1990s, Australians Philip and Roger Bell suggested another perspective: "one might think of 'Americanization' as a linguistic infiltration. It does not so much replace or displace the local lexicon as supplement it."[1] Applied to antitrust internationalization, these metaphors described a process whereby societies *selectively* acquired a language of market competition. At the more familiar instrumental level of enforcement, of course, antitrust engages private business practices to achieve particular social and market outcomes in a capitalist economy. Thus, symbolically and instrumentally, antitrust creates a particular consciousness about what constitutes legitimate individual or corporate conduct as well as the appropriate scope and substance of policy enforcement. Adopting antitrust as a governmental regime involves, then, not only making basic policy choices but also the acquisition of a mental stance and a mode of communicating. To other societies American antitrust represents a praxis: a model or practical example for emulation embodying theories of accountability and competition that societies must follow if antitrust is to be translated into customary market conduct.[2] The praxis idea also suggests the degree to which antitrust reflects a distinctive institutional culture committed to enforcing certain policies toward competitive and noncompetitive behavior. Though substantive rules and procedures governing restrictive practices and monopolies vary among jurisdictions, antitrust regimes possess a common institutional culture defined by relative bureaucratic autonomy, due process standards, and judicial review.

Such institutional and symbolic autonomy did not happen randomly. Instituting an antitrust regime required officials to choose to enforce its legitimacy within the changing indigenous business, governmental, and social order. Whether the regime was effective enough to actually shape conduct depended, moreover, upon the extent to which the consciousness sustaining it became imbedded. According to the praxis imagery, therefore, antitrust gained enforcement authority in America and spread abroad when it possessed sufficient bureaucratic and symbolic autonomy through procedures, rules, and policies that the dominant capitalist enterprise was more or less held accountable to external public and private interests. Clearly, the principle of accountability lacks formal force when compared with established antitrust doctrines such as the per se prohibition against cartels or the

---

[1] Philip Bell and Roger Bell, "Introduction," in Philip Bell and Roger Bell, eds., *Americanization and Australia* (Sydney, 1998), 6.
[2] Antonio Gramsci, ed., *Further Selections from the Prison Notebooks*, trans. Derek Boothman (Minneapolis, 1997), 395, 430, 579.

rule of reason distinguishing "efficient" mergers from those creating unlawful monopolies. Understood as a consciousness and institutional culture embracing competition over collaboration, however, accountability acquires a sharper policy content underlying all formal antitrust rules and process. Approached in this way, the numerous doctrines and procedures comprising antitrust as an autonomous field of law constitute a general policy of accountability fostering the public consciousness that some degree of market competition enforceable by law was preferable to having the law sanction collusive market behavior.

Conceiving of antitrust as praxis that promotes and enforces competition consciousness must take into account the basic changes in managerial capitalism. Shortly after World War II, in 1947 Joseph A. Schumpeter identified the difference between firms that adapted to and those that innovated in response to market and technological imperatives. The adaptive firm simply attempted to minimize costs within a market environment it took as given. The innovative firm pursued strategies within a process of change. Shortly after World War I, in the early 1920s and then increasingly during the Great Depression, certain American managers in innovative firms discovered that more efficient administrative coordination could be achieved by separating the strategic decision-making process from the operational process, instituting a multidivisional structure. Chief executives in separate divisions fashioned strategies to develop new products or markets and monitored profitability. By the Depression, historians found, a few firms had adopted a similar multidivisional structure in such diverse capitalist systems as liberal Britain and Australia or fascist Germany and Japan. That such versatile managerial innovation arose among different governments and cultures possessing conflicting ideologies confirmed Chandler's general theoretical insight: Most economic theory assumed that divisional specialization within the corporation was a "natural response to improved technology and markets." He concluded, however, that "increasing specialization must, almost by definition, call for more carefully planned coordination."[3]

This book argues that to varying degrees antitrust shaped managerial capitalism's global expansion, especially as it refined the multidivisional structure. Although managers implemented a unified investment and operational strategy, each corporate unit was bound by the local laws and regulations of the sovereign state or states where it did business. Both authoritarian and liberal-democratic governments imposed conflicting laws and regulations upon multinational corporations, circumscribing the manager's control. During the Great Depression and World War II, U.S. antitrust authorities exposed the extensive involvement of U.S.

---

[3] Alfred D. Chandler, Jr., *The Visible Hand: The Managerial Revolution in American Business* (Cambridge, MA, 1997), quote at 489–90.

multinational corporations in cartels and other anticompetitive agreements benefiting big business and governments in Germany, Britain, Japan, Australia, and elsewhere. After the war multinational corporations maneuvered within the new liberal international order to manipulate or avoid government restrictions. Ultimately, however, the proliferation of antitrust regimes proved difficult to escape. At the same time, the manager's ability to preserve centralized control had profound social and political consequences. The separation between owners and managers heightened labor's, small business', and consumers' market vulnerability, exacerbating class conflict. Big business became the object of political struggles defining socialism, fascism, and John M. Keynes's "middle-way" between unfettered laissez faire and authoritarianism. During the final decades of the twentieth century, similar struggles exacerbated the economic and cultural clashes identified with globalization.

From World War II on, trade policies and antitrust increasingly presented distinct approaches to competition. Trade policies embraced wide-ranging government controls through tariffs, currency exchange rates, taxes, investment, antidumping regulations, commodity agreements, and patent monopolies. Antitrust dealt with private business conduct. Before the war the U.S., Japanese, German, British, and Australian governments countenanced or even promoted international cartels in order to protect themselves from foreign competition and to project their power against other nations. During the war the United States and its Allies replaced the protectionist system with the liberal international financial order maintained through the International Monetary Fund and the World Bank. Controversy nonetheless arose over whether the International Trade Organization (ITO) should include antitrust provisions targeting international cartels, patents, and other anticompetitive behavior. The General Agreement on Tariffs and Trade (GATT) went into effect without antitrust provisions in 1947–48. Although the United States had proposed the antitrust provisions, it proved unwilling to create international antitrust regulation over private business' anticompetitive practices exercising authority that was comparable to that applied by the government through control of employment, technological innovation, agricultural or industrial commodity prices, and the balance of payments within the international trade system. This book offers new evidence explaining the ITO's defeat and its implications for the coexistence of antitrust and trade policies under the WTO.

Trade policies and antitrust also applied changing economic theories over time in divergent approaches to competition. Trade officials applied economic theory to protect industries and jobs from international competition; they achieved these goals primarily through domestic politics and international diplomacy. Antitrust authorities, by contrast, applied much the same economic theory on behalf of consumer welfare, exemptions for organized labor and farm groups, and, under certain circumstances, the defense of small business. Compared with trade authorities, stricter procedural autonomy and judicial review nonetheless constrained antitrust officials. Placed within changing political and cultural contexts and public discourse, this book attempts to show how and why contemporary officials, big and small businesses, industrial and agricultural groups, and legal–economic experts constructed on their own terms, through three distinct phases from the 1930s to the turn of the century, the meaning and outcomes of antitrust's and trade policies' use of economic theories. In the following chapters, accordingly, an effort is made to allow the participants themselves to define legal and economic terms and to explain what they believed were the issues at stake in doing so. In this sense this book is a policy history.

The first internationalizing phase was the Great Depression and World War II. This period witnessed the reconstitution of American antitrust and its rejection abroad, especially through international cartels, amidst the intractable struggle between liberal and protectionist trade systems. In the initial postwar period from 1945 through the early 1970s, American antitrust experienced its most active enforcement ever within a liberal consensus. As a result, international cartels became exceptional whereas American managers developed strategies leading to diversification and conglomerate mergers on a global scale. Over this period, too, European and Japanese firms gradually became more competitive against U.S. multinational corporations. The European Community's Commission employed antitrust to integrate a common market based on equal economic opportunity and a new respect for competition whereas Australia's antitrust revival paved the way for instituting an effective antitrust regime in the 1970s. Meanwhile, Japanese antitrust survived by preserving some market competition and protecting small business, thereby exercising surprising influence on the economic miracle engineered by the powerful finance and trade ministries. Even so, up to the 1970s, antitrust authorities everywhere sought to balance social welfare objectives and market efficiency through theories of "workable competition."

The third phase was the second postwar period continuing from the 1970s until after the millennium. The oil shocks of 1973 and 1979 facilitated new U.S. investment strategies defining "efficiency" solely in terms of consumerism and increased shareholder values. A chaotic business cycle of recession and boom recurred. American managerial capitalism was transformed; its effectiveness tied to the short-term performance of the stock market whereas advocates of the Chicago School of Economics remade antitrust. Over the same period, multinational corporations in Western Europe, Japan, and Australia increasingly competed effectively with their U.S. counterparts for global advantage. The United States experienced weakened antitrust enforcement in the 1980s; in the following decade,

European, Australian, and Japanese antitrust enforcement became more active. The end of the cold war and the emergence of antiglobalization ideology facilitated the internationalization of antitrust. The United States reinvigorated antitrust enforcement, targeting international cartels rather than monopoly. Although the European Commission's decisions were stronger than that of its American counterparts, international cooperation increased as never before, prompting persistent, if unfulfilled, demands for an antitrust authority at the level of the WTO. Antitrust praxis thus achieved new force in the growing effort to impose accountability on global capitalism.

1

Reconstituting American Antitrust, 1937–1945

On April 29, 1938, Franklin Roosevelt put aside pressing foreign policy concerns to present an antimonopoly message. Roosevelt declared that activist antitrust enforcement was essential in order to defend American liberal democracy and free enterprise from becoming a "fascist-collective" system on the European "model." The dramatic foreign imagery and conspiratorial overtones contrasted sharply with the monopoly problem that Roosevelt defined in technical terms such as patents and cartels.[1] A remedy of vigorous enforcement and investigation seemed tame when compared with the Progressive trust-busting ideology that Louis Brandeis had popularized to combat the "curse of bigness." Contemporary and later observers sharing the Brandeisian perspective concluded that the message resulted primarily in the disappointing investigation of the Temporary National Economic Committee (TNEC) and Thurman Arnold's flamboyant but narrowly bureaucratic antitrust campaign.[2] Given the context of economic foreign policy and New Deal liberalism's evolving business–government relations, however, Roosevelt's antimonopoly message reconstituted antitrust policy, imposing accountability on the expansion of American managerial capitalism in peace and war.[3]

---

[1] "Recommendations to Congress to Curb Monopolies and the Concentration of Economic Power, April 29, 1938," *The Public Papers and Addresses of Franklin D. Roosevelt, 1938, Volume 7, The Continuing Struggle for Liberalism* (New York, 1941), 305–32; for the foreign policy context, see Robert Dallek, *Franklin D. Roosevelt and American Foreign Policy, 1932–1945* (New York, 1979), 160.

[2] Thomas K. McCraw, *Prophets of Regulation Charles Francis Adams, Louis D. Brandeis, James M. Landis, and Alfred E. Kahn* (Cambridge, MA, 1984), 80–142; Alan Brinkley, *The End of Reform, New Deal Liberalism in Recession and War* (New York, 1996), 86–200; Ellis W. Hawley, *The New Deal and the Problem of Monopoly* (Princeton, NJ, 1974), 270–455.

[3] Dallek, *Roosevelt and Foreign Policy*, 101–70; David M. Kennedy, *Freedom from Fear the American People in Depression and War, 1929–1945* (New York, 1999), 323–464; Robert A. Divine, *The Illusion of Neutrality* (Chicago, 1962), 162–228; Tony A. Freyer, "Antitrust and Bilateralism: The US, Japanese, and EU Comparative and Historical Relationships," in Clifford A. Jones and Mitsuo Matsushita, eds., *Competition Policy in the Global Trading System* (The Hague, 2002), 3–52; Thomas K. McCraw, "Government, Big Business, and the Wealth of Nations," in Alfred D. Chandler, Jr., Franco Amatori, and Takashi Hikino, eds., *Big Business and the Wealth of Nations* (Cambridge, UK, 1999), 522–45.

Placing the New Dealers' bureaucratic struggles within the context of national security and liberal trade politics, this chapter argues that Arnold built better that either he or the historians imagined.[4] Section I examines Robert Jackson's proposals for an antitrust study committee which located patent, cartel, and corporate finance issues within the context of domestic and international economic policies before the recession of 1937 diminished New Dealers' reform hopes. Section II traces how Roosevelt's approval of Jackson's study committee affected the Antimonopoly Message of 1938. Section III follows Thurman Arnold's implementation as he shifted from enforcement policies aimed at promoting social welfare to a policy focusing on preserving accountability in the defense build up prior to 1941. Section IV explores the scope and impact of Arnold's compliance strategy during the period preceding Pearl Harbor. Section V examines how this expanded strategy influenced war and peacemaking from 1941 to 1945. The chapter suggests that the continuity linking Jackson's antitrust study committee, Roosevelt's Antimonopoly Message, and Arnold's initial enforcement record reflected the New Dealers' wider struggle to keep reform alive. The defense build up and the war compelled Arnold to institute an antitrust regime capable of holding American managerial capitalism accountable to American democracy. His success shaped the future image of antitrust.

I. ROBERT JACKSON AND THE ANTIMONOPOLY STUDY COMMITTEE

Robert Jackson did much to shape Roosevelt's decision to deliver an antimonopoly message. He became one of Roosevelt's inner circle during 1937. In January he left the post of general counsel for the Internal Revenue Service to become the Justice Department's assistant attorney general of the Antitrust Division.[5] The move coincided with the administration's search for ways – including an active antimonopoly campaign – to revive the New

---

[4] The evidence concerning Arnold is presented below. Compare this evidence with the secondary works discussed within the notes and text below: John Morton Blum, *V Was for Victory Politics and Culture during World War II* (San Diego, CA, 1976); Brinkley, *End of Reform*, 106–25 Susan Ariel Aaronson, *Trade and the American Dream, a Social History of Postwar Trade Policy* (Lexington, KY 1996); Patrick J. Hearden, *Architects of Globalism Building a New World Order during World War II* (Fayetteville, AR, 2002); Wyatt Wells, *Antitrust and the Formation of the Postwar World* (New York, 2002). But see the pioneering study by Graham D. Taylor, "Debate in the United States over the Control of International Cartels, 1942–1950," III *The International History Review* (July 1981), 385–98. See also Tony A. Freyer, *Regulating Big Business Antitrust in Great Britain and America 1880–1990* (Cambridge, UK, 1992).

[5] File, "Justice Jackson's Story," manuscript of tape recording taken by Dr. Harlan B. Phillips, Oral History Research Office, Columbia University, 1952–53, RHJ Papers, Box 190, Library of Congress (LC), 256–638.

Deal reform programs the Supreme Court had struck down. Yet, by the summer and fall opposition to Roosevelt's court-packing plan and a pronounced recession stalled the reform drive. Even so, the National Recovery Administration's (NRA's) suspension of antitrust laws in favor of federally enforced cooperation within manufacturing and labor sectors, like the anticompetitive practices the AAA instituted, had for the first time imposed upon peacetime America the sort of cartelized order prevailing in Europe and Japan. Thus, although the court had overturned the early New Deal's cartel policies, the government's sanction of those policies exposed anticompetitive market conduct pervading corporate relations.[6] In early 1937, moreover, the *Alcoa* case publicized international cartel practices, revealing larger security and trade issues.[7] Some liberals nonetheless persistently advocated a neo-NRA policy. Jackson quietly addressed these conflicting demands, proposing an antimonopoly study committee to explore corporate accountability within New Deal liberalism.[8]

As the government's leading antitrust official, Jackson confronted liberals who favored the NRA approach. The NRA's rise and fall represented the influence of those who believed that the Depression presented an opportunity to transform American capitalism into a scientifically planned cooperative economy. Prominent business leaders had promoted this approach, particularly Gerard Swope of General Electric and Henry I. Harriman of the Chamber of Commerce.[9] By 1937–38, liberals such as Donald Richberg, the NRA's former general counsel, urged reconstructing the New Deal on the basis of cooperative planning. Some of the president's closest advisors accepted this view, including Harold Ickes, who generally favored a vigorous antitrust campaign except in the petroleum industry over which he presided. Jackson later recalled that Roosevelt himself was "not too clear" on the difference between the NRA approach and antitrust laws; the president generally conceived of economic issues "in terms of rights and wrongs." He believed that if he talked with businessmen and "made them see that their course was morally wrong, they would do something about it." Enforcing the antitrust laws was for Roosevelt, accordingly, "punishing a conspiracy, thinking of a conspiracy as a dark

[6] Merle Fainsod and Lincoln Gordon, *Government and the American Economy* (New York, 1941), 557–620; Hawley, *New Deal*, 286–87, 374–8, 389–94; Kennedy, *Freedom from Fear*, 352–3; Brinkley, *End of Reform*, 55–61, 88, 92–3, 101, 110–11, 267.

[7] *U.S. v. Aluminum Co. of America*, 44 F.Supp. 97 (Dis. Ct. S.D.N.Y., 1941); "Memorandum For Attorney General, Re: U.S. v. Aluminum Co. of America et al., March 16, 1937," RHJ Legal File, *Alcoa*, Box 77, LC.

[8] File, "Justice Jackson's Story," Columbia University Oral History, 1952–53, RHJ, Box 190, LC; Jackson to Leon Henderson, July 20, 1937, RHJ Legal File, Box 77, LC.

[9] Freyer, *Regulating Big Business*, 218–20; Mira Wilkins, *The Maturing Multinational Enterprise: American Business Abroad from 1914 to 1970* (Cambridge, MA, 1974), 49–244; Wyatt Wells, *Antitrust*, 4–37.

cellar operation in which evil men got together in masks and plotted something."[10]

Jackson's opposition to neo-NRA policies framed his own questions regarding the formation of effective antitrust policy. He hoped to have antitrust proposals included in the president's 1938 annual message. In July 1937, before the recession descended upon the nation, Jackson wrote to New Deal economic expert Leon Henderson setting out possible policy questions for Roosevelt's consideration. Jackson located his assessment of the antitrust policies within a context of rising prices behind which consumers' and workers' purchasing power and wages lagged, "retarding full recovery and provoking strikes." The wage/price imbalance fostered a "political demand for anti-monopoly activity." The "cumbersome and dilatory" slowness accompanying the antitrust enforcer's reliance upon judicial proceedings – as well as institutional constraints due to "inadequate staffing" – were "little understood limitations [that] may cause the criticism that the administration is indifferent to monopoly." Pointing out that statutory policies were "conflicting," Jackson noted that the "basic philosophy" of antitrust had "not been thoroughly examined for forty years." Jackson urged Roosevelt to "anticipate the demand for anti-monopoly action by naming a committee to study the problem and report to him."[11]

The research questions Jackson suggested touched domestic and international dimensions of antitrust enforcement. An underlying issue was the "relation between rigid price industries and unemployment." Getting at that large issue required broad study. Thus he queried whether the courts had "faithfully executed" the antitrust laws, particularly considering the "economic difference between the government's legal victory over Standard Oil and its defeat by United States Steel." In its decision of 1911, the Supreme Court had broken up the Standard Oil Company. In the *US Steel* decision of 1920, however, the court decided that, despite being one of the largest corporations in the world, the company evidenced no intentionally pernicious behavior toward competitors, against whom, indeed, it competed "fairly." Jackson's focus upon "economic" results suggested that the toleration of bigness had fostered mergers and acquisitions among firms, raising issues regarding "our monopoly problem." The interdependency of these issues had a bearing on the movement of American companies abroad through patent licensing agreements and the creation of foreign subsidiaries organized through bank holding companies.[12]

[10] File, "Justice Jackson's Story," Columbia University Oral History, 1952–53, RHJ, Box 190, LC, quotes at 431–2, 432–3; Brinkley, *End of Reform*, 42–6, 90, 91, 267; Hawley, *New Deal*, 149, 153, 164, 271, 395–6, 401–2,

[11] Jackson to Leon Henderson, July 20, 1937, RHJ Legal File, Box 77, LC.

[12] *Ibid.*; *U.S. v. U.S. Steel Co.*, 251 US 417 (1920); *Standard Oil Co. v. United States*, 221 US 1 (1911); Freyer, *Regulating Big Business*, 76–195; Hans B. Thorelli, *The Federal Antitrust Policy, Organization of an American Tradition* (Baltimore, MD, 1955).

Jackson also expressed concern about industries in which price competition had ceased, particularly involving cartels. A chief goal of the NRA had been the stabilization of prices through the federal government's enforcing price-fixing agreements. The demise of the NRA left a contradictory record. The exemption from antitrust laws for organized labor and direct federal supervision of unions and businesses were enduring outcomes of the NRA. The NRA revealed the extent to which anticompetitive practices pervaded the nation's domestic economy and the increasingly significant operations of corporations doing business abroad. Henderson and others argued that such market restraints hurt consumers and workers, breeding social discontent. This assessment led Jackson, in turn, to question whether Americans had "in fact a submerged and secret and hence unregulated Cartel system" and, if so, what "would be the effect of recognizing and regulating the right to establish cartels as is done abroad?"[13]

The focus on cartels reflected the divergence of American and foreign law. Except during the NRA's brief reign and the war, American antitrust laws generally declared cartel practices to be per se illegal without having to show moral intent. Other nations employed cartels throughout their economies. Indeed, America's chief international trade rivals, including the British Empire, Germany, and Japan, sanctioned wide-ranging cartel combinations. In addition, American managers from DuPont, General Electric, and the leading science-based electrical equipment and chemical industries, petroleum firms, the automobile industry, and nonferrous metal producers like Alcoa, maintained membership in international cartels.[14]

Jackson's focus upon patents and bank holding companies suggested the need for imposing legal accountability upon changing corporate organization. Since the 1920s managers had been pioneering a decentralized corporate organization designed to accommodate the product diversification necessary for supplying growing consumer demand. The structure gave increased autonomy to corporate divisions to administer operations within expanding domestic and international markets. Financial holding companies and patents were vital components of this organizational restructuring.[15]

Jackson's perception that research into these diverse fields of law could be "made to help the anti-monopoly policy" arose from the transformation occurring in corporate capitalism.[16] In 1932 Columbia University's A. A. Berle and Gardiner C. Means published *The Modern Corporation and Private Property* in which they described the United States as experiencing a "silent revolution" whereby the "translation of perhaps two-thirds of the industrial wealth of the country from individual ownership to ownership by

---

[13] Quotes cited in note 11 above; on NRA, see note 6 above.   [14] See note 9 above.

[15] See notes 6 and 9 above.

[16] Jackson to Henderson, July 20, 1937, RHJ Legal File, Box 77, LC.

large, publically financed corporations vitally changes the lives of property owners, the lives of workers, and the methods of property tenure." The magnitude of such a "divorce of ownership from control" raised significant questions: "Is this organization permanent? Will it intensify or will it break up?" The authors described Brandeis as "struggl[ing] to turn the clock backward" and Frankfurter as "inclined to believe even now that it cannot last." They believed nonetheless that the "process will go a great deal further than it has now." By 1937, Berle favored cooperative business–government relations along the lines of a modified NRA.[17]

The conflicted policy outcomes Berle's and Means' findings suggested reflected an economic theory of imperfect competition. Economists increasingly agreed that oligopoly or monopoly had displaced classical competition defined as rivalry between small units. Thus, Britain's Joan Robinson and America's E. H. Chamberlin rejected the classical assumption that monopoly and competition were exclusive, showing that both factors influenced pricing practices. Economists nonetheless had mixed views regarding the implications of imperfect competition. Concerned primarily with such macroeconomic issues as government intervention to alleviate unemployment, Britain's John Maynard Keynes and his followers did not object to cartel practices. In America supporters of a neo-NRA employed Keynesian principles to argue that extensive government planning rather than mere antitrust prosecution was required to end the unemployment and prevent corporate "autocracy."[18]

The program Jackson described to Henderson incorporated theories of imperfect competition in conjunction with institutional economics. For institutionalists the legal rules governing the marketplace determined market outcomes: an autonomous market apart from what legal rules constituted did not exist. Classical economists contended that market relations functioned according to preexisting universal laws. Neoclassical economists, in turn, accepted theories of imperfect competition while rejecting the institutionalist's denial of universal laws. Institutionalists, by contrast, incorporated theories of imperfect competition into their discourse as consistent with the view that diverse and often irrational motivations drove market conduct. Thurman Arnold – who according to Max Lerner epitomized institutional economic ideas – described "Mordecai Ezekiel of the Department of Agriculture, Ben Cohen of the Department of

[17] Adolf A. Berle, Jr. and Gardiner Means, *The Modern Corporation and Private Property*, (New York, 1932) vii–viii; Freyer, *Regulating Big Business*, 204–5.
[18] Freyer, *Regulating Big Business*, 204–5; Robert Skidelsky, *John Maynard Keynes: The Economist as Savior, 1920–1937*, vol. 2 (New York, 1992), 229–30, 236, 483–536, 608–9; Brinkley, *End of Reform*, 128–35, 232–3; William Lee Baldwin, *Antitrust and the Changing Corporation* (Durham, NC, 1961), 77–117; Rudolph J. R. Peritz, *Competition Policy in America, 1888–1992 History, Rhetoric, Law* (New York, 1996), 145, 148–54, 157, 170–1, 184–5, 236, 241–2, 258–9.

Interior, William O. Douglas of the Securities and Exchange Commission, and Assistant Attorney General RHJ" as "friends of mine with economic philosophies which I think are *inevitable*." Noting that they generally lacked "economic training," Arnold nonetheless declared, "I believe that the economists in colleges are too far out of touch with governmental affairs to have the grasp on the problems which these men have."[19]

Two institutional imperatives further shaped the ideas that Jackson presented to Henderson. Jackson realized how limited the Antitrust Division's resources were. Prior to his appointment in January, he had talked with Attorney General Homer Cummings and Roosevelt about his commitment to pursue active antitrust enforcement. Both men affirmed Jackson's goal in principle, though all three understood that their support did not reflect a clear understanding of precisely what that might entail. Once in office Jackson reorganized the Antitrust Division focusing especially upon bringing together the resources of the economic advisor with those of the complaints section. Jackson's predecessor had hired three economists to handle the growing demand for economic data. In addition, virtually all antitrust matters came to the division as a result of complaints from business people. In order to strengthen the Division's policy and enforcement effectiveness, Jackson established closer cooperation between the two sections.[20]

In April, however, Roosevelt announced that "reduced expenditures" were necessary throughout the executive branch. Shortly thereafter Jackson wrote Cummings a memorandum detailing the "increasing strains" facing the division. Rising prices engendered a demand for more investigation of "claims of unlawful activities" and new statutory provisions threatened a "deluge" of cases. "I am beginning to appreciate the pitiful inadequacy of our appropriation," he wrote. "Anything like a satisfactory or reasonably complete effort to enforce the law is impossible." But pursuing "only partial enforcement" requiring the "selection of cases ... always involves the claim of discrimination. We are under such pressure that the very best job we can do is likely to prove inadequate," and "we will certainly be

---

[19] Lerner, "Shadow World of Thurman Arnold," *Yale Law Journal* 47 (March 1938), 698–700; Thurman Arnold to Porter Sargent (August 6, 1937), in Gene M. Gressley, ed., *Voltair and the Cowboy, The Letters of Thurman Arnold* (Boulder, CO, 1977), quote at 263–4.

[20] File "Justice Jackson's Story," Columbia University Oral History, 1952–53, RHJ, Box 190, Folder 3, 350–3, 426–30; "Office Order General No. 7 (a) 1937, Organization (February, 19, 1937)," Folder, RHJ Legal File, Reorganization and Operation of the Division, Box 79, LC; "Report of Assistant Attorney General John Dickinson, Antitrust Division, *Annual Report of the Attorney General of the United States, Fiscal Year, 1936* (Washington, DC, 1936), 22–3; "Report of Assistant Attorney General Robert Jackson, Antitrust Division," *Annual Report of the Attorney General of the United States, Fiscal Year, 1937* (Washington, DC, 1937), 36–63.

humiliated." Jackson was impelled, accordingly, to let go a number of attorneys and to consider closing the New York office.[21]

The second institutional imperative arose from Jackson's decision to initiate antitrust action against Alcoa. During the Wilson administration, the government and Alcoa had agreed to a consent decree employing the rule of reason. By the Depression, Alcoa's adjustments to international price instability had resulted in the company's gaining a monopoly in the domestic market. Studies of the international cartel movement, in conjunction with NRA and other data, reveal the extent of Alcoa's monopoly. In 1936, Jackson's predecessor considered making an inquiry into the company's conduct.[22] When Jackson took over the Antitrust Division, he moved ahead with the *Alcoa* case despite significant challenges. Collecting thousands of pages of documents located in the United States and foreign nations placed an enormous investigative burden on the division. The standard of proof the rule of reason imposed was difficult enough to meet. Alcoa's international cartel membership maintained under patents, licensing, and other anticompetitive agreements created still more difficult evidence problems. Unlike American doctrine declaring cartel practices per se illegal, antitrust law's jurisdiction over international cartel arrangements was unclear. The earliest case held that U.S. antitrust possessed virtually no extraterritorial authority. During the late 1920s and early 1930s, the Antitrust Division had won cases somewhat eroding this rule; nevertheless, Jackson's decision to test the rule further against Alcoa was a policy gamble.[23]

Several factors nonetheless confirmed Jackson's judgment. Alcoa's primary owners and stockholders included the powerful A. W. and R. B. Mellon brothers of Pittsburgh and the Trustees of the Duke Endowment.

[21] Franklin D. Roosevelt, "To the Heads of Executive Departments, Independent Establishments and Other Government Agencies," April 7, 1937; Jackson, "Memorandum for the Attorney General," April 24, 1937, RHJ Legal File, Reorganization and Operation of the Division, Box 79, LC.

[22] Freyer, *Regulating Big Business*, 141; George David Smith, *From Monopoly to Competition the Transformation of Alcoa, 1888–1986* (Cambridge, UK, 1988); John Wattawa, "Memorandum for the Attorney General, Re: The Aluminum Company of America," December 30, 1936, Folder, RHJ File, Ass. Att. Gen. A.D., Roosevelt's Monopoly Message, Box 77, LC; William Tandell Elliott et al., *International Control in the Non-Ferrous Metals* (New York, 1937), 257–73, 497.

[23] Elliott et al., *International Control*, 257–73, 497; *American Banana Co. v. United Fruit Co.*, 213 US 347 (1909); Paul Matsuo Matsushita, "Application of US Antitrust Laws to Foreign Commerce," Unpublished Ph.D. Dissertation, Tulane University, 1963, 1–85; see cases and decrees, 1920–32, Wilbur Lindsay Fugate, *Foreign Commerce and the Antitrust Laws*, 2nd edn (Boston, 1973), 502–5; "Report of Assistant Attorney General Antitrust Division, Antitrust Division," *Annual Report of the Attorney General of the United States for Fiscal Year 1928* (Washington, DC, 1928), 26–7; John Lord O'Brian, "Report of the Assistant Attorney General, Antitrust Division," *Annual Report of the Attorney General of the United States Fiscal Year 1931* (Washington, DC, 1931), 28–9.

Public association of such big business leaders with nefarious corporate financial manipulations and the Depression facilitated political support for a vigorous antimonopoly campaign. Indeed, Attorney General Cummings received a letter encouraging the case because the "Vicious Mellon Circle" dominated the entire Pittsburgh community. "They are so grasping, greedy, and underhanded that everybody ... is afraid of them." As "Shy-locks ... every act on their part should be unveiled. They form 'corporations' ... in each field for deeper control purposes." Their domination, the letter claimed, reached even the Orphans' Court. Alcoa's lawyers reinforced the image by getting a restraining order from a federal judge in Pittsburgh – who was allegedly sympathetic to the Mellon interests – on the ground that the old Alcoa consent decree established jurisdiction in Pittsburgh, not in New York, where the Justice Department had filed the present suit. The dispute received national attention. Bills challenging the judge's order were introduced in Congress and the matter received Roosevelt's personal attention. Finally, Jackson won an order from the Supreme Court sustaining the case in New York.[24]

The *Alcoa* case also aroused vague yet potent images touching national security. By 1937 Hitler's expansion, the Spanish Civil War, and Japan's aggression against China had heightened public support for an isolationist foreign policy. Public discussion included the material necessary for national defense, including aluminum. According to Justice Department records, Alcoa's international cartel agreements demonstrated that aluminum's use "expanded until at the present time this metal is indispensable in the economic and industrial life of the Nation and in its military and naval defense." Accordingly, during the summer of 1937, the State Department undertook for the Justice Department "confidential investigations in England, Canada, France, Germany, Austria, Switzerland, Italy, Norway, Sweden and Russia to obtain evidence of restraints upon production, liquidation of surplus stocks, allocation of markets and price fixing" involving Alcoa's international cartel operations and their bearing on the firm's monopoly within the domestic U.S. market.[25]

[24] Quotes from Pittsburgh Citizens and Property Owners to Homer S. Cummings, May 7, 1937 (see other letters, same file, criticizing Alcoa); "US Aluminum is Blocked by Federal Judge," May 15, 1937 (Associated Press); Joseph B. Keenan to Cummings, May 17, 1937 ("The President is anxious to see what can be done to meet the situation brought by Judge Gibson's action in issuing a temporary injunction."); Cummings to Roosevelt, June 1, 1937; Wright Patman to Cummings, July 26, 1937; Walter L. Rice to Jackson, August 10, 1937; House Resolution 287, US House of Representatives "Authorizing The Committee of the Judiciary to investigate various practices in the inferior courts of the United States and for other purposes," 75th Congress, 1st Session, August 5, 1937; Jackson to Joseph B. Keenan, December 17, 1937, RHJ Legal File, Ass. Att. Gen. A.D., *Alcoa*, Box 77, LC.
[25] Cummings to Cordell Hull, secretary of state, August 17, 1937; Walter L. Rice, "Foreign Investigation of Aluminum Cartel," August 17, 1937; John Wattawa, "Memorandum for the Attorney General," quote at 48, cited above.

Jackson's letter to Henderson in July 1937 thus engaged at several levels Roosevelt's decision concerning an antitrust initiative. As the recently appointed head of the Antitrust Division – then a minor agency – Jackson was working to give antitrust enforcement a higher priority during Roosevelt's second term. The scope of Jackson's proposed policy inquiry had wide-ranging instrumental and symbolic implications. Ultimately, the proposals suggested contrary images of New Deal liberalism and its meaning within a dangerous world. The neo-NRA proponents favored a corporatist liberal capitalist state having cartelized business–government relations similar to the European model. New Dealers like Jackson envisioned a liberal regime in which the government used antitrust to hold big business accountable. The focus on accountability touched the nation's isolationist foreign policy debate, the global expansion of American corporations, and the American attempt to institute a liberal trade order in a world dominated by autarkic protectionism, international cartels, colonialism, and ideological militarism. These were the stakes in Jackson's effort.

II. THE NEW ANTIMONOPOLY MESSAGE, APRIL 1938

Jackson's antitrust proposals were increasingly contentious. By 1937 an economic recession engulfed the nation. As a result, organizing an antimonopoly study committee became part of a wider political conflict. Jackson wrote to Thurman Arnold that "the 'big business' crowd and the conservative Democrats and Republicans formed a loose sort of coalition to destroy the work of this administration." Those advocating neo-NRA policies gained heart that Roosevelt might again turn to them to reconstitute a less controversial program. A series of speeches that Jackson and Ickes delivered blaming big business, the wealthy, and their political acolytes for a "capital strike" against expanding New Deal reforms inflamed the political scene even more. Their rhetoric implied that a conspiracy with fascist overtones was at work. Roosevelt aggravated the situation by appointing Jackson to the higher position of solicitor general and naming the controversial Arnold his successor to lead the Antitrust Division. In foreign affairs, the recession and Roosevelt's embattled political position intensified the neutrality debate. Uncertainty also masked Secretary of State Hull's liberal trade polices. Accordingly, by April 1938 Roosevelt's decisions about the antimonopoly message had acquired profound meaning for liberalism at home and abroad.[26]

In October 1937, Roosevelt had approved Jackson's idea of forming an antimonopoly study committee. Anticipating his annual message before Congress in early 1938, Roosevelt authorized Jackson to "assemble

---

[26] Jackson to Arnold, December 31, 1937, RHJ Legal File, Ass. Att. Gen. A. D., Antitrust Division Matters, Miscellaneous, Box 77 , LC; notes 5 and 6 above.

material" concerning antimonopoly "abuses" and "possible remedies" that
could be employed to "select a program" and be used in "messages, bills,
and speeches." As the committee did its work, the president sent Jackson
various letters he received from those hoping to establish an economic
policy modeled after a revived NRA. Thus, one letter Jackson read was
from Donald Richberg urging Roosevelt that "in anything" said about the
antitrust issue "you will leave the door open to consideration of legislation,
which will not only strengthen the anti-trust laws, but will also provide
protection and encouragement to the cooperative efforts of enlightened
business men to increase production and employment, to improve working
conditions and to furnish better service to consumers." Generally, Roosevelt asked Jackson to comment on these NRA-like ideas as "we come to
prepare the anti-monopoly part of my message."[27]

Henderson's input on the committee undoubtedly sharpened Jackson's
negative perception of cartels. Henderson had been director of the NRA's
Research and Planning Division, where he gathered materials concerning
the protection of consumers from the abusive conduct of cartels. Upon
coming to power in 1933, the Nazis revised the system of cartel regulation
initiated under the Weimar republic. Henderson received reports analyzing
the "new" German cartel policy. He also read a *Barron's* article entitled
"German Cartels and the NRA, Their Economic Effects Reveal Pitfalls to
Be Avoided." In addition, Henderson's staff prepared memoranda comparing the NRA with cartel regulations in Germany, Norway, Hungry, and
Poland. These materials presented a mixed image of cartel regulation in the
"public interest." Broadly, Henderson's materials revealed the challenges
involved in holding cartels accountable to public interest standards. Indirectly, the Japanese evidence suggested a similar conclusion. European
chemical exporters belonging to an international cartel complained that the
Japanese government's sanction of national cartel practices disrupted
international "cooperation." A *Business Week* article appearing in 1934
indicated that Japan's cartel law was "like the NRA in spirit."[28]

---

[27] Franklin D. Roosevelt to Jackson, October 22, 1937; [Handwritten] "Memo. on visit to
Pres.," [October] 21, 1937, RHJ Legal Files, Ass. Att. Gen. A.D., Antitrust Division
Matters, Miscellaneous, Box 77, LC; Donald R. Richberg to Roosevelt, October 28, 1937;
Roosevelt to Jackson, October 30, 1937; Charles H. Weston to Jackson, "Re. FTC
Proposals for Revising Section 7 of the Clayton Act," September 30, 1937, RHJ Legal File,
Ass. Att. Gen. A. D., Antitrust Division Matters, Miscellaneous, Box 77, LC.

[28] Gustav Seidler, "Protection of Consumers against abuse of Economic Powers by Cartels and
Similar Industrial Agreements," NRA, Research and Planning Division, Leon Henderson,
director; Anon., "Comparison of Codes under the National Industrial Recovery Act and
Germany Cartels"; Henry P. Leverich, vice counsel [US] Berlin, "Cartels under the National
Socialist Government in Germany," August 18, 1934; Louis Domeratzky, "New German
Cartel Policy," November 1, 1933; Mabel S. Lewis, "German Cartels and the NRA,"
Barron's, January 22, 1934, p. 18; "Japan Will Regulate Industry," *Business Week*, August

Throughout the winter Jackson and the antimonopoly message gained a higher profile. A news story had designated Jackson the "New Deal's Legal Ace."[29] He and Harold Ickes delivered speeches vigorously attacking big business leaders with explosive images like those deployed earlier against the Mellons and Alcoa. The speeches received national attention. Jackson was either praised as a champion of New Deal reform or condemned as a socialist or worse. Jackson wrote to Arnold that the December speeches "changed the whole atmosphere in Washington. Instead of asking what they can do to the New Deal, 'big business' is now asking what the New Deal is going to do to them." He criticized General Motors' executives who defended the company's fall profits of "$419,790,657.00 at the time they turned 30,000 men into the streets." According to Jackson, that "traces the cause of the recession directly to the lack of purchasing power of the lowest income classes."[30]

In January, the president's annual address indicated that an anti-monopoly message was in the works. Roosevelt was vague about the substance the message might take, suggesting that he had not yet decided between the NRA-like cooperative approach such as Richberg's or Jackson's broad antitrust attack. Still, New Dealer Connecticut Congressman William M. Citron assured Jackson that the president's noncommital tone was "perfect, and hit the nail on the head, following the masterly speeches" of Ickes and Jackson "whose remarks were timely and also definitely put the opposition and the Republicans on the defensive."[31]

Roosevelt's nomination of Jackson as solicitor general was controversial. The October meeting concerning the formation of the antitrust study committee had included the subject of Jackson's resigning no later than January 1938, in order to move from the Antitrust Division to a higher position. Thus, in February 1938, the Senate took up Roosevelt's nomination of Jackson as solicitor general. The nomination coincided with the Supreme Court's consideration of the revised Agricultural Adjustment Act and the Public Utilities Holding Company Act of 1935. Despite the defeat of the court packing plan, the reconstitution of the court was underway as a result of Roosevelt's appointment of Hugo Black and Stanley Reed. The *Alcoa* case also received attention. Utah Senator William H. King opposed Jackson raising images of Stalin, Hitler, and militarist Japan, intimating that democratic mass support for the New Deal could be manipulated for

18, 1934, Leon Henderson Papers, Cartels, Box 2, Franklin D. Roosevelt Presidential Library (FDRPL).

[29] "'Country Lawyer' New Deal's Legal Ace," *Record*, Folder Fishing Trip with President Roosevelt [Philadelphia, PA], November 27–December 6, 1937, RHJ Legal Files, Ass. Att. Gen. A. D., Box 78, LC.

[30] Jackson to Arnold, December 31, 1937, cited above

[31] William M. Citron to James Roosevelt [cc Robert Jackson], January 7, 1938, RHJ Legal Files, Ass. Att. Gen. A. D. Antitrust Division Matters, Miscellaneous Box 77, LC.

evil purposes and implying that Jackson's speeches were typical of such manipulation. Senator William E. Borah of Idaho and other supporters of antitrust activism responded favorably to the nomination, and Jackson was confirmed.[32]

Roosevelt's March nomination of Thurman Arnold to head the Antitrust Division further politicized the antimonopoly issue. As a Yale Law professor, Arnold had attained a national reputation with the publication of *The Symbols of Government* (1935) and *The Folklore of Capitalism* (1937), which employed behavioral psychological ideas to criticize America's leading governmental institutions. He was particularly known for mounting a withering attack upon the antitrust laws. During the confirmation hearings, Borah sharply questioned making such a powerful critic the nation's chief antitrust enforcer. Displaying smooth rhetorical skills, Arnold convinced even Borah that his assault upon the antitrust laws had been intended to expose underlying weaknesses which if properly addressed could lead to more effective policy. Arnold was thus confirmed as Jackson's successor.[33]

The substance of Roosevelt's antimonopoly message remained unsettled. In a press conference on March 1, 1938 Roosevelt was asked, "Do you think the antimonopoly drive will achieve a breakdown into small operating companies?" The president replied, "Oh, my lord, I don't know. That is too big a question." When asked, at another point, when the message might be presented, Roosevelt said, "I don't know when. Do not assume it will be up this week or next."[34] As Jackson prepared to leave the Antitrust Division, he continued to consider materials for inclusion in what was increasingly expected to be a major presidential address.[35]

Jackson knew that any effective antitrust initiative demanded addressing the patent and financial holding company issues. He embraced Evan A. Evans's recommendations that "patents should be issued" only to U.S. subjects and that the government "should grant to an alien," especially

---

[32] [Handwritten] "Memo. on visit to Pres.," [October] 21, 1937; Nomination of Jackson Solicitor General, Part 1, January 31, February 10 and 11, 1938, Hearings before Subcommittee of the committee of the Judiciary US Senate, 75th Congress, 3rd Session (Washington, DC, 1938), 1–39, Wendall Berge Papers, Folder Judge Greiger Hearings, Box 44, LC.

[33] Nomination of Arnold to be Assistant Attorney General, Hearings before Subcommittee of the Committee on the Judiciary US Senate, March 11, 1938, 75th Congress, 3rd Session (Washington, DC, 1938) 1–11, Wendall Berge Papers, Folder Judge Greiger Hearings, Box 44, LC.

[34] *Complete Presidential Press Conferences of Franklin D. Roosevelt* (New York, 1972), vol. 11, no. 438, (March 1, 1938), 196, 198.

[35] Evan A. Evans to Jackson, February 21, 1938; Jackson to Evans, March 2, 1938; Herman Oliphant to Jackson, March 26, 1938; "Draft of Antitrust and Bank Holding Company Message," RHJ Legal File, Ass. Att. Gen. A.D., Antitrust Division Matters, Miscellaneous, Box 77, LC.

British or German subjects, "only such patent protection ... and upon exactly the same conditions as are given to an American inventor in the foreign country." Documents from Herman Oliphant contained wide-ranging recognition of the need for strengthened antitrust laws and enforcement to combat the evils resulting from employing bank holding companies as shelters for the anticompetitive manipulation of patents, tax laws, and tariffs. Such "over-elaboration of corporate organization" reduced "opportunities by destroying small business" and revealed the "great economic power that might be wielded" by a "group which may succeed in acquiring domination over banking resources in any considerable area of the country."[36]

In April a flurry of publicity suggested that Roosevelt's antitrust message finally might be forthcoming. Richberg wrote Roosevelt that he did not believe press reports stating that Roosevelt and Borah had expressed "substantial agreement on the monopoly issue" or that their "opinions on all its phases coincide largely." Richberg exclaimed that the NRA's "philosophy" and the New Deal were "wholly consistent." The "philosophy of the fanatic trust busters, their hostility to all large enterprise, their assumption that cooperation is always a cloak for monopolistic conspiracy – this philosophy is wholly inconsistent with the New Deal." The "present need is not one of more vigorous enforcement" of the antitrust laws, as Jackson and Arnold were urging, but merely "sound, clear statement of law" so to "make clear the areas of lawful conduct wherein business men can promote more and better business." Finally, Richberg asked – echoing the totalitarian images critics employed to equate fascist and communist regimes with Roosevelt's liberalism – "Is the policy of business regulation to be consistent with the New Deal philosophy by which we rely upon democratic cooperation to solve problems which could not be solved by laissez-faire and for which, in other lands, solutions are being sought by dictatorial, undemocratic methods?"[37]

Significant international and domestic events coincided with the drafting of the address. By the end of March, Benjamin Cohen and Thomas Corcoran had worked up drafts in Charleston; Cohen then met Jackson in Atlanta and boarded the president's train returning to Washington from Warm Springs, Georgia, where Roosevelt had discussed the need for increased federal expenditures to counter the recession. On the train Roosevelt confirmed that he would deliver the antimonopoly message soon. On April 14, the president asked Congress to appropriate several billion dollars "to stimulate recovery." The announcement was followed that evening with a Fireside Chat, Roosevelt's first in 6 months. He suggested

---

[36] *Ibid.*
[37] Richberg to Roosevelt, April 23, 1938, RHJ File, Ass. Att. Gen. A.D., Antitrust Division Matters, Miscellaneous, Box 77, LC.

that the spending program was necessary in order to strengthen the nation's defense. Hitler had taken over Austria.[38] Nazi domination led to the expulsion of 190,000 Jews which in turn created for Roosevelt a refugee crisis, aggravating the neutrality debate. An April *Fortune* poll showed that a majority of Americans supported ending America's military presence in China.[39] These developments shaped the rhetorical images Roosevelt's Fireside Chat conveyed; the title later assigned to it was "Dictatorships Do Not Grow Out of Strong and Successful Governments, but Out of Weak and Helpless Ones."[40]

On the evening of April 28, 1938, Jackson, Cohen, and Corcoran met with Roosevelt at the White House. Referring to the draft they had discussed weeks before on the Washington-bound train and to the memoranda received from Attorney General Cummings, Arnold, and Oliphant, Roosevelt dictated a rough copy of the antimonopoly message. Significantly, Jackson recalled, Richberg's proposals were absent, as was the neo-NRA "proposition to open" the antitrust policies "so as to allow industries to agree on production schedules." Further discussion ensued; then near midnight Roosevelt asked to have a final copy ready to sign the next morning for transmission to Congress by noon. The president retired. The three men worked through the night, and the message was ready.[41]

The message employed conflicted international imagery to assert that antitrust activism promoted and defended American welfare. "Unhappy events abroad" taught Americans "two simple truths about the liberty of a democratic people." The "liberty of a democracy is not safe if the people tolerate the growth of private power to a point where it becomes stronger than their democratic state itself. That, in its essence, is Fascism." Similarly, "a democracy is not safe if its business system does not provide employment and produce goods in such a way as to sustain an acceptable standard of living." Since the Great Depression in 1929, he continued, the American people had gradually perceived that the "danger" arose from "concentrated private economic power." A "cluster of private collectivisms ... masking itself as a system of free enterprise after the American model ... [was] becoming a concealed cartel system after the European model."[42]

Roosevelt presented an image of individual opportunity and consumer welfare imperiled by monopolistic power. Cartels and monopoly were not necessarily a problem because they spawned corporate bigness: indeed, he said, "we have some lines of business, large and small, which are genuinely competitive." He noted, too, that "modern efficient mass production"

[38] Brinkley, *End of Reform*, 100–1; compare File "Justice Jackson's Story," 533–9, Folder 4, Box 190, LC.
[39] Dallek, *Roosevelt and American Foreign Policy*, 167; Kennedy, *Freedom from Fear*, 402.
[40] As quoted in Brinkley, *End of Reform*, 101.   [41] Ibid., and note 38 above.
[42] "Recommendations to Congress," 305–6, 308.

could "require one or more huge mass production plants." But the efficiencies of volume production were "not furthered by a central control which destroys competition among industrial plants each capable of efficient mass production while operating as separate units. Industrial efficiency does not have to mean," he emphasized, "industrial empire building." The danger arose when "[c]lose financial control, through interlocking spheres of influence over channels of investment, and through the use of financial devices like holding companies and strategic minority interests, creates close control of the business policies of enterprises which masquerade as independent units." Honest investors were harmed by this "banker control of industry." According to Roosevelt, "[i]nvestment judgment requires the disinterested appraisal of other people's management. It becomes blurred and distorted if it is combined with the conflicting duty of controlling the management it is supposed to judge." Moreover, the "small business man is unfortunately being driven into a less and less independent position." Generally, then, the "individual must be encouraged to exercise his own judgment and to venture his small savings, not in stock gambling but new enterprise investment. Men will dare to compete against men but not against giants."[43]

Roosevelt linked public anxieties about domestic economic concentration to a nefarious "cartel" threat. During a recession, the "practices of monopolistic industries make it difficult for business or agriculture which is competitive ... to find a market for its goods even at reduced prices" because many customers "are being thrown out of work by those noncompetitive industries which choose to hold their prices rather than to move their goods and to employ their workers." And while the return to market competition was necessary, the president cautioned, it could "be carried to excess." Unfair trade, consumer, and labor practices should be administered "intelligently," including the federal government's providing business competitors, consumers, farmers, and workers alike with adequate information and programs to address problems of overproduction or giving "special treatment to chronically sick industries which have deteriorated too far for natural revival." Thus "power should not be vested in any private group or cartel." Instead, it "must be diffused among the many or be transferred to the public and its democratically responsible government."[44]

Although Roosevelt described in expansive terms the evils facing America, the remedy offered was moderate. In order to furnish "jobs or income or opportunity for over one-third of the population" directly hurt by the Depression, it was essential, he said, "to preserve the system of private enterprise for profit." Yet as a "democratic people" possessing strong "traditions of personal liberty," Americans would not "be content to

---

[43] *Ibid.*, 308–9.   [44] *Ibid.*, 307, 311, 313.

go without work or ... to accept some standard of living which obviously and woefully falls short of their capacity to produce." And a people with such a heritage would never "endure the slow erosion of opportunity for the common man, the oppressive sense of helplessness under the domination of a few, which are overshadowing our whole economic life." The centerpiece of Roosevelt's proposals was, accordingly, the allocation to the Justice Department's Antitrust Division and the Federal Trade Commission the largest ever federal budget appropriations so that they could develop and implement a new antitrust enforcement program.[45] To strengthen this expanded antitrust regime, Roosevelt asked Congress to fund "a thorough study of the concentration of economic power in American industry and the effect of that concentration upon the decline of competition."[46]

Jackson's vision of antitrust activism significantly shaped Roosevelt's message. Reflecting institutional economics and behavioral theories, his prognosis of the legal doctrines underpinning big business power resonated with the distinction Roosevelt drew between American and European capitalist "models." Countries as culturally different as Japan and Britain sanctioned cartels for nationalistic purposes. That liberal Britain and Nazi Germany countenanced similar cartel practices suggested, moreover, how grave the conflict between American "free enterprise" and the European "cartel system" was. Roosevelt's imagery linked the domestic monopoly problem to foreign business–government cartelization; those same images conveyed a "collectivist fascist" evil threatening American liberalism. In order to impose accountability upon this dual monopoly danger, the nation required an effective antitrust regime. Thus, the national and foreign "monopoly problem" possessed a protean meaning for Americans' perception of the liberal state. Defining this meaning was now the duty of Thurman Arnold.

III. THURMAN ARNOLD AND THE NEW ANTITRUST ACTIVISM

Roosevelt's selection of Arnold to implement the antitrust program had unexpected results from 1938 to 1941. Initially, Arnold reconstituted antitrust process employing images promoting the welfare, security, and consumer opportunity of ordinary Americans beset by the recession. In numerous public statements and during the early proceedings of TNEC, he explained that an approach to enforcement using consent degrees as well as a litigation strategy focusing on patents and cartel practices would achieve these goals.[47] Once Germany invaded Poland in September 1939, however,

---

[45] *Ibid.*, 312–13.   [46] *Ibid.*, 315.

[47] Brinkley, *End of Reform*, 106–36; Hawley, *New Deal*, 420–55. Hawley contrasts Arnold's enforcement policy with the Brandeisian approach; his analysis of cases within the national

Arnold gradually reshaped antitrust policy, incorporating the consumer and social welfare goals into the escalating American defense effort within the tenuous limits of neutrality and liberal free trade. Unlike the demise of antitrust occurring during the World War I, Arnold deftly reconciled the institutional and symbolic images reflecting the domestic welfare and defense policy demands to win increased budget appropriations for the Antitrust Division. With these resources he enlarged enforcement capabilities. The Supreme Court rejected his attempt to impose greater accountability upon organized labor, but the most vigorous prosecution ever mounted against international cartels succeeded. Supported by Jackson, who became attorney general in 1940, antitrust gained a central if contested place in the defense effort.[48]

Arnold's eclectic pragmatism facilitated the adaptability of his antitrust enforcement strategy. Born in 1891 in Laramie, Wyoming, Arnold spent his early career there practicing law; he also served as the town's mayor and was elected as the only Democrat in the state legislature. He was educated among the nation's elite at Princeton University and Harvard Law School. In 1927, he returned east to take up the deanship of West Virginia Law School, which had offered the appointment on the recommendation of Harvard Law School dean, Roscoe Pound. While Arnold's Western origins engendered a general irreverence toward prevailing dogmas, he proved to be an able administrator. His combination of talents and temperament led him to active involvement in the legal realist movement; in 1930, Arnold was appointed professor at Yale Law School, a center of the legal realists. His two well-known books exposing the cultural symbolism and institutional economics sustaining American government and capitalism revealed the legal-realist and behavioral psychological assumptions Arnold employed to reshape antitrust enforcement policy.[49]

In 1938 Max Lerner, *The Nation*'s editor, analyzed these assumptions. Possessing a "contempt for the virtues of logical consistency" combined with a "fierce pragmatism," Lerner observed, Arnold rejected the ideological coherence of both capitalism and totalitarianism, "a concern possible

market is invaluable, but has little about international cartel prosecutions. Wells (*Antitrust*, 37–72) examines selected cartel prosecutions, though consideration of the institutional impact is limited.

[48] The discussion below draws upon two primary documents: Edythe W. First, *Industry and Labor Advisory Committees in the National Defense Advisory Commission and the Office of Production Management, May 1940 to January 1942* (Civilian Production Administration Bureau of Demobilization, Historical Reports on War Administration: War Production Board Special Study No. 24, December 9, 1946); Bureau of Demobilization Civilian Production Administration, *Industrial Mobilization for War History of the War Production Board and Predecessor Agencies, 1940–1945, Program Administration Volume I* (Washington, DC, 1947). I am indebted to Lincoln Gordon for the latter citation.

[49] Gene M. Gressley, ed., *Voltaire and the Cowboy, the Letters of Thurman Arnold* (Boulder, CO, 1977), 7–54.

only in an age in which the rationale of industry has yielded place to the manipulations of corporate finance, the propaganda machines of nations in mortal combat, the power-diplomacy of fascist adventurers." A seminar Arnold taught at Yale with pioneering behavioral psychologist Edward S. Robinson further confirmed the certain belief in the "complete and utter irrationalism of man as a political animal," a conviction strengthened by the "experience with war propaganda and the study of the techniques that the fascist and communist movements have used in manipulating the effective symbols for mass persuasion."[50]

Arnold's depiction of capitalism drew from the "revolt against" classical and neoclassical economists that Thorstein Veblen, Walton Hamilton, Berle and Means, and others mounted in order to "break ... down economics itself as a category so that it becomes merely the most significant point at which law, custom, technology, psychology, and property traditions meet and cross." This institutional economics rejected Marxist theories. Thus, Arnold's critique of antitrust policy held that the "prevailing economic opinion favoring the small productive unit and the competitive market" clashed with the "economic reality" that the "large-scale industrial technique, demand large-scale methods of distribution." Exploiting Americans' faith in the symbolic force of the old antitrust regime, financial managers established the "monopoly form." Countering this manipulation, Arnold epitomized a "middle-class radicalism" that was either "gloriously opportunistic" or represented merely the New Deal's "amorphous experimentalism."[51]

Arnold applied activist social consciousness to reconstitute the nation's antitrust regime. Prior to 1937, the Antitrust Division's annual congressional budget appropriation averaged about $200,000; after the Supreme Court's overturning of the NRA's cartelization plan made renewed antitrust enforcement inevitable, the Roosevelt administration authorized $440,000 for 1937–38. Under Arnold's leadership, however, Congress appropriated $780,000 for fiscal year 1938–39. World War II threatened the continuation of these budget increases. But Arnold displayed promotional skill: in the budget years of 1939–40 and 1940–41, the Antitrust Division received an annual appropriation of $1,325,000. America's slide from neutrality to war during 1941 tested Arnold; the Senate cut an additional $750,000 funding increase the House had approved. Nevertheless, after appealing directly to Roosevelt, Arnold reported that the division was receiving an $875,000 increase for fiscal year 1941–42. Arnold justified the increased resources by emphasizing that under the old antitrust regime, the funding was simply too limited to permit meaningful enforcement. He gave the

---

[50] Lerner, "The Shadow World of Thurman Arnold," 47 *Yale Law Journal* 47 (March 1938), 692, 694–5.
[51] *Ibid.*, 698–9, 701.

example that a single successful criminal prosecution of Midwestern oil companies cost about $175,000. After the fall of 1939, he strengthened his argument by urging that antitrust activism was essential to overcoming the dark image of German-dominated cartels endangering America.[52]

In numerous public statements, Arnold promoted the achievements of effective enforcement. The growing annual budget appropriations enabled the Antitrust Division to enlarge its staff from a few dozen lawyers and a handful of economists to about 250 personnel. The increased staff implemented an enforcement policy emphasizing market "results" over moralistic intent. Even so, in 1937–38, the division had instituted only eleven cases and fifty-nine "major" investigations. During 1939–40, however, these numbers jumped to 92 cases and 215 investigations and a record of winning 31 of 33 cases. By 1941, Arnold reported winning 58 of 64 cases, while having begun 88 new cases and 180 new investigations. Perhaps the most conspicuous measure of fiscal success was that during Arnold's tenure the division was "self-sustaining, collecting [in 1941] a total in fines of $2,239,056.06 as against an appropriation of $1,325,000."[53] Building on organizational changes begun under Jackson, Arnold further restructured the Antitrust Division. In 1937 the linkages between patents and the sorts of antimonopoly issues the *Alcoa* litigation presented resulted in Jackson's authorizing more extensive collection of data involving international cartels. Arnold expanded this initiative establishing a section whose members possessed the expertise to disentangle thousands of patent and other anticompetitive agreements by U.S. corporations and their foreign subsidiaries and affiliates.[54]

In order to strengthen results-focused case analysis, Arnold recruited individuals possessing economic training. One non-lawyer was Cornell University–trained Corwin Edwards. Initially his work involved market

---

[52] Fainsod and Gordon, *Government and the American Economy*, 609–14; Arnold to Jackson, May 17, 1941, Arnold to Roosevelt, May 17, 1941, in Gressley, *Voltaire and the Cowboy*, 319–22; "Report of Assistant Attorney General Thurman Arnold in Charge of the Antitrust Division," *Annual Report of the Attorney General of the United States for Fiscal Year Ended June 1941* (Washington, DC, 1942), 58–67 [confirms $875,000 increase at 63]; "Report, Ass. A.G., A. D., Thurman Arnold," *Annual Report* (1939), 36–45; "Report, Ass. A.G., A.D. Thurman Arnold, *Annual Report* (1938), 54–69; "Report, Ass. A.G. A. D., RHJ," *Annual Report* (1937), 35–63 (see RHJ to Arnold, January 31, 1938, RHJ Legal File, Ass. Att. Gen. A. D., Miscellaneous, Box 77, LC, confirm Arnold wrote the 1937 *Annual Report*); "Report, Ass. Att. Gen. A. D., John Dickinson," *Annual Report* (1936), 21–51.

[53] Brinkley, *End of Reform*, 111; "Report, Ass. Att. Gen. A.D., Arnold," *Annual Report* (1941), 63.

[54] "Report, Ass. Att. Gen. A. D., Arnold," *Annual Report* for 1941, 61–3; Werner J. Kronstein to Tony A. Freyer, May 17, 2002 (phone interview); Alfred Kahn to Tony A. Freyer, June 6, 2001 (phone interview); "Antitrust Enforcement in the War Emergency General Work of the Division during the War Years," (1939–41), 3–6, Wendell Berge Papers, Folder Statements, October 15, 1943 to January 21, 1947, Box 43, LC.

restraints in the food distribution sectors; as the Antitrust Division developed an intensive investigation into patents, however, Edwards turned to disentangling the intricate monopoly practices in order to promote competition. Edwards, in turn, drew upon the work of academic economists such as Harvard's Edward S. Mason.[55] In a *Yale Law Journal* article of 1937, Mason observed that at least until World War I, courts and economists held that monopoly was the "antithesis of free competition, unregulated monopoly was always necessarily a public evil, and its remedy was, in the Wilsonian phrase, 'a fair field with no favor.'" By the Great Depression, however, a conceptual gulf widened between the thinking of lawyers and economists. Generally, lawyers and judges were slow to incorporate theories of imperfect competition into their analyses. At the same time, economists had failed to adapt economic theories to the evidence procedures and standards of proof driving the court's definition of the "public interest." Mason began reshaping economic theory to develop legal "tests" of the sort lawyers and judges used in litigation, especially to establish whether the "existence of price discrimination, of price rigidity, advertising expenditures, price leadership and other practices are sufficient to indicate the presence of monopoly elements."[56]

Heinrich Kronstein added international law and economics expertise to the division's result-oriented enforcement policy. A Jewish convert to Catholicism, who before fleeing the Nazi regime in 1935 was already an established authority on German cartel law and policies, Kronstein received a law degree from Columbia University in order to establish American credentials. During the summer of 1938, Kronstein first worked at the Antitrust Division; after graduating from law school in 1939, he became a leading member of the patent and cartel section. The ominous foreign cartel threat cited in Roosevelt's antimonopoly message that Arnold repeated, aroused American fears. Kronstein's deep legal and economic understanding of European cartel practices and their impact enabled the Antitrust Division to counter the international cartel threat at both the levels of enforcement and as a symbol contrasting American and foreign ideologies regarding capitalist accountability and national identity. The TNEC hearings focusing on cartels and patents periodically generalized from technical matters to consider whether Germany's cartel system was a precondition for the Nazi's triumph. German émigrés presented conflicting TNEC testimony, but Kronstein maintained that the system had facilitated Hitler's rise.[57]

[55] Arnold, *The Bottlenecks of Business* (New York, 1940), 224, 239; Kronstein to Freyer, May 17, 2002 (phone interview); Alfred Kahn to Tony A. Freyer, June 6, 2001 (phone interview) cited above.

[56] Edward S. Mason, "Monopoly in Law and Economics," *Yale Law Journal* 47 (November 1937), 34–5, 47, 49.

[57] Kronstein to Freyer, May 17, 2002 (phone interview); David J. Gerber, "Heinrich Kronstein and the Development of United States Antitrust Law," in Marcus Lutter, Ernst C. Stieful,

Arnold applied these institutional resources to examine the bearing patents had on improving American social welfare. At the start of the TNEC hearings, he observed that by "increasing the distribution of goods through competitive prices," the antitrust laws could facilitate a "lowering of prices" for the "five and one-half million families not on relief." Acknowledging that the purpose of antitrust was "customarily referred to as an antimonopoly policy," Arnold observed that a "more accurate description would be to call it a policy against such restraints of trade as unreasonably hamper the free flow of goods in commerce at competitive prices." The basic "assumption" was that "free and independent enterprise is able to distribute goods with efficiency, provided that small groups without public responsibility are prevented from eliminating competition and exercising arbitrary power over prices and distribution." Since reshaping the law of "monopoly power" had no "inevitably logical starting point," the Justice Department was "beginning with patents." The law's technical complexity "affords to the patent owner such a wide choice in exploiting a new industrial art that it offers wide opportunities for the restraint of trade." The Justice Department would focus its attention on the patent practices of the glass and automobile industries, "because they illustrate typical situations" and "involve products which are of interest to every consumer."[58]

Arnold grilled corporate executives concerning their company's domestic and foreign patents. The Corning Glass company employed patent technology in the manufacture of clear-glass and inside frosted-glass bulbs for incandescent lamps. Arnold probed the company's international price competition with Japanese lamp makers and the anticompetitive patent relationship Corning had with General Electric, which also made lamps. Arnold's queries suggested linkages between Corning's patent arrangements and European cartel practices. Arnold affirmed that he was "not saying" that Corning's patent agreements were "illegal, because that is not the purpose of this inquiry." Still, Arnold asked, was the Corning executive "familiar with the cartel system in Europe?" Responding to the executive's protest that there was a technical distinction between lawfully granted patent licenses and other restrictive contracts, Arnold insisted that "I was

and Michael H. Hoeflich, eds., *Der Einfluss deutscher Emigranten auf die Rechtsentwicklung in den USA und in Deutschland* Vorträge und Referate des Bonner Symposions im September 1991 (Tübrngen, 1993), 155–69; *Cartels Part 25, Investigation of Concentration of Economic Power*, Hearings before TNEC, 76th Congress, 3rd Session, January 15–19, 1940 (Washington, DC, 1941), 13038–81, 13161, 13213, 13311–29, 13347–63. On the "Patent/Cartel" section, see Joseph Borkin, "Patents and the New Trust Problem," *Law and Contemporary Problems* 7 (Winter 1940), 74–81.

[58] *Patents Automobile and Glass Container Industry Part 2 Investigation of Concentration of Economic Power*, Hearings before TNEC, 75th Congress, 3rd Session, December 5–6, 12–16, 1938 (Washington, DC, 1939), 254, 255, 256.

only suggesting that you had something under patents which was very similar to the European cartel system under contracts." Moreover, testimony from an Owens-Corning Fiberglass manager admitted that, consistently with their exclusive international patent arrangements with German, Dutch, French, Italian, British, and Canadian companies, the firm's technological advantage was such that it "had no fear of any foreign competition."[59]

The TNEC inquiries facilitated Arnold's broader enforcement strategy. The testimony revealed how interdependent patented technology and corporate organization were. In the *Socony-Vacuum Oil Co.* case, the nation's leading oil companies raised a defense combining technological and organizational efficiencies to justify their cooperative purchasing of "surplus" gasoline from independent refiners to prevent the surplus from being introduced into the market. The companies argued that because the industry's high fixed costs made cut-throat competition ruinous cooperation to fix prices was reasonable. Indeed, the NRA had approved the program. The Supreme Court, however, extended the per se rule against cartel practices, upholding the Justice Department's argument that the companies were engaged in an illegal price-fixing conspiracy.[60]

Antitrust authorities further addressed such "efficiency" claims through broader use of consent decrees. Over assertions that the wide-ranging discretion the decree sanctioned was arbitrary, courts approved Arnold's assurance that sufficient oversight existed to prevent abuse. Thus, the Justice Department fashioned a consent decree restricting Ford's and Chrysler's control of dealer financing; GM challenged the decree in federal court but lost. Even so, Arnold made an analogy with Germany, where a "[s]imilar argument, based on lack of legal precision in decrees directed at monopoly, was an important factor in stopping effective enforcement by logically-minded Germany until it drifted into direct price-fixing as a more precise substitute."[61]

Arnold's activist enforcement had uneven results, especially regarding labor. The Supreme Court's *Apex Hosiery* decision held that a union's strike for a closed shop was not an antitrust violation, but where the strike interfered with business competitors, the union's antitrust exemption did not prevent prosecution. Arnold hoped the decision would facilitate using antitrust litigation to limit labor's unfair practices. In the *Hutcheson* decision of 1941, however, the court dismissed the Justice Department's indictment of Carpenter Union officials' interference with Machinist Union

[59] *Ibid.*, 646–7, 652–3, 656, 664.
[60] *U.S. v. Socony-Vacuum Oil Co.*, 310 US 150 (1940); known as Madison Oil case, see Fainsod and Gordon, *Government and the American Economy*, 550–2; Spencer Weber Waller, "The Language of Law and the Language of Business," *Case Western Reserve Law Review* 52 (Fall 2001), 294–5.
[61] *Ibid.*; Arnold, *The Bottlenecks of Business*, 138.

members. One observer questioned the impact the decision would have on the efforts to curb all "forms of labor racketeering."[62]

In letters, however, Arnold concluded, that the case "throws doubt over all our labor prosecutions excepting where labor has combined with employers." Moreover, for the flood of criticism those prosecutions received, he blamed liberals who were "unable to see any individuals. They see unions and they see labor movements. When individuals are crushed they think no more of it than Mr. Hitler does." By contrast, he noted that after the Supreme Court affirmed the government's prosecution of an agricultural association, the "powerful and influential American Farm Bureau" publically approved the "prosecution policy with respect not only to industry and labor but to agriculture."[63]

The *Hutcheson* decision suggested how contentious antitrust activism was within American liberalism. The court's holding strengthened organized labor's antitrust exemption, Arnold wrote, so that "we are not going to get the enforcement effect out of bringing these [labor conspiracy] cases which we got before. This is a tremendous loss." Until the court's decision, "the mere calling of a grand jury was enough to stop a vicious labor practice. I suspect that labor is going to be pretty cocky." Replying to Attorney General Jackson's queries concerning the impact prolabor congressional legislative proposals might have, Arnold described still broader consequences: the decision not only "in effect allows one union to destroy another regardless of the wishes or choice of the employees and regardless of the willingness of the employer to be fair to organized labor," but it also "raised problems which not only concern defense but also the distribution of food and housing to low income groups." The court's decision seemed to confirm the view that Dan Tobin of the International Teamster's Union reportedly expressed, that Arnold was "making a serious legal mistake, which has not added to his prestige."[64]

The nation's defense build up offered Arnold the political opportunity to offset the labor problems. The controversy over labor cases mounted through 1940–41 during the same time the Roosevelt administration searched for an effective defense policy. The debate over neutrality

[62] *Apex Hosiery Co. v. Leader*, 310 US 658 (1940); Arnold, *The Bottlenecks of Business*, 254; Arnold to Westbrook Pegler, June 9, 1940, in Gressley, *Voltaire and the Cowboy*, 307; *U.S. v. Hutcheson*, 312 US 219 (1941); Fainsod and Gordon, *Government and the American Economy*, 158.
[63] Arnold to Edward A. Evans, February 17, 1941; Arnold to Reed Powell, February 21, 1941, in Gressley, *Voltaire and the Cowboy*, quotes at 311, 317; and Arnold, *Bottlenecks of Business*, 256.
[64] Arnold to Edward A. Evans, February 17, 1941; Arnold to Jackson, February 17, 1941, in Gressley, *Voltaire and the Cowboy*, 312; [no author], "The I.B.T.C.W.H. of A.... Meaning the Teamsters' Union," 23 *Fortune* No. 5 (May 1941), 99–100, 135–6, 140–2 quote at 135.

converged with the political and economic costs engendered by growing
foreign aid and Americans' demand for affordable consumer goods as the
recession finally receded. Arnold's bureaucratic maneuvers resulted in
establishing the Antitrust Division as an independent defender of fair consumer prices. *Fortune's* commentary on price controls offered a positive
measure of Arnold's success in this role. "For, except in cases of defense
necessity, his hands are free to maintain the government's traditional attitude
toward price and the functioning of the profit system: maintenance of competition," the article stated. He was "one of the very few" who "had the nerve
to treat agriculture, industry, and labor on the same impartial terms and judge
them by the same criteria." Thus, Arnold achieved the difficult political
gymnastic feat of turning the loss in the labor cases into a gain. He did so,
however, because the testimony of corporate executives before the TNEC and
the Antitrust Division's work on cartels and patents facilitated reshaping the
social welfare goals of the antitrust enforcement policy to exploit "foreign"
images of international cartels threatening the national defense program.[65]

IV. ARNOLD, INTERNATIONAL CARTELS, AND MOBILIZING AMERICA'S DEFENSES

The initial years of World War II challenged Arnold's ability to establish
antitrust activism's enduring place within New Deal liberalism. Arnold
gradually reoriented the antitrust enforcement policy beyond social welfare
goals to strengthen business accountability and promote American individual opportunity within the growing defense effort. He combined policing
consumer prices with the aggressive prosecution of international cartels. In
the process he used increased budget appropriations to strengthen the
Antitrust Division, raising the stature of antitrust within the Washington
establishment. Arnold's grasp of institutional economics and of the psychological dynamics driving individuals and institutions alike enabled him
to fashion a coherent enforcement strategy adaptable to the incremental
phases of Roosevelt's defense program before Pearl Harbor. Although the
government lost at trial in the *Alcoa* case, its appeal reflected a growing
mastery of the complex issues involving international cartels and their
relation to a liberal trade policy. Aided by Jackson's collaborations with
leaders of successive defense bureaucracies – especially John Lord O'Brian
and the Office of Production Management – Arnold's antitrust activism
achieved what its World War I predecessor had not: a central place in
mobilizing the nation's defense.[66]

[65] [no author], "Price Control: 1941," 23 *Fortune* No. 1 (January 1941), 65–7, 78, 80, 82, quote at 82.
[66] Lincoln Gordon to Tony A. Freyer, interview, April 29, 2002. Dr. Gordon noted that his contributions to Fainsod and Gordon, *Government and the American Economy*, including

The progress of the *Alcoa* case revealed the international ramifications of Arnold's antitrust policy. A *Yale Law Journal* student note observed that the government filed the suit in 1937 after the travails of the NRA had heightened public awareness that "the ever-increasing cartelization of European business enterprise, with its concomitant elimination of competition, division of world markets and limitations upon total productive output, has an important effect on American industry." The case came to trial in June 1938. The federal court addressed the rule established in the *American Banana* decision of 1909 denying the antitrust law's extraterritorial impact within U.S. borders. Although previous Supreme Court decisions had eroded the rule, the *Alcoa* case presented the most direct argument yet for establishing antitrust jurisdiction on the basis of extraterritorial effects. In "extraterritorial conspiracies, the debatable issue has been whether effect on American commerce is sufficient to bring them within" the jurisdiction of the antitrust laws. The federal trial judge accepted the government's argument that direct evidence did not establish Alcoa's participation in a conspiracy involving the international aluminum cartel, but the facts did reveal "constructive intent" having an extraterritorial effect upon the U.S. market that established antitrust jurisdiction. In 1940 the federal court nonetheless rejected the government's broader argument to break up Alcoa, whereupon the government appealed. The war delayed a final decision.[67]

The *Alcoa* appeal coincided with Arnold's effort to maintain the antitrust program's momentum during wartime. Just as Arnold had generalized from the TNEC patent evidence to establish the nexus between technological efficiency and the abuse of big organizations, he publicized an image of America threatened by an "international cartel movement" loosely associated with Nazi Germany. In order to meet the danger, strengthened antitrust enforcement was essential. He pointed out that "every single instance of German influence" on the international operations of U.S. corporations was "uncovered by an antitrust investigation or prosecution," including "military optical instruments, tungsten carbide, aluminum, magnesium, beryllium, chemicals and drugs." From August through December 1941, the *Fortune* survey of public opinion revealed that a majority favored continuing doing business with the combatants within the restrictions imposed by the neutrality laws. Even so, after Germany conquered Western Europe, Arnold emphasized, the German government had

the material relating Arnold's antitrust regime to the defense build up, were written prior to the Jackson-O'Brian letter discussed below. See also notes 6 and 48 above.

[67] Robert T. Molloy, "Application of the Anti-Trust Laws to Extra-Territorial Conspiracies," 49 *Yale Law Journal*, (May 1940) 1312–19, quotes at 1312, 1315; *American Banana Co. v. United Fruit Co.*, 213 US 347 (1909); *U.S. v. Aluminum Co. of America*, 44 F.Supp. 97 (Dis. Ct. S.D.N.Y., 1941); *U.S. v. Aluminum Co. of America*, 148 F.2d 416 (C.C. App. 2d Cir., 1945). See also John Wolff, "Business Monopolies: Three European Systems in Their Bearing on America Law," 9 *Tulane Law Review*, (April 1935) 325–77.

exploited for strategic purposes, the numerous anticompetitive patent and other agreements German firms had with companies throughout the world, particularly U.S. multinational corporations. Thus, Arnold quoted one article that stated, "by cleverly playing upon the profit motive (which is suppressed inside Germany)" the Nazis had "gulled businessmen in the democracies into limiting production of the very articles that the democracies were to need most urgently in their own defense. In this way Germany induced Europe's democracies to 'stabilize' aluminum production ... while German production shot forward at top speed. The consequences of this have since become all too plain."[68]

Arnold's prosecution of U.S. multinational corporations represented a major change in enforcement priorities. Between the end of World War I and 1930, the Justice Department had prosecuted seventeen antitrust cases involving international anticompetitive conduct. Major corporations producing petroleum, potash, or quinine – or in one instance, the Radio Corporation of America – were parties; a large proportion were firms engaged in fishing or the making of sisal cordage, or soap and toiletries. The government's record of winning was mixed, as it had a modest impact on the international expansion of American corporate capitalism.[69] From 1932 to 1937, the *Alcoa* suit was the only international antitrust prosecution. Under Arnold's leadership, however, prosecutions against multinational corporations accelerated. In 1939, he brought five suits including a prosecution of U.S. and Dutch firms engaged in the monopolization and price-fixing of potash production. Two other cases involved the anticompetitive conduct of Dow Chemical and the Chilean governmental cartel in the manufacture of nitrate derivatives. A fourth case – also related to the nitrate cartel – challenged a synthetic nitrogen producer, and the last case concerned a tariff violation in newspaper sales between the United States and Canada.[70]

---

[68] "Report, Ass. Att. Gen. A. D. Arnold," *Annual Report Att. Gen. US, 1941*, Arnold quoting *Fortune*, at 59; see also "Fortune Survey," 24 *Fortune* (August 1941), 75–8; *Fortune* (October 1941), 105–8; 24 *Fortune* (December 1941), 119–22.

[69] Fugate, *Foreign Commerce and Antitrust Laws*, 502–5; Sumatra Purchasing Co. [US wins 1920]; Walter Moore [*nolle prosequi* 1920]; Walter Moore [dismissed 1920]; Railway [US won 1923]; Standard Oil Co. [appeal 283 US 163 (1931) filed 1924, complaint dismissed 1931]; Sisal Sales Corp. [US wins]; Lay Fish Co. [US wins 1926]; Leibner & Co. [US wins 1926]; Deutsches Kalisyndikat Gesellschaft [US wins 1929]; Asbestos Corp. [case filed 1928, dismissed for mootness 1931]; Amsterdamsche Chininefabriek Eq. [US wins consent decree 1929]; [same defendant, *nolle prosequi* 1928]; 383, 340 Ounces of Quinnine-Derivatives [consent decree 1928]; Radio Corp. of America [consent decree 1932]; 5,898 Cases Sardines [US wins consent decree 1931]; A. B. C. Canning Co. [US wins consent decree 1931].

[70] Fugate, *Foreign Commerce and Antitrust Laws*, 506–7; American Potash & Chemical Corp. [filed 1939, *nolle prosequi* 1940]; Crown Zellerbach Corp. [filed 1939, defendants plead *nolo contendere*, and indictment dismissed as to others 1941]; Allied Chemical & Dye Corp. [*nolle prosequi* as to all defendants in view of consent decree in civil case 1941]; Chilean nitrate Sales Corp. [filed 1939, consent decree 1941 and 1942, including Chilean

These cases provided an important leaning experience. The Justice Department won the newsprint case. The government agreed not to prosecute the potash case on the basis of the court's holding of *nolle prosequi*. Even though there was no conviction, the case publicized the involvement of four U.S. companies and one Dutch firm, as well as fifty-seven individuals in an alleged monopolization, price-fixing, group boycott, and market division of the international potash trade. Exposing the extent of the cartel undoubtedly influenced the favorable outcome in the three nitrate cases where the government employed intricate procedural negotiations to get all parties to accept a comprehensive consent degree ending the cartel. The settlement included a foreign governmental agency, the Chilean Nitrate Sales Corporation. At the request of the State Department, the Justice Department agreed to a *nolle prosequi* determination as long as the Chilean government otherwise obeyed the consent decree.[71]

The nitrate settlement received less attention than the *Alcoa* case, but it represented a major step in Arnold's international cartel prosecutions. The cartel members included DuPont; Allied Chemical; the Chilean government; the German firm, I.G. Farben; the British corporation, ICI; and the Norwegian company, Norsky Hydro. The last three companies maintained ties with their governments and with other governments throughout Europe. Assembling complex evidence of such cartel practices was a precondition the Antitrust Division had to master in order to mount more cases during the next two years.[72]

The seven international prosecutions initiated in 1940 indicated that the government had learned its lessons well. Two of these cases were against Bausch & Lomb; Corning Glass, General Electric, and the American potash producer were the parties, respectively, in three suits, while two cases concerned the business–labor conspiracies of firms manufacturing waste paper for foreign distribution. The government won each of these cases, including the renewed prosecution of the potash cartel suspended the previous year. In four of the seven cases, the firms ultimately pleaded no contest (*nolo contendere*). A guilty verdict was rendered against General Electric and a German producer of tools, dies, and composition made from hard metals; the cartel was broken up, though GE contested the verdict for years afterward. *Fortune* suggested the favorable impact of these decisions, declaring that Arnold's "department has done excellent work in ending the division of the world market for military optical instruments between Bausch & Lomb and Carl Zeiss, and in cutting through the tie- up between General Electric and Krupp."[73]

government following intervention US State Department]; Synthet Nitrogen Products Corp. [*nolle prossed* in view of consent decree in civil case 1939].
[71] *Ibid.*   [72] Wells, *Antitrust*, 58–9.
[73] Fugate, *Foreign Commerce and Antitrust Laws*, 507–8; Bausch & Lomb Optical Co. [2 cases, *nolo contendere*, consent decrees entered 1940]; American Potash & Chemical Corp. [consent decree 1940]; Corning Glass Works [*nolo contendere*, fines $47,000]; General Electric [guilty

Antitrust prosecutions against the international cartels reached a higher level in 1941. Twenty-three cases involved such diverse commodities and industries as incandescent lamps, magnesium alloys, magnesite brick, fertilizer nitrogen, battery separators, pharmaceuticals, lumber, sheet music, evaporated milk, canned fruits and vegetables, rice, sardines, hard metal alloys, hormones, photographic materials and film, and dyestuffs. Leading American firms were targeted, including General Electric, Alcoa, Dow Chemical, and Bayer; the German chemical giant, I.G. Farben, was the most conspicuous foreign firm. Some cases were straightforward conspiracies, such as the California rice industry's price-fixing on Japanese rice. In other instances complicated patent and cartel agreements were being litigated, such as the prosecution against Alcoa's and I.G. Farben's attempt to monopolize the trade in magnesium alloys and products. The government won most of these suits. To be sure, in only a few cases were fines substantial and while the companies often pleaded no contest, the final decision did not occur until after the war.[74]

Still, the international cartel cases gave the Antitrust Division a national security role in the defense effort. *Fortune* assessed positively Arnold's independence and effectiveness, observing that he "has been a kind of *enfant terrible* to industry because of his antitrust suits. But ... [he] has not been raised by the exigencies of the defense program to a position where he must join hands with industrial bigness or must readapt the smoke-filled room technique to getting the nation its guns. Arnold's attitude toward the Defense Commission is one of full co-operation."[75]

---

verdict, fines 1941]; Levine Waste Paper Co. [filed 1940, *nolo contendere* 1942]; Wholesale Waste Paper Co. [filed 1940, *nolo contendere* 1942]. 25 *Fortune* (January 1941), 82.

[74] Fugate, *Foreign Commerce and Antitrust Laws*, 509–13: Harbison-Walker Refractories Co. [filed 1941, *nolo contendere*, fines $76,500]; General Electric Co. [filed 1941, consent decree 1942, and for another defendant, 1946]; Broadcast Music Inc. [consent decree 1941]; Alcoa [I.G. Farben, filed 1941, *nolo contendere*, total fines $104,993, 1942]; American Magnesium Corp. [filed 1941, *nolo contendere* 1942]; Dow Chemical Co. [filed 1941, *nolo contendere* 1942]; American Society of Composers, Authors, and Publishers [*nolo contendere* 1941]; National Fertilizer Association [filed 1941, *nolo contendere* 1942, fines, $259,852]; Allied Chemical [consent decree 1941, effective 1945]; Dried Fruit Association [filed 1941, directed verdict of not guilty 1944]; Evaporated Milk Association [filed 1941, *nolo contendere* and dismissals 1943]; Canners League of California [filed 1941, 45 defendants pleaded *nolo contendere*, 3 dismissed, 2 *nolle prossed*, after trial 14 others found not guilty 1943]; Monterey Sardine Industry, Inc. [*nolo contendere* 1941]; Battery Separator Mfgs. Ass. [*nolo contendere* 1941]; California Rice Industry Co. [*nolo contendere* to 4 defendants and *nolo prosequi* as to others 1941]; Alba Pharmaceutical Co. [*nolo contendere* 1941]; Bayer Co. [consent decree primary complaint 1941]; General Electric [filed 1941, general verdict, fines imposed 1948]; Schering Corp. [consent decree 1941]; Swiss Bank [consent decree 1941]; General Dyestuffs [3 defendants dismissed, 1 *nolle prossed* 2 pleaded *nolo contendere* and were fined, 1 found not guilty 1941]; General Auile & Film Corp. [filed 1941, *nolo contendere* 1950, fines $1,000 and $500]; Dietrich A. Schmitz Cr. [filed 1941, 1 defendant dismissed 1944, others, *nolo contendere* fines $1,000, $2,000, 1950].

[75] *Fortune* (January 1941), 82.

The large-scale assault upon U.S. multinational corporations' involvement in international cartels thus sustained antitrust activism's credibility. The government's victories promoted the vigorous antitrust campaign – at least within the Washington establishment and among big business – despite the defeats Arnold faced in the high-profile labor cases and the construction industry investigations.[76] The unprecedented scope of the international cartel prosecutions coincided, moreover, with the TNEC's ongoing revelations of Standard Oil's, DuPont's, General Electric's, Alcoa's, and other major corporations' extensive patent and cartel agreements with foreign companies, especially I.G. Farben, the firm most associated with Nazi Germany. The successful prosecution of these giants reinforced Senate committee investigations of defense matters relating to corporate America, including the dangers international cartels posed to the enormous defense build up beginning in October 1940.[77]

Prosecuting international cartels involved antitrust in the nation's "economic warfare," and the linkages between antitrust enforcement and the national defense program grew incrementally. From the uncertain months preceding Germany's invasion of Poland to the German conquest of Western Europe, Arnold struggled over the labor cases and other issues. Indeed, angered by the lack of support from Attorney General Frank Murphy, he contemplated resigning his post.[78] Even so, in September 1939, he urged the defense agencies to establish "conditions under which otherwise illegal action might be legal in a war emergency and the circumstances in which national defense interests would make postponement of prosecution desirable."[79]

Meanwhile, Roosevelt searched for an effective defense organization within the executive branch that could balance competing demands for improved consumer welfare and military expansion.[80] Initially, Roosevelt considered tailoring the defense bureaucracy to the policy of business–labor–government collaboration and the suspension of the antitrust laws associated with the NRA and Bernard Baruch's administration of the War Industries Board in World War I. As the new defense effort evolved, Baruch advocated reviving the old policies, particularly immunizing business leaders from the sort of aggressive prosecutions Arnold was pursing in the *Socony Vacuum Oil* case.[81]

---

[76] Brinkley, *End of Reform*, 118–21.

[77] Wilkins, *Maturing of Multinational Enterprise*, 204, 259, 263; Wells, *Antitrust*, 73–9.

[78] Arnold to Jackson, January 23, 1940, in Gressley, *Voltaire and the Cowboy*, 300–3.

[79] First, *Industry and Labor Advisory Committees* (reference to "Conference with Mr. Thurman Arnold, 3 p.m., September 14, 1939"), 7, note 19.

[80] Ibid., 1–64; *Industrial Mobilization for War*, 3–88.

[81] First, *Industry and Labor Advisory Committees*, 5, 11; *Industrial Mobilization for War*, 13, 51–2. See also Jordon A. Schwarz, *The Speculator: Bernard M. Baruch in Washington, 1917–1965* (Chapel Hill, NC, 1981) 289–93, 327–8, 358–63, 409–32.

Between May 1940 and early 1941, Roosevelt formally rejected Baruch's approach, authorizing two successive defense organizations. Initially, the National Defense Advisory Commission endeavored to balance defense and consumer demands while maintaining effective antitrust enforcement. Roosevelt's chief advisors overseeing this effort were General Motors President William S. Knudsen, union leader Sidney Hillman, and US Steel executive Edward R. Stettinius, Jr. The TNEC hearings and the *Socony-Vacuum Oil* decision undercut whatever preference the commission may have had for Baruch's policies. Addressing the "antitrust problem," members of the commission's various committees agreed that "[i]f we keep this thing in the right channel, there is not likely to be a bad aftermath, but if we can't we all know from the post-NRA-Department of Justice round what we may expect." In addition, Arnold's announcement of pending investigations or prosecutions in related defense industries aroused considerable "wariness" among Stettinius, Knudsen, and others. Some business leaders were also concerned about avoiding criticism that the commission was permitting big firms to abuse small ones in the administration of public contracts.[82]

The Office of Production Management (OPM) took over administering the defense effort in January 1941. The leadership changed little except that Roosevelt appointed John Lord O'Brian to be the OPM's general counsel. A prominent Republican lawyer from New York, O'Brian had served in many government positions, including the assistant attorney general of the Antitrust Division in the Hoover administration. As the government's top antitrust official, O'Brian had reversed the lenient policy of his predecessor, William Donovan, toward advance clearance of international cooperative agreements. O'Brian also had a close working relationship with fellow New Yorker, Robert Jackson, who had become attorney general in February 1940. O'Brian provided exceptional leadership, establishing the legal policy governing the entire defense allocation process. In addition, Leon Henderson, head of the Office of Price Administration, administered pricing policies.[83]

Antitrust enforcement gained further importance under the Office of Production Management. The OPM took over responsibility for administering the mounting resource allocation demands of civilian and military authorities which, in turn, converged with foreign aid pressures from Britain and the Allies.[84] As a result, Jackson and O'Brian reached agreement on a more formal system of Justice Department oversight. While necessary

---

[82] First, *Industry and Labor Advisory Committees*, 11–12, quote at 30; *Industrial Mobilization for War*, 3–88.

[83] First, *Industry and Labor Advisory Committees*, 56–229; *Industrial Mobilization for War*, 89–200; Lincoln Gordon to Tony A. Freyer, interview, April 29, 2002; Schwarz, *Speculator Baruch*, 369–78, 387, 408, 426. For O'Brian, see the oral history, *The Reminiscences of John Lord O'Brian* (New York, 1972), 331–4, 463–600. Compare Donovan and O'Brian at Antitrust Division; Freyer, *Regulating Big Business*, 218–19.

[84] *Ibid.*

cooperation between business and government and among business leaders themselves to further the purposes of national defense generally would not be subject to antitrust prosecution, they agreed, "[i]n the case of all plans and procedures," the Justice Department "reserves complete freedom to institute civil actions to enjoin the continuing of acts or practices found not to be in the public interest."[85]

Jackson confirmed a procedure he and O'Brian had evolved to counter dissenters within the defense organizations who supported Baruch's policies. Even so, a steel official suggested that a dominant business attitude was one of "extreme diffidence," featuring "prosecution under the anti-trust laws, if not now at some future time." This prevailing view recognized Arnold's ruling "that so long as the [OPM] demands information from the industry committee rather than simply to accept its recommendations, the industry committee will avoid legal entanglements." Thus, when the OPM ended following Pearl Harbor, O'Brian wrote to Arnold concluding that the organization had "proved very satisfactory both as a method of securing the cooperation of industry and at the same time of enabling us to prevent infringement of the law."[86]

Arnold thus successfully established the image of antitrust as defending economic democracy from an ominous "foreign" threat. As long as "individual freedom" was the prevailing ideal, the *"main* method of distributing goods and services must be by free exchange in a free market." (emphasis in the original)This was the "American ideal." A second way to attain technological and organizational efficiency in order to maintain high consumption was, however, the "destruction of competitive domestic markets by private combinations, cartels, and trade associations ... illustrated by Germany today." He presented the antitrust program as a "middle way" of "practical reform" capable of preserving American freedom. The Weimar Republic attempted to regulate the traditionally cartelized German economy by enacting a modest antitrust law. German business claimed that antitrust enforcement fomented market "uncertainty," unions asserted that "large and prosperous cartels" paid higher wages, and trade associations contended that governmentally enforced cartel agreements afforded "protection against the chiseler." Above all, however, Germany's "socialist planners" repudiated antitrust as contrary to the "planned economy." In such a culture, the emergence and triumph of a Hitler was "inevitable."[87]

---

[85] Jackson to John Lord O'Brian, April 29, 1941, "Report, Ass. Att., A. D., Thurman Arnold," *Report Fiscal Year 1941* (1942), full text at 65–7. See also *The Reminiscences of John Lord O'Brian*, 463–600.

[86] First, *Industry and Labor Advisory Committees*, 73, 85, 167–8.

[87] *Bottlenecks of Business*, 5, 10–11, 14–15, 17–18.

Similarly, despite the protestations of Winston Churchill, Britain's parliamentary democracy was held in the grip of "a static civil service and a set of industrial cartels. Even after Munich, these cartels were busy pursuing their own private interests and actually arming Germany against England." Arnold ranked himself among those "practical reformers" who "always ha[d] to fight not only reactionary opposition to reform, but also the politically impractical ideas of liberal economic planners." Neither conservatives nor liberals nor antidemocratic autocrats grasped, he declared, that

institutions respond to pressures, not to logical thinking. They are like human personalities. The direction they take depends on the necessity of adjustment to outside forces. If you are going to make that adjustment easier and less painful, you must use methods which do not create fear and distrust by attacking revered traditions. And there lies the strength of the Sherman Act. It is a symbol of our traditional ideals.[88]

V. ANTITRUST AT WAR: INTERNATIONAL CARTELS AND THE ORIGINS OF THE ITO, 1941–1945

The Japanese attack on Pearl Harbor altered the international cartel issue. From 1941 on, the Justice Department faced repeated assertions from the military service departments and big business leaders that antitrust undercut the war effort. Echoing Baruch, the critics argued that the agreement reached by Jackson and O'Brian with Roosevelt's authorization on April 29, 1941, requiring certification and postponement of antitrust violations jeopardized efficient mobilization and procurement of economic and military resources. On March 20, 1942, Roosevelt nonetheless approved a letter signed by Attorney General Francis Biddle, Secretary of War Henry L. Stimson, Secretary of the Navy Frank Knox, and Thurman Arnold which essentially continued the earlier system as long as hostilities lasted. This agreement only ensured persistent contention among the parties regarding particular cases as well as the Antitrust Division's ongoing campaign to expose links among U.S. multinational corporations, international cartels, and the Axis powers. Amid such opposition, Arnold and other Antitrust Division officials received favorable notice in well-publicized congressional hearings: the Bone committee's examination of patents, the Truman special committee investigation into the national defense program, and the Kilgore Senate subcommittee inquiry into military affairs. And yet, during the transition from war to peace in 1945, the international cartel issue

---

[88] *Ibid.*, 80–1, 92.

aggravated the formation of the ITO and the Allies' Occupation policy toward Germany and Japan.[89]

From 1941 to 1943, antitrust authorities successfully maneuvered to avert their predecessors' fate in World War I. Historians later focused on Roosevelt's elevation of Arnold to the federal court in 1943 as indicating a disruption of antitrust activism amidst executive department bureaucrats' early uncertainty over the means of attaining military victory. Preoccupation with Arnold's departure ignored the reality that the Antitrust Division's regular congressional budget appropriation *after* Pearl Harbor remained at the same historic levels Arnold had achieved during 1939–41. This emphasis upon congressional willingness to allocate relatively high budget appropriations indicated its wartime role. Accordingly, the change in the Antitrust Division's leadership from Arnold to Wendell Berge in early 1943 signaled not that the "antitrust drive seemed dead." Rather, facing "representations ... to Congress to relax antitrust legislation on the grounds that the government's defense program would thereby be facilitated. ... the Department of Justice immediately directed attention toward the pro-Nazi political activities of German cartels with which American companies had relations." As a result, "[n]ot merely was the movement for curbing the antitrust program forestalled, but Congress came forward with substantially increased appropriations to expand the work of the Anti-trust Division."[90]

Within the Antitrust Division, Heinrich Kronstein developed intelligence information about international cartels. Since 1938, Kronstein had employed a deep understanding of German cartels in work with both the Antitrust Division and the Alien Property Custodian (APC). On December 23, 1941, he authored a memorandum for the latter agency describing evidence he had collected about patents revealing linkages between German and U.S. firms; he also suggested the ramifications this fact-finding had for broadly conceived antitrust operations during wartime. Noting that the "problems discussed in this memorandum involve many economic and technical questions of antitrust policy, of defense capacity, of the future

---

[89] Memorandum for Assistant Attorney General Berge, "Antitrust Enforcement in the War Emergency," April, 22, 1947; Biddle, Stimson, Knox, and Arnold to Roosevelt, March 20, 1942; President's approval, March 20, 1942, in Appendix F, March 28, 1942, "Antitrust Enforcement in the War Emergency," Wendell Berge Paper (WBP), File A/Berge, Box 43, LC; *Industrial Mobilization for War*, 201–966; Samuel I. Rosenman to Roosevelt, March 14, 1942, and Biddle, "Memorandum for the President," March 20, 1942, recognizing "John Lord O'Brian ... in whom all parties have confidence," Official File #277, Anti-Trust Laws, FDPL; Dale B. Furnish, "A Transnational Approach to Restrictive Business Practices," 4 *The International Lawyer* #2 (January 1970), 317–52, especially 321–2 [the committee chairmen's names, respectively, are Homer T. Bone, Harry Truman, and Harley Kilgore].

[90] Wells, *Antitrust*, 96 and Charles R. Whittlesey, *National Interest and International Cartels* (New York, 1946), 14.

international relations and of banking," Kronstein urged the establishment of procedures and structures "which make it absolutely certain that all these aspects of the problems are sufficiently considered." Four months later, Kronstein won Arnold's support for instituting within the Antitrust Division a continuing commitment to collecting and dispersing data about international cartels. Kronstein gathered from the Treasury and Commerce Departments, the Alien Property Office, and elsewhere "information concerning international cartels and international patent agreements" pertaining to future "antitrust investigations," issues involving "South American connections," and the need for "knowledge to prepare a policy in regard to international cartels during the war and post-war period."[91]

Arnold's authorization of the more centralized investigation of wartime international cartels was timely. During July 1942, he used these data in a nationally broadcast talk presented to the American Business Congress in New York and a speech transmitted to Nazi Germany. Condemning the "abuse of patents," Arnold said, "this evil is illustrated by the fact that recently the Antitrust Division uncovered a list of 162 cartel agreements affecting American business, penetrating nearly every great industry, made with I.G. Farben, of Germany." In this connection, he attacked Standard Oil's as well as General Electric's involvement with the "German Electric Bulb Company." Kronstein gave congressional testimony addressing why Germany had emerged as the "homeland of cartels," and how Hitler used the "cartel and patent system" in "preparing for and waging the war." Even antitrust proponents such as Harvard's Edward Mason considered that the Antitrust Division's claims regarding the impact on Germany's war-making capacity were exaggerated. Nevertheless, from 1942 until the initial postwar years, Arnold and his successor, Wendell Berge, used the evidence Kronstein and others gathered to perpetuate among federal bureaucrats, Congress, prominent journalists and academics, and even officials within Allied governments the evil image of Germany's international cartels.[92]

By early 1943, the Antitrust Division had established its wartime role as Roosevelt promoted the nation's economic power and strategic diplomacy. Thus, the Antitrust Division's institution of 315 cases from 1941 to 1946

[91] Heinrich Kronstein, "Memorandum to Mr. Fowler Hamilton," December, 23, 1941, 13, Box 3, Folder "Patents," and Heinrich Kronstein to Arnold, April 22, 1942, Box 10, Folder "German Cartels Law," 1–3 (Heinrich Kronstein Papers [HKP] Georgetown University Special Collections [GUSC]).

[92] Thurman Arnold, "The Abuse of Patents" (July 28, 1942), 5; Box 3, Folder "Patents," and Heinrich Kronstein, "The Dynamics of German Cartels and Patents," 1, Box 10, Folder "HK on patents" (HKP/GUSC); Arnold, "Cartels, a Short Wave Broadcast Message to Germany," July 22, 1942 (note, while this address went through several drafts, certain of Kronstein's key points were retained) (Thurman Wesley Arnold Papers [TWAP,] American Heritage Center, University of Wyoming [AHCUW]).

had impact beyond the built-up pressures resulting from numerous post-ponements granted during the war. In 1942, the Justice Department won a consent decree against Standard Oil and a partial decree concerning Alcoa, though the long-running appeal in that case was not decided until 1945. These and other decrees affirmed a liberal transfer of patent technology under use agreements benefiting U.S. firms during and after the war. In addition, the participation of Antitrust Division officials in several inter-departmental committees furthered "foreign economic policy for the United States and in preventing cartel practices." Thus, the Board of Economic Warfare found the Antitrust Division's international cartel data vital in locating strategic targets, the "bombing of which would seriously impair enemy war potential." Yet, the antitrust authorities' role was especially noteworthy beginning in spring 1943 as the State Department's Special Committee on Monopoly and Cartels geared up under Assistant Secretary of State Dean Acheson. The committee's members included Deputy Chairmen Edward Mason of the Office of Strategic Services and the Anti-trust Division's Hugh Cox. Also, Corwin Edwards moved from the Anti-trust Division to the State Department to advise the committee on monopoly and cartel matters. Another member was Under Secretary of Commerce William Clayton, a wealthy cotton broker and expert on com-modity trading.[93]

From early 1943, the Cartel Committee influenced U.S. foreign economic policy and peacemaking. A "Summary" memoranda dated October 14, 1943, described the work accomplished since the first meeting in May; it identified an ongoing study of "three problems": "enemy property" in South America, including Mexico and Colombia; "enemy property affect-ing industry and industrial organization in the occupied and enemy coun-tries of Europe" spurred by the invasion of Italy; and the "problems of international industrial combinations." These "three problems" reflected, moreover, the revelations about international cartels that were being pub-licized in congressional hearings and court cases; they involved, too, the aid negotiations with the British beginning in September 1943. The "three problems" also had a bearing on the massive wartime procurement process overseen by the General Council for the War Production Board, John Lord O'Brian, who successfully preserved basic antitrust competition values despite resistance from the military departments. Even so, the Cartel Committee understood the military's diverse operational "missions." These

[93] For "Antitrust Enforcement in the War Emergency" (5–9, quotes at 8, 9, WBP, File A/Berge, Box 43, LC) and on the origins and outcome of the cases, see discussion below; for the Cartel Committee's membership, see "A Review of the Work of the Special Economic Committees for the Week, Ending December, 21, 1943," December 23, 1943, in Edward S. Mason, deputy chairman, Special Committee on Private Monopolies and Cartels (hereafter, Mason, Cartel Committee, Notter Files, Record Group [RG] 59, Box 34, National Archives [NA]).

missions shaped each service's procurement demands – which concerned the productive capacity of many of the same major multinational corporations whose ties to German industry were being exposed by the Justice Department.[94]

By November 1943, these issues had acquired a shape that would persist into the initial postwar period. Broadly, the Committee's internal reports on international cartels confirmed the complex interrelationships existing among the investment and technology transfers of U.S. and foreign multinational corporations and their close connection with government economic policies. The intricate interdependency linking private and government investment indicated the need for a comprehensive international agreement embracing antitrust. Thus, the committee fashioned a "draft memorandum enumerating specific restrictive practices which might be prohibited by international agreement." Cartel agreements around the world engendered committee reports calling for international policies toward vital regulated industries such as aviation, petroleum, banking, and related commodities like minerals, rubber, and agricultural staples. "Concern was expressed" in one report, "lest policies in these fields crystallize before the Cartel Committee" determined the scope of cartel "prohibition dealing with patent licensing and patent agreements" and the "relation of American foreign investment policy to cartel problems."[95]

Discussion of an international agreement coincided with concerns about investment flows and Allied occupation of enemy territory. During 1943, the committee's consideration of the draft proposal of "A Positive International Cartel Program" resulted in the decision "that enforcement of a prohibitions convention must be left to individual governments which become parties to the agreement." The enforcement question coincided with the committee's framing of "cartel provisions for inclusion in the charter of an international bank." The interdependencies meant "that no new cartel connections involving American capital and participation should develop or old ones be reestablished before an international cartel policy has been formulated .... otherwise investment funds would flow to areas of least regulation." Still, if an international bank were established, it could "deny loans to cartelized firms or to governments not adhering to an appropriate international cartel policy." These matters arose as the committee examined the monopoly and cartel issues Allied governments and military forces faced in occupying Italy. In the aid negotiations from September through October, the committee undertook discussions with members of a British "cartel discussion group," while it initiated "a review

---

[94] "Special Committee on Monopoly and Cartels," October 14, 1943 (Mason, Cartel Committee, Notter Files, RG 59, Box 34, NA); Blum, *V Was for Victory*, 140.

[95] Quotes in "Special Committee on Monopoly and Cartels," November 5 and 19, 1943, 1 (Mason, Cartel Committee, Notter Files, RG 59, Box 34, NA).

of European administrative experience, an examination of changes brought about by war and German domination, a study of the relation between cartel problems and national security and special consideration of the Soviet Union's interest in cartel questions."[96]

By December 1943, the committee had formalized its "positive program" for dealing with international cartels. The committee called for an "international convention" signed by participating nations. In order to comply with this convention, Congress would have to rewrite various "national patent and trade mark laws … so that licensing contracts may no longer provide legal cover for what would otherwise be prohibited agreements and so that technological improvements may be more accessible." Another "international convention" was called for "to facilitate the development of scientific research" through "international machinery for cooperation so that new technology will be made widely and speedily available to business firms." Finally, the committee proposed an International Office for Industrial Studies devoted to seeking international cooperation among governments in order to address problems of "inherently unstable industries," to prepare international conferences, and to promote study of international economic problems. "Power of decision would, however, be reserved to individual countries." Still, the committee suggested neither how the U.S. government might achieve congressional ratification of such wide-ranging conventions which limited national sovereignty, nor how to mobilize the necessary congressional support for the sorts of contentious changes in antitrust legislation that seemed too divisive to attain.[97]

These proposals coincided with recommendations for canceling cartel agreements with "enemy" companies. As the committee grappled with the mazes of anticompetitive agreements, the Alien Property Custodian saw the need for legal authorization from the Justice and State Departments "for the cancellation of cartel contracts with enemy firms." The Cartel Committee's deputy chairman, Edward Mason, transmitted through its superior, the Committee for Coordination of Economic Policy Work chaired by Myron Taylor, for approval by Acheson, Berge, and the Alien Property Custodian, a report stating the "various procedures available to the APC by which substantial progress might be achieved in eliminating illegal contracts which restrict the use of technology or access to markets by American firms", and which could "so far as possible make available to American industry, without restriction, the patents, and technical know-how

---

[96] Quoted in, successively, "Special Committee on Monopoly and Cartels," November 29, 12, 5, 1943, 1 (Mason, Cartel Committee, Notter Files, RG 59, Box 34, NA).

[97] Quoted in "Special Committee on Private Monopolies and Cartels," December 11, 1943, 1, 2, Mason, Cartel Committee; see also Cartel Memo.16A, "A Positive International Cartel Program," December 7, 1943, both in Notter Files, RG 59, Box 34, NA.

involved." Mason observed that invalidating of the enemy firms' "cartel contracts" and opening their technology to American industry "would contribute to the security and economic welfare of the United States." The program would also provide a reference point in discussions with Canada and Britain, which confronted similar situations.[98]

Since the Lend-Lease Act of 1941, aid negotiations between Britain and America had wide-ranging implications for war and peacemaking. Roosevelt had narrowly won congressional authorization of Lend-Lease in return for amendments ensuring congressional accounting of the aid appropriations. After Pearl Harbor, congressional influence steadily expanded into areas affecting virtually all economic foreign policy. In 1943, Roosevelt attempted to retain control within the executive bureaucracy of the State Department's program for aid to war-torn areas of Europe through the establishment of the United Nations Relief and Rehabilitation Administration. Ultimately, however, in order for the organization to receive funding, Roosevelt and Secretary of State Hull had to defer to congressional oversight and accept amendments. These realities provided the context for the U.S.–British aid negotiations of September–October 1943, and for the Cartel Committee's contemporaneous work on the "positive program for dealing with international cartels." Mason and Edwards engaged British officials, including economist James E. Meade, regarding antitrust issues. Meade had dealt with international cartel issues as a British member of the League of Nation's economic policy bureau. After the war began, he became a civil service economist in the British government's economic warfare ministry.[99]

Meade's personal diary recounted the positions of officials during the aid negotiations. Prior to arriving in Washington, British diplomats had prepared negotiating positions on state-trading and agricultural subsidies, the complex interconnections between competition and cooperation involving commodity agreements, and an international development bank and monetary policy. But London's senior government ministers had not developed, Meade noted, an official stance on the international cartels "problem." Even so, since the 1930s, Meade had been one of small group of British academics and civil servants who, influenced by the League of Nation's cartel work, had discussed establishing some sort of British and even international antitrust regime. This work gained immediacy in reaction to the Nazis' deployment of the "German cartel system" to mobilize war-making capabilities through the New Economic Order they imposed

[98] Mason to Myron Taylor, December 28, 1943, 1, 2, Mason, Cartel Committee, Notter Files, RG 59, Box 34, NA.

[99] Blum, *V Was for Victory*, 305–8; James E. Meade Diaries, Mission to US, vol. 1, section 1/ 1, September–October 1943, British Library of Political and Economic Science Archives/ London School of Economics (BLPESA/LSE).

on conquered European nations. As a result, the British government did consider the value of instituting a competition policy regime in the Keynesian "mixed economy" of postwar Britain. Accordingly, as the aid negotiations proceeded, senior London ministers provided Meade, Sir Percivale Liesching, and other colleagues no formal instructions on the cartel and monopoly issue, encouraging a reactive role as they consulted with the Americans.[100]

Meade's diary revealed the contrasting perceptions of the "cartel problem." Within the British delegation's "group ... dealing with Cartels," he was assigned leading responsibility, even though "[u]nfortunately we cannot say much" given that "our ministers at home" had not "made up their minds on the problem." In initial meetings with the Americans, discussions involved the "prospects of anti-monopoly action in the U.K." and the difficult "distinction between Commodity Agreements and Cartels." At the State Department he heard Mason give an "introductory speech, followed by the super-trust buster Edwards." Meade assessed as "superb" Edwards's "wealth of illustrative detail" distinguishing among the "regular cartel," the "giant concern" and the "patent pool." While the British "adopted a passive listening role" and did not address directly Mason's "point-blank" questions whether "the British were willing to discuss ... the matter of international cartels," Meade found Edwards's presentation "certainly a very strong one." Even so, Meade was chosen "to draw up a revised agenda with Mason for the future discussions" of the "Anglo-American Cartels Committee." Shortly thereafter in a meeting which included economist Paul Sweezy, one of Mason's Harvard students, Meade's topical agenda was accepted. "I think," his diary entry read, "we have made a very unexpectedly favorable impression by fuzzeling an Agenda which is really forthcoming on the subject." The effort dissipated the "impression of [British] 'crazyness' " on these issues.[101]

By early October, the respective views came into sharper focus. At a meeting of the joint "Cartels group," Meade "made a general statement emphasizing that the U.K. after the war might ... adopt a 'mixed economy,' " including an antitrust regime possessing five policy objectives: "fact finding and publicity"; the distinguishing of substantive policy choices toward "Patent Laws, Company Laws, Restraint of Trade"; authority to pursue "Trust-busting"; state-owned or -operated companies requiring "Public Regulation"; and state intervention in the form of "Public Management." Instituting this national antitrust regime provided the basis for an "economic organization" capable of establishing an "international solution of the problem, as in the case of commercial policy," concerning

[100] Meade Diaries, Mission to US, vol. 1, section 1/1, September–October 1943, BLPESA/LSE, 12, 58, 66, 73–4, 87–8, 99, 121.
[101] *Ibid.*, 58, 66, 73–4, 87–8.

commodity agreements tariffs and trade. Edwards, the "god-like prophet of trust-busting on the American side," Meade observed, "made some extremely good interventions on the general problem of monopoly control." The British responded "with a searching cross-examination of Edwards to see how far American trust-busting law relied on precise definitions of prohibited monopolistic practices" as opposed to "case-made law by legal interpretations of what is 'unreasonable' in restraint of trade." Favoring the "latter" rule of reason approach, Meade perceived that, as Mason had implied initially, the "Americans are thinking of suggesting" many "precise prohibitions for external policy when these have not been found to work in [U.S.] internal policy."[102]

As the meetings closed, Meade's diary recorded his personal, not official, reaction to the American proposals. "The Americans are just about 100% right in their diagnosis of the dangers of uncontrolled monopoly organization," he wrote, though he did not support an enforcement regime based on per se prohibitions. Nevertheless, the Americans' faith in such prohibitions was clear. At the Treasury Department, members of the Anglo-American Cartels Group heard "an impassioned speech" about the "security aspects of international cartels, asserting that most cartels have been the instrument for German exchange, etc." In that context, the group considered the "possibility of action in the international sphere." In addition, they "suggested a number of legal arrangements (patent law, company law etc) which they would like to see reformed; and suggested the institution of an international body to fact find, police and regulate international cartel management." In responding officially, Meade was "careful to be very non-committal and cagey without appearing non-cooperative. This is a role I like, – particularly when I agree so thoroughly with the Americans!" Drafting the final document was a "tricky job": it must offer qualified approval of international cartel regulation in principle "but refrain" from "making any suggestions" to London Ministers concerning the "touchy subject of international monopolies."[103]

Meade's diary also suggested wider long-term outcomes of the aid negotiations which proved to be prophetic. On September 9, he wrote that "American 'imperialism' would be much preferable to American isolationism and complete withdrawal and that we cannot hope for a new international order without [an] ... interventionist force of which the USA, one hopes, would form the core." Thus, amidst the qualified internationalist sentiments arising from the U.S. Congress by late 1943, Meade observed that "[a] mixture of American 'imperialism,' Anglo-American Alliance, United Nations organization, and full-blooded Wilsonian idealist universalism is probably the best for which we can hope. Of these the essential first thing to work for is, I am sure, a close Anglo-American

[102] *Ibid.*, 99–100.   [103] *Ibid.*, 100, 109, 116–17, 121.

understanding." Even so, during the summer of 1944, the British and other Allies won at Bretton Woods some limits on U.S. domination of the International Monetary Fund and the International Bank for Reconstruction and Development. Similarly, the United States made modest concessions in the Charter of the United Nations negotiated at Dumbarton Oaks in August 1944. In each case, while powerful business groups and their congressional representatives offered general support, they contended that these organizations threatened U.S. sovereignty. Accordingly, after Roosevelt's death and Truman's succession to the presidency, these international agreements received congressional approval at least in part because they formally accepted the budget oversight authority of Congress.[104]

While Meade and his colleagues contributed to the Anglo-American discussions regarding international cartels, Mason, Edwards, and the other Cartel Committee members worked on the "Positive Program Dealing with International Cartels" and the recommendations for vesting the Alien Property Custodian with authority to terminate patent and cartel agreements involving enemy companies. Meade's references to an international body possessing the powers of fact gathering – geared to specified prohibitions which required extensive "reform" of American as well as foreign patent, corporate, and commercial law – corresponded to the particular provisions and rationales stated in the "Positive Program." Moreover, Edwards's vigorous antitrust activism suggested that one goal Americans surreptitiously pursued was an international order capable of enforcing a stronger antitrust regime. Indeed, Edwards soon became a foremost exponent of the activist view; Mason, by contrast, fashioned economic theories to improve the enforcement efficiency of antitrust litigation.[105]

Finally, Meade's references to British concerns about distinguishing commodity or patent agreements from cartels reflected a larger context. Throughout the interwar period, officials and business leaders of industrial nations, as well as League of Nations authorities and academic experts, observed that commodity agreements, involving agricultural products and industrial goods such as coal or finished steel possessed a dual character: private firms entered into anticompetitive agreements that received direct or indirect legal sanction from governments. In addition, through patents and other devices, governments authorized various anticompetitive practices facilitating private firms' development of technology – especially in chemicals and electronics – which in turn could be transferred through license agreements to firms in other nations. These arrangements imposed contractual obligations. But in policy terms, a dichotomy existed between anticompetitive contracts involving the state as well as private parties, and

[104] *Ibid.*, 42; Blum, *V Was for Victory*, 302–16; Aaronson, *Trade and the American Dream*, 34–49; Heardon, *Architects of Globalism*, 39–64, 147–200.
[105] Compare notes 97–8 and 100–3 above.

those to which only private firms agreed. The state-supported contracts often arose in commodity agreements receiving tariff or currency exchange protection which contributed to the nationalist-militarism and racial identity politics of Germany and Japan. Moreover, the attention Meade and his colleagues gave to commodity agreements indicated that liberal Britain and its empire, including Australia, Canada, and New Zealand promoted or otherwise authorized anticompetitive trade and cartel preferences.[106]

Broader political tensions shaped U.S. wartime and postwar trade policy. Secretary of State Hull's famous support for trade liberalism did not ameliorate his doubts regarding the multilateral approach linking full employment and commercial policy. State Department experts incorporated the multilateral approach into what became the ITO during 1945 in preparation for the London Conference of 1946. But as early as the Lend-Lease aid negotiations of fall 1943, State Department experts divided between proponents of the comprehensive trade organization approach and those who favored giving the president greater discretion under the Reciprocal Trade Agreements Act (RTAA). Political conflicts within the executive branch and between it and Congress undermined passage of the ITO charter while the GATT eventually became the basis of postwar policy.[107]

The contentious cartel issues further agitated trade politics. The RTAA encountered repeated criticism during periodic congressional renewal; Clayton and other State Department officials resisted tying the GATT and ITO too much to congressional authority. The confrontation paralleled the disputed passage of the UN, International Monetary Fund, and the Development Bank during 1944–45 that tested the divergent powers of Congress and the executive toward budgetary authority and national sovereignty. Moreover, the ITO and GATT enmeshed Congress and the president in the clash of farm and industrial special interests that had bedeviled national politics and foreign commercial policy since the nation's beginning. Nevertheless, the GATT's jurisdiction over tariff and trade policies involving only governments was less contentious than the ITO's dual authority which – primarily due to the antitrust provisions – embraced the interconnections between private and state anticompetitive commodity agreements. The GATT ultimately prevailed in 1947–48 primarily because it "was tailored to fit the grant of legislative authority to the executive under the 1945 extension of the RTAA." Thus, the Truman administration's trade officials argued, the "RTAA did not authorize the executive branch to sign a treaty or build an international organization." Indeed, they were "careful to portray the GATT simply as a trade agreement."[108]

Less conspicuous bureaucratic politics further reshaped the struggle over internationalizing antitrust. The Justice Department had won from the

[106] *Ibid.*; see notes 77 and 104 above.
[107] Aaronson, *Trade and the American Dream*, 38–49.   [108] *Ibid.*, 82, 83.

federal district court initial criminal indictments against DuPont and National Lead on June 28, 1943. In mid-1944, Roosevelt supported the Department's prosecution despite vigorous opposition from the military departments. Roosevelt's approval went against the British government's strong appeals on behalf of Imperial Chemical Industries (ICI), a leading contractor of both the British procurement authorities and several American firms under federal indictment. Historians later argued that the improved military and strategic imperatives over the months culminating in D-day explained the antitrust "revival." The service departments won one delay and sought another. Meanwhile, beginning in late 1943, the Antitrust Division had been giving publicized testimony before the Kilgore committee. The revelations that DuPont and other U.S. multinational corporations had recently had extensive international cartel connections not only with German firms, but also with ICI, legitimized the Justice Department's image as a defender of U.S. wartime security. The publicity undercut the service departments' credibility in asserting that they should dominate compliance.[109]

Still more obscure bureaucratic maneuvering benefited the Justice Department. In November 1943, a memorandum for Roosevelt's legal advisor, Samuel I. Rosenman, queried, "Don't you think the Administration ought to take the leadership on doing something about cartels?" Prompting the question was legislation that Wyoming Senator Joseph C. O'Mahoney had introduced in October mandating the registration of any foreign contracts, including commodity agreements of multinational corporations and their subsidiaries. Although the bill did not pass, it encouraged various officials to offer the president, through Rosenman, their expertise regarding cartels. During January and February 1944, two members of the Board of Economic Warfare, Irene Till and Jean Pajus – pursuing contacts with Eleanor Roosevelt – presented to Rosenman their evidence. They revealed the international cartel issues' complex bearing on the O'Mahoney Bill, bureaucratic relations within the executive branch and between it and Congress impinging on the service departments' procurement demands and foreign policy concerns arising from the DuPont–ICI case, and relations with enemy nations. Till and Pajus saw the need for an office within the State Department to monitor the complex cartel interrelationships; the proposed office would provide ongoing fact-gathering but

---

[109] Compare Wells, *Antitrust*, 96–107; Blum, *V Was for Victory*, 136–140 with Wendell Berge, to D. J. Brady, August 18, 1944, at the White House, Official File #277, Anti-Trust Laws, FDRL, which includes correspondence among Attorney General Biddle, Secretary of the Navy Forrestal, and Acting Secretary of War Patterson concerning postponements in the cases against National Lead, DuPont, and others; these documents summarize litigations, June 1943–July 1944, and include Lord Halifax to Cordell Hull, April 27, 1944 appealing on ICI's behalf and Roosevelt, Memorandum for the Attorney General, August 14, 1944, authorizing the Justice Department to proceed.

would not displace the policy role of Cartel Committee. Till and Pajus also suggested that Roosevelt should author a public letter calling upon Hull to deal with the cartel issue.[110]

Roosevelt acted on these solicitations. In late January, he discussed the Till–Pajus materials with Rosenman; by early March he advised the director of the budget accordingly. Roosevelt learned from Attorney General Biddle that the Army's Civil Affairs Division, the State Department, and the OSS were "more or less actively engaged in investigations of cartels." The president decided that "[a]s the Antitrust Division of the Department of Justice has been active in this field for several years, and it is well staffed to do the investigation work, I suggest that the work should be concentrated there." By March 22, Roosevelt approved an Executive Order creating an "interdepartmental" Executive Committee on Economic Foreign Policy. "Since cartel policies affect the operations of a dozen or more Government units, the Committee ... will facilitate consistency between cartel and other economic policies," the memorandum stated, especially given the "confusion in our many-sided foreign economic policies" and "interagency rivalries." In April, the Bureau of the Budget reported to Roosevelt as follows: "In order that Justice may operate as the central repository of cartel data, within the United States, all agencies should transmit such data to Justice." Moreover, "Investigation abroad of cartels will have expanded importance as new sources of information are opened up in liberated and enemy areas. The Foreign Service of State should be prepared to render investigatory assistance to all agencies concerned."[111]

Among Roosevelt's cabinet members, the cartel issue gained momentum throughout 1944. During the summer, after attempting to have James Byrnes resolve the interdepartmental clash over the Justice Department's prosecutions of high profile cases, Roosevelt personally intervened in favor of Attorney General Biddle. In addition, while the Kilgore Committee publicized the cartel issue, Treasury Secretary Henry Morgenthau began formulating his idea for imposing upon conquered Germany an agricultural economy in order to prevent its revival as an industrial, militaristic, and racist power. By September, Morgenthau wrote to Eleanor Roosevelt thanking her for "transmitting the memorandum on German cartels

---

[110] Oscar Cox, Memorandum for Judge Samuel I. Rosenman, November 1, 1943 and attached bill O'Mahoney introduced into the Senate, October, 25, 1943; Till and Pajus to Eleanor Roosevelt, January 12, 1944, and Till and Pajus Memorandum for Rosenman, February 19, 1944, Rosenman Papers [SIRP], Folder 6, Cartels, FDRL.

[111] Franklin D. Roosevelt Memorandum to S.I. Rosenman, January 24, 1944, referring to attached letter, Till and Pajus to Eleanor Roosevelt, January 12, 1944, SIRP, Folder 6, Cartels, FDRL; Draft Memorandum from the President to Harold Smith, March 3, 1944; Donald C. Stone Memorandum to Judge Rosenman, March 22, 1944; H.S. Memorandum for the President, "Cartel Work of Federal Agencies," April, 15, 1944, Official File, #277, Anti-Trust Laws, FDRL.

prepared by Mr. Pajus. I found his recommendations of special interest … and I have turned over the material to my staff" for "their use." As
Morgenthau's plan gained Roosevelt's approval but divided the Cabinet,
opponents argued that its harshness would strengthen German resistance.
Meanwhile, Vice President Henry Wallace's "attacks on cartels and his
advocacy of stringent enforcement of the antitrust laws" angered business
leaders and their political allies. As Roosevelt prepared to run for a fourth
presidential term, a memorandum from Rosenman stated, "I think it would
be advisable for you, some time in early September, to make a statement … on the subject of *international cartels* (emphasis in the original)."[112]

Meanwhile, the State Department and its Cartel Committee addressed
the issues raised by Rosenman. Between February and June 1944, Under
Secretary of State Edward R. Stettinius, Jr., evaluated reports of "Allegations Concerning Cartel Matters," which closely paralleled Till's and
Pajus's critical assessment, an "Inventory of Economic Policy Recommendations" on "Monopolies and Cartels" expanding upon the "Positive
Program" generated by Deputy Chairman Mason's Cartel Committee in
1943, and finally, a "Tentative Program for Dealing with International
Cartels." This last proposal regarded cartels as "harmful in general and
contrary to the liberal economic policy we would like to see after the war."
It rejected both "unilateral prohibition" by the United States as "ineffective" and any "acceptance of cartels in principle." Favoring instead an
"International Agreement with other nations to eliminate objectionable
cartel activities," the "Tentative Program" advocated "a coordinated
program under which each nation would undertake to regulate cartels
coming within its jurisdiction." It advised that "[n]ational laws regarding
patents, trade marks, etc. would be adjusted to make restrictive cartel
practices more difficult," and an "international office of business practices
might be established to coordinate efforts to restrict cartels." Conceding
that "some cartel activities in the interest of international security, con-
servation of national resources, … might not be offensive," the program
recommended that they "be carried on by intergovernmental agreements
rather than by agreements between individuals."[113]

---

[112] Michael Beschloss, *The Conquerors Roosevelt, Truman, and the Destruction of Hitler's Germany, 1941–1945* (New York, 2002), 63–215; Eleanor Roosevelt to Morgenthau, September 22, 1944, and Morgenthau to Roosevelt, September, 29 1944, and attached Pajus Memorandum to Frank Coe, "A Policy toward German Cartels," September, 14, 1944, Morgenthau Diaries, Microfilm, Diary 777: 99–101, Reel 225, 9/29–10/9, 1944; Diary, 777: 103–10, Reel 225, 9/29–10/9, 1944, FDRL; Blum, *V Was for Victory*, 287; Rosenman Memorandum to the President, August 17, 1944, SIRP, Folder 6, Cartels, FDRL.

[113] Compare evidence in note 110 above with "Memorandum re: Allegations Concerning Cartel Matters," February 3, 1944, and see other memoranda titles noted in text, including

In September, Roosevelt transmitted a letter to Hull urging action on the cartel issue. Since January, Rosenman had effectively promoted the cartel issue with the president. He encouraged Roosevelt's support for appropriations to fund the Justice Department's fact-gathering and litigation work despite the military departments' procurement demands. Thus, the president's decision favoring Attorney General Biddle in the court cases of summer 1944 was part of wider bureaucratic maneuvering reflecting the letter's contentious origins. Roosevelt's support of Biddle suggested, however, that the Justice Department's influence depended upon maintaining links through the Cartel Committee to the State Department's war and peacemaking objectives. Accordingly, Rosenman's August 17 memorandum precipitating Roosevelt's public letter of September cast the issue in terms of the divided but generally sympathetic British attitude toward cartels. Crediting Secretary Hull with getting the British to "carry on cartel discussions" despite their desire to "postpone them entirely until after the war," he said, "I think it should be pushed now while the cohesive force of the war is in effect." Rosenman noted that Roosevelt's antimonopoly policy proclaimed in 1938 was consistent with the work of the State Department's "very good Inter-departmental Committee ... on the subject of cartels."[114]

The relationship between the State and Justice departments, however, became strained. On September 6, 1944, Herbert J. Seligmann published through the Overseas News Agency a story, "Crushed Reich Pins Hope on Cartels." The story publicized the Kilgore Committee's revelations of the Justice Department's evidence exposing the ongoing influence of German cartelized big business despite the inevitable German military defeat, suggesting conspiracies to maintain American multinational corporations' involvement in these cartels. Seligmann publicized, too, certain British business leaders' stated preference for the postwar perpetuation of international cartels. The story reported the Justice Department's resistance to the State Department's willingness to countenance government sanction of private international cartel agreements. Seligmann noted the clash over allowing an international anticompetitive agreement in the petroleum industry authorizing the "exclusion of low-priced Middle East oil from the United States." If allowed, the agreement could promote government–business "monopoly control" of "chemical, rubber, steel, tanning material, and other

"DIGEST OF PWC DOCUMENTS 169 AND 178 – CARTELS," June 30, 1944, quote at 1, Edward R. Stettinius Papers (ERSP), Box 720, Folder Committees-Cartels, University of Virginia Library Special Collections (UVLSC); compare his evidence with "A Tentative Program," April 29, 1944, Notter Files, RG 59, Box 35, NA. But see Wells, *Antitrust*, 107–16.

[114] Roosevelt to Hull, September 6, 1944, Official Files, Box 3, 1944–45, FDRL; Rosenman Memorandum to the President, August 17, 1944, SIRP, Folder 6, Cartels, FDRL, quotes at 1, 2.

colossi … as they did before the war." He warned that "unscrambling this Nazi spider web is no child's play" and that "German business is on the march." He thought that only the president could achieve the "State Department's policy alignment with that of the Justice Department."[115]

Notwithstanding its conspiratorial overtones, Seligmann's story reflected widely accepted images within and outside the government. During September, Morgenthau read and incorporated into his plan Pajus's anti-German cartel insights. In a phone conversation discussing the conclusions of his committee report recommending the decentralization and demilitarization of Germany, Kilgore told Morgenthau that "your plan and mine fairly well coincide." Morgenthau replied, "There's no question about it." Days before, critical of Republican Governor Thomas E. Dewey's charge that Morgenthau had put "'fight into the German army,' prolonging the war and killing American boys," the *New York Post* declared that the Kilgore Committee's report and the "Morgenthau Plan" supported the evidence in the "statements and proposals of Justice Department experts who have been studying German industry ever since the war first started." Every source reinforced the conclusion that unless the Allies' postwar peace programs destroyed the militaristic "cartel tradition" forever, German instigation of "World War III" was inevitable. Indeed, in May, California Congressman Jerry Voorhis delivered a speech which, he told Truman, "deals with the danger to future peace inherent in the resumption of cartel agreements with German firms and in the attempts, already underway, on the part of German industry to escape from allied controls."[116]

Defenders of big business had also publicized their views. Since the *Alcoa* case began, the State and Justice departments wrestled with a policy issue: U.S. multinational corporations were accountable to the antitrust laws at home, whereas abroad, national laws and culture presumed the legitimacy of cartels and other anticompetitive practices. Milo Perkins, former head of the Board of Economic Warfare, urged the State Department to institute a process for authorizing cartel agreements among foreign firms, governments, and U.S. multinational corporations so that American business would not lose its export advantage. In congressional testimony during June 1944, a senior executive for Standard Oil and former ambassador, James W. Gerard, speaking as a corporate stockholder, agreed. The Justice Department's antitrust enforcement activism compounded the disadvantage, they asserted, because managerial operations, investment decisions, and product research and technology were caught between contrary

---

[115] Story located at WBP Box 43, File A/Berge, LC.

[116] Morgenthau Diaries, Microfilm, Diary 796: 21–2, Reel 230, 11/17–11/28, 1944, Transcript of conversation between Senator Kilgore and Morgenthau, November 17, 1944, and Diary 794: 277–8, Reel 229, 11/5–11/16, 1944, reprint from *New York Post*, November, 14, 1944, "The Kilgore Conclusions," and quotes from Voorhis to President Truman, May 19, 1945, HSTP, White House Central Files, HSTL.

rules as to what constituted legitimate business. The testimony of international commercial lawyer Gilbert Montague, whose clients included these interests, observed pointedly that "[i]f American nationals, under these circumstances, are liable to prosecution by the Department of Justice they will be as completely debarred by the United States from doing business abroad as were the nationals of China and Japan during the centuries when these were the 'hermit nations.'"[117]

During the transition from war to peace, strategic postwar peacemaking further exacerbated the issue. At the Yalta Conference, Roosevelt, Churchill, and Stalin agreed to postwar objectives, which included eradication of cartels and monopolies defined by images equating Nazi militarism with the cartel tradition. After Germany's surrender, the Potsdam Declaration included anti-cartel language: "At the earliest practicable date,.the German economy shall be decentralized for the purpose of eliminating the present excessive concentration of economic power as exemplified in particular by cartels, syndicates, trusts, and other monopolistic arrangements." Moreover, although the influence of the Morgenthau Plan.steadily dissipated under Truman's administration, the Potsdam Declaration stated, "[i]n organizing the German economy, primary emphasis shall be given to the development of agriculture and peaceful domestic industry." The surrender terms that Japanese leaders signed accepted the Potsdam Declaration, including the antitrust language. Still, regarding Japan, the antimonopoly and anticartel imagery applied to eradicating the ties between *zaibatsu* family holding companies whose alliance with Japanese militarists, many experts believed, had fostered war with America.[118]

The Cartel Committee confronted the divisions over the Allied occupation governments' policies. As early as August 1945, General Lucius Clay, the military commander of the U.S. zone of Occupied Germany, received reports from his field units that hunger and social tensions threatened implementation of the peace programs imposed by the Potsdam Declaration. He confronted divided counsel from his subordinates regarding the enforcement of the Potsdam Declaration's anticartel and antimonopoly provisions. One group, reflecting the sentiments of big business and influential congressional Republicans, argued that any antitrust policy would undercut the reconstruction of the German economy, which in turn would open the way to radical political influences. An opposing group urged Clay

---

[117] Whittlesey, *National Interest and International Cartels* (1946), 55–75, quote at 58, 59, 59–60.

[118] Quotes from "Agreed Report of the Tripartite Conference of Berlin," August 3, 1945, Isador Lubin Papers, Box 104, German Reparations, FDRL, 6; ch. V, part I.

to pursue active antitrust enforcement upon which a more competitive capitalist economy could be built.[119]

Division among occupation authorities also emerged in Japan regarding the bearing antitrust had on postwar recovery. General Douglas MacArthur established a unique role in the occupation of Japan. Unlike Clay, who within Germany shared authority with French, Russian, and British zonal commanders, MacArthur was the Supreme Commander Allied Powers. In November 1945, he enforced the Potsdam Declaration, ordering the Japanese government to enact antimonopoly measures. The most conspicuous target was the *zaibatsu* family holding companies and their alliances with the nation's defeated militarists. The policy toward the *zaibatsu* nonetheless split authorities within MacArthur's General Headquarters. Those sharing the views of Joseph C. Grew, the ambassador to Japan before Pearl Harbor, thought that a limited dismantling of the *zaibatsu* was indeed necessary to eradicate the militarist influence but that antimonopoly policy should not threaten the recovery of Japan's postwar economy. An opposing group of self-described New Dealers advocated creating a competitive capitalist economy by subjecting the *zaibatsu* to massive trust busting.[120]

The Cartel Committee reported similar contentiousness concerning the emerging ITO. Indeed, Truman had not approved the Executive Committee's entire ITO program by September 1945. Accordingly, the Truman administration developed a multiple strategy toward Congress and foreign governments, publically supporting the RTAA, the ITO, and what became the GATT. The equivocation toward commodity agreements emerging in 1945 proved fatal to the ITO in the long run.[121]

VI. CONCLUSION

In the same September 1945 memorandum proposing the revised ITO, Acheson noted that negotiations with the British were about to begin. By March 1946, the Truman administration's preference for the GATT approach was apparent. James Meade wrote in his diary, "We did not want to encourage the American view that a reduction of trade barriers was all that was necessary to preserve full employment," a central goal of the Labour government's postwar "mixed" Keynesian economy. Suggesting a view not inconsistent with the ITO, Meade concluded, "our view" should be "that domestic policies were necessary to ensure full employment and

[119] Robert P. Terrill, executive secretary to members of the Committee on Private Monopolies and Cartels, Cartel Memo 167, November 1, 1945, Notter Files, RG 59, Box 35, NA; ch. V, part I.

[120] See ch. IV, part I; on Ambassador Grew, see ch. II, part IV.

[121] Dean Acheson, Memorandum for the President, "Proposal to Establish an International Trade Organization," September 7, 1945, HSTP, White House Files, Confidential Files, HSTL, 1–4, quote at 3.

that an effective application of such policies was almost a necessary condition for the successful carrying out of a policy of reduction of tariffs and other trade barriers." Even so, by the fall of 1947, after a dispute with Australia, the Departments of State and Agriculture agreed to reduce the U.S. tariff duties on wool. The government's "provisional" authorization of the GATT which followed in January 1, 1948, "did not include the ITO's articles on the maintenance of employment and subsidies ... The GATT did not even include all of the commercial policy provisions covered in the ITO charter!"[122]

As the ITO's fate emerged, antitrust activists increasingly pursued a unilateral enforcement policy with mixed success. Acheson reminded Truman that the ITO "provisions regarding cartels were concurred in by you in a conversation with Mr. Clayton and Mr. Mason on May 17, 1945." Yet that same year, several significant cases postponed during the war reached decision. Most importantly, in the long-running *Alcoa* litigation, federal appellate judge Learned Hand reversed the lower court, upholding the Justice Department. The decision strengthened monopoly doctrines limiting big business within U.S. territory and extended the extraterritorial application of antitrust. The U.S. judiciary expanded both the monopoly and extraterritorial doctrines to impose antitrust abroad. During the same period, the divisions between antitrust activists and their opponents agitated occupation governments. In Germany, Clay followed the State Department's call to reject activist enforcement; this action in 1948 precipitated media criticism, a War Department investigation, and congressional inquires. Ironically, Clay's shift encouraged German proponents to develop their own antitrust regime. In Japan, although the *zaibatsu* breakup was more moderate than what either the New Dealer antitrust activists or Corwin Edwards – who authored a special report supporting their position– had hoped, the Japanese did pass the strong Antimonopoly Law of 1947. Within two years, however, antitrust critics supported weakening the law through amendments to foster Japan's economic recovery as a cold war bastion.[123]

Meanwhile, Mason left his wartime dual positions in the Office of Strategic Services (OSS) and the Cartel Committee. Back at Harvard he organized graduate student research projects to study how antitrust enforcement at home and in the U.S. Occupation government of Germany affected the State Department's proposed ITO, including the administration of the commodity agreements. His book, *Controlling World Trade Cartels and Commodity Agreements* expressed qualified support for the ITO if efficient bureaucratic planning prevailed. In this connection, he criticized,

---

[122] *Ibid.*; James E. Meade Cabinet Office Diaries, vol. IV, March–September 1946, BLPES/ LSE, quotes at 2–3; Aaronson, *Trade and the American Dream*, 80–3, quote at 82.

[123] Dean Acheson, Memorandum for the President, 3; *U.S. v. Aluminum Co. of America*, 148 F. 2d 416 (C. C. App. 2d Cir., 1945); ch. IV, part I; ch. V, part I.

Thurman Arnold's, the Justice Department's, and the Antitrust Division's aggressive campaign to expose the national security threat engendered by U.S. big business' involvement in international cartels and patent agreements. It was a "real question," Mason exclaimed, "whether over-exaggeration of the cartel problem has not already gone far toward discrediting antimonopoly policy in general and, by confusing legitimate with illegitimate business practices, has not contributed materially to an unsound relationship between business and government in the United States." Since the 1930s, Mason promoted economic efficiency theories to improve antitrust enforcement. At the same time, he believed in expanded bureaucracies like the ITO to offset the power of big business. Thus, trusting in efficient big bureaucracies, Mason opposed the activist antitrust campaign Arnold and his successors mounted against international cartels and monopolies. Arnold, by contrast, consistently distrusted bureaucratic "planners."[124]

The divergence between Mason and Arnold suggested an emerging postwar compromise consensus. As a federal judge, Arnold periodically delivered public addresses reaffirming the belief that, notwithstanding certain exceptions pertaining to commodity agreements, the courts provided the most effective remedies against cartels and monopolies. Moreover, from 1943 to 1945, Arnold's decisions on patents, observed one commentator in 1946, "may be accepted as embodying advanced judicial thinking on the relation of patents to competition and monopoly." Although Justice Hugo Black and other dissenters basically accepted Arnold's views, the Supreme Court generally did not. Nevertheless, beginning with the *Alcoa* decision of 1945, the court reshaped the economic efficiency theories pioneered by Mason, employing antimonopoly and extraterritorial doctrines to mount an aggressive and ultimately successful attack on international cartels. Meanwhile, during the initial postwar years, Edwards, Kronstein, and others attempted to reconcile Arnold's activism to the multinational approach epitomized by the ITO. As these efforts gradually failed, the activists turned to a judicially enforced unilateral antitrust policy. Finally, the State and Justice departments agreed that within this unilateralism, the government would, on a case-by-case basis, authorize anticompetitive agreements involving governments while it promoted other nations' adopting antitrust regimes.[125]

[124] (New York, 1946), 98–9; Arnold, *Bottlenecks of Business*, 92, 15–19.
[125] "Address by the Honorable Thurman Arnold, Associate Justice of the Court of Appeals for the District of Columbia," February 8, 1944; Thurman Arnold, "Speech to American Business Congress," March 17, 1944, Waldorf-Astoria Hotel, NYC, TWAP, Box 4, AHCUW; "Let's Face the Issue – Are Cartels Necessary?" February 25, 1945, radio show script and transcript, TWAP, Box 106, AHCUW; see also Thurman Arnold, "The A-B-C of Cartels," *Credit Executive* (January–February 1943), TWAP, Box 81, AHCUW, 196–8, 227–8; Whittlesey, *National Interest and International Cartels* (1946), 86–93, quote at 88–9.

2

Protectionism Over Competition:
Europe, Australia, and Japan 1930–1945

The Great Depression tested the strength of capitalist institutions in the world's industrial nations, fostering war. The economic policies that governments imposed reflected a divergent liberal and fascist public discourse. Government bureaucracies held capitalist enterprise accountable to conflicting images of national welfare. Each nation's bureaucracy possessed its own institutional culture and professional discourse shaping protectionist tariffs, currency restrictions, and cartel practices. The following discussion locates within political and cultural contexts the policies instituting protectionism over competition in German, British, Japanese, and Australian capitalism during the Great Depression and World War II. The argument is that each nation's bureaucrats and legal–economic experts implemented cartel and trade policies which held U.S. multinational corporations accountable to either liberal-democratic or fascist images of capitalism. In all four nations, the dominant policy enforced protectionism over competitive markets; within each nation, however, individuals possessing greater or lesser influence contested this triumph, thereby offering the image of a different capitalist order in the future.[1]

Section I considers the liberal-democratic and fascist policy discourse – reflecting not only the rejection of American style antitrust but also images of national identity – that British and German officials and economic experts applied to international cartels and U.S. multinational corporations. Focusing on British expert opinion toward international cartel regulation and Australia, Section II briefly explores the impact the British imperial system of trade preference had on promoting the latter's cartelized market capitalism and radical egalitarian social consensus between Conservative and Labor parties. Australia's experience was noteworthy because during

---

[1] The idea that competition and protectionist policy making reflect distinct and often contested images of capitalist order and national identity is suggested in Jeffrey R. Fear, "Constructing Big Business: The Cultural Concept of the Firm," in Alfred D. Chandler, Franco Amatori, and Takashi Hikino, eds., *Big Business and the Wealth of Nations* (Cambridge, UK, 1999), 546–74; Kevin M. Doak, "What Is a Nation and Who Belongs? National Narratives and the Ethnic Imagination in Twentieth-Century Japan," 102 *American Historical Review* (April 1997), 283–309; and Benedict Anderson, *Imagined Communities Reflections on the Origins and Spread of Nationalism* (London, 1991).

the Commonwealth's early history it had enacted and attempted to enforce an antitrust law whose language was borrowed in part from the Sherman Antitrust Act.

The discussion then turns to the distinctive culture and institutions defining Japan's unusual capitalist order and bureaucratic system. In Section III, the cartelization of the nation's capitalist order and militarization of society provides context for the economic discourse of two Japanese academics and a British economist who explain *zaibatsu* family capitalism's disputed dominance of small business, farmers, and workers. Section IV examines more closely how the Japanese bureaucracy's institutional culture – including the use of a comparative legal discourse which among other sources drew upon U.S. regulatory experience – permitted the *zaibatsu* wide autonomy in the administration of the Mobilization Laws, despite opposition from militant nationalists. This chapter considers the images of capitalist enterprise that each nation's public officials enforced during the Depression and World War II, including the rejection of American-style antitrust. German and Japanese fascists imagined a peace maintained through protectionist trade and cartel policies; British and Australian liberals, however, realized the need for constructing a peace built on a competitive international order, though the Americans and British disagreed over how to achieve that future.

I. EUROPEAN COUNTERPOINT: GERMANY AND GREAT BRITAIN

In contrast to American policies during the Depression and early war years, most German and British commentators employed a discourse defending cartel policies. Some commentators urged creating a transnational authority capable of regulating multinational corporations and the cartel movement, but political tensions rooted in national sovereignty defeated the effort.[2] In 1933, the Weimar government's fall and Adolf Hitler's ascendancy began Europe's slide toward the democracies' appeasement policy and World War II. Proclaiming a superior national identity, the National Socialists restricted foreign corporations. Asserting Keynesian economics and social welfare liberalism, Britain imposed trade protectionism through the system of imperial preference. In both nations, stronger competition policy had supporters, but only in Britain did they influence professional discourse.[3]

---

[2] "Report of the Delegation on Economic Depressions, Part II," No. C.I.M.I.1945.II.A., *Economic Stability in the Post-War World the Conditions of Prosperity after the Transition from War to Peace* (Geneva, 1945), 30, 31, 97, 108.

[3] Wyatt Wells, *Antitrust* (New York, 2002), 4–89, and see notes 4, 16, and 20.

The League of Nations disagreed about the international cartel issue, reflecting wider contention among European economic experts. Following years of dispute, the Depression shattered the faith British economists and policy makers had in laissez faire's self-regulating market relations, engendering a broad acceptance of anticompetitive business "rationalization" defined as "industrial self-government" promoting efficient technologies and preventing "wasteful" labor disorder and class conflict. In Germany, the Depression confirmed, by contrast, the dominant theories of historical economists who accepted government intervention in the marketplace – including enforcement of cartel agreements – as economically efficient and necessary to prevent social-class struggle. Economic experts from both nations were well informed about the contrasts between their countries' divergent experience with cartels and monopoly and the distinctive record of the United States. They rejected the judiciary-centered U.S. antitrust tradition which ironically promoted numerous giant corporations – like the ubiquitous U.S. multinational firms – while the United States declared cartels per se illegal within the domestic market. At the same time, however, British and German economic policy discourse increasingly recognized that some sort of cartel and monopoly regulation was necessary in order to prevent abuse. By 1937–39, the search for a regulatory regime capable of balancing "efficient" business cooperation against abuse in each nation converged with militarization and armament programs.[4]

Robert Liefmann, a leading cartel authority, explained the causes and consequences of the "ineffectual" U.S. antitrust system. He traced the early history of state and federal antitrust legislation as a reaction against the "trust" device S. C. T. Dodd fashioned to promote John D. Rockefeller's Standard Oil company. The nation's federal system – especially the failure to enact a national incorporation law – fragmented subsequent attempts to regulate big business and left ultimate authority to the courts. Fundamentally, however, the problem was corruption. "Anyone who is familiar with the economic and above all the *political* influence exerted in America by these tremendous concentrations of property is amazed to hear," Liefmann declared, "Americans maintain that their country is a genuine democracy." In addition, German cartels lacked the organizational capability to stop the production of all members. But U.S. big business "shut down some of their works completely, throwing the American workers on the streets with an incredible ruthlessness."[5]

German trade unions, often working in conjunction with cartels, checked the arbitrary power of business. In America big corporations exploited small shareholders, and promoted "private speculation." Also, the "accumulation

---

[4] Robert Liefmann, *Cartels, Concerns, and Trusts* (New York, 1932), 273–339, and for general argument 280, 282, 286–7 (especially U.S. antitrust legislation), 289, 292–7.
[5] Liefmann, *Cartels, Concerns, and Trusts*, quotes at 298.

of a considerable portion of the whole capital of the country in a few hands is one of the great dangers that threaten the State and its social life through the development of trusts – especially in America, where everything whatever is bought and sold for money." This materialism led to Germany's defeat in World War I. "The socialists are perfectly right in their assertion that it was these great capitalistic interests that were responsible for America's entry into the war," Liefmann affirmed. "The whole war was for them a stroke of business and America's whole attitude to Europe after the war has been and will continue to be regarded purely as a business proposition."[6]

Germany epitomized the problems associated with regulating cartels and corporate mergers. Prior to 1933, Liefmann stated, protective tariffs encouraged cartel agreements in order to stabilize prices and transfer patent technology among firms operating in both national and international markets. In addition, lawyers contended that companies combined cartel participation with merger strategies to avoid national tax laws or the weak cartel regulations such as those existing under the Weimar Republic. In 1931, Heinrich Kronstein published a study of the separation between corporate parent and subsidiary firms, arguing that managers employed the rules pertaining to incorporation to escape government regulation. A common form of merger throughout Europe was the holding company, which enabled families to retain dominant control. The German government vigorously enforced tariff, currency, and shareholder restrictions against multinational corporations; to reduce the impact of these protectionist policies, other nations' multinational corporations joined cartels. Thus, for political as well as legal reasons, the complex market interdependency between huge unified corporate organizations like I.G. Farben and extensive domestic and international multimember cartels impeded establishing effective regulatory policies. Liefmann observed that the "question as to how a country is to prevent itself being exploited by a few big international concerns [corporations] is one of the most difficult which foreign policy has to deal with."[7]

Yet German cartel regulation was not static. Responding to the cartels' manipulation of currency during the period of hyperinflation following World War I, the Weimar government instituted the nation's first formal cartel ordinance in 1923. The government faced political pressures divided among liberals opposed to both cartels and strong government, the proletarian parties of socialists and communists who resisted cartels but favored

---

[6] Ibid., 285, quotes at 294, 301, 308, 311–12.

[7] Ibid., concerning tariffs, 214, and quote at 272; David J. Gerber, "Heinrich Kronstein and the Development of United States Antitrust Law," in Marcus Lutter, Ernst C. Stiefel, and Michael H. Hoeflich, eds., *Der Einfluß deutscher Emigranten auf die Rechtsentwicklung in den USA und in Deutschland Vorträge und Referate des Bonner Symoposions im September 1991* (J.C.B. Mohr [Paul Seibeck] Tübingen, 1993), 155–69, reference to study at 159.

strong state control, and the Federation of German Industries advocating cartelized business self-regulation.[8] Constrained by compromises among these groups, the Ordinance of 1923 instituted a provisional regime generally sanctioning cartels but only moderately capable of restraining abuse. The primary regulatory body was a cartel court empowered to review cartel agreements.[9]

The Depression forced the Weimar government to impose more direct cartel controls. During 1929–30 the government sponsored an extensive review of the nation's entire economic order, especially its policy toward cartels. The Social Democrats advocated stronger government supervision of and intervention in cartel affairs, though they remained supportive of market cartelization in principle. A few liberal lawyers and economists urged vigorous policies restricting cartels. Addressing these pressures between the summers of 1930 and 1932 – with the support of centrist, socialist, and communist parties – the Weimar government instituted a series of emergency edicts expanding its authority to implement price reductions through closer regulation of cartel agreements. The new system gave primary enforcement authority to the Ministry of National Economy; it reached more cartel agreements than had been covered under the 1923 ordinance, including resale price maintenance and import duties on "cartel-controlled commodities." The prices established under international cartel agreements received an exemption. The emergency measures were generally unsuccessful, provoking considerable political opposition that the Nazis exploited during their rise to power in 1933.[10]

The Nazis reshaped the cartel regulation in their own image. Building upon the Weimar government's emergency edicts, the Nationalist Socialists enacted in July 1933, the Compulsory Cartels Law. It authorized the Minister of Economics to establish new cartels or to compel firms to enter into presently existing cooperative agreements, when doing so served the national economic interests and the general welfare. The minister was empowered to dissolve cartel agreements when necessary and otherwise to

---

[8] Gustav Seidler, "Protection of Consumers against Abuse of Economic Powers by Cartels and Similar Industrial Agreements," NRA Research and Planning Division, Leon Henderson, director; Anon., "Comparison of Codes under the National Industrial Recovery Act and German Cartels"; Henry P. Leverich, vice counsel [US] Berlin, "Cartels under the National Socialist Government in Germany," August 18, 1934; Louis Domeratzky, "New German Cartel Policy," November 1, 1933; Mabel S. Lewis, "German Cartels and the NRA," *Barron's*, January 22, 1934, p. 18, all in Leon Henderson Papers, Cartels, Box 2 FDRPL; Gustav Stolper, *German Economy, 1870–1940* (New York, 1940), 209–25; Theodore F. Marburg, "Government and Business in Germany: Public Policy toward Cartels," XXXVIII *Business History Review* (1964), 83–8.

[9] William C. Kessler, "German Cartel Regulation," 50 *Quarterly Journal of Economics* (1936), 680–93, especially 688; David J. Gerber, *Law and Competition in Twentieth Century Europe: Protecting Prometheus* (Oxford, 2001), 114–64.

[10] Gerber, *Law and Competition*, 145–8.

regulate the obligations and rights of all parties to cartel agreements. In 1934, Hitler affirmed that the intent of the law was not to eviscerate private initiative; rather, its purpose was to encourage business's voluntary adoption of cartels without direct intervention from the government. The minister did establish compulsory cartels in select cases. In these instances the goal was to prohibit creation of enterprises which, by reducing potential new production, decreased the production quotas being imposed among cartel members; this, in turn, strengthened weak cartels and facilitated efficiency through reorganization, including limiting the adoption of technologies that might promote unemployment. Generally, however, the number of cartels formed *voluntarily* increased, particularly in the finished goods industries. Ultimately, the cartel policy enabled the Nazi government to use controlled prices to maintain high employment; still more broadly – in conjunction with the complementary policy cartelizing agriculture – it fostered the full mobilization of the nation's resources for war.[11]

The Nazis employed the cartel policy to distinguish "good" and "bad" capitalist enterprise. A provision of the law passed in July 1933 authorized the Cartel Court to approve a boycott by cartel members against a business "managed by persons of insufficient reliability." Clearly, the provision facilitated maintaining stable prices, but it could also be used to favor Germans over foreigners or to define market relations in racial terms. According to German liberal politician and economic historian Gustav Stolper, an "anti-capitalist yearning" permeated the National Socialists' "unalterable" party program. The program reflected, in turn, the amorphous but fundamental association German public discourse established between the evils of hyperinflation and "foreign" finance. The Nazis defined "finance and trade capital" as "rapacious capital." Giving into this form of capital controlled by foreigners, the Weimar Republic "subjected the [German] people to interest slavery." In the name of the German nation, the Nazis promoted industrial or "creative" capital like that which the cartel law protected.[12]

Stolper explained how the Nazis applied the distinction between legitimate and illegitimate capital to reinforce national identity. Writing from America in 1940, he declared that the "Nationalist Socialist movement had realized that the redemption of the people could be achieved only by breaking the bondage of this interest slavery. And by another logical shortcut, finance capital was characterized as Jewish, the creative capital as 'Aryan.'"[13] Reasoning of this sort undoubtedly sustained boycotts against the many Jewish-owned companies which the government subsequently expropriated. Similarly, German members of the international viscose cartel regulating German prices and imports received the Cartel Court's approval to withdraw without notice from the agreement with Italian,

---

[11] Ibid., and note 8 above.   [12] Stolper, *German Economy*, 236.   [13] Ibid.

Dutch, Swiss, Belgian, and French producers.[14] Though the official reasons given for the action involved claims of unequal treatment, the imagery underlying "creative" and "rapacious" capital probably also encouraged the German cartel members' claims. Finally, despite the anticapitalist rhetoric, Hitler approved the removal of Nazi leaders who had promoted small business and labor against large corporations, such as I.G. Farben; instead, these firms gained a leading role in building and maintaining the Nazi war machine.[15]

Once Germany began the war, its propaganda machine used cartel imagery to help justify instituting a "new order in Europe." German propagandists proclaimed a continental economic program in conjunction with the political and military occupation it established in conquered nations. Despite the imposition of slave labor, the assault upon Jews and other ethnic minorities, and the massive deprivation of civil liberties, the Nazis emphasized the economic prosperity German victory would make possible for all Europeans. Every vestige of the Depression would be eradicated under German leadership through efficient market planning, an expansionary monetary policy, stable currency tied to the German mark, generous capital resources administered from Berlin, managed agricultural production, and beneficial labor relations based on each nation's industrial strengths. Cartel policy, central to Germany's national economy, had a vital role in the "New Order."[16]

English critic Paul Einzig of London's *Financial News* exposed the domination underlying the Nazis' transnational cartel system. There "will be extensive rationalization of industries on an international scale over the whole territory under German control, with the aid of industrial cartels," he asserted. In order to overcome the problems of balkanized global trade,

[14] Louis Domeratzky, "New German Cartel Policy," November 1933; Henry P. Leverich, vice counsel [US] Berlin, "Cartels under the National Socialist Government in Germany," August 18, 1934, Leon Henderson Papers, Cartels, Box 2 FDRPL.

[15] Contemporary economic experts agreed on the outcome, but disagreed as to whether it was good or bad; compare Stolper, *German Economy*, 229–74; Maxine Y. Sweezy, *The Structure of the Nazi Economy* (Cambridge, MA, 1941); Guenter Reimann, *The Vampire Economy Doing Business under Fascism* (New York, 1939); Paul Einzig, *Hitler's "New Order" in Europe* (London, 1941); G. W. Guillebaud, *The Economic Recovery of Germany from 1933 to the Incorporation of Austria in March 1938* (London, 1939); W. F. Bruck, *Social and Economic History of Germany from William II to Hitler 1888–1938 a Comparative Study* (Oxford, UK, 1938); A. P. Laurie, *The Case for Germany a Study of Modern Germany* (Berlin, 1939), which concludes, "I thank God that the Peace of Europe is in the guardianship of the Führer and therefore, in spite of the frantic efforts of all those here and in Europe and America who want war, secure" (quote at 179)

[16] Compare with Robert Skidelsky, John Maynard, *Keynes Fighting for Freedom 1937–1946*, vol. 3 (New York, 2000), 179–232; Scott Newton, "Cartels," and Helen Mercer, "Rhetoric, and Reality of Antitrust Policies," in Carlo Morelli, ed., *Cartels and Market Management in the Post War World* (Business History Unit Occasional Paper No. 1 London School of Economics, 1997), 3–17, 40–77.

"German-controlled Europe will negotiate trade agreements, barter agreements, and cartel agreements with other continents as one huge economic unit." Einzig aimed his criticism at English academic economists like G. W. Guillebaud who were sympathetic toward the bureaucratic planning and market rationalization the German program made possible. Even so, German propagandists attempted in part to legitimatize their nation's conquests by drawing upon old images of a "United States of Europe" and the regulatory ideas that League of Nations officials had proposed to deal with international cartels.[17]

Germans opposing the Nazi regime resisted the Nazis' cartel law. Liefmann's Jewish heritage doomed him to death, while in government custody in 1940; but among legal–economic experts throughout the world his writings and those of others publicized the idea of a regulatory regime capable of restraining abuse while it promoted the cartel's positive role in preserving "ordered" markets. The feasibility of regulating cartels in the public interest ultimately had more enduring influence upon European cartel policy making than the Nazis' exploitive "new order."[18] German émigrés emphasized, by contrast, the evils of the Nazis' and weaknesses of the Weimar Republic's cartel policies; they nonetheless asserted a continuity between the economic policies of the two regimes. After coming to America in 1933, Stolper especially influenced American policy makers such as Thurman Arnold to understand Hitler's triumph as inevitable because it drew upon a militarist Prussian past shaped by the cartel-dominated economic order. Also, Harvard economist Edward S. Mason accepted Stolper's interpretation of the continuity between Weimar and Nazi economic policies, including exploitive uses of cartel policies.[19]

Heinrich Kronstein was affiliated with a small group of liberal German academics generally identified with Germany's Freiburg University. This Freiburg "School" of academic discourse included lawyer Franz Böhm – who between 1925 and 1931 served in the Ministry of Economics' Cartel Department in Berlin – and economist Walter Eucken, whose studies in corporate and other commercial law fields argued that weak regulation of

---

[17] Einzig, *Hitler's "New Order,"* 23–34, quotes at 27; Guillebaud, *Economic Recovery of Germany*; compare Skidelsky, *Keynes Fighting for Freedom*, 195; Derek W. Urwin, *The Community of Europe: A History of European Integration since 1945* (London, 1997), 1–12; John Laughland, *The Tainted Source: The Undemocratic Origins of the European Idea* (London, 2000).

[18] Gerber, *Law and Competition*, 147–62; I thank Professor Gerber for tracking Liefmann's tragic end.

[19] For the German emigres' – including Kronstein's and Stolper's – influence in the United States see ch. I, section IV and V; W. F. Bruck, author of *Social and Economic History of Germany from William II to Hitler*, formerly a professor of Political Economy at the University of Münster, Westphalia, before becoming a visiting professor and research scholar in Industrial Relations at the University College of South Wales and Monmouthshire, Cardiff.

private cartel and monopoly power undermined liberal government and promoted autocracy. These ideas continued to influence Kronstein after he arrived in the United States, especially his work for the Justice Department's Antitrust Division beginning in 1938. Remarkably, despite the Nazis' rule Böhm, Eucken, and others benefited from Freiburg's relative geographic isolation on Germany's southwestern border with Switzerland, to develop a comprehensive liberal-market philosophy based primarily upon a free government's enforcement of competition policy. Despite periodic Nazi harassment, this group of lawyers and economists possessed relative autonomy to develop their liberal philosophy in secret, for use in a freer postwar era they hoped would emerge.[20]

Britain's search for a regulatory regime consistent with its national cartel and monopoly experience was also contested. Since World War I British business and labor leaders, economic experts, and policy makers disagreed about the appropriate scope of government intervention to maintain industrial self-government or market competition. Once Britain imposed a protective tariff through the Import Duties Act of 1932, the Import Duties Advisory Committee used its authority to approve cartel agreements in select industries, including iron and steel. Academic economists and labor and consumer groups debated whether this limited rationalization facilitated stable class relations and technological efficiencies more effectively than market competition. Nevertheless, the dominant business opinion identified with the Federation of British Industries (FBI) and the Tory Party supported business self-regulation in the form of cartel agreements and rationalization sustained by ad hoc government intervention. This approach prevailed despite opposition from smaller durable consumer goods and food and drink industries and some Labor Party groups. Broadly, certain smaller manufacturing firms resisted government's pursuing a "compulsory" policy because it fostered mergers, while the FBI's ad hoc approach left most firms somewhat freer to decide how much "self-regulation" they might accept.[21]

---

[20] On the Freiburg School, see Gerber, *Law and Competition*, 233–61; Viktor J. Vanberg, "Freiburg School of Law and Economics," in Peter Newman, ed., *The New Palgrave Dictionary of Economics and the Law*, 3 vols (London, 1998), 2: 172–9. Gerber, "Heinrich Kronstein and the Development of United States Antitrust," discusses Kronstein's place in the Freiburg School, 158–9.

[21] Helen Mercer, *Constructing a Competitive Order* (Cambridge, UK, 1995), 48–50; Freyer, *Regulating Big Business Antitrust in Great Britain and America 1880–1990* (Cambridge, UK, 1992), 213–17, 234–9; J.D. Gribbin, *The Post-War Revival of Competition as Industrial Policy*, Government Economic Service Working Paper No. 19 (London, December 1978), 6–15; J.D. Gribbin to Tony A. Freyer, Interview, July 6, 1989; J.D. Gribbin, "The Contribution of Economists to the Origins of UK Competition Policy," in P. de Wolf, ed., *Competition in Europe Essays in Honour of Henk W. de Jong* (Dordrecht, 1991), 138–41.

The FBI's "industrial self-government" policy prevailed, favoring British firms' involvement in international cartels. During the 1930s, various government departments within the Board of Trade managed the nation's participation in oil, tea, rubber, and other major commodity agreements. On the Import Duties Advisory Committee the Board of Trade's officials expanded this role, cooperating with British business to counteract foreign competition through international cartels rather than relying on tariff protectionism. The government's facilitation of international cartel agreements coincided during 1937–39 with Britain's evolving appeasement diplomacy toward Germany. The Board of Trade encouraged the FBI to apply its influence to broaden British participation in international cartels. Consequently, with Foreign Office approval, the government and the FBI sought to revive exports by pursuing economic rapprochement with the National Socialist government. The cartel policy focused especially on third countries where British and German manufacturers competed. British business hoped to escape the "unfair" competitive advantage the Nazi government's exchange-rate adjustments and export subsidies provided German firms in these third-nation markets. Early in 1939, representatives from each nation's coal industries agreed on quotas regulating coal exports throughout Europe. In March at Dusseldorf, the FBI and its German equivalent, Reichsgruppe Industrie, signed an agreement to end "destructive competition" and achieve a "more ordered system of world trade" by negotiating to fix prices. Perceiving U.S.–South American trade to be the object of the Dusseldorf Agreement's "third country" clause, the U.S. State Department protested violation of America's liberal trade policy, though with little effect.[22]

When the war began, British and German firms were party to 133 restrictive trade agreements. During the "phony war" of 1940, British and German government and business officials continued discussing global partition of trade through international cartels as part of peacemaking diplomacy. By the time Winston Churchill's coalition government came to power in 1940, British oil executives had contacted Herman Goering; President Roosevelt had criticized the Cable and Wireless executive, Lord Inverforth, for "peace-mongering"; and officials in the International Electrical Association and the International Electric Lamp Cartel had employed the British offices of Swedish Electrolux to discuss peace with Berlin. Meanwhile, ICI maintained its cartel agreements with I.G. Farben, British and German firms stayed in the International Lamp cartel (switching headquarters from Amsterdam to Geneva), and British Cable and Wireless and German Telefunken continued to lead the telecommunications cartel in South America. Finally, the Nazi victory on the continent and Britain's

[22] Mercer, *Constructing a Competitive Order*, 49–51, quote at 51; Newton, "Cartels," in Morelli, ed., *Cartels and Market Management*, 8–11.

desperate struggle in the fall of 1940 ended the government's countenancing British involvement in these international cartels. In the United States, cartels had become associated with appeasement.[23]

When Britain abandoned laissez faire for trade protectionism early in the 1930s, Cambridge economist D. H. MacGregor suggested that British officials faced a "new monopoly problem." The Depression heightened awareness of the organizational transformation large-scale business enterprise had been undergoing for decades throughout the world's industrial nations. Vertically integrated firms or "fusions" such as Britain's ICI and the many similar American corporate giants "belong to the study of big business, but in themselves, unless combined with trusts or cartels, they are nothing which a democratic community needs to watch or control." Basically, MacGregor categorized fusions as "efficient" because they represented management's ability to approach full capacity; "they may also make for economies of continuous or related operation, and for a distribution of risk." Looser business organizations including trusts were, by contrast, "problematic to the community by their *horizontal* reach over the outlets of particular products; problematic, that is because monopoly and higher [efficient] organization look much the same, and the community has to find ways of ensuring that the latter is not becoming the cloak of the former." He noted that differing national policies had resulted in divergent corporate structures: "In America, the cartel is illegal, so that industry has sought its administrative solution in fusions; in England trusts and cartels coexist; in Germany, they are interlaced, great trusts having their feet in one cartel, their shoulders in another, and their heads in a third."[24]

MacGregor's assessment reflected British policy makers' desire to find a middle way between American and German extremes. As a result of Britain's protective trade policies, the "extension of cartels and trusts into the international field has placed in the hands of these organizations the power, if not to cancel, at any rate greatly to modify the protection given to the consumer by international commerce." He acknowledged that the operation of these agreements remained obscure, "But we are undoubtedly approaching a new phase of market control, in which international operations depend on the strength of national [private business] organization, so that we have to be more sure than ever that the latter are real economic administrations, and that we obtain their advantages." MacGregor suggested that the "law of one country may have a different prejudice from that of another . . . a differing business psychology, derived" in America

---

[23] Newton, "Cartels," in Morelli, ed., *Cartels and Market Management*, 12–14, quoted phrase at 12; Mercer, *Constructing a Competitive Order*, 51–3. For Britain's dependence on U.S. aid, see Skidelsky, *Keynes Fighting for Freedom*, 91–134.

[24] D. H. MacGregor, "Introduction," to Liefmann, *Cartels, Concerns and Trusts*, vii–viii; Tony Freyer, *Regulating Big Business*, 78–9, 121–2, 124–9, 136, 140, 148, 154, 179, 215, 296, 324.

"from the size or conditions of evolution of the home market," in Germany from a "national bias that is more or less favourable to discipline and order," and in Britain from "a tradition of family business." Other than suggesting a "public interest" standard based on "reasonableness," he defined the problem without proposing a regulatory remedy.[25]

Other British economists offered different analyses of the nation's "monopoly problem," but regulatory solutions remained elusive. Denying that national "psychologies" explained divergent policies, Hermann Levy in 1937 argued that anticompetitive conduct arose from objective market conditions accompanying the swings of the business cycle, especially the Great Depression. Conceding that some form of government action fostering greater market competition was necessary, Levy proposed no institutional regime to address the problem. Early in 1941, Cambridge professor E. A. G. Robinson published a historical survey comparing British, German, and U.S. policies toward monopoly and cartels. He, too, applied an objective standard to argue that distinctive national regulatory polices reflected the practical and often reasonable demands of each nation's business–government relations during a particular period.[26]

The war, moreover, aroused pressures to reevaluate the British policy toward "industrial self-government" versus competition. Collaboration among business groups, organized labor, and government officials raised the stakes in the nation's social-class power struggle. British "revolutionists" contended, Robinson declared, that there "must ... inevitably come a painful struggle between the class that represents monopoly and privilege, and the class that represents the ordinary wage or salary earner, and consumer." British expert opinion representing "evolutionists" who continued to "believe that the British genius can best be defined as an infinite capacity for muddling through," by contrast, fell into three groups: those advocating no change, a few favoring a procompetitive approach, and those supporting moderate government intervention based on a "reasonable" standard defined in the "public interest." Among these groups there was some support for a commission empowered to investigate and publicize business conduct, somewhat like the American Federal Trade Commission.[27]

---

[25] MacGregor, "Introduction," to Liefmann, *Cartels, Concerns and Trusts*, xiv; for case law defining "reasonableness" and "public interest," see Freyer, *Regulating Big Business*, 207–11.

[26] Hermann Levy, *Industrial Germany a Study of Its Monopoly Organizations and Their Control by State* (Cambridge, UK, 1935); E. A. G. Robinson, *Monopoly* (Cambridge, UK, 1948, first published 1941), 274–89, quotes at 286, 287, and note 25.

[27] Robinson, *Monopoly*, 286, 287, and see 289 for FTC reference.

II. BRITAIN AND AUSTRALIA: A GLOBAL CONTEXT FOR PROMOTING PROTECTION OVER COMPETITION

James E. Meade and Lionel Robbins added to this commentary. Meade's book *The Economic Basis of a Durable Peace* (1940) drew upon his experience in the League of Nations' Economic Policy section; it urged creating an international organization devoted to maintaining peace by regulating global trade. Members from both "liberal" and "planned" economies would oversee administration of international currency, variable foreign exchange rates, international migration movements, colonies and raw materials supplies, exchange control and clearing agreements, international capital flows, and international trade, including cartels. Like John Maynard Keynes, Meade emphasized the importance of achieving full employment. Keynes' primary concern, however, was macroeconomic theories and monetary policy which did not include direct analysis of cartel issues; Meade, by contrast, developed linkages between macroeconomic theories and trade policies, including international cartels. During the interwar years Lionel Robbins of the London School of Economics also advocated international and domestic regulation aimed at restricting abuse within relatively free markets. These works reflected the continuing influence of British and League of Nations civil servant, Arthur Salter's internationalist regulatory discourse, though unlike him neither Meade nor Robbins defended international cartels as a positive good.[28]

After the war began, this regulatory thinking acquired practical force when Meade joined the Economic Section under the Reconstruction Unit of the Board of Trade. Following Hitler's declaration of the "New Economic Order" in October 1940, Keynes prepared "Proposals" opposing the German system and favoring a liberal postwar international monetary regime dominated by America and Britain. In November 1941, Meade contributed a memorandum to the Board of Trade's internal policy discussions arguing that achieving postwar full employment required addressing the anticompetitive practices of business and workers. Meade's work was part of an interdepartmental committee structure responsible for administering wartime and postwar policies. The Board of Trade relied on the Central Committee for Export Groups, composed of about three hundred representatives, to manage foreign trade, factory space, allocation of raw materials, the utilization of labor, and price controls. Meade was

---

[28] *The Economic Basis of a Durable Peace* (New York, 1940); Lionel Robbins, *Economic Planning and International Order* (London, 1938); for Keynes and Meade, see Skidelsky, *Keynes Fighting for Freedom*, 11–12, 139, 146, 208, 217–18, 236, 270–81, 310–14, 339; see also David Vines, "James Edward Meade," in John Eatwell, Murry Milgate, and Peter Newman, eds., *The New Palgrave a Dictionary of Economics*, vol. 3 (London, 1988), 410–17. Arthur Salter, *Recovery the Second Effort*, (New York, 1933).

one of the few economic experts or government officials advocating pro-competitive policies within this committee structure.[29]

During 1940–41 among the Board of Trade committees three distinct policy positions emerged concerning anticompetitive conduct. Throughout the interwar years, the FBI's promotion of industrial self-government was indicative of how broadly trade associations shaped Britain's turn toward restrictive markets. Thus, Sir Charles Innes advocated forming an Industrial Council or Commission in which business worked through trade associations to enforce mandatory anticompetitive conduct under government oversight. Innes stressed the need for strong trade associations to negotiate with the government about exports, prices and output restrictions, and redundancy schemes during the postwar transition. Essentially representing the position of the committees' business members, Innes' views reflected economic "rationalization" theories government officials and academic economists had used since World War I to justify expanded cooperation within industry and between business and government. Cambridge economist Ruth L. Cohen, however, favored a procompetitive regime. She pointed out the incentives trade associations had to maintain high prices when consumer demand declined, to restrict entry of new firms, and, overall, to hamper reducing costs through improved organizational efficiency. Cohen suggested the risks to parliamentary democracy resulting from too close an association between government and business. Henry Clay took a middle position. Emphasizing diversity among industries, he contrasted the difference between industries controlled by looser trade associations and the "big merger organization" such as ICI, whose organizational efficiencies outweighed their economic weakness and political threat.[30]

British court decisions suggested a similar policy dispute. By the late nineteenth century British courts generally allowed anticompetitive agreements among firms, but declined to enforce them except in the rare case where it could be shown that the agreement was "reasonable" in light of the "public interest." After the turn of the century, however, British judges increasingly reinforced the prevailing move toward industrial self-government and rationalization. The trend climaxed with two leading cases. In *Thorne v. Motor Trade Association* (1937) the House of Lords declared that certain forms of blacklists a trade association enforced against outsiders were reasonable in order to maintain the continuing existence of weak as well as strong firms, which, in turn, facilitated employment.

[29] Mercer, *Constructing a Competitive Order*, 55–6; Freyer, *Regulating Big Business*, 234–8; Skidelsky, *Keynes Fighting for Freedom*, 179–232, 264–374.

[30] Freyer, *Regulating Big Business*, 234–8, quote at 236; Gribbin, "Contribution of Economists," in de Wolf, ed., *Competition in Europe*, 138–41, and Gribbin to Freyer, interview, July 6, 1989; for a contrary view, see Mercer, *Constructing a Competitive Order*, 55–6.

Similarly, in the *Harris Tweed* case (1942) the Lords sustained restrictive agreements between business and labor against another business. On Scotland's Harris Island some mill owners qualifying under the Harris Tweed trademark had their yarn spun on the mainland using cheaper techniques, but then had the Harris Island cottage crofters weave the cloth into a finished product. The Harris Mill Owners' Association, however, controlled the industry. The Association and the dock-workers' union entered into an agreement refusing to import yarn from the mainland. The Association wanted to maintain a minimum selling price, while the workers sought to protect a collective bargaining agreement with the Association. The mills relying upon the imported yarn challenged the agreement, alleging conspiracy, but the Lords upheld its reasonableness.[31]

This British official discourse reflected ambivalence toward American trade and antitrust policy and international cartels. German authorities generally repudiated American antitrust as alien to European culture and institutions; they favored Liefmann's "regulated" cartel approach, though the Nazis distorted the principle and the Freiburg School rejected it. Robinson's 1941 survey suggested, by contrast, that some British commentators perceived the need for stronger government intervention if it could be reconciled with the "public interest" standard accepting "reasonable" cartels and mergers. Most British economists and government officials, however, supported a compromise between business interests that demanded compulsory cartelization through trade associations and groups whose opinion was that a regulatory system relying upon publicity would be sufficient to restrain cartel and monopoly abuses. The division among British officials encouraged the government's sanction of international cartels right up to the early part of the war.[32]

Britain's growing dependence on U.S. foreign aid from the fall of 1940 onward ensured that the international cartel issue would arise in British–American trade negotiations. The United States pressured Britain to replace the imperial preference system with an American style liberal trade policy. The trade program that Keynes proposed in opposition to the German New Order focused on monetary policy without addressing the cartel issue. At the Board of Trade, Meade not only advocated a stronger anticartel and monopoly policy for Britain at home, but his work in the League of Nations' Economic section equipped him to address the international cartel issue as well. As a result, members of the Board of Trade were prepared to

[31] Freyer, *Regulating Big Business*, 215–17; case cites, *Thorne v. Motor Trade Association* [1937], A.C. 797, overruling *R. v. Denver* [1926], 2 K.B. 258; *Crofter Hand Woven Harris Tweed Co., Ltd. v. Veitch and Another* (1942), 1 All E. R. 142. See also W. Friedmann, "The Harris Tweed Case and Freedom of Trade," VI *Modern Law Review* (December 1942), 1–21; W. Arthur Lewis, "Monopoly and the Law: An Economist's Reflections on the *Crofter* Case," VI *Modern Law Review* (April 1943), 97–111.
[32] Ibid.

negotiate with the Americans on the connections between international cartels and the liberal trade policy, whereas Keynes led the British regarding the larger struggle about the monetary system which would overcome the nationalistic trade protectionism represented by the German New Order. Even so, during 1943–45 the U.S.–British discussions gradually focused on the antitrust provisions which were eventually incorporated into the International Trade Organization (ITO). The negotiations, nonetheless, continued to proceed along separate tracks regarding trade policy and international cartels.[33]

Between 1930 and 1941, German and British policy discourse promoted trade and cartel protectionism over competition. As a result of the Great Depression, each nation imposed stringent nationalistic tariff and currency controls. The market restrictions exposed and strengthened cartel cooperation among leading U.S., German, and British multinational corporations, though ICI and I.G. Farben were among the few European firms experiencing the managerial revolution and the divisional restructuring that characterized American big business. Private anticompetitive agreements so permeated national markets that political, business, and labor groups increasingly supported regulation. International regulation also received consideration if not action. Although German and British authorities were aware of the American antitrust tradition, they rejected it, favoring the European policy which formally sanctioned cartels. A small group at Freiburg University advocated stronger competition despite Nazi harassment; in Britain, the proponents of such policies were more influential but were clearly on the defensive. Both nations turned trade protectionism and cartel regulation to war-making purposes. The Nazis, however, constructed their New Economic Order around an Aryan self-identity manifested through planned cartelized markets freed from Jewish and foreign influences. Britain's dependence on U.S. aid, by contrast, intensified the debate among British authorities over whether a stronger competition policy was compatible with either the American or Keynesian image of liberal-democratic capitalism and mixed economy at home and within the Empire. Yet by 1945, despite U.S. pressure for the ITO, only a few well-placed officials like Meade advocated establishing a British or an international antitrust regime.[34]

Australia's abandoned antitrust heritage suggested that conflicting policy pressures shaped anticompetitive conduct within the British Empire. Britain's adoption of the imperial preference system in 1932 exacerbated the long-existing trade rivalry among America, Britain, and members of the

---

[33] Note 23, and ch. I, section V.
[34] Kessler, "German Cartel Regulation," 680–93; Gerber, *Law and Competition*, 114–64; Stolper, *German Economy*, 236; Marburg, "Government and Business," 78–101; Robinson *Monopoly*, 274–89.

Empire, including Australia. These trade tensions only indirectly involved cartels, but that issue lurked in the background, particularly concerning the numerous restrictive commodity agreements to which U.S. firms belonged. Many of these agreements involved U.S. corporate subsidiaries and affiliates which during the 1930s restructured themselves to operate under the incorporation laws of Britain or the British Dominions of Australia and Canada. Around the turn of the century these dominions enacted weak antitrust measures.[35] The Australian government enforced its antitrust law – which when passed in 1906 specifically drew language from the Sherman Antitrust Act of 1890 – against the nation's cartelized coal industry. But the Australian appellate court overturned the trial court's decision favoring the government, and the Empire's Judicial Committee of the Privy Council in London did the same in 1913, establishing a leading precedent. By World War II, the international cartel issue compounded the uncertainties driving British–American trade relations; it also accentuated Australia's policy choice favoring cartelized home markets within the empire's protectionist trading system, despite the nation's unusual early experience with Americanized antitrust.[36]

During the interwar period, primary farm producers and small manufacturers dominated the Australian economy. Especially after the system of imperial preference took hold, the exchange rate favored agricultural producers, who maintained home consumption and exports as the leading sector. Small and medium-size manufacturing, by contrast, included textiles, automobile assembly, and chemicals. The states of New South Wales, Victoria, Queensland, South Australia, Western Australia, and Tasmania regulated the domestic transportation sector as public utilities. The national government authorized the shipping conference cartel's control of the nation's international transport of goods to the principle markets of Britain, continental Europe, the United States, and Japan; it also managed the "Northern Territories" and exploited the indigenous aboriginal population in a manner favoring "white Australia." Despite the use U.S. and other multinational firms made of Australian incorporation laws for restructuring purposes, little merger activity and limited vertical integration of firms

[35] Skidelsky, *Keynes Fighting for Freedom*, 187–8; Capling, *Australia and the Global Trade System*, 14; Mira Wilkins, *The Maturing of Multinational Enterprise American Business Abroad from 1914 to 1970* (Cambridge, MA, 1974), 62–7, 82–5, 138–41, 156–62, 190–2, 204–7, 234–50; Freyer, *Regulating Big Business*, 95.

[36] Andrew Hopkins, *Crime Law & Business The Sociological Sources of Australian Monopoly Law* (Canberra, 1978), 17–32; [Justice] R. S. French, "Judicial Approaches to Economic Analysis in Australia," 9 *Review of Industrial Organization*, Special Issue (October 1994), 551–3; Geoffrey de Q. Walker, *Australian Monopoly Law: Issues of Law, Fact and Policy* (Melbourne, 1967), 31–5; J. E. Richardson, *Introduction to the Australian Trade Practices Act* (Sydney, 1967), 20–3; Freyer, *Regulating Big Business*, 130–1; Neville R. Norman, "Progress under Pressure: The Evolution of Antitrust Policy in Australia," 9 *Review of Industrial Organization* (October 1994), 529.

took place. Meanwhile, the nation's tariff facilitated stable cartels. The protectionist regime sustained, moreover, industry-wide self-government enabling inefficient firms to survive, which in conjunction with the broader labor arbitration system gave workers a preferred position compared to Europe and the United States. Indeed, the system worked so well that Australian public discourse combined a radical social-class consciousness with a transcendent egalitarian ethos embracing "mateship."[37]

World War II promoted change. During the war, Australian officials mildly supported the U.S. campaign against international cartels, even though they advocated most strongly the trade preference policy. The opportunities increased for foreign-owned industry operating on a national scale. A significant boom in wool, wheat, and mineral exports developed; a new immigration policy fostered extensive (white) population growth. The wartime cooperation between government and business reshaped, within the continuing tariff regime, the nation's cartel structure on the basis of proliferating trade associations. Australians accepted the British Empire's protectionist trade system in large part because it benefited the exports of the nation's primary producers not only against the United States and Japan, but against Britain. Even so, protected foreign trade facilitated the ongoing home market stability, maintained through trade associations' anticompetitive agreements. The benefits of standardized products, quality control, and maximum output seemed more important than restricted entry, fixed prices, and other unfair trading practices. In addition, unlike Americans who historically distrusted the giant trusts, the "Australian tends to associate all big business with the Broken Hill Proprietary Co. Ltd. [BHP], a benevolent monopoly." Also, the "smaller" national market permitted fewer firms to adopt the most efficient innovations; accordingly, "many industries must be organized as monopolies or oligopolies in order to utilize the most up-to-date machinery." In addition, the Australian "states owned the railways, which were historically the most obnoxious monopolist in America; labor organizations, foreign competition, modern standards of fair play ... all helped to limit monopolistic exploitation."[38]

---

[37] Chapter VI, section I; and Barrie Dyster and David Meredith, *Australia in the International Economy in the Twentieth Century* (Cambridge, UK, 1990), 72–163; Louis Hartz, "A Theory of the Development of the New Societies" and Richard N. Rosecrance, "The Radical Culture of Australia," in Louis Hartz, ed., *The Founding of New Societies Studies in the History of the United States, Latin America, South Africa, Canada, and Australia* (New York, 1964), 12, 13, 275–318; Braham Dabscheck, "Industrial Relations," in Philip Bell and Roger Bell, eds., *Americanization and Australia* (Sydney, 1998), 148–63; James Walter, "Australian Democracy and the American Century" and Peter Beilhartz, "Civilizing Capitalism? Game Over, Insert Coins," in Harold Bolitho and Chris Wallace-Crabbe, eds., *Approaching Australia* (Cambridge, MA, 1998), 199–216, 217–24.

[38] John A. Bushnell, *Australian Company Mergers 1946–1959* (Melbourne, 1961), 167; S. J. Butlin and C. B. Schedvin, *War Economy 1942–1945* (Canberra, 1977), 655, 659.

The same British imperial order that earlier facilitated Australia's unique antitrust policy ultimately sanctioned its displacement by trade protectionism. The Australian Industries Practices Act's rise and fall after 1906 nonetheless had wider implications for Britain's and the empire's negotiations with the United States about the liberal international economic order each hoped to emerge from the chaos of World War II. Australia's antitrust policy reflected the early Commonwealth's emerging national consciousness and producer economy – including an unusual institutional and social settlement combining social-class radicalism and egalitarianism – confronting threats from foreign and domestic capitalist enterprise. A constitutional order blending American and British liberal institutions encouraged, in turn, the coincident enactment of antitrust and protectionist trade policies in order to preserve that national settlement. Despite early repeated efforts by Isaac Isaacs and others to maintain the competition policy, protectionism prevailed. It did so prior to World War I because both the Australian High Court judges and the Privy Counsel Lords shared the belief that cartelized business–labor relations diffused social-class conflict better than "cut-throat competition." During the interwar period the same faith sustained an even more aggressive protectionism amidst proliferating state nationalism and the increasingly balkanized world economy. The political and cultural evils fostering World War II shook the faith of some Australian and British officials in the social and market benefits of cartelized capitalism. By 1941, the Americans, British, and Australians disputed international cartels and liberal monetary policy as they contested a more competitive capitalist order. As the proposals for international cartel regulation evolved into the ITO during 1943–45, the Australians gave more support than the British, though maintaining the imperial preference remained the primary goal for both.[39]

III. JAPANESE COUNTERPOINT AND CULTURAL DISTINCTIVENESS, 1930–1945

The triumph of protection over competition followed the most distinctive course in Japan. It was the only nation which successfully engrafted Western capitalist markets and legal principles onto eastern relational culture to the point of challenging European and American political and industrial primacy. An isolated agricultural state in 1868 when the Meiji Emperor regained full power from feudal clans, Japan extended its imperialist reach. During the 1930s, Japan embarked upon a new phase of expansion, first seizing Manchuria (renamed Manchukuo), and then entering into a protracted war against China in 1937. These conquests aggravated

---

[39] Ibid., and ch. VI, section I, including consideration of Isaacs's role. Regarding Australia's contribution to the ITO's demise, see ch. I, section V, conclusion.

long-simmering tensions involving America's anti-Japanese immigration policies. Once World War II began, the Japanese–American conflict escalated as the United States gradually tightened trade restrictions.[40] During the summer of 1941, the United States imposed a partial embargo that soon coalesced into a complete freeze on trade between the two nations; Japan then pursued a strategic gamble culminating in the attack on Pearl Harbor. Sustaining this decision was a protectionist economic order established during the 1930s in support of the increasingly militarized society. Nevertheless, Japanese small and big business, government officials, political and military parties, and academics contested the system of market control. The contingent character of Japan's protectionist regime grew out of the unusual cultural and institutional settlement evolving under the Meiji Constitution up to and including World War II.[41]

Since 1853, when the United States forced open Japan to foreign trade, the nation's officials had maneuvered to preserve independence. They pursued a consistent strategy of industrialization through selective adoption of European and American technology, education, and institutions, while successfully avoiding the grip of Western imperialism. From the Meiji Restoration on, Japan developed a unique capitalist system in which private property rights and contract coexisted with extensive government promotion maintained through obscure yet pervasive personal obligations and cultural imagery. After the turn of the century big business emerged as the *zaibatsu*, an unusual form of family capitalism closely controlled within holding companies. Despite the *zaibatsu's* market dominance, peasant

[40] Edwin O. Reischauer and Marius B. Jansen, *The Japanese Today Change and Continuity* (Cambridge, MA, 1995), 41–102, 295–309, 347–50; Akira Iriye, "East Asia and the Emergence of Japan, 1900–1945," in Michael Howard and William Roger Louis, eds., *The Oxford History of the Twentieth Century* (Oxford, UK, 2000), 50–62, 103–16, 139–50, 205–15; Taichiro Mitani, "The Establishment of Party Cabinets, 1898–1932," Gordon M. Berger, "Politics and Mobilization in Japan, 1931–1945," Mark R. Peattie, "The Japanese Colonial Empire, 1895–1945," Ikuhiko Hata, "Continental Expansion, 1905–1941," Takafusa Nakamura, "Depression, Recovery, and War, 1920–1945," and Peter Duus and Irwin Scheiner, "Socialism, Liberalism and Marxism, 1901–1931," in John W. Hall, Marius B. Jansen, Madoka Kanai, and Denis Twitchett, eds., *The Cambridge History of Japan the Twentieth Century*, vol. 6 (Cambridge, UK, 1988), 55–96, 97–153, 271–314, 451–93, 654–710; Walter LaFeber, *The Clash* (New York, 1997), 132–213; Doak, "What Is a Nation and Who Belongs?" 287–99.
[41] John O. Haley, "Consensual Governance," in Shumpei Kumon and Henry Rosovsky, eds., *The Political Economy of Japan Cultural and Social Dynamics*, vol. 3 (Stanford, CA, 1992), 32–62; Bernard S. Silberman, "The Structure of Bureaucratic Rationality and Economic Development in Japan" and Michio Muramatsu and T.J. Pempel, "The Evolution of the Civil Service before World War II," in Hyung-Ki Kim, Muramatsu, Pempel, and Kozo Yamamura, eds., *Japanese Civil Service and Economic Development*, (Oxford, 1995), 135–73, 174–87; Johnson, *MITI*, 83–156; John O. Haley, *Authority without Power Law and the Japanese Paradox* (New York, 1991); John O. Haley, *The Spirit of Japanese Law* (Athens, GA, 1998).

agriculture and small business remained strong, especially in the export sectors, which by the interwar period gained Japan a leading role in global trade. During the era of Taisho democracy (1912–26) an active labor movement emerged, reflecting the nation's tentative acceptance of liberal-democratic institutions and Marxist radicalism.[42]

Purposefully managed business–government relations protected Japan's home market from foreign penetration more effectively than tariff or currency restrictions. Seeking Western technology and managerial techniques, the government generally relied on joint ventures to allow foreign firms access to the Japanese market. A leading example was the government's promotion of cooperation between Mitsubishi Oil and various American and British petroleum firms during the Japanese military build-up of the 1930s. Among other goals, the Japanese government hoped to learn the process of hydrogenation (producing gasoline from crude oil and coal). Similarly, German chemical companies and other members of international cartels bemoaned how effectively the Japanese government protected the nation's export sectors. By the 1930s, the government nonetheless faced the difficult challenge of balancing these interests against the demands of militarizing Japanese society.[43]

Although the Japanese government promoted cartelized business organization, its control was incomplete. In 1925, the Ministry of Commerce and Industry had prepared and the Diet had enacted the Export Cooperatives Law and the Significant Exporting Products Industry Cooperative Law. This legislation empowered small and medium-sized firms involved in export markets to replace the prevailing cut-throat competition with price-fixing agreements and production quotas. The Ministry monitored these agreements, but compliance was often problematic. Over the same period, the family-controlled *zaibatsu* generally avoided such cartel agreements; instead, they dominated much of the nation's economy through an oligopolistic organizational structure subject to government oversight but minimum regulation. During the early Showa period (1926–45), by contrast, private market conduct gradually receded before increased government intervention.[44]

The government's ascendancy was nonetheless contested and even in wartime was never absolute. In 1940, G. C. Allen, a British economist and Japan specialist, observed that it "is always dangerous in Japan to take

[42] See note 40 above.
[43] Wilkins, *Maturing of Multinational Enterprise*, 231–3; Scott P. O'Bryan, "Economic Knowledge and the Science of National Income in Twentieth-Century Japan," 6 *Japan Studies Review* (2002), 2–9; O'Bryan, "Growth Solutions," Unpublished Ph.D. Dissertation, Columbia University, 2000, 64–97.
[44] Alex Y. Seita and Jiro Tamura, "The Historical Background of Japan's Antimonopoly Law," 1994 *University of Illinois Law Review* (1994), 115–85, especially 133–35; and note 41 above.

legislation at its face value, for the Government is inclined to take for itself wide powers which it often uses only in the last resort, or not at all." In addition, "Japanese business men show ingenuity in evading the restrictions imposed on them, and there is evidence that the earlier control measures were not effectively enforced in many industries." Similarly, as late as March 1941, an American studying at Tokyo Imperial University, Thomas L. Blakemore, used the term "darkness market" to describe the term the Japanese employed in discussing violations of the supply and price-fixing laws.[45]

Throughout the 1930s, formal bureaucratic authority over business clearly increased. The Ministry of Commerce and Industry drafted and the Diet enacted the Significant Industries Control Law of 1931. The law authorized the Ministry to enforce price-fixing agreements, output restrictions, joint-sales practices, and other market restraints. By the end of the following year, cartels existed throughout the nation's economy: heavy industry had thirty-three cartels, the chemical industry had thirty-one, while in textiles, food processing, and finance there were eleven, eight, and eighteen cartels, respectively. Altogether, the total number of cartels authorized under the Control Law was 108. The law was amended in 1933 imposing upon firms the requirement to register investment proposals with The Ministry of Commerce and Industry; government authorization was also necessary in order to establish production goals and pursue plant expansion. In the 1930s, the jurisdiction established over the economy's export sectors during the Taisho period was expanded, giving bureaucrats authority to administer and enforce anticompetitive practices among manufacturing firms, wholesalers and retailers, and importers as well as exporters. Further strengthening these measures was the General Mobilization Law passed in spring 1938 that "gave the State almost unlimited powers of control, in an emergency, over the country's resources, human and material." Most significantly, perhaps, the law embraced the *zaibatsu*, eventually empowering the Ministry of Finance to regulate even corporate dividends, reserves, and depreciation accounts.[46] According to Allen, Japan's economy was being reshaped "from a private capitalistic to a totalitarian system" similar to Nazi Germany's. The broad economic policy the government imposed through the Mobilization Law of 1938 sought to control inflation.[47]

Even so, as was the case in the European fascist states, the Japanese government's market restrictions coincided with the disruption and then

[45] Allen, *Japanese Industry* (New York, 1940), 179; Thomas L. Blakemore to W. S. Rogers, March 10, 1941, in John H. Wigmore, T.L.B. from Japan 1939 to 1941, Japan Correspondence, Special Collections, Northwestern University, SC, NWU, Box 1, File 2, Folder 8.

[46] Seita and Tamura, "Historical Background," 135–8; Allen, *Japanese Industry*, 75.

[47] Allen, *Japanese Industry*, 76.

disbanding of liberal political party and labor organizations. The government's action included even smaller liberal or leftist groups, such as Ikuo Oyama's Labor-Farmer Party. Like many Japanese intellectuals, Oyama reshaped Western ideas in order to reimagine Japanese society. Oyama used the social democratic thought of Austrian Otto Bauer to advocate a collective national identity freed from the influences of bourgeois capitalism. Although Japanese militarists often attacked liberal groups and the *zaibatsu* in the name of anticapitalist collective national identity, they condemned leftist radicalism to the point that, fearing for his life, Oyama fled to the United States.[48] Ultimately, notwithstanding their anticapitalist rhetoric the militarists depended on big business to pursue the war effort. As a result, the government's enforcement of the Mobilization Law actually encouraged – though steadily constricted – the *zaibatsu's* dominance.[49]

The steady expansion of government authority over private market conduct was disputed. In 1938, Uyeda Teijiro, president of Tokyo University of Commerce, rebutted international claims that low wages and "sweat shop" conditions among Japan's small businesses resulted in the "social dumping" of cheap exports abroad. Small family firms produced as much as 60–70 percent of the nation's exports comprising cotton, rayon textiles, woolens, rubber goods, bicycles, enameled iron ware, and electric lamps. Paternalistic relations between employers and workers generally ameliorated the hard conditions in small to medium-size workplaces, Uyeda affirmed. The "traditional policy" of the government, moreover, was to "encourage and promote" small industries; "small ones are in need of protection and guidance from above." Accordingly, during the 1930s the government promoted "Hundreds of *Kogyo-Kumiai* or manufacturers' associations ... in order to apply co-operative principles to buying and selling, transporting, finishing, etc." The government's sanction of trade associations and other cartel arrangements also enabled many rural firms to adopt electricity. Such examples suggested "how far small-scale industries can be made effectively to compete with large-scale industries." Uyeda concluded, however, that "if we take into consideration the financial side of business, the question remains whether these small manufacturers will combine in co-operative organizations or come under the control of more powerful capitalists."[50]

Applying Marxist theory Fujita Keizo declared more pointedly that government action hurt small enterprise. A professor at Osaka University of

---

[48] Doak, "What Is a Nation and Who Belongs?" 291–5; for Oyama's exile and fate in America, see Wigmore to James L. Houghteling, September 13, 1938; Kenneth Colegrove to Wigmore, September 1938, in JHW, Japan Correspondence, Box 1, File 2, Folder 4, SC, NWU.

[49] Notes 43–7 above.

[50] Teijiro Uyeda, *The Small Industries of Japan, Their Growth and Development* (New York, 1938), 1, 4, 18, 19.

Commerce, Fujita published a wide-ranging examination of this "control" system as it had evolved by the end of 1935. Before the Depression "Japanese industries were feeling the need for ... reorganization, adjustment for self-sufficiency and well-planned control in preparation for international trade rivalry," he wrote. "Therefore, the advent of that intense depression made it imperative for the government to enforce certain industrial control laws." Factions within the military, bureaucracy, and the political parties urged that such "control" should support smaller enterprises. Fujita observed that the United Sates and European nations had instituted a similar market "rationalization" through cartelization. Moreover, like these other industrial powers, Japan had formulated its cartel regime in conjunction with various "commissions" of experts. Fujita declared, however, that "in reality this body of experts was already in the position of dominating the economic and financial affairs of the country," constituting a sort of "Industrial General Staff Office" under the Ministry of Commerce and Industry. Even so, as Japan extended its imperialist expansion into Manchukuo and northern China, small- and medium-size industries producing "peacetime" goods primarily for export were displaced by demand for military production dominated by the large firms, especially the *zaibatsu*.[51]

The deteriorating status of small business was nonetheless contested within bureaucratic policy-making channels. Fujita observed that where the "capitalist axiom of private property prevails with its corollary of freedom of enterprise, there inevitably occurs conflict of interests within and without cartels, whether voluntary or compulsory." In regard to the case of the leading carbide, superphosphoric acid (fertilizer), cement, and electric bulb industries the bureaucrats were unable or unwilling to enforce full compliance with the control laws. In the first case, Fujita observed, the "power of large financial cliques" was the "great obstacle" hindering effective enforcement of the cartelization effort. Concerning the next case, various smaller producers in the fertilizer industry sought production quotas from the Ministry of Agriculture and the Imperial Agricultural Association. But the larger Taki interests refused to comply. Accordingly, Fujita declared, a "political factor took the teeth out of the coercive strength of the compulsory cartel." The Taki clique exploited a "conflict of opinion" between the Ministry of Agriculture and the Ministry of Commerce and Industry; a compromise forced Taki into the Taiwan market, but, Fujita concluded, the end result was that "large financial interests"

---

[51] Fujita, "Cartels and Their Conflicts in Japan," III *Journal of the Osaka University of Commerce* (December 1935), 68, 73, 109. An international study grant from Japan's Ministry of Education enabled Fujita to study in Germany during the Weimar Republican era; he witnessed the operation of the Cartel Law of 1923. Throughout his career, Fujita supported small business.

employed the compulsory cartel to "prevail upon small and middle-sized rivals."[52]

Equivocal bureaucratic action also diffused the administration of the cement industry cartels, hurting smaller firms. Within the Cement Union, Asano Portland Cement and Onoda Cement disagreed concerning how much to restrict an increase in output. Although the Ministry of Commerce and Industry presented "an arbitration plan ... under the implicit threat of legal coercion" Onoda rejected it, "resist[ing] compulsion by establishing subsidiary companies" in colonial territories "which lie beyond the jurisdiction of the cartel law." The cartel members urged the government to bring the colonies within the cartel law's jurisdiction, but the government declined to do so. At the same time, there was "an internal clash of interests between the Asano clique and small and middle-sized concerns." Fujita predicted that the conflict would continue until Onoda "gains hegemony both in Japan and the colonial territories. Such aggression of large independent concerns against smaller rivals and financial cliques constitutes an outstanding feature of cartel conflicts ... enforced cartelization is a process through which a powerful financial group asserts its dominance."[53]

In the electric bulb producer's case the struggle possessed an international dimension. Tokyo Electric was, according to Fujita, a "large outside rival representing foreign capital," General Electric. It clashed with the cartel whose members included Tokyo, Imperial, and Ebisu Electric Bulb companies and various "small and middle-sized makers." Within the cartel the large and small producers were also at odds. Exploiting the internal conflict, Tokyo Electric joined and immediately dominated the cartel. "As an outcome of this fusion," Fujita noted, "the cartel that had been organized by emotional antagonism against this outsider, now became dominated by that very rival." Despite protests from small firms and other cartels the government did not intervene. Thus, Fujita concluded, weak bureaucratic intervention through the control laws favored large over small enterprise. He conceded that conflicting interests existed among the big capitalists themselves, so that "even the legal system created by their own will does not represent their interests to their hearts' content." The *zaibatsu* nonetheless possessed sufficient political autonomy that the bureaucrats rarely attempted to coerce them, at least directly, for "no capitalist would consent to a system of powerful control."[54]

Small business, however, lacked such advantages. Even though the government created the cartel control system in 1930–31 so that small enterprise might overcome the "cut throat" competition unleashed by the Depression, these groups complained that by 1935 the laws were not being enforced on their behalf. They blamed the large capitalists' influence over the bureaucrats' administration for the failure to protect smaller cartel

[52] Ibid., 84, 92.   [53] Ibid., 93, 94.   [54] Ibid., 94, 95.

members. Among the most exploited groups were those enterprises caught in the "systems of temporary employment and sub-contract which are now widely adopted." While the military promoted the comparatively insecure short-term contracts in response to the growing procurement demands following the Manchurian incident, its increasing "prevalence" was "due more largely to the special interests that industrial capital" established. To remedy such exploitation small business interests urged the government to establish an independent cartel court or commission capable of adjudicating the abuses resulting from the large capitalist's market domination. But the government remained unresponsive.[55]

Although Fujita focused on conflict, he hoped that "public" pressure might encourage a changed official policy. The "position of small and middle-sized enterprises within the capitalist system is entirely precarious, despite numerous efforts made for their protection," he concluded. Indeed, the evidence suggested that the unequal condition would continue. Fujita nonetheless observed that the "only bright prospect seems to lie in the hope that the public may eventually realize the limitations involved in technical improvement" and that future "conflicts between large and small capital may lead to a fundamental change in government policies." Thus, Fujita perceived that altered policy might result not from the consistency of governmental policy but rather because that policy was equivocal.[56]

The militarists' increasing control following the bloody "incident" of 1936 altered the balance of power Fujita described. On February 26 of that year approximately fourteen hundred army troops led by young officers associated with the Imperial Way faction mutinied, occupying the Diet, the Army Ministry, and other places in downtown Tokyo. The rebels killed some leading government officials before the authorities reestablished order; after hesitation, the government executed the rebels. The following year, the military embarked upon the conquest of China, heightening nationalist enthusiasm throughout Japan. The militarists' ascendancy seemed straightforward enough. G. C. Allen cautioned, however, that "Japanese policy is full of surprises," because it was "determined not by political campaigns and elections, but as a result of alliances and compromises among groups whose activities are not always known to outsiders."[57]

These conflicts were complex. Many members of political parties in the Diet – reflecting the greater liberalism of the Taisho era – were allied with large capitalists, particularly members of the *zaibatsu* families. Opposing

[55] Ibid., 98–107, quotes at 99, 107.   [56] Ibid., 109.
[57] Berger, "Politics and Mobilization, 1931–1945," in Hall et al., eds., *Cambridge History of Japan*, 119–20; Allen, "Japanese Industry Its Organization and Development to 1937," in E. B. Schumpeter, ed., *Industrialization of Japan and Manchukuo, 1930–1940* (New York, 1940), 786.

the party-capitalist group were numerous military – particularly younger – officers who championed the cause of farmers or small enterprises since those sectors provided most recruits. A second important group resisting the party-capitalists consisted of younger "progressive reformers" for whom "reform" meant the institution of a centrally managed "new" economic and political order constructed along fascist lines. Many of them occupied important positions within the bureaucracy. Each group also contained senior leaders, especially those with family ties to the old feudal clans. Representative of this group was Prince Konoe Fumimaro, who supported the centralized wartime economic mobilization the reformers demanded without accepting the complete fascist program.[58]

The group struggles had consequences for Japan's system of business–government relations. The exploitation of small business worsened as a result of the increased centralized control instituted under the Mobilization Law of 1938. Yet, as Allen observed, "the political groups which wished to strengthen the small producers against the great capitalists," have by "their [war mobilization] policy ... largely contributed to their decline. In a word, the triumph of the military extremists in Japan's Government has been fatal to that section of the country's economic life which they most favored." Moreover, although political, military, and bureaucratic factions opposed the *zaibatsu* families, the demands the mobilization laws imposed were of such large scope that the "machinery for administering many of those measures is in the hands of the large firms."[59]

Meanwhile, from 1939 to 1941 further conflict arose. The factional struggles shaping business–government relations engendered wage and price controls, and workers came under compulsory restrictions in virtually all business sectors. Corporate dividend rates and finance were subjected to full control. Nevertheless, when in late 1940 the government advanced the New Economic Order patterned after the progressive reformers' plan for a thoroughgoing fascist state, business groups balked, condemning the idea as a "communistic" repudiation of Japanese capitalism. A compromise was reached, but according to the later assessment of Nakamura Takafusa, the factional conflict contributed to the Japanese government's being "behind in its efforts to organize a wartime economic mobilization."[60]

---

[58] Berger, "Politics and Mobilization, 1931–1945," in Hall et al., eds., *Cambridge History of Japan*, 118–50; Bai Gao, *Economic Ideology and Japanese Industrial Policy from 1931 to 1965* (Cambridge, UK, 1997), 66–120; Masao Maruyama, *Thought and Behaviour in Modern Japanese Politics* (Oxford, UK, 1963), 25–83.

[59] Allen, *Japanese Industry*, 78–80, quote at 80; compare Fujita, "Cartels and Their Conflicts in Japan," 65–109.

[60] Nakamura, "Depression, Recovery, and War, 1920–1945," in Hall et al., eds., *Cambridge History of Japan*, 480–8, quotes at 485, 488; compromise confirmed, Gao, *Economic Ideology and Japanese Industrial Policy*, 115–16.

The relative independence the *zaibatsu* maintained during the war mobilization reflected their social and economic distinctiveness. While the term applied to approximately a dozen large business groups in Japan, the four leading *zaibatsu* ranked in order of significance were Mitsui, Mitsubishi, Sumitomo, and Yasuda. Unlike the large corporations found in America and Europe, Allen observed, these four business organizations were "pre-eminent at once in finance and also in industry." The combination of manufacturing, trading, and banking functions under a unitary corporate structure controlled by a single family enabled the *zaibatsu* to dominate the credit sources and business decision-making of most large and small firms throughout the nation. Even so, these giant corporate conglomerates manifested the same prevailing orientation toward group identity that pervaded Japan's entire sociopolitical and cultural life. Thus, Allen noted, the *zaibatsu* were "family businesses. Control is centered upon a partnership (Mitsui Gomei, Mitsubishi Goshi, Sumitomo Goshi, and Yasuda Hozensha), the capital of which is owned entirely by a family or group of families with a common ancestor." The central familial partnership "exercises its control through the holding of shares in other companies and through the appointments of directors and managers."[61]

Each *zaibatsu* was organized through a series of holding companies. Allen employed Mitsui to illustrate the complex property relationships maintained through familial shareholding within these holding companies. Securities held in many firms constituted Mitsui Gomei's assets. The familial partnership's control of the entire structure began with the direct capitalization of six companies: Mitsui Bank, Mitsui Life Insurance, Mitsui Mining, Toshin Warehouse, Mitsui Bussan, and Mitsui Trust. "Each of these concerns in turn controls, through security holdings or other financial connections and through appointment of directors, a large number of other companies." Thus, Mitsui Bussan ran subsidiary companies in such diverse industries as oil-refining, condensed milk, rayon, engineering, flour-milling, electrical apparatus, cotton-merchanting, loom, and marine and fire insurance. Each subsidiary, in turn, had financial and managerial interests in other firms. Mitsui Gomei also controlled major individual enterprises, including Shibaura Engineering Company, Electrochemical Industry Company, the Hokkaido Mining and Steamship Company, and the Japan Steel Works. Finally, Mitsui's possession of "small capital holdings"

---

[61] Allen, "Japanese Industry Its Organization and Development to 1937," in Schumpeter, ed., *Industrialization of Japan and Manchukuo*, 630, 635–45, quotes at 630, 635; Morikawa, "Japan: Increasing Organizational Capabilities of Large Industrial Enterprises, 1880–1980s," and Hikino, "Managerial Control, Capital Markets, and the Wealth of Nations," in Chandler et al., eds., *Big Business*, 307–35, 480–96.

enabled it to influence one of Japan's largest firms, Oji Paper Company, and the Kanegafuchi Spinning Company.[62]

The families delegated administration of the holding companies to select individual managers known as *Banto*. Generally, these managers were recruited from Japan's top universities – especially Tokyo Imperial University – or the higher technical and commerce schools. Broadly, they were chosen on the basis of merit with little regard for social-class background. The senior *Banto*, in turn, trained individual subordinates who competed to become their senior's successor. Thus, personal loyalties bound the managers to one another and to the *zaibatsu* family. According to Allen, the *Banto* and his retainers were "not so much employees ... as fellow-clansmen who devote themselves to the service of their overlord, or rather to that of the *batsu* or group to which they belong, and in this respect the organization of the business house is characteristic of the social, political, military, and economic life of present-day Japan." Competition was intense within the *batsu* groups and among the various leading *Bantos*. The rivalry was nonetheless, Allen affirmed, "subordinated in theory, and generally in practice, to the welfare of the House, and the dominance of a particular group or a particular policy will last only so long as it contributes to the prosperity of the whole." The organization built on inter-personal loyalties gave managers considerable autonomy within the holding company structure while it insured against failure, for all losses were "borne by the House as a whole."[63]

The cooperative rivalry within each *zaibatsu* matched the intense yet bounded competition between the great houses themselves. The organizational diversity of each *zaibatsu* enterprise ensured that interests clashed throughout most of the nation's leading market sectors. Generally, the great Houses and their subsidiary companies did not provide capital to rival *zaibatsu* enterprises. Indeed, as Fujita suggested, the rivalries persisted even as the government increasingly relied upon *zaibatsu* control of the cartel system in order to meet the escalating demands arising from the nation's wartime mobilization. Nevertheless, the inexorable military exigencies engendered cooperative initiatives. During the Depression some *zaibatsu* jointly developed trust companies that provided increased capital for various undertakings. Each *zaibatsu* invested in the government's effort to rationalize the nation's iron and steel industry through the organization of Nippon Seitetsu (Japan Iron Manufacturing Company); they also joined the Industrial Bank of Japan in securing the debentures of electricity producers. Despite initial opposition from the military, many of the *zaibatsu* acquired shares in quasi-state enterprises operating in Korea, Manchukuo, Taiwan, and elsewhere.[64]

---

[62] Allen, "Japanese Industry Its Organization and Development to 1937," in Schumpeter, ed, *Industrialization of Japan and Manchukuo*, 637–69, quote at 637–8.
[63] Ibid., 636.   [64] Ibid., 639–40.

The *zaibatsu's* control was nonetheless disputed. The conflicts between the large and small capitalists Fujita described reflected the expanding dominance the *zaibatsu* established over small enterprise during the 1930s. The big family houses broadened their capital base in response to the Depression and the mounting demands of wartime mobilization. They exploited the government's promotion of a consolidated banking system that had been underway for decades. Eventually, smaller independent banks were displaced by a few big *zaibatsu*-controlled banks. The "smaller merchants and manufacturers who were the chief customers of the minor banks have suffered from this change," declared Allen. "To an increasing extent they have been forced within the financial orbit of *Zaibatsu*, and they have resented it." Similarly, the move into foreign trade by house-affiliated companies such as Mitsui Bussan forced either a dependent status or bankruptcy upon the smaller merchants and manufacturers who previously had controlled international commerce. Moreover, groups associated with the Army and Navy and their allies among small enterprise and peasant farmers linked their criticism of the political parties to the "further extension of the power of the great concerns that were known to control the parties. Frequent political scandals fomented this discontent." Claims surfaced that the *zaibatsu* were behind the deflationary policy the party-based Minseito Government instituted at the onset of the Depression. The militarists exploited the discontent. In 1932 the popular anger provided the pretext for the murder of the leading *Banto*, Takuma Dan.[65]

This conflict had mixed results. The *zaibatsu* attempted to hide their business activities behind names not associated with the big families and otherwise to mollify public criticism by funding welfare relief and providing easy credit terms for smaller firms operating within the cartel system; they also funded development of war-related industries that the military favored. In some instances the families sold shares in certain holding company subsidiaries on the public market. As one Japanese commentator explained, however, these actions constituted merely a "Camouflage Policy" which did not diminish the controlling influence the *zaibatsu* and their political party allies exercised. After 1937, such criticism shaped the complex intergroup compromises resulting in the incomplete implementation of the New Economic Order. While the compromise policies preserved the capitalistic base underlying the *zaibatsu* market power, this power was subjected to ever more complete military purposes.[66]

Meanwhile, the military encouraged a younger generation of big business leaders. Identified with large firms such as Nissan (Nippon Sangyo Kaisha), these enterprises received the military's support – generally in the

[65] Allen, "Japanese Industry Its Organization and Development to 1937," in Schumpeter, ed., *Industrialization of Japan and Manchukuo*, text and quotes at 640, 641.
[66] Ibid., 642–6, quote at 643.

form of large procurement contracts – to counter the *zaibatsu's* political and economic influence. Initially, the new military–business collaboration emerged in Manchukuo and the north China war zone. As the old *zaibatsu's* central role gradually increased in the operation of the cartel "control associations" instituted under the War Mobilization Law of 1938, however, the military promoted Nissan and other newcomers in the home market. Allen emphasized that the "capital of the Nissan holding company, unlike that of the *Zaibatsu's* holding companies, has been subscribed by many thousands of shareholders, and in this respect it apparently possesses a very different financial foundation from that of the other capital groups." The Army "bitterly opposed" what it regarded as the old houses' subordination of nationalist interests to capitalist exploitation; even so, it was "willing to compromise to the extent of admitting a capital group ostensibly outside the great families." Allen cautioned that the public shareholding might ultimately prove insufficient to preserve the "younger" capitalists' independence, especially if family ties existed. Similarly, Fujita's and Uyeda's earlier analyses confirmed that multiple images and meanings characterized the bureaucracy's central role in shaping Japanese capitalism and society throughout the protracted era of war ending in the 1945 defeat.[67]

IV. JAPANESE BUREAUCRACY AND CULTURE: AUTHORITY WITHOUT POWER TO 1945

Under the War Mobilization Laws the bureaucracy's exercise of authority was ambiguous. Fujita's description of the Ministry of Commerce and Industry's and the Ministry of Agriculture's enforcement of the cartel laws was consistent with Allen's observation regarding the Mobilization Law of 1938: while Japanese government officials possessed formal authority, their uses of it was often contingent.[68] Under the Meiji Constitution the bureaucrats had institutional independence as "servants of the emperor" whose authority was ultimately defined by imperial decree rather than parliament. Bureaucrats were selected on the basis of competitive examination open to individuals regardless of social class and home region; they were recruited from the nation's top universities, particularly Tokyo Imperial University's Law Department. It was apparent, however, that traditional group loyalties and origins coexisted with the system of merit selection. Moreover, like the Army and Navy, the economic ministries formulated national policies through participation in the uncertainties of Imperial cabinet politics. Parliament enacted legislation, but the bureaucrats drafted virtually all laws and were primarily responsible for

[67] Ibid., 645; and notes 50 and 51 above.
[68] Allen, *Japanese Industry*, 179; Fujita, "Cartels and Their Conflicts in Japan," 84, 92.

enforcement.[69] Thus, although bureaucratic autonomy was such that officials remained firmly loyal to their ministry, members from various ministries could constitute a group such as the "progressive reformers" who collaborated to further a consistent policy program dominated by a coherent nationalist ideology up to 1945.[70]

Several factors explained how Japanese bureaucrats could possess, to use John O. Haley's phrase, authority without power. As traditional group affiliations declined in importance during the twentieth century, bureaucratic identification with one's own ministerial department increased, fostering intense interministry competition. As the enforcement of the Mobilization Laws suggested, each ministry developed an enforcement policy for approaching small business, peasants, or the *zaibatsu* as "clients." As long as the bureaucracy's administration of the cartel control laws was broadly consistent with national security interests, each ministry exercised considerable discretion in determining the scope and limits of official power. In addition, divergent relational interests – such as those Fujita noted concerning the bureaucratic enforcement of cartel restrictions governing the fertilizer industry – fostered contrary interpretations among various ministries.[71] Also, the powerful institutional rivalries and jealousies included not only the leading economic ministries, but also the Army, the Navy, and the Ministry of Home Affairs, which exercised significant control over local law enforcement and public project construction. Moreover, the Mobilization Laws established a degree of governmental authority over cartelization that was new, facilitating competitive experimentation and flexibility in compliance policies.[72] Thus, bureaucratic competition impeded implementing the Mobilization Laws according to the progressive reformers' coercive fascist ideology.[73]

A unique Japanese legal consciousness further shaped the separation between authority and power. The Meiji Constitution sanctioned superimposing Western legal institutions and ideas upon the deeply rooted customary rules of social and market conduct identified with Japan's rural village *(mura)*, upon Confucian bureaucratic duties, and upon judicially enforced feudal obligations. Fundamentally, the profound tensions underlying the process of institutional and cultural amalgamation gave public

---

[69] Muramatsu and Pempel, "The Evolution of the Civil Service before World War II," in Kim et al., eds., *Japanese Civil Service*, 174–87, quoted phrase at 175.
[70] Compare, Gao, *Economic Ideology and Japanese Industrial Policy*, 71–117; Johnson, *MITI*, 35–82, 116–56; Haley, *Authority without Power*, 139–68.
[71] John O. Haley, "Japan's Postwar Civil Service: The Legal Framework," in Kim et al., eds., *Japanese Civil Service*, 80–1; Haley, *Authority without Power*, 13.
[72] Muramatsu and Pempel, "The Evolution of the Civil Service before World War II," in Kim et al., eds., *Japanese Civil Service*, 177–9.
[73] Gao, *Economic Ideology and Japanese Industrial Policy*, 116; Nakamura, "Depression, Recovery, and War, 1920–1945," in Hall et al., eds., *Cambridge History of Japan*, 485–8.

officials wide scope to exercise discretion in determining legal authority.[74] While the cultural force of customary traditions shaped the legitimate uses of discretion, by the 1930s two distinct visions – emphasizing the paternal image of the emperor – contested the sources and substance of those traditions. The first was the "organ" theory identified with Minobe Tatsukichi, Professor of Constitutional Law at Tokyo Imperial University. Drawing upon the patriarchal values dominating Japanese culture, Minobe argued that the emperor was the paternal head of the nation to the same extent that the father was the head of the family. Even so, under the power arrangements enshrined in the Meiji Constitution the patriarchal imagery meant that the Emperor, though possessing primary leadership, nonetheless exercised that leadership in relation to the other centers of constitutional power, especially Parliament. This "organic" ordering of authority further envisioned that ultimately the government would enact and enforce rules according to the received consensual norms of custom, just as the essence of the father's authority derived from respecting ancestral heritage.[75]

The second vision embraced an absolutist image of the emperor which indirectly facilitated the *zaibatsu's* influence under the Mobilization Laws. Those supporting the militarization of Japanese society reshaped the uses of custom to legitimize the theory that the emperor was supreme, embodying the qualities of a god. At one level the imagery reenforced the patriarchal authority possessed not only by heads of households from the great *zaibatsu* families to the numerous small businesses and peasants, but also "such persons [who] exercised paternal authority over the members of their groups, over assistants, clerks, laborers, craftsmen, servants, tenants, and other subordinates." According to Murayama Masao, "their standard of living was not very high, being scarcely different from that of their subordinates. Nevertheless, they were the undisputed rulers of their own microcosms, in which they had the authority of petty emperors." In 1935 the proponents of the absolutist vision attacked Minobe, resulting in his removal from the House of Peers and the censorship of his works although they had previously enjoyed wide acceptance. At a more instrumental level, however, the social conflicts underlying the implementation of the absolutist's vision – particularly the *zaibatsu's* contested status with the military, small business, and farmers – encouraged fragmented bureaucratic enforcement which the *zaibatsu* exploited to retain limited but sufficient

---

[74] Haley, "Consensual Governance," in Kumon and Rosovsky, eds., *Political Economy of Japan*, III, 42–50.

[75] J. A. A. Stockwin, *Japan: Divided Politics* (New York, 1982), 22–3; Reischauer and Jansen, *The Japanese Today*, 100–1; Maruyama, *Thought and Behaviour in Modern Japanese Politics* (1963), 59–61, 313.

autonomy within the constraints of the Mobilization Laws even after Japan attained full war mobilization.[76]

Thomas Blakemore, the American student attending Tokyo Imperial University, further suggested the interstitial character of Japanese law enforcement. In progress reports to his benefactors during 1939–41, Blakemore periodically noted the equivocal outcome of the Mobilization Laws. Thus in April 1940, he wrote that "infractions of these control regulations are being reported on a scale which indicates a wide-spread willingness to dispense with governmental aid in bargaining for scarcer commodities. As the Minister of Justice pointed out in a recent speech, the curbing of such illicit transactions now is the chief problem before Japan's law administration agencies."[77] Blakemore's visit to a District Court indicated the underlying cultural assumptions shaping public as well as business compliance with Mobilization Laws. The "judge urged us not to be misled by the western appearance of Japanese legal institutions," Blakemore reported, "for he assured us that behind the facade, the operations are different."[78]

At roughly the same time, Allen published his appraisal of the increasingly "totalitarian" implementation of the Mobilization Laws noted above. Coincidentally, Blakemore's description of pervasive noncompliance confirms Allen's cautionary note regarding the tendency of Japanese bureaucrats to enforce such laws interstitially, leaving much space for private action defined as the Japanese "way of life." Inferentially, the District Court judge defined the ultimate goals of law enforcement in similar terms: "Attorneys, judges, those accused, and prosecutors alike join in the spirit of patriotism and filial respect for Imperial authority which is the foundation of all law, so thus the decisions and sentences take more the form of paternal settlements and reprimands than adjudications."[79]

A comparative method of legal discourse taught in Japanese law schools shaped policy making and enforcement. Tokyo Imperial University's Law Department was the principal recruiting ground for the ministerial departments of Home Affairs, Commerce and Industry, and Finance. Since the Meiji Restoration, officials borrowed extensively from European and American sources as they continuously reconstituted Japan's civil, economic, and military institutions; routinely, too, the government sent its officials abroad to study foreign practices. Blakemore encountered the patterns of this "comparative" legal discourse in his course work. He

---

[76] Maruyama, *Thought and Behaviour in Modern Japanese Politics*, 60.

[77] Thomas L. Blakemore to W. S. Rogers, May 15, 1940, T. L. Blakemore Letters from Japan, 1939–41, File 2, Folder 8, JHW Papers, Japan Correspondence, Box 1, SC, NWU; Gao, *Economic Ideology and Japanese Industrial Policy*, 111.

[78] T. L. Blakemore to W. S. Rogers, April 1, 1940, T. L. Blakemore Letters from Japan 1939–41, File 2, Folder 8, JHW Papers, Japan Correspondence, Box 1, SC NWU.

[79] Ibid.; Allen, *Japanese Industry*, 75.

commented upon the "relatively heavy use of comparisons of Japanese legal rules with those of other countries" and the "frequent reference to foreign laws." Given that "Japan's codes are to a considerable extent blends of foreign statutes," he reflected, "it may be necessary to explain the parent systems in order to give a true picture of present-day law." The professor "constantly writes out citations and terms in German, English, French, and Latin." At the same time, Blakemore found that the teaching included "a good deal more of historical sidelights, both Japanese and western, and much more speculating on underlying social conditions and trends," which in "an American law class would be regarded as interesting but extraneous." This instructional mode well suited the large proportion of law students who "most frequently" used law degrees as "springboards to the civil service," and it "bears out the Law Department's reputation for being the great training ground for the civil service."[80]

Comparative legal discourse reinforced the bureaucracy's discretionary independence in implementing the Mobilization Laws. The progressive reformers fashioned their "new" political and economic orders after studying and comparing Nazi, Soviet, and American New Deal policies. The principal architect of the program nationalizing the electric power industry in 1938, for example, visited the Tennessee Valley Authority (TVA) and Britain's grid system. Moreover, in order to better understand the electric power issue in the context of the New Deal as a whole, progressive reform bureaucrats "imported all the major business magazines published in North America and collected many volumes of the *United States Government Manual*." The Japanese gleaned from those sources the larger organizational dynamics the New Deal revealed which could be selectively employed to shape the Mobilization Laws according to Japan's distinctive bureaucratic separation between power and authority. Thus, the Japanese found instructive the unique constitutional balance the New Deal struck between bureaucratic centralization and decentralization which the TVA epitomized. The lesson regarding bureaucratic balancing had implications, moreover, for a dispute among progressive reformers over whether to institute an agency capable of imposing uniform policy and budgetary constraints upon the diverse ministries. The proposal clashed with the ministerial tradition of jurisdictional competition (*nawabari arasoi*), a tradition resonating with the New Deal analogy. Accordingly, with the Army's and Navy's support the Ministry of Finance – maintaining its ultimate control of national budgetary process – defeated the proposal.[81]

---

[80] Muramatsu and Pempel, "The Evolution of the Civil Service before World War II," in Kim et al., eds., *Japanese Civil Service*, 175–8; T. L. Blakemore to W. S. Rogers, June 16, 1941, T. L. Blakemore Letters from Japan 1939–41, File 2, Folder 8, JHW Papers, Japan Correspondence, Box 1, SC, NWU.

[81] Gao, *Economic Ideology and Japanese Industrial Policy*, 109–13, quote at 110; Haley, "Japan's Postwar Civil Service," in Kim et al., eds., *Japanese Civil Service*, 92.

Blakemore's experience suggested that reliance upon comparative legal discourse sustained Westernized liberal thinking among some academics. With the aid of Takayanagi Kenzo, professor of Anglo-American Law, Blakemore became one of only a few foreign students to study at Tokyo Imperial University during the 1930s and early 1940s. Despite the mounting U.S.–Japanese tensions and militarist power, Blakemore encountered a group of liberal-minded professors. In addition to Takayanagi, he received support from Takagi Yasaka, who taught American Constitutional Law and American History and Tanaka Kotaro, the Law Department's former dean and one of Japan's leading authorities on commercial law.[82] Takagi pioneered the Japanese study of American constitutional institutions and the ideas of personal responsibility underlying the Declaration of Independence. Reflecting faith in Taisho democracy, Takagi's first book published in 1931, *Amerika seijishi jostu*, argued that, in order for Japan to adopt Anglo-American parliamentary institutions, its people should first develop Protestant Christianity's individualistic spiritual consciousness. His argument was significant in part because it suggested that Japanese culture and institutions could incorporate on their own terms Anglo-American liberal constitutional and economic values.[83]

Tanaka employed transnational comparisons to advocate a more liberal legal discourse. In a prize-winning study published in 1932 entitled "A Theory of Global Law" Tanaka applied Western natural law theories to Japanese national and imperialist experience. He refuted the growing influence of those who argued that law should embody and enforce Japan's distinctive cultural and racial patterns of conduct. Tanaka agreed with his opponents that the "ethnic nation" (*minzoku*) embraced a distinctive way of life; he argued, however, that the state's legal rules were part of a multiethnic constitutional regime which both transcended and legitimated this "ethnic nation." He drew an analogy between Japan's incorporation of Korea and Taiwan into a multiethnic imperial state and the multiethnic empires of Great Britain and the United States. Moreover, natural law provided the underlying theoretical legitimacy sustaining a relative degree of liberalism throughout these imperial states. Tanaka used this transnational natural law reasoning to sanction a liberal interpretation of the Meiji Constitution and the law it sanctioned. His argument enabled him to distinguish cultural imperatives such as language reflecting the "ethnic nation" from the constitutional and legal order instituting the Japanese state, which embraced this cultural entity but transcended it. Consistent with the

---

[82] T. L. Blakemore to W. S. Rogers, December 10, 1939, T. L. Blakemore Letters from Japan 1939–41, File 2, Folder 8, JHW Papers, Japan Correspondence, Box 1, SC, NWU; for Tanaka, see Doak, "What Is a Nation and Who Belongs?," 295–7.

[83] Tadashi Aruga, "The Declaration of Independence in Japan: Translation and Transplantation, 1854–1997," 85 *The Journal of American History* (March 1999), 1418–20.

distinction between nation and state Tanaka declared, "I do not hesitate in encouraging politicians to carry out the legislative policy of the state in a fundamentally different manner than national language policies, that is, in a purely rational technical spirit."[84]

The liberal ideas these teachers applied to institutions obliquely reinforced the progressive reformers' study of the New Deal. In order to institute government control of electrical power the bureaucrats collected U.S. governmental documents about the TVA and the New Deal, some of which even included references to American antitrust.[85] Moreover, a few German studies of cartels made reference to American examples.[86] Almost certainly, these sources had no practical bearing on the progressive reformer bureaucrats' policy making; very likely, however, the comparative and historically minded teaching method the two professors used in their classes did refer to such sources and as such would have encouraged a willingness on the part of students to approach policy making from a comparative perspective. As former Dean of the Law Department and recognized authority on commercial law – one of the required subject fields included in the civil service examination – Tanaka was particularly influential as a teacher. The comparative legal discourse he employed to distinguish between Japan as an ethnic-nation and as an imperial-state resonated, moreover, with the analogies the progressive reformers found in the decentralized constitutional order underlying the TVA and the New Deal generally.[87]

Meanwhile, Takayanagi actively promoted the broader Western rule of law ideal reflected in comparative legal discourse. Following World War I, he received legal training at Harvard and Northwestern, establishing friendships with two of the nation's prominent legal academics, Roscoe

---

[84] Doak, "What Is a Nation and Who Belongs?," 295–7, quote at 297, note 44.

[85] Note 81.

[86] Takayanagi's use of U.S. sources, including those pertaining to antitrust, is suggested by two articles he wrote during the occupation of Japan: "The Sherman Act," Monday, November 12, 1945 (part I) and (part II), November 13, 1945, *Nippon Times* (both appear on the front page). For discussion of both articles, see ch. IV, section I. In addition to his law studies in America, he researched "foreign law" in Britain, France, Germany, and Italy. The two articles appearing in the *Nippon Times* were extracted from his lectures at Tokyo University's Law Department, indicating further the character of the comparative legal discourse. Following the earthquake of 1923, Takayanagi circulated an appeal for Western books and periodicals to restore the University's library collections. The U.S. campaign is well documented in correspondence with Pound (located at Harvard Law School), and Wigmore (note 89). The correspondence included lists of the acquired materials and their source. Takayanagi's effort affirmed the internationalized character of the university. Kenzo Takayanagi to Wigmore, January 16, 1924, Japan Correspondence 1935, File 2, Folder 1, JHW Papers, Box 1, SC, NWU.

[87] For reference to commercial law and the Civil Service Examination, see Muramatsu and Pempel, "The Evolution of the Civil Service before World War II," in Kim et al., eds., *Japanese Civil Service*, 176.

Pound and John H. Wigmore. Both men pioneered the international study of comparative law. During the 1890s, Wigmore had been among the first Americans to teach law at a Japanese university; at that time, he began a study of the development of law and legal institutions in the Tokugawa period. In the 1920s, Takayanagi employed these and other personal contacts to collect U.S. and European law books and materials for Tokyo Imperial University's library.[88] By 1935 – amidst the struggle over Minobe's constitutional doctrines – Takayanagi fostered liberal legal ideas by gaining government approval for Wigmore's brief return to Japan to lecture and resume the uncompleted study of the Tokugawa legal order. Two years later, Pound received authorization to deliver a lecture on jurisprudence. These visits involved high level government approval, requiring Takayanagi to maneuver carefully within the tightening formal constraints of nationalistic ideology and power.[89]

Wigmore's return to Japan was symbolic. His early research had direct implications for efforts to construct images of national identity. Tanaka and Takagi, as well as Oyama for that matter, fashioned that identity for liberal ends, while the nationalists attacking Minobe promoted the absolutist image of the emperor.[90] In addition, Wigmore provided Oyama minimal employment at Northwestern University after he fled Japan and intervened on Oyama's behalf when the State Department questioned his continued residence as an alien. Wigmore was a strong critic of U.S. immigration laws which discriminated against the Japanese.[91] Accordingly, the Japanese government authorized Wigmore's visit on the understanding that his lectures and research would involve no political concerns. At Tokyo University, Wigmore's lecture was entitled the "Evolution of Law" which Takayanagi translated into Japanese. Wigmore suggested that among the world's early legal orders only England and Japan, despite pronounced religious and racial differences, developed "their systems by the same mode,

---

[88] Background on Takayanagi and Wigmore appears in William R. Roalfe, *John Henry Wigmore Scholar and Reformer* (Evanston, 1977), 21–31, 267–9. See also notes 86 and 89.

[89] The issues involving Takayanagi's securing approval for Wigmore's visit appear, Roalfe, *Wigmore*, 267–9, and Wigmore to Kenzo Takayanagi, February 15, 1935; Kenji Nakauchi to Wigmore, March 8, 1935; John H. Wigmore [?] to Kenzo Takayanagi, May 21, 1935; C. Burnett to Wigmore, August 1, 1935; Wigmore to Setsuichi Aoki, June 26, 1935, in correspondence from Japan, File 2, Folder 1, Box 1, JHW Papers, SC, NWU. On the Pound visit, see Roscoe Pound to Kenzo Takayanagi, September 3, 1937, Microfilm Reel 95:0540. Manuscripts Division Harvard Law School.

[90] Compare notes 81, 83, and 84 with Shinzo Koizumi, "Dr. John Wigmore: The Panorama of the World's Legal Systems" (an abridged translation of a review of the book in the Chuo Koron for August 1935, Tokyo [typescript]), Count Ayské Kabayama to Wigmore, June 5, 1935, in correspondence from Japan, File 2, Folder 1, Box 1, JHW Papers, SC, NWU.

[91] Note 48; Wigmore to editor of Asia, December 1, 1939, Wigmore to Cordell Hull, October 20, 1939, Wigmore to Shinzo Koizumi, July 10, 1939, in Japan Correspondence, File 2, Folder 5, Box 1, JHW Papers, SC, NWU.

that of official judges." The lecture was consistent with the comparative legal discourse shared among Japanese legal experts and bureaucrats; it left to the imagination of the listeners what bearing the transnational comparison had on the authoritarian principle of emperor worship. Within the complex relational politics of the government, the visit received added symbolic force because the Japanese government conferred on Wigmore a high imperial honor.[92]

A distinguished Tokyo lawyer also urged employing Western legal values to reshape the legal culture. At his estate in Tokyo's Asabu neighborhood Dr. Masujima Rokuichiro established a library "dedicated to the use of Japanese students of the Anglo-American Common Law," containing the reports of the U.S. Supreme Court, lower federal courts, and some state courts, along with "many text books." In 1933, he prepared a lecture read before the Chicago Bar Association which used Justice Oliver Wendell Holmes's common-law writings to defend an independent legal profession as a bulwark against Japan's rising authoritarian power. Masujima believed that an autonomous legal profession bound by the rule of law could "direct and control state and municipal affairs according to nothing but a due sense of justice," in contrast to the "pernicious activities and insincere motives of politicians and officials misguided in judgment and miscalculated in design." The Anglo-American bar operated to "obey justice and depart not from it," he asserted, and as a result it "transcends the Bars of all other nations." The "Oriental Bar" should adopt the same common-law ideals of justice "to hold politics in check." Indeed, he exclaimed, "Party politics poison the State; no nation can be rightly governed so long as partizans [*sic*] predominate in State affairs." Additionally, "Official parasites and book worm professors abuse the law and misconstrue it to serve the need of the passing moment." Equating the ideal of the autonomous legal profession with the independent stature accorded Japan's historic warrior class, Masujima asked his fellow lawyers, "Why stain the sacred sword of the Samurai?"[93]

Foreign critics assessing Japan's imperialist expansion generally ignored the comparative legal discourse and the liberal strains it contained. Northwestern University political science professor Kenneth W. Colegrove was representative of the relatively few American academics possessing a

---

[92] Wigmore [Translation, Takayanagi], *Evolution of Law* (May 24, 1935) quote at 10, pamphlet in the International Law Library, Harvard Law School. Reference to terms of government's authorization is in Kenji Nakauchi to Wigmore, March 8, 1935, and to the "decoration," Takayanagi to Wigmore, September 9, 1935, in correspondence from Japan, File 2, Folder 1, Box 1, JHW Papers, SC, NWU.

[93] [Printed text, date June 28, 1933], in Oliver Wendell Holmes, Jr., Papers Microfilm Reel 35:0001, Harvard Law School, 1–15, quotes at 12–13; see also R. Masujima to Wigmore, April 10, 1935, in correspondence from Japan, File 2, Folder 1, Box 1, JHW Papers, SC, NWU.

deep understanding of Japanese politics and language. He emphasized how nationalists and militarists manipulated ideas of racial superiority inherent in "Emperor loyalty" and the *Bushido* code of military honor associated with *samurai* warriors to impose a European-style fascist state upon Westernizing liberal intellectuals, political party groups, and government officials. Joseph C. Grew, who became ambassador to Japan in 1932, held similar views. He stressed not only the militarists' exploitation of patriotism and economic distress to dominate farmers, workers, and the middle classes, but also the corrosive impact the Mobilization Law of 1938 had on Japanese business. In 1932, he observed, "Japanese business was still a model of comparative efficiency, drive, and inventiveness," but as the decade advanced it became the tool of fascist war making. Grew observed that the "Japanese generals follow policies not unlike those of Hitler in Europe. Trade was cartelized. Foreign enterprises were tied in with the domestic war economy. Foreign exchange became the subject of repressive regulation." Back in Washington, 1942–45, Grew staunchly advocated these views, influencing policies toward peace and Allied occupation.[94] Other foreign commentators disagreed over claims that Japanese racial self-identity was so ideologically distinctive that it was impenetrable to Western liberal democratic ideas.[95]

A *zaibatsu*-affiliated company president describing Japan's war mobilization regime defended, however, Japan's cultural and military destiny. Fujihara Ginjiro of Oji Paper Company and a member of the House of Peers published a memoir on Japan's rising national and economic success. Despite the protectionist policies of European nations and the trade rivalry with the United States, Japanese business had expanded throughout the world and increasingly dominated East Asia. The "most important cause," declared Fujihara, was the "spiritual element. I mean the mental discipline cultivated by the Japanese for centuries, and technical superiority largely due thereto. I would also point out the diligence of our people and the whole-hearted devotion to their work."[96]

According to Fujihara, this cultural superiority justified Japan's "leading China on the way to prosperity." Regardless of the political party leadership, moreover, the "duty of the Japanese Government" was to promote "industrial expansion" as the most effective way to "feed our increasing

[94] Kenneth W. Colegrove, *Militarism in Japan* (Boston, 1936), 9; Joseph C. Grew, *Report from Tokyo: A Message to the American People* (New York, 1942), 42–5, quotes at 44. See also Harold G. Moulton and Junichi Ko, *Japan: An Economic and Financial Appraisal* (Washington, DC, 1931); and ch. IV, section 1.

[95] Compare Westel W. Willoughby, *Japan's Case Examined* (Baltimore, 1940); and Wigmore to editor of Asia, December 1, 1939, Japan correspondence, File 2, Folder 5, Box 1, JHW Papers, SC, NWU.

[96] Ginjiro Fujihara [translated by Yasunosuke Fukukita], *The Spirit of Japanese Industry* (Tokyo, 1936), 8–52, quote at 61.

population." Such policies included cartelization of the cotton, electrical, chemical, dyestuffs, nitrogenous fertilizers, and rayon industries. He disclaimed proposing the "use of armed forces for economic expansion in an aggressive way," but Fujihara depended on the military to defend "our foreign trade needs. No nation in the world can curb the progress of Japan's foreign trade if it is supported by the whole nation and all branches of the government. We have a splendid opportunity to expand abroad; it is the manifest destiny of the Japanese nation."[97]

Japanese bureaucrats and legal experts reshaped these opposing cultural images within a distinctive comparative legal discourse. Thus, one group of progressive reformers affirmed jurisdictional discretion over another group's attempted centralized action. The struggle revealed the complex institutional culture shaping the bureaucracy's authorization of the *zaibatsu's* dominant role in enforcing the Mobilization Laws, despite the militant nationalists' anticapitalist rhetoric and professed sympathy for small business and farmers. The bureaucrats encountered comparative legal discourse at such prestigious institutions as Tokyo Imperial University. Blakemore's student experience suggested that as late as 1941 a small group of professors remained active who possessed a wide understanding of and accesses to materials about Anglo-American liberal constitutional and economic ideas and the rule of law. Takayanagi, Tanaka, and Takagi, of course, possessed no direct influence against the militarist and nationalist ideology dominating public affairs. The wider comparative legal discourse the bureaucrats employed to legitimize their policy making and enforcement indirectly sanctioned, however, some of these liberal ideas; within the unique Japanese institutional culture which held "authority without power" residual legal liberal values persisted for use in peacetime.

V. CONCLUSION

Japan's place within the balkanized world economy of the Depression and the war era was institutionally and culturally distinctive. The nation responded to European trade protectionism, international cartels, and war through a unique institutional culture whereby bureaucrats employing discretionary authority enforced market cartelization under the Mobilization Laws. Following the selective reception of Western experience dating from the Meiji Restoration, Japanese bureaucrats drew upon European and American regulatory examples to construct a system that protected the unusual capitalist order from unrestricted market competition. Despite the military's and many bureaucrats' professed sympathies favoring small business and farmers, the *zaibatsu* retained a dominant if increasingly restrained place within the militarizing economy and society prior to Pearl

[97] Ibid., 117, 131.

Harbor and throughout the Pacific war. The unique Japanese institutional and cultural path nonetheless resulted in an end similar to that occurring elsewhere: big business prevailed in totalitarian Germany contrary to the Nazis' expressed "anticapitalist yearning," in the United States notwithstanding the antitrust tradition, and in Britain and Australia where governments applied protectionist trade over competition policies to ameliorate class tensions and balance the interests of big and small business and labor. On July 21, 1940, newly appointed Foreign Minister Matsuoka Yosuke expressed in an interview the ideological assumptions prevailing within the Japanese government. "In the battle between democracy and totalitarianism the latter adversary will without question win and will control the world. The era of democracy is finished and the democratic system bankrupt," Matsuoka declared. "There is no room in the world for two different systems or two different economies. ... Fascism will develop in Japan through the people's will. It will come out of love for the Emperor."[98] Nevertheless, some Japanese and German authorities were ready to contest these views should peace bring defeat, while some British and Australians did the same in pursuit of victory.

[98] As quoted, Herbert P. Bix, *Hirohito and the Making of Modern Japan* (New York, 2000) at 374.

3

American Antitrust Since 1945

After World War II containing American managerial capitalism's national and international hegemony was a continuing struggle. Policy makers and corporate managers grappled with how to maintain a dynamic consumer society and economic growth amidst mounting competition from the market-based economies of developed nations – including former enemies, Japan and Germany – as well as persistent civil rights conflicts at home, the communist threat from abroad, the emergence of developing nations as colonialism collapsed, and after the end of the cold war, challenges identified with globalization.[1] This chapter examines how postwar American antitrust and trade policies shaped corporate investment and restructuring strategies through the discourse of public authorities and legal/economic experts. Managerial capitalism's hegemony was more contested and the accountability imposed on multinational corporations more effective than critical images of regulatory capture or arbitrage suggested.[2] Section I considers the interaction between the institutions and elite cultural opinion legitimating the liberal state and corporate diversification strategies at home and abroad from the mid-1940s to the end of the 1960s. Section II focuses on the liberal antitrust policies and institutional culture during the initial

[1] For consumer society and its broad domestic and international significance, see Oliver Zunz, *Why the American Century?* (Chicago, 1998), 77–140; James T. Patterson, *Grand Expectations The United States, 1945–1974* (New York, 1997), 343–74, 410, 738, 684–5, 789; Alan Brinkley, *New Deal Liberalism in Recession and War* (New York, 1996); Nelson Lichtenstein, "From Corporatism to Collective Bargaining: Organized Labor and the Eclipse of Social Democracy in the Postwar Era," in Gary Gerstle and Steve Fraser, eds., *The Rise and Fall of the New Deal Order, 1930–1980* (Princeton, NJ, 1989), 122–52; Margaret Weir, Ann Shola Orloff, and Theda Skocpol, eds., *The Politics of Social Policy in the United States* (Princeton, NJ, 1988).

[2] For business, legal, and academic texts as elite official "discourse," see Spencer Weber Waller, "The Language of Law and the Language of Business," 52 *Case Western Reserve Law Review* (Fall 2001), 283–338. The idea that antitrust and trade policies reflect distinct, contested images is suggested in Jeffrey R. Fear, "Constructing Big Business: The Cultural Concept of the Firm," in Alfred D. Chandler, Jr., Franco Amatori, and Takashi Hikino, eds., *Big Business and the Wealth of Nations* (Cambridge, UK, 1999), 546–74; Kevin M. Doak, "What Is a Nation and Who Belongs?" 102 *American Historical Review* (April 1997), 283–309; and Benedict Anderson, *Imagined Communities Reflections on the Origins and Spread of Nationalism* (London, 1991).

postwar phase. Section III explores the triumph of government deregulation and market fundamentalism reflected in public and professional discourse during the pronounced swings of the business cycle from the 1970s to the turn of the century. Section IV examines changes in and the sporadic tension between antitrust and trade policies during this period. The chapter shows that postwar internationalization of antitrust gradually imposed contingent accountability on American managerial capitalism which foreign antitrust regimes selectively adopted; globalization as a historical process was, accordingly, the culmination of policy choices rather than simple destiny.

I. THE LIBERAL STATE AND CORPORATE DIVERSIFICATION, 1945–1969

During Truman's presidency, the liberal administrative state and business organization attained a distinctive relationship. Truman said that the combination of economic opportunity and political democracy which constituted the postwar American way of life should spread throughout the world; but he also affirmed that the American people were weary of social or governmental experiments.[3] Truman's assessment reflected a New Deal cultural and institutional settlement that accepted several principles[4]: (1) big business's oligopolistic domination of leading industries, including automobiles, chemicals, electronics, and steel, of primary wholesalers such as Sears, Roebuck & Company; and of major service sector enterprises; (2) retention of competitive small business markets, including such enterprises as machine tools, venture capital firms, and retail establishments; (3) close regulation of public utilities and telecommunications and supervision of markets through the Securities and Exchange Commission and the Federal Reserve; (4) mitigation of labor unrest through a process of governmental dispute resolution which included exempting unions from antitrust laws; (5) a guarantee of social welfare, especially Social Security; (6) financing the governmental regulatory apparatus and social welfare through deficit spending and a progressive tax; (7) bankruptcy policy that protects corporate managers and employees, shareholders, and consumer debtors, so that bankruptcy is largely a business device; (8) trade policy promoting a liberal system of international agreements; and (9) antitrust policy to promote these policies by ensuring opportunity and preserving accountability.

---

[3] Patterson, *Grand Expectations*, 139; Philip Bell and Roger Bell, "Introduction: The Dilemmas of 'Americanization'" in Phillip Bell and Roger Bell, eds., *Americanization and Australia* (Sydney, 1998), 3.

[4] See note 1 above; for bankruptcy as a business device, see David A. Skeel, *Debt's Dominion: A History of Bankruptcy Law in America* (Princeton, NJ, 2001), 71–244.

Elsewhere in the world, communist regimes or liberal democracies either owned industrial operations outright or exercised extensive control without meaningful review by an independent judiciary. The American administrative state differed in the virtual absence of state ownership and the delegation of regulatory functions to governmental agencies possessing limited authority. What most distinguished the American regulatory state was its ultimate accountability to the judicial establishment. In a series of decisions during the 1930s and 1940s the Supreme Court announced a constitutional presumption favoring individual rights, while leaving to the legislature and administrative agencies greater authority to regulate the economy. The Court formally declared this policy in footnote 4 of the *Carolene Products Co.* decision of 1938. Thus, among constitutional lawyers footnote 4 became famous for signaling that the Court would examine civil rights and liberties claims according to a standard of strict scrutiny; when economic regulations were at issue the Court would generally defer to the authority of the government. After World War II, the Supreme Court's historic promotion of rights consciousness – particularly under the leadership of Chief Justice Earl Warren – highlighted the irony that attaining greater democratic inclusiveness depended on a nonelected judiciary. Even so, the federal judiciary generally sanctioned liberal trade and antitrust policies.[5]

Antitrust epitomized the ambivalent relationship between big business and liberal policy making. Business-government relations in other capitalist economies reflected images of cooperation; in the United States such images emphasized conflict growing out of the culture's ingrained resistance to unchecked economic and political power. In addition, the nation's deep popular attachment to individualism favored business enterprise and innovation at the same time it embodied the faith that capitalist initiative could be held accountable to a wider public interest.[6] Throughout the initial postwar years those possessing Thurman Arnold's activist antitrust philosophy in the Justice Department and the Federal Trade Commission (FTC) continued enforcing the spirit of Roosevelt's antimonopoly message of 1938, which generally conformed to these same cultural values. This liberal antitrust policy attempted to strike a balance between promoting

---

[5] Reuel E. Schiller, "Enlarging the Administrative Polity: Administrative Law and the Changing Definition of Pluralism, 1945–1970," 53 *Vanderbilt Law Review* (October 2000), 1389–453; Edward A. Purcell, Jr., *Brandeis and the Progressive Constitution Erie, the Judicial Power and the Politics of the Federal Courts in Twentieth-Century America* (New Haven, CT, 2000); Mark Tushnet, ed., *The Warren Court in Historical and Political Perspective* (Charlottesville, VA, 1993); Tony Freyer, *Hugo L. Black and the Dilemma of American Liberalism* (Glenview, IL, 1990). *U.S. v. Carolene Products Co.*, 304 US 144 (1938).

[6] Alfred D. Chandler, "The Adversaries," 57(6) *Harvard Business Review* (November–December 1979), 88–92; Freyer, *Regulating Big Business*, 15, 25, 98, 102.

and restraining big business. But antitrust authorities fervently disagreed among themselves and with business leaders regarding control of subsidiaries in the domestic and growing global markets.[7]

As the Truman administration ended, Commerce Secretary Charles Sawyer publicized a report, "Effective Competition." Prepared by the Department's Business Advisory Council, which was composed mainly of corporate executives, the report reflected prevailing attitudes toward the role of antitrust in American capitalism. Sawyer affirmed that the "great material progress made by the United States is due largely to the unparalleled and unprecedented success of our business operation. It has given prosperity in time of peace and victory in time of war." Sawyer declared that the "basic job of our competitive business system is to provide more and better goods and services. ... The test of competition is its effect upon the consumer." He emphasized that the "old Adam Smith type of simple competition no longer exists" and that the "organization of business presents a kaleidoscope of movement," resulting from the "destruction of old ways ... and the creation of new patterns." Meanwhile, in domestic and international markets the American businessman continuously confronted a "real struggle" to "satisfy his customers, outwit his competitors, and conform his activities to governmental restraint and regulation." This conflict demanded, accordingly, "a new, modern definition of competition."[8]

Reconstructing the meaning of competition required reimagining antitrust. Although Americans "have the most effective economic system the world has ever seen," they simultaneously "worship bigness" and "are afraid of it." They "are apprehensive of the giant corporation, fearful about the large labor union, and have a deep dislike for big government," Sawyer concluded. Many possessed "sentimental objections" rooted in a yearning for "small government, small business, small unions, and a nation of neighborly small towns." Antitrust reflected these popular images. Even so, Sawyer observed, "[t]here has, within the years since the Sherman Act became law, grown up a network – if not a jungle – of administrative rulings, conflicting laws, and judicial decisions which have made incredibly difficult the task of the businessman and his lawyer honestly trying to obey the law."[9] Thus, the report urged changing procedures, publicizing guidelines, and broadening the use of the rule of reason to displace the more aggressive policies associated with Thurman Arnold's activist antitrust philosophy. The report estimated that if in place of consent decrees

[7] Raymond Vernon and Debora L. Spar, *Beyond Globalism Remaking American Foreign Policy* (New York, 1989), 115, 131; and Chapter 1, this volume.
[8] Charles Sawyer to Business Advisory Council (December 18, 1952), quotes at 1, 2, 3, accompanying *Effective Competition Report to the Secretary of Commerce by His Business Advisory Council with a Letter of Comment from the Secretary of Commerce* (Washington, DC, 1952).
[9] Ibid., 1, 2.

antitrust enforcement officials relied upon consultation with business they "might well get rid of 90% of all potential cases of the Department of Justice *without their being instituted in the first place.*"[10]

A decade later *Fortune* editors endorsed this liberal antitrust consensus while recognizing the need for continuing reevaluation. Since the end of the war antitrust had become a "sacred cow" muffling the need for constructive discussion. The editors "emphatically disagreed" with extreme condemnation of antitrust; they especially opposed imposing classical economic theory upon the historical process, which resulted in a selective reading of business development and antitrust enforcement. Still, the *Fortune* editors published divergent views of antitrust in order to "stimulate debate." They conceded that problems arose from the Robinson-Patman Act's fair-pricing practices protecting small business and from the Court's "extraordinary" merger decisions, such as divesting DuPont of its share in GM and the blocking of one shoe company's take-over of another in the *Brown Shoe* case. Such decisions undercut the broadly positive market competition antitrust had promoted since Arnold's time, a procompetition policy *Fortune* had generally supported. "Unless it is kept under constant review," the editors concluded, "antitrust can become dangerously antibusiness."[11]

The incorporation of internationalized antitrust into the subject reflected a new phase of policy contentiousness. In 1939 Arnold launched the ultimately successful campaign against international cartels. U.S. authorities won from the courts precedents imposing antitrust's reach outside American territory; they also effectively encouraged foreign nations to create antitrust regimes. However, in 1955 the American Chamber of Commerce in London published a pamphlet hotly condemning as contrary to international law various court decisions which established the principle of extraterritorial antitrust.[12] In the same year the contributors to the Eisenhower administration's attorney general's *Report* on the antitrust laws were sharply divided over the extraterritoriality principle.[13] During the 1950s and 1960s newspaper stories, pamphlets, and books addressed the issue, while business publicists and elite international corporate lawyers lobbied

[10] *Effective Competition Report*, 19–20.
[11] Editorial, "Antitrust: The Sacred Cow Needs a Vet," 66 *Fortune* (November 1962), 104, 106.
[12] The American Chamber of Commerce in London, *The American Anti-Trust Laws and American Business Abroad* (December 31, 1955); the pamphlet attacked the *Timken*, *3M*, and *GE* cases discussed below.
[13] In *The Report of Attorney General's National Committee to Study the Antitrust Laws* (Washington, DC, 1955), 98–114, Eugene V. Rostow and Wendell Berge published a critical dissent arguing for expanded extraterritorial antitrust jurisdiction and U.S. support for an organization modeled on the ITO. A rejoinder prepared by Gilbert H. Montague vigorously defended the committee majority's decision to maintain the status quo.

Congress against extraterritorial antitrust jurisdiction; they also appealed to the White House to establish a process of consultation permitting the advanced clearance of international investment arrangements.[14]

Antitrust's increasing international impact coexisted with trade policy. The Truman administration failed to procure congressional support for the International Trade Organization (ITO). By 1948 it became increasingly apparent that Congress would not support a liberal international trade order incorporating antitrust institutions. The U.S. negotiators won support at home and abroad, however, for a narrower trade program dubbed the General Agreement on Tariffs and Trade; the GATT sought to end the nationalistic tariff and currency discrimination which had sustained the autarkic global economic order of the 1930s associated with the rise of fascist militarism in Germany and Japan.[15]

The ITO's antitrust provisions would have encouraged governments to attack directly *private* restrictive and monopoly practices such as international cartels. The GATT, by contrast, promoted only liberal trade agreements implemented or authorized by governments themselves. Nevertheless, during the initial postwar era U.S. antitrust activism and the episodic adoption of antitrust institutions by other nations converged with the development of the GATT's liberal trade policy. Meanwhile, as antitrust and trade polices evolved separately, the original ITO ideal remained alive – despite continued U.S. opposition – as advocates repeatedly urged adopting an international antitrust regime under United Nations' auspices. Developing nations in particular condemned U.S. opposition, declaring it to

---

[14] Kingman Brewster, Jr., *Antitrust and American Business Abroad* (New York, 1958); W. Friedmann, ed., *Anti-Trust Laws: A Comparative Symposium* (Toronto, 1956), 469–515; A. D. Neale, *The Antitrust Laws of the United States: A Study of Competition Enforced by Law* (Cambridge, UK, 1960); Andre Simmons, *The Sherman Antitrust Act and Foreign Trade* (Gainesville, 1962); The Special Committee on Antitrust Law and Foreign Trade of the Association, Bar, New York City, *National Security and Foreign Policy in the Application of American Antitrust Laws to Commerce with Foreign Nations* (New York, 1957). "US Antitrust Curb Easing," *Journal of Commerce* (November 8, 1955); "Policy on Cartels Getting Tough in Europe," *Journal of Commerce* (October 15, 1959); "Euromart Warned on Cartels" (October 15, 1959); "Business Globe," *Fortune Magazine* (January 1956). On the business and commercial lawyer's congressional lobbying effort, see "Foreign Trade and the Antitrust Laws," Subcommittee on Antitrust and Monopoly, Committee on the Judiciary US Senate, Hearings July 22, 23, and 29, 1964, 88th Congress, 2nd Session (Washington, DC, 1964), part 1, 1–315. For White House lobbying efforts, see Joseph Rand Records, Committee on Foreign Economic Policy, Box 12, Folder 3; Antitrust Task Force, Box 3, and White House Office Staff Justice Department, Boxes 12 and 13, Eisenhower Presidential Library (EPL), 1–100, 101–832; on the "advance clearance" issue, see Freyer, *Regulating Big Business*, 302–5.

[15] Joel Davidow, "The Seeking of a World Competition Code: Quixotic Quest?" in Oscar Schachter and Robert Hellawell, eds., *Competition in International Business* (New York, 1981), 361–5; and Aaronson, *Trade and the American Dream*, 34–132; Chapter 1, Sections IV and V, this volume.

be yet another example of imperialism. The principal forum for this contention became the UN Conference on Trade and Development (UNCTAD) established in Geneva in 1964. Gradually, the developing or "southern" nations – designated the Group of 77 – focused on the proposition that "restrictive business practices" harmed their growth and trade. These weaker nations endeavored to restrict the power of multinational corporations, but they also sought to maintain the employment and technology transfers those firms made possible.[16]

Antitrust and other liberal policies promoted an organizational transformation within postwar American managerial capitalism. Prior to the Great Depression two corporate organizational structures had emerged within American big business. The first was a "unitary" or "U" organizational form in which vice presidents for sales, production, purchasing, and research and development, as well as staff officials such as those heading the Law Department and publicity, reported directly to the president. Henry Ford's motor company was probably the most famous example of the "U" form. Ford not only pioneered assembly line production; he also sought to avoid dependence upon parts suppliers and raw materials producers by purchasing plants and mines, thereby establishing a vertically integrated organization directly under his centralized control. The historic contraction of demand during the Great Depression, however, revealed a fundamental weakness in the unitary organization and its underlying investment strategy: Ford's costly investment in fixed capital stock such as coal and iron ore mines or steel mills brought the company to the verge of bankruptcy.[17]

The second organizational structure was pioneered by DuPont and General Motors. Managers in these firms realized that the U-form corporate organization inefficiently regulated the costs of producing the widely diversified products needed in the growing consumer economy of the 1920s. At the start of that decade, DuPont acquired a controlling share in GM, delegating primary managerial authority to Alfred Sloan. Sloan's experience equipped him to understand how organizational restructuring could make GM more competitive than Ford. Sloan and his counterparts at DuPont developed, accordingly, the multidivisional organization known as the M-form, promoting an investment strategy of product diversification sustained by functionally independent divisions that were monitored by a centralized administrative office. The M-form structure established within the firm an internal administrative balance between divisional chiefs possessing considerable initiative for independent action and the centralized

---

[16] Ibid.; *Attorney General's National Committee to Study the Antitrust Laws* (1955), 65–114; Brewster, *Antitrust and American Business Abroad*, 31–6; W. Friedmann and P. Verloren van Themaat, "International Cartels and Combines," in W. Friedmann, ed., *Anti-Trust Laws*, 469–515.

[17] Richard S. Tedlow, *The Rise of the American Business Corporation* (Paris, 1991), 55–60.

assessment process which maintained accountability. The circumscribed autonomy of each division was particularly suited to a diversification investment strategy of acquiring firms that had developed specialized products whose production and sale could be integrated in the dominant firm.[18]

The multidivisional organization prevailed after 1945. It proved particularly adaptable to the postwar commercialization of technological innovation. Increasingly after the war the unusual American system of university, governmental defense, and industrial R&D took hold, constituting an "institutionalization of research" whereby U.S. antitrust policies limited the right of firms to employ patent licenses to form cartel agreements like those which European governments often sanctioned in order to restrict the public use of technological innovation. An important outcome was that the Truman administration's federal prosecution eventually compelled IBM to publicize its applications of computer technology the government had developed during the war, creating competition in the computer-leasing business. Even so, while universities and the defense establishment provided basic research vital to maintaining American capitalism's technological edge, the industrial laboratories of RCA, AT&T, IBM, DuPont, GM, Kodak, GE, and other corporations – whose divisional specialization the M-form promoted – applied this research. During the 1950s corporate America spent 78 percent of its research on product development and only 22 percent for applied and basic research. Management's preoccupation with commercialization of technological innovation ensured returns to the corporation itself, rather than profits distributed to patent holders.[19]

Thus, by the early 1950s links between liberal state policies and corporate investment were firmly established. In the domestic American market, antitrust's patent and merger policies facilitated the adoption of the of M-form structure. Liberals Adolf A. Berle and Gardiner C. Means in their classic study, *The Modern Corporation and Private Property* (1932), had revealed a fundamental separation between corporate owners and

---

[18] Ibid.

[19] For "institutionalization of research," see David Mowery and Nathan Rosenberg, "Twentieth-Century Technological Change," in Stanley L. Engerman and Robert E. Gallman, eds., *Cambridge Economic History of the United States*, vol. III (Cambridge UK, 2000), 803–925, 908–9. Also, according to Sylvia Ostry, *Governments & Corporations in a Shrinking World Trade & Innovation Policies in the United States, Europe & Japan* (New York, 1990), 67–8, "antitrust litigation against AT&T's Bell Laboratories and IBM during the 1950s played a major – if largely unintended – role in stimulating semiconductor and computer innovation." See also J. W. Markham, "The Constraints Imposed by Antitrust" and D. F. Turner and O. E. Williamson, "Market Structure in Relation to Technical and Organizational Innovation," in J. B. Heath, ed., *International Conference on Monopolies, Mergers, and Restrictive Practices, Papers and Reports, Department of Trade Industry, Cambridge, 1969* (London, 1971), 98–105, 132, 138.

decision-making managers. Joseph A. Schumpeter predicted that this managerial capitalism was doomed primarily because the larger governmental bureaucracies and corporate organizations sustaining it would stifle ongoing technological innovation. Writing in 1954, however, Berle argued that the separation between owners and managers constituted an enduring capitalist revolution making big business more socially benign. Berle also pointed out that liberal antitrust and securities policies promoted the rise of institutional investors such as pension trusts and mutual funds which eventually might dominate the investment strategies of the leading corporations, further strengthening their societal accountability.[20]

Berle's analysis suggested how profoundly liberal government polices shaped the early cold war's corporate diversification process. During the Truman administration Ford Motor Co. adopted the multidivisional form. Meanwhile, the managerial control that the M-form instituted enabled DuPont, Westinghouse, Sears, Standard Oil, and GM to pursue successful investment strategies that enlarged domestic market penetration. Especially in the American South, New Deal labor and agricultural policies – sustained in numerous Supreme Court decisions – – promoted the postwar movement of northern-based corporate subsidiaries southward, which in turn began to erode the economic incentives for maintaining the Jim Crow labor system. As a result, during the 1950s, southern promoters competed to attract to their communities the employment and investment fostered by northern-headquartered corporate subsidiaries.[21]

A similar institutional pattern characterized the investment sustaining the movement of American corporations abroad. A "parent corporation normally operates through subsidiary corporations each organized in the state where it is to operate." In order for the U.S. multinational firm's subsidiary to do business it was necessary that the foreign state's laws authorize the "parent corporation" to "own shares of the stock of another corporation ... and ... it must be possible for the shares of the subsidiary to be owned by one corporation to an extent sufficient to confer effective control." As a practical matter, these legal and investment imperatives created a troubled corporate "divided personality." The parent corporation's

[20] Adolf A. Berle, Jr. and Gardiner Means, *The Modern Corporation and Private Property* (New York, 1932); Adolf A. Berle, Jr., *The 20th Century Capitalist Revolution* (New York, 1954); Joseph A. Schumpeter, *Capitalism, Socialism and Democracy*,3rd edn (New York, 1975); William Lee Baldwin, *Antitrust and the Changing Corporation* (Durham, 1961), 118–226; Thomas K. McCraw, "In Retrospect Berle and Means," *Reviews in American History* 18 (1990), 578–96; Jordan A. Schwarz, *Liberal Adolf A. Berle and the Vision of American Era* (New York, 1987).

[21] Gavin Wright, *Old South, New South* (New York, 1986), 52–75; Elizabeth Jacoway and David R. Colburn, eds., *Southern Businessmen and Desegregation* (Baton Rouge, LA, 1982); Adam Fairclough, *Better Day Coming Blacks and Equality, 1890–2000* (New York, 2001).

"home country (in particular the United States) finds it hard to resist the temptation to extend its authority over the foreign subsidiaries and to treat them as mere extensions of the parent." At the same time, "host countries ... may deny 'domestic' treatment to corporations not qualifying by tests of local shareholding or management." The host state's authority over subsidiaries enabled local officials to impose demands upon the subsidiary's operation "even where that plan of operation conflicts with the parent's plan that the subsidiary be operated in the interests of the overall enterprise. Finally, host countries are often tempted to use their grasp upon the subsidiary to assert regulatory authority over the operations of the system as a whole."[22]

The liberal state's promotion of corporate diversification had other unintended outcomes. Berle had argued that the increasing separation between managers and owners left stockholders only the right to collect dividends; by contrast, in early nineteenth-century America and in postwar Europe, these shareholder owners had possessed authority to control corporate investment strategies. Berle underestimated the significance of well-publicized proxy battles during the 1950s and later, which suggested the increasing clout of institutional investors. But he was clearly correct that even as postwar Wall Street volumes reached new heights, American corporate management's general policy of fighting for market share, especially through advertising, rather than maximizing profits for investors, was the least risky strategy under oligopolistic competition.[23]

Moreover, commentators representing such diverse views of postwar corporate expansion as critic John Kenneth Galbraith and defender Peter Drucker acknowledged that profit maximization was secondary to the manager's personal motivations involved in winning power and creative influence resulting from running a bigger division or groups of divisions of the sort the M-form organization facilitated. The contradictory institutional pressures working on the multinational corporation's "dual personality" meant that "shareholders will even more rarely exert a discernable influence on operations" and, given "different currency perspectives," it was "simplistic" to assume that corporate managers were devoted primarily to

[22] Detlev Vagts, "The Multinational Enterprise: A New Challenge for Transnational Law," 83 *Harvard Law Review* (February 1970), 739–92, quotes at 742, 743. See also Mira Wilkins, *The Maturing of Multinational Enterprise American Business Abroad from 1914–1974* (Cambridge, MA, 1974); Paul N. Doremus, William W. Keller, Louis W. Pauly, and Simon Reich, *The Myth of Global Corporation* (Princeton, NJ, 1998).

[23] Baldwin, *Antitrust and the Changing Corporation*, 206–9; on the rising stock market and inflationary pressures, see Wyatt Wells, "Certificates and Computers: The Remaking of Wall Street, 1967–1971," 74 *Business History Review* (Summer 2000), 193–235; Tony A. Freyer, *Producers Versus Capitalists Constitutional Conflict in Antebellum America* (Charlottesville, VA, 1994).

"profit-maximizing." However, the overriding goal driving management's early postwar investment strategy was its own well-being.[24]

The liberal state, accordingly, both ensured and challenged managerial security. The period from the end of World War II to 1970 witnessed the most active antitrust enforcement yet. Not only did federal antitrust authorities bring more cases, but during the 1960s private suits initiated by plaintiffs against corporate interests increased sevenfold. Most government and private cases involved price fixing and other cartel practices, such as the enormous electrical equipment litigation which resulted in record civil damages and the imprisonment of executives. The government and private litigants also initiated more cases challenging mergers, solidifying a socially responsive managerial capitalism like that which Berle and other liberals condoned. Increased activism against mergers resulted in managers such as Harold Geneen, who pioneered vigorous corporate take-over strategies. Clearly responding to the constraints of liberal antitrust policy, Geneen instituted a diversification investment strategy at International Telephone and Telegraph (ITT). He diversified beyond ITT's telecommunications field to establish a conglomerate of functionally unrelated firms, including Avis Rent-a-Car, Levitt and Sons, Sheraton, Rayonier, Continental Baking, and Hartford Insurance. Geneen's use of the M-form to incorporate such diverse companies made financial accounting the leading department within the conglomerate, facilitating growing managerial attention to cost efficiency and shareholder values.[25]

Thus, early postwar merger and cartel policy channeled financial management's diverse motivations regarding corporate takeovers. Geneen declared that the "most important aspect" of antitrust policy was that the "concentration of markets within – I repeat – within industries" was of primary concern to authorities and the courts, until "horizontal and vertical mergers" had "virtually ceased." Therefore, "only the so-called diversification or conglomerate mergers remain to business as a method of seeking more effective forms of management efficiency and growth, which could be translated into stockholder values without concentration of markets within industry." Geneen referred directly to the government's antimerger activism pursued by both Democratic and Republican administration authorities during the 1950s and 1960s.[26]

Corporate lawyers also recommended increased diversification, especially through conglomerate mergers. "In the post-war years, there have been some special pressures and temptations to diversify," reported *Fortune*

[24] Baldwin, *Antitrust and the Changing Corporation*, 169–79, 229–31, especially 208–9, 259; Vagts, "Multinational Enterprise," 753, 755.

[25] Freyer, *Regulating Big Business*, 298–310; Neil Fligstein, *The Transformation of Corporate Control* (Cambridge, MA, 1977), 221, 249–51.

[26] Geneen, *Vital Speeches*, October 23, 1969, at 149 in Fligstein, *Transformation of Corporate Control*, 250.

magazine in 1954. "The trend of antitrust enforcement has made it difficult for many corporations to expand in their own industries." Similarly, a commentary on mergers in *Business Week* noted, "whatever happens, it won't be because all recent mergers were entered into blindly. There's plenty of evidence that they have been made only on careful advice of counsel. Most of the current deals do not look as though monopoly has been their goal. Rather, they seem aimed at some legitimate aims such as diversification." Commenting upon the appointment of Harvard Law professor Donald Turner to head the Antitrust Division, *Business Week* reported that he was trying "to channel the merger movement away from 'horizontals' ... and, to a lesser extent, vertical mergers ... into the conglomerate stream. Private lawyers are well aware of this attitude and advise corporate clients, 'If you're thinking about conglomerate mergers, do it now.' "[27] Geneen and other managers followed this advice.

The Truman administration's trade policies had an unintended long-term impact on international corporate expansion. The Marshall Plan aided in the postwar recovery of Western European capitalist economies, while the United States dominated Allied Occupation did the same for the Japanese economy. In addition, the United States promoted the postwar liberal trade order maintained under the GATT, the International Monetary Fund (IMF), and the World Bank. These liberal trade programs and policies stabilized international markets so that American firms expanded by adopting the M-form organization to the operation of the multinational corporation. As the initial cold war era unfolded, the success of this global corporate expansion was known abroad as the "American challenge." By the late 1950s, however, the culturally and institutionally distinctive European and Japanese capitalist economies – which sustained much higher levels of government supported social welfare policies – had sufficiently recovered from the war's devastation that they too were increasingly enjoying impressive economic growth. Indeed, a few foreign firms began employing direct investment in the domestic U.S. market. More generally, European and Japanese governments promoted the growth of their indigenous capitalist systems through favorable tariff, exchange rate, and pricing or cartel practices – as well as the formation of state supported "national champion" enterprises.[28]

By the 1960s, American managerial capitalism's international competitive advantage was eroding. European and Japanese firms steadily cut into American corporations' international market dominance: between the first and second half of the sixties the annual average of the U.S. merchandise

[27] *Fortune* (April 1954), 155; *Business Week* (December 1951), 120; *Business Week* (March 12, 1966), 168.
[28] Raymond Vernon and Debora L. Spar, *Beyond Globalism Remaking American Foreign Economic Policy* (New York, 1989), 109–39.

surplus was reduced from $5.4 billion to $2.8 billion. Economic experts and trade-policy bureaucrats recognized, moreover, that U.S. steel companies did not invest in the cost-saving oxygen furnace, an Austrian invention, until foreign firms had employed it. Similarly, the U.S. textile industry lost market share to cheaper Japanese goods. This declining competitiveness undercut the market power of U.S. corporations abroad.[29]

Thus, despite American managerial capitalism's impressive global reach, its international dominance was vulnerable. In a significant *Foreign Affairs* article Harvard Professor Raymond Vernon argued that the multinational corporation's autonomy held governments' "sovereignty at bay." At another level, however, the multinational corporation's multidivisional structure worked against its competitiveness. American managers had to decide between U.S. or foreign capital markets to finance their foreign subsidiaries, which by 1969 received approximately twenty percent of the manufactured products that U.S.-based firms exported. Nevertheless, the transnational diversification investment strategies the M-form structure fostered also brought American managers up against the reality that the operations of their firm's foreign subsidiaries were tied to the local laws and trade policies.[30]

As a result, internationalized antitrust acquired increased significance. The liberal trade order allowed nations to sanction a wide range of anticompetitive practices in which American managers of foreign subsidiaries collaborated in order to implement their investment strategies. In response, despite opposition from American corporate executives – and various foreign governments – U.S. officials increasingly initiated and won extraterritorial antitrust prosecutions challenging the transnational anticompetitive conduct of such firms as Schlitz Brewing Co., Monsanto, Alcoa, 3M, GE, and Singer. The U.S. Senate's Antitrust and Monopoly Subcommittee chaired by Michigan Democrat Philip Hart conducted hearings on the issue, while experts such as Berle and Corwin Edwards disputed the policy.[31]

---

[29] Harry N. Scheiber, Harold G. Vatter, Harold Underwood Faulkner, *American Economic History* (New York, 1976), 435, 436. Walter Adams, "The Antitrust Alternative," in Ralph Nader and Mark J. Green, eds., *Corporate Power in America* (New York, 1973), 136 [steel example]. Norton E. Long, "The Corporation, Its Satellites, and the Local Community," in Edward S. Mason, ed., *The Corporation In Modern Society* (Cambridge, MA, 1960).

[30] "Economic Sovereignty at Bay," 47 *Foreign Affairs* (October 1968), 110–22; for 20% figure, see *Fortune* (August 15, 1969), 73. A contemporary view of the multinational corporation's diversification investments is H. W. Wertheimer, "The International Firm and International Aspects of Policies On Mergers," in Heath, ed., *International Conference on Monopolies*, 171–206.

[31] Vernon and Spar (*Beyond Globalization*, 116–17) argue that the Eisenhower administration fundamentally restricted the government's campaign against international cartels. Section II below offers a revision of that view; for the number of cases, see Fugate, *Foreign Commerce and Antitrust*, 372–92, 520–41. Compare Berle, *20th Century Capitalist Revolution*,

The U.S. government's trade policies in other ways indirectly weakened corporate America's international advantage. The U.S. steel and textile firms, unable to match foreign competition, lobbied for and received protectionist measures. As Schumpeter predicted, government protection undercut the competitive incentives for "creative destruction" through investment in technological innovation.[32] Similarly, in order to reduce the declining balance of payments that the Vietnam War aggravated, the Johnson administration instituted the Foreign Direct Investment Program, limiting the American multinational corporation's use of U.S. currency to pursue direct investment abroad. Accordingly, many U.S. multinational firms relied on European capital markets to finance foreign mergers and acquisitions.[33] These mergers, in turn, increased the U.S. multinational corporations' involvement in the local law and culture of foreign nations, including incentives to engage in foreign anticompetitive practices.[34]

These governmental policies engendered discussion about managerial capitalism's legitimacy within cold war liberalism. Liberals like Berle argued that corporate management's apparent responsiveness to diverse goals beyond merely profit making suggested the embrace of "social responsibility" and "corporate conscience." The liberals' recognition of corporate America's social ethic was part of what social theorist Talcott Parsons described as a displacement of the older Progressive and New Deal discourse emphasizing economic conflict with one in which social relations predominated. The Supreme Court's use of psychological and sociological evidence as a basis for overturning the South's racially segregated school system in the *Brown* decision of 1954 was perhaps the most conspicuous instance of this shift toward behaviorist concerns as a central criterion. Similarly, J. K. Galbraith, Berle, and others published influential books arguing that the New Deal settlement instituted a benign interest-group pluralism that held big business in check as it maintained the productive capacity and technological innovation necessary to promote the American consumer society. Galbraith's image of big labor, large-scale mechanized agriculture, and big business jockeying against each other as "countervailing

---

118–44, and Corwin D. Edwards, *Control of Cartels and Monopolies an International Comparison* (Dobbs Ferry, NY, 1967).

[32] See note 29 above and compare Alfred E. Eckes, Jr., "U.S. Trade History," in William A. Lovett, Alfred E. Eckes, Jr., and Richard L. Brinkman, eds., *U.S. Trade Policy* (New York, 1999), 78–83; Peter H. Lindert, "U.S. Foreign Trade and Trade Policy in the Twentieth Century," in Engerman and Gallman, eds., *Cambridge Economic History of the U.S.*, 407–58.

[33] Wertheimer, "The International Firm and International Aspects of Policies on Mergers," in Heath, ed., *International Conference on Monopolies*, 195.

[34] H. Kronstein, "Multinational Corporations and Restrictive Practices," and Fugate, "The International Aspects of the United States Anti-Trust Laws," in Heath, ed., *International Conference on Monopolies*, 207–10, 227–33.

powers" efficiently sustaining the world's most "affluent society" epitomized this elite public discourse.[35]

The pluralist discourse explained how international investment and antitrust influenced labor's social welfare concerns.[36] Hart's Senate committee's inquiry into business claims that antitrust hurt U.S. foreign investment included testimony from Nathaniel Goldfinger, director of Research, AFL–CIO. He conceded that the issue had a direct bearing on three million "export-related jobs." Nevertheless, business appeals to institute what amounted to a process for selectively exempting international firms from the nation's antitrust laws, "must be weighed in terms of their impact on our domestic economy and our entire society." Goldfinger doubted the business argument that antitrust activism contributed to the nation's balance-of-payment problems and shrinking export competitiveness. He urged that "[i]n our efforts to expand exports, let us be careful not to dismantle our economic and social legislation or so alter them as to undermine valuable parts of our economic and social structure." Goldfinger resisted altering the status quo which by the early 1960s affirmed a liberal policy of antitrust activism and an antitrust exemption for organized labor.[37]

A comprehensive study by the Twentieth Century Fund suggested the dimensions of this liberal pluralist consensus. Since the interwar period, independent social science research centers like the Brookings Institute, the Bureau of Economic Research, and the Twentieth Century Fund had influenced policy making. From the 1930s on, the Twentieth Century Fund supported research about market concentration and antitrust; in 1951 it published *Monopoly and Free Enterprise*, the last of three large studies focusing on the immediate postwar era. Prepared by the Fund's

[35] Berle, *20th Century Capitalist Revolution*, 61–115; Berle, "Property, Production, Revolution, a Preface to the Revised Edition," in Berle and Means, eds., *Modern Corporation*, xxvi; J. K. Galbraith, *American Capitalism: The Concept of Countervailing Power* (Boston, 1952), and *The Affluent Society* (Boston, 1958); references discussed in Baldwin, *Antitrust and the Changing Corporation*, 178–85, 218–21, 280–1. Concerning Parsons, see Howard Brick, "Talcott Parson's 'Shift Away from Economics,' 1937–1946," 87 *The Journal of American History* (September 2000), 490–514; on the use of social science evidence, see G. Edward White, "Earl Warren's Influence on the Warren Court," in Tushnet, ed., *Warren Court*, 48–9.

[36] For uses of "pluralism," see Eugene V. Rostow, "To Whom and for What Ends is Corporate Management Responsible?" and Kingman Brewster, Jr., "The Corporation and Economic Federalism," in Mason, ed., *Corporation in Modern Society*, 53, 75, 76. Baldwin, *Antitrust and the Changing Corporation* does not use the term but works from similar assumptions. See also Zunz, *Why the American Century*, 115–36, 138–9, 148–50, 161; Robert A. Dahl, "After the Triumph: What Next?" 40 *Public Affairs Report Institute of Government Studies* (Berkeley, November 1999), 7–10; Schiller, "Enlarging the Administrative Polity," 53 *Vanderbilt Law Review* (October 2000), 1390–453.

[37] Sen. Hart, "Foreign Trade and the Antitrust Laws," Hearing July 22, 23 and 29, 1964, 88th Congress, 2nd Session, subcommittee on Antitrust and Monopoly Subcommittee Hearings, 138–9.

International Cartels and Domestic Monopoly committee the study reflected a compromise in postwar liberal policy making. Harvard Law School's James M. Landis, Standard Oil's consulting manager Frank M. Surface, and economists George W. Stocking and Myron W. Watkins were representative of the professional expertise molding the study's conclusions.[38]

The study affirmed the benefits big business brought America as well as the need for imposing accountability. Suggesting the degree of interest-group compromise favoring consumer values and faith in technological innovation, the committee concluded that despite the degree of concentration throughout U.S. business, "American industry as a whole has shown itself remarkably dynamic, achieving a steady flow of new products, a continuous development of new tastes, constant improvement of quality and repeated shifting of methods of production and distribution to offer an ever-widening array of goods and services." Amidst assaults from conservatives opposing the sort of antitrust intervention identified with the Brandeisians and advocates of liberal government planning such as Berle, the report recommended a "middle-course," between "the two extreme points of view that concentration in industry should be altogether prohibited or ... that it should be accepted as inevitable, and brought under public regulation or ownership." *Dun's Review* equated the exploration of contemporary capitalism appearing in the third volume with Adam Smith's classic study of capitalism, observing that its policy proposals were "an ingenious attempt to reconcile the need for active competition with the most efficient forms of production." The *Economist* of London lauded the skillful use of oligopoly theory to draw important conclusions for the antitrust policies emerging in Great Britain.[39]

The "middle-course" policy recommendations proposed modest substantive changes. Increased funding for the FTC and closer cooperation with the Justice Department's Antitrust Division were called for, as well as stronger penalties for Sherman Act violations and replacing criminal with civil remedies in cases where precedents were unsettled. The study urged the creation under executive order of an interdepartmental body which included business representatives to provide greater consultation. The

---

[38] The work of the Fund's International Cartels and Domestic Monopoly Committee (1948–51) is traceable in the James McCauley Landis Papers (JMLP), Library of Congress Manuscripts Division (LCMD): JML Office Files, 1948–51, Cartels and Monopoly Committee 20th Century Fund, Box 62. See also Donald A. Ritchie, *James M. Landis Dean of the Regulators* (Cambridge, MA, 1980), 176. The three volumes are George W. Stocking and Myron W. Watkins, *Cartels in Action Case Studies in International Business Diplomacy* (New York, 1947); Stocking and Watkins, *Cartels or Competition? The Economics of International Controls by Business and Government* (New York, 1948); Stocking and Watkins, *Monopoly and Free Enterprise* (New York, 1951).

[39] "For Release," *News from the Twentieth Century Fund*, January 15, 1951, Landis Papers, LCMD, 1–5, quotes at 1, 3. Reviews of *Monopoly and Free Enterprise* are in *Dun's Review* (April 1951), and *The Economist* (April 14, 1951), both located in Cartels and Monopolies Committee, 20th Century Fund, Box 62 Landis Papers, LCMD.

recommendations included restricting the system of antitrust exemptions through: repeal of the Webb-Pomerene Act's authorization of export trade associations, repeal of the Miller-Tydings provision permitting state-fair trade laws, amendment of the Robinson-Patman Act's tying of price competition to a showing of "cost-differences," limiting labor's immunity to "those markets in which it sells its services," and "revision of agricultural marketing agreements legislation." A. S. Goss of the Grange opposed the final recommendation. Standard Oil's Frank Surface dissented from the recommendation to amend the Sherman Act to establish a threshold to the level of industrial concentration that big firms could exceed only by proving in court that "their largeness was in the public interest."[40]

The liberal pluralism that the Twentieth Century Fund report embodied was nonetheless challenged. Conservative management theorist Peter Drucker argued as early as 1946 that profit making, social welfare, and personal freedom were compatible without excessive liberal state intervention because the dynamics driving American management to adopt the multidivisional form undercut monopolistic tendencies. "All this is attainable only in a *decentralized* big business," Drucker affirmed. "Hence decentralization is the condition for the conversion of bigness from a social liability into a social asset." Many conservatives condemned postwar liberal antitrust activism as unnecessary and harmful because it undermined the manager's incentives to pursue single-mindedly the technological innovation essential to maintaining consumer welfare, international competitiveness, and defense of the anticommunist world. Radicals, by contrast, claimed that liberal pluralist policies ultimately ensured conservative outcomes. Contending that the liberal regulatory state had been captured by big business, leftist thinkers asserted that the "countless laws, such as the antitrust bills, pure food and drug acts, and the Taft-Hartley Law," as well as the "complex system of quasi-judicial regulatory agencies ... systematically favor the interests of the stronger against the weaker party in interest-group conflicts and tend to solidify the power of those who already hold it. The government, therefore, plays a conservative, rather than a neutral, role."[41]

Neither radical nor conservative business critiques questioned that American business–government policy making was adversarial rather than cooperative, though radicals argued that the ultimate policy outcome harmed weaker groups and perpetuated inequality. Finally, radicals said, the liberal's sanction of capitalism enabled business to prevent meaningful regulatory initiatives through "capture." However, the policy disputes engendered compromises aiding organized labor, agricultural groups,

---

[40] For Goss and Surface, see *News* (January 15, 1951), 3.
[41] Drucker, *Concept of the Corporation* (New York, 1946), 228; Robert Paul Wolff, "Beyond Tolerance," in Robert Paul Wolff, Barrington Moore, Jr., Herbert Marcuse, eds., *A Critique of Pure Tolerance* (Boston, 1969), 46.

southern blacks engaged in the civil rights struggle, technological innovation, and national security by preserving – and in the case of antitrust, strengthening – the New Deal settlement. As a result, institutional accountability was imposed upon postwar managerial capitalism; but the tensions underlying the international antitrust issue, trade policies, and big business's domestic and global investment diversification strategy revealed how contentious policy making diffused the various interests at home, while it blunted the demand from developing nations to institute an international organization restraining multinational corporations.

II. ANTITRUST ACTIVISM AND CORPORATE INVESTMENT, 1945–1969

A professional culture of legal and economic experts employed antitrust policies and symbols to shape postwar managerial capitalism. Richard Hofstadter wrote in 1964 that earlier in the nation's history, antitrust had been "largely an ideology," but since World War II it had become "differentiated, specialized, and bureaucratized." According to Hofstadter, "the business of studying, attacking, defending, and evaluating oligopolistic behavior and its regulation has become one of our small industries," the "almost exclusive concern of a technical elite of lawyers and economists." In particular, these experts oversaw the bureaucracy that guided the "potentialities of antitrust action." The social and market conflict this bureaucratic order channeled, moreover, was part of an ongoing readjustment in discourse about the legitimacy of the liberal administrative state and big business. Hofstadter noted in accord with leftist criticism, big business understood that the antitrust process "can be considered an alternative to more obtrusive regulations as outright controls on prices," and in any case the "pieties at stake are too deep to risk touching." By contrast, liberals, including defenders of small business, advocated stronger antitrust enforcement; "they retained their old suspicion of business behavior." Conservatives and liberals nonetheless essentially agreed that the "state of the public mind ... accepts bigness but continues to distrust business morals."[42]

Antitrust lawyers in particular constituted a professional culture. Since the late nineteenth century big-city firms had served corporate giants as litigators, counselors, and lobbyists. After World War II such firms underwent further specialization. Former American Bar Association (ABA) president Bernard G. Segal argued that as a result of the Supreme Court's general sanction of activist antitrust policies, postwar corporate managers

---

[42] Richard Hofstadter, "What Happened to the Antitrust Movement? Notes on the Evolution of an American Creed," in Earl Frank Cheit, ed., *The Business Establishment* (New York, 1964), 113–51, quotes at 150, 151.

had developed respect for and dependence upon the antitrust bar. Also, the "revolving door" phenomenon became increasingly common, whereby after a number of years government lawyers took their expertise into the private sector. In addition, the antitrust community was strengthened through the formation of the ABA's antitrust section, which maintained close and generally cordial ties with the FTC and the Antitrust Division. Washington, DC, became the haven for firms possessing such connections. Numerous periodicals, provided a steady flow of opinion and analysis. In addition, prominent lawyers, such as Thurman Arnold and John J. McCloy had active international practices involving antitrust issues, while Harvard Law School's Kingman Brewster pioneered academic research and teaching in the field of international antitrust. The ABA's International Commercial Law Section published its own journal which included articles involving international antitrust issues.[43]

This legal culture maintained a close if uneasy collaboration with economists. In 1937 Harvard economist Edward S. Mason noted the considerable degree to which the technical discourses of law and economics had diverged, especially concerning antitrust. From the 1930s on, Mason and other economists worked with lawyers to reshape theoretical assumptions and analyses to the imperatives of the legal process. In professional cultures as diverse as Europe and Japan rule-making and enforcement were largely dependent upon administrative process which facilitated predictable outcomes reflecting general cooperation between government and business. Under the American constitutional system, however, rule-making was subject to judicial review and the adversarial process dependent upon lawyers. Even after the Supreme Court sanctioned the principle of deferring to liberal state authority, the judiciary continued shaping the substance of those policies. Judicial intervention was especially significant in the field of antitrust. Thus, while economists such as Mason succeeded in adapting to the legal process, this process was more disputed and contingent than was the case in other capitalist economies.[44]

Kingman Brewster suggested the differing professional cultures in a comment delivered at the meeting of the American Economic Association in 1955. The successful melding of legal process and economic theories, Brewster observed, clearly "suggests an agenda for creative economic and legal architecture ... [which] seems ... more fruitful than lawyers' efforts to stretch words out of their popular and legislative sense in order to

---

[43] Freyer, *Regulating Big Business*, 281. On Arnold as founding partner of Arnold and Porter, see testimony in Hart, Antitrust and Monopoly Subcommittee Senate Hearings, 123–37; for McCloy, see *National Security and Foreign Policy in the Application of American Antitrust Laws*, 6.

[44] For discussion of Mason's earlier work, see Baldwin, *Antitrust and the Changing Corporation*, 133–5, 214–18; Chandler, "The Adversaries," 57 *Harvard Business Review* (November–December 1979), 88–92.

accomodate [sic] economic concepts," or "economists' efforts to criticize decisions by criteria which the courts do not or should not purport to apply." Most U.S. economists, business people, and the courts agreed that the per se rule against cartel practices generally made sense. Considerable dispute arose, however, concerning an appropriate theory governing mergers. Since the end of war business leaders and their lawyers, as well as certain economists, complained that judges applying economic theories emphasizing market results or "effects" had imposed the "curse of uncertainty." The answer was not, Brewster exclaimed, doing away with antitrust; he urged instead "requiring advance governmental permission for some, if not all, acquisitions." A rigorous application of economic theory could foster "more objectivity of administration ... by making competitive necessity rather than competitive effects the standard of a merger's legality."[45]

Nevertheless, postwar economic theory diverged concerning the degree to which deductive mathematical assumptions underlying perfect price competition should incorporate heterogeneous values. Most American economists built on the work of Schumpeter, Joan Robinson, and E. H. Chamberlin, incorporating into theories of technological innovation and imperfect oligopolistic competition a primary emphasis upon efficiency. One group applied efficiency assumptions to determine whether business scale and anticompetitive practices affected social-welfare interests. Gradually, this group developed a theory of "workable competition," aiming for a balance between efficiency and broader social values. According to Vanderbilt University economist George W. Stocking, workable competition assumed that "pure competition is not generally attainable and that pure monopoly rarely exists." The policy goal of experts was, accordingly, to analyze the structure of an individual industry in relation to the conduct and performance of the firms within it. "If an industry is dynamic, if business firms are efficient, if prices respond quickly to changes in the conditions of demand and supply, if entrepreneurs pass on to consumers promptly the cost reductions that follow technological innovation, and if profits are reasonable, an industry is workably competitive regardless of the number and size of the firms that comprise it." Stocking himself admitted the practical difficulties of applying the theory; he urged not employing it in particular cases.[46]

Another group of experts, however, approached from a narrower standpoint of market efficiency. Many sources contributed to this criticism,

---

[45] Brewster, "Enforceable Competition: Unruly Reason or Reasonable Rules? (Draft for discussants, American Economic Association, December 29, 1955)," Brewster Papers, HLS, Manuscripts Division, 12.

[46] George W. Stocking, *Workable Competition and Antitrust Policy* (Nashville, TN, 1961), 180–1, 267 quote at 190.

but the most influential was the University of Chicago's economics department and its law school's Law and Economics program, led by economist Aaron Director. Legal scholar Robert Bork was a prominent exponent of applying Chicago law and economics theories to antitrust. Bork said, "[I]t is the essential mechanism of competition and its prime virtue is that more efficient firms take business away from the less efficient." Bork conceded that where "certain business behavior is likely to result in monopoly profits and mis-allocation of resources. . .[it] should be illegal." The leading example of legitimate antitrust policy was the per se rule against cartels. But Bork insisted that such behavior was exceptional. "All other behavior should be lawful so far as antitrust is concerned, since, in relation to consumer welfare, it is either neutral or motivated by considerations of efficiency. The market will penalize those that do not in fact create efficiency."[47]

Proponents of libertarian philosophy asserted that Chicago economics did not go far enough in rejecting antitrust. Alan Greenspan applied classical price theory, declaring that the "ultimate regulator of competition in a free economy is *the capital market.* So long as capital is free to flow, it will tend to seek those areas which offer the maximum rate of return." The theory reinterpreted the whole history of the business regulation, showing that the "entire structure of antitrust statutes in this country is a jumble of economic irrationality and ignorance. It is the product: (a) of a gross misinterpretation of history, and (b) of rather naive, and certainly unrealistic, economic theories." New York University law professor Sylvester Petro applied this critique to reinterpret the Supreme Court's antitrust decisions; he concluded that the "New Deal legacies" of "[c]rippling taxation, overwhelming union power, and the strangling grip of antitrust and other regulatory systems" were jeopardizing American capitalism. "If our economy were to lose its drive, the record ought to show the real cause of the stagnation. Free enterprise and free competition have not failed. The failure would lie in the principle of government control and tutelage that the antitrust laws, properly understood, exemplify so clearly."[48]

These disputes reflected the experts' efforts to shape the content and outcomes of antitrust policy. The distinction Brewster drew between the lawyer's and economist's expertise suggested the search for a discourse removed from overt political ramifications. A policy based on "objective"

[47] Freyer, *Regulating Big Business,* 278, 320; *Fortune* (September, 1963), 200–1; *Fortune* (September, 1969), 104. A useful summary of the Chicago Law and Economics antitrust theory is Robert H. Bork and Ward S. Bowman, Jr., "The Crisis in Antitrust," in "The Goals of Antitrust: A Dialogue on Policy," 65 *Columbia Law Review* (March 1965), 363–760.

[48] Alan Greenspan, "Antitrust," in Ayn Rand, ed., *Capitalism: The Unknown Ideal* (New York, 1967), 63–71, quotes at 68, 70; Sylvester Petro, "The Growing Threat of Antitrust," *Fortune* (November 1962), 128–30, 188, 191–2, 197–8, 203–4, quote at 208.

economic principles would have a greater chance of acceptance given the popular culture's contradictory fears of unchecked power and attachment to consumer benefits identified with bigness, individualism, and free markets. Although postwar economists had firmly established that their discipline was grounded on scientific assumptions, the disputed analysis and theories of Mason, Bork, Stocking, and Greenspan indicated that the choice of "objective" principle was contingent. Bork and Ward Bowmen pointedly described the need for educating legislators, courts, and business people in what was at stake in choosing among these scientific economic principles: "The courts and the legislature preside like a body of medicine men, giving the tribe a new set of chants ... in order to make the mysterious mechanism [free market competition] behave."[49]

Legal-economic discourse admitted the contingency of this policy choice. Economists Joel B. Dirlam and Alfred E. Kahn critiqued antitrust policies arising from postwar government prosecutions, Supreme Court decisions, and Congressional powers established to regulate mergers in the Celler-Kefauver Amendment of 1950. "Economics is not an exact science; in many ways it is not a science at all. Yet to hear some economists predicting dire consequences of antitrust decisions ... one would think that the tools of the economic analysis were keen indeed," they observed. The central problem was how "to measure the ... economic costs, if any, of requiring 'fair dealing' for competitors." Determining "fairness" was a matter of choices. They cautioned, however, that "[a]ll the economist can do is to indicate where, if at all, a decision in the interest of equity involves a sacrifice of the interests of others. And he has an obligation, in doing so, to avoid overstating the ability of economics to predict the direction, let alone to measure the dimensions, of these consequences." Similarly, Chicago-trained, Duke University economics professor Donald Dewey wrote concerning the impact of antitrust on the nation's economy, "Given the difficulty of defining – much less measuring – economic welfare and the problems inherent in any effort to apportion credit for economic progress, it is unlikely that any amount of empirical work will yield answers that satisfy even the fraternity of specialists."[50]

Central to this disputed discourse were disagreements over how much liberal antitrust intervention business could bear. Tennessee Senator Estes Kefauver and New York congressman Emmanuel Celler, as well as business publicists like Theodore K. Quinn, kept alive the "curse of bigness" tradition associated with Louis Brandeis. But their views had modest impact

---

[49] Robert H. Bork and Ward S. Bowman, Jr., "The Crisis in Antitrust," *Fortune* (December 1963), 138–40, 192, 197–8, quote at 201.

[50] Joel B. Dirlam and Alfred E. Kahn, *Fair Competition the Law and Economics of Antitrust Policy* (Ithaca, NY, 1954), 21; Donald Dewey, *Monopoly in Economics and Law* (Chicago, 1959), 302.

within the legal-economic discourse dominating policy making.[51] Mason dismissed classical economic theory of the sort Greenspan espoused – including its outright rejection of antitrust – as the "apologetics of managerialism." He expressed sympathy if not enthusiasm for the principle of liberal pluralism that "big-business competition can and should be kept 'workably' competitive in the public interest," finding it "more persuasive than the views of those who like Berle, rejoice in the disappearance of competition in favor of industry planning."[52] Bork and Bowmen argued, however, that antitrust policy shaped by the liberal theories associated with Stocking, Kahn, or Mason – rather than the pro-market principles of Chicago economics – was in a state of "crisis." The "best short run hope is the more active and direct participation of the business community" to "inform itself of what is taking place and take an active, intelligent role in the political arena in support of competition." Unless business acted, the "antitrust laws are condemned to become parodies of themselves and the most potent political symbol of the free market ever known to our society will be lost to the forces of economic regimentation."[53]

The professional discourse concerning antitrust internationalization generally condoned economic theories like workable competition rather than the narrower Chicago efficiency principles. At Harvard, Mason developed an active seminar and research program which introduced international students to U.S. antitrust institutions and doctrines; throughout the initial postwar period Mason's preference for strong regulatory theories and distrust of classical economics shaped the understanding of American antitrust these students carried back to their nations.[54] In addition, the Justice Department and FTC offered foreigners the opportunity to study the practical operation of antitrust from an enforcement perspective. Corwin Edwards assisted such visitors; an authority in the antitrust field

---

[51] Estes Kefauver, *In a Few Hands Monopoly Power in America* (New York, 1965); Theodore K. Quinn, *Giant Corporations Challenge to Freedom the American Economic Revolution* (New York, 1956). For the modest long-term impact of Celler's and Kefauver's work despite their success in amending Clayton Act, see Freyer, *Regulating Big Business*, 231–2, 299–304.

[52] Edward S. Mason, "The Apologetics of 'Managerialism,'" XXXI *The Journal of Business* (January 1958), 1–11, quotes at 8, 11. Compare Mason's comments with Greenspan's, note 48 above.

[53] Bork and Bowman, "Crisis in Antitrust," 201.

[54] On Mason's research program at Harvard, see John Kenneth Galbraith Interview, May 9, 2003; Robert Bowie Interview, April 30, 2002, and, as an example of a funded conference resulting in publication of fifteen papers turned into book, see Mason, ed., *The Corporation in Modern Society*; on the seminar I am grateful to Maureen Brunt; on the influence of "workable competition" theories, see Brunt, "The Trade Practices Bill II Legislation in Search of an Objective," Extract from the Economic Record, *The Journal of the Economic Society of Australia and New Zealand* (September 1965), 357–86.

since joining Arnold's campaign against international cartels in 1939, Edwards actively championed procompetition economic theories.[55]

Brewster's international business seminar at Harvard Law School suggested how the understanding of international antitrust grew. Throughout the 1950s Brewster's class work explored the full range of issues impinging upon the multinational corporation's operations in North America, Europe, and Latin America. Conflicts between transnational tax and antitrust laws engendered case problems concerning the "allocation of expenses between the American and ... [foreign] country operations," with the foreign "officials ... claim[ing] the authority to subject the books and records of the entire operations of the American company to their scrutiny." Generally, the manager of the international branch advised establishing a subsidiary to "solve these problems." Gradually, the internationalization of antitrust became enmeshed in growing diplomatic and cold war security matters; Brewster expanded the range of issues that the seminar treated accordingly. In 1958 he published *Antitrust and American Business Abroad*, a pioneering study of international antitrust. Brewster argued that American capitalism's global competitiveness as well as national security required a more internationally encompassing antitrust policy. Such a policy could be implemented, he stated, with modest adjustments, such as strengthening collaboration between antitrust enforcers, the White House and State Department, and the repeal of the antitrust exemption for U.S. export firms.[56]

Similarly, Corwin Edwards, published studies advocating competition. Throughout the period he focused on the connections between the multinational corporation's investment and international cartels; he also promoted the UN's efforts regarding antitrust. Senator Hart's Antitrust and Monopoly sub-committee recognized Edwards' expertise in its investigation of antitrust's impact on international business. A government's "policy toward restrictive business practices," was, Edwards wrote, "intimately related to ... policy toward matters as diverse as foreign trade and investment, industrial growth, patents, ... the degree of separation between government and private action, personal and contractual freedom, and the division of powers within government." For international purposes, then, a state's antitrust regime was "partly a participant in supra-[national] developments and partly a peculiar national entity." A state's competition policy, in turn, reflected its "political, legal, economic, and cultural

---

[55] Corwin D. Edwards, *Maintaining Competition Requisites of a Government Policy* (New York, 1949); Baldwin, *Antitrust and the Changing Corporation*, 121–5, 161–2; Thorelli, *Federal Antitrust Policy*, viii–ix; Neale and Goyder, *Antitrust Laws*, xv; Walter Damm, "National and International Factors Influencing Cartel Legislation in Post-War Germany," Unpublished Ph.D. Dissertation, University of Chicago, 1958, v.

[56] Brewster, *International Business Legal Problems Doing Business Abroad*, 1957–58, HLS, Manuscripts Division, 179, 180. Compare the teaching "problems" Brewster developed to his analysis in *Antitrust and American Business Abroad*, 267.

history," current institutions, and "the whole range of relevant government policies. The ideological barriers to understanding are more formidable than the language barriers."[57]

This public discourse suggested the growing significance of antitrust in international business and foreign relations. The disputes about what constituted legitimate competition in the domestic market paralleled contentiousness about corporate management's international diversification. The interplay between cold war foreign policy and its reliance upon corporate investment made macroeconomic issues involving multilateral tariff reduction, exchange-rate equilibrium and price stability the most conspicuous and publicized concerns confronting American trade bureaucrats and business interests alike. Still, corporate managers in chemicals, electronics, and petroleum appealed to the White House and Congress for relief, urging that strong antitrust enforcement at home against international cartels, patent agreements, and mergers undercut American firms abroad, while most national governments either tolerated or actively promoted widespread anticompetitive business cooperation. In addition, the proliferation of state-owned or authorized companies designated "national champions" were emerging as another source of competition.[58]

The issue of extraterritorial jurisdiction was perhaps most controversial. After losing at trial, the government won the *Alcoa* decision of 1945, fostering greater antitrust activism *within* U.S. borders by holding that monopoly practices could be prosecuted for the abuse of economic power. In addition, the decision affirmed that violations under the Sherman Act occurring in Canada were within U.S. jurisdiction if there were provable anticompetitive "effects" across the border. In *National Lead* (1947) the Supreme Court affirmed the lower court decision holding that patent licensing agreements among DuPont and other U.S. firms and French and German companies dividing the global titanium market violated the Sherman Act. Shortly thereafter a federal district court in New Jersey invalidated similar anticompetitive agreements between General Electric and Philips company of the Netherlands to restrict the international market for incandescent lamps; and a New York federal district court limited the antitrust export exemption of Webb-Pomerne Act in the Alkali Export Association case. During the early 1950s federal judges struck down anticompetitive practices involving, respectively, a market-sharing cartel between DuPont and ICI, and the Minnesota Mining & Manufacturing[3M]

[57] Davidow, "Seeking of a World Competition Code: Quixotic Quest?" in Schachter and Hellawell, eds., *Competition in International Business*, 361–5; Edwards's testimony before Hart, Antitrust and Monopoly Senate Subcommittee, 17–44. Corwin D. Edwards, *Trade Regulations Overseas the National Law* (Dobbs Ferry, NY, 1966), quote at iii–iv.

[58] See note 14 above.

Company's use of international subsidiaries to control four-fifths of the export trade in coated abrasives.[59]

The Supreme Court's *Timken* decision affirmed extending antitrust jurisdiction over the multinational corporations' use of subsidiaries. The U.S. producer of tapered roller bearings joined with its British competitor to control the market leader, French Timken and its British counterpart. The Court declared the anticompetitive outcome of the arrangement to be illegal, dramatically expanding antitrust's jurisdiction. Such procompetitive outcomes continued throughout the following decade, though the number of cases declined. Thus, during 1946–47 the Justice Department handled 12 and 10 international antitrust cases, respectively. After 1948, however, except for 1954 and 1964, the average number of international cases was fewer than five, though in the two exceptional years 11 and 10 cases were litigated. In addition, throughout the initial postwar era the government not only won most cases, but the courts established and broadened the doctrines associated with *Timken* that curbed the power of multinational corporations to pursue anticompetitive practices.[60]

The *Singer* cases suggested how this doctrinal innovation persisted into the 1960s. By the late 1950s Japanese sewing machine manufacturers were challenging Singer's U.S. domestic market share in the sale and distribution of household zigzag sewing machines, a patented technology. Following complex maneuvers Singer entered into patent sharing agreements with Italian and Swiss competitors which enabled them to control market share within North and South America. The Justice Department did not challenge in principle the lawfulness of entering into a patent agreement in order to block competitors. It argued, however, that the three manufacturers pursued an illegal conspiracy to form a number of ancillary arrangements in addition to the basic patent agreements with the express intent of excluding Japanese firms. The issue before the trial court was whether the government's evidence proved that such a conspiracy existed. The issue raised anew the question of broadening antitrust's extraterritorial jurisdiction associated with the *Alcoa* decision. The lower court held that the government had not met the burden of proof; upon appeal in 1963, however, the Supreme Court

[59] *U.S. v. ALCOA*, 44 F.Supp. 97 (Dis. Ct. S.D.N.Y., 1941); *U.S. v. ALCOA*, 148 F.2d 416 (C.C. A.2d, 1945); *U.S. v. National Lead Co.*, 63 F.Supp. 513 (Dis. Ct. S.D.N.Y., 1945), affirmed 332 US 319 (1947); *U.S. v. General Electric Co.*, 80 F. Supp. 989 (Dis. Ct. S.D.N.Y., 1948); *U.S. v. General Electric Co.*, 82 F.Supp. 753 (Dis. Ct. NJ, 1949); *U.S. v. U.S. Alkali Export Ass'n.*, 86 F.Supp. 59 (Dis. Ct. S.D.N.Y., 1949); *U.S. v. Minnesota Mining & Manufacturing Co.*, 92 F.Supp. 947 (Dis. Ct. MA, 1950); *U.S. v. Imperial Chemical Industries*, 100 F.Supp. 504 (Dis. Ct. S.D.N.Y., 1951); *U.S. v. Imperial Chemical Industries*, 105 F.Supp. 215 (Dis. Ct. S.D.N.Y., 1952).

[60] *Timken Co. v. U.S.*, 341 US 593 (1950). Justice Black wrote for the majority; Justices Frankfurter and Jackson dissented; the court affirmed with modified decree, *U.S. v. Timken Roller Bearing Co.*, 8 F.Supp. 284 (Dis. Ct. N.D. Ohio, E.D., 1949). The figures are taken from Fugate, *Foreign Commerce and Antitrust Laws*, 498–551.

reversed in the government's favor. More broadly, the decision increased competition within and outside the U.S. market by authorizing the use of technology by foreign multinational corporations.[61]

Cases challenging U.S. multinational corporation's and their subsidiaries' patent transfers and related conduct led to diplomatic protests from Canadian, British, Swiss, and other governments. Several nations enacted "blocking" laws, and a British court handed down a decision preventing the enforcement within its borders of U.S. extraterritorial antitrust actions. Moreover, implementing U.S. foreign aid programs in Western European nations following the Marshall Plan, American officials adhered superficially to the formal policy requiring that these agreements comply with antitrust laws. Informally, American aid officials dismissed the policy as contrary to the culture and market behavior of the nations in which they worked.[62]

The extraterritorial antitrust issue became directly involved, too, in the cold war security clash over Iranian oil. The eight leading oil companies of the world – five U.S. and British, Dutch, and French firms – formed an agreement with the Iranian government and the state-owned National Iranian Oil Company in September 1954. The Justice Department attempted to subpoena records of parties to the consortium, but, facing resistance from the State Department, White House, and foreign governments it issued opinions asserting that the agreement did not violate antitrust laws. The Justice Department nonetheless affirmed, that "such immunity would not extend to any other agreements or understanding among the participants, or to marketing distribution, further manufacturing or transportation agreements relating thereto."[63]

These conflicts fostered policy outcomes curbing the power of U.S. multinational corporations. Foreign governments, American business, the Commerce Department, and their allies criticized internationalizing antitrust, while officials in the State, Justice, Treasury, and Defense departments, the White House, and a leading group of antitrust professionals supported the process.[64] The State Department's defense of the government's policy revealed the play of clashing interests. In a statement delivered to the Senate's Antitrust subcommittee the State Department's representative for Economic Affairs, Thorsten V. Kalijarvi, affirmed that by

---

[61] *U.S. v. Singer Manufacturing Co.*, 374 US 174 (1963), reversed, 205 F.Supp. 394 (Dis. Ct. S.D.N.Y., 1962).

[62] The British case is *British Nylon Spinners Ltd. v. Imperial Chemical Industries Ltd.* [1953], 1, ch. 19; and see Brewster, note 56 above.

[63] Compare Friedmann and van Themaat, "International Cartels and Combines," in Friedmann, *Anti-Trust Laws*, 504–10, quote at 506; and Alexander DeConde, *A History of American Foreign Policy* (New York, 1963), 749.

[64] For the position of the various executive agencies, see Eisenhower's Commerce Department Task Force and the response of the Council on Foreign Economic Policy, Freyer, *Regulating Big Business*, 302–3.

"promot[ing] an expanding world economy" through liberal international trade and private investment – as well as "our espousal of competition as an alternative to cartelism or socialism" – the U.S. government enhanced the nation's security and "helps to achieve the desires of peoples abroad to share more broadly in the advantages of industrial techniques and progress."[65]

Because American business interests were divided and foreign critics weak, U.S. officials successfully rebuffed them. The State and Justice departments could afford to resist pressures from American international business for an antitrust exemption because antitrust was only one of several policy concerns influencing private investment abroad. Thus, international business and its allies found it difficult to bring unified lobbying pressure to bear, each separate governmental entity having its own goals regarding economic and security issues.[66] On the international level, another division of interests enabled the U.S. government to resist an international antitrust regime modeled on the defeated ITO. Kalijarvi admitted that the UN's Economic and Social Council facilitated the spread of a competition consciousness and antitrust institutions. This consciousness building was not advanced, however, by a proposed international agreement to create an agency empowered to research and publicize findings concerning, and if necessary solicit national government action against, restrictive business practices.[67]

Opposition stymied an agreement but had unintended consequences. Kalijarvi asserted that the United States opposed the UN agreement "on the grounds that the substantial differences in national policies and practices which still exist in this field would make the agreement ineffective in accomplishing its purpose of eliminating restrictive business practices which interfere with international trade." Instead, the United States urged the UN to promote the development of antitrust "national programs," and, thereby to address the international problem of restrictive trade practices by supporting cooperation among national antitrust regimes.[68] Indeed, the United States was pursuing this strategy through various bilateral agreements. However, U.S. promotion of national regimes fostered competitive

---

[65] Statement by Thorsten V. Kalijarvi, September 15, 1955, Council for Foreign Economic Policy (CFEP), Box 12, Folder 2, EPL, quote at 1.

[66] Ibid.; this paragraph draws upon the CFEP correspondence and memoranda Box 4, Folder 6; Box 12, Folder 2; and Joseph Rand Records Box 12, Folder 2, EPL. Kalijarvi's presentation of the State Department's views is consistent with Attorney General Brownell's and the White House's regarding the Commerce Department's representation of the position of international business interests favoring "advance consultation"; Freyer, *Regulating Big Business*, 302–3. The outcome favors the "middle course," and Vernon and Spar, *Beyond Globalism*, 116–17.

[67] Compare with note 65 above Kalijarvi, quote 6; Davidow, "The Seeking of a World Competition Code: Quixotic Quest?," Timothy Atkeson, "Commentary," Samuel Wex, "Commentary," in Schachter and Hellawell, eds., *Competition in International Business*, 361–403, 416–21, 422–4.

[68] Ibid.

national economies in which foreign multinational corporations were increasingly able to meet the global American challenge. In addition as the liberal Democratic presidencies of the 1960s adopted the Eisenhower administration's basic international antitrust policies, continuing opposition to the UN agreement facilitated "southern" developing nations' antiimperialist rhetoric.[69]

Within this context Democratic and Republican administrations shaped the liberal antitrust policy. In keeping with Twentieth Century Fund's and the Business Advisory Council's mixed view toward concentrated industries, this policy did not in principle repudiate a few big corporations' controlling a given market. Basically, the prevailing liberal-pluralist stance applied a structure-conduct-performance analysis. It assumed that concentrated markets fostered anticompetitive conduct, particularly by stimulating inflation, encouraging "inefficient" cartel practices and mergers, facilitating needless product multiplication employing advertising techniques to reduce price competition, and accentuating wealth inequities benefiting producers at the expense of consumers. Workable competition theories did not alone reflect this analysis: indeed, in certain cases Stocking rejected using that theory because it seemed to sanction the conduct of large corporations; experts working for big business, such as Frank Surface favored it for that very reason. The central assumption underlying the structure-conduct-performance analysis which workable competition theory epitomized, however, was that antitrust policy should encompass multiple values rather than the narrower preoccupation with market efficiency which could be "proven" by rigorously applying price theories such as Bork or Greenspan advocated.[70]

The extraterritorial antitrust decisions suggested contrary outcomes of the dominant legal analysis. Throughout the initial postwar era, the disputes focused on antitrust prosecutions of multinational corporations' diversification investment strategies, including the controversial Timken, 3M, DuPont/ICI, and GE decisions, as well as the action against IBM and RCA, enforcing increased competition.[71] Thus, Princeton economist J. W. Markham wrote that "firms obviously prefer above-competitive to

[69] Lee Loevinger, "Antitrust Law in the Modern World," VI *International Comparative Law Bulletin* [ABA Section, International and Commercial Law] (May 1962), 20–33; Loevinger comments, Hart Senate Antitrust and Monopoly Subcommittee (1964), 107–22; William H. Orrick, Jr. [Assistant Attorney General, Antitrust Division, Justice Department], "Address, United States Inter-American Council," December 7, 1964, W. H. Orrick Papers, Box 15, John F. Kennedy Presidential Library (JFKPL), 1–12; Davidow, "The Seeking of a World Competition Code: Quixotic Quest?" in Schachter and Hellawell, eds., *Competition in International Business*, 361–403.

[70] On "structure–conduct–performance" analysis, see Waller, "Language of Law and Language of Business," 52 *Case Western Reserve Law Review* (Fall 2001), 296–300.

[71] Peter H. Lindert, "U.S. Foreign Trade and Trade Policy in the Twentieth Century," in Engerman and Gallman, eds., *Cambridge Economic History of the U.S.*, 451; Freyer, *Regulating Big Business*, 302.

competitive rates of return on capital, and will pursue whatever legal (occasionally even illegal) means as are available to attain such returns." Without procompetitive patent and antimonopoly policies, accordingly, "such activities as price-fixing, monopolization and cartel formation may compete with innovational effort (research and development)as means for attaining the higher rates of return." But when these practices were made illegal the incentives for abandoning them improved. Thus as patent and antimonopoly policies "are administered more vigorously, as has been the case in the United States over the past two decades, business managers have very likely increased their respective firms' innovational effort (R and D) outlays."[72]

This same analysis facilitated reshaping merger doctrines. Truman administration's antitrust authorities had attempted a proactive merger policy, instituting the *Columbia Steel* litigation which for the first time sought to block a merger before it was completed. By a 5–4 vote the Supreme Court decided against the government. In what became a famous dissent, William O. Douglas condemned the majority opinion for reasons that expressly drew upon Brandeisian philosophy that bigness was bad. The Celler-Kefauver Amendment of 1950 enabled the Eisenhower administration's Justice Department to win cases limiting vertical monopolistic restraints following the Supreme Court's affirmation of the federal government's order requiring DuPont to divest its share in GM. Eisenhower's Justice Department prepared the even more controversial *Brown Shoe* litigation which applied the *Alcoa* "effects" theory to prevent a merger between the fourth and twelfth largest shoe producers which would have established retail control of a market share totaling only 8 percent. The Kennedy administration's Justice Department won the case; the Court decided that because the firm's increased horizontal and vertical concentration enlarged its share in various local markets the merger violated the Celler-Kefauver law. The precedent shaped the course of the Court's antimerger decision making for nearly a decade.[73]

Even so, by the late 1960s imposing accountability upon conglomerates fostered policy conflicts. President Lyndon B. Johnson supported an extensive enquiry into antitrust enforcement, the Antitrust Task Force was headed by University of Chicago Law School Dean Philip Neal. The Neal Report, published in May 1969 after Richard Nixon took office, proposed legislation to support a broad attack on conglomerate mergers through

[72] J. W. Markham, "The Constraints Imposed by Anti-Trust," in Heath, ed., *International Conference*, 97–8.
[73] *U.S. v. Columbia Steel Co.*, 334 US 495 (1948) (Douglas, W.O., Justice dissenting in which Justice Black, Murphy, and Rutledge concur); *U.S. v. E.I. duPont de Nemours and Co.*, 366 US 316 (1961); *Brown Shoe Co. v. U.S.*, 370 US 294 (1962). See also Neale and Goyder, *Antitrust Laws of the U.S.A.* (3rd edn, 1982), 174–5, 186–8, 195–7; Freyer, *Regulating Big Business*, 303–9.

extensive divestiture. The legislation reflected the FTC's application of Turner's policy blocking the merger of Consolidated Foods and Gentry; applying the same policy, the Justice Department prevented General Dynamics and Liquid Carbonic Company from merging.[74] Task Force member Robert Bork dissented from Turner's focus upon such conglomerates and the approval of legislation aimed at policing them. Early in the group's proceedings Bork wrote Neal urging research into Donald Turner's suggestion that "many conglomerate mergers (the suggestion would seem to apply to horizontal and vertical mergers as well) are motivated by factors other than the search for increased efficiency or the desire for market size that makes restriction of output profitable." As the Task Force completed its work, Bork concluded that its "major recommendations seem to me to rest on erroneous analysis and inadequate empirical investigations. Their net effect seems more likely to injure consumers than to aid them."[75]

Liberal antitrust activism also reshaped procompetition doctrines to promote the interests of private plaintiffs. By 1960 the number of private actions was the highest in history, at 228; over the next eighteen years the number rose to 1,611. Plaintiffs' lawyers employed economic theories to convince federal judges that corporate conduct hurting private litigants was anticompetitive or monopolistic. In 1950 Congress promoted such litigation, enacting the Celler-Kefauver Amendment which closed the merger loop-hole, section 7a of the Clayton Antitrust Act. Harvard Law School's Donald Turner melded law and economic theories into concepts that extended the grounds for applying the law in private and government actions challenging mergers. In addition, the electrical equipment litigation created remedies and sanctions for antitrust violations, including the imprisonment of managers from General Electric and treble-damage verdicts totaling nearly $1 billion. Finally, the postwar corporate expansion resulted in a market for the services of antitrust lawyers who served a class of private plaintiffs.[76]

The empowerment of private antitrust plaintiffs reflected the postwar liberal-pluralist consensus antitrust authorities implemented. The Truman administration's unsuccessful *Columbia Steel* litigation, followed by the

---

[74] Freyer, *Regulating Big Business*, 308, 317, 320; *F.T.C. v. Consolidated Foods Corp.*, 380 US 592 (1965); *U.S. v. General Dynamics Corp.*, 258 F.Supp. 36 (Dis. Ct. S.D.N.Y., 1966); Neale and Goyder, *Antitrust Laws of the USA*, 199–200.

[75] Robert H. Bork to Phil C. Neal, January 3, 1968; Separate Statement of Robert H. Bork [draft, n.d.], in Office Files of James Gaither, Antitrust General, Box 387, Folder R.H. Bork, Lyndon Baines Johnson Presidential Library (LBJPL).

[76] Freyer, *Regulating Big Business*, 282, 308–9; Baldwin, *Antitrust and the Changing Corporation*, 133–5, 155, 158, 214–18; Charles A. Bane, *The Electrical Equipment Conspiracies the Treble Damage Actions* (New York, 1973); J. W. Markham, "The Constraints Imposed by Anti-Trust," in Heath, ed., *International Conference on Monopolies*, 103.

Business Advisory Council's and the Twentieth Century Fund's reports on big business and antitrust, prescribed the "middle-course" policy toward competition which balanced the culturally conflicted triumph of oligopoly in American capitalism and the persistent popular resistance to inequities associated with concentrated markets. Despite pressures, the Eisenhower administration antitrust enforcers hewed to the "middle-course" fashioning doctrines that imposed accountability upon managerial capitalism's domestic and international investment strategies.[77] The Kennedy administration's Antitrust Division head, Lee Loevinger suggested the policy making continuity: "I don't think there was any dramatic change in policy." The former Minnesota Supreme Court Justice said that his Republican predecessor, Robert T. Bicks, "did pretty well. I think that he ran away with it a little bit, and he probably went beyond what the Eisenhower administration really wanted as an antitrust policy."[78]

Under the Johnson administration Turner's Antitrust Division pursued the restrained enforcement policy against conglomerates. Turner instituted guidelines applying to domestic and international antitrust enforcement. The Merger Guidelines of 1968 were among the most important innovations in postwar merger policy; they proposed statistical concentration levels that determined the basis for bringing an antitrust suit. The Guidelines permitted enforcement against conglomerates on the basis of "reciprocity," a theory that defined corporate concentration in terms of the market pressure the "parent company" such as Geneen's ITT could bring to bear on the firms it purchased even though those firms operated in seemingly unrelated markets. Notwithstanding Bork's contrary assertions, Turner declared that neither the Guidelines nor the "reciprocity" theory sanctioned more than a limited restraint. "One cannot support an attack of much greater depth on conglomerates without trenching on significant economic and other values, and therefore without an unprecedented reliance on judgments of an essentially political nature."[79]

A draft of the Department of Commerce paper attacking conglomerates suggested its subject's broad social impact. The paper's recommendation of increased prosecution reflected the government's and the judiciary's success in limiting horizontal and vertical mergers and the disruption of international cartels.[80] By the end of the 1960s liberal antitrust policies sustained the New Deal settlement which tied the welfare of American society to

---

[77] See notes 66, 70, and 73 above.
[78] "Oral History Interview with Lee Loevinger," May, 13, 1967, JFKPL, 4, 7, 8, 9, 12, 22–3.
[79] Freyer, *Regulating Big Business*, 308–9; Fligstein, *Transformation of Corporate Control*, 205–6.
[80] Compare note 81 below with Freyer, *Regulating Big Business*, 317, 320. Regarding antitrust prosecutors' success against horizontal and vertical mergers, see Victor H. Kramer, "Antitrust Today: The Baxterization of the Sherman and Clayton Acts," 1981 *Wisconsin Law Review* (1981), 1287–302.

maintaining entrepreneurial oligopolistic competition among the nation's largest firms, especially multinational corporations. "The challenge to this power structure presented by the irresponsible rioting of the last few years, as well as by the more responsible approaches adopted by the bulk of the Negro community, has caused nearly all our citizens to re-examine that structure," the draft of the report declared. "The relevance of the antitrust laws – a remote and little understood area – to these problems should not be overlooked." Accordingly, "insofar as the problem is definitely an economic one – assuring that any member of our society can enter into a small business venture which can be developed into a large one – an antitrust evaluation is appropriate."[81]

Liberal antitrust policies thus shaped ambiguous images of corporate America's accountability. In 1969 economist Markham presented data revealing that between the decades of 1946–57 and 1958–67 the 187 leading U.S. multinational corporations' investment in foreign subsidiaries more than doubled while the number of acquired subsidiaries rose from 635 to 2,442. Markham concluded that the "stricter United States merger policy has apparently had the consequence of inducing large United States corporations to substitute acquisitions and joint ventures abroad for expansion through domestic acquisitions." He noted, too, that the impact of prosecutions of conglomerates was unclear. Harvard law professor Detlev Vagts concluded that notwithstanding its many critics, the multinational enterprise's "political power does not seem particularly formidable ... it pays its way in the host countries – to the point where one might argue that, particularly in its tendency to diffuse technology with great speed, it relatively disadvantages the home country." Nevertheless, repeated assertions that international corporations constituted a "malevolent influence" promoting "economic vassalage" throughout the developing world posed a legitimate demand for accountability which Vagts predicted would be achieved through bilateral agreements sustaining cooperation among national antitrust regimes. From the 1970s on, the trends Markham identified acquired unforeseen dimensions while Vagts proved to be a prophet.[82]

III. THE VICISSITUDES OF MARKET FUNDAMENTALISM SINCE THE 1970S

Challenges to managerial capitalism's hegemony gradually changed during the second phase of the postwar era. A market-centered discourse

---

[81] "Antitrust Regulation of Concentrated American Business in the 1960s: 'Technological Imperatives' v. Preservation of Competition, [draft]," in Office Files of James Gaither-Antitrust General, Separate Folder, LBJPL, quote at 10.

[82] J. W. Markham, "The Constraints Imposed by Anti-Trust," in Heath, ed., *International Conference on Monopolies*, 102–3; Vagts, "The Multinational Enterprise," 739–92, quotes at 791.

dominated public perceptions of and policy prescriptions regarding the chaotic business cycle prevailing from the mid-seventies to the turn of the century. Weaker groups were more dependent than ever on corporate America's investment entrepreneurialism.[83] As the cold war dissipated and suddenly ended, trade policy increasingly symbolized insecurities Americans associated with the "unfair" competitive advantage of nations such as Japan. Increasingly, these fears culminated in widespread ambivalence toward globalization and its symbols: the World Trade Organization (WTO), the IMF, and the World Bank. Even so, American capitalism – identified with multinational corporations and an expansive consumer culture – was praised or condemned for technological and organizational innovation.[84] Lauding the efficiency gains that greater managerial accountability fostered, experts aggressively pursued the corporate take-over investment strategy, exploiting the ever-rising stock market. Business groups, liberal labor and consumer interests, and representatives of state and local governments argued, however, that the take-over and merger mania sacrificed American capitalism and the nation's sovereignty to greedy financial speculators and allied foreign governments and corporations.[85] Meanwhile, diverse radicals and their critics either denied

---

[83] Compare "Survey: The World Economy, the Unfinished Recession," 364 *The Economist* (September 28–October 4, 2002), 3–28; Eugene N. White, "Banking and Finance in the Twentieth Century," in Engerman and Gallman, eds., *Cambridge Economic History*, III, 785–802; Joseph E. Stiglitz, *Globalization and Its Discontents* (New York, 2002), xii, 38, 65, 104–15, 120–7, 137, 218; McCraw, "American Capitalism," in McCraw, ed., *Creating Modern Capitalism*, 341–50; Skidelsky, "The Growth of a World Economy," in Howard and Louis, eds., *Oxford History of the Twentieth Century*, 50–62.

[84] Geza Feketekuty and Bruce Stocks, eds., *Trade Strategies for a New Era, Ensuring U.S. Leadership in a Global Economy* (New York, 1998); Lovett et al., eds., *U.S. Trade Policy*, 4, 7–9, 11, 83, 136, 141, 155–9, 161–2; Chalmers Johnson, "Japanese 'Capitalism' Revisited," *JPRI Occasional Paper No. 22* (August 2001), 1–11; R. Taggart Murphy, *The Weight of the Yen* (New York, 1997); Gary Burtless, Robert Z. Lawrence, Robert E. Litan, and Robert J. Shapiro, eds., *Globaphobia Confronting Fears about Open Trade* (Washington, DC, 1998); Thomas K. McCraw, ed., *America Versus Japan* (Boston, MA, 1986); Joseph S. Nye, Jr., *The Paradox of American Power: Why the World's Only Superpower Can't Go It Alone* (New York, 2002); Stiglitz, *Globalization and Its Discontents*, 23–52; Thomas L. Brewer and Stephen Young, *The Multilateral Investment System and Multinational Enterprises* (Oxford, UK, 1998).

[85] See Fligstein, *Transformation of Corporate Control*, 248, 258–94; George P. Baker and George David Smith, *The New Financial Capitalists: Kohlberg, Kravis, Roberts and the Creation of Corporate Value* (Cambridge, UK, 1999); Murphy, *Weight of the Yen*, 170, 220, 235; Margaret Cox Sullivan, *The Hostile Corporate Takeover Phenomenon of the 1980's* (Washington, DC, 1997); Choong Soon Kim, *Japanese Industry in the American South* (New York, 1995), 136, 139–40; Joel F. Henning, "Corporate Social Responsibility: Shell Game for the Seventies?" in Nader and Green, eds., *Corporate Power in America*, 151–70.

or mounted an international campaign against the joint "evils" of globalization and capitalism.[86]

The public discourse shaping the legitimacy of managerial capitalism triumphed during the 1970s. The shock of the 1973 oil embargo rippled through a nation adjusting to defeat in Vietnam, the emerging Watergate crisis, five years of mounting inflation, and nearly a decade of northern urban racial unrest and campus disorders. The combination of painful events – in conjunction with "stagflation" – repeatedly drove home how vulnerable America's consumer culture had become to forces beyond its control. Stagflation epitomized the nation's anxious condition. In the past, Americans had experienced periods of inflationary price rises which eroded savings and the value of fixed assets but also resulted in higher cost-of-living salary increases; they had also encountered economic depression. These two conditions had generally not existed in the nation simultaneously. In the 1970s, however, spiraling inflation and the highest unemployment since the Great Depression gripped the nation. Polls indicated that growing numbers of Americans, including baby-boomers who had known only relative prosperity, doubted the nation's future. During the long period of postwar growth, managerial capitalism generally received support because it had effectively adapted technological innovation and investment to promote America's consumer culture against the cold war threat. Now that culture faced challenge, "searching for self-fulfillment in a world turned upside down."[87]

The declining share of U.S. international trade became a growing source of public anxiety. In 1950 the U.S. share was 16.6 percent of world exports; the share was 15.9 percent in 1960 and by 1973 it was 12.2 percent. As long as postwar growth persisted, corporate America's declining international competitiveness was of concern primarily to trade-policy bureaucrats and other economic experts. On August 15, 1971, President Richard Nixon

[86] Compare Jerry Mander and Edward Goldsmith, *The Case against the Global Economy and for a Turn toward the Local* (San Francisco, 1996) and John Lloyd, *The Protest Ethic How the Anti-globalization Movement Challenges Social Democracy* (London, 2001). For the cultural diversity of globalization discourse, see Peter L. Berger and Samuel P. Huntington, eds., *Many Globalizations: Cultural Diversity in the Contemporary World* (New York, 2002).

[87] James Patterson, "The United States since 1945," in Howard and Louis, eds., *Oxford History of the Twentieth Century*, 165–6; Patterson, *Grand Expectations*, 710–90; Louis Galambos, "The US Corporate Economy in the Twentieth Century" and Richard H. K. Vietor, "Government Regulation of Business," in Engerman and Gallman, eds., *Cambridge Economic History of the United States* III, 927–68, 969–1012; Joseph Stanislaw, *The Commanding Heights: The Battle between Government and the Market that Is Remaking the Modern World* (New York, 1998), 60–6, 129, 131, 149; examination of Alfred Kahn in Thomas K. McCraw, *Prophets of Regulation Charles Francis Adams, Louis D. Brandeis, James M. Landis, Alfred Kahn* (Cambridge, MA, 1984), 222–99; Daniel Yankelovich, *New Rules: Searching for Self-Fulfillment in a World Turned Upside Down* (New York, 1981).

announced an end to the dollar's convertibility into gold. This action precipitated a crisis in the Bretton Woods monetary system leading to new global arrangements during the 1970s. As a result, international monetary readjustment and stagflation converged, sharpening public perceptions of a dangerous interdependency between what big business did at home and abroad. Developing nations' assaults upon U.S. imperialism, centered in the United Nations but expressed most powerfully through Organization of Petroleum Exporting Countries (OPEC), further aroused American anger.[88]

As the nation's competitiveness deteriorated during the 1970s, corporate management's investment strategy came under renewed attack. In 1972 the biggest 200 corporations held 60 percent of the nation's manufacturing assets, up from roughly 48 percent in 1948. In this same manufacturing sector, moreover, the concentration of profit shares was even greater than asset shares: in 1974, of more than 200,000 manufacturing corporations the 422 largest ones received 71 percent of the profits while the assets held were 68 percent. Adhering to economic doctrines of workable competition one group urged Congress to enact legislation facilitating a broad attack on conglomerate mergers through extensive divestiture. Led by University of Chicago economist George Stigler, another group expressed doubt that conglomerate mergers possessed anticompetitive consequences, opposed divestiture, and resisted the need for legislation.[89]

The Nixon administration's controversial ITT settlement presaged the defeat of efforts to contain conglomerates. After initial vacillation – during which the government reached a settlement in the ITT litigation resulting in a divestiture of corporate assets worth $1 billion – Nixon reversed course, supporting conglomerate mergers. Nixon's embrace of the Chicago

[88] The export picture is presented in Scheiber, Vatter, and Faulkner, *American Economic History*, 432–7; especially concerning Nixon's action, Lindert, "US Foreign Trade and Trade Policy in the Twentieth Century," in Engerman and Gallman, eds., *Cambridge Economic History of the US*, III, 488–503. For the wider interactions between trade/energy policies and society, see Daniel Yergin, *The Prize: The Epic Quest for Oil, Money and Power* (New York, 1991). McCraw, "American Capitalism," in McCraw, ed., *Creating Modern Capitalism*, 343; Brewer and Young, *Multilateral Investment System*, 86–91; Johnson, "Japanese 'Capitalism' Revisited," *JPRI Occasional Paper* No. 22 (August 2001), 4; for the issue of "trade," of concern primarily to Congress and the president, as distinct from the wider culture of insecurity, see Susan Ariel Aaronson, *Taking Trade to the Streets: The Lost History of Public Efforts to Shape Globalization* (Ann Arbor, MI, 2001), 58–91.

[89] Concentration numbers from Scheiber, Vatter, and Faulkner, *American Economic History*, 437–9. For the corporate restructuring and a comparative perspective, see W. F. Mueller, "Commentary," in Schachter and Hellawell, eds., *Competition in International Business*, 344–51; W. F. Mueller, *The Celler-Kefauver Act: The First 27 Years* (1978), Published by the Subcommittee on Monopolies and Commercial Law of the Committee on the Judiciary, House of Representatives, 95th Congress, 2d Session (Washington, DC, 1980); Williard F. Mueller, "The ITT Settlement: A Deal With Justice?," 1 *Industrial Organization Review* (1973), 67–86. Concerning Nixon's turning to the Chicago theorists, Freyer, *Regulating Big Business*, 307–9, 317–19; and Fligstein, *Transformation of Corporate Control*, 205–12.

theorists' condemnation of the government's prosecutions coincided with dramatic allegations linking the ITT settlement to a $400,000 political contribution the company made to the Republican party. The government's antitrust triumph itself received little public notice; however, columnist Jack Anderson's revelation of its apparently scandalous entanglements was front page news for weeks. The episode closed inconclusively and was soon forgotten in the burgeoning Watergate crisis.[90] The outcome suggested the government's declining willingness to pursue activist antitrust policies against the rising influence of Chicago economic theories. Indeed, when the conglomerate regulation bill was revived under the Carter administration it was defeated.[91]

Although the conglomerate merger wave ended by 1974, it had a lasting impact. Contentiousness over the conglomerate investment strategy reflected a growing demand among corporate managers and investors alike for market efficiency. The persistent cycle of bust and boom after 1973 promoted an increasing reliance on market costs and gains as the primary measure of economic effectiveness. The U.S. Steel Company exemplified the adaption of the diversification investment strategy to this market environment. Since World War II, U.S. Steel's performance steadily deteriorated, especially against mounting competition from Western Europe and Asia. By the 1970s, while steel production remained primary, U.S. Steel had separate divisions managing commercial real estate and coal properties, as well as divisions making cement, pails, and drums. In 1979, the company hired David Roderick, a finance manager possessing no expertise in steel manufacturing. Roderick initiated an investment strategy aimed at reducing reliance on steel. He sold off the old divisions unrelated to the steel business itself in order to help finance the purchase of a major petrochemical firm, Marathon Oil; he then bought a leading oil and gas producer, Texas Oil and Gas which controlled a large pipeline network. Within six years, the steel division generated only about thirty percent of the restructured company's revenues. Profits from the petrochemical and oil and gas divisions were needed to fund a $1.8 billion debt that the steel division carried. The company had reimagined itself, even changing its name to USX.[92]

The economic expert's newly ascendant "efficiency" discourse reshaped the public image of the regulatory state. In accordance with New Deal liberalism, the Nixon administration initially expanded regulatory control,

[90] Mueller, "ITT Settlement: A Deal with Justice," 1 *Industrial Organization Review* (1973), 67–86; Freyer, *Regulating Big Business*, 317–19; Fligstein, *Transformation of Corporate Control*, 205–12.

[91] Edwin M. Epstein, "PACs and the Modern Political Process," in Betty Bock, Harvey J. Goldschmid, Ira M. Millstein, and F. M. Scherer, eds., *The Impact of the Modern Corporation* (New York, 1984), 399–405; Fligstein, *Transformation of Corporate Control*, 18–19, 203–16, 256–62, 295–300.

[92] Fligstein, *Transformation of Corporate Control*, 257–8.

establishing the Environmental Protection Agency and the Occupational Health and Safety Administration. The dislocation of the business cycle beginning in the 1970s was too disruptive, however, for the reliance upon liberal regulatory policy making to persist unchallenged. As a result, leaders in and out of government seized upon market-oriented efficiency theories supporting deregulation. Notwithstanding a general rhetorical condemnation of government control, this reform effort to bring laws and regulations more in line with market efficiencies actually substituted one regulatory regime for another.[93]

Indeed, the substance of deregulation policies varied among nations depending on culture and history. In the United States, direct bureaucratic intervention declined in leading market sectors, including telecommunications, trucking and railroads, financial services, oil and gas, electrical power, and aviation; the role of civil litigation as a regulatory device grew apace. Even so, the complexities of stagflation enlarged the role of economists who were equipped to apply cost theories to rate making. Initially, Alfred Kahn's original synthesis of earlier economic ideas into a marginal-cost theory dominated deregulation public discourse. Employing a dramatic public relations style, he used a position on the New York Public Service Commission and then the chairmanship of the federal Civil Aeronautics Board during Carter's administration to popularize his approach to deregulation.[94]

After the second oil shock and Ronald Reagan's election the following year, however, the Chicago School's pro-market theories were ascendant. On the defensive in the 1960s against such theories as "workable competition," Chicago market fundamentalism thrived during the following decade. Reagan's reliance on Chicago economic efficiency theories dominated the deregulation movement during the 1980s.[95] Under Reagan, antitrust cases against mergers declined to the lowest point in eight decades. William Baxter, the Assistant Attorney General in charge of the Antitrust Division, did break up AT&T on the ground that it was a monopoly, but the Reagan administration's approach to market concentration allowed most mergers. Meanwhile, the Reagan antitrust authorities dramatically increased the prosecution of price-fixing agreements in the domestic market but displayed less concern about international cartel practices involving U.S. multinational corporations.[96]

During the postwar era of growth, management's domestic and global corporate diversification and merger strategy was driven less by profit-maximization than by other institutional and psychological factors. As a result, liberal-pluralist discourse affirmed that a more socially responsive

---

[93] Compare notes 87, 125, and 126.   [94] McCraw, *Prophets of Regulation*, 222–99.

[95] Freyer, *Regulating Big Business*; 320–3.

[96] Ibid.; Marc Allen Eisner, *Antitrust and the Triumph of Economics Institution, Expertise, and Policy Change* (Chapel Hill, NC, 1991).

corporate consciousness prevailed. During the 1970s, however, there was a reversion to anti–big business popular discourse reminiscent of earlier periods of American history. Thus, an associate of consumer advocate Ralph Nader dismissed "corporate social responsibility" as a hollow myth hiding the corporate "shell game."[97] A conspicuous voice for reform, Nader publicized the dangers corporate power posed to America. Moreover, he and other liberals won impressive legal victories improving consumer, environmental, and other regulatory protections. Nevertheless, the policy remedies embodied such conflicted ideological tensions that they proved vulnerable to the rising popular distrust of liberal big government and faith in the more efficient "free market." Nader himself suggested the contrariness of liberal reform policy prescriptions in 1972: "Some look to the courts, other[s] dismiss the judiciary; some value regulation, others disdain it; some value 'corporate democracy,' others disparage it; some opt for public enterprise, others for competitive capitalism."[98]

New Left radical discourse was still more diffuse. Social theorist Talcott Parsons had argued that underlying the mid-twentieth century American liberal consensus was a broad shift from a cultural discourse focusing on economic conflict to one emphasizing social relations. New Left advocates accepted the fundamental logic of social relations, but they rejected liberalism's Vietnam foreign policy, racial desegregation efforts, and compromising affirmation of gender equality. Liberalism was inadequate because it co-opted popular feeling and masked the domination of conservative forces. The radicals enlarged the social relational imperatives to embrace more meaningful forms of self identity and community solidarity favoring absolute racial and gender equality, while their critique of capitalism dismissed America's preoccupation with consumerism as contrary to authentic social relationships. Still, the radical discourse did little to explain the cultural malaise and pervasive sense of impotence accompanying the onslaught of stagflation. The recession of 1981–82 and the success of the Federal Reserve's subsequent use of high interest rates to reduce inflation facilitated a growing public acceptance of the need for market efficiency. The vacillating economic conditions persisting into the early 1990s – and then the long boom that followed – further undermined whatever broader cultural appeal the New Left may have had.[99]

[97] Joel F. Henning, "Corporate Social Responsibility: Shell Game for the Seventies?" in Nader and Green, eds., *Corporate Power in America*, 151–70.

[98] Nadar, "Preface," in Nadar and Green, eds., *Corporate Power in America*, vii; David Vogel, *Fluctuating Fortunes: The Political Power of Business in America* (New York, 1989); David Vogel, "A Case Study of Clean Air Legislation 1967–1981," in Bock et al., eds., *Impact of the Modern Corporation*, 309–86, and "Commentators" Remarks: Ernest Gellhorn, Charles Lindblom, Robert Pitofsky, 387–98.

[99] Howard Brick, "Talcott Parson's 'Shift Away from Economics,' 1937–1946," 87 *The Journal of American History* (September 2000), 490–514.

The public discourse concerning the multidivisional corporation's impact on domestic and global markets also changed. In 1971, Raymond Vernon pointed out that not unlike the transfer of industrial corporate divisions and plants from the northern states to the American south, the international divisions of General Electric, Ford, the oil companies, and IBM brought technological innovation which increased a foreign nation's exports and employment. But from the mid-1970s on, a more critical view gained influence, stressing the harm corporate autonomy did to American and foreign local communities, families and workers. Within the U.S. market, this criticism condemned the environmental degradation that corporate diversification caused, the racial and gender discrimination that corporate managers practiced, and above all, the threat to local employment that corporate mobility posed. Domestically, the empty steel mills and automobile plants in Indiana or Ohio and their removal to the Sun Belt sustained the force of this critical discourse. The international critique was similar in its condemnation of environmental destruction and the ease with which corporate management shifted jobs from American communities abroad; it also drew attention to the readiness of multinational corporations to engage in anticompetitive conduct and cartels to the detriment of economic opportunity and social welfare.[100]

The efficiency discourse legitimating corporate America's entrepreneurial take-over strategy was disputed. Broad public opposition arose against corporate take-overs. A Harris poll showed that 58 percent of those surveyed believed that hostile take-overs did "more harm than good," while nearly that percentage of stockholders and corporate employees stated the same opinion. Moreover, 78 percent of the respondents endorsed the assertion that "most hostile takeovers are engineered by groups of big investors who are trying to drive up the price of the stock just to make a profit for themselves." Business defenders such as Drucker, Lee Iacocca, the Business Round Table and the National Association of Manufacturers, as well as liberals like Galbraith and the consumer organization, Stockholders of America Foundation, united in opposing take-over investment strategies. Business interests and liberals were too divided among themselves, however, to stem the corporate take-over tide.[101]

[100] Raymond Vernon, *Sovereignty at Bay the Multinational Spread of US Enterprises* (New York, 1971); Mark J. Green, "The Corporation and the Community," Nadar and Green, eds., *Corporate Power in America*, 42–66; McCraw, "American Capitalism," in McCraw, ed., *Creating Modern Capitalism*, 339–48; R. J. Barnet and R. E. Müller, *Global Reach: The Power of the Multinational Corporations* (New York, 1974); Aaronson, *Taking Trade to the Streets*, 58–91; Eric Alterman, *Who Speaks for America? Why Democracy Matters in Foreign Policy* (Ithaca, NY, 1998), 101–80; and note 85 above.
[101] For diverse critics, see generally, Sullivan, *Hostile Corporate Takeover Phenomenon of the 1980s*, 242–4, Harris poll data cited 237.

The 1987 stock market crash, financial scandals, and recurring recessions, made evident the insecurity of corporate investment. The crash in October, 1987, was the worst stock market plunge since 1929, though by the millennium an even broader collapse had occurred. The puncturing of the speculative investment bubble demonstrated the profound risk underlying the global equities market. The Savings and Loan crises of the late-1980s revealed, moreover, the unintended opportunities for corruption following financial deregulation. With American taxpayers footing the bill for a $300 billion bail out, the Bush administration supported congressional legislation reestablishing some meaningful regulation of financial intermediaries. Even so, despite the recession of 1990–91, the increased managerial responsibility implicit in the efficiency discourse seemed vindicated by the long boom that followed in the Clinton administration.[102] During the decade the dominant American public discourse embraced images of U.S. triumphalism. Assorted international critics, however, employed anti-American rhetoric to denounce the global proliferation of consumerism and the free-market model of entrepreneurial corporate governance which threatened indigenous cultures.[103]

As Federal Reserve Chairman Alan Greenspan noted, the tightened links between a firm's asset base and the stock market imposed upon corporate executives an overriding demand for short-term profitability. This led in turn to Enron's becoming the world's largest bankrupt firm. It conceded that it had fraudulently shifted debts to corporate divisions to claim enormous profits. Similarly, at the time of its take-over of MCI in 1999–2000, WorldCom claimed a grossly inflated rate of profits; similarly, the company had fraudulently declared $3.8 billion profits in other large acquisitions during the 1990s.[104]

Globalization exacerbated the American consumer culture's interdependence with foreigners. Throughout the eighties the direct investment resulting from the diversification of foreign-based corporations within the United States went from $50 billion in 1979 to $200 billion in 1986. The expansion drew upon two fundamental transformations in the structure of the global economy. First, the growing impact of knowledge-based

---

[102] Institute for International Economics, Special Report G, *Resolving the Global Economic Crisis: After Wall Street a Statement by Thirty-Three Economists from Thirteen Countries* (Washington, DC, 1987); and note 110.

[103] Compare notes 88, 107, 108, and 111.

[104] For Greenspan, "Survey: The World Economy, The Unfinished Recession," 364 *The Economist* (September 28–October 4, 2002), 23–4. Concerning scandals, see Douglas M. Branson, "Enron and Its Aftermath," Unpublished; Richard Waters and Philip Coggan, "WorldCom on the verge of collapse," *Financial Times* (Thursday, June 27, 2002); "Subpoenas Issued to Top WorldCom Executives," *Financial Times* (Friday, June 28, 2002); "Bush Pledges to Crack Down on Corporate Crime," *Financial Times* (June 29/30, 2002); "WorldCom Investigators Look for Link to Ebbers," *Financial Times* (July 13/14, 2002).

industries firmly took hold during the 1980s, constituting a revolution in Information Technology; second, the precipitous growth in private domestic and international investment was made possible largely through the creation of a global capital market.[105]

As consumers, Americans readily embraced the international merchandise market that globalization represented. As citizens and workers, however, they shared a sense of national and personal vulnerability. In 1988, "75% of U.S. adults surveyed in a poll conducted. . . for a group of Japanese firms agreed that foreign acquisitions have boosted U.S. economic growth, employment, and competitiveness. Nevertheless, nearly 75% viewed the increased foreign presence as undesirable." Tennessee, for example, was a leading recipient of foreign direct investment: in 1994 manufacturing, sales, and distribution of 113 Japanese firms accounted for 26,840 jobs as a result of $4.8 billion investment. According to Tennessee Governor Lamar Alexander, the "English, the Germans, and the Dutch each own about as much of us as the Japanese do. Altogether, foreign investment in Tennessee is about the same as GM's investment in the new Saturn Plant ... only about five per cent of our manufacturing base."[106]

By the 1990s, a policy discourse of market fundamentalism and globalization prevailed. Increasingly, U.S. officials and legal–economic professionals debated the need to incorporate cultural and institutional factors into policies affecting the nation's global competitiveness. The transition from a public discourse of "decline" to one of American "triumphalism" maintained a consistent preoccupation with the U.S. competitive position in relation to Europe and Pacific rim nations. One group of policy makers – including those espousing the IMF's Washington consensus toward developing and newly developed nations – embraced an overriding faith in market fundamentalism. At its most useful level, this approach was consistent with the institutional ideas of Douglass C. North who emphasized the importance of incentives in the operation of economic markets or political and legal systems; accordingly, imperfect information, transaction costs, and other factors brought about outcomes that were neither optimal nor beneficial to those who purportedly sought such results through manipulation of the rules. Not unlike Corwin Edwards' assessment of the importance of ideology to explaining the diverse international pattern of antitrust regimes, North argued that groups pursued contrary views of self-interest because religious and ideological conflicts fostered opposing perceptions of property rights.[107]

---

[105] The foreign direct investment figure is from Vernon and Spar, *Beyond Globalism*, 137.

[106] Choong Soon Kim, *Japanese Industry in the American South* (New York, 1995), 136, 139–40, Lamar, as quoted at 138.

[107] Douglas C. North, *Institutions Institutional Change and Economic Performance* (Cambridge, UK, 1993); Paul Kennedy, "The (Relative) Decline of America," 260 *The Atlantic* (August 1987), 29–38; Chalmers Johnson and E. B. Keehn, "A Disaster in the

Another group of experts urged fashioning policies that took cultural and institutional distinctiveness more directly into account. Thus, a public discourse emphasizing cultural imperatives challenged the dominant belief in market fundamentalism. Even so, *The Atlantic* in 1990 observed, "China and Japan as examples," and suggested "what American business may be doing wrong overseas." It was not a problem of "resolve," but of "cultural blindness. Although the specific experience in China and Japan differ greatly in detail, Americans in both countries in recent years have ... failed to understand the character and the mechanics of the local political and economic regime. As American business confronts new markets in the formerly communist nations of Europe – and continues trying to penetrate markets in Asia – it must bear some lessons in mind."[108] Inferentially, such warnings reflected American political economist Francis Fukayama's underlying assumption stated in another context, that Chicago neoclassical economic and related "macro-economic growth models ... cannot account for 30% to 40% of actual observed economic growth that goes on in the world." According to Fukayama, "it is cultural factors that account for that residual." Moreover, "[e]verybody is embedded in a whole series of overlapping social groups, including the family, the workplace, the local community, and the state."[109]

Other commentators focused on the anticompetitive behavior impinging on liberal trade among distinctive capitalist regimes. The ongoing U.S.–Japanese trade dispute exacerbated international concerns that currency exchange, tariff, and pricing policies were no longer sufficient to preserve the postwar liberal trade order. Accordingly, Raymond Vernon observed, U.S. trade policy makers should understand that multinational corporations were increasingly involved in anticompetitive practices that in order to be remedied demanded international antitrust action. Since 1947 successive GATT rounds lowered macroeconomic trade barriers throughout the world, facilitating the integration of domestic economies into a global business order based on internationally deregulated capital markets, which nonetheless remained rooted in the multinational corporation's host state. A measure of this market globalization was that in 1995 the world Gross National Product (GNP) was $25,223 billion, with 200 multinational corporations turning over $7,850 billion. Thus, multinational

---

[108] Editors, "Innocents Abroad," 266 *The Atlantic* 4 (October 1990), 55. For the wider "cultural" perspective, see Sheila Johnson, *The Japanese Through American Eyes* (Tokyo, 1988); Endymion Wilkinson, *Japan Versus The West Image and Reality* (London, 1990); James Day Hodgson, Yoshihiro Sano, and John L. Graham, *Doing Business with the New Japan* (Lanham, MD, 2000).

[109] Francis Fukayama, "Culture and the Market Process," in *Market Process Update: News from the Center for Market Processes at George Mason University* (Fairfax, VA, Spring 1997), 1.

corporations' anticompetitive practices were an unintended consequence of effective trade liberalization which macroeconomic trade policies left unregulated.[110]

Meanwhile, a critical discourse opposing globalization disputed this growing international order. Conservative journalist Patrick J. Buchanan argued that the U.S. government's rejection of trade protectionism and sanction of the global regime associated with the WTO constituted the "Great Betrayal" harming America's workers, families, constitutional sovereignty, and national security.[111] Starting with the 1999 Seattle meeting of the WTO, more radical antiglobalization groups became increasingly active. Condemning international capitalism, the protestors represented a loose alliance, including nongovernmental organizations such as Oxfam, radical environmentalists such as Greenpeace, advocates of consumers and workers throughout the developed and underdeveloped nations, assorted right and left wing defenders of traditional society, and nihilists. While the antiglobalization and anticapitalist discourse condemned the relentless proliferation of American consumerism with an internationalist rhetoric, it was reminiscent of the New Left's yearning for more authentic, humane, and equitable social relations. Also joining the visionary chorus were members of the international establishment such as Nobel–prize winning economist Joseph Stiglitz, whose book *Globalization And Its Discontents* (2002) argued that the IMF was destroying poor nations.[112]

IV. THE GLOBALIZATION OF ANTITRUST SINCE THE 1970s

Despite all criticisms, the practice and symbol of antitrust gradually acquired international force. In 1968 Turner had instituted merger guidelines intended to draw a clearer line between legal and illegal conduct in mergers, including anticompetitive effects resulting from conglomerates. Antitrust policy was nonetheless changing to facilitate national and international diversification investment strategies favoring corporate takeovers. Initially, the Nixon administration supported aggressive antitrust

[110] Vernon and Spar, *Beyond Globalism*, 139; Tony A. Freyer, "Regulatory Distinctiveness and Extraterritorial Competition Policy in Japanese–US Trade," 21 *World Competition Law and Economics Review* (September 1998), 5–53, figures quoted at 9; Organization for Economic Co-Operation and Development, *Antitrust and Market Access, The Scope and Coverage of Competition Laws and Implications for Trade* (Paris, 1996); Edward M. Graham and J. David Richardson, eds., *Global Competition Policy* (Washington, DC, 1997); Jagdish Bhagwati and Mathias Hirsch, eds., *The Uruguay Round and Beyond* (Ann Arbor, MI, 1998); John Whalley and Colleen Hamilton, *The Trading System After the Uruguay Round* (Washington, DC, 1996).
[111] Patrick J. Buchanan, *The Great Betrayal: How American Sovereignty and Social Justice Are Being Sacrificed to the Gods of the Global Economy* (Boston, 1998).
[112] See notes 86 and 107.

prosecutions as a way of preserving "Mom and Pop" stores. Soon, however, Nixon switched course in favor of Bork's vigorous condemnation of the conglomerate prosecutions. Under the Ford and Carter administrations congressional opponents defeated stronger antimerger legislation, such as the "no-fault" Monopolization Bill, the Industrial Reorganization Act, and the Monopolization Reform Act. Over the coming decades, however, U.S. antitrust officials increasingly prosecuted multinational corporations through cooperation with antitrust regimes abroad.[113]

Gerald Ford signed the Hart-Scott-Rodino Antitrust Improvement Act of 1976 (HSR). Reflecting growing community and state agitation over corporate diversification resulting in the loss of local jobs, taxes, and resources, the law included the *parens patriae* provision authorizing federal funds for state attorneys general to prosecute antitrust actions. The law also made managements' merger decisions more transparent and thus open to takeover strategies. The HSR act required firms to inform the Justice Department and the FTC before going ahead with mergers that exceeded the size limits the Turner guidelines had established; it imposed, too, a mandatory waiting period before certain acquisitions and tender offers could proceed. Also, the Justice Department and the FTC maintained a lenient policy toward mergers. The Supreme Court's *GTE Sylvania* decision underlined the shift: in 1977 it applied the rule of reason to allow a territorial vertical restraint on the basis of economic efficiency. The decision reversed a Warren Court precedent which had held that such restraints were illegal. While the Carter administration vacillated on the matter of mergers, Antitrust Division head Donald I. Baker rejected a 10-million dollar congressional appropriation to strengthen the state antitrust prosecutions. The refusal corresponded with the Supreme Court's *Illinois Brick* decision which imposed limitations on state actions.[114]

By the mid-1970s Chicago efficiency theories achieved growing power over the thinking of legal–economic experts. Broadly, policy makers and experts systematically repudiated the pluralist economic theories associated with "workable competition" and Turner's policies limiting conglomerate mergers.[115] In 1978 Bork published what became an influential statement of the Chicago School antitrust vision, *The Antitrust Paradox*. Dismissing pluralistic policy goals as merely "a jumble of half-digested notions and mythologies," Bork affirmed that antitrust policy had one legitimate purpose: "consumer welfare maximization." For courts, legislatures, and legal-economic professionals the "important point" was that the "ultimate goal

---

[113] See notes 89–91; and see below.

[114] Freyer, *Regulating Big Business*, 319–23; *Continental T.V. Inc. v. G.T.E. Sylvania, Inc.*, 433 US 36 (1977); *Illinois v. Illinois Brick Co.*, 431 US 720 (1977).

[115] Compare the divergent analysis of "efficiency" in John E. Kwoka, Jr. and Lawrence J. White, *Antitrust Revolution Economics, Competition, and Policy* (New York, 1999) to Neale and Goyder, *The Antitrust Laws*. Also see notes 89–91 and 96.

of consumer welfare provides a common denominator by which gains in destruction of monopoly power can be estimated against losses in efficiency, and economic theory provides the means of assessing the probable sizes of the gains and losses." He asserted, moreover, a "high probability," that "dissolving any oligopolistic firm that grew to its present size would inflict a serious welfare loss." Nevertheless, Bork attested, contradictory court decisions sustained an antitrust policy "at war with itself." Although Bork protested "ideological" antitrust values, he recognized that antitrust symbols shaped policy making, including corporate take-over rules. Antitrust law had, Bork wrote, a "unique symbolic and educative influence over public attitudes toward free markets and capitalism." Accordingly, he condemned the Nixon administration's prosecutions of conglomerate mergers because they undercut "efficient" corporate diversification strategies.[116]

Reagan administration antitrust officials entrenched the Chicago free market theories, though not without opposition. Antitrust Division head William Baxter, a Stanford Law professor, did win a major victory under monopoly doctrines, breaking up A T & T. In the merger and cartel field, however, he significantly altered the proportion of cases. Following policy priorities reaching back decades, the Carter Justice Department brought 67.5 cases annually, 30 civil and 37.5 criminal. Baxter and his successors, however, initiated 94 cases annually, 80 criminal and 14 civil. The shift had considerable enforcement significance. Unlike its predecessors, the Reagan Antitrust Division generally declined to prosecute either price or non-price vertical restraints, a policy the federal courts sanctioned; at the same time these officials took a lenient policy toward mergers. The enforcement record of the FTC was similar. The laxity toward mergers aroused criticism even from Republican antitrust authorities who embraced the ABA Task Force report. The report suggested that Reagan antitrust officials had too easily assumed that most mergers were "efficient" because market entry barriers were generally unimportant according to the dictates of price theory.[117]

The policy dispute grew among antitrust professionals. The Chicago theories assumed that: antitrust's primary goal was to "maximize allocative and productive efficiency;" oligopolistic markets were generally efficient; in the unusual case of monopoly market pressures would normally dislodge it without government action; "natural barriers to entry are more imagined than real;" and firms attain economies of scale more readily than "workable competition." Other Chicago theories understood that the central goal is profit maximization and that the "decision to make the neoclassical market efficiency model the exclusive guide for antitrust policy is

---

[116] Robert Bork, *The Antitrust Paradox: A Policy at War with Itself* (New York, 1978), 3, 7, 54, 79, 196.
[117] Freyer, *Regulating Big Business*, 322–3; and note 96.

nonpolitical."[118] By the early 1990s, however, Dewey concluded that the price-theory could not sustain antitrust policy. Also, the critics Harry First, Eleanor Fox, and Robert Pitofsky sought to "revitalize" antitrust through a return to the principles of the 1960s, which promoted more vigorous action against horizontal and vertical mergers and some restriction of conglomerates. Another analysis emerging from the market access issue focused on the "international contestability of markets," wrote Edward M. Graham: "A contestable market is one in which barriers to new entrants are sufficiently low that incumbent firms must behave competitively in order to foreclose new entry by rival firms. This implies competitive pricing."[119]

Even so, Chicago market efficiency doctrines shaped a fundamental restructuring. At one level, state and federal courts adopted these theories to reduce dramatically the accountability private suits imposed on corporate enterprise: well into the 1980s there were as many as 1, 052 such suits in a single year, but by the end of the decade the number dropped to 654.[120] Perhaps the most profound impact of the Chicago doctrines was to promote corporate mergers and acquisitions. Indeed, applied across the whole field of antitrust, tax and securities law, free market efficiency theories gave broad symbolic and instrumental legitimacy to corporate takeovers.[121] A case in point was the diversification of Stern Metals during the 1970s. Originally a small dental and gold refining supply company, Kohlberg Kravis Roberts used leveraged buyout (LBO) finance techniques to acquire a diverse investment portfolio including Thompson Wire, Boren Clay Products, Barrows Industries, and Eagle Motors. By the 1980s and 1990s GE's Jack Welch and his counterparts throughout corporate America employed this entrepreneurial manipulation of merger/acquisitions and securities law to pursue more complex mergers and sell-offs; moreover, in the boom of the nineties these techniques were used to reconstitute many firms that had been sold off because of low profits. Imbedded in these commercial transactions were numerous opportunities to pursue corrupt practices of the sort exposed in the Enron scandals.[122]

The Chicago antitrust doctrines facilitated a proliferation of mergers which included multinational corporations. From the late 1970s on, the

---

[118] This summary follows closely that of Waller, "Language of Law and Language of Business," 52 *Case Western Reserve Law Review* (Fall 2001), quote at 301–2.

[119] Donald Dewey, *The Antitrust Experiment in America* (New York, 1990), 131–58; Harry First, Eleanor Fox, and Robert M. Fox, eds., *Revitalizing Antitrust in Its Second Century: Essays on Legal Economic, and Political Policy* (New York, 1991); Edward M. Graham, "Contestability, Competition, and Investment in the New World Order," in Feketekuty and Stokes, eds., *Trade Strategies for a New Era*, 204–22, quote at 205.

[120] Freyer, *Regulating Big Business*, 282.

[121] Kwoka and White, *Antitrust Revolution*, 1–5.

[122] Baker and Smith, *New Financial Capitalists*, 43, 53–4; Fligstein, *Transformation of Corporate Control*; see note 104 above.

Supreme Court applied Chicago theories to mitigate per se rules against joint ventures. The FTC pursued the same policy change; the Reagan administration and Congress followed suit. The Foreign Trade Antitrust Improvements Act of 1982 granted procedural limitations on extra-territorial antitrust jurisdiction. The Export Trading Act Company Act of 1982 established procedures permitting the Commerce and Justice departments to certify export agreements which provided protection from private suits by imposing single rather than treble damages. The National Cooperative Research Act of 1984 held transnational R&D joint ventures to a standard of reasonableness. Suggesting the practical impact of this general policy change was the FTC's sanction in 1984 of a joint venture between GM and Toyota to produce a compact car at the former company's unused factory in Fremont, California.[123]

Although advocates asserted that international markets operated according to neoclassical price theories, ambivalent deregulation policies challenged this assumption. Proponents of efficiency argued that market pressures would moderate profits and that the actual or possible entry of new producers would readily spread entrepreneurial profits. The invisible hand of the market was thought to be working so well that private anticompetitive business conduct seemed irrelevant compared with declining macroeconomic trade barriers under GATT. As late as 1983 President Ronald Reagan's Assistant Attorney General of the Antitrust Division told the National Association of Manufacturers that the cartel practices and "lax antitrust laws" of "our trading partners" neither aided their international competitiveness nor disadvantaged American business.[124] The divergent course of the international deregulation movement indicated, however, that global markets operated differently. At the theoretical level, deregulation meant that governments reduced formal constraints in favor of market liberalization. The practical result of deregulation, however, was paradoxical: a theory aimed at reducing regulation actually fostered it; a theory driven by internationalized markets facilitated national regulatory distinctiveness; and a theory based upon limiting governmental control of private business conduct depended upon the government itself.[125]

---

[123] Initial cases include *Broadcast Music, Inc. v. Columbia Broadcasting System, Inc.*, 441 US 1 (1979), *NCAA v. University of Oklahoma Bd. of Regents*, 468 US 85 (1984), *Northwest Wholesale Stationers, Inc. v. Pacific Stationary & Printing Co.*, 472 US 284 (1985); Fox, "Competitors Collaboration – A Methodology for Analysis," in First et al., eds., *Revitalizing Antitrust*, 324–6. See also Freyer, *Regulating Big Business* 322–3; especially interviews William Baxter/Tony Freyer, April 1, 1988 and Tony Freyer/Terry Calvani [former FTC commissioner] July 31, 1990.

[124] Address by William F. Baxter to the National Association of Manufacturers (May 10, 1983); see also William Baxter/Tony Freyer, interview, April 1, 1988.

[125] Steven K. Vogel, *Free Markets, More Rules: Regulatory, Reform in Advanced Industrial Countries* (Ithaca, NY, 1996); McCraw, *Prophets of Regulation*, 22–31.

America expressed one version of this paradox. Its economy was, said Pietro S. Nivola, "singularly unfettered," as a result of the deregulation movement since the 1970s. But at the same time, "American entrepreneurs face a profusion of legal fine points and perils different from, but not necessarily less exacting than, the regulatory rigors in other places." In addition, because "private litigants do much of the enforcing in the US ... we wind up with smaller government but millions of civil suits. Swapping a somewhat lower level of public control for a high degree of privatized legal wrangling is not always an advantage." John O. Haley suggested that these particular characteristics of the American deregulation movement exacerbated a growing tension between United States trade and antitrust laws, including whether a unilateral, bilateral, or multilateral policy should govern their application.[126]

The Archer-Daniels Midland (ADM) antitrust litigation suggested the benefits of such transnational cooperation among antitrust authorities. In 1996 the Justice Department's Antitrust Division sought grand jury indictments against ADM and seven other defendants, including two Japanese companies, a Korean firm, a United States subsidiary of another Korean firm, a Korean national, and two Japanese citizens. Cooperating with antitrust officials in those nations, U.S. authorities obtained the evidence needed to prove significant collusive conduct. A federal court decided that the defendants had entered into a criminal conspiracy to fix the worldwide price of lysine, an amino acid essential in the nutrition of animals and man. In a related case, ADM, a United States subsidiary of a German company, two Swiss firms, and a German and an Austrian citizen pleaded guilty to a charge that they had conspired to fix the global price of citric acid. The fine ADM paid for its part in both conspiracies was $100 million; for its role in the citric acid conspiracy, Haaman & Reimer, a United States subsidiary of Bayer AG, paid $50 million. The Justice Department won these cases in part because it procured evidence from abroad proving that the guilty parties had entered into a conspiracy affecting consumers within U.S. borders. Thus, the ADM case demonstrated how the dual international and domestic character of globally operating firms could violate a nation's antitrust law.[127]

[126] Pietro S. Nivola, "When It Comes to Regulations, US Shouldn't Cast the First Stone," *Wall Street Journal* (May 15, 1996), A15; John O. Haley, "Competition and Trade Policy: Antitrust Enforcement: Do Differences Matter?" in Haley and Iyori, eds., *Antitrust*, 303–26.

[127] Joel I. Klein, "Anticipating the Millennium: International Antitrust Enforcement at the End of the Twentieth Century," Fordham Corporate Law Institute 24th Annual Conference International Antitrust Law & Policy (New York, October 16–17, 1997), 1–17. See also Kurt Eichenwald, *The Informant a True Story* (New York, 2000); James B. Lieber, *Rats in the Grain: The Dirty Tricks and Trials of Archer Daniels Midland, The Supermarket to the World* (New York, 2000).

This new campaign against international cartels instituted meaningful corporate accountability, winning historic fines. The proportion of Justice Department's cases involving multinational corporations jumped from just 5 percent to, on average, 29 percent between 1993 and 1997. Effective cooperation among antitrust regimes, in conjunction with the federal government's leniency program designed to encourage corporate managers to provide evidence, reinforced this strong enforcement record. In 1999 the Justice Department's antitrust enforcers won, largely from international cartel prosecutions, a record $1.1 billion in criminal fines. Suggesting the international scope of these decisions, the department won from a single Swiss company a $500 million fine, from a German firm a $225 million fine, and a "record" fine of $10 million dollars from an individual corporate executive (a German). In addition, through the cooperation of European officials, a precedent was established when two European executives pleaded guilty to violating U.S. antitrust laws; in at least one of these cases the executive served a prison sentence in the United States. Moreover, of the "top 100 Corporate Criminals of the 1990s," declared Joel I. Klein of the Antitrust Division, "three of the top four firms on the list and six out of the top ten were multinational firms that had been convicted of Sherman Act violations."[128]

The *Nippon Paper* case indicated the unsettled limits of the extraterritorial antitrust principle. In 1995, as a result of the Justice Department's action, a federal grand jury indicted Nippon Paper, a Japanese producer of thermal facsimile paper, for an alleged conspiracy to fix the price of facsimile paper purchased by consumers in the United States and Canada. Unlike the companies in the ADM case, Nippon Paper was principally a domestic Japanese firm which relied upon trading companies to sell its product abroad. The price-fixing conspiracy thus occurred within Japan, but those affected were foreign consumers. Accordingly, the principal issue before the federal court was whether the criminal provisions of U.S. antitrust law applied to collusive conduct taking place exclusively within Japan. More particularly the doctrinal question was: did the *effects* of the price fixing conspiracy upon American consumers justify giving extraterritorial reach to American antitrust law? The precedents were sufficiently unclear that in 1996 the trial court decided against the Justice Department's claim of extraterritoriality. But the following year the U.S. Court of Appeals reversed, establishing an extraterritorial rule in criminal antitrust cases.[129]

[128] Percentage quoted in "Reno Forms Antitrust Advisory Panel," *Tuscaloosa News*, November 25, 1997; and Joel I. Klein, "The War against International Cartels: Lessons from the Battle Front," in Barry E. Hawk, ed., *Fordham Corporate Law Institute, International Antitrust Law & Policy Annual Proceedings* (Irvington-on-Hudson, 2002), 13–29, quotes at 16–17.
[129] *U.S. v. Nippon Paper Industries Co., Ltd.*, 944 F.Supp. 55 (Dis. Ct. MA, 1996), revised, 109 F.3d 1 (1st Cir. 1997).

Even so, the procedure underlying extraterritorial antitrust doctrines raised difficult practical problems. The evidence required to prove legal violations usually was located abroad.[130] In the *Nippon Paper* case U.S. and Canadian prosecutors gathered sufficient evidence to initiate the suit only because they cooperated with Japanese prosecutors to raid the offices of two Japanese firms. But as the case proceeded, the Japanese government intervened as an amicus curiae on behalf of the same Japanese companies, declaring that the U.S. government's suit violated Japanese sovereignty. The federal trial court decided against the United States, in part, because of this defense; the appeals court reversed, creating a farther reaching extra-territorial criminal antitrust doctrine.[131]

In some important merger cases cooperation failed to establish agreement. In the *Boeing/McDonnell Douglas* case of 1997 the European Commission and the FTC disagreed over the rule to apply in the market for large commercial airplanes. The case demonstrated that the two agencies with the most extensive record of cooperation could reach opposing policy decisions; U.S. and European Commission authorities agreed, nonetheless, that the disputed outcome would actually encourage stronger cooperation in future.[132] A more striking conflict resulted when one American company, General Electric, petitioned each antitrust authority to approve the take-over of another U.S. firm, Honeywell, for $43 billion. U.S. officials approved the merger, but the European Commission, applying a stricter merger rule, did not. Blocking the merger between two U.S. firms drama-tically expanded the Commission's extraterritorial antitrust jurisdiction; so much so that the United States protested and GE appealed to the European Court of Justice. The case dramatically underlined the difference between

[130] *Timberlane Lumber Co. v. Bank of America*, 549 F.2d 597 (9th C.C.A. 1976); *Hartford Fire Insurance Co. v. California*, 509 US 764 (1993).

[131] Concerning shifting of cooperation, see Michael H. Byowitz, "Unilateral Use of US Antitrust Laws to Achieve Market Access: A Pragmatic Assessment," *International Antitrust in a Global Economy* (International Association of Young Lawyers, New Orleans, LA, April 24–27, 1997), 1–27; Mark A. A. Warner's views summarized in Tony A. Freyer, "Restrictive Trade Practices and Extraterritorial Application of Antitrust Legislation in Japanese-American Trade," 16 *Arizona Journal of International and Comparative Law* (1994), 154–84; Harvey M. Applebaum and Thomas O. Barnett, "Sherman Act Can Apply to Criminal Antitrust Actions Taken Entirely Outside the Country, If These Actions Have Foreseeable, Substantial Effect on US Commerce," *The National Law Journal* (April 21, 1997), B4; and Klein, *Anticipating the Millennium*, 1–17; Office for Trade Policy Review, Ministry of Economy, Trade and Industry, *2002 Report on the WTO Consistency of Trade Policies by Major Trading Partners* (Tokyo, 2002), 477–8.

[132] In Re the Proposed Acquisition of McDonnell Douglas Corp. by the Boeing Co., FTC File No. 971–005 (July 1, 1997); Boeing/McDonnell Douglas, O.J.L. 336/16 (1997) (Comm'n.); Joel I. Klein, "Anticipating the Millennium," Robert Pitofsky, "Vertical Restraints and Vertical Aspects of Mergers – A US Perspective," and Alexander Schaub, "EC Competition Law – The Millennium Approaches," in Hawk, ed., *Fordham Corporate Law Institute Proceedings*, 7–8, 120–1, 239–40.

U.S. merger doctrine reflecting "efficiency" theories and the European "market domination" theory which held that "companies with a strong position in one market can use mergers to gain a stronghold in a related market."[133]

In the Microsoft case U.S. and European Commission antitrust authorities again disagreed. The 1994 U.S./Commission settlement had no direct bearing on the better known prosecution that the Clinton administration had initiated arguing that the company was exerting monopoly control in the domestic market. Microsoft attempted to rebut clear evidence of predatory and monopolistic conduct by asserting that its investment strategy of internal growth had permitted extraordinary technological innovation. Economic and legal experts disagreed as to whether the anticompetitive behavior should outweigh the efficiency gains. Federal trial and appellate courts decided against Microsoft on the merits resulting in large damage awards and continued monitoring of the company's inner operations. The U.S. appeals court, however, overturned the lower court's decision to break up the company. Although Microsoft applauded its victory, the most likely long-term outcome was continuing state and private suits, as well as foreign litigation, drawing on the proven record of abusive conduct and the transparency of the company's affairs that government monitoring ensured. Indeed, applying stricter monopoly doctrines than were enforced in the United States, the European Commission ultimately won a decision from the European Court of First Instance ordering a strong remedy like that which the U.S. appeals court had rejected. Thus, Microsoft was defending itself against the sort of disruptive remedy it had resisted for years. Ultimately, the likelihood of ongoing litigation against the company facilitated the sort of oligopolistic competition among a few firms prevailing throughout so many other market sectors.[134]

These difficulties nonetheless encouraged more formal inter-governmental cooperation in international antitrust cases. According to one observer, "a culture and bureaucracy favoring effective antitrust enforcement in purely domestic contexts is increasingly present in various countries.

[133] Case No. Comp/M. 2220 – *General Electric/Honeywell* (3/07/2001); Francesco Guerrera, "Brussels Appeals Over Merger Ruling," *Financial Times* /(December 21/22, 2002).
[134] Consent decree, *U.S. v. Microsoft Corp.*, 1995–2 Trade Cases para. 71,096 (D.D.C. 1995); Richard J. Gilbert, "Networks, Standards, and the Use of Market Dominance: Microsoft (1995)," in Kwoka and White, *Antitrust Revolution*, 409–29; Francesco Guerrera, "Antitrust Chief Warns EU over Microsoft Case," *Financial Times* (May 16, 2002), 6; Francesco Guerrera and Birgit Jennen, "Microsoft Faces Tough EU Action," *Financial Times* (front page, May 10, 2002); Francesco Guerrera, Peter Spiegel, and Andrew Hill, "EU Plans Hard Line on Microsoft," *Financial Times* (May 10, 2002), 6; Francesco Guerrera, "Microsoft Set to Take Tough Line with Europe," *Financial Times* (front page, November 4, 2002); Paul Abrahams and Richard Waters, "Microsoft Tries to Play Down Its Court Triumph," *Financial Times* (November 4, 2002), 2; see Chapter 5, Section IV, this volume for the EC's court victory.

Such a culture and bureaucracy are prerequisites to the possibilities of having the host jurisdiction challenge private restraints that deny market access to non-host country firms." Thus, in spite of the *Boeing/McDonnell Douglas* merger case, Antitrust Division director, Joel I. Klein, declared that "for both US and EU antitrust enforcers, our discussions would have been far more difficult had we not already established a strong relationship based on common antitrust enforcement interests." The Chicago theories were sufficiently undermined that by the 1990s the modest regulatory outcome in the U.S. Microsoft case was possible; even so, antitrust's enforced competition promoted sufficient technological innovation to maintain a competitive advantage.[135]

Tensions between trade and antitrust authorities complicated the growing international effort to impose accountability on multinational corporations. Historically trade and antitrust occupied distinct policy spheres within the constitutional order, as shown by the struggle over commodity agreements which resulted in the GATT displacing the ITO. Since the 1970s, however, institutional frictions between the two channels of dispute resolution increased. Section 301, established in the Trade Act of 1974, provided American business interests an official process implemented through the United States Trade Representative (USTR) by which the government could employ its diplomatic power to act against foreign market behavior unilaterally. Over the years under various revisions of section 301, firms from such industries as semiconductors, pharmaceuticals, automobiles, photography, and entertainment mobilized support to target primarily Japan, but also India and Brazil. Moreover, antidumping regulations operated as a protectionist trade device sheltering firms in the national market from competition with foreign multinational corporations. The United States won discretionary authorization for these unilateral enforcement policies through the GATT's and WTO's dispute resolution process, though not without resistance.[136]

Separating the trade and antitrust policy processes and goals were differing enforcement standards and bureaucratic administration. The procedural standards governing antitrust were more rigorous than those applied under the trade laws. Moreover, protecting domestic industries and jobs from international competition were the principal objectives of trade policies; antitrust laws, by contrast, promoted competition fostering consumer welfare. In addition, the executive and legislative branches of government cooperated with trade bureaucrats to fashion and implement trade laws, which, in turn had more leeway for interpretation without judicial

[135] Byowitz, *Unilateral Use of Antitrust Laws*, 1–27, quote at 9; Klein, "Anticipating the Millennium," 1–17, quote at 8.
[136] Compare Young, *U.S. Trade Law and Policy* (2001), 51–114; Office for Trade Policy Review, METI, *2002 Report on WTO* (Tokyo, 2002), 269–88, 447–86.

review. Antitrust actions were more bureaucratically autonomous because they were limited by judicial review, engendering stricter due process rules, legal damage systems, the claims of private litigants, and various long-recognized defenses such as foreign sovereign immunity, foreign sovereign compulsion, and the act of state rule.[137]

As globalization transformed international economic order, however, the trade-antitrust policy distinction became increasingly conflicted as foreign anticompetitive private conduct impinged upon America's strategic economic security. For policy experts the technical issues exposed clashing institutional and cultural images of national sovereignty and American capitalist market power. Thus, one trade expert declared in 1998, "Differences in tradition, intellectual outlook, and operational approach contribute to misunderstanding and even hostility between policy makers on opposite sides of the trade/antitrust divide." Moreover, the "institutional fissure between trade and antitrust is itself working to undermine the ability of the United States to deal with the new forms of protectionism that jeopardize the world trading system, most notably the 'privatization' of market areas abroad." Such rhetoric echoed nationalistic imagery reflected in the earlier attack on international cartels and struggle over the ITO.[138]

The WTO added a multilateral dimension to frictions between U.S. trade and antitrust laws. The WTO, like the old GATT, had no direct jurisdiction over the sorts of private anticompetitive conduct which antitrust laws traditionally sought to combat. The WTO dealt solely with "government measures" which included not only national protectionist trade barriers such as tariffs, but also domestic laws and regulations having the same effect. A question arose, however, over the scope and limit of "government measures" which could justify one nation's bringing a case against another nation before the WTO's dispute resolution process. Under Article XXIII 1.(b) of the WTO, one sovereign state could institute the dispute resolution process against another if government action by that nation promoted or permitted private anticompetitive practices which "nullified or impaired" the other state's multilateral guarantees. An opposing view rejected a construction of "government measures" which incorporated such private anticompetitive effects. In 1996 the United States government's decision to turn Eastman Kodak's unilateral claim against Fuji under section 301 into an Article XXIII 1.(b) appeal gave the WTO's dispute resolution process an opportunity to consider the matter.[139]

[137] Harvey M. Applebaum, "International Harmonization of Antitrust and Trade Laws," *International Antitrust in a Global Economy* (New Orleans, LA, April 24–25, 1997), 1–12.
[138] Thomas R. Howell, "The Trade Remedies: A US Perspective," in Feketekuty and Stokes, eds., *Trade Strategies for a New Era*, 299–323, quote at 313.
[139] Edward M. Graham, "Contestability, Competition, and Investment in the New World Order," in Feketekuty and Stokes, eds., *Trade Strategies for a New Era*, 204–22.

The USTR's appeal of Kodak's claim against Fuji suggested the potential significance the WTO had for resolution of international antitrust disputes. The WTO, of course, had no direct authority over purely private claims. Thus Kodak could not enter the WTO's dispute resolution process contending that Fuji conspired with Japanese film distributors and retailers to limit the American firm's access to Japan's home market. Instead, under section XXIII 1.(b) it could ask the United States government to argue on the firm's behalf that particular Japanese government policies either expressly permitted or at least did not prevent anticompetitive collusion by Fuji throughout the Japanese distribution system. As represented by USTR, Kodak's principal WTO claims were, therefore, that the Ministry of International Trade and Industry (MITI) had used administrative guidance under the Large Scale Retail Store Law to sanction Fuji's anticompetitive conduct; and that the Japan Fair Trade Commission (JFTC) had encouraged the same outcome by inadequately enforcing Japan's antitrust laws.[140]

Kodak's WTO appeal thus revealed the complex multilateral dimensions of competition policy. Initially, Kodak went to USTR hoping that the United States government would use unilateral pressure sanctioned under section 301 to defeat Fuji in Japan. In response, Fuji employed a leading American law firm which not only rebutted the section 301 claims concerning the closed nature of the Japanese market but also argued that Fuji faced the same economic pressures in the domestic American market that Kodak encountered in Japan. Neither private collusive conduct nor government action, Fuji's lawyers argued, but legitimate economic competition determined the market outcome in each nation. Faced with increasing legal ambiguity, USTR suspended the 301 action and appealed to the WTO under section XXIII 1.(b). The question arose, however, whether the WTO's dispute resolution process, which historically had dealt with more clearly defined governmental trade barriers, was capable of addressing claims involving a less transparent connection between governmental action and private business conduct.[141]

In December, 1997, the WTO decided against the U.S. government's argument. The *Oriental Economist* suggested that the decision implicitly

[140] Compare Charles Lake, *The US Government's Photographic Film and Paper Case against the Government of Japan*, JPRI Critque III (January 1996), 1–2; Toshihiro Yamada, *Camera Obscura: Fuji, Konica, Kodak All Using Shady Practices* (Tokyo, October 1995), 36–7; Akio Shimizu, *Analysis of GATT Non-Violation Cases, Selected GATT/WTO Panel Reports Summaries and Commentaries*, III (Tokyo, April 1997), 155–9; see Chapter 4, Section V.
[141] "Fuji US Lawyer Confident of Victory in Trade Row," *Japan Times* (October 4, 1995). "Kodak Practices May Affect Fuji Probe," *Japan Times* (August 9, 1995). "Japan Greets US WTO Move, Complaint Says Tokyo Erected Barriers to Kodak's Sales and Complaint to FTC too," *Japan Times* (June 15, 1996); Edward M. Graham, "Contestability, Competition, and Investment in the New World Order," in Feketekuty and Stokes, eds., *Trade Strategies for a New Era*, 205 note 1.

sanctioned the broader theory which brought private anticompetitive conduct facilitated by government action within the WTO's dispute resolution jurisdiction. "Indeed, some of the legal breakthroughs in this case" could foster "a successful case against government-created structural barriers in Japan." The defeat of USTR's defense of Kodak demonstrated, however, "that the next few test cases had better be narrow, clear-cut and simple. And there'd better be a very direct and irrefutable causal connection between government measures and market patterns." Because of the factual problems noted by the U.S. law firm representing Fuji, the "Kodak-Fuji dispute was not that case."[142]

The *Fuji/Kodak* case confirmed that maintaining international market competition required reconciling trade and antitrust policy frictions. American, European, and Japanese officials agreed that transnational cooperation among antitrust authorities was essential.[143] The Americans, however, resisted European efforts to codify a prohibition of cartel practices under a WTO multilateral agreement. New York University law professor, Eleanor Fox proposed that such an agreement might incorporate "trade-related antitrust measures or TRAMS," much like already functioning WTO trade-related provisions governing investment and intellectual property disputes. Fox suggested that there could be an agreement concerning "hard core" cartel practices of the sort which were often the focus of the burgeoning transnational antitrust enforcement. She conceded, however, that attaining international consensus on other competition policies was problematic, especially regarding vertical restraints.[144]

Contention among antitrust professionals converged with the assertion that international antitrust enforcement threatened national sovereignty. Trade policy makers' implementation of unilateral actions perpetuated the power of multinational corporations often without instituting meaningful market accountability. Above all, seeking to enforce accountability, U.S. antitrust professionals circumscribed the potent claims of sovereignty and national economic self-interest trade policy affirmed by agreeing with European and Japanese commentators that an acceptable alternative was greater international reliance upon positive comity. Rooted in principles articulated in the Organization of European Cooperation and Development's report of 1967, positive comity as a term was used first by European

[142] Richard Katz, "Big Loss at the WTO: Kodak's Moment: Not a Pretty Picture," *The Oriental Economist*, 66 (January 1998), 7–9, quote at 8.

[143] Tony A. Freyer, "Regulatory Distinctiveness and Extraterritorial Competition Policy in Japanese–US Trade," 21(5) *World Competition Law and Economics Review* (September 1998), 5–53, especially 18–20.

[144] Eleanor Fox, "Towards World Antitrust and Market Access," 91 *American Journal of International Law* (1997), 1–25; Edward M. Graham, "Contestability, Competition, and Investment in the New World Order," in Feketekuty and Stokes, eds., *Trade Strategies for a New Era*, 216–18.

antitrust experts. During the 1990s the Justice Department's Charles Stark drew on the principle to encourage bilateral antitrust agreements.[145]

By the turn of the century, WTO-centered initiatives and bilateral antitrust cooperation achieved uneasy complementarity. Despite the disruption of the Seattle meeting, WTO authorities established a working group devoted to hammering out solutions to the trade/antitrust frictions; the group was to encourage developing nations to adopt competition policies in harmony with indigenous institutions and culture. The United States continued to resist both the international – code idea and a multilateral proposal like TRAMs, because of underlying concerns about national sovereignty and practical problems involving confidential business information.[146] American antitrust officials and professionals generally accepted, however, the recommendation of the International Competition Advisory Committee, to create a Global Policy Initiative. The Initiative created a structure to provide technical assistance and institutional resources – much as the United States had done during the cold war in Europe and elsewhere – but on a more integrated global scale supporting developed as well as developing nations. Clearly, the goal was to strengthen indigenous institutions in order to enforce greater accountability and market competition.[147]

V. CONCLUSION

American, European, and Japanese authorities agreed that expanded channels of multinational antitrust collaboration could pave the way to a more centralized global enforcement regime. The future of such an organization remained problematic at the turn of the new century. At the same

[145] Charles S. Stark, "The International Application of United States Antitrust Law," Paper delivered, International Antitrust in a Global Economy (International Association of Young Lawyers, New Orleans, LA, 1997) 1–14.
[146] Klein, "Anticipating the Millennium," Karel van Miert, "International Cooperation in the Field of Competition: A View from the EC," Hideaki Kobayashi, "The World Trade Organization and Competition Policy," and Mitsuo Matsushita, "Reflections on Competition Policy/Law in the Framework of the WTO," in Hawk, ed., *Fordham Corporate Law Institute Proceedings*, 8–12, 13–26, 27–30, 31–52. On Seattle protests, see Joseph S. Nye, *Paradox of American Power* (New York, 2002), 41, 100, 103, 108.
[147] Robert Pitofsky, "Antitrust Cooperation, Global Trade, and US Competition Policy," Shogo Itoda, "Competition Policy of Japan and Its Global Implementation," Mario Monti, "Cooperation between Authorities – A Vision for the Future," Charles S. Stark, "Improving Bilateral Antitrust Cooperation," Frédéric Jenny, "Globalization, Competition, and Trade Policy: Convergence, Divergence and Cooperation," Joel Klein, "Expanding Our Web of Bilateral Agreements," Merit E. Janow, "A Need for New Multilateral Initiatives?" and Clifford A. Jones and Mitsuo Matsushita, "Global Antitrust in the Millennium Round: The Ways Forward," in Jones and Matsushita, eds., *Competition Policy in the Global Trading System*, 53–60, 61–8, 69–82, 83–94, 295–334, 335–40, 387–96, 397–406.

time, conservative nationalists as well as antiglobalization radicals contended that the multinational corporation had transcended the bounds of formal state sovereignty and had escaped the limits of accountability. Nevertheless, growing global cooperation among antitrust authorities, the effectiveness of the international cartel campaign, the ability of the European's' stronger merger and monopoly doctrines to hold their own against limited microeconomic price theories, the gradual proliferation of antitrust regimes among developed as well as underdeveloped nations, and the willingness of trade policy officials at the WTO to embrace enforced competition at least in principle suggested that antitrust's traditional concern with curbing economic power had achieved global force. Thus, working through the process of globalization, antitrust reshaped the discourse contesting managerial capitalism's hegemony.

4

Japanese Antitrust Since 1945

Japanese antitrust achieved growing significance by the millennium. Prior to 1945, antitrust policy reflected alien images of market competition. Some Japanese authorities nonetheless understood that antitrust's underlying values of economic democracy resonated with their opposition to the wartime control system and the *zaibatsu's* dominance. During the occupation, the same sort of indigenous resistance contributed to shaping key provisions of the Antimonopoly Law of 1947 and its subsequent enforcement until Japan regained full sovereignty in 1952. As the postwar era unfolded, the Japanese continually contested the process of accommodating antitrust policy and institutions. The few antitrust defenders struggled to preserve competition values against the industrial policy discourse government and big business leaders employed to justify "high speed" growth. Even so, antitrust officials defended small business and influenced the restructuring of Japan's corporate order into the unusual *keiretsu* system which attained global trade leadership by the 1980s. But this international success soon dissolved amidst profound economic and political dislocation and foreign criticism; for the first time, Japanese business and government leaders promoted deregulation and antitrust. Possessing official legitimacy, Japan's antitrust regime tested the limits and meaning of this reversal in the public stance toward competition policy.[1]

---

[1] For the dynamic interaction among Japanese policy discourse, corporate structure, electoral politics, ideology, and global trade, see Bai Gao, *Japan's Economic Dilemma: The Institutional Origins of Prosperity and Stagnation* (Cambridge, UK, 2001); Junnosuke Masumi *Contemporary Politics in Japan* [trans. Lonny E. Carlile] (Berkeley, CA, 1995); J. A. A. Stockwin, *Japan: Divided Politics in a Growth Economy* (London, 1982); T. J. Pempel, *Regime Shift: Comparative Dynamics of the Japanese Political Economy* (Ithaca, NY, 1998); Paul N. Doremus, William W. Keller, Louis W. Pauly, and Simon Reich, *The Myth of the Global Corporation* (Princeton, NJ, 1998); Bai Gao, *Economic Ideology and Japanese Industrial Policy Developmentalism from 1931 to 1965* (Cambridge, UK, 1997); Kent E. Calder, *Crisis and Compensation Public Policy and Political Stability in Japan* (Princeton, NJ, 1988); John O. Haley, *Antitrust in Germany and Japan: The First Fifty Years, 1947–1998* (Seattle, 2001); John Haley, *Authority without Power: Law and the Japanese Paradox* (Oxford, UK, 1991); Chalmers Johnson, *MITI and The Japanese Miracle: The Growth of Industrial Policy, 1925–1975* (Stanford, CA, 1932); Chalmers Johnson, "Japanese 'Capitalism' Revisited," 22 *JPRI Occasional Paper* (August 2001), 10–11; Marie

Some Japanese and American commentators have noted that despite the preeminent influence of Japanese bureaucrats' industrial policy it always evolved in relation to competition policy.[2] This chapter reexamines that interaction from the perspective of the antitrust regime itself and the extent to which its institutional culture has facilitated accommodating competition values to Japanese society. Section I presents new evidence suggesting why the Japanese were well prepared during the occupation for the negotiations resulting in the Antimonopoly Law of 1947. Section II

Anchordoguy, "Whatever Happened to the Japanese Miracle?" 80 *JPRI Working Paper* (September 2001), 1–6; Thomas K. McCraw, ed., *American Versus Japan* (Boston, 1986); Morikawa Hidemasa, "Japan: Increasing Organizational Capabilities of Large Industrial Enterprises, 1880s–1980s," in Alfred D. Chandler, Franco Amatori, and Takashi Hikino, eds., *Big Business and the Wealth of Nations*, 307–35; Jeffrey R. Bernstein, "Japanese Capitalism," in Thomas K. McCraw, ed., *Creating Modern Capitalism: How Entrepreneurs, Companies, and Countries, Triumphed in Three Industrial Revolutions* (Cambridge, 1997), 441–91; Gerald M. Meier, *The International Environment of Business Competition and Governance in the Global Economy* (Oxford, UK, 1998), 264–95: Jones and Matsushita, ed., *Competition Policy*; Steven K. Vogel, ed., *U.S.–Japan Relations in a Changing World* (Washington, DC, 2002); Freyer, "Regulatory Distinctiveness and Extraterritorial Competition Policy in Japanese–US Trade," *World Competition Law and Economics Review*, 5–53.

[2] Frank K. Upham, "Privatized Regulation: Japanese Regulatory Style in Comparative and International Perspective," 20 *Fordham International Law Journal* (December 1996), 396–511; Johnson, *MITI*, 175–6; Pempel, *Regime Shift*, 179, 202; Jones and Matsushita, eds., *Competition Policy*; Kristina Leigh Case, "An Overview of Fifteen Years of United States – Japanese Economic Relations," 16 *Arizona Journal of International and Comparative Law* (Winter 1999), 11–28; Leonard J. Schoppa, *Bargaining with Japan: What American Pressure Can and Cannot Do* (New York, 1997); Restrictive Trade Practices Specialist Study Team, *Control of Restrictive Trade Practices in Japan* (Japan Productivity Center, Tokyo, 1958); Hiroshi Iyori, *Antimonopoly Legislation in Japan* (New York, 1969), 1–38; H. Iyori and A. Uesugi, *The Antimonopoly Laws and Policies of Japan* (Federal Publications, New York, 1994), 1–66; Corwin D. Edwards, "Japan," *Trade Regulations Overseas the National Laws* (Oceana Publications, Inc., Dobbs Ferry, New York, 1966), 647–726; Eleanor M. Hadley, *Antitrust in Japan* (Princeton University Press, Princeton, NJ, 1970); Haley, *Antitrust in Germany and Japan*, 52–63; Kozo Yamamura, *Economic Policy in Postwar Japan Growth Versus Economic Democracy* (University of California Press, Berkeley, CA, 1967); Michael L. Beeman, *Public Policy and Economic Competition in Japan Change and Continuity in Antimonopoly Policy, 1973–1995* (Routledge, London, 2002); Amaya Naohiro, "Harmony and the Antimonopoly Law," and Yasuda Osamu, "Strange Ideas on the Antimonopoly Law," VIII(1) *Japan Echo* (1981), 85–95, 96–102, especially 85, 91, 92, 97; Hosoya, Masahiro, "Selected Aspects of the Zaibatsu Dissolution in Occupied Japan, 1945–1952: The Thought and Behavior of Zaibatsu Leaders, Japanese Governmental Officials, and SCAP Officials," Unpublished Ph.D. Dissertation, Yale University, 1982; Mark Tilton, *Restricted Trade: Cartels in Japan's Basic Materials Industries* (Cornell University Press, Ithaca, NY, 1996); Ulrike Schaede, *Cooperative Capitalism Self-Regulation, Trade Associations, and the Antimonopoly Law in Japan* (Oxford University Press, Oxford, UK, 2000); Lonny E. Carlile and Mark C. Tilton, Editors, *Is Japan Really Changing Its Ways Regulatory Reform and the Japanese Economy* (Brookings Institution Press, Washington, DC, 1998); Robert M. Uriu, *Troubled Industries Confronting Economic Change in Japan* (Cornell University Press, Ithaca, NY, 1996).

examines the conflicted interaction between industrial policy and anti-monopoly policy emerging after the occupation as a result of the business–government collaboration instituted by the "system of 1955." Section III contrasts the institutional and political tensions promoting divergent images of activist antitrust enforcement from the 1970s to the 1990s. Section IV considers foreign and Japanese interest-group tensions, symbolic imagery, and the ambiguities of foreign pressure that shaped the reconstitution of Japan's antitrust regime. In light of the changing postwar international trade order and domestic political economy, Section V explores the Japanese antitrust regime's enforcement record following the Structural Impediments Initiative (SII).

I. THE JAPANESE INFLUENCE ON ENACTING THE ANTIMONOPOLY LAW OF 1947

During General Douglas MacArthur's tenure as the Supreme Commander Allied Powers (SCAP), Japanese and foreign commentators observed, the new Constitution and the Antimonopoly Law of 1947 were important democratic reforms. Others contended, however, that the Antimonopoly Law was so alien to Japan's cooperative culture when SCAP imposed it beginning in 1945 that Japanese bureaucrats readily defeated its enforcement once the occupation forces withdrew. These commentators did not appreciate the degree to which Japanese officials in 1946–47 helped to shape the Antimonopoly Law. Recent studies show that the transformation it represented has been misunderstood. The following examines why, after a false start, the Japanese drafters were well prepared to confront SCAP officials in the negotiations engendering the Antimonopoly Law. The impact of these origins on the early enforcement of the Antimonopoly Law up to 1952 in defense of "democracy" is also suggested. John W. Dower's seminal work, *Embracing Defeat*, argues that despite the imperial tendencies of MacArthur's regime and the national bureaucracies' enduring power, a pacific democratic consciousness took hold within early postwar Japan. The following offers further examples of such a democratic consciousness expressed in a public discourse linking antitrust to the promotion of democratic economic opportunity.[3]

---

[3] Imamura, S., "Consumer and Competition Policy," in M. Ariga, ed., *International Conference on International Economy and Competition Policy* (Tokyo, 1973), 289–92; Johnson, *MITI*, 175–6; H. Iyori and A. Uesugi, *The Antimonopoly Laws and Policies of Japan* (New York, 1994), 285–300; Eleanor M. Hadley, *Antitrust in Japan* (Princeton, NJ, 1970); Haley, *Antitrust in Germany and Japan*; Gao, *Japan's Economic Dilemma*; Harry First, "Antitrust in Japan: The Original Intent," 9 *Pacific Rim Law & Policy Journal* (February 2000), 1–71; John W. Dower, *Embracing Defeat: Japan in the Wake of World War II* (New York, 2000).

On November 6, 1945 SCAP issued a directive ordering the Imperial government to begin dissolution of the *zaibatsu* and to establish an antitrust regime. Following the language of the Potsdam Declaration announced in August, the Japanese government was ordered to present for SCAP authorization: "Its program for the enactment of such laws as will eliminate and prevent monopoly and restraint of trade, undesirable interlocking directorates, undesirable intercorporate security ownership and [ensure] the segregation of banking from commerce industry and agriculture as well as provide for equal opportunity to firms and individuals to compete . . . on a democratic basis." Japanese government officials also were immediately to "take such steps as are necessary effectively to terminate and prohibit Japanese participation in private international cartels or other restrictive private international contracts or arrangements." While Japanese authorities responded expeditiously to SCAP's *zaibatsu* dissolution order with the Yasuda Plan, they approached the antimonopoly measure less successfully. The Japanese presented SCAP a proposal as early as January, 1946, called the Industrial Order Bill, but it was rejected as unsatisfactory.[4]

Meanwhile, on November 12, 1945, Tokyo's English-language newspaper, *Nippon Times*, published an article entitled "The Sherman Act." The author was Takayanagi Kenzo, professor of Anglo-American Law in Tokyo Imperial University. The article began: "The proposed dismemberment of the Zaibatsu seems to have revived in some quarters an interest in the Sherman Antitrust Act, the Great Charter of American industry." Takayanagi's essay summarized the standard history of the origins, enactment, and initial development of the Sherman Antitrust Act of 1890 and the Clayton Antitrust Act of 1914. Regarding the first of these antitrust measures, Takayanagi described bills "drafted in a highly crusading spirit," and "introduced in the Fifty-first US Congress in response to popular clamor about smashing the 'trust'. . . of the 'Robber Barons,' of 'giant octopi,' whose long and relentless arms encircled the farmers, the employees and the consumers in the grip of an all-absorbing greed." He stated that after many changes Senator John Sherman's original proposal emerged from the Senate Judiciary Committee as a significantly revised bill, which included expansive yet vague provisions against *every* trade restraint and monopoly.

[4] Ray A. Moore and Donald L. Robinson, *Partners for Democracy: Crafting the New Japanese State under MacArthur* (Oxford, UK, 2002); Alex Y. Seita and Jiro Tamura, "The Historical Background of Japan's Antimonopoly Laws," 1994 *University of Illinois Law Review* (1994), 115–85. See also Hiroshi Iyori, "Competition Policy and Government Intervention in Developing Countries: An Examination of Japanese Economic Development," 1 *Washington University Global Studies Law Review* (2002), 35–48; Hiroshi Iyori to Tony Freyer, "On the Japanese Antimonopoly Law," August 7, 2003; SCAP Directive No. 244, November 6, 1945, "Dissolution of Holding Companies," in Hiroshi Iyori, ed., *Antimonopoly Legislation in Japan* (New York, 1969); Haley, *Antitrust in Germany and Japan*, 17, 22; Hadley, *Antitrust in Japan*, 122.

Takayanagi explained further that after much conflict the law's general language fostered the triumph of an interpretation known as the rule of reason, established by the Supreme Court in Chief Justice White's famous *Standard Oil* and *American Tobacco* decisions of 1911.[5]

Takayanagi cited by name former president William H. Taft's 1914 study of antitrust and the Supreme Court. Taft's critique suggested how the rule of reason and the popular reaction against it resulted in the Clayton Act's more precise phraseology. But Takayanagi quoted directly from Taft and Chief Justice Charles Evans Hughes, to show that ultimately the court-centered, "case-by-case" process prevailed. In this way, the court applied antitrust legislation as a Charter of Freedom, to determine whether "ingenious measures adopted by American industrialists, farmers, and labor groups" were reasonable. Citing early leading cases, Takayanagi displayed a clear understanding of how the rule of reason enabled American courts to overcome the artificial distinction between holding companies employed for production purposes (established in the *Knight Sugar Trust* decision of 1895) – that were lawful – and looser, cartel arrangements, that were illegal. From 1911 on, the court developed a per se rule against cartel practices and a more flexible approach toward mergers. He revealed a sophisticated awareness of how, by the 1930s, the "modern trust problem" involved "mergers and consolidations," employing "more refined tactics for major purposes of monopoly – security manipulations, patent pools and cross-licensing systems, and dominance of large industrial units through price market leadership."[6]

Takayanagi's conclusions stipulated antitrust's long-term impact culminating in Thurman Arnold's activism. "Americans generally believe," he said, that "a regime of free economic competition is part and parcel of the American way of life, and that a society of independent competing businessmen, farmers, and laborers is an essential ingredient of Democracy." Nevertheless, he emphasized, not "[u]ntil recently" was the "fight against the movement toward economic concentration and monopoly" other than a "sporadic and unsystematic . . . series of crusades . . . consisting not in preserving competition itself but in dramatizing the ideal of a competitive regime." The focus upon U.S. antitrust symbolism recalls Arnold's image-making discourse denigrating antitrust in his two books published during the 1930s. Yet, although his name is not mentioned, Takayanagi revealed a clear grasp of Arnold's sophisticated use of consent decrees and injunctions combined with media campaigns "conducted in a spirit of a Roman circus," dramatizing the fundamental need to reinvigorate enforcement of antitrust. Takayanagi even mentioned the historic expansion of the Antitrust Division's personnel to "some 400." Most importantly, Takayanagi recapitulated the national identity imagery Arnold and Roosevelt had used to

---

[5] "The Sherman Act," *Nippon Times* (November 12, 1945), 4.   [6] Ibid.

promote antitrust activism, in order to address the "fear of the American people," that without the Sherman Act "America will be on the royal road to an industrial autocracy like Germany."[7]

Clearly, Takayanagi's articles did not reflect an understanding of U.S. antitrust that many Japanese shared. The article was significant, however, because it suggested the resources available to some officials when they confronted SCAP's antitrust directive. Since the rise of prewar Japanese militarism, the influence of Takayanagi and the study of Anglo-American law he promoted had declined within Tokyo University's Law Department, the school from which most of the nation's civil service came. Still, Takayanagi had built an American law curriculum and faculty that included three Japanese professors. The historical and legal detail Takayanagi's November articles displayed was consistent with the Tokyo University Law Department's U.S. law sources and pedagogical techniques. Ultimately, Takayanagi employed his wide understanding of comparative law and institutions in the defense of the new Constitution, SCAP's legitimizing of the emperor, and the Japanese war-crimes trials.[8]

Yazawa Atsushi, one of Takayanagi's former students, used the Tokyo University Library's U.S. materials to inform Japanese officials' response to SCAP's antitrust directive. Graduating from the Law Department in 1943, Yazawa had an academic class standing sufficiently high that he received a dispensation from military service to study economic law issues involving Japan's peacetime recovery and, ultimately, the consequences of defeat. As the occupation began, Yazawa was a graduate student holding a research position in the Ministry of Commerce and Industry, which drafted the Industry Order Bill subsequently rejected by SCAP. By early 1946, Yazawa turned his attention to U.S. antitrust materials. In addition to Takayanagi's article, he was familiar with numerous English language sources published between 1913 and 1941. Yazawa relied extensively on an American textbook by Harvard academics Merle Fainsod and Lincoln Gordon. Preparing his reports for government officials, Yazawa employed the comparative law technique learned at the university, which incorporated into the Japanese text numerous technical legal terms *in English*, such as "holding company," "injunction," "National Recovery Administration," and "competition." For the early period of U.S. antitrust development, Yazawa tracked generally Takayanagi's historical sources. Concerning what he subsequently described as the "Fourth Antitrust Movement and Revival of Antitrust"

[7] Ibid.

[8] See Chapter 2, Section IV, including T. L. Blakemore Letters from Japan, 1939–41, JHW Papers Japan Correspondence, Box 1, File 2, Folder 8, SC NWU. On Takayanagi's wider role during the occupation see, Moore and Robinson, *Partners for Democracy*, 285, 298, 301–4, 307, 313, 376, 379.

identified with Arnold's Antitrust Division, Yazawa drew extensively on Fainsod's and Gordon's book.[9]

Another Japanese academic aiding the government officials' response to SCAP's antitrust directive was Wakimura Yoshitaro. A professor of Economics at Tokyo University, Wakimura was a member of the Special Survey Committee (SSC) composed of Japanese bureaucrats, business people, and academics. This unofficial yet quite influential group developed a comprehensive plan for Japan's postwar economic revival. He was also a member of the Holding Company Liquidation Commission (HCLC) under SCAP which oversaw the dissolution of the *zaibatsu*. In each of these roles, Wakimura advocated freeing Japanese middle-class investors and small business from the *zaibatsu*'s influence. Wakimura also favored weakening, if not actually abolishing, the *zaibatsu* holding company structure in order to give younger middle managers leadership opportunities and to increase investment possibilities for average Japanese stock purchasers. Wakimura later explained that his approach was influenced by his study of American economic history, including the struggles against "monopoly capital," much as Takayanagi and Yazawa described that conflict in relation to U.S. antitrust history.[10]

[9] I've pieced together the material about Yazawa's work in preparation for and during the negotiations of the Antimonopoly Act from the following sources, all of which were translated from Japanese originals: Interview Professor Yazawa Atsushi (Professor, Tokyo University, Faculty of Law) in Dokusen Kinshi Seisako Sanjunenshi [A Thirty-Year History of Antimonopoly Policy], Kosei Torihiki Iinkai Jimukyoku (Fair Trade Commission Secretariat) ed., 1977, 421–8; Yazawa Atsushi, Reports, "The Development of Antitrust Law in the US (n.d., but likely 1945 or 1946)," and "Formation of Antitrust Law in the US (1947)." Also, Tony Freyer interviews with Matsushita Matsui and Murakami Masahiro [Yazawa's former students], cited below; Hiroshi Iyori to Tony Freyer – written comments entitled, "On Japanese Antimonopoly Law," and accompanying spoken remarks – delivered August 7, 2003 [Mr. Iyori also was one of Yazawa's students]; Tsugue Sano, "Research Report to Tony Freyer," April 19, 2001. Merle Fainsod and Lincoln Gordon, *Government and the Economy* (New York, 1941). Yazawa said he received the Fainsod and Gordon book from the Japanese economist, Tsuru Shigato in 1946; in my interview with Professor Gordon, he confirmed that he gave Professor Tsuru a copy of the book. The point is noteworthy because Yazawa says that his first report was based upon his research in earlier materials located at Tokyo University and the Ministry of Commerce and Industry and it was received by Yoshikuni Ichiro, in conjunction with preparing the Industrial Order Bill. In this report he concluded that the influence of antitrust was weak even in the United States. However, once he received the Fainsod and Lincoln book, he revised his conclusions to take into account the impact of Arnold's "Antitrust Revolution" which provided the basis of his subsequent report used during the negotiations of 1946–47.

[10] Wakimura Yoshitaro, "The Financial World during Occupation," in Ando Yoshio, Testimony for the Showa Government Economic History [Showa Seiji Keizaishi e no Shogen] (*Mainichi Shimbunsha*, Tokyo, 1972), 177–211; Scott Patrick O'Bryan, "Growth Solutions: Economic Knowledge and Problems of Capitalism in Post-War Japan, 1945–1960," Unpublished Ph.D. Dissertation, Columbia University, 2000, 13–21, especially 21; Gao, *Economic Ideology*, 150, 237. See also Tony Freyer interview Ariga Michiko, cited below.

These factors undoubtedly had little or no influence upon the Japanese bureaucrats who submitted to SCAP the Industrial Order Bill in January 1946. The bill was drawn by the planning unit of the Ministry of Commerce and Industry (the predecessor of the famous Ministry of International Trade and Industry or MITI), in response to the SCAP directive. The bill was modeled on the government's wartime control legislation, which had sanctioned official enforcement of cartels. The measure clearly did not represent a realistic grasp of American antitrust. Indeed, Morozumi Yoshihiko, a bureaucrat involved in drafting the bill, later indicated that German and continental civil law had influenced the Ministry of Commerce and Industry's Bill. During the 1930s, the Japanese government had enacted a cartel regulation law in part employing German precedent; the Industrial Order Bill reflected this influence. By contrast, Morozumi stated, U.S. antitrust law's cartel prohibition was difficult for Japanese bureaucrats to understand.[11]

In January 1946, as SCAP rejected the Industrial Order Bill, a U.S. *zaibatsu* study mission led by economist Corwin Edwards arrived in Japan. From January to March, his mission prepared a report on *zaibatsu* dissolution and its relationship to creating a more democratized economic order. The mission reflected disagreement among Washington policy makers as to whether a plan drawn up by Yasuda Osama was sufficient to facilitate economic democratization. A group of American diplomats and businessmen with close ties to prewar Japan favored accepting the limited Yasuda Plan. The selection of Edwards to lead the *zaibatsu* study task force represented, however, the temporary ascendancy within the State Department of an aggressive approach. The Northwestern University economist was a prominent New Deal bureaucrat who had helped to shape the campaign against international cartels which Arnold had begun in 1939. Edwards and others believed that such anticompetitive practices had fostered the rise and triumph of German Nazism and Japanese militarism. Edwards also influenced the transnational antitrust provisions subsequently incorporated into the ITO. Regarding Great Britain and the Allied occupation of Germany, he advocated the creation of antitrust institutions in order to ensure a more competitive international trading system. The mission to Japan thus complemented his wider purpose. While *zaibatsu* dissolution was the primary goal, the mission's recommendations for an antitrust regime coincided with SCAP's rejection of the Industrial Order Bill.[12]

---

[11] Iyori and Uesugi, *Antimonopoly Laws*, 16; Morozumi Yoshihiko, "How the Antimonopoly Law Got Started," *Nihon Keizi Shimbun*, March 1960. See also Morozumi quoted in Johnson, *MITI*, 175, citing *Tsusan Jyanaru*, May 24, 1975, at 44–5, 175–6.

[12] Corwin Edwards et al., *Report of the Mission on Japanese Combines*, 2 vols (March 1946) (original in Justice Department, Antitrust Division, I am grateful to Stuart M. Chemtob for procuring this document); Haley, *Antitrust in Germany and Japan*, 16, 22, 24, 29, 33, 40, 174; First, "Antitrust in Japan: Original Intent," *Pacific Rim Law & Policy Journal*, 21–9.

As the Americans carried through their own initiatives, the SSC worked on its own report. The committee's influence spread throughout Japan's Ministry of Foreign Affairs and among leading academics who subsequently provided theories used by political parties and business groups, including Keidanren (Federation of Economic Organizations), the spokesman for Japanese big business. Active SSC members included the prominent Marxist Wakimura, whose affiliation with the Labor and Farmer (*Rono*) political faction had resulted in imprisonment; Nakayama Ichiro of Hitotsubashi University, a follower of "modern" neoclassical and marginalist economic theories who was also familiar with Keynesian economics; and Ishikawa Ichiro, the leader of the Federation of Chemical Industry Associations and, later, of Keidanren. From August 1945 to March 1946 the SSC met. Recalled Okita Saburo, "Although our Committee contained members with widely differing political views, each member participated freely in the debates and discussions . . . and everyone was eager to build a new society from the ashes of the old." In March 1946, more than ten thousand copies of the committee's 145-page final report went into circulation. Meanwhile, Yazawa's research on U.S. antitrust moved forward. By the autumn of 1946, these factors converged to guide Japanese negotiators' response to SCAP's demand for the antimonopoly law.[13]

Edwards suggested his general approach in a letter written shortly after he landed in Japan. Following three weeks of investigation in January, Edwards asked a colleague in Northwestern University's Economics Department to assist him "in locating those Japanese who have been close students of economic and industrial organization and, if possible, have had some sort of administrative and business responsibilities yet are capable of envisaging an industrial Japan not dominated by the millionaire families." He recalled that Northwestern professors Kenneth Colegrove and John H. Wigmore had helped support the former leader of Japan's Farmer-Labor Party, Oyama Ikuo, after he had fled Japan. Edwards hoped Oyama could recommend individuals like himself to aid the mission's work. "One of the difficulties in democratization, with the Japanese Government used as intermediary, is that too many of the Japanese who are brought to our attention are wedded by ideas and interest to the regime which we are trying to replace," Edwards explained.[14]

[13] *Basic problems for Postwar Reconstruction of Japanese Economy, Translation of a Report of Ministry of Foreign Affairs Special Survey Committee September 1946* (Tokyo, 1977) (copy located in Coolidge/Widner Library System, Harvard University; I thank Frank Schwatz, Program on US–Japan Relations); O'Bryan, "Growth Solutions," Unpublished Ph.D. Dissertation, 2000, 13–21; First, "Antitrust: Original Intent," *Pacific Rim Law & Policy Journal*, 16–21.

[14] Corwin Edwards to Professor James W. Bell, January, 29, 1946, Kenneth Colegrove Papers (KCP)/Northwestern University Archives (NUA) Series #11/3/22/4.

Still, he and the study-team members found the "problem fascinating. The complexities of the Japanese corporate structure and the peculiarities of Japanese business and accounting methods are difficult to grapple with." The "effort to devise some way of creating a middle class out of nothing, of decentralizing a highly concentrated credit system as well as industrial system, and of developing in Japan an understanding and sympathy with what we are doing has launched us upon a sea of intangibles." Edwards's own "democratic instincts" made the "position of conqueror . . . unpleasant." But its "sharp edges" were "rubbed off by the easy-going kindliness" of the Americans and the "acceptance of the situation by the Japanese."[15]

The reports of Edwards's team and the SSC possessed significant continuities and contrasts. In keeping with the commitment to "democratization" that Edwards suggested in his letter, the Mission's report recommended that, except for firm expansion achieved through technological and managerial efficiencies, a general policy establishing limits on company size was preferable. The report's condemnation of size in relation to the *zaibatsu* nonetheless departed from traditional American antitrust analysis. Holding companies controlled by the *zaibatsu* impeded the opportunity of smaller enterprise – as well as the emergence of trade unions and modern agriculture – because their size and structure created "substantial disparities in bargaining power." Law professor Harry First later noted that the "idea that firms with monopoly position might use their power to exclude rivals was well-accepted at the time in U.S. antitrust law, but this concept had never been detached from monopoly and put into a context of absolute firm size or multi-market occupancy." Even so, this novel policy formulation "led the [Edwards] report not only to advocate the dissolution of the *zaibatsu*, but also continuing antitrust prohibitions on conduct that might exclude firms from markets."[16]

The SSC Report accepted the basic need for dissolution in order to destroy the *zaibatsu's* monopoly power. The "problems of smaller business including medium-sized enterprises in particular" resulted from "the concentration of capital in a limited number of *zaibatsu* . . . to so high a degree in the Japanese economy that even the medium enterprises cannot hold complete independence and have relations subordinate to and dependent on large capital in the aspects of capital, technology, and sales of products." The SSC Report recognized that the occupation's policies aimed at eradicating the "main prop of militarism . . . centering around the dissolution of *zaibatsu*" was "not necessarily clear." Still, "overwhelming their medium- and small-sized competitors," the *zaibatsu* holding companies "seized and monopolized the greater part of Japanese economy. Further such large

[15] Ibid.
[16] Compare *Edwards Mission Report* (v. 2, 1946); First, "Antitrust in Japan: Original Intent," *Pacific Rim Law & Policy Journal*, 28–9.

capital joined hands with the feudalistic [militaristic] State power." Thus, in order to promote small-scale enterprise, encourage trade unions, modernize agriculture, and "free competition in the private sector" from the "direct intervention of the government in the economy," the SSC in principle condoned SCAP's "directive . . . issued to dissolve the *zaibatsu*." Even so, the SSC contended that replacing the family holding companies with large-scale enterprise would strengthen postwar Japanese capitalism once economic growth displaced the initial period of starvation and personal deprivation.[17]

Edwards's report expressly argued against employing the American antitrust experience as the model for a Japanese law. United States antitrust law, the report stated, "has been insufficient to prevent the rise of giant industrial combines possessing excessive power because of their size. Moreover, the American statutes are framed in language so general that, against the background of traditional Japanese thinking, the interpretation of a law based exclusively upon similar phrases would likely violate an antitrust program." Furthermore, the American system of checks and balances facilitated "a willingness to use quasi-judicial commissions, and independence of the judiciary in matters of statutory and constitutional interpretation. The Japanese government has none of these features." The report urged as a "starting point" for Japanese antitrust "principles of business freedom from private restrictions which are likely to be generally accepted among democratic industrial countries." Edwards's report cited "principles" the U.S. government had proposed "in the hope that they may become a basis for the work of an international office for business practices to be attached to the United Nations' Organization." In order to perpetuate the benefits attained through *zaibatsu* dissolution the same principles "should be adapted to Japanese institutions and problems."[18]

SCAP was not receptive to the Edwards report's recommendations. The mission left Japan in March 1946. A commentary was prepared by GHQ asserting that "the practical execution" of its "program, except in broad outline and along general lines, is quite beyond the size and organization of the Occupation Forces." The scope of social transformation attending the proposed scale of *zaibatsu* dissolution incorporated "Utopian aspects" of the "most advanced refinement in the fields of finance, economics, commerce and industry – subjects which are now agitating the governments of the world and ones that are in a constant state of flux and unbalance." Accordingly, the "basic question" was "whether the purpose of the occupation is to establish an ideal economy here or whether it is merely to provide the introduction of such democratic methods and the abolition of such menaces as to insure the disability of Japan to make future war." The

[17] *Basic Problems for Postwar Reconstruction Japanese Economy*, 23, 54–5, 58.
[18] Edwards Mission Report (v. 2, 1946), 238, 239.

postwar government in Washington imposed "budget restrictions" which "definitely limit the structure of the SCAP organization to a mere controlling echelon to provide and enforce broad principles." The Edwards report's "many details of refinement" would "be of great difficulty or even unpracticability of accomplishment."[19]

Thus, SCAP did not accept the novel theory linking general distrust of firm size to traditional antitrust concepts. Instead, SCAP officials stipulated a more modest policy against the "practice of pyramiding ownership by means of a chain of intermediate holding companies. . . . [which made it] possible for a holding company to control assets with a value of approximately ten times its initial investment." Consistent with the New Deal's Public Utilities Holding Company Act (PUHCA) of 1935, SCAP advocated imposing a 50 percent "equity capital (common stock)" limit on the "total capitalization of any company which wishes to issue senior capital (bonds or preferred stock)." Also in line with the PUHCA's policy, SCAP urged a "prohibition against any corporation holding shares of another corporation which itself owns any corporate securities." Employing a narrower policy approach toward holding companies, SCAP contended, actually gave more realistic protection to smaller shareholders. While SCAP's policy objectives arose independently from its own practical bureaucratic contingencies – evidencing no direct awareness of the SSC's acceptance of the need for *zaibatsu* dissolution – the two policy recommendations nonetheless coincidently possessed similarities.[20]

SCAP concurred in some but not other recommendations. It favored the use of stringent rules against unfair trade practices. It resisted as "too liberal," however, the "proposal to prohibit banks from investing as much as 25 percent of their capital and reserves in securities and advances to any other company." SCAP also concluded that the prohibition of "interlocking directorates be applied only in the case of competing companies." Mindful of its reliance upon Japanese authorities for administering reforms, SCAP diluted the report's effort to "prohibit employees of the Ministry of Finance from accepting positions with private financial institutions [later known as *amakudari*]." In addition, SCAP accepted "in principle" the idea that the Japanese government's "control associations" should be "abolished" at some point, but that currently "the economy of Japan is in a critical condition and means must be developed to stimulate the production of badly needed commodities and to encourage their distribution in areas where they are most in demand."[21]

[19] SCAP (Confidential) Comments on the Report of the Edwards Mission (n.d.), GHQ/SCAP Records, RG 331, section 3–402 NND no. 775019, National Archives (NA). See also same source cited, First, "Antitrust in Japan: Original Intent," *Pacific Rim Law & Policy Journal*, 34 note 157, located in Diet Library, Tokyo, Japan.

[20] SCAP Comments, 3, 4; First, concerning PUCHA, 22–8; and notes 13 and 17.

[21] SCAP Comments, 6, 7.

During 1946–47, drafting antitrust legislation and *zaibatsu* dissolution diverged. The Edwards mission's recommendations became enmeshed in a dispute pitting the "old-Japan hands" against the New Dealers. The former won, resulting in a modest scale of *zaibatsu* dissolution. The confrontation also ensured that even the limited dissolution program did not have significant effect until a year or more *after* Japan's Diet enacted the Antimonopoly Act on March 31, 1947. Accordingly, promulgation of the antimonopoly law followed an independent path involving primarily Japanese and SCAP negotiations with no direct input from Washington. During the summer and fall of 1946 each side developed its proposals; in December, Japanese and American negotiators began the formal process of hammering out a statute.[22]

Initially, the Japanese responded to a draft developed by Posey T. Kime, a lawyer from the Justice Department's Antitrust Division on temporary assignment to the Antitrust and Cartels Division. Kime's draft precipitated the Japanese side's first serious attempt to fashion an antitrust measure. Following Kime's departure in October, his successor, Lester N. Salwin, handled the negotiations. According to Professor First, the Japanese possessed a more informed grasp of U.S. antitrust than previously has been understood. This was the case, however, largely because the Imperial cabinet authorized the Japanese Economic Stabilization Agency to establish an Antimonopoly Law Study Committee chaired by Hashimoto Ryogo. Other committee members included Wakimura and Yazawa. Equipped with these resources Hashimoto led the Japanese side's negotiations with Salwin.[23]

SCAP officials had already begun work on an antitrust proposal. Within the Economic and Science Section, the chief of the Antitrust and Cartels Division was James M. Henderson. A lawyer detached from the West Coast Office of the Antitrust Division and a member of the Edwards mission, Henderson allotted more resources to *zaibatsu* dissolution than to drafting antitrust legislation. The Zaibatsu Branch included eleven officials; the Antitrust Legislation Branch had only Kime. He had been an active Indiana lawyer and New Deal liberal who had served eight years on the state appellate court. After working several years as a staff attorney for the Federal Power Commission, Kime came to Arnold's Antitrust Division in 1942. Kime's legal background and social experiences in Japan undoubtedly influenced the proposal he had prepared by August 1946. He brought to bear a thorough understanding of common-law decision making, public

[22] For divergence, compare citations note 12, and chronology in First, "Antitrust in Japan: Original Intent," *Pacific Rim Law & Policy Journal*, 35–67.
[23] Ibid.; Iyori, "Competition Policy and Government Intervention," *Washington University Global Studies Law Review*, 5–7; Hiroshi Iyori to Tony Freyer, "On the Japanese Antimonopoly Law," August 7, 2003.

utilities policy, and antitrust doctrine. His academic bent facilitated syn-
thesizing long-standing antitrust principles and the innovative ideas of such
advanced New Dealers as Corwin Edwards. Associations with and empathy
for the entrepreneurial potential of postwar Japan's businessmen gave
concrete meaning to the drafting process.[24]

Meanwhile, other units within SCAP – including Government Section,
which was promulgating Japan's new democratic Constitution, and Labor
Section which was attempting to establish freer labor organizations –
commented upon Kime's draft. By the time he left Japan, the Americans and
Hashimoto's Antimonopoly Study Committee finally had a clear starting
point from which to begin formal negotiations.[25]

Kime's synthesis of the Edwards report's recommendations and GHQ's
critique resulted in an advanced and original proposal. In the coverage of
conduct subject to criminal violations involving exclusive dealing, predatory pricing practices, and unfair competition generally, the Kime Draft
follows closely the language of the Sherman, Clayton, and Federal Trade
Commission acts.[26] Prohibitions against joint action and cartel-devices such
as price-fixing were presented in long lists of offenses made per se illegal. In
standard U.S. antitrust law, by contrast, such offenses were generally
covered by case law and, in certain instances, were governed by a rule of
reason rather than a per se standard. The Japanese government's control
associations which authorized cartel practices had no parallel in U.S. law.
In addition, U.S. law protected American export trade and included
exemptions for export cartels, whereas the Kime Draft abolished existing

[24] Theodore Cohen, in Herbert Passin, ed., *Remaking Japan: The American Occupation as
New Deal* (New York, 1987), 353–77, especially 356–7; Haley, *Antitrust in Germany and
Japan*, 29, 33. Yazawa notes meeting Henderson and Kime, see note 9 above. On the
numbers of officials, see *Occupation Forces Telephone Directory*, September 1946 and
July–August 1947, and interview Eleanor M. Hadley, Tony Freyer November, 9, 1995,
Seattle, Washington (I am indebted to Dr Hadley for access to the phone directories). A
report prepared at the request of Professor Maurice Baxter by the Alumni Office, Indiana
University for my use is the source of the basic biographical information on Judge Kime. His
daughter, Mrs Helene Kime Lewis, gave me an interview, December 14 and 15, 1996, and
provided access to family memorabilia, the judge's passport, a photo album – including the
comments noted in my text – and several news clippings he had saved from Japan; I am
indebted to Mrs Lewis and her husband, Stanley R. Lewis, for access to these materials.
Judge Kime had a signed photograph of Arnold.
[25] The copy of the Kime Draft in my possession [thanks to Professor T. Nogimura] was signed
"Kades," for Charles L. Kades, the official in SCAP's Government Section who authored
much of the U.S. draft of what became Japan's postwar Constitution; see Moore and
Robinson, *Partners for Democracy*. On labor section's role, see Cohen, Passin, ed.,
Remaking Japan, 353–77.
[26] First refers to the two copies of Kime's draft of the Antimonopoly Law located among the
SCAP records Diet Library Micro Films, Tokyo; the shorter version contains marginal
notation "Kime, 8/6/46," in "Antitrust in Japan: Original Intent," 9 *Pacific Rim Law &
Policy Journal* (February 2000), 35.

Japanese import/export companies, made illegal unfair practices in foreign trade, and required Japanese companies to file with the government their contracts with foreign firms.[27]

Comparing the structural provisions, Kime's language criminalizing monopolization itself copies the Sherman Act. But subsequent sections added the far stricter rule prohibiting "substantial disparities in bargaining power" that had no parallel in U.S. antitrust law. Also, stock or asset acquisitions were banned among competing firms; the language echoed – but its scope of application was broader than – the PUHCA. Similarly, mergers and amalgamations of competitors were banned, though non-competitors could seek exemptions on the basis of the "public interest." Again, the language paralleled, but was stricter than, the Clayton Act which allowed treble damages plus attorney's fees; it departed from U.S. law, however, capping attorney's fees at between 1/4 and 1/3 of awards of ¥20,000 or more. In the Kime Draft, criminal penalties were tougher than those of the Sherman Act and the range of alternative penalties greater. Finally, the Kime Draft instituted an antitrust agency with three commissioners possessing extensive investigatory powers. In conjunction with the agency, a separate Fair Trade Practices Court was established.[28]

Key provisions of this ambitious draft reflected the diverse sources Kime drew upon. Kime linked "substantial disparities of bargaining power," to the "potential ability to monopolize"; the Edwards report, by contrast, had extended the concept to include large firms in oligopolistic markets that dominated or excluded smaller enterprise. Second, the Kime Draft established an absolute "yen-limit" on the size of Japanese corporations, something the Edwards report had argued against doing. These differences reflected the backgrounds of Kime and Edwards: one was a lawyer, the other an economist. Any explanation should note, however, that generally the conceptual distinctions followed GHQ's critique of the Edwards report. Thus, Kime's provisions exceeded U.S. antitrust law to a certain extent, maintaining the basic policy toward undue bargaining power and monopoly.[29]

The scope of innovation was perhaps most apparent in the Kime Draft's structural provisions banning stock and asset acquisition among competing firms. The ban was similar to GHQ's prohibition of holding company investments among competitors. Kime adopted, however, the Edwards report's forthright abolition of the government's control associations over the tacit approval they received from GHQ. Finally, Kime went farther than either the Edwards report or GHQ in constructing an independent antitrust enforcement commission under the prime minister. Although the

---

[27] See the comparative tables in First, "Antitrust in Japan: Original Intent," *Pacific Rim Law & Policy Journal*, 37–41, and especially on provisions regarding monopolization, "substantial disparities in bargaining power," and "public interest" and fees at 39, 40.

[28] Ibid.   [29] Ibid.

commission was not subject to the direct control of individual ministries it had no direct representation in the cabinet. Thus, within Japan's cabinet system of government – where the powerful ministries such as Finance or Trade and Industry were constantly at odds – support for the Antimonopoly Law and its commission could be subject to intense bureaucratic rivalry.

Upon receiving the Kime Draft in August 1946, the Japanese responded with a two-pronged strategy. Within a month they prepared and submitted to SCAP a memorandum entitled "Japanese Government's Views and the Suggested Legislation relating to Economic Order." Japanese officials resisted the Kime Draft's "sweeping character," arguing that a measure of such scope was "unparalleled even in the countries like the United States with a highly developed economy." Consistent with the substantive concerns the SSC Report had articulated regarding the war-damaged economy, the Japanese "[f]rankly fear[ed]" that applying such a law rigorously to the nation's "still undeveloped and . . . struggling" economic order "might not only defeat the ultimate objectives of the proposed legislation . . . but also produce results inimical to the public interest." The memorandum opposed the Kime Draft's imposition of per se prohibitions relying on court-centered enforcement rather than the European style, bureaucratic approach with which the Japanese were familiar. Similarly, the memorandum objected to an enforcement regime – particularly involving criminal cases – located in an independent agency separate from the ministerial bureaucracy. The memorandum criticized the draft's provisions against price-cutting and the ban on the control associations; it denied vigorously the draft's structural provisions proscribing substantial disparities in bargaining power and prohibitions against stock or asset acquisitions and mergers that generally inhibited the creation of large firms, which, the Japanese believed, was "not an evil in itself."[30]

The memorandum's second strategic prong was to urge delaying the enactment of an antitrust law, giving a proposed bureaucratic commission time to develop a measure better suited to the nation's needs. The Japanese strategy linking focused, counter-recommendations to in-depth study of American antitrust proved effective. Shortly before departing, Kime received from the Japanese the "Views" memorandum. SCAP took no action until Salwin arrived in Tokyo in early December. The change in the leadership coincided with Edward C. Welsh's replacing Henderson as chief of the Antitrust and Cartels Division. *Zaibatsu* dissolution remained the division's priority: personnel responsible for that program were increased from eleven to sixteen. Like Kime, however, Salwin was the only senior official assigned to drafting antitrust legislation. The personnel changes

---

[30] Ibid., 41–4, discusses the "Views" memorandum. The text cites the original, "The Japanese Government's Views on the Suggested Legislation Relating to Economic Order," SCAP, 1205, section 3–402 NNDG no. 775019, NA, 1–7, quotes at 1, 2, 6.

meant that neither the new division chief nor the head of Antitrust Legislation Branch had firsthand experience with either the Edwards mission and GHQ's response or the original Japanese-American exchanges.[31]

Salwin apparently never met Kime. Thus Salwin, who was not an antitrust lawyer, approached the Kime Draft and the Japanese disapproval of it with less experience and preparation than the Japanese. As direct negotiations began in mid-December, the initiative lay with the Japanese. They informed Salwin that the Cabinet had appointed an eight-man "Study Committee on Anti-Trust Legislation," chaired by Hashimoto which included Wakimura; no mention was made that they benefited from the extensive U.S. antitrust materials provided by Yazawa. In initial meetings, Salwin rejected the proposals set forth in the "Views" memorandum but left to the Japanese responsibility for drafting a preliminary antitrust proposal. From late December to March the Japanese retained the initiative. In December they gave Salwin an "Outline of Antitrust Law" which went beyond the basic policy goals of the "Views" memorandum. Although Salwin rejected the "Outline," he called it a distinct improvement and urged the Japanese to prepare a more comprehensive proposal.[32]

Shortly thereafter, Japanese negotiators submitted a memorandum entitled "Questions Pertaining to the Interpretation of Antitrust Laws." Citing a handful of American sources, the "Questions," according to First, "showed considerable sophistication in terms of U.S. antitrust law, right down to an appreciation of the distinction between protecting competition and protecting competitors." Basically, the authors of the "Questions" had perceived "apparent inconsistencies" resulting from the Kime Draft's attempt to "rationalize" within a single statute the substance and standards of U.S. antitrust law's "three separate statutes enforced by two different kinds of enforcement agencies," the Antitrust Division and the Fair Trade Commission, all of which depended ultimately on judicial interpretation. The depth of understanding this analysis evidenced undermined later Japanese and American contentions that "antitrust belonged" to a "culture that was so foreign that the concepts could not be understood." On the contrary, First says, it demonstrated, "that US antitrust legislation, and common law development were not perfectly clear, and . . . that the Kime draft only exacerbated the interpretive problems by putting all US antitrust into one piece of legislation."[33]

[31] Ibid., First, "Antitrust in Japan: Original Intent," *Pacific Rim Law & Policy Journal*; on changes in the personnel, see Yazawa's comments and the SCAP phone books cited in notes 9 and 24 above.

[32] For an incisive analysis, see First, "Antitrust in Japan: Original Intent," *Pacific Rim Law & Policy Journal*, 44–9; and notes 4, 9, and 10 above.

[33] Ibid., 45–53, quote at 52–3. Yazawa's recollections cited in note 9 corresponds to this chronology and confirms Professor First's insight.

During the start of 1947, Japanese negotiators pursued an effective strategy. At Salwin's urging, the Japanese produced by early February a tentative draft of legislation entitled "Law Relating to Prohibition of Private Monopoly and Preservation of Lawful Trade." In part, the tentative draft's provisions stipulating per se violations, substantial disparities of bargaining power, and enumerated types of unfair methods of competition significantly modified the coverage of the Kime proposal. Similarly, the tentative draft retained an independent enforcement agency, as had Kime, but it had increased membership and enhanced procedural authority. The draft had new provisions subjecting the conduct of "entrepreneurs" to standards of "unreasonable" monopolization and "unreasonable" restraints of trade. In addition, although both the tentative and Kime drafts authorized a private right of action, the Japanese proposal reduced the penalty from treble to single damages. Also, private plaintiffs had to rely primarily upon the new antitrust agency which was authorized to proceed on their behalf following a petition. Generally, each of these provisions was included in final versions of the bill that ultimately became law. Overall, the negotiations altered the Kime Draft. The Japanese succeeded in getting adopted "vague" provisions in keeping with "Japan's desire to retain bureaucratic discretion, particularly in the area of cartel behavior, rather than create a system with clearly delineated offenses to which no exceptions could be made."[34]

During February and March, Salwin, joined by Eleanor Hadley from Government Section, responded to the Japanese initiative. On Japan's side were Hashimoto and fluent English-speaker Kashiwagi Ichirō, an experienced international banker attached to the Ministry of Finance, who had been involved in *zaibatsu* dissolution. Behind them were Wakimura, equipped with the work of the SSC and Yazawa's U.S. antitrust research. In what eventually became daily meetings, Salwin and Hadley gained important points. While Salwin apparently did not mention specifically any of the Kime Draft's provisions, often, the substance of his "objections were consistent with that approach." The Ministry of Justice wanted to weaken further private damage actions by leaving them to the regular courts. Closer to the Kime provision, Salwin insisted upon, and the Japanese accepted, a distinct "antitrust panel" on the Tokyo District Court. In keeping with the independence the Kime Draft conferred upon the antitrust agency's enforcement authority, Salwin favored a criminal indictment procedure controlled by the antitrust agency itself. The Japanese compromised somewhat, proposing a "provision requiring the Public Procurator General, in cases where prosecution was requested but declined, to give to the Prime Minister, through the Minister of Justice, written reasons explaining the

---

[34] First, "Antitrust in Japan: Original Intent," *Pacific Rim Law & Policy Journal*, 53–6, quote at 55–6.

failure to prosecute. This provision subsequently became law," making the commission a "bureaucratic agency."[35]

Significant agreements concerned the antitrust commission's autonomy and restrictions intended to limit international cartels and the scale of corporate enterprise. Five months earlier the "Outline" had proposed, in keeping with the Kime Draft, that the antitrust agency's independence might be preserved by making it responsible to the prime minister. In mid-February, however, Hashimoto and Kashiwagi argued that the Ministry of Justice should have direct authority over the commission. In a meeting of Japan's cabinet – and after winning the approval of Government Section, which perceived the issue in terms of the checks and balances it was attempting to establish in the Constitution – Salwin prevailed. The Japanese accepted locating the commission under the prime minister, without granting it ministerial standing *within* the cabinet. Meanwhile, regarding intercorporate stockholding and international cartels the Japanese had not accepted the strict limitations imposed in the Kime Draft, and their approach to mergers was quite lax. Hashimoto and Kashiwagi endorsed a compromise on intercorporate stockholding: the pure holding company was banned, but stock purchases potentially creating "mixed holding-operating companies" of unrestricted size were subject to approval by the antitrust commission. The Japanese agreed to maintain an initial prohibition of international cartels but requested giving the commission power to authorize such agreements in future. They also acquiesced to Salwin's substitution of a weak premerger notification process for a "mandatory provision requiring Commission pre-merger approval."[36]

During much of March, either Salwin or Hadley or both met almost daily with Hashimoto and Kashiwagi. Through successive drafts the negotiators refined their statutory proposal into a bill. Regarding stockholding and mergers other than the significant ban on holding companies, the outcome Salwin accepted favored the Japanese position that a flexible standard should govern the amount of "share control" necessary for establishing large companies. "If we are to determine a monopoly by the ratio of total domestic production," stated a memorandum written by a Japanese negotiator, "the size of the enterprise may be too small to enable it to stand on its own feet economically." The policy incorporated into the statute was, then, that a merger should not be judged on the basis of "share control" but whether it could not "restrict substantially competition within a certain field of trade." The Japanese side promoted the interests of small business and economic democracy by actually increasing the prohibitions against unfair competition. The commission's basic independence and the scope of its enforcement authority were incorporated into the final statute.[37]

---

[35] Ibid., 56–8, quote at 57–8.   [36] Ibid., 58–9, quote, at 59.
[37] Ibid., 61–5, quote at 61, 64.

At a meeting on March 18, the cabinet accepted provisions pertaining to cartels and corporate holding of stock in subsidiaries. The bill was ready for submission to the Diet, but opposition from "certain political leaders" suddenly arose seeking to prevent passage before the session ended. Japanese negotiators and the cabinet, joined by Salwin, argued forcefully against delay. With the help of SCAP's Government Section, resistance was overcome. The last Imperial Assembly under the Meiji Constitution ended on March 31, 1947. Introduced into the Diet on March 25, the Antimonopoly Act became law on the final day of the old Imperial constitution. The symbolism reflected what became an enduring public discourse which linked the new Constitution and the Antimonopoly Law of 1947 as embodying the ideals of a peaceloving Japanese nation committed to liberal capitalist democracy.[38]

Eventually, foreign and Japanese "revisionist" critics disputed the validity of this imagery because the bureaucracy, which had exercised such power prior to the war, retained its guiding influence throughout the postwar era. Nevertheless, the members of the new Fair Trade Commission (FTC) constituted under the Antimonopoly Law took seriously the commitment to "economic democracy." Although Hashimoto departed for a political career, many of the staff composing the Antitrust Study Committee joined the FTC. Among these individuals was Mrs Ariga Michiko; having worked with Kashiwagi as a translator during both Kime's and Salwin's tenure in the occupation, she became a commission attorney and eventually, the FTC's first female commissioner. Yazawa was appointed the first professor of Antimonopoly and Commercial Law at Tokyo University; for some decades, he introduced students to careers in the FTC.[39]

In July 1947, the FTC began operation. The Cartel Division's Edward C. Welsh worked with the FTC's first chairman, Nakayama Kikumatsu, who served until the occupation ended. At the same time, SCAP's proposed Trade Association Act went into effect enforced by the FTC, though certain cooperatives received exemption. Under Nakayama's leadership, the FTC handled more than forty cases, a higher caseload than that administered by the U.S. Justice Department. The FTC's Japanese staff handled this large work load with "relative vigor." Antitrust was clearly not too foreign to be grasped within Japanese culture. Instead, the issue was whether Japanese

---

[38] Ibid., 65–7, quote at 66. Just exactly who the opposition "political leaders" were is not clear. But see Iyori and Uesugi, *Antimonopoly Laws*, 16, stating that the Antimonopoly Act of 1947 was discussed in Parliament on March 28, "without much argument."

[39] Concerning Mrs Ariga, see interview and other materials cited below. In our interview, August 7, 2003, Iyori elaborated upon the career paths of Hashimoto and other members of the Antitrust Study Committee. The FTC's commitment to "economic democracy" is confirmed in Mrs Ariga's interview. For Professor Yazawa's career, see note 9 above, especially Tsugue Sano's "Research Report."

authorities and business chose to support the active enforcement of the Antimonopoly Law or a bureaucratic approach to economic regulation.[40]

In an essay published in English and Japanese, Welsh described anti-monopoly legislation as a "Test of Democracy in Japan." Whether the legislation proved to be "a permanent or temporary asset depends in large measure upon how much" a "sense of 'fair play' has developed" among the Japanese, rather than being "mere 'lip service' or expediency." Struggling over the "permanency of democracy . . . it will take great courage to defend" the laws and "to make them work fairly and objectively. Contrariwise, it will (and does) take no courage to attack them and to attempt to make them ineffectual." He acknowledged that neither the Anti-monopoly Law nor the Trade Association Law was an "indigenous product," but "able and informed Japanese" supported "the creation and effectuation of these important pieces of legislation. Moreover, it is no reflection upon the Japanese for them to have acquired improvements from other cultures, other economies." Condescension notwithstanding, Welsh conceded that Japan's "most respected persons and companies" gathered "economic power for the purpose of economic control." By contrast, "if democracy is to succeed" there must be "distinct practical benefits to the people as a whole from successful enforcement of anti-monopoly principles." Failure to implement the "legislation, objectively and fairly, would stand out as a neon sign" revealing the Japanese government's publicized "democratic objectives" as "mere opportunistic camouflage. This point cannot be over-emphasized. Anti-monopoly legislation in Japan has become more than legislation against monopolies and unfair trade practices. It is a symbol of practical democracy in action!"[41]

Nevertheless, the cold war shift toward the more conservative SCAP policies of 1948 resulted in the first amendment to the Antimonopoly Law in 1949. The amendment relaxed the strictures against stockholding or interlocking directorates among potentially competing firms, loosened the notification rules pertaining to international contracts and national mergers, and incorporated a more economically precise definition of "competition." The amendment's passage nonetheless revealed that despite strong

---

[40] Iyori, "Competition Policy and Government Intervention," *Washington University Global Studies Law Review*, 6–8; Harry First, "Antitrust Enforcement in Japan," 64 *Antitrust Law Journal* (Fall 1995), 137–82, especially at 156 for quoted phrase; Iyori, *Antimonopoly Legislation in Japan*, 16–17, 246–7, 254–6; First, "Antitrust in Japan; Original Intent," *Pacific Rim Law & Policy Journal*, 59 note 253, quoting the *Official SCAP History* which reported for 1949–50 in response to an active media campaign that business peoples' complaints "began to poor in." But see Wells, *Antitrust*, 185–6 assessing the enforcement effort as "a qualified failure."

[41] Edward C. Welsh, "Anti-Monopoly Legislation: The Test of Democracy in Japan," 1, 2 (copy located at the University of Washington, Marian Gould Gallagher Law Library, Seattle, n.d.).

lobbying pressure, Japanese big business and ministry bureaucrats achieved only limited modification of the Antimonopoly Law, modifications which even the law's proponents agreed were necessary. Meanwhile, the FTC's enforcement continued, including the protection of opportunity for small enterprises and agricultural cooperatives by addressing big business' abusive power.[42]

Nakayama stated the motivations driving the FTC's enforcement. " 'Economic democratization' means an economic situation where faithful and fair people are respected and honored, and where their abilities can be freely, highly and fully developed, so that people are able to have a chance to enjoy a happy social life." Enforcing the Antimonopoly Law thus promoted the "denial of munitions industries, dissolution of Zaibatsu, popularization of capital, cooperation and participation in the management of workers, reforms of farmland," whereby the "fundamental idea is the establishment, maintenance and development of a humane economy based on egalitarianism, freedom and fraternity. Frankly speaking, it is an economic situation where there is universally diffused and growing real income without inequal distribution or the binding of capital." Rejecting Japan's war-torn recent past, Nakayama exclaimed that "[a]n economy which contains the causes for an imperialistic economic invasion should not be called a wholesome national economy. A wholesome national economy is a 'peaceful economy,' . . . where there is no more struggle and exploitation." In summary, he said, the "wholesome" growth of political and economic democracy "means the maintenance and development of an economic situation in which the opportunity of developing the faithful and true power of a human being in correspondence with his/her talents can be equally recognized." As former FTC commissioner Hiroshi Iyori observed, Nakayama had provided "an excellent expression of the Japanese free market economy combined with popular Confucian Philosophy."[43]

During the years following Japan's surrender, a few officials responded to SCAP's directives with increased understanding of antitrust principles. The Industrial Order Bill SCAP rejected in January 1946 was based upon a bureaucratic system of wartime market controls rooted in Japanese and German precedent. The measure evidenced virtually no awareness of the principles Takayanagi had publicized in his "Sherman Act" article some months earlier. By the time the Japanese received the Kime Draft, however, they were prepared to give an informed critique. They assembled a support

[42] On the "cold war shift," compare Haley, *Antitrust in Germany and Japan*, 33–4; Cohen and Passin, ed., *Remaking Japan* (1987), 359–77; Wells, *Antitrust*, 185–6. For the Antimonopoly Act amendment of 1949, see Iyori, *Antimonopoly Legislation in Japan*, 18–19; Iyori and Uesugi, *Antimonopoly Laws*, 30–1; Iyori to Freyer, interview, August 7, 2003, for quoted phrase.
[43] Iyori, "Competition Policy and Government Intervention," *Washington University Global Studies Law Review*, quote at 6–7, and Iyori's assessment at 7.

apparatus that brought to bear extensive research into the history of American antitrust and economic and constitutional institutions. In a lengthy article about U.S. antitrust development from 1890 to the early 1940s published just six weeks after the Diet passed the Antimonopoly Act, Yazawa suggested the depth of this research. He cited a committee that as early as 1943 had been studying the American economy. Yazawa's citations to English-language books and articles included at least forty items published from 1905 to 1941. He was familiar with Arnold and the National Economic Committee, which epitomized the New Deal antitrust activism of Corwin Edwards. His article also cited German sources on cartels and monopoly. Thus, like Wakimura, Yazawa was well equipped to support the team that negotiated with SCAP to produce the Antimonopoly Act.[44]

This understanding enabled Japanese negotiators to win from SCAP concessions altering the Kime Draft so as to correspond to an image of postwar Japanese economic democracy. The compromises Salwin agreed to regarding stockholding, mergers, and the holding company ban reinforced the *zaibatsu* dissolution policy. Eleanor Hadley, John Haley, Theodore Cohen, and Kozo Yamamura have well documented how removing the *zaibatsu* families transformed Japan. Through the holding companies, the "millionaire families" Edwards described had dominated Japanese industry's management and stock investment. SCAP's dissolution program successfully removed the powerful families from their controlling place in Japan's economic order. The Antimonopoly Law's holding company ban undercut the families' long-standing financial and managerial control; its flexible shareholding and merger provisions increased the opportunity for smaller investors and the organizational authority of middle managers, just as Wakimura had hoped. Once the occupation ended, the middle-management structure and its working relationships with government ministries were reconstituted as the distinctive form of group enterprise or *keiretsu*.[45]

Juxtaposing the public discourse of the SSC Report, Nakayama's blend of "economic democracy" and "Confucian philosophy," the interdependency Takayanagi and Yazawa established between American democracy and antitrust, and the negotiations resulting in the Antimonopoly Act exposed further dimensions of the search for a more democratic political and economic order. The negotiations weakened the Kime Draft's strict prohibitions against cartels and diluted enforcement through private actions. The Japanese negotiators strengthened, however, the Antimonopoly Act's unfair business practices provisions and did not oppose the holding company ban, which enabled the FTC better to defend small and medium-sized enterprises. The protectionist policy reflected – much as the SSC Report had

---

[44] See notes, 9, 30, and 32–8 above.
[45] Compare notes 4 and 10 with text and citations to public discourse in Section II which follows.

urged – the necessity of ameliorating the abuse of dominance arising from the "double industrial structure" pitting efficient corporate giants emerging as *keiretsu* against the traditional smaller enterprises. In response to economic dislocation engendered by the Korean War, moreover, the Japanese enacted the Temporary Measures for the Stabilization of Specific Medium and Small Enterprises and the Export Trading Law. This protection of smaller enterprise perpetuated a more egalitarian, pro-producer social order than the expressly consumer-oriented system of American capitalism. The changes in Japanese society that the occupation's Antimonopoly Act fostered in the name of "economic democracy" impeded the achievement of an Americanized consumer economy.[46]

II. JAPANESE POLITICAL DEMOCRACY AND THE VICISSITUDES OF ANTIMONOPOLY POLICY AFTER 1952

During the initial decades following the occupation, Japanese antimonopoly policy achieved tenuous permanence. In 1953, Japan's Diet enacted amendments relaxing certain provisions of the original Antimonopoly Law. By 1958, the government of Prime Minister Kishi Nobusuke, big business, and MITI promoted further revisions seeking to eviscerate the law altogether. The effort failed, but the struggle defined the future course of antimonopoly policy making. Over the same period, the government exempted coal mining, textiles, and other depressed industries from the Antimonopoly Law, enabling MITI to authorize "rationalization" cartels as the remedy for "excessive competition." The exemption-authorization process nonetheless generally required consultation between MITI and the FTC; although initially MITI usually dominated, a negotiational relationship eventually evolved benefiting the FTC. In 1962–63 the government submitted to the Diet a bill challenging the FTC's role, but opposition again prevented passage. Thus, FTC commissioner Ashino Hiroshi's assessment concerning the revision struggle of 1958 was prophetic: "The Anti-Monopoly will remain, on the statute book indefinitely . . . and the Fair Trade Commission will continue its forlorn existence. The destiny of the Law in the future is closely tied to that of political democracy in Japan, and the anti-monopoly policy will either rise or fall with democratic government."[47]

---

[46] On the Temporary Measures for the Stabilization of Specific Medium and Small Enterprises and The Export Trading Law, see Hiroshi Iyori, "Cartels in Japan," *The Oriental Economist* (January 1964), 25–9, especially 25. I am grateful to former FTC official Professor Hirabayashi Hidekatsu for his many insights.

[47] Ashino, Hiroshi, "Experimenting with Anti-Trust Law in Japan," 3 *The Japanese Annual of International Law* (1959), 31–51, quote at 51; Haley, *Antitrust in Germany and Japan*, 52–3, 56–8; Iyori and Uesugi, *Antimonopoly Laws of Japan*, 30–41; [n.a.] "Anti-Monopoly

Ashino's perception reflected Japan's volatile political environment. He identified the Kishi government as promoting the antimonopoly revision proposals. Kishi gained power following the merger of Japan's two major conservative, probusiness parties to form the Liberal Democratic Party (LDP). A personal foe of Japan's most prominent conservative leader, Yoshida Shigeru, Kishi received credit for instituting the LDP-dominated "system of 1955," a complex alliance linking diverse, often opposing groups, including big and small business and agriculture. He made the LDP's electoral success dependent upon maintaining unity among divergent factions. Kishi's governance system widened the conservative power base throughout Japan, ensuring the LDP's enduring hold on power; the system nonetheless fostered persistent factional competition within the party. Displacing Yoshida as the conservatives' leader, Kishi was prime minister from 1957 to 1960; one of his primary goals was implementing the Antimonopoly Law revisions proposed in 1958. Despite the LDP's persistent Diet majorities, however, individual LDP factions periodically voted independently on particular issues and could prevent passage of government-sponsored bills.[48]

Given this political disharmony Ashino assessed the fate of Kishi's assault on the Antimonopoly Law. Recognizing that the "scheme may mean complete emasculation of the Law . . . roars of protest" arose from consumer and small business groups which since 1953 had been at odds over various cartel exemptions, including those authorized by the Medium and Small Scale Enterprise Organization Law. These two groups "now joined hands in fighting the common foe. Agriculture, too, dismayed at the prospect that the price of what it sells would be depressed and its cost increased, joined the fight" along with the Socialist Party. Ashino frankly acknowledged that the "interests" of the various parts of the economy "are extremely complex, and consequently their attitudes vary according to the particular issue." The Kishi government's staunchest supporter of the

Law Revision," XXVI *The Oriental Economist* (January, 1958), 567–71; Yanaga Chitoshi, *Big Business in Japanese Politics* (New Haven, CT, 1968), 152–76; Yasusuke Murakami, "Toward a Socioinstitutional Explanation of Japan's Economic Performance," in Kozo Yamamura, ed., *Policy and Trade Issues of the Japanese Economy American and Japanese Perspectives* (Seattle, 1982), 3–46; Yamamura, *Economic Policy in Postwar Japan*; Edwards, "Japan," *Trade Regulations Overseas*, 647–726; Ariga Michiko, and Luvern v. Reike, "The Antimonopoly Law of Japan and Its Enforcement," 39 *Washington Law Review* (August 1964), 437–78; Restrictive Trade Practices Specialist Study Team, *Control of Restrictive Trade Practices in Japan*, 1–112; Johnson, *MITI*, 226–7.
[48] Ashino, "Experimenting with Anti-Trust Law," *Japanese Annual of International Law*, 46; Masumi, *Contemporary Politics in Japan*, 17–56, 85–6, 107–15, 135, 166, 208, 220; Stockwin, *Japan: Divided Politics*, 68–75, 127, 135, 256–68; Haley, *Antitrust in Germany and Japan*, 52–8, 85, 100; Johnson, *MITI*, 53, 122, 144, 171, 226, 238, 251, 291; Iyori and Uesugi, *Antimonopoly Laws of Japan*, 34–7; Richard J. Samuels, "Kishi and Corruption: An Anatomy of the 1955 System," 83 *JPRI Working Paper* (December 2001), 1–12.

revision proposals was "large scale industry, producing basic materials, which is easy to cartelize," identified with the leading big business organization, Keidanren. "On the other extreme," Ashino located "the consuming public, which has nothing to gain and all to lose by cartelization," but it was a "force . . . most difficult to organize." The middle groups' interests were "not so simple and consequently their attitudes cannot be so clear cut." Labor was divided, and so "only half-heartedly" supported consumers.[49]

The "political parties reflect this complex relation," Ashino observed. "[F]inancially dependent upon big business . . . [and] close to it in mental attitude," the LDP "must listen primarily to its voice, but is not immune from the pressure of small business and agriculture." Meanwhile, the Socialist Party did not support the "cause of anti-monopoly . . . necessarily out of love for or faith in the virtues of free competition" but rather from "antagonism against big business and against the ruling party which tends to put the interests [of] big business first." Some Socialist Party "theorists" also considered that, eventually, "further cartelization of industry . . . might . . . make the task of nationalization simpler."[50]

Moreover, Ashino declared, the Antimonopoly Law's origins in "American experience without any precedent in Japan" meant that "comparatively few people understand its underlying philosophy." Thus, "[o]nly slowly" did Japanese business leaders who persistently resisted the "American dictated Anti-Monopoly Law and its guardian angel, the Fair Trade Commission," perceive that "some sort of self-disciplinary devices for the capitalist economy may be inescapable." Ashino concluded that a "paradoxical situation" resulted whereby the conservative "free enterprise" champion LDP opposed the FTC and antimonopoly policy, while the Socialist Party, which in principle advocated "greater governmental control of business and even nationalization of key industries," defended "this fundamentally individualistic law."[51]

The complex political struggle influenced the FTC's enforcement priorities in relation to MITI's administrative guidance. Following release from prison as a war criminal, Kishi combined a program of political party building with promotion of MITI's expanded use of administrative guidance to overcome what he described as the "condition of our economy" to "fall into the bad habit of excessive competition." First as political insider and then as prime minister, Kishi promoted MITI's industrial policy – including the reliance upon cartel exemptions – over the FTC and the Antimonopoly Law, advocating the 1953 amendments and the 1958 revisions. Accordingly, as the FTC struggled amidst the Diet's successful and

[49] Ashino, "Experimenting with Anti-Trust Law," *Japanese Annual of International Law*, 49, 50.
[50] Ibid. [51] Ibid., 50, 51.

attempted revisions of the Antimonopoly Law and the coincident proliferation of cartel exemptions, it shifted its enforcement efforts toward
unfair business practices which broadly favored smaller enterprises.[52]

Ashino acknowledged that the FTC's increased emphasis on unfair
business practices aided smaller firms. Under pressure from a mass movement seeking to organize them along lines of labor unions, the LDP and the
opposition parties "with an eye to the tremendous votes of small business"
supported passage of the Medium and Small Scale Enterprises Organization
Law of 1957, which permitted cartelization among small firms and along
vertical lines between small and large companies. While MITI regulated the
cartel relationships through administrative guidance, it generally favored
big business. The discriminatory treatment clashed with several measures
enacted to protect against "unfair business practices." But while cartel
legislation sanctioned MITI's use of administrative guidance, the same
measures generally empowered the FTC to enforce the unfair trade provisions. Thus, Ashino observed, "unfair methods of trade . . . claim[ed] more
and more of the FTC's time and attention, and often receive the liveliest
publicity in the newspapers and over the radio." Broadly these enforcement
efforts involved protecting "weak suppliers or independent stores" from
department stores abusing their position, "or with speeding up payment by
big companies to their subcontractors." Also, the FTC ensured that small
firms' uses of lotteries and premiums to draw customers were not unreasonable in sectors "ranging from soya sauce and rubber foot wares to
department stores, newspapers and school book publishers."[53]

The occupation's deconcentration program had forbidden the business
use of famous family names, but when the occupation ended the Diet
repealed the prohibition against *zaibatsu* names, and during the next decade Japanese business was reconstituted under that symbolic imagery. This
restructuring occurred through a process of mergers, acquisitions, and
technology transfers monitored by the FTC. According to Ashino, by fall
1958 more than 3,500 merger notifications had been filed with the FTC in
conjunction with almost 1,500 business acquisition agreements. Accompanying the process of merger and acquisition, more than 1,000 international agreements were filed with the FTC, the "bulk of which relate to
licensing of patents and other forms of technological co-operation." The
FTC also reviewed trade associations, which by 1958 numbered nearly
17,600.[54]

[52] Haley, *Antitrust in Germany and Japan*, 57.
[53] Ashino, "Experimenting with Anti-Trust Law," *Japanese Annual of International Law*, 42,
      45; Yanaga, *Big Business in Japanese Politics*, 152–76; Edwards, "Japan," *Trade
      Regulations Overseas*, 647–726; Ariga and Reike, "Antimonopoly Law of Japan," 39
      Washington Law Review, 437–78; Iyori, "Cartels in Japan," *Oriental Economist*, 25–9.
[54] Ashino, "Experimenting with Anti-Trust Law," *Japanese Annual of International Law*
      (1959), 35, 45.

Ashino's discourse thus linked Japan's business restructuring to the struggle over antimonopoly policy. Suggesting the widespread disapproval the Japanese media and fascist-militarists alike had directed at the *zaibatsu* holding companies from 1931 to 1945, Ashino observed that "[o]pen criticism has never been voiced against outlawing of holding companies" in Article 9 of the Antimonopoly Act. The diverse Japanese political party, and bureaucratic interests publically "accepted as reasonable in principle" the "prohibition of private monopolization" and, inferentially, the regulation of unfair trade practices. Significantly, these latter areas were those in which Japanese negotiators had most directly shaped the provisions during the drafting of the law. Even so, Ashino declared, the Japanese expressed "grievances" most "strong[ly] . . . against the categorical condemnation of cartels and the too severe restrictions on freedom regarding such matters as mergers, stock holdings and multiple directorates." The occupation government itself – under pressure from *American* interests representing multinational corporations – supported the law's revision in 1949, especially removing the original stipulation imposing prenotification for any international agreement.[55]

MITI, big business, and their conservative party allies developed proposals for emasculating the Antimonopoly Law through the amendment of 1953. The FTC did its best to dilute the revisionist proposals by insisting upon counter-recommendations. The resulting amendment embodied compromises, Ashino suggested, by which the law was "made more moderate in order to facilitate the nation's economic recovery." Broadly, it "repealed" the original law's "provisions making certain concerted activities illegal per se, the provisions relating to undue and substantial disparities in bargaining power," and the "restrictions on intercorporate stockholdings and multiple-directorates." It also "moderated" the provision's pertaining to the "merger of companies."[56]

Viewed as a contested compromise, the amendment symbolized a continuing struggle for economic democracy. The corporate shareholding revisions arose from unsatisfied public desire to increase investment opportunity. The original Antimonopoly Law's holding company ban had furthered this public purpose, but its cross-shareholding restrictions left much to be desired. The cartel exemptions were, according to an informed commentary, "modeled" on drafts of a contemporary West German law. Under the German regulatory tradition "crisis" or "rationalization" cartels theoretically balanced the interests of large and small business and

[55] Ibid., 35.
[56] Ibid., 37; Gao, *Japan's Economic Dilemma* 136–7; Restrictive Trade Practices Specialist Study Team, *Control of Restrictive Trade Practices*, 9–18; Haley, *Antitrust in Germany and Japan*, 53–4; Iyori and Uesugi, *Antimonopoly Law of Japan*, 32–4; Murakami, "Toward a Socioinstitutional Explanation of Japan's Economic Performance," in Yamamura, ed., *Policy and Trade Issues*, 4–11.

consumers. These considerations give sharper focus to the amendment's provisions, which sanctioned cartel exemptions so that firms might mitigate recessions or gain organizational and technological efficiencies through rationalization; broadened the meaning of "unfair methods of competition" into new "unfair business practices"; established procedures for authorizing resale price maintenance; made easier intercorporate shareholding, interlocking directorates, and mergers; and repealed particular trade prohibitions, the FTC's authority to address "undue disparities" in bargaining power by reconstituting firms, and the prohibition against government authorizing control organizations.[57]

Ashino's focus on the FTC's enforcement regime and Japan's shifting politics thus reflected a disputed policy discourse. Policy makers especially contested the meaning of "competition" and "public interest," which, in turn, determined the actual enforcement of the Antimonopoly Law's unfair trade practices, cartel, and merger-intercorporate shareholder provisions after 1953. In 1957, a Keidanren publication stated that it was "too narrow to believe that keeping free competition coincides with" the "public interest" which "should be naturally judged from the higher point of view, that of the broad national economy, which may include naturally both entrepreneurs and consumers." However, the FTC's "Commentaries" published following the amendment's passage stated that the "purpose" continued to be encapsulated in the phrases "to promote free and fair competition" in order to "heighten the level of employment, and thereby to promote the democratic and wholesome development of the national economy as well as to assure the interest of the general consumer."[58]

Prime Minister Kishi attacked antimonopoly policy as part of a larger program aimed at broadening police powers over public education, instituting warrantless searches and seizures, and strengthening Japan's control of national defense. The defense measures especially clashed with the U.S.– Japan Security Treaty and, most importantly, the Constitution's very popular Article 9, denying Japan's sovereign right to use military force. The Antimonopoly Law revisions did not pass the Diet when initially introduced in 1958, despite the LDP's "comfortable majority . . . in both Houses," Ashino asserted, because it became entangled with the "sudden appearance of the Police Duties Bill . . . a political issue of the first magnitude. The functioning of the Diet was for the time being paralyzed." Ashino's assessment ended with the outcome in doubt, but the revisions died amid the mixed results of Kishi's program. The Police Bill and the

---

[57] Haley, *Antitrust in Germany and Japan*, 53–4.
[58] *Keidanren Ikensho* (*Opinions of the Federation of Economic Organizations*, 1957), and "Kaisei Dokusen Kinshi Ho Kaietsu (The Commentaries on Reformed Antimonopoly Act, 1954)," discussed in Imamura, "Consumer and Competition Policy," in Ariga, ed., *International Conference on International Economy*, 290.

constitutional changes touching Article 9 never passed. However, despite hundreds of thousands of demonstrators against alteration of the Security Treaty, Kishi achieved limited modifications preserving U.S. control of Okinawa while enlarging Japanese authority over the Self-Defense Forces. Following these equivocal results, Kishi resigned in June 1960; the LDP's Ikeda Hayato became prime minister advocating the "high growth" economic policy.[59]

International trade frictions influenced the government's economic growth program, including the role of antimonopoly policy. By the early 1960s, Japan increasingly liberalized its international trade, despite increasing calls for protection within the domestic market. Buffeted by a relatively declining U.S. trade surplus, U.S. officials pressured the Japanese government to enter into bilateral trade agreements on textiles and steel. Fearing foreign imports might exacerbate the recurring "excessive competition" which Japanese business repeatedly complained of, business groups, bureaucrats and the LDP-promoted government policies permitting easier mergers and acquisitions, technology transfers, and, of course, cartel formation.[60]

MITI bureaucrat Morozumi Yoshihiko summarized the public debate shaping industrial policy within these conflicting demands. During 1946–47, Morozumi had been charged with explaining drafts of the Antimonopoly Bill to his superiors; throughout the rest of his career he formulated industrial policy by minimizing wherever possible the influence of antimonopoly law principles. In 1962, Morozumi published an analysis of administrative guidance under industrial policy. Rejecting the "classic belief that the public welfare will be promoted by the invisible hand of free competition," he declared that "free competition" resulted in "excessive competition" which "neither provides the most suitable scale nor a guarantee of proper prices." Morozumi borrowed from U.S. antitrust policy the term "workable competition" to describe a "moderate" level of concentration "result[ing] in greater specialization from a technical point of view and from the management aspect, the elimination of inefficient enterprises. In other words we have the conditions for workable competition." He emphasized that the "pressing, urgent business is the formation of a business system which will promote economic growth." Spreading the "benefits of high growth – prices, wages, profits – must not be awarded to the law of free competition which stifles the conditions of growth."[61]

Only limited action was necessary to address market concentration, Morozumi insisted, in order to further technology transfers. If there arose a "problem in the suitable distribution of the economies of scale, it is an ex

[59] Ashino, "Experimenting with Anti-Trust Law," *Japanese Annual of International Law*, 50.
[60] Gao, *Japan's Economic Dilemma*, 114–51.
[61] Hadley, *Antitrust in Japan*, translated from Morozumi, quote at 397, 398.

post facto inspecting function, for the Fair Trade Commission or the results should be corrected through public finance measures." Understandably, Morozumi and his fellow bureaucrats would not "wait to theorize about" the effect "a policy of concentration will have. To the extent that our export strength is assured, the growth of our economy is assured." Moreover, he linked the economy's "recent splendid technical advances" to the international "postwar technical agreements . . . with large enterprises," benefiting Japanese firms. Indeed, "53 Japanese companies have entered into technical arrangements with RCA. Peabody and Co. receives royalties from 17 Japanese companies on the Sanfordizing process. Thus can one conclude there is an 'invisible hand?'" In addition, the interdependency between lax merger policy and technology agreements enabled Japan to maintain a protectionist regime even while liberalizing trade.[62]

Morozumi applied the idea of "middle way" to Japan. Following the occupation, the nation's system of business–government collaboration "represents the middle way between the 19th century laissez-faire [in the West] and the controls of the war period of the 1930s in Japan," he affirmed. Industrial policy replaced the "strife under freedom and the compulsion under controls." Between these extremes Japan developed an economy based on consent: "Out of discussions between government and private enterprise, mutually determined national targets are worked out. Private enterprise pledges to carry these out. Government, on its side, pledges special favors . . . such as subsidies and taxation measures. . . . Mutual consent and bilateral methods, obviate the need for legal compulsion."[63]

Nevertheless, advocates of antimonopoly policy resisted the dominant industrial policy discourse. The government had long drawn upon the expertise of scholars in "study groups" to establish the intellectual legitimacy for policy making. The Study Group reporting on the 1958 proposals generally supported the procartel position advocated by MITI, big business, and LDP. The Study Group's work coincided, however, with Japanese academic periodicals publishing a debate in which various scholars vigorously opposed the procartel approach. These academic critics provided rationales supporting the idea that the Antimonopoly Law and the FTC

---

[62] On Morozumi's role during the occupation, see Section I, this chapter; and Johnson, *MITI*, 175; during the initial postwar era, he published two works discussing the tension between antitrust and industrial policy: *Kyoso to dokusen no banashi* (The Story of Competition and Monopoly, Nikei Bunko, Tokyo, 1962) and, "Keizai seicho to dokukin seisaku," (Economic Growth and the Antitrust Policy), in Kosei Torihiki Kyokai, ed., *Kokusai Kyoso to dokukinho* (Nihon Keizai Shinbunsha, Tokyo (1963), 15–45. See also Imamura, "Consumer and Competition Policy," in Ariga, ed., *International Conference on International Economy*, 290. Hadley, *Antitrust in Japan*, translated from Japanese to English, quote at 397.

[63] Ibid., including Hadley's translated text, quote at 398.

shielded small business and consumers form the sort of exploitation prevailing during the wartime era. Under the occupation, moreover, the FTC's antimonopoly law enforcement benefited weaker groups. The scholarly debate concerning the 1958 revisions represented the continuing struggle to preserve antimonopoly policy in order to promote market competition and protect small business and consumers in the name of economic democracy.[64]

Indeed, dissatisfied consumers attempted to compel stronger antimonopoly enforcement. The FTC procured evidence revealing that representatives of leading newspapers had met in order to discuss a simultaneous price increase. The newspaper firms submitted a letter to the FTC claiming, however, that while prices were clearly uniform each company had set the price "independently," not as a result of collusion. Asserting that its evidence was not strong enough to prove in court the existence of a formal collusive agreement, the FTC terminated the investigation. Although previous court decisions had established a high standard of proof in such cases, scholars condemned the FTC's "docility." In addition, a consumer group brought suit, seeking a court order requiring the FTC to continue proceedings against the Yomiuri Newspaper Company. The group's lawyers also attempted to recover damages under the Japanese Civil Code's general tort provision, section 709. The court rejected these claims. Nevertheless, the case revealed a strategy advocating vigorous antimonopoly enforcement that consumer groups and scholars would pursue.[65]

Defenders attempting to enhance antimonopoly policy's legitimacy through wider international recognition had mixed success. Foreign legal–economic experts furthered this cause by publishing and holding international meetings including studies of Japanese antitrust.[66] However, a *Business International* report declared in 1965 that the FTC's "chief activity . . . seems to be the sanctioning and registering of exceptions to the [Antimonopoly] Law, rather than enforcing it." By contrast, the preceding year FTC official Iyori Hiroshi published an article indicating that antimonopoly enforcement depended upon institutional authority as well as

---

[64] Ashino, "Experimenting with Anti-Trust Law," *Japanese Annual of International Law*, 46–7; Edwards, "Japan," *Trade Regulations Overseas*, 709–26; Yanaga, *Big Business in Japanese Politics*, 152–76; Iyori and Uesugi, *Antimonopoly Laws of Japan*, 34–6.
[65] Ariga and Reike, "Antimonopoly Law of Japan," *Washington Law Review*, 453–5; Edwards, "Japan," *Trade Regulations Overseas*, 709–26.
[66] Arthur Taylor von Mehren, ed., *Law in Japan the Legal Order in a Changing Society* (Cambridge, MA, 1963), xv–xxxviii; J. B. Heath, ed., *International Conference on Monopolies, Mergers, and Restrictive Practices Cambridge, U.K., 1969* (London, 1971), 117–24, 155–60. The article, Ariga and Reike, "Antimonopoly Law of Japan," *Washington Law Review*, 437–78, grew out of a major Japan-East Asian Program at the University of Washington [phone interview T. A. Freyer and Professor Luvern V. Reike, March 26, 2003].

political contingencies. Most cartel exemptions benefited small and medium-sized firms involved in export sectors vulnerable to the international liberalization measures. These groups were among the FTC's few political supporters in Japan, as demonstrated by their role in defeating the revision proposal in 1958 and in 1963. Iyori suggested, accordingly, that while small business cartelization was "not without problems, the impact in these cases is relatively small." The greater problem arose from imposing "production cut-backs" through bureaucratic administrative guidance.[67]

Iyori's policy discourse, like Ashino's, located the FTC's enforcement within a wider political context. He observed that Prime Minister Ikeda had recognized the need to lessen tensions between the trade liberalization policies and the bureaucrats' expanding use of administrative guidance. Ikeda's statement reflected the public's growing concern about rising prices as the country's economic miracle unfolded during the 1960s. FTC chairman Watanabe Kikuzo seized upon the price issue, Iyori suggested, to cultivate broadened government support to redress the cut in staff by one-third the agency had suffered. Watanabe won a special budget increase enabling the FTC to pursue more active enforcement. Iyori admitted that while "consumers, farmers, small business enterprises, and scholars" were increasingly "aware" of the FTC's defense of competition, "an influential body of opinion, particularly in the financial and business world," stressed "the evils of excessive competition in order to justify further cartelization and joint action." He nonetheless concluded on an optimistic note, exclaiming that "though the traditional and social environment has not been favorable for the anti-monopoly policy and in spite of numerousness of cartels . . . in consideration of the above recent trend, a healthy milieu for the anti-monopoly system is taking root and will thrive."[68]

International contingencies sometimes reinforced antimonopoly policy's survival. Japan's acceptance of the International Monetary Fund's program for currency exchange required restricting a power bureaucrats had long exercised. Japan's compliance with the GATT's tariff-reducing measures had a similar impact on bureaucratic authority. Accordingly, from 1961 to 1963 MITI again supported enacting Antimonopoly Law exemptions, this time fostering its influence over the National Federation of Banker's Association and the Ministry of Finance. Defending market competition, the FTC objected with the support of small business, consumers, and scholars. More importantly, however, big business and its bureaucratic and LDP allies prevented passage of the exemption on the ground that it

---

[67] Hadley, *Antitrust in Japan*, 445; Iyori, "Cartels in Japan," *Oriental Economist*, 25–9, quote at 29.

[68] Iyori, "Cartels," 29. See also Hadley, *Antitrust in Japan*, 386; Imamura, "Consumer and Competition Policy," in Ariga, ed., *International Conference on International Economy*, 290–1.

encouraged a return to wartime controls. This rationale suggested that formally strengthening MITI's authority would disrupt the delicate balance it and big business maintained. Similarly, later in the decade automobile manufactures successfully resisted MITI's attempt to employ administrative guidance to consolidate the industry through merger.[69]

The FTC's enforcement pattern reflected these policy constraints. The *Noda Soy Sauce* case (1955) was one of only five arising during the period under the Antimonopoly Law's provision against private monopolization, and though the *Soy Sauce* case sustained both competition values and the interests of small business, it was exceptional. As Ashino noted, the FTC devoted much of its limited resources to "monitoring" cartels, technology transfers, and shareholding resulting from mergers and acquisitions. The FTC's most active enforcement field concerned unfair business practices which often involved small business. Ariga Michiko, who had contributed to the Japanese side's antimonopoly law negotiations and subsequently rose from being FTC counselor to commissioner, revealed a change in enforcement patterns. By July 1963, of the 191 complaints the FTC had issued, "78 involved some form of unfair business practice." A shift in enforcement priorities was "especially noticeable . . . after the 1953 amendments. From 1947 through 1953 the Commission issued 82 decrees dealing with monopolization or restraints and only 11 involving unfair trade practices. From 1954 through 1960, there were as many decrees dealing with unfair practices [as] with . . . [other] problems – 17 in each category." The actions covered thirteen industries, ranging from the protection of vital consumer items like foodstuffs to preventing department store domination of wholesalers and the stopping of bribes to influence school textbook selections.[70]

Japan's international trade liberalization nonetheless fostered challenges to mergers and technology licensing agreements. During the 1960s, the FTC's merger policy gradually came into conflict with MITI's industrial policy of promoting big business. In 1969, Keidanren's Anti-monopoly Study Group set out the big business position in its report *Mergers and Anti-monopoly Policy*. Japan's leading industries were "in the world-wide movement of economic internationalization as expressed by liberalization of capital transactions and removal of trade barriers," the report declared. The "unavoidable task" of Japan's "world-wide enterprises" was to "insure their independence and future development" throughout the "arena of international markets." Consequently, "consideration should be given so

[69] Hadley, *Antitrust in Japan*, 400–1; Gao, *Japan's Economic Dilemma*, 96, 189–90, 199, 206, 257; Johnson, *MITI*, 258, 268, 278, 286–8.

[70] Ariga and Reike, "The Antimonopoly Law of Japan and Its Enforcement," 39 *Washington Law Review* (August 1964), 455–62, quotes at 456; Iyori, *Antimonopoly Legislation in Japan*, 69–83.

that the Anti-monopoly policy, which is a part of the economic policy, does not work as a hindrance to the necessary reorganization of industries and to the endeavors for strengthening of enterprises."[71]

Following the 1953 Amendment, the FTC increasingly considered merger actions. In the *Snow Brand Dairy* case (1958), the *Chuo-Sen'i* fiber manufacturer's case (1959), and the *Mitsubishi Heavy Industry Co.* (1963) case the FTC allowed the merger. Even so, the last case aroused public comment expressing fears that the *zaibatsu* were being reconstituted. It preceded a publicized controversy in 1965 over MITI's use of informal administrative guidance (*kankoku sotan*) to enforce major steel firms' mutual request to maintain production restrictions. After initial vacilation, Sumitomo Metals defied the cartel agreement, whereupon MITI – supporting the major steel companies' demands – compelled Sumitomo's compliance. MITI "threatened" to use its authority under the Foreign Exchange and Control Act to curb Sumitomo Metals' coking coal imports. The FTC received favorable publicity for its criticism of MITI's heavy-handed conduct. The perception of the FTC's increased activism undoubtedly influenced several leading paper firms to "terminat[e] their merger plans" upon learning that the FTC's investigation would likely result in "rejection."[72]

These developments preceded a major turning point in enforcement, the *Yawata-Fuji Merger* case. A single steel firm prior to 1946, under the occupation it was broken in two, becoming Japan's number one and two steel companies that symbolized the nation's postwar economic miracle. The two firms announced plans to merge in 1968. Aggravating images of *zaibatsu* revival, the proposed merger received international media attention; it also fostered extended debate in the Japanese press among legal–economic professionals and between MITI and the FTC policy makers. The policy discourse of merger opponents contended that Japan's place within the liberalizing global economy could be promoted on the basis of competition values which, though borrowed from the United States, were adaptable to Japan's capitalist economy. A group of non-Marxist economists issued a public statement condemning the merger. Merger proponents asserted Keidanren's and MITI's position that Japanese business should be protected from competition at home in order for it to compete successfully abroad.[73]

---

[71] Y. Kanazawa, "Firm Behavior and Policy on Mergers in Japan," in Heath, ed., *International Conference on Monopolies*, translation Japanese to English text, 118.

[72] Ariga Michiko, "Merger Regulation in Japan," 5 *Texas International Law Forum* (Spring 1969), 112–26, quotes at 113; Iyori and Uesugi, *Antimonopoly Law of Japan*, 167–9. On the Sumitomo case, see contrasting views of MITI's coercion: Uriu, *Troubled Industries*, 108–9; Johnson, *MITI*, 268–71, 277, 279, and Frank K. Upham, *Law and Social Change in Postwar Japan* (Cambridge, MA, 1987), 176–84.

[73] Ariga, "Merger Regulation in Japan," *Texas International Law Forum*, 112–13; Kanazawa, "Firm Behavior and Policy on Mergers in Japan," and H. Suzuki, "Big Business Mergers

Ultimately, the FTC authorized the merger requiring the firms to accept a procompetitive remedy. Following a drawn out process, the FTC entered a consent decision in which Yawata-Fuji Steel agreed to twenty-four remedial measures intended to maintain oligopolistic competition through continuing technological innovation: sixteen of the twenty-four measures promoted competitive "technology assistance." Iyori later wrote that despite the controversy, the "case sent a strong message to business that the Antimonopoly Act could prevent big mergers even if they were supported by competent ministries." More significantly, "after this case, relevant companies tended to seek advance clearance from the FTC." He concluded that, "Viewed with hindsight" the FTC "became for the first time, a well known name throughout the nation."[74]

The *Amano* case had particular bearing on foreign investment involving patent licensing agreements. In 1966, the Japanese firm Amano and the Danish company Novo Industrial agreed not to compete in the sale and distribution of alkaline bacterial proteinase (a cleaning agent ingredient) within Japan, Okinawa, Taiwan, and Korea. Although the agreement formally ended in 1969, the FTC found that two restrictive clauses remained in effect, which after further proceedings, the FTC invalidated as unfair. In a separate proceeding, the Danish company initiated suit in the Tokyo High Court challenging the FTC's decision, but the court held that the firm lacked standing, a decision which on appeal the Supreme Court affirmed. These decisions were consistent with Japanese and U.S. perceptions of the market protectionism prevailing throughout Japan's economy. As one law review declared, in the *Amano* case the FTC evidently held the "view that in an effort to preserve orderly competition in the Japanese market and to place some controls on the present internationalization era the Antimonopoly Law will be utilized for controlling the foreign induction of technology and capital tie-ups under terms and conditions which might be unreasonable and unfair to Japanese companies."[75]

and Anti-Trust Laws: A Businessman's Point of View," in Heath, ed., *International Conference on Monopolies*, 117–24, 155–61; Uriu, *Troubled Industries*, 109; Iyori and Uesugi, *Antimonopoly Laws of Japan*, 166–7 (October 30, 1969, 16 KTIS 46).

[74] Iyori and Uesugi, *Antimonopoly Laws of Japan*, quote at 48, and decree as quoted, 166–7. See also Tony A. Freyer/Iyori Hiroshi interview, cited infra. The controversy was heightened when FTC Chairman Yamada resigned. He denied that public criticism was the reason for stepping down, asserting that "I laid a rail" (i.e., that he set a straight future course).

[75] Initial stages of the case: Matsushita Mitsuo and James L. Hildebrand, "Antimonopoly Law of Japan – Relating to International Business Transactions," 4 *Case Western Reserve Journal of International Law* (Spring 1972), 124–62, especially 135–7, and quote at 157–8. For outcome see: John Owen Haley, "Antitrust in Japan: Problems of Enforcement," in John Owen Haley, ed., *Current Legal Aspects of Doing Business in Japan and East Asia* (Seattle, 1977), 127–33.

Despite the precarious path toward legitimacy antimonopoly policy followed, its substantive doctrines were comparable to foreign practice. Although the Antimonopoly Law had no direct prewar precedent, the unfair trade practices, private monopolization, and the holding company ban provisions reinforced Japanese opposition to the wartime control system and the *zaibatsu*. As a result, the FTC's enforcement regime retained some legitimacy after the occupation ended. Japanese antimonopoly defenders noted that the Amendment of 1953 authorized the FTC and the courts to enforce antimonopoly policy on the basis of "reasonableness" and "substantial restraint" doctrines that were roughly comparable to contemporary U.S. standards.[76] According to Ariga, "An American comparison with the genus, if not the species, can be found for almost every exemption from the Japanese law." As H. W. Tanaka explained, in Japan the enforcement doctrines were geared to "regulating the exercise of power through continuing administrative guidance rather than imposing a limitation upon the possession and accumulation of power as under the United States antitrust laws. Like the Europeans, the Japanese authorities place faith in administrative control over the exercise of market power."[77]

By the 1960s, an uneasy status quo characterized antimonopoly policy in Japan. Despite the enduring influence of Kishi's "1955 system," the failures to revise the Antimonopoly Law in 1958 and 1963 institutionalized a public dispute about competition. But international trade liberalization coinciding with Ikeda's high growth economic program engendered a relative increase in cases being brought, though Japanese and foreign critics agreed that the law's enforcement remained weak. Echoing Ashino, FTC's Ariga nonetheless suggested that democratic contingency continued to shape the future. Perceiving a "new attitude" among "Japanese businessmen and others affected by" the Antimonopoly Law, she insisted that the "hostility and suspicion" derived from "its genesis in the mandate of the occupation forces, has disappeared" and there had "developed" an "appreciation of the contributions which free competition can make" to Japan's "postwar reconstruction," including "combating rising prices." She declared finally, that "Antimonopoly Law is in Japan to stay."[78]

---

[76] Oskadani, "Japan," in Friedmann, ed., *Anti-Trust Laws*, 238–57, quoted at 257.

[77] Ariga and Reike, "Antimonopoly Law of Japan," *Washington Law Review*, 471 [Ariga as source confirmed in Freyer and Reike, phone interview, March 26, 2003]; Hajime William Tanaka, "Comments on Selected Japanese Laws Bearing on United States Trade with and Investment in Japan," 7 *The Patent, Trademark, and Copyright Journal of Research and Education* (1963–64), 418–30, quoted at 424.

[78] Ariga and Reike, "Antimonopoly Law of Japan," *Washington Law Review*, 478 [Ariga as source confirmed in Freyer and Reike, phone interview, March 26, 2003].

III. CHANGING ANTIMONOPOLY POLICY AND POLITICAL CULTURE: THE 1970s AND THE 1990s

Antimonopoly law enforcement followed a cycle reflecting Japan's shifting sociopolitical environment. As the economic miracle gave way to decades of decline or no growth following the first oil shock of 1973 – exposing fissures within the social security system sustaining the generally conservative political regime – the alliance among big business, bureaucrats, and the LDP periodically became vulnerable. Episodic scandals disrupted the LDP's electoral power, facilitating struggles about antimonopoly policy resulting in stronger rather than weaker enforcement in the 1970s and then from the 1990s on. Meanwhile, the tension between industrial policy and antimonopoly policy shaped the corporate order identified with *keiretsu*, which temporarily fostered the image of global Japanese economic dominance during the 1980s.[79] That image proved to be a fragile "bubble," and its demise during the 1990s led Keidanren, MITI, and LDP leaders to support a vigorous antimonopoly enforcement by the FTC. The expansion of the bubble economy, moreover, engendered foreign demands for access to the Japanese home market epitomized by the SII, which resulted in growing of selective promotion of antimonopoly principles.[80]

The U.S. government's ending of fixed exchange rates in 1971 and the oil shock of 1973 promoted protectionist demands in Japan. Oligopolistic competition intensified among groups of firms forming *keiretsu*. The steady injection of technology heightened business rivalry, as corporate subsidiaries aggressively pushed for market share. "In emphasizing product competition, in contrast to price competition," Eleanor Hadley explained using Joseph Schumpeter's metaphor, the "difference" was "a bombardment in comparison to forcing a door. In Japan . . . competition has been of

---

[79] On politics, see Stockwin, *Japan: Divided Politics*; Pempel, *Regime Shift*; Gao, *Japan's Economic Dilemma*. For *keiretsu* and economic policy, see Morikawa, "Japan: Increasing Organizational Capabilities of Large Industrial Enterprises, 1880s–1980s," in Chandler et al., eds., *Big Business and the Wealth of Nations*, 307–35; Bernstein, "Japanese Capitalism," in McCraw, ed., *Creating Modern Capitalism*, 441–91; Meir, *International Environment of Business*, 264–95; Kozo Yamamura and Yasukichi Tasuba, eds., *The Political Economy of Japan the Domestic Transformation Volume I*, 3 vols (Stanford, 1987); Takashi Inoguchi and Daniel I. Okimoto, *The Political Economy of Japan, the Changing International Context Volume 2*, 3 vols (Stanford, 1988); Doremus et al., *Myth of the Global Corporation*.

[80] Compare Gao, *Japan's Economic Dilemma*; Anchordoguy, "Whatever Happened to the Japanese Miracle?," 80 *JPRI Working Paper*, 1–6; Edward J. Lincoln, *Arthritic Japan the Slow Pace of Economic Reform* (Washington, DC, 2001); Pempel, *Regime Shift*. For antitrust and SII, see Beeman, *Public Policy and Completion*; Schoppa, *Bargaining with Japan*; and Charles Stewart Markham, "The Japan Fair Trade Commission and the Evolving Framework of Antitrust Enforcement," Senior Thesis, BA, East Asian Studies Department, Princeton University, 1993. I thank Mr Markham for permission to cite his work.

bombardment proportions." Business repeatedly sought from government remedies for "excessive" competition implemented through administrative guidance and cartel exemptions. In addition, said Corwin Edwards as a result of the Antimonopoly Law's holding company ban and the 1953 Amendments, Japanese big business was reconstituted through increased numbers of mergers, acquisitions, and technology transfers, which were monitored but "seldom opposed" by the FTC. Indeed, from the mid-1960s to the mid-1970s, FTC surveys revealed, mergers worth 10 billion yen or more increased from thirty to seventy-five.[81]

More particularly, Japanese big business took advantage of the Amendment of 1953 legalizing intercorporate shareholding identified with *keiretsu*. Firms procured capital by developing expanded reciprocal shareholding among corporations to establish closer ties with banks. In 1949, a survey of 473 corporations stated, 25 percent held more than 5 percent of stock in other corporations; within two decades the percentage rose to 78.4 percent. In addition, between 1950 and 1973 the percentage of shares held by individuals as compared to institutions shifted from 61.3 and 23.66 percent, respectively, to 32.7 and 60.4 percent. Automobile companies exemplified this growth. In the late 1960s, Toyota was unconcerned if U.S. automakers opened factories in Japan, a situation not unlike that existing prior to 1941. "What is threatening is that Toyota's stocks can be bought or taken over by foreign companies. Toyota cannot compete with this strategy," an executive manager declared. MITI responded in 1970 to GM's purchase of Isuzu stock, accordingly, by channeling investment into joint ventures. "In the joint venture, it is extremely important that the Japanese side protects its autonomy in management," said Minister Miyazawa Kiichi. "It is necessary to have Japanese shareholders and create stabilizing forces that are strong enough to compete effectively with foreign capital in order to prevent the management's being taken over."[82]

Within the expanding *keiretsu* system, antimonopoly policy reconstituted the relation between big and small business. This tension had international policy implications. Since small business sectors dominated more than half of Japan's export industries, the international financial and trade liberalization instituted during the 1960s accentuated those enterprises' market vulnerability once a more chaotic business cycle and declining growth took hold.[83] Accordingly, the nation's protective policy toward big and small business aggravated Japan's trade relations. In 1973,

[81] Hadley, *Antitrust in Japan*, 424; Edwards, "Japan," *Trade Regulations Overseas*, 695, 696; Gao, *Japan's Economic Dilemma*, 109–10.

[82] Gao, *Japan's Economic Dilemma*, 92–7, quoted at 94, 96.

[83] Tanaka, "Comments on Selected Japanese Laws," *Patent, Trademark, and Copyright Journal of Research and Education*, 419, declares that by 1958, "52.7 percent of total product output of Japan," was "accounted for" by medium and small enterprises employing 300 or fewer persons.

Professor Matsushita articulated the policy dilemma: It was "not always safe for Japanese export industries to utilize export cartels to avoid conflicts with the manufacturers of importing countries" because "it is likely that the importing countries will have to resort to some measures to control imports from Japan and to protect domestic industries." As a result, there was "a policy conflict inside the importing countries. On the one hand, domestic industries demand that imports from Japan be restricted. On the other hand, from the stand point of combating inflation and protecting consumers, imports from Japan may be desirable." He concluded that either a "government agreement or at least some kind of communication channel" to "deepen mutual understanding" might be "helpful." Indeed, Japan supported an international antitrust regime like the ITO as a way to counter U.S. extraterritorial antitrust jurisdiction.[84]

Matsushita's commentary reflected a wider Japanese policy discourse urging stronger antimonopoly enforcement. In 1973, the FTC, several government ministries, and private groups sponsored in Tokyo an international conference on the global economy and competition. Antitrust authorities from Japan, the United States, European nations, and the OECD explored global competition issues, including those which impinged on Japan's protectionist market. The proceedings, which former FTC Commissioner Ariga edited, focused on the growing influence international trade and financial liberalization had on the operation of multinational corporations – including technology transfers and the administration of antidumping policies – within increasingly oligopolistic national markets. Ariga frankly expressed the hope that the "conference might serve as an impetus to those persons, particularly those Japanese persons, responsible for the control of restraints on competition in the fields of enterprises, oligopolies, use of technology, and consumer protection." She recognized that "Several countries have strengthened their [antitrust] laws" at the very time Japan's controversial new FTC chairman, Takahashi Toshihide, "stated that the present" Antimonopoly Act was "too weak to maintain competitive market order in Japan and revision to strengthen the law is necessary."[85]

The timing of the conference was propitious regarding Chairman Takahashi's ambitious agenda for reconstituting antimonopoly policy. Previously a senior Ministry of Finance official, Takahashi was appointed FTC Chairman in October, 1972 by his former MOF associate, Prime

---

[84] M. Matsushita, "The Japanese Antimonopoly Act and International Transactions," in Ariga, ed., *International Conference on International Economy*, 261–71, quote at 270. Joel Davidow, "The Seeking of a World Competition Code: Quixotic Quest?" in Oscar Schachter and Robert Hellawell, eds., *Competition in International Business Law and Policy on Restrictive Practices* (New York, 1981), 367–8.

[85] Ariga, "Report of the Conference," in Ariga, ed., *International Conference on International Economy*, 15, 16.

Minister Tanaka Kakuei, who the same year had launched the LDP's ambitious Plan to Remodel the Japanese Archipelago. Although Tanaka represented the pro-big business LDP mainstream which clearly opposed Takahashi's activism, it resonated with LDP faction leader Miki Takeo's advocacy of "social justice (shakaiteki-kosei)" to promote the welfare of ordinary Japanese. Even LDP Dietman Miyazawa Kiichi demanded "social justice."[86] On September 13, 1973, Takahashi disclosed a proposal to strengthen the Antimonopoly Law's enforcement authority, which immediately became "a highly controversial business and political issue." At a press conference in October, he received more attention, proposing to strengthen by amendment the Law. The economy was steadily deteriorating; during 1974–75 it registered the first negative growth rate of the postwar era. The LDP's Diet majority soon reached a postwar low, sparking grassroots, civil society, consumer, and environmentalist activism. During the same period, diplomatic problems and scandal led to Tanaka's resignation and Miki's election as prime minister. Miki's support for strengthening the Antimonopoly Law gave Takahashi's proposal new impetus.[87]

As Japan's political and economic conflict intensified, Takahashi articulated his activist enforcement program. He noted public anger over rising prices reflecting the "dilemma" of worldwide spiraling inflation combined with the "internationally strong but domestically weak yen." The price increases accompanied growing concern about "narrow roads and serious traffic jams," as well as the doubling of imports and "gradually diminishing" export surplus. From the standpoint of "competition policy," he asked foreign governments to "tolerate our export cartels as an inevitable and temporary policy," while he promised a "strict policy to eliminate" unauthorized international cartels. During the "high growth" era, Japan's "antitrust policies were obliged to take a few steps backwards," Takahashi admitted. Now, however, the nation experienced major yen "revaluation, while industry has moved toward oligopoly," which in turn exposed connections between oligopoly and "grave problems of environmental pollution which directly affect national life." The resulting "market inflexibility" roused the Japanese "people's anti-business feelings," which if they grew "stronger" could "retard seriously future development of the industry."[88]

[86] Beeman, *Public Policy and Competition*, 40–96, quotes at 41; Markham, "The Japan Fair Trade Commission and Antitrust Enforcement," 60–74.

[87] Ariga, "Report of the Conference," in Ariga, ed., *International Conference on International Economy*, 16; Stockwin, *Japan: Divided Politics*, 77–9; Hirabayashi to Freyer, "Comments," August 29, 2004.

[88] T. Takahashi, "Opening Speech," in Ariga, ed., *International Conference on International Economy*, 22.

Takahashi echoed earlier and contemporary Japanese antitrust policy discourse. In Japan as elsewhere, Takahashi declared, the "social anxiety which threatens human existence" promoted diverse public demands to "strengthen" antimonopoly policy. Like civic groups in other nations, Japanese consumer organizations advocated antitrust action to remedy not only unfair business practices but also rising prices generally. Takahashi stated that the FTC would address these consumer group demands primarily through investigation to expose abuse under the Act Against Unjustifiable Premiums and Misleading Representations, which the commission would in turn remedy by "recommending that each industry establish its own fair competition rules." The price-rise issue was symptomatic, moreover, of a problem "peculiar" to Japanese *keiretsu*, the "dominant position of 'general trading firms' both in trade and distribution." Possessing "sufficient funds from banks and utilizing their advantageous position, they have expanded into many fields and now have enormous influence over the distribution and production system."[89]

Takahashi's proposals had significant political ramifications. Small business groups clearly supported provisions aimed at big business concentration, but were concerned about eroding their hard-won protectionist status. Consumer interests perceived the opportunity to improve the civil damage system by overcoming the obstacles to private actions like that which had failed in 1961. Big business, by contrast, had the most reason to resist change.[90] The facility to pursue ever "more ingenious" methods raised procedural questions concerning the use of "circumstantial evidence" making prosecutions difficult, Takahashi stated. One remedy for the "peculiar" Japanese enforcement problems could be, he suggested, the revival of the corporate divestiture power – which was intended as a remedy for oligopoly rather than cartels – in the original Antimonopoly Law prior to the Amendment of 1953; regarding more general evidence issues he favored implementing "special enforcement measures, considering the character of economic crimes." These proposals exposed antimonopoly policy and the FTC to the sort of wide-ranging political conflict the revision struggle of 1958 epitomized. Takahashi mentioned the need to rely on "assistance from specialists," an oblique reference to Japanese bureaucrats' use of "study groups" to promote support for policy proposals. Seeking legitimacy from abroad he declared, "We place our hope on the future activities of the OECD" to facilitate competition policies based on "international cooperation."[91]

[89] Ibid., and compare texts cited in note 67 above.
[90] Beeman, *Public Policy and Competition*, 77–83; Markham, "The Japan Fair Trade Commission and Antitrust Enforcement," 50–115.
[91] Takahashi, "Opening Speech," in Ariga, ed., *International Conference on International Economy*, 23.

Takahashi's program and Miki's support of it as prime minister engendered ongoing public attention and conflict. During the mid-1970s, the FTC issued sixty-seven decisions against cartel practices: "a record number." Moreover, meeting Japanese legal procedure's high standard of evidence the FTC initiated what was essentially the "first criminal accusation" under the Antimonopoly Law, providing the Public Prosecutor's Office with the "names of 12 oil wholesalers and five of their directors accused of price-fixing, and the Japanese Petroleum Federation and its four representatives for production quantity restrictions."[92] The FTC case prompted three consumer groups to bring a rare private action. The shadow of the bureaucrats' administrative guidance complicated these cases, delaying the court's decision until the early 1980s. Within this flow of events, the FTC, drawing upon German precedent for what became the Japanese surcharge system, drafted an amendment embodying Takahashi's proposals to fortify the commission's enforcement capabilities.[93]

The Antimonopoly Law's friends and foes seized the opportunity the proposed amendment offered to press their own demands. Consumer groups argued that the amendment should include provisions strengthening damage claims like those currently being litigated in the petroleum cartel private action; small enterprises favored a system imposing higher penalties on big business but wanted to be exempt from the stockholder and divestiture provisions. Economists and law scholars constituted study groups which generally favored fortifying the FTC's enforcement capabilities. Opposition parties such as the Japan Socialist Party supported effective reporting and transparency provisions. Big business, the dominant LDP factions, and bureaucrats such as MITI attempted to emasculate the measure and undermine the FTC.[94]

Takahashi's public statements proved to be prophetic regarding mounting social welfare tensions throughout Japan, especially once the high growth era dissolved. The "Lockheed scandal" of 1976, in which the U.S. company bribed "unnamed" Japanese politicians, further weakened the LDP's Diet control. Although Miki remained personally untainted, he resigned, paving the way for the LDP's narrow election of Fukuda Takeo. Miki and Fukuda supported the FTC's amendment proposals strengthening the surcharge system and imposing corporate divestitures and stockholding

[92] Iyori and Uesugi, *Antimonopoly Laws of Japan*, 51.
[93] Ibid., 49–61; Beeman, *Public Policy and Competition*, 69–96; Markham, "The Japan Fair Trade Commission and Antitrust Enforcement," 65–74; Gao, *Japan's Economic Dilemma*, 216–20, 230–5; Haley, *Antitrust in Germany and Japan*, 59–60; and Hirabayashi to Freyer, "Comments," August 29, 2004.
[94] Iyori and Uesugi; *Antimonopoly Laws of Japan*, 49–61; Beeman, *Public Policy and Competition*, 69–96; Markham, "The Japan Fair Trade Commission and Antitrust Enforcement," 65–74; Gao, *Japan's Economic Dilemma*, 216–20, 230–5; Hirabayashi to Freyer, "Comments," August 29, 2004.

restrictions. After extensive debate, the third revision of the amendment finally became law in June, 1977. Despite compromises among the lawyer-economist study group's recommendations and those of the opposition parties, the FTC achieved its basic proposals; in addition, small business received protection but neither consumers nor big business, MITI, or the dominant LDP factions gained their primary demands.[95] Takahashi did not witness the outcome of his activist program. In 1976 because of failing health, he resigned and soon died.[96]

Takahashi's departure left an institutional vacuum readily filled by the long dominant triangle of the LDP, big business, and the bureaucracy. During the early 1980s, in the petroleum cartel cases, the courts upheld the FTC. The petroleum cartel private suits resulted in two consumer groups' agreeing to a modest settlement, while the court decided against a third group holding that the evidence did not sustain their damage claim. In this last litigation the consumers nonetheless won a partial victory when the lower court upheld a favorable theory of damages that consumer lawyers subsequently employed in future cases. Meanwhile, throughout the 1980s the FTC applied the authority the amendment of 1977 conferred to pursue administrative compliance rather than the more activist enforcement the petroleum cartel cases epitomized. Professor Hirabayashi Hidekatsu, a former member of the FTC, later assessed the Amendment's impact: it "turned out to be ineffective, except [the] surcharge system, because the amendment became too much a political issue."[97]

As a result of the SII and the collapse of the "bubble economy" Japan's Antimonopoly Law received fresh support. Since the early 1980s, the LDP's leadership repeatedly undercut deregulation proposals identified with the *Rincho* administrative reform movement.[98] But during the 1990s, the LDP's continuing dependence on coalitions with smaller parties to retain a tenuous hold on power facilitated the party's embrace of deregulation and antitrust. Historically, to be sure, Japanese deregulation rhetoric was without substance, but the rhetoric of the 1990s was different in that it promoted an active role for antitrust. Thus, although Keidanren initially opposed SII, by the mid-1990s it publicized a deregulation program that

---

[95] Iyori and Uesugi, *The Antimonopoly Laws of Japan*, 50–3, Beeman, *Public Policy and Economic Competition in Japan*, 40–96; Stockwin, *Japan: Divided Politics*, 80–7, quoted phrases at 80; Haley, *Antitrust in Germany and Japan*, 148–9.

[96] See note 113 below; for Takahashi's resignation, see Beeman, *Public Policy and Economic Competition in Japan*, 87.

[97] Iyori and Uesugi, *The Antimonopoly Laws of Japan*, 56–61. On the outcome in the private action, see Murayama Makoto, "Private Enforcement of Antitrust Law in Japan," in Jones and Matsushita, eds., *Competition Policy in the Global Trading System*, 246–7 [the favorable private action decision in Akita branch Sendai High Court (March, 26, 1985, "Ne" No. 65, 1985), reversed, Supreme Court (December 14, 1988, "o No. 933 and No. 1162). Hirabayashi to Freyer, "Comments," August 29, 2004.

[98] Carlile, "The Politics of Japanese Regulatory Reform," 23–52.

envisioned a capitalist market order. Japan's globally competitive corporate sectors would especially benefit. MITI's official pronouncements also urged the FTC's vigorous enforcement of competition law. Admittedly, observers like the *Oriental Economist* concluded that Japan's reform efforts were "going nowhere." Still, groups which were close to, or members of, a principal LDP faction publicly supported the essentials of Keidanren's deregulation plan, including effective enforcement by a strengthened FTC. Ultimately, these changes in policy were consistent with the *Oriental Economist's* view that global "economic trends" working within Japan "will force change. But Japan's political leaders are unlikely to move until they have no other choice."[99]

Keidanren's "Deregulation Promotion Plan" suggested changing public perceptions regarding business–government relations. The plan acknowledged Keidanren's central role as facilitator concerning policy making and the need to "seek a consensus among related industries on exactly which areas of deregulation needed to be addressed." The plan called upon bureaucrats to impose a maximum 5-year limit upon the operation of "new rules or regulations," urged greater public participation in the formulation of regulatory measures in the Diet under clear due-process standards, and prescribed "zero-based" principles according to which "all regulations must be abolished and recreated based on the needs of current economic conditions." These principles left much discretion to bureaucrats to maintain the *status quo*; Keidanren proposed to limit the bureaucrats' options, however, by setting out specific "Requirements for Deregulation."[100]

The plan set out explicit prescriptions as to what deregulation meant for particular business sectors. Reflecting broad-based domestic and international concerns regarding the price-gap problem – the higher prices for the same goods charged in Japan as compared to Western nations – the Plan asserted that "[e]limination of all price regulations is a fundamental and essential reform." Also targeted for initial abolition were "non-supply-and-demand related entry" restrictions and import regulations not directly subject to international agreement. In the financial services and insurance industries only regulations involving accreditation procedures were to be maintained. The plan had detailed lists of particular business sectors requiring deregulation, including agriculture, trade, and basic materials. In many cases, the Keidanren Plan recognized that a limited degree of bureaucratic authority would continue to apply; still, the underlying purpose of holding regulatory intervention to a minimum was clear.[101]

[99] See Freyer, "Regulatory Distinctiveness," 5–53. These points are developed in this and the following section; see also Peter Ennis "Impasse Inc. Japan's Economy, Reform Efforts Going Nowhere," 65(10) *The Oriental Economist* (December 1997), quotes at 1, 2.

[100] "Deregulation Promotion Plan," 148 *Keidanren Review* (February 1995), 4, 5.

[101] Ibid., 6.

Finally, Keidanren proposed rigorous enforcement of Japan's Anti-monopoly Law. Specifically, this requirement aimed to abolish the many cartel practices and resale price maintenance that existed based on various exemptions and cartels established under the Antimonopoly Law. More broadly, the plan recognized that as deregulation moved forward competition would cause social friction by, for example, weakening the group-oriented relational networks which supported less efficient, small enterprises, increasing unemployment. These negative consequences might undermine the deregulation movement by fostering more rather than less popular support for a system of bureaucratic protection. Effective and fair implementation of the antimonopoly policy could, by contrast, facilitate orderly transition from protectionism to competition. Thus, Keidanren's plan stated that "[i]n order to ensure that the positive effects of deregulation are experienced throughout society (*and that the conflicts it causes are eased*), the government must promote free and fair competition through the aggressive application of the Anti-Monopoly Law, and through adoption of a progressive competition policy."[102]

Keidanren's deregulation reforms potentially benefited large firms competing in a global market the most. "Simply put," Keidanren officials stated privately, the "manufacturing sector competing in the world market must play the game at whatever the yen rate is; they have to export." At the same time, Japanese government policies protected the electrical, gas, and financial intermediary industries from international competition. These protected industries produced as much as 60 percent of Japan's GNP, the officials estimated, whereas the globally competitive manufacturing sector produced 40 percent. Even so, global competition forced the generally larger, multinational corporate sectors such as automobile manufactures to operate more efficiently. As a result, the efficient competitive international business sectors were subsidizing the less efficient, protected ones. Confirming this view, the *Oriental Economist* observed that anticompetitive "[r]egulations raise domestic prices in Japan, which serve as a subsidy to low-productivity, protected sectors of the economy." By ending protection, deregulation would level the playing field within Japan for Japanese as well as foreign firms.[103] Similarly, "liberalization for competition is necessary to adjust the price differences between the Japanese market and the international market," Nakauchi Isao, the leader of the distribution sector, asserted. "We Japanese should not look at the other economies of the world such as the US and Asian countries only from our side. Instead,

---

[102] Ibid., quoted phrase, italics added.
[103] Quoted statements and paragraph substance, author's interview, Keidanren officials, October 6, 1995; see also Richard Katz, "Pass on By: East Asia Set to Recover Faster than Japan," 65(10) *The Oriental Economist* (December 1997), quote at 9.

we should look at Japan from the outside, Japan as a member of the world economy."[104]

Among Keidanren's business constituents a deregulation strategy emphasizing rigorous enforcement of antimonopoly policy was nonetheless controversial. Keidanren officials who advocated the Deregulation Plan explained that until the 1990s Keidanren's official position resisted competition in favor of the more protectionist orientation of MITI's industrial policy. Not only business but Japanese society as a whole was unsupportive of antimonopoly policy and the FTC. As the changing economy culminated in the prolonged recession of the 1990s, however, market data collected by Keidanren revealed widespread consumer dissatisfaction with pervasive high costs identified with the price gap, officially sanctioned cartels, and related problems, which in turn were seen as the outcome of protectionism. At the same time, many Japanese business sectors, nonetheless, benefited from the protectionist policy. Thus, the old system was, said Keidanren officials privately, to "some players very comfortable but not to others." Most importantly, many larger, multinational firms competing in the global economy perceived that their profitability was constrained by, in effect, subsidizing those less efficient sectors enjoying protection. Reflecting the consumer demands and market efficiencies which were consistent with the multinational corporate firms' competitive environment, Keidanren publicly disassociated itself from the old order, and despite internal criticism, switched to advocating a deregulation program emphasizing the FTC's vigorous enforcement of antimonopoly policy.[105]

In 1994, MITI indicated further support for Keidanren's general position. Guided by the industrial policy of the past, Japan's economy had experienced "spectacular performance." But by the 1990s, "many Japanese individuals question the claim that this country is affluent." This "paradox of prosperity" was the outcome of a "Corporate Society in which the producer's perspective – from policy making to company attitude – has prevailed over that of the consumer, thus affecting the quality of life for each individual." "Irritation" and "frustration" grew on the "part of the Japanese people . . . [who] thought that the effort they have made to ensure Japan's economic growth has not been fully rewarded." Public dissatisfaction reflected concerns about "poor housing; . . . long working hours spent in overcrowded cities; the lack of sufficient opportunities for women and elderly in terms of self-fulfillment; consumers who do not benefit from the system."[106]

[104] Nakauchi, Isao, "Top Japanese Distributor," 5 *Journal of Japanese Trade and Industry* (1995), 34.

[105] Quoted phrase and paragraph generally, author's interview, Keidanren officials, October 6, 1995; "Building a Dynamic and Creative Society, May 1995," and "A Message from the Chairman, September 1995," *Keidanren* (Tokyo, 1995).

[106] *Japan: A Perspective on Industrial Policy* (October 1994) (the source is listed as "ACORN, an independent research/consulting firm in Tokyo, on commission by the Japan Economic

To meet this challenge MITI was "now shifting" its industrial policy. The change reflected a division between the ministry's Industrial and Policy bureaus: The Industrial Bureaus were "nostalgic" for the old protectionist regime, whereas the Policy Bureau favored competition-based deregulation. The new "emphasis" was upon "deregulation, the reform of existing systems and the promotion of competition." Like Keidanren's plan, the 1994 MITI-statement conceded that the government's "regulations and business practices" which had "served as the linchpin of Japan's socio-economic structure" also "have tended to serve as barriers to imports and smooth market entry. This has resulted in the undermined competitiveness of Japanese industries as well as price disparities. These problems hamper the healthy growth of the economy and pose a serious problem for the consumer." It was therefore necessary to examine "across the board" business conduct and the bureaucracy's regulations and to "encourage the business community to act on its own initiative."[107]

The policy reorientation within MITI reflected tensions buffeting Japan's bureaucracy. The favorable views toward transnational cooperative antitrust measures and multilateral resolution of competition issues indicated the influence of procompetition bureaucrats inside MITI's Policy Bureau.[108] They nonetheless welcomed outside pressure. As Hitotsubashi University economist Nakatani Iwao observed, during the auto dispute of the mid-1990s "bureaucrats at MITI were actually quite pleased at the prospect of the WTO condemning Japan's auto market – because it is pressure from abroad that makes market-opening happen."[109] Similarly, the *Oriental Economist* concluded that while some "bureaucrats oppose reform, of course," Japan's "much-criticized bureaucracy . . . is not the huge obstacle to reform that it is often accused of being." Instead, the "mood in the bureaucracy" showed "drift and demoralization" rather than "spunky arrogance." Thus the "cause of today's sense of impasse in Japan" was not the bureaucrats; it was the " '*zoku-giin*' – special interest – politics of the LDP, and the broader ambivalence about reform."[110]

Keidanren's and MITI's support for deregulation and antitrust coincided with a changing market for lawyers' services. As long as business interests generally turned for guidance first to bureaucrats, they had little reason to seek advice from the fully licensed *bengoshi* or the numerous quasi-lawyers

Foundation, a non-profit organization, based primarily on materials provided by MITI and a series of interviews with MITI and other government officials)," 22.
[107] Ibid. For the division between the two MITI bureaus, see author's interviews with senior MITI (whence comes the "nostalgia" quote) and FTC officials.
[108] Ibid.
[109] Iwao Nakatani, quoted in "How to Get Out of the Rut," 63(10) *Tokyo Business* (October 1995), 25.
[110] Peter Ennis, "Impasse Inc.," 64(10) *The Oriental Economist* (December 1997), quote at 2.

which constituted Japan's legal practitioners. By the late 1980s, however, many of Japan's largest corporations began consulting *bengoshi* in Japan's handful of leading commercial law firms about industrial policy and the Antimonopoly Law. The most noteworthy change was that corporations asked for legal advice *before* they approached the bureaucrats. This trend indicated that large multinational corporations wanted greater independence from industrial policy in order to operate efficiently in the competitive global market. At the same time the *bengoshi* began "appearing" as representatives of big corporations during informal negotiations which resulted in administrative guidance. In addition, *bengoshi* represented big Japanese companies and consumers alike in antitrust suits. A greater reliance upon lawyerly understanding impinged upon the bureaucrats' authority and was consistent with the gradual expansion of a private market that deregulation symbolized.[111]

Indirectly, the growing market for legal services reinforced the move toward antimonopoly among consumers. From the occupation on, many organizations claiming to represent "consumers" consisted of small and medium-sized businesses or agricultural cooperatives using the Antimonopoly Law to counteract the cartel power of big business. The law's provisions regulating premium offers and the big firms' abuse of their dominant position protected these smaller enterprises. Throughout the period, however, groups identified with housewives (Shufuren), "local women" (Chifuren), and others formed into the Forum for National Consumer Associations (Shodanren) were more truly representative of consumers in Japan's urban mass society. These consumers became most concerned about the price gap and related problems. The Japan Federation of Bar Associations responded to this expanded consumer culture with a committee on consumer law. During the 1990s, it pressed for increased consumer protection through deregulation, improvements in the Antimonopoly Law, and more stringent enforcement by the FTC, as well as attempting to exert further pressure by appealing to U.S. experts for assistance. Yamaguchi Hiroshi, an active member of the committee, brought the first major private action involving competition issues in more than a decade, representing sixty-one citizens of Saitama prefecture. The suit charged that sixty-three construction firms and three former prefectural-government officials colluded to bid for public works projects at exorbitant prices, wasting the taxpayers' money. Although the case

---

[111] Interviews with five Japanese *bengoshi*, three of whom are members of Japan's leading commercial law firms and two who are consumer lawyers; four in Tokyo (one in Osaka): September 11, 1995; September 14, 1995; June 28, 1996; July 2, 1996; July 16, 1996; July 18, 1996; July 24, 1996. During the 1990's there were between fifteen and twenty Japanese *bengoshi* who practiced in the antitrust field. The general picture is confirmed by interviews with FTC and MITI officials.

moved slowly through the court system, its symbolic significance was noteworthy.[112]

In the Osaka-Kyoto area Murayama Makoto and a group of some thirty lawyers cooperated to bring ten antitrust suits by 1997. The Saitama case raised various legal challenges under the Antimonopoly Law and other laws as well. The multiplicity of procedural and substantive issues undoubtedly contributed to the gradual progress of the case. The Murayama group also represented consumers. With the start of SII in 1989, the group formulated a program based on Antimonopoly Law provisions by which the FTC, upon receiving a private complaint, has a discretionary power to initiate an investigation. By the millennium judges received, under an amendment of the Civil Code, discretionary power to decide the amount of damages. In 1996, Murayama won such a private action. His client was a news dealer who had been excluded from the Kansai Airport by an anticompetitive arrangement between several major newspapers and distributors.[113]

The essentials of Keidanren's Deregulation Plan received support from The Anti-Trust Law Study Council headed by Saito Eizaburo. Suggesting further the expanding market for antitrust legal services among *bengoshi* during the 1990s, growing numbers of law professors and public officials, who as politicians or bureaucrats had been involved with the Anti-monopoly Law and the FTC, established study groups which, usually as a money-making enterprise, disseminated antitrust information among lawyers. A lesser known group, established March 7, 1992, was chaired by Saito, an LDP elected official and sometime government minister. Though Saito's group was of marginal significance, it indicated that as a result of political expediency LDP leaders were voicing support for, rather than opposition to, the Antimonopoly Law and the FTC. Throughout much of the postwar era Saito had been involved in antitrust problems, especially those bearing on bid rigging in the construction industry. For 18 years, he worked at the cabinet level as a member of the Diet subcommittee

[112] Hirata, Keiko, *Civil Society in Japan the Growing Role of NGOs in Tokyo's Aid and Development Policy* (Palgrave Macmillan, NY, 2002). Interviews, Yamaguchi Hiroshi September 26, 1995, Tokyo Kydo Law Offices and Murayama, Makota Osaka Law Offices, July 16, 1996. See also "Proposed Antitrust Law, Japan Federation of Bar Associations, March 28, 1990;" "Proposed Antitrust Law Amendment Concerning Civil Damage Claims based Upon Antitrust Law Violations, June 15, 1990"; Yamaguchi Hiroshi to S. Linn Williams, deputy USTR, May 13, 1991; "Press Release", July 1, 1993, Eigi Iwaki, Representative Plaintiff, Group of Saitama Residents seeking to unveil the Dango Suspicion of 'Saitama Doyokai.' " Further, see Kumiko Makihara, "Cleaning up the Construction Site. Can the Government Change a Tradition of Bid Rigging?" *Time* (October 4, 1993). For all these sources, I am indebted to Mr. Yamaguchi. See also Hirabayashi Hidekatsu to Freyer, "Comments," August 29, 2004.
[113] Interview, Murayama, Osaka, July 16, 1996; *FTC/Japan Views*, no. 28, June 1997, 20. See also Ramseyer, "Costs of Consensual Myth," *Yale Law Journal* (1985), 604–45, and Hirabayashi Hidekatsu to Freyer, "Comments," August 29, 2004.

responsible for antimonopoly policy and, as a member of the LDP's Nakasone faction, had led attempts to weaken the Antimonopoly Law.[114]

Similarly, Hashimoto Ryutaro, a member of the LDP's Tanaka faction, was during the mid-1990s, successively, MITI's minister and LDP president, and in 1996, Japan's prime minister. Saito and Hashimoto – whose political constituents represented the cosmetics industry and the medical industry – had often resisted meaningful deregulation reform and effective antitrust enforcement. The two men's' advocacy of a strengthened antimonopoly policy and FTC suggested that the LDP leadership's antitrust policy discourse was changing. Thus, Saito's Study Council, though ostensibly a "private" body rather than a government entity, defended the Antimonopoly Law: "In line with the recent sweeping changes in the economic situation both in and outside Japan," including "economic globalization" the Antimonopoly Law was "perhaps equivalent in importance to the Constitution . . . it is designed to improve the nation's standard of living by serving general consumers' interests and by promoting democratic and free competition." Saito nonetheless remained vague as to what precisely his reversal of position meant.[115]

During the spring of 1995, Japan's coalition party cabinet adopted a Deregulation Action Program. According to the *Tokyo Financial Review* the government's Deregulation Action Program was not inconsistent with Keidanren's plan. In addition to targeted deregulation measures in eleven areas, the *Review* reported, "The Program makes it clear that an active approach should be taken toward competition policy, including the stringent and appropriate application of the Anti-Monopoly Law." Reflecting Japanese consumer and international foreign interests regarding the price gap and cartels, the program "calls for a review and clarification of the system that allows special [i.e., exemption] cartels to operate outside the Anti-Monopoly Law, the resale price maintenance system, restrictions on holding companies and regulations concerning promotional gifts." The last two items had been suggested in passing but not emphasized in the Keidanren Plan; Saito's Antitrust Council also supported them. Coincidently, the period in which the government prepared the program corresponded with Keidanren's preparation and publication of its own deregulation plan.

[114] Interviews with *bengoshi*, noted above, confirmed the emergence of antitrust study groups, one of which the author visited. For Mr. Saito's quote, see "Prospectus of the Anti-Trust Law Study Council," March 7, 1992. For this source and other information, I am indebted to Mr. Eizaburo Saito, interview, September 26, 1995.
[115] Ibid. Press reference to the Council as a "private-sector study group" was "Anti-Monopoly Law Study Group Proposes Upgrading Fair Trade Commission to 'Fair Trade Agency' to Strengthen Organization," in Mainichi, Daily Summary of Japanese Press, August 4, 1995. Loosely, the "private-sector" terminology is correct; nevertheless, Saito himself, *bengoshi*, and other specialists recognized the continuing influence of the LDP point of view. Also Hirabayashi to Freyer, "Comments," August 29, 2004.

Over the same months, Keidanren officials exchanged views in periodic meetings with representatives of the bureaucracy including MITI and the FTC.[116]

Reaction to the cabinet's action program ranged from cautiously optimistic to highly skeptical. Suggesting the view of those within Keidanren who supported their organization's plan, the *Tokyo Financial Review* observed that "Potentially, the Action Program could prove to be quite effective, though this will depend on the government's stance toward its implementation." Even so, the *Review* set out extensive evidence analyzing how the program's support of competition could reduce the price gap and cartel practices, thereby benefiting Japanese consumers and international market interests. Yet, it noted the failure to address such "significant measures" as "abolition of the Large-scale Retail Store Law and the price maintenance scheme for agricultural goods." A freelance writer in *Japan Update* dismissed the program as ineffective, "like fanning the sun with a peacock's feather." The fundamental problem was "administrative inertia" whereby bureaucrats had no incentive to support deregulation because ultimately it threatened not only their jobs but the traditional guarantee of "promotion" to a retirement position (*amakudari*). The critic suggested "a system in which officials can be promoted for contributing to administrative reform and deregulation." That such an action was unlikely, however, indicated a basic "illness" of Japanese society.[117]

Tokyo Business presented a similarly skeptical view. Pro-deregulation reform "undergrounds" existed among Diet politicians and even within MITI, the article conceded. The "forces of change," however, confronted an "immovable object" in the Diet and the bureaucracy. Too many elected politicians, often former bureaucrats themselves, maintained close ties with the ministries and the industries which those ministries protected. At the same time bureaucratic rivalry and fragmentation reenforced inertia. The problem was that the powerful Ministry of Finance and other protection-oriented ministries were "not particularly thrilled about the idea of having MITI lead the charge on reforming the economy." Moreover, fundamentally "this honing of industry would hurt many vested interests, squeeze inefficient domestic business, and even bankrupt some, which is a political non-starter these days." The initiative for change most likely rested, then, with deregulation-reform supporters in the Diet; yet the forces of conservatism were so strong throughout Japanese society that such a "transformation" seemed "almost impossible."[118]

---

[116] Nishimura, "Deregulation and Structural Problems," 20(8) *Tokyo Financial Review* (August 1995), 3. For Mr. Saito's support, see note 114 above; see also note 119 below.

[117] Ibid.; Nakazawa, Takao, "Administrative Inertia, Bureaucracy Avoids Deregulation," *Japan Update* (June 1995), 11.

[118] Mike Millard, "The Forces of Change Meet the Immovable Object," 63(10) *Tokyo Business* (October 1995), 10–13, quoted phrases at 11.

Nevertheless, opponents and supporters of change agreed that foreign pressure favoring antimonopoly policy challenged the status quo. In private interviews, a Keidanren official admitted that it used "outside pressure" to achieve its deregulation goals. Indeed, without "outside pressure Keidanren would not have achieved what deregulation they had." This "use" of "outside pressure to [bring about] change inside is strange," the official said, and it is "sad that Japan cannot solve problems itself."[119] A high official in the Ministry of Finance resisted reform identified with the FTC's vigorous enforcement of the Antimonopoly Law. Although formal cartels and the price gap problem required positive action consistent with moderate deregulation, a strong implementation of the Antimonopoly Law and an active FTC threatened collectivist values which were fundamental to Japanese society. The only way the more aggressive approach to deregulation policy would prevail, was through the intervention of foreign pressure.[120] Meanwhile, consumer lawyers Yamaguchi and Murayama privately solicited support from foreigners. Finally, news stories reported that, as a "private sector" organization, Saito's Anti-Monopoly Study Group announced during July 1995 support for a plan to strengthen the FTC so that it might enforce a number of deregulation proposals which broadly paralleled those included in the cabinet's action program (and Keidanren's plan).[121]

IV. STRENGTHENING JAPANESE ANTITRUST'S ENFORCEMENT CAPABILITIES AND THE AMBIGUITIES OF FOREIGN PRESSURE

As long as antimonopoly policy was subordinate to industrial policy, the FTC's authority within the bureaucracy and toward big business was weak. During the 1980s, a greater awareness of antitrust issues inherent in Japan–U.S. trade disputes emerged – especially those concerning the FTC's enforcement capabilities – culminating in the SII. "Like the Anti-Monopoly Law, which had been ignored as a result of the priority given to industrial policies," remarked FTC official Uesugi Akinori in 1995, the FTC had been "regarded as a minor organ." Following the LDP's historic electoral defeat in 1993, a succession of LDP-dominated coalition governments formally endorsed deregulation principles, including restriction and ultimate elimination of the cartel exemption system. "Finally the cartel loses its status as a tool for industrial policy," said Uesugi. More broadly, the outcome was that as "deregulation measures proceed" the "business sectors covered by" the Antimonopoly Law increased; at the same time the FTC's "jurisdiction

---

[119] Quoted statements and rest of text, author's interview, Keidanren officials, October 6, 1995.
[120] Interview, MOF senior official.   [121] Notes 111–13, 115.

is enlarged automatically and the room for competition among business expands."[122] As a result, the LDP-led coalition governments and MITI supported fortifying the FTC's enforcement regime. The bundle of anti-monopoly issues pertaining to the FTC's institutional strengthening over-lapped with, but were distinguishable from, disputes concerning government action and private conduct covered by Japan–U.S. bilateral agreements or the WTO multilateral order.

Economic disputes under the postwar liberal trade order could raise antimonopoly policy issues because of voluntary export restraints. FTC authorities defined these policies as "private or governmental voluntary acts to restrain exports to a particular region or a country to avoid trade friction." Moreover, when government–business negotiations resulting in export restraints established a mandatory export quota, "allocat[ing] a fixed export quantity among exporters," they could not be strictly "voluntary" but rather were "compelled by either the exporting country or the importing country." The importing nation could exercise this com-pulsory authority if the business failed to comply with the "voluntary" export restraint; such failure might "trigger protectionist measures," the avoidance of which could operate as "a sufficient sanction" to ensure that the "voluntary" action maintained practical force. Regarding anti-monopoly policy, voluntary export restraints were "indistinguishable from international cartels. When competitors petition the government, and the government negotiates" voluntary export restraints "on their behalf, in essence it is equivalent to an international cartel." In other instances, governments and business may agree to the restraint to establish "minimum export prices" in order to offset antidumping charges. In Japan, MITI generally possessed jurisdiction to enforce such anticompetitive outcomes through formal export cartels, licenses, and administrative guidance.[123]

From the 1960s to the 1990s, the political and economic context of Japanese–U.S. trade and antitrust policy changed. In the 1960s, firms such as Singer Sewing Machine Co. and American television manufacturers employed U.S. antitrust laws to challenge Japan's growing influence within the U.S. market. After protracted litigation, the U.S. Supreme Court ulti-mately decided these cases in favor of the Japanese companies. The com-parative legal consciousness taught in Japanese universities equipped some MITI bureaucrats, a few legal–economic experts, and FTC officials with a deeper understanding of antitrust law. In addition, as Japanese multi-national corporations increasingly penetrated the U.S. market during the

[122] Uesugi, Akinori, "New Directions in Japanese Antitrust Enforcement," in Barry E. Hawk, ed., *Annual Proceedings of the Fordham Corporate Law Institute International Antitrust Law & Policy 1994* (transnational juris publication, Irvington-on-Hudson, NY, 1995) quoted at 35, 36.
[123] Iyori and Uesugi, *The Antimonopoly Laws of Japan*, quotes at 371, 372.

1970s and 1980s, some Japanese chief executives in companies like Toyota became sensitive to antitrust's role. Initially, Japanese executives denied that antitrust policy was appropriate for their nation. As Japan's global competitiveness declined in the 1990s, however, executives from multinational corporations dominating Keidanren asserted that deregulation and antitrust were essential to reviving Japan's international economic power.[124]

Among officials and legal–economic experts the comparative competition consciousness nonetheless grew slowly. In the 1970s, even activist FTC Chairman Takahashi had asked foreign trade officials to accept Japan's temporary use of export restraints. In addition, Japanese business relied upon U.S. law firms to defend their conduct in antidumping disputes arising within the American market.[125] But over the course of U.S.–Japan trade disputes involving potash, electrical products, steel, automobiles, and semiconductors each nation's trade policy makers gradually recognized that avoiding antitrust risk could be part of larger bilateral settlements. The interdependency between trade and antitrust policy emerged during the automobile case. Under provisions of the Trade Act of 1974 the United Auto Workers of America petitioned U.S. trade officials in June 1980 seeking limits on Japanese car imports. Although the U.S. International Trade Commission decided that direct action was not appropriate, bilateral discussions followed, facilitating MITI's implementation of a "voluntary" export quota. Japanese automobile exporters made monthly reports to MITI under the Foreign Exchange and Foreign Trade Control Act of 1949. Employing administrative guidance, MITI informed exporters that it would enforce a quota by limiting the number of export licenses.[126]

The discourse among U.S.–Japanese officials in the automobile case suggests how trade conflicts gradually incorporated antitrust concerns. Concerning MITI's "unprecedented" construction of the export law to justify imposing the automobile quota through the licensing system, FTC authorities later declared, "it was clear that no one would raise serious objection to such action in Japan."[127] Japanese exporters, however, might assert that enforcing the quota through administrative guidance was invalid under U.S. antitrust law. To address such questions, a U.S. trade official observed, "Japanese Government officials consulted regularly with

---

[124] Compare: On comparative legal consciousness during World War II and the occupation, see Chapter 2, this volume; for statements contemporary with postwar era, see Katsuta Aritsunne, "The Functions of Japanese Hybrid Legal Culture: Western and Japanese Law," 4 *Journal of Japanese Trade & Industry* (July/August 1996), 8–11; see Chapter 2, Section IV; Chapter 1, Section II; and discussion below.

[125] See notes 91, 107, and 110 above; W. Tanaka, "Antidumping, Antitrust and the Consumer Interest in the United States," in Ariga, ed., *International Conference on International Economy*, 293–9.

[126] Iyori and Uesugi, *The Antimonopoly Laws of Japan*, 378–80.   [127] Ibid., 379.

representatives of the Antitrust Division . . . and the Office of the General Counsel, United States Trade Representative. These meetings could best be characterized as technical consultations concerning the subtleties of anti-trust law, and the vagaries of Japanese commercial statutes." In 1981, the U.S. Attorney General presented a letter stating "we believe that the Japanese automobile companies' compliance with export limitations directed by MITI would properly be viewed as having been compelled by the Japanese government, acting within its sovereign powers." Thus, the U.S. Justice Department's view was that the Japanese government's "implementation of such an export restraint," including MITI's "division among the companies . . . of the maximum exportable number of units, and compliance with the program by Japanese automobile companies, would not give rise to violations of [U.S.] antitrust laws."[128]

Throughout the 1980s, antitrust issues became increasingly significant in trade disputes. As the global competitiveness of the American economy declined, business and labor groups pressured the U.S. Government to limit liberal trade policies on a selective basis. The government vigorously implemented antidumping regulations against foreign "unfair practices" inside American territory, which the GATT broadly authorized. Although Japanese and other exporters condemned antidumping measures as con-trary to antitrust principles, American policy makers treated the system as politically sacrosanct. Concerning other trade issues, however, interests were less clearcut. Friction often resulted when individual American interests petitioned for reciprocal trade concessions maintained through the threat of unilateral action authorized under revisions of the Trade Act of 1974. Congress generally proved responsive to such political demands. The executive, by contrast, had to balance these pressures against wider political interests and international expectations. Mounting trade disputes rein-forced U.S. officials' support for strengthening Japan's antitrust regime through SII. Buffeted by the large trade deficit and political agitation regarding unfair barriers within Japan's home market, the Reagan Administration pursued the bilateral Market-Oriented Sector Selective negotiations. By the end of the decade, political demands to extend unilateral trade authority led Congress to enact the Omnibus Trade and Competi-tiveness Act and the SII. Congress sought pledges from the Japanese – the terms of which a Justice Department lawyer drafted – to address the weak enforcement of the Antimonopoly Law by increasing the FTC's budget, staff, and investigation authority, enhancing provisions for private actions, and improving institutional transparency of the enforcement process.[129]

---

[128] Ibid., quoted at 378, 379.
[129] Case, "An Overview of Fifteen Years of United States–Japanese Economic Relations," 16(1) *Arizona Journal of International and Comparative Law* (1999), 12–21; Schoppa,

During SII's implementation after 1989, the process of strengthening the FTC's enforcement structure acquired symbolic and practical importance. On periodic annual visits to Japan, a member of the Justice Department's Antitrust Division regularly supported the bureaucratic upgrade proposal. Foreign pressure converged with Keidanren's switch from opposing to advocating improved enforcement as part of Japan's deregulation movement; the ruling political party coalition's endorsement further aided the FTC's cause.[130] Indeed, Hashimoto Ryutaro observed that "Deregulation and the strengthening of the FTC are like the two wheels of a cart. They should be treated as a set."[131] In addition, the coalition government's Administrative Reform Project Work Team involved in the deregulation process considered a restructuring plan prepared by the FTC. "It is significant that Japanese and U.S. cabinet ministers confirmed the policy line of strengthening the FTC's mechanism," observed a senior FTC official.[132]

During auto trade talks pressures converged dramatically to favor the FTC. By summer 1995, the autotrade negotiations appeared on the verge of collapse. In the final hours before the end of the June deadline, however, U.S. Trade Representative, Mickey Kantor, and the top Japanese negotiator, MITI minister Hashimoto, reached an agreement which called for strengthening the FTC in regard to the Japanese automobile market. The American media virtually ignored the proposal as a component of the negotiations. But according to a Japanese press report, in the "last minute talks with the deadline for sanctions against Japan near at hand" Kantor proposed that "[i]n order to secure fair-market access and competition in the automobile area, it is necessary to strengthen FTC's functions." Hashimoto replied that the "Japanese government is willing to improve [the

Bargaining with Japan, 49–253. The article which informed the Justice Department lawyer's antitrust proposals incorporated into SII was J. Mark Ramseyer, "The Costs of the Consensual Myth: Antitrust Enforcement and Institutional Barriers to Litigation in Japan," 94 *Yale Law Journal* (January 1985), 604–45. Shogo Itoda, a senior FTC official and future commissioner, was the Justice Department official's counterpart during the SII negotiations; and see Itoda, "Competition Policy of Japan and Its Global Implementation," in Jones and Matsushita, eds., *Competition Policy in the Global Trading System*, 64.

[130] Ibid.; see Section III above; Yoshikazu Kawai, "Competition Policy and Industrial Policy in Japan," and Makoto Kurita "Recent Developments of Competition Policy in Japan and Their Implications for International Harmonization of Competition Laws," in Chia-Jui Cheng, Lawrence S. Liu, and Chih-kang Wang, eds., *International Harmonization of Competition Laws* (Martinus Nijhoff Publishers, Dordrecht, 1995), 47–57, 361–79; Haley, "Japan's Postwar Civil Service," in Kim et al., eds., *Japanese Civil Service*, 85–6.

[131] "Fair Trade Commission Taking Steps to Increase Power to Thoroughly Apply Anti-Monopoly Law; Crackdown and Policy-Planning Capability to be Broadly Strengthened," Sankei, Daily Summary of Japanese Press, August 26, 1995, 2.

[132] "Fair Trade Commission Aiming to Strengthen Functions; US Request Provides Favorable Tailwind; Tug of War Continued Over General Secretariat Concept, between Ruling Parties and Management and Coordination Agency, Issue Intertwined with Administrative Reform," Nihon Keizai, Daily Summary Japanese Press, August 29, 1995, 3–4.

FTC's] structure and increase the fixed number" of personnel.[133] Another Japanese press report stated that Hashimoto had telephoned from Geneva to obtain a "go-ahead sign" directly from Prime Minister Murayama Tomiichi.[134] An informed source within the FTC indicated further that Kantor actually received the FTC-strengthening idea from the Japanese side. Coincidentally, the coalition government's project work team on Deregulation and Administrative Reform, which included one of Hashimoto's MITI officials, had been considering issues involving improvement of the FTC's structure and power since at least March 1995. The MITI official had supported the FTC throughout the process.[135]

As a result of the Hashimoto-Kantor agreement the controversy over enforcement capabilities became more focused. On one level, groups aligned with LDP members of the government's ruling coalition seized the opportunity to push for ending the Antimonopoly Law's prohibition against holding companies, Article 9. An incorporation device which enabled firms to grow in size and scale through certain stock purchases, the holding company was permitted under the law of every major industrial nation except Japan's. When written in 1947, the law imposed this unique restriction in part because some *Japanese* draftsmen believed that it would prevent the revival of the *zaibatsu*, but it seemed unlikely that *zaibatsu* might return nearly fifty years after dissolution.[136] As a result, Keidanren, certain LDP leaders and their allies such as the Antimonopoly Study Group chaired by Saito, *bengoshi* who represented major corporations, and legal academics linked the FTC's organizational strengthening to the repeal of Article 9.[137] The chairman of the government's Administrative Reform Project Team agreed: "If FTC proposes strengthening its mechanism in a bid to ease the restriction on holding companies, I can understand, but it is hard to approve the idea, with the issue of holding companies left undecided."[138]

---

[133] Ibid.

[134] "Fair Trade Commission Taking Steps to Increase Power to Thoroughly Apply Anti-Monopoly Law; Crackdown and Policy-Planning Capability to be Broadly Strengthened," Sankei, Daily Summary of Japanese Press, August 26, 1995, at 2.

[135] Ibid.; and Interviews, senior MITI official and senior FTC official.

[136] Interview, senior FTC official. Also, on *zaibatsu* dissolution generally, see Hadley, *Antitrust in Japan*, and Section I, this chapter; points about Japanese investors and managers, author's interview, Eleanor M. Hadley, November 9, 1995 (Seattle, WA); confirmed further by author's interview, Michiko Ariga, July 22, 1996 (Tokyo). As noted above, Section I, Mrs Ariga was involved in drafting the AML on the Japanese side and was the first woman to serve as an FTC commissioner.

[137] See note 115 above.

[138] "Fair Trade Commission Aiming to Strengthen Functions; US Request Provides Favorable Tailwind; Tug of War Continued over General Secretariat Concept, between Ruling Parties and Management and Coordination Agency, Issue Intertwined with Administrative Reform," Nihon Keizai, Daily Summary of Japanese Press August 29, 1995, 3–4. *Fair*

Further complicating such seemingly straightforward political tradeoffs were struggles involving resource allocations within the bureaucracy. The Diet imposed by law a limit on the number of Japanese bureaucrats. The Management Coordinating Agency (MCA) – with input from the various agencies and ministries, including the FTC – was formally responsible for apportioning personnel and corresponding budget expenditures within that limit. As a result of deregulation, the Diet imposed upon many agencies a lower overall personnel number. At the same time, the MCA received approval to give precedence to a few agencies deemed vital to the national interest, especially the Ministry of Foreign Affairs and the FTC. Beginning in 1994, these specially designated agencies were to receive additional personnel and resources. Because of the Diets' absolute limit, however, the MCA could achieve the approved increase only by taking personnel slots and budget from other agencies.[139]

The FTC's proposed expansion plan of 1994–95 made still more sensitive the MCA's apportionment function. The plan sought to raise its own organization closer to that of the cabinet-level ministries. The proposal meant more staff and a specific increase in the number of grade-one, career people. The grade-one positions would include a general secretariat responsible for executive functions, a competition bureau, an economic and trade practices bureau which would draft and disseminate antimonopoly guidelines among business firms, and an investigation bureau possessing greater resources for prosecuting violations. During the 4 years preceding the start of SII in 1989 the average annual number of new positions assigned to the commission was 3.5, remaining close to the number for 1953, which was just 2. The average annual number of new positions during the six years after SII began, however, was ten. Indeed, as public pressure within Japan and from abroad increased by the budget years of 1994 and 1995 the FTC's personnel allocation rose to thirteen and fourteen, respectively. Meanwhile, as a result of deregulation the FTC was negotiating with other government agencies to end the cartel exemption systems; the widely held perception of its lower status, however, placed it at a disadvantage. "In some cases, we found it difficult to engage in negotiations," said a senior official, "for as we do not have a director general, we are regarded as lower." In addition, "a shortage of managerial posts is dampening the morale of the staff."[140]

Related to these factors of morale and intrabureaucratic status were considerations involving recruitment. In Japan, individuals generally remained in the career they chose at college graduation, though career entry

---

Trade Commission Taking Steps to Increase Power to Thoroughly Apply Anti-Monopoly Law; Crackdown and Policy-Planning Capability to be Broadly Strengthened, Sankei, Daily Summary of Japanese Press, August 26, 1995, 2.
[139] Ibid., and interview, senior official, FTC.   [140] Ibid.

depended on examination scores. The prestige of the university from which one graduated was also significant. Yet, many Japanese condemned the popular regard for academic hierarchy, and even the coalition government cabinet publicly opposed it. Thus, selection of a career in the bureaucracy, especially at level one, depended on individual choice and a high enough test score. Still, as a practical matter, powerful ministries such as Finance and MITI were the first choice of the graduates from Tokyo and the other top universities. Indeed, about 95 percent of the grade-one level people Finance recruited were Tokyo graduates. By contrast, in 1995 at the FTC of the eighty-six grade-one positions thirty-six were filled by Tokyo graduates. The FTC was confident that its personnel performance was excellent. Nevertheless, given the realities of Japanese cultural perceptions, because of its lower organizational status, the FTC was said to be less competitive for the top graduates from the leading universities, which further contributed to diminishing its influence. The FTC's upgrade plan was intended, then, to remedy organizational and symbolic deficiencies.[141]

Informing the government's view of the FTC's upgrade plan was another influential factor of bureaucratic culture. A basic characteristic of Japanese culture was the pervasive reliance upon official relations and decision making that gave precedence to long-term personal contacts. This was the more profound implication of a senior FTC official's statement that "contacts are important in Japan." A working manifestation of this relational characteristic was the practice of *shukko*. As a principle of personnel administration, the practice meant simply that the Diet sanctioned extensive short-term, interagency transfers: in the case of the FTC during a given year approximately sixty personnel from various agencies and ministries received temporary assignment for on average two years to the FTC, after which they returned to their "home" bureaucracy. At the same time as many as twenty FTC personnel were transferred temporarily to other agencies. From the politician's and the bureaucrat's point of view, the virtue of *shukko* was that it increased the personal contacts among individuals at all levels throughout the bureaucracy. To be sure, while assigned to a given agency, an official did his or her best for that agency. Even so, a complementary result of *shukko* was that it extended an agency's informal influence. FTC officials stated privately that temporary transfers facilitated more effective and persuasive communication about competition law and policy, something which clearly benefited the FTC, especially as deregulation threatened to reduce certain ministries' jurisdiction. Thus, if successful, the FTC upgrade proposal would *formally* strengthen the commission's position; because of *shukko* its *informal* influence would correspondingly increase as well.[142]

[141] Interviews senior officials, FTC.   [142] Ibid., including quoted phrase.

The FTC proposal raised further issues involving the commission's political and bureaucratic independence. Since the end of the Allied occupation, it was the tradition that most of the commission's members, including the chairman, were generally retired senior bureaucrats from the major ministries. Since the 1960s, one commissioner usually had risen through the ranks of the FTC's grade-one officials, such as Iyori Hiroshi. The commission's chairman, moreover, was virtually always a former senior official from the Ministry of Finance. As the government considered the upgrade plan, the issue of independence engendered controversy. Critics argued that maintaining the old order compromised the FTC's institutional standing within the bureaucracy. A particular object of concern was the continued allocation of the chairmanship to a retired Finance bureaucrat. Publicly, consumer advocates, the media, academics, and Keidanren called for diversifying the commission's membership. The commission should include, they said, one or two people from outside the government such as an academic or someone from business. Privately, some senior officials within the FTC favored change; others were more cautious, aware that, much like the practice of *shukko*, the traditional membership pattern might enhance the commission's influence within the bureaucracy, cabinet, and Diet. In private, certain MITI officials supported the principle of recruiting non-bureaucrats for the commission, though the primary concern involved the practice of drawing the commission's chair from Finance. Meanwhile, a representative of the U.S. Antitrust Division during periodic post-SII visits to Japan supported both the need for a diversified commission membership and a non-Finance chair.[143]

Perhaps the most important factor influencing the success of the FTC upgrade plan was the role of the LDP. Although the LDP lost its governing majority, it remained the largest single party in the Diet, and its members constituted a majority of ministers in successive coalition cabinets. The LDP exerted pressure on the commission's proposal partially because it required ministerial support at the cabinet level. MITI, whose minister had been LDP president Hashimoto, favored the FTC plan in principle. MITI and its former minister, however, did not oppose the repeal of the prohibition against holding companies. In addition, within the Diet, members of the LDP's antimonopoly subcommittee privately favored linking passage of the upgrade plan to repeal of Article 9. In the 1970s, when the commission began actively pursuing authority to impose higher civil penalties and won passage of the surcharge amendment of 1977, the LDP established its antimonopoly policy subcommittee which met periodically with FTC

---

[143] The points summarized in this paragraph recurred throughout the interviews. Concerning the input of the Antitrust Division, the DOJ lawyer negotiated directly with FTC, MITI, and other ministerial officials during at least three separate visits to Japan between September 1995 and January 1996.

officials. By 1994–95 the two regularly discussed the organizational upgrade plan and the holding company provision. The commission's senior officials noted that they listened "very carefully" to what the LDP members had to say. From both the cabinet and the Diet, the FTC thus was made aware that the approval it received from the LDP's powerful faction was at least partially conditioned upon the repeal or relaxation of article 9.[144]

Still broader political conflicts shaped the fate of the FTC and deregulation reform generally. During the mid-1990s, the continuing recession exacerbated the fragmentation of the political party structure and its links to the bureaucracy and business, as economic tensions heightened the importance of uncommitted voters in big cities, this floating "gray zone" of salary men's wives, working wives, and youths constituted two-fifths of Japan's voters. They were also the core consumer groups potentially most affected by the price gap and other problems involving deregulation. A senior LDP leader admitted that "whether the LDP wins or loses . . . is decided by whether new customers can be gained in new markets." About three-fifths of the voter "markets and customers" were already settled before an election. The LDP was "strong in the primary industries and among retail store and factory operations," groups with direct linkages to various protectionist bureaucracies. The floating voters, however, changed camps in each election. During the mid-1990s these voters' skepticism toward the old order contributed to keeping the LDP from control of the government. Accordingly, most LDP representatives, whose constituencies nonetheless had a stake in the traditional system of bureaucratic protection, could not publicly oppose either deregulation generally or the FTC in particular, at least not as long as the recession persisted. The few LDP officials who publicly favored the FTC component of deregulation had reason to do so, by contrast, not only in order to win the narrow repeal of the holding company prohibition. They were mindful that defending the Antimonopoly Law was of interest to the same uncommitted urban voters who were most concerned about the price gap problem and related consumer issues. These political considerations influenced minority party support for deregulation and the FTC's organizational strengthening.[145]

MITI's advocacy of fortifying the FTC was not inconsistent with the wider political pressures. Undoubtedly, MITI's interest in pursuing a quid pro quo of eliminating or at least relaxing the article 9 owed much to Keidanren's influence. Keidanren pushed for deregulation and improving the FTC's enforcement as a way to lessen the market pressure on those leading industries confronting international competition. And MITI shared

---

[144] See Section III, this chapter; and interviews with senior FTC officials, including quoted phrase. See also Schoppa, *Bargaining with Japan*, 215–53.

[145] Masumi, *Contemporary Politics in Japan*, 424–6, quoted phrases at 425; and discussion below.

with Keidanren a concern for the competitiveness of these industries. Similarly, officials in both organizations favored reducing price fixing and other structural barriers to foreign competitors. The urban consumers who were the floating voters that the LDP and such coalition members as the Social Democratic Party and the Sakigake Party hoped to win had an interest in reducing barriers in so far as they contributed to keeping prices high. Thus, practical concerns binding together leaders within Keidanren and MITI overlapped with those of the coalition government's leaders who were appealing to Japan's large uncommitted voter constituency.[146]

After months of intensive negotiations a law strengthening the FTC's enforcement capabilities passed. In February 1996, the Diet received a bill drafted by the FTC which upgraded the commission's secretary general to a level just below minister and established two new enforcement bureaus. Moreover, within the Investigation Bureau a "special investigation department" was created to crack "down on serious wrongdoers, such as bid-riggers in public works projects or companies that form clandestine cartels to fix prices." The law went into operation on June 14. Skeptics and supporters alike described the outcome as largely a symbolic victory. Knowledgeable sources within the FTC noted, however, that the general secretary represented higher bureaucratic status, which enhanced the commission's effectiveness in dealing with ministries whose jurisdiction would shrink as a result of a deregulation.[147]

Most importantly, perhaps, the law increased the incentives for the new Investigation Department to pursue criminal cases. Keidanren officials, Japanese business executives, and the *bengoshi* which advised and represented them emphasized repeatedly in private interviews that the commission's criminal accusations were an effective means of achieving Antimonopoly Law compliance. The administrative resources required for criminal cases, even with increased personnel, meant that the FTC could sustain only a small number of criminal cases annually. Even so, Japanese business lawyers noted, the annual prosecution of a few such cases had broad ramifications, in part because they fostered private litigations and shareholder suits. Thus, large corporate firms within major industries and their employees faced a minimum of a few years of litigation costs as a result of the FTC's criminal accusation; defending against private claims could lengthen the time costs. These factors facilitated the perception that ongoing criminal accusations against cartel practices, "rather than merely fining them or ordering them to stop anticompetitive" conduct, were a significant measure of the FTC's effectiveness. A further incentive influencing the Investigation Department's actions was that, since criminal cases

[146] Ibid.
[147] "Antitrust Law Boosts FTC's Powers," *Japan Times* (Saturday, June 15, 1996); and interviews with FTC officials.

were resource intensive, they provided a major justification for continuing growth in personnel allocations from the MCA.[148]

The appointment of Negoro Yasuchika as FTC chairman in 1996 reinforced these expectations. The FTC's chair had generally been held by a former senior official from Finance. Negoro, by contrast, was the former Tokyo superintendent public prosecutor, a post second in authority to the chief public prosecutor and identified with "officials directly responsible for investigative duties." Suggesting the informal influence associated with *shukko*, Negoro also possessed "a broad personal network with politicians and bureaucrats, not to mention with judicial officials."[149]

Despite the success of the FTC's enforcement plan, a relaxation of the holding company ban in Article 9 initially did not pass. By 1996, the FTC, MITI, Keidanren, and the coalition government reached an agreement in principle that weakening Article 9's absolute ban against holding companies was appropriate. The LDP's and the Social Democratic Party's conference memorandum endorsed the principle without stipulating the scope of change. Meanwhile, the FTC, which received diverse proposals from its study group, incorporated into the upgrade bill presented to the Diet a revision of Article 9. This change continued to ban the largest corporations from forming holding companies by establishing a capital limit. Companies whose assets placed them below the limit could form holding companies, with the commission's authorization. As a practical matter, the ban applied only to Japan's largest firms, many of which were heirs of the *zaibatsu* families. Essentially, the relaxation of the prohibition in Article 9 would enable smaller venture capital companies and certain banks to achieve greater organizational efficiencies like those which firms enjoyed in other major industrial nations. At the same time, maintaining restrictions ameliorated fears that the *zaibatsu* might revive in some modern guise.[150]

Once the Diet began considering the holding company revision, however, party consensus dissolved. Some LDP and Social Democratic Party representatives questioned linking the upgrade plan and the Article 9 alteration within the same bill. There was no effective resistance to the plan strengthening the FTC's enforcement regime, but increasing numbers of Diet members did not feel the same about weakening the holding company ban. Presented with the FTC's specific language for revising Article 9, the Social Democratic Party especially was opposed. In Japan, labor unions

---

[148] See notes above for reference to attitudes of Keidanren, *bengoshi*, and senior FTC officials (whence comes quoted phrase).

[149] Quoted passages from "Yasuchika Negoro, FTC Chairman-Designate; Expectations for His 'Cooperation' with Prosecutors; Has Broad Personal Networks with Political and Bureaucratic Worlds," Sanki, June 12, 1996, Daily Summary of Japanese Press, June 22–24, 1996.

[150] "Parties Agree Not to Submit Bill on Holding Companies," *Japan Times* (June 15, 1996); and interviews with FTC, Sakigake Party, and Keidanren officials.

were organized within separate companies, and unions were important constituents of the Social Democratic Party, which realized that a company's reorganization as a holding company might weaken the union's as well as the party's influence. Less vocal criticism came from some LDP and Social Democratic Party members representing smaller retailers who feared that the holding company device might give discounters price advantages through improved economies of scale. In February 1996, the coalition parties split the FTC's bill in two; they voted to enact the upgrade plan, but the holding company matter was turned over to a project team. For roughly two months, the team intensely debated the revision issue. A Sakigake member of the project team (who felt that alteration of Article 9 should occur as part of a wholesale revision of Japan's commercial code) and the Social Democratic Party blocked ending the holding company ban. As a result, the issue was left for settlement in the Diet session of the following year, when the holding company prohibition was relaxed.[151]

National and international perceptions informed evaluations of the SII and its role in strengthening antimonopoly policy enforcement. During the 1990s, U.S. observers considered the SII in terms of American trade interests and whether Japanese business and government authorities were developing a market consciousness more favorable to competition values, including the opening of Japan's protected market. Leading American business commentators and trade policy experts criticized the Bush administration for pursuing SII rather than the result-oriented, unilateral power authorized under section 301 of the Trade Act; it was, they argued, a delaying tactic to build support amid disagreements over the U.S. government's promotion of the GATT Uruguay Round and the World Trade Organization (WTO). The antitrust provisions of SII were one focus of contention. American skeptics claimed that strengthening Japan's antitrust enforcement regime would have little effect against its collaborative culture. Those defending SII's antitrust provisions perceived within that very culture, however, opportunities to reinforce Japanese proponents of stronger antitrust enforcement.[152] FTC official Sugiyama Yukinari gave qualified support to the latter view, declaring: "SII perhaps played a significant role in getting some fines passed, as well as in the improvement in recognition for antimonopoly policy and respect for the importance of free competition among the Japanese public."[153]

---

[151] Ibid.; 29 *FTC/Japan Views* (July 1997), 1–4; 28 *FTC/Japan Views* (June 1997), 35–40; 26 *FTC/Japan Views* (November 1996), 1–6.

[152] Schoppa, *Bargaining with Japan*, 1–17; Case, "An Overview of Fifteen Years of United States–Japanese. . . Economic Relations," 16(1) *Arizona Journal of International and Comparative Law* (1999), 18–19; Iyori and Uesugi, *The Antimonopoly Laws of Japan*, 61–6; and citations, Chapter 2, Sections III and IV.

[153] Markham, "The Japan Fair Trade Commission and the Evolving Framework of Antitrust Enforcement," quoted at 86, note 176.

Indeed, over the decade following SII antitrust provided noteworthy indicators of Japan's changing political economy. By the mid-1990s, although the strengthened antitrust enforcement regime and relaxation of the holding company ban passed into law, the Hashimoto government was unable to enact more comprehensive deregulation reforms. This pattern of antitrust success coinciding with larger unfulfilled economic reform became conspicuous under Prime Minister Koizumi Junichirô. Backed by a considerable electoral mandate, Koizumi announced an impressive economic reform program in April 2001. Nevertheless, within a short time his efforts stalled amid bureaucratic inertia and political party fragmentation. During the same period, however, the government reshaped the legal framework governing the finance and structure of Japan's big corporations in order to make them more globally competitive. The corporate restructuring fostered increased antitrust activism.[154]

V. JAPANESE ANTITRUST ENFORCEMENT SINCE SII

The SII transformed Japanese antitrust from a symbol of comparative legal consciousness into working policy. SII reflected increased international cooperation among antitrust authorities which in turn facilitated comparative understanding of effective antitrust enforcement within and among nations. Thus, over the same period when U.S. antitrust authorities initiated the SII provisions seeking to strengthen the FTC's enforcement capabilities, the United States concluded the cooperative enforcement agreement of 1991 with the European Community. Although most American officials regarded U.S., German, and the Community's antitrust enforcement to be comparable, they generally contended that the FTC's enforcement was weak. A few specialists challenged this view, however. Employing a deep understanding of the extensive German influences upon Japanese legal culture, John O. Haley argued that a realistic standard for measuring the FTC's enforcement effectiveness was German civil law practice. Unlike the American antitrust tradition, which relied upon judicial process, the civil law employed primarily an administrative approach. Applying this civil administrative standard to Japan's legal culture, Haley concluded, the FTC's enforcement efforts were reasonably effective. Japanese antitrust experts such as former FTC commissioner Iyori Hiroshi and Professor Matsushita Mitsuo agreed, though Professor and former FTC official Hirabayashi Hidekatsu remained skeptical.[155]

---

[154] Aurelia George Mulgan, *Japan's Failed Revolution Koizumi and the Politics of Economic Reform* (Asia Pacific Press, Canberra, Australia, 2002); Lincoln, *Arthritic Japan*.

[155] See Moritani Kazuo, "Comparison of Competition Law in the US and Japan," Unpublished Paper for Program on US–Japan Relations, Harvard University, 1994, in possession of the author); and Haley, *Antitrust in Germany and Japan*. On the US–European Community Cooperative Agreement of 1991, see Chapter 5, Section 4; Professor

Harry First of New York University Law School took the comparative method one step further. He found that using American standards the FTC's efforts approached the U.S. government's level of enforcement by the 1990s. Since SII, there was a significant increase in the FTC's formal "recommendations" holding that business conduct violated the Antimonopoly Law. The amount of administrative (surcharge) fines the FTC imposed on conduct under the amendment of 1977 rose markedly; the level of fines "has been either roughly comparable to, or at times has exceeded U.S. fines. This is so despite the fact that the number of criminal cases brought in the United States has been four to six times greater than the number of cartel cases brought in Japan." Finally, First recognized the need to adjust for the respective size of each nation's economy, since it was reasonable to expect that more antitrust problems would occur in large economies than in smaller ones. Again, the "level of government antitrust enforcement" in the two nations was "very close." Professor Hirabayashi noted, by contrast, that the amount of surcharges the FTC imposed in fiscal 1990 totaling 12.5 billion yen was due primarily to the cement cartel case. After 1990, the amount of surcharges imposed returned to the previous level.[156]

U.S. pressure implemented through SII supported Japanese translation of antimonopoly symbols into enforceable rules. As one senior MITI official wrote in 2002, "Now, deregulation is under way in every sector and discretionary powers of the bureaucracy are phased out where possible." A new order based on "*post facto* monitoring of compliance with general rules" was displacing the old system of "*ex facto* regulations." Bureaucratic reliance on "[a]dministrative guidance . . . must change," he declared. "In the *post facto* monitoring type of governance, corporate activities will not be restricted as long as they are compliant with laws. If problems arise, they must be resolved in court. As we go through the deregulation process, we need to review laws to create transparent rules that encourage competition."[157]

Significantly, the deregulation discourse did not suggest terminating bureaucratic intervention; instead, it reimagined bureaucrats as promoters of competition rather than protection. A U.S. Congressional Research Report asserted that the FTC "is to monitor the transactions among *keiretsu* firms to determine whether or not they are being conducted in a manner that impedes fair competition." Periodically, the FTC should analyze and publish the results of surveying "various aspects of the *keiretsu*

Hirabayashi Hidekatsu to Freyer, "Comments," August 29, 2004; Iyori/Freyer interview; Matsushita/Freyer interview, August 19, 2003.

[156] "Antitrust Enforcement in Japan," 64 *Antitrust Law Journal* (1995), quotes at 139, 142; Professor Hirabayashi Hidekatsu to Freyer, "Comments," August 29, 2004.

[157] Sections 2–4, this chapter; and Moriya, "Creating a New Competitive Business Environment in Japan," in Jones and Matsushita, eds., *Competition Policy in the Global Trading System*, 163.

groups, including supplier–customer transactions, financing arrangements, personal ties, and the role of trading companies" and "take steps, including stricter enforcement of the Antimonopoly Act, to address anti-competitive and exclusionary practices uncovered." Aided by an "advisory group" the FTC would "establish guide lines to insure that transactions among companies in the *keiretsu* groups do not discriminate against foreign firms." By subjecting the *keiretsu* relationship to greater transparency maintained through ongoing FTC oversight, the United States hoped to expose anticompetitive practices impeding the access of American firms to the Japanese market. Antitrust authorities in the United States nonetheless conceded that "*Keiretsu* organizations, in and of themselves, do not appear to violate U.S. antitrust law. Neither vertically integrated nor diversified business organizations, per se, are prohibited except as they violate laws governing monopolies, restraint of trade, or other specific behavior. The question appears to be one of behavior, not structure."[158]

The greater transparency reinforced the deregulation discourse Japanese business, LDP, and bureaucratic leaders adopted following SII. After 1989, the coincident deterioration of the LDP's electoral dominance and the bubble economy converged with the end of the cold war, subjecting Japanese multinational corporations to increased costs of operating in the protected home market even as they faced increased competition resulting from financial and technological globalization. SII focused the attention of some bureaucrats, business leaders, and politicians on the need to expand the monitoring function in order to facilitate restructuring the *keiretsu* system. Thus, the Japanese multinational corporations' global competitiveness required establishing market competition inside Japan. Burdened with huge bad loans, banks were unable to maintain their central place as suppliers of credit, forcing many of the nation's leading corporations to compete for capital in the stock and bond markets. These market pressures threatened to overwhelm small business subcontractors working within the *keiretsu* system. They also accentuated the costs of lifetime employment. The Japanese nonetheless used the SII pressure to reconstitute antitrust enforcement capabilities on their own terms. The economic dislocation was of such magnitude that an FTC official declared in 1992: "Even if there weren't any SII talks, the enhancement of deterrence is necessary in the near future, so it would have happened anyway." Still, "Japanese society is a stable one, with various vested interest groups. *Gaiatsu* makes negotiation among these smoother."[159]

---

[158] Dick K. Nanto, "Japan's Industrial Groups: The *Keiretsu*," *CRS Report for Congress, November 5, 1990* (Congressional Research Service, Library of Congress, Washington, DC, 1990), quotes at 18 and 19.

[159] Markham, "The Japan Fair Trade Commission and the Evolving Framework of Antitrust Enforcement," quoted at 101, note 215, and 105–6.

Within this conflicted political and cultural context the Japanese Diet enacted laws strengthening the FTC's authority to enforce higher civil and criminal fines. Under Japanese law only criminal penalties could be punitive, meaning that civil "surcharges are considered to be administrative measures aimed at requiring simple disgorgement of illegal overcharges, without any punitive component." Even so, consistently with SII stipulations and ongoing U.S. pressure, a law of 1991 increased the surcharge rates imposed as civil penalties. Following political maneuvering among LDP factions and smaller political parties, business groups, and MITI and the Construction Ministry, the FTC compromised. The legislation established a two-tier system with a 6 percent surcharge rate generally applicable to big business, whereas the rate for small firms was 3 percent, for wholesale firms it was 1 percent, for larger retail firms the rate was 2 percent, and for smaller retail firms it was 1 percent. The lower rates applied because the profit/sales ratios were lower in those sectors. In 1999, another law enlarged the definition of small enterprises governed by the lower rate.[160]

Similar political compromises shaped the increase in criminal fines. The passage of the stronger civil surcharge system was followed the next year by legislation raising criminal fines. The Antimonopoly Act included criminal penalties, but between the close of the occupation and SII the only significant criminal prosecution the FTC won was the petroleum cartel case instituted under Takahashi. As a result of interest group pressures, however, the FTC compromised on the law of 1992. Predictably, business groups such as Keidanren declared that the existing low fines were high enough. By contrast, critical commentary from the Social Democratic Party, to which MITI indirectly acquiesced, asserted that maximum criminal fines proposed by the construction industry and its *zoku* factional allies in the LDP and Ministry of Construction were too low to constitute a meaningful deterrent. The FTC nonetheless accepted the construction *zoku* demands, lowering the proposed maximum criminal fine from ¥300 million to ¥100 million.[161]

During the 1990s the FTC prosecuted six criminal accusations, but the policy impact was ambiguous. The first case challenged price-fixing on polyvinyl chloride stretch film (1991), and another case invalidated a market-sharing agreement on ductile iron pipe (1999). Four cases involved bid rigging: on seals ordered by the Social Insurance Agency (1993), on

[160] Chemtob, "Antitrust Deterrence in the United States and Japan," in Jones and Matsushita, eds., *Competition Policy in the Global Trading System*, 195–210, quoted at 202; Beeman, *Public Policy and Economic Competition in Japan*, 141–3; Iyori and Uesugi, *The Antimonopoly Laws of Japan*, 256–63; Professor Hirabayashi Hidekatsu to Freyer, "Comments," August 29, 2004.

[161] Chemtob, "Antitrust Deterrence in the United States and Japan," in Jones and Matsushita, eds., *Competition Policy in the Global Trading System*, at 205 note 29; Iyori and Uesugi, *The Antimonopoly Laws of Japan*, 250–5; Beeman, *Pubic Policy and Competition in Japan*, 144–6.

Japan Sewage Agency electrical equipment contracts (1995), on water meters the Tokyo Metropolitan Government purchased (1997), and on the Defense Agency's procurement of an oil product (1999). Whether this record number of criminal accusations was sufficient to stem collusive conduct pervading Japanese business, especially in the notorious field of bid-rigging, remained unclear. Under Japanese criminal jurisprudence prosecuting criminal accusations was the job of the Public Prosecutors Office. Although that office and the FTC cooperated during the 1990s, it was not enough to overcome the fundamental institutional conservatism making Japanese prosecutors reluctant to proceed without irrefutable evidence of guilt sustainable in court. The same conservatism determined the judiciary's requirement for a high showing of proof in criminal cases. These constraints were such that after 2000 the FTC shifted its investigative resources into civil cases which did not require cooperation with the Prosecutor's Office; the LDP-dominated government reinforced this decision by empowering the FTC to encourage whistle blowers under a leniency program and by strengthening its power to procure evidence from businesses through onsite raids.[162]

Perhaps the clearest difference between the U.S. and Japanese enforcement regimes involved private actions. Suits initiated by private individuals were a vital component of American antitrust enforcement; in Japan, such actions were rare. Private actions did not begin to exceed government cases even in the United States, however, until the 1950s, after which they rose steadily. In Japan, as in Europe, neither treble damages nor American-type contingent fees were allowed. During the early 1980s, moreover, the Japanese courts established a leading precedent against private plaintiffs in the petroleum cartel case. As a result, although the 1990s witnessed a noteworthy "revival" of private suits in Japan, litigated by such consumer advocates as Yamiguchi and Murayama, there were only a small number of cases. As Professor First observed, it "is the resources brought to antitrust by private litigants that marks the most significant difference between the level of antitrust enforcement in the two countries."[163]

Still, despite repeated setbacks some Japanese consumer lawyers pursued private actions. In 1958, consumer advocates initiated but lost a court case promoting private actions. Similarly, in the private price-fixing petroleum cartel cases initiated in the 1970s, consumer groups reached only modest

---

[162] Chemtob, "Antitrust Deterrence in the United States and Japan," in Jones and Matsushita, eds., *Competition Policy in the Global Trading System*, 206, note 3; Iyori and Uesugi, *The Antimonopoly Laws of Japan*, 250–5; T. A. Freyer's interview with member of the Justice Department's Antitrust Division, March 28, 2003.

[163] First, "Antitrust Enforcement in Japan," 64 *Antitrust Law Journal* (1995), quoted at 163–4. See also Sections II and III, this chapter; and Murayama, "Private Enforcement of Antitrust Law in Japan," in Jones and Matsushita, eds., *Competition Policy in the Global Trading System*, 243–54.

settlements or lost on appeal to the Supreme Court. By contrast, with FTC acquiescence during the 1980s consumer advocates representing taxi companies in Kyoto prefecture got the Ministry of Transportation to allow some nationwide competition in fares. By 1990, antitrust subcommittee members of the Japan Federation of Bar Associations sought U.S. support for private actions during the SII negotiations. As a result of this and other considerations SII included provisions urging more private actions. Even so, Murayama, the subcommittee's sometime chair noted the rarity of Japanese private suits. Such limited antitrust enforcement in Japan, he said, "delays the growth of an ethical sense, the sense that violations of antitrust law are not only prohibited by law, but also should be felt as a shame. Some still assume hit and run is good to do."[164]

Following SII, by contrast, consumers achieved noteworthy successes. The Ministry of Finance ended the discriminatory practice of securities firms' covering major but not smaller clients' losses. Also, under the Antimonopoly Law's section 17–2, which required firms to report reasons for simultaneous price increases, the FTC warned beer companies to end unfair resale price maintenance agreements. As a result, the beer companies indicated in advertising that their suggested prices were not binding but just for reference, resulting in lower prices. And in a regular tort case Japanese law's failure to provide for injunctive relief resulted in Toyota Trading Corporation's paying a ¥200 billion damage award to elderly people suffering losses because they had authorized purchases without being adequately informed about the risks of gold futures trading. Moreover, the Citizens' Ombudsman filed a number of damage suits nationwide in collusive tendering cases against local governments, which were reluctant to recover damages from violators. By the late 1990s, MITI established a study group chaired by Professor Matsushita; the FTC instituted its own group as did the Japan Federation of Bar Associations. The FTC prepared a bill that became law in May 2000. Murayama declared that the law "did not adopt some suggestions," of the Japan Federation of Bar Associations, "therefore the revision is not enough, but it did accept a large part of them."[165]

Interest-group pressures shaped the new injunctive relief law's two main provisions. The MITI Study Group's proposals most directly influenced this outcome. The law authorized private litigants – such as consumers and entrepreneurs – to obtain from courts injunctions against unfair trade practices. The injunction embraced trade associations as well as single

---

[164] Section III, this chapter; Murayama, "Private Enforcement of Antitrust Law in Japan," in Jones and Matsushita, eds., *Competition Policy in the Global Trading System*, 243–54, quote at 245.

[165] Murayama, "Private Enforcement of Antitrust Law in Japan," in Jones and Matsushita, eds., *Competition Policy in the Global Trading System*, quote at 250; Professor Hirabayashi Hidekatsu to Freyer, "Comments," August 29, 2004.

businesses. The law extended the injunctive-relief power to courts throughout Japan, not just the Tokyo High Court system, which had sole jurisdiction for cases appealing FTC's decisions, antitrust criminal cases, and damage suits under section 25. Japanese scholar critics argued that while the law facilitated private suits, its definition of unfair trade practices reached only indirect purchasers or consumers rather than competitors or direct purchasers. The issue was contentious because unfair trade practices could be construed to reach competitors in cases involving unjust low prices or direct purchasers such as in resale price maintenance. In addition, the law did not significantly expand potential damage claims beyond those sanctioned under the limited general tort system of the Civil Code's section 709. Moreover, the FTC did not wish to promote too much private litigation competing with the commission's central role as Japan's primary antimonopoly law enforcer.[166]

MITI actively supported policies and laws promoting the restructuring of Japan's corporate order, including *keiretsu*. The significant weakening of the holding company ban was part of the Japanese government's systematic revision of the Antimonopoly Law, the nation's Commercial Code, and various tax and accounting provisions in order to encourage freer financial restructuring through mergers and acquisitions (M&A), corporate divestitures (spin-offs), management friendly bankruptcy, and corporate takeovers. The government's leading ministries basically altered the legislative framework sustaining financial arrangements. According to one MITI official, a "remarkable" increase in mergers and acquisitions had taken place from 621 to 1,169 cases between 1995 and 1999. He noted "several big bank" mergers and "a merger between Nippon Oil and Mitsubishi Oil. Sony has taken advantage of the 'stock-for-stock swaps' provisions and turned Sony Music and others into 100%-owned subsidiaries. These are good examples of the improved restructuring process in Japan." Ito-Yokado, one of the nation's supermarket chains, benefited from deregulation to establish ATMs; in addition, Sony was developing electrical banking on the Internet. Moreover, Japan adopted a U.S. style chapter bankruptcy provision, which "allows restructuring without changing the old management." MITI also took the lead in policies aimed at weakening *keiretsu* by reducing the number of company directors and

---

[166] Murayama, "Private Enforcement of Antitrust Law in Japan," in Jones and Matsushita, eds., *Competition Policy in the Global Trading System*, quote at 250–1. On the perceived strengths and weaknesses of the Injunction Law, see Murakami Masahiro, "Competition Rules and Enforcement in the US, EU, and Japan," Tamura, "Market Access Issues in Japan's Antimonopoly Law," Moriya, "Creating a New Competitive Business Environment in Japan," and Seryo Shingo, "Private Enforcement and New Provisions for Damages and Injunctions," in Jones and Matsushita, eds., *Competition Policy in the Global Trading System*, 101–2, 152–6, 166–77, 287–91.

supporting Keidanren's "announcement that it is trying to dissolve cross-shareholding."[167]

This legislative program promoted the corporate restructuring necessary to make Japanese multinational corporations more globally competitive. A MITI official declared that "M&A between foreign companies and Japanese companies has been increasing – by 67% in 1998 and by 52% in 1999, which surpassed the increases of M&A among Japanese companies in both years." In some cases takeovers involved failed Japanese firms. Thus, the bankruptcy provision encouraged GE Capital to purchase Japan Lease and Ripplewood Partners (USA) to acquire Long Term Capital Bank of Japan. The MITI official noted that foreign companies acquired "healthy" Japanese firms, such as the Cable & Wireless takeover of the Japanese communication firm, IDC and the merger of the German and Japanese pharmaceutical companies, Boehringer-Ingelheim Co. and SSP Co. Following SII, moreover, MITI facilitated the publicized loosening of the Large Scale Store Law resulting in American Toys R Us to enter the Japanese market. Another outcome of financial deregulation was that Merrill Lynch and other leading multinational financial firms obtained access to Japan. "These acquisitions are 'transparent,' indicating," the MITI official affirmed, "that business transactions are now made on the basis of economic rationalism in Japan."[168]

The Japanese automobile industry suggested, moreover, how major multinational mergers loosened *keiretsu*. Leading examples were the restructuring of Daimler Chrysler/Mitsubishi, General Motors/Fuji Heavy Industries [Subaru]/ Isuzu/ Suzuki, and Ford/Mazda.[169] Perhaps the most conspicuous merger was Renault/Nissan. Through the skillful intercultural managerial leadership of Renault's Carlos Ghosn, Nissan once more became a thriving multinational corporation. Ghosn explained the impact such mergers had on *keiretsu*. "Under the system manufacturing companies maintain equity stakes in partner companies. This, it's believed, promotes loyalty and cooperation." Nevertheless, he found that the "majority of these shareholdings were far too small for Nissan to have any managerial leverage on the companies." Accordingly, "soon after I arrived, we started dismantling our *keiretsu* investments." Notwithstanding "widespread fears" that suppliers were concerned about "sell-offs. . . . It turns out that

[167] Moriya, "Creating a New Competitive Business Environment in Japan," in Jones and Matsushita, eds., *Competition Policy in the Global Trading System*, quotes at 164, 169, 172–3.
[168] Ibid., quotes at 173.
[169] Alexander Harney, "A Difficult Meeting of Cultures," *Financial Times* (June 1, 2000), p. 1; Rahul Jacob and Naoko Kakamae, "Prospects Promising in Year of the Deal," *Financial Times*, May 19, 2000, vi; Carlos Garcia-Pont and Nitin Nohria, "Local Versus Global Mimetism: The Dynamics of Alliance Formation in the Automobile Industry," 23 *Strategic Management Journal* (2002), 307–21.

our partners make a clear distinction between Nissan as customer and Nissan as shareholder. They don't care what we do with the shares as long as we're still a customer," he concluded. "Although breaking up the Nissan *keiretsu* seemed a radical move at the time, many other Japanese companies are now following our lead."[170]

The global financial interconnectedness of Japanese and foreign multinational corporations facilitated, in turn, Japan's endorsement of transnational cooperation among antitrust regimes on the basis of "positive-comity." Accordingly, Japanese officials from the FTC, Ministry of Foreign Affairs, and METI (MITI was renamed the Ministry of Economy, Trade, and Industry in 2001) supported "a positive comity process" to encourage antitrust regimes' "cooperating to deal with the anti-trust activities occurring beyond the borders." Although since the 1970s Japan had refused three times to conclude such an agreement, in 1999 Japan and the United States signed a bilateral cooperative antitrust agreement, indicating how the Japanese officials' environment had changed. In 2002, Japan provisionally entered into a similar agreement with the European Union and began negotiations to do the same with Canada and Singapore.[171]

The global interdependence in multinational corporate finance reinforced Japan's growing transnational antitrust cooperation. During SII, the U.S. Justice Department began developing a policy to "sue US-based subsidiaries of foreign companies engaged in unfair trade practices, even if those practices occurr[ed]" in foreign markets, including "antitrust violations by *keiretsu* in Japan." The policy raised anew the controversial issue of extraterritorial antitrust jurisdiction. The Japanese supported bilateral antitrust cooperative agreements, declared a government-authorized report, "to provide a framework for preventing clashes caused by extraterritorial application of competition laws." Yet in the *Thermal Fax Paper* case of the mid-1990s the Japanese government argued before U.S. courts that under international law extraterritorial jurisdiction should be limited in principle. In an earlier phase of that same litigation, the Tokyo District Public Prosecutor's Office had nonetheless assisted the United States, conducting an investigation based on the Antimonopoly Law's criminal provisions. FTC officials also cooperated with U.S. and European officials in major international cartel cases, including in 1999 the warning issued against

[170] "First Person Saving the Business Without Losing the Company," *Harvard Business Review* (January 2002), 37–45, quotes at 38, 39; Harry Korine, Kazuhiro Asakawa, and Pierre-Yves Gomez, "Partnership with the Unfamiliar: Lessons from the Case of Renault and Nissan," 13(2) *Business Strategy Review* (Summer 2002), 41–50; Victoria Emerson, "An Interview with Carlos Ghosn, President of Nissan Motors, Ltd. and Industry Leader of the Year (Automotive News, 2000)," 36(1) *Journal of World Business* (2001), 3–10.
[171] Industrial Structure Council, Ministry of Economy Trade and Industry, *2003 Report on the WTO Consistency of Trade Policies by Major Trading Partners* (Tokyo, 2003), 397–401, quotes at 397.

Japanese members of the electrodes cartel. In addition, they raided the offices of firms participating in the vitamin cartel. In neither case, however, did the FTC take legal action.[172]

The interdependency of global trade reinforced Japanese support for the WTO. The WTO could only indirectly address private anticompetitive conduct involving government action. Still, the *Kodak/Fuji* decision of 1997 highlighted the extent to which more effective transnational antitrust enforcement ameliorated potential extraterritorial antitrust confrontations. While the results of the *Kodak/Fuji* decision favored Japan, the intractability of underlying issues concerning anticompetitive conduct of multinational corporations demonstrated the need for international agreement on standards defining just what such conduct might entail. Reaching agreement nonetheless proved difficult. In 1997, senior FTC official Kobayashi Hideaki endorsed "enabling the WTO to handle" antitrust "related problems," because "it entrusts the settlement of bilateral dispute to a neutral third party. It makes the process of the dispute settlement less emotion-provoking and more transparent at least on an *ex post facto* basis. This is due to the fact that the WTO is the only more or less universal international organization that has a reasonably well functioning dispute settlement mechanism." He emphasized, however, that establishing international standards was problematic in part because most WTO members had little or no experience with competition policy. The most "worthwhile" course was thus "working step by step," beginning with the WTO's taking "the initiative, in close co-operation with the OECD, in attaining certain international convergence among competition laws and policies."[173]

An annual breakdown of cases suggested the overall pattern of FTC enforcement. In fiscal year 1993 its investigation Department handled 222 cases. In two cases, through a proceeding of open public hearing, the Department prepared for criminal accusation. In addition, the commission settled twenty-seven cases through recommendation, twenty-five at the warning level, and seventy-nine through caution; fourteen cases were dropped, and seventy-five were deferred to the following year. During the 1990s, the FTC imposed the increasingly costly fines identified with recommendation decisions because in each case it had collected sufficient evidence to prove a violation in court. By contrast, the FTC employed a warning or caution when the evidence of violation was significant but not

---

[172] Nanto, "Japan's Industrial Groups: The *Keiretsu*," *CRS Report for Congress* (1990), 18; *2003 Report on the WTO Trade Policies*, 397–401, quote at 397; Chemtob, "Antitrust Deterrence in the United States and Japan," in Jones and Matsushita, eds., *Competition Policy in the Global Trading System*, 209.

[173] Kobayashi Hideaki, "The World Trade Organization and Competition Policy," in Berry E. Hawk, ed., *Fordham Corporate Law Institute International Antitrust Law & Policy Annual Proceedings, 1997* (Juris Publishing, Inc., Yonkers, NY, 1998), 27–30, quote at 30.

enough for judicial prosecution. The Trade Practices Department dealt on a routine basis with another 1,000–2,000 cases regulating premium offers and abuse of dominant position, which were of interest primarily to small firms. The FTC's seven regional offices were responsible for proportionally more cases falling within these two categories.[174]

A sample of cases indicated the commission's enforcement priorities following SII. Foreign pressure and the interests of Japanese consumers converged with dramatic consequences in bid-rigging cases. Since the early 1980s, the commission had compiled data and issued guidelines aimed at extensive price-fixing and corruption maintained through bid-rigging in the construction industry. A social welfare justification for these cartel practices was that they sustained employment by keeping afloat thousands of small contractors. But the losers undoubtedly were the consumers. As SII targeted the harm done to Japanese consumers the FTC initiated significant prosecutions against bid-rigging *dango*. Meanwhile, the U.S. Department of Justice won similar cases against the construction industry's *dango* operating on American military installations. The consumer group in Saitama Prefecture also began its private damage action against a cartel of sixty-six construction companies known as the Saitama Saturday Society for rigging sixty-three construction contracts valued at ¥81 billion. In this case, the commission authorized providing supportive evidence to plaintiffs bringing private actions, something consumer lawyers and advocates had long urged. These bid-rigging prosecutions coincided with the corruption scandal involving construction industry leaders and powerful politicians that contributed to the LDP's electoral defeat in 1993.[175]

Conflict of such dimensions inevitably engendered criticism that the commission's prosecutions were inadequate. In one conspicuous bid-rigging case involving the Ministry of Construction there were unsubstantiated claims that by relying upon civil penalty instead of criminal accusation the commission had buckled to LDP pressure. Commission officials responded, however, that the failure to seek criminal indictments involved bureaucratic negotiation with the government prosecutor's office. The FTC had power to *accuse* only; it was the responsibility of the prosecutor's office to decide whether to prosecute. In the controversial bid-rigging case the media pressed the commission to make the accusation, but as long as the prosecutor's office declined to act the commission had little reason to move

[174] Interviews with senior FTC officials. See also Yamada, Akinori, "Recent Development of Competition Law and Policy in Japan," in Berry E. Hawk, ed., *Fordham Corporate Law Institute International Antitrust Law & Policy, Annual Proceedings, 1997* (Juris Publishing, Inc., Yonkers, NY, 1998), 53–82.

[175] Beeman, *Public Policy and Economic Competition in Japan,* 114, 143, 158, 161–70; Haley, *Antitrust in Germany and Japan,* 71, 143, 161–72; Iyori and Uesugi, *The Antimonopoly Laws of Japan,* 86–93.

on its own. Instead, the FTC settled for imposing one of the largest civil fines ever.[176]

Even so, the bid-rigging prosecutions indicated an important policy shift favoring consumers. "Industrial policy that has restricted competition to protect failing firms during periods of temporary recession has often indirectly fostered competition," Iyori wrote in 1986, "by preserving a sufficient number of firms to provide competition in an industry once the economic conditions have improved." According to First, however, during the 1990s a "much more vigorous" enforcement began under SII with the bid-rigging cases and "[t]his vigor spread to price fixing cartels in other industries." Thus, despite the social welfare costs and political pressures, the FTC began during the 1990s to pursue a policy against cartel practices which increasingly benefited Japanese consumers as well as Japan's own multinational corporations and small business. This policy shift ameliorated foreign criticism stemming from the market-access issue.[177]

The commission's efforts to reduce the prices that Japanese consumers paid for basic products achieved compliance but not without resistance. During the mid-1980s, Hitachi Chemical Co. and seven other makers of resin components of circuit boards for electrical and electronic household appliances maintained a price-fixing agreement. Cartel member Toshiba Chemical Co. joined in a price hike. In 1987, the FTC ordered the eight firms to dissolve the cartel: seven complied but Toshibia Chemical refused. The commission issued a decision against the company in 1992, whereupon Toshiba appealed to the court, challenging the FTC's impartiality. During the complaint process the head of the Investigation Department handling the case was appointed as a new commissioner. Toshiba Chemical claimed that a commision which included the former Investigation Department official could not make a fair determination. The court ordered the FTC to reconsider the case in February 1994. The following year, the commission, with the new commissioner not participating in the decision, again ruled that Toshiba Chemical had violated the Antimonopoly Law. When the company appealed, the court sustained the ruling.[178]

[176] First, "Antitrust Enforcement in Japan," *Antitrust Law Journal*, 64 (1995), 164–6. Jeffrey P. Clemente, interview, Tokyo, September 4, 1995. Hired by DOJ, Mr Clemente assisted in the military base, bid-rigging cases for the U.S. government. The explanation regarding the commission's failure to bring criminal accusations was given to the author by a senior FTC official. The most balanced treatment of this matter is in Beeman, *Public Policy and Economic Competition in Japan*, 167–9.

[177] Iyori, "Antitrust and Industrial Policy in Japan," in Gary R. Saxonhouse and Kozo Yamamura, eds., *Law and Trade Issues American and Japanese Perspectives* (Seattle, WA, 1986), 64; First, "Antitrust Enforcement in Japan," 64 *Antitrust Law Journal* (1995), 166.

[178] "Ruling against Toshiba Chemical Upheld," *Japan Times* (Wednesday, October 4, 1995); interview, senior FTC official.

In the distribution sector, the FTC's proconsumer policy again confronted uneven compliance. As part of the "revolution" that shook Japan's distribution system in the 1990s, the two price-cutters, Daiei and Jusco, planned to discount their cosmetics in 1993. Shiseido, the nation's largest cosmetics producer, urged the discounters not to do so in exchange for a promise to provide them with free cosmetic samples and other sales promotion assistance. An undisclosed source informed the FTC (such informants remain confidential), however, that Shiseido's program, which depended on extensive use of its sales personnel, kept cosmetics prices high and generated excess profits for both the producer and some retailers specializing in cosmetics. The commission's investigation revealed, moreover, that the price-cutters were forced to end their bargain sales plans for fear that Shiseido might retaliate by halting shipments of its products. The FTC ordered the company to end its interference with the discounters. Shiseido backed down under a bureaucratically enforced plan to ease the transition from producer-imposed sales techniques to a system of price discounting. Meanwhile, in unrelated private actions discounters alleged that Shiseido had stopped supplying cosmetics because of breach by discounters of face-to-face selling obligations. The Supreme Court sustained Shiseido's conduct, however, finding that the practices were distinguishable from resale price maintenance despite the pricing effect. The FTC case, by contrast, raised more directly an issue of resale price maintenance.[179]

The FTC's willingness to use bureaucratic enforcement raised the specter of USTR intervention in the *Kodak* case. As noted above, in 1995 Kodak charged that Fuji film, its chief competitor in Japan, used "underhanded" tactics to keep Kodak out of the domestic market. The principal object of complaint was a system of rebates Fuji paid to film retailers. Under the AML (and U.S. antitrust law as well) many rebate practices were legal. Following published guidelines, the FTC used bureaucratic guidance to bring the industry's rebate practices within legal limits. Ironically, Kodak itself employed these same lawful rebates in the Japanese market. Initially, Kodak declined to seek redress through the FTC, claiming that the commission "did nothing." Instead, Kodak petitioned USTR to intervene.[180] Represented by a leading U.S. law firm, Fuji presented evidence showing

---

[179] "Shiseido Will Abide by FTC Order," *Japan Times* (Tuesday, October 3, 1995); Professor Hirabayashi Hidekatsu to Freyer, "Comments," August 29, 2004.

[180] See Chapter 3, this volume, and following: Charles Lake, "The US Government's Photographic Film and Paper Case against the Government of Japan," III (1) *JPRI Critique* (January 1996), 1–2; Toshihiro Yamada, "Camera Obscura: Fuji, Konica, Kodak All Using Shady Practices," *Tokyo Business* (October 1995), 36–7; "US Kodak and Fuji Photo Film to Launch Joint Development While Engaging in Dispute with Each Other; Is It Revolution to Revitalize Industry or an Unproductive Attempt? Concerns about Price Destruction Becoming Entrenched; Expansion of Share Aimed at Stagnant Sales," Yomiuri, Daily Summary of Japan Press, July 31, 1995.

that no clear violations existed. Fuji's American lawyer pointed out that the FTC "did not conclude that Fuji's rebates were illegal or exclusionary or anticompetitive. Fuji changed its rebates in order to be squeaky clean."[181] Meanwhile, the U.S. Antitrust Division made a preliminary investigation to determine whether Kodak had violated the antitrust laws at home. By late summer 1996, the Clinton Administration decided to submit Kodak's claim to the WTO's dispute settlement authority. Meanwhile, Kodak filed its own complaint with the FTC. Neither the WTO nor the commission would reach a decision until after the November U.S. presidential election.[182]

Kodak's defeat in the WTO decision of December 1997, had ambiguous implications. The *Oriental Economist* correctly concluded that Kodak lost because USTR could not prove the profoundly difficult factual issues upon which the company's claims rested. But loss on the merits obscured the question of what theory should govern the construction of Article XXIII 1(b.) in the WTO's dispute resolution process. The "US captured an extremely significant legal beachhead for future cases. For the first time ever, the WTO ruled that actions other than subsidies, e.g. nontariff barriers of various sorts, can 'nullify' a tariff." As the convergence of opinion among Japanese, European, and American antitrust officials suggested, moreover, sanctioning the WTO's expanded authority to challenge state-supported, private anticompetitive conduct facilitated increased cooperation among national antitrust authorities.[183]

Meanwhile, even Japanese advocates of deregulation reform suggested that Kodak's case was problematic. *Tokyo Business* observed that "[b]y essentially copying Fuji's strategies instead of attacking Fuji aggressively with some radically new approach, Kodak . . . ha[s] played the role of the 'permanent No. 2' so common in other Japanese industries." Once Kodak understood this, it "decided to play its only ace in the hole and petitioned USTR." *Tokyo Business* concluded that " 'Fuji bashing' alone will not open the market. Kodak . . . and the retailers as well need to re-think their own approaches to this market and break Fuji's stranglehold from the inside. It can be done." The contention was reasonable because the FTC had already laid the basis for increased competition. Coincidently, during the same time Kodak petitioned USTR, it launched a joint development program with Fuji. Understandably, a Japanese newspaper expressed surprise. "The picture of two firms shaking hands together with their right hands, while

[181] "Fuji US Lawyer Confident of Victory in Trade Row," *Japan Times* (Wednesday, October 4, 1995).
[182] "Kodak Practices may Affect Fuji Probe," *Japan Times* (Friday, September 8, 1995). "Japan Greets US WTO Move, Complaint Says Tokyo Erected Barriers to Kodak's Sales"; "Complaint to FTC," *Japan Times* (Saturday, June 15, 1996).
[183] Richard Katz, "Big Loss at the WTO: Kodak's Moment: Not a Pretty Picture," 66(1) *The Oriental Economist* (January 1998), quote at 8; see Chapter 3, Section IV; Chapter 5, Section IV; see also Chapter 6, Section IV, all in this volume.

repeatedly pummeling each other with their left hands, is so puzzling that one feels as if in a dark room."[184]

Another conspicuous case involved Japan's automobile distribution system. The last minute settlement Kantor and Hashimoto reached at the end of June 1995 was the culmination of a protracted dispute. Basically, the American position was that Japanese auto manufacturers controlled their dealer networks through financial ties, including rebates, market allocations of particular models, and other cooperative methods such as technical assistance which "virtually preclude[d] the establishment of direct franchise agreements between foreign automakers and Japanese dealers." A further charge was that Japanese authorities, especially the FTC, did not adequately enforce the AML "to require that dealerships be freely open to all manufacturers." At least two years before the final settlement, however, there had already been considerable action. The commission had conducted a major investigation of the automobile distribution sector and published its findings. In March 1994, the cabinet approved, as part of an External Economic Reform package, a policy supporting FTC enforcement of the Distribution and Business Practices Guidelines in the automobile sector.[185]

Based on its data, the FTC was already pursuing bureaucratic enforcement by the time Kantor and Hashimoto reached agreement. Although most of the evidence revealed few actual violations, there were practices nonetheless that required adjustment. For example, Toyota sought approval from the FTC to increase its holding of Daihatsu stock from 15 to 35 percent. The commission approved the purchase but "requested" that Toyota not interfere with Daihatsu's internal affairs. Since 1991, Japanese and American manufactures had already responded to certain market incentives including lower prices and innovations such as introducing an American vehicle with a right-hand steering wheel in 1992. Accordingly, the actual market share of foreign car imports in Japan had risen from 4.5 in 1991 to 8.7 in 1994. The FTC's reliance upon bureaucratic guidance reflected an understanding of organizational and market pressures already at work within the distribution sector facilitating increased competition.[186]

Under the 1995 autotrade agreement, the FTC became responsible for monitoring and enforcing compliance. The Toyota-Daihatsu order suggested how the FTC could use its authority to facilitate the opening of Japanese dealers to American auto manufactures. The use of bureaucratic enforcement in the monitoring process also coincided with social welfare tensions. After 1991, the market pressures within the autodistribution system

[184] Yamada, Toshihiro, "Camera Obscura: Fuji, Konica, Kodak All Using Shady Practices, Kodak," *Tokyo Business* (October 1995), 36–7.
[185] Uesugi, "New Directions," *Fordham Corporate Law Institute*, 24–35, quotes at 25.
[186] Ibid., 30–1. The reference to the Toyota–Daihatsu purchase comes from a senior FTC official, including use of the quoted word "requested."

heightened concerns that *keiretsu* relationships which helped marginal dealers avoid bankruptcy were breaking down. Larger automobile manufacturers, like big firms elsewhere in the Japanese distribution system, were feeling cost constraints caused by the status quo. In 1991 a trade journal survey reported that 33.6 percent of Japanese dealers had "suffered a loss." Not surprisingly, many firms looked upon the increasingly competitive market as providing little more than the "freedom to die." One way the FTC could ease the transition was to use its monitoring authority to encourage American manufacturers to develop their own marketing and service networks with Japanese distributors. The FTC's report showed that 78.8 percent of the dealers preferred American auto producers to create an automobile parts supply system, 73.3 percent needed a repair service system, and 53.5 percent called for the development of a secondhand car market. By comparison, 42.9 percent of the dealers felt that reducing the American automobile's price was most important. Thus, the FTC's role in monitoring the 1995 agreement suggested a flexible compliance strategy favoring increased competition between foreign and Japanese auto manufacturers while easing the market transition confronting Japanese dealers.[187]

The FTC achieved further success with a monitoring-compliance strategy in the pharmaceutical industry. Throughout the world governments limited the full operation of the market in order to maintain the price, content, and quality standards of pharmaceutical goods. Japan's version of this regulated industry employed a reimbursement system in which doctors and hospitals dispensed between 80 and 90 percent of the nation's prescription drugs, purchased at a discount from the nationwide price fixed by the health ministry. The difference between the fixed reimbursement price and the price at which the drugs were actually sold to consumers was a profit margin (*yakkasa*). Thus, doctors and hospitals bought drugs from wholesalers, which in turn purchased them from the manufacturers at prices which were determined more directly by the discount than by the fixed reimbursement price. This pricing mechanism was to a certain extent characteristic of the industry throughout the world. In Japan, however, cultural traditions involving gift-giving enmeshed the system in various illegal practices from rebates to social inducements such as golf outings.[188]

[187] Uesugi, "New Directions," *Fordham Corporate Law Institute*, 30–5 for statistics. For reference to social welfare concerns (including the quoted phrase) and their relation to the larger autotrade dispute, I am grateful to Professor Mitsuo Matsushita. On the FTC's role in enforcing the autotrade accord, see "Japan–US Auto Accord Revealed; Seven Items as Subject to Quantitative Criteria," Nihon Keizai, Daily Summary of Japanese Press August 4, 1995, 2–3; and see also senior FTC official for *Toyota-Daihatsu* case.
[188] Interviews, senior officials in Pharmaceutical Manufacturers Association (PMA) and Japan's PMA (JPMA) September 5, 1995; September 6, 1995; September 26, 1995; October 5, 1995; I wish to thank Mr Tadaharu Wakabayashi, whose initiative made possible those interviews; I am grateful too for his insights.

The FTC took more than a decade to transform the pharmaceutical industry's system of self-governance. In 1981, buffeted by inflationary pressures, the health ministry reduced the national reimbursement price by 18.6 percent. When the industry formed a cartel to protect itself, criticism came from U.S. pharmaceutical firms and Japanese wholesalers. As a result, the FTC challenged the cartel; after three years of legal dispute, the Japanese manufacturers surrendered. Instead of fines or other penalties, the FTC instituted an industry-wide council system which the commission monitored. The council made detailed regulations for the industry based on FTC guidelines. Assisted by lawyers, the top executives of the individual firms belonging to the council formulated rules which in turn required certification by the commission. Through a committee structure within the industry, rule infractions were investigated and adjudicated, subject to commission supervision. When questions or disputes arose, further consultation with the commission was mandated.[189]

As the industry became more attuned to competition policy, the FTC refined the system, maintaining necessary oversight. In 1986, the Pharmaceutical Manufacturers Association (PMA) representing U.S. firms opened a Tokyo office, facilitating more effective collaboration with Japan's PMA within the council system. The FTC published its guidelines concerning the distribution system in 1991, which prohibited manufacturers from negotiating with hospitals, doctors, or other dispensers over prices. During the early 1990s, the industry increasingly developed and enforced its own codes within individual firms. Under FTC guidance, according to one company's internal statement, these rules became "more specific over time. The core Rules and Regulations that were initially enacted contained vague standards that could be and often were freely interpreted by some members without regard to the spirit of the regulations." But "[a]s a result of . . . changes, a higher and more consistent level of compliance will likely be expected of all association members in the future." The statement concluded that although "the regulations make a good case-study for the regulatory gradualism that is so common in Japan, the trend of the . . . regulations towards greater specificity and compliance should also not be underestimated."[190]

The FTC also broadened its scope by asserting extraterritorial antitrust jurisdiction against a Canadian multinational corporation. In 1998, the FTC found evidence to prove that MDS Nordion of Canada, a leading producer of molybdenum 99 – a component of radioactive medical products – had implemented long-term supply contracts making the sale of its product to Japanese pharmaceutical firms contingent on their agreement to

---

[189] Ibid., "Overview of the Fair Competition Rules of the Prescription Pharmaceutical Industry Limiting the Offering of Premiums."
[190] Ibid.; see note 188 above.

purchase solely from the Canadian company. Nordion had no offices in Japan, though it authorized a Japanese lawyer to handle documents and transactions with Japanese firms. Following an investigation, the FTC issued a recommendation decision against Nordion which the company accepted "without complaint."[191]

Perhaps the most important criminal cartel case the FTC won was the Tokyo High Court's decision against nine businessmen from Hitachi, Toshiba, and other leading Japanese drainage equipment manufacturers. The court upheld the commission's accusation that the companies' employees and local governments, which purchased drainage equipment for public sewage construction, had joined in collusive tendering. The individuals' prison sentences ranged from 8 to 10 months (suspended for two years), while the fines imposed upon the separate companies were between ¥40 and ¥60 million. The decision was significant in part because it opened government officials to criminal prosecution if they were found guilty of collusive procurement practices.[192]

The FTC also entered the controversy over the restructuring of Japan's telecommunication's giant, Nippon Telegraph and Telephone Corporation (NTT). The NTT controversy engendered many technologically complex and politically difficult problems, which the coalition government dealt with slowly and episodically during the turn of the century. The FTC nonetheless took the position that the AML applied to NTT prior to as well as after any restructuring or possible division.[193] An FTC report, which a leading LDP official endorsed, affirmed that the NTT "group be restructured to encourage competition among group companies" and that NTT's "control" over the affiliated mobile communications firm, DoCoMo, "be eased by reducing NTT's holding of DoCoMo stocks so that the DoCoMo can compete with NTT." By 2001 such pressures had influenced two significant developments: an "extraordinary" alliance between AT&T and DoCoMo, and a Japan–U.S. dispute over NTT's connection fees which a MITI official declared should be addressed "by further deregulating Japan's telecommunications industry and encouraging competition."[194]

---

[191] Itoda, "Competition Policy of Japan and Its Global Implementation," in Jones and Matsushita, eds., *Competition Policy in the Global Trading System*, 63; Professor Hirabayashi Hidekatsu to Freyer, "Comments," August 29, 2004.

[192] Interviews with senior FTC officials and *bengoshi*, who were informed about the cases.

[193] "Fight over NTT Putting Drag on Competitiveness," *Nikkei Weekly* (May 6, 1996) and interview with senior FTC official.

[194] Itoda, "Competition Policy of Japan and Its Global Implementation," in Jones and Matsushita, eds., *Competition Policy in the Global Trading System*, quote at 66; "NTT's Nasty Surprise," *The Economist* (October 28, 2000), 61; Michiyo Nakamoto, "Top Japanese Official Warns NTT over Charges," *Financial Times* (June 2, 2000), 8; Michiyo Nakamoto, "NTT Faced with Review of Operations and Rates," *Financial Times* (May 31, 2000), 6; Korine et al., "Partnering with the Unfamiliar," 13(2) *Business Strategy Review* (Summer 2002), 41.

The FTC continued to protect the interests of small business. Thus, the commission was sensitive to the complaints of small electrical appliance dealers and modest-sized retailers that large discount stores were competing unfairly by offering to sell television sets at a price of ¥1. Consistent with public outcry from small and medium business associations and their elected representatives in the LDP and SDP, the FTC issued orders holding that such sales violated unfair trade provisions. The commission thus condemned such "market anarchy" as counterproductive to achieving the healthy competition the cartel and criminal prosecutions promoted.[195]

VI. CONCLUSION

Japanese and foreign authorities evaluated differently SII's impact on antitrust enforcement within Japanese society. Although American multinational corporations increasingly gained access to Japan's market after the early 1990s, U.S. trade officials and experts continued to contend that the traditional Japanese collaboration between government and business impeded developing an American-style competition consciousness. This view, reflected in the *Kodak/Fuji* argument assumed that Japanese big business, bureaucratic, and LDP leaders pursued basically the same policy goals between the 1950s and the millennium. Considering SII's practical and symbolic significance within the wider disrupted political and economic context circumscribing Japan's antitrust regime since the 1990s, by contrast, American antitrust authorities concluded that the FTC employed bureaucratic enforcement as well as stronger civil and criminal cartel prosecutions. Even so, the FTC's enforcement record may be seen as relatively effective, though the paucity of private actions was a major problem in Japan.

While Japanese antitrust authorities generally agreed with their American counterparts on these points, they compared the improved enforcement record to the longer struggle waged against the antagonistic political culture dominating Japan since the occupation. Thus, the deregulation and antitrust discourse – especially the fundamental shift from opposing to supporting stronger antitrust enforcement – suggested a search for policy consensus to sustain bureaucratic implementation of market-conforming legal rules and promote the financial restructuring of Japanese multinational corporations, even at the cost of weakening the *keiretsu* system. The new policy legitimacy encouraged, moreover, FTC bureaucratic and judicial actions facilitating the continuing defense of small business and proconsumer private suits. During 2003–04 Keidanren's and the LDP's support ebbed, however, leaving in doubt the fate of yet another round of

---

[195] Senior FTC official; *Japan Times* (June 6, 1996).

amendments strengthening the Antimonopoly Law.[196] The FTC's enforcement capabilities – already having attained the highest level since the occupation – may well have reached a new limit.

[196] Shigeyoshi Ezaki, Etsuko Hara, and Vassili Moussis, "Merger Control in Japan," *The Asia Pacific Antitrust Review 2004* (Global Competition Review, Special Report, London, 2004), 49–52, especially quote at 51–2: "The Amendments to the AMA were expected to be enacted in April 2004 but recent very strong opposition to the amendments, especially from the Japan Federation of Economic Organizations, 'Keidenien,' means that it is now uncertain when, and if, such amendments will be adopted." I am also grateful to professor and former FTC official Hirabayashi Hidekatsu for material in the text.

5

Antitrust in Postwar European Social Welfare Capitalism

The postwar immigration of antitrust to Europe followed a middle course. During and after the cold war the European Community accepted a degree of bureaucratic interventions into the market to promote social welfare that was closer to the Japanese and Australian forms than to those of the United States. The European Community nonetheless adopted antitrust more readily than did Japan, primarily because of the overriding commitment to market integration.[1] Still, envisioning the rise of antitrust in Europe as resulting from the subordination of nationalist ideology and political contingency to Americanized efficiency-seeking political economy raises significant questions. The argument that follows is that throughout the postwar era of uneven economic growth, the public discourse constituting competition policy not only shaped European market integration, but also engendered a competition consciousness promoting the broader goal of equal treatment among private as well as public enterprises. This in turn reinforced bureaucratic independence and discretion. Except for giving much attention to the German system and passing reference to the British, French, and Polish regimes, the following discussion does not focus on the axis of development: the interaction between national and European Union (i.e., integration) experience. Rather, the story emphasizes the core institutional, political, and ideological interactions which enabled the European Commission to impose upon business stronger social welfare accountability as compared to U.S. antitrust.

Section I presents evidence showing that during the Allied occupation of Germany, although the United States did not succeed in imposing an antitrust regime, the collaboration among officials in the administration of

---

[1] Clifford A. Jones and Mitsui Matsushita, eds., *Completion Policy in the Global Trading System Perspectives from the EU, Japan and the USA* (The Hague, 2002); Thomas K. McCraw, ed., *Creating Modern Capitalism How Entrepreneurs, Companies, and Countries Triumphed In Three Industrial Rovolutions*; (Cambridge, MA, 2000); Daniel Yergin and Joseph Stanislaw, *The Commanding Heights: The Battle between Government and the Marketplace that is Remaking the Modern World* (New York, 1998); Alfred D. Chandler, Franco Amatori, and Takashi Hikino, eds., *Big Business and the Wealth of Nations* (Cambridge, UK, 1999); Andrew Moravcsik, *The Choice for Europe: Social Purpose and State Power from Messina to Maaestricht* (Ithaca, NY, 1998), 90, 136, 147–59, 181–4, 204, 218–19, 233–6, 479–87.

the "decartelization program" promoted a competition policy compromise consistent with Ordo Liberalism and the social market economy. Section II suggests how this compromise influenced the European Coal and Steel Community (ECSC) and the Federal Cartel Law of 1957.[2] Section III considers how each of these factors shaped the creation of the European Economic Community and its Commission's role in promoting social welfare capitalism from 1957 to 1986. Section IV examines how amid the struggle for competitive advantage and the end of the cold war the commission managed the transition from community to union. It also considers the growing tension between trade and competition policies, the accession of ten new member states in 2004, and significant modernization reforms.[3]

I. ANTITRUST AND THE ALLIED OCCUPATION OF GERMANY, 1945–1949

Most studies of the Allied occupation's antitrust regime focus on the administration of the U.S. program. Contemporary critics concluded that a pro-U.S. business military command – confronting, first, massive material destruction and hunger, and, then, the political struggle resulting from the partition of Germany at the onset of the cold war – undermined antitrust enforcement advocated by "zealous trust busters."[4] Less conspicuous, however, was the confrontation of the Germans with the Allies' divided institutional regime. German business, government, and academic policy makers disagreed among themselves whether antitrust policy could be

---

[2] In addition to the citations below (including "Decartelization Program"), I am grateful for interviews with participants Robert R. Bowie, April 30, 2002 and John Kenneth Galbraith, May 9, 2003; and Sydney Willner's permission to cite his unpublished, *The First Step in European Integration: A U.S. Role, A Personal Reminiscence*; I thank, for assistance, Karen Ferguson, Mr. Willner's daughter.

[3] In addition to the citations below, I thank the following participants for interviews: Charles S. Stark, May 30, 2003; Professor Anna Fornalczyk, April 5, 2000; Geza Feketekuty, June 17, 1999; Zbigniew Lewicki, June 19, 2000; and Alfred and Eve Micron, March 8, 2000. See also, *Economist* (July 31, 2004), 51.

[4] Compare Robert Wolfe, ed., *Americans as Proconsuls: United States Military Government in Germany and Japan, 1944–1952* (Carbondale, IL, 1984); James Stewart Martin, *All Honorable Men* (Boston, 1950); Lucius D. Clay, *Germany and the Fight for Freedom* (Cambridge, MA, 1950); *Report of Committee Appointed to Review the Decartelization Program in Germany* (April 15, 1949), Garland S. Ferguson, chairman, and "Supplemental Report of Samuel Isseks," University of Wyoming American Heritage Center, Copy of report located in Joseph J. O'Mahoney Papers, Box 341; Wyatt Wells, *Antitrust and the Formation of the Postwar World* (New York, 2002), 137–86; John Kenneth Galbraith, *A Life in Our Times: Memoirs* (Boston, 1981), 240, 246–55; Michael Beschloss, *The Conquerors: Roosevelt, Truman and the Destruction of Hitler's Germany, 1941–1945* (New York, 2002), 260–96; and Robert Bowie, interview, April 30, 2002, including quoted phrase; Willner, *First Step in European Integration*; John Kenneth Galbraith, interview, May 9, 2003.

adapted to the postwar nation's capitalist economy. Studies that considered the German perspective disagreed about the success of the Allied effort on its own terms, but they nonetheless suggested that, ironically, divisions among the Allies ultimately provided the procompetition German policy makers with sufficient legitimacy to institute an effective German antitrust regime, despite considerable business opposition.[5]

At the war's end in Europe, the Allies possessed divergent images of antitrust. The Americans perceived a direct connection between instituting an antitrust regime – aimed especially at eradicating German cartels – and the creation of a nation capable of living peaceably with the world. General Lucius Clay, the military governor of the U.S. zone of occupied Germany until 1949, summed up the multiple peacemaking goals as "the four D's": denazification, demilitarization, democratization, and decartelization.[6] Yet even the Americans disagreed over how vigorously to pursue antitrust among these four objectives. The British Labour Government, which came to power a few months after Germany's surrender, supported antitrust as a punitive principle, because it affirmed that German big business had fostered Hitler's rise to power and because government officials believed decartelization could facilitate Britain's postwar trade advantage. French authorities vaguely linked antitrust to procuring reparations from Germany and ensuring its weakened influence within the postwar European economy. Russian officials held similar views, though their policies were more exploitive. Even so, as the Soviets steadily pursued an independent course, U.S., British and, eventually, French cooperation prevailed in the antitrust field.[7]

The Germans, too, were divided about antitrust. Many business people, government officials, and academics favored administrative regulation of cartel and monopoly *abuse* like that which had existed during the Weimar Republic. For them, anticompetitive conduct could promote technological efficiency, protect small business, and ameliorate labor radicalism; they defined "abuse" as behavior undercutting these values. Still, most popular opinion equated antitrust with punitive measures designed to limit Germany's economic revival, most particularly U.S. Treasury Secretary Morgenthau's plan to democratize and demilitarize Germany by reconstituting it as an agricultural economic order. Among those holding this

---

[5] Volcker R. Berghahn, *The Americanization of West German Industry, 1945–1973* (Bennington Spa, NY, 1986), 1–111; Walter Damm, "National and International Factors Influencing Cartel Legislation in Post-War Germany," Unpublished Ph.D. Dissertation, University of Chicago, 1958; David J. Gerber, *Law and Competition in Twentieth Century Europe Protecting Prometheus* (Oxford, 2001) 254–76; H. K. Bock and H. Korsch, "Allied Decartelization and Deconcentration Laws," in W. Friedmann, ed., *Anti-Trust Laws: A Comparative Symposium* (Toronto, 1956), 138–75, 189–237; Hagen Schulze, *Germany: A History* (Cambridge, MA, 1998), 288–320.

[6] Beschloss, *Conquerors*, 273, 285.

[7] Damm, "Factors Influencing Cartel Legislation," 129–32.

critical view were Germany's big business leaders, such as the electrical equipment manufacturers, the Krupp steel dynasty, and the managers of the giant chemical conglomerate, I.G. Farben. By contrast, the Social Democrat Party (SDP), like the British Labour Government, believed that many of these industrialists had aided the Nazis, who in turn had persecuted the SDP, condemning members to death in concentration camps. Thus, SDP leaders supported punitive uses of antitrust against big business. Finally, some Christian Socialists and the small group of Ordo Liberals – who despite Nazi rule maintained a theory of competitive market constitutionalism embracing antitrust theories – resisted American antitrust activism as relying too much on courts instead of administrators.[8]

The Germans had encountered Allied antitrust policy statements prior to surrender. Following the Fourth Principle of the Atlantic Charter announced by Roosevelt and Churchill in 1941, the United States consistently pushed for an antitrust policy against international cartels. After Pearl Harbor, the United States consistently pressured its Allies to support antitrust measures, both as a condition for receiving military and economic aid and in conjunction with the unconditional peace terms to be imposed upon defeated Germany and Japan. At the Tehran Conference of December 1943, and the Yalta Conference of February 1945, allied leaders divided Germany into zones of occupation. In part to enforce political policy the Yalta Accords reaffirmed the need for a "radical decartelization" program. Thus, on the road to defeat Germans repeatedly confronted official references to an Allied antitrust policy. These provisions were, however, cryptically framed as the means to attaining major political goals. Nazi propaganda noted "decartelization" primarily as a tool by which the Allies would implement a punitive peace. Only some legal–economic experts remaining under cover since the Weimar era understood antitrust to be anything else.[9]

Following the Allied victory, "decartelization" acquired more concrete meaning. As Allied military authority spread throughout Germany, the U.S. Joint Chiefs of Staff issued JCS-1067 on April 26, 1945, though its terms did not receive general publicity until months later. In order to "decentralize" and "demilitarize" the economy, military authorities should "prohibit all cartels or other private business arrangements and cartel like organizations" and "effect a dispersion of ownership and control of German industry." In order to implement this policy Allied authorities "were to make a survey of combines and pools, mergers, holding companies, and interlocking directorates and communicate the results, together with the recommendations for action, to the governments through the JCS."

---

[8] Ibid., 157–69; Schulze, *Germany*, 286–97; Gerber, *Protecting Prometheus*, 254–76.
[9] Damm, "Factors Influencing Cartel Legislation," 132–4, quote at 133; Schulze, *Germany*, 279–85; Gerber, *Protecting Prometheus*, 259–61.

Between mid-July and early August of 1945, Truman, Stalin, and Clement Attlee, who had just replaced Churchill as British prime minister, endorsed the decartelization program as part of the Potsdam Declaration. Decartelization references supported the main goals which sought not to "destroy and enslave" Germany, but to assist the nation's people to "prepare for eventual reconstruction of their life on a democratic basis." By the summer of 1946, however, the Russians rejected the U.S. demand to unify the four zones' economic administration. Ultimately, the military commanders of each occupation zone determined policy, including the decartelization program.[10]

The Nuremberg war-crimes trials that convened in 1945 legitimized the decartelization program, indirectly. The prosecution of the Nazi authorities responsible for "war crimes and crimes against humanity" included business people who had exploited foreign slave laborers. These business men reinforced the negative images of exploitive cartels, which the United States in particular used to justify inclusion of "decartelization" among the 4-Ds. Thus, the images of economic exploitation, like the "crimes committed by Germans during the war and in the extermination camps received the widest possible publicity, with no attempt to cover them up." The effect of the "trials was their elimination of any possibility that Germans could take refuge in legends of betrayal and a 'stab in the back' as had happened after World War I." Inferentially, that logic undercut German claims that the 4-Ds embodied nothing more than the putative motives identified with the Morgenthau Plan. A *US Military Government Weekly Information Bulletin* article entitled "Decartelization" depicted the ideological implications: an image included various industries entangled in the coils of an enormous octopus bearing the Nazi Swastika.[11]

Implementing the 4-Ds facilitated the influence of non-Nazi labor, business, academic, and government authorities. As required by JCS-1067, investigators from the branches of the military government conducted "decartelization" surveys. One investigator was Heinrich Kronstein, a German émigré lawyer. During the war, Kronstein aided Arnold's efforts to fashion the U.S. Antitrust Division's campaign against international cartels. Early in the occupation he informed military authorities about the Ordo Liberals who had espoused antitrust ideas despite Nazi persecution.[12]

---

[10] JCS 1067, part I, section 3(e), and part II, no. 37; Berlin Protocol of the Potsdam Conference, section B, paragraphs 12, 13, 15 (August 2, 1945); Damm, "Factors Influencing Cartel Legislation," 132–4, Beschloss, *Conquerors*, 262–70, quoted at 267–8; Schulze, *Germany*, 293–4.

[11] Schulze, *Germany*, 289; and Willner, *First Step in European Integration*, 3–4, 10–12. Damm, "Factors Influencing Cartel Legislation," 160–1, citing the issue dated March 3, 1947, at 33.

[12] I am grateful to Heinrich Kronstein's son Werner for a telephone interview, May 17, 2002, and for permission to quote from the papers. Damm, "Factors Influencing Cartel

During August and September 1945 investigators, including Kronstein, reported that "closer coordination is required between the activities of the German agencies and those of the Military Government." Because the "de-Nazification policy as applied to industry and commerce is considered difficult of application," some "German officials" suggested that "a committee might be formed consisting of the Military Government de-Nazification teams, several government officials, several prominent businessmen, and several representatives of labor for ... recommendations based on a study." Thus the "implementation of the de-Nazification policy in industry might be ... partially assumed by the German people themselves in the form of advisory councils created to assist the special de-Nazification Sections."[13]

Kronstein's interviews with German businessmen revealed the ambiguous early impact of the Allied decartelization program. The military governments did not implement a uniform policy of breaking up or "deconcentrating" industry; instead, zone commanders pursued piecemeal dismantling or reorganization of corporate giants such as I.G. Farben and the coal and steel firms. These episodic deconcentration efforts were distinguishable from the Allied policy toward cartels. Thus, Kronstein's investigations revealed that certain international cartels controlling light bulbs and suppliers of I.G. Farben were endeavoring to reconstitute themselves. For example, two managers of Metallgesellschaft – which supplied I.G. Farben with aluminum and nickel – who were advising the military government, were "deeply concerned" about whether they could return to the "friendly" prewar "relations" with British Metal. A "case pending between a British and Swiss company ... will determine whether the shares will be held by the British or the Swiss." The German firm had "lost control over the Swiss company in connection with the compromise between the Swiss firm and the US Government." In addition, given that the prewar "nickel business was completely controlled by" the International Nickel cartel, a manager was now "quite concerned ... that the Russians may disturb the market."[14]

Kronstein's interviews revealed how the denazification program directly threatened certain managers. Kronstein told one informant involved in the

Legislation," 137–9; Berghahn, *Americanization of West German Industry*, 155–9; Schulz, *Germany*, 290; David J. Gerber, "Heinrich Kronstein and the Development of United States Antitrust Law," in Marcus Hutter, ed. (full cite, ch. II, section I).

[13] [A. J. Gottlieb, Henrich Kronstein, investigators], "German Agencies in Bavaria," Georgetown University Special Collections (GUSC), Heinrich Kronstein Papers (HKP), Box 1, Folder General, quotes at 1, 9.

[14] H. Kronstein, "Report on Interview with Dr. Peterson and Mr. Euler of Metallgellschaft," September 24, 1945, Box 1, quotes at 1, 2; Heinrich Kronstein, "Cartels and Combines (Decentralization of Economic Structure)," Box 10, Cartel, HKP/GUSC [no pagination, n.d., but internal evidence indicates late 1946–early 1947].

electrical equipment cartel that his "resignation is unavoidable and should come soon" because he was "in the 'mandatory dismissal' class." Under such pressure business managers and executives provided investigators with useful information about cartel relations. The same informant, Kronstein reported, "remains greatly interested in going into the bulb field. Braun-Boveri and Bosch are both convinced that they should oppose the resurrection of A.E.G.–Siemens monopoly." In addition, "unsolicited," he "called my attention to the conditions" showing that "Siemens and A.E.G. controlled the field completely and are understood to have brought prices to a ridiculously high level. The position of Siemens–A.E.G. is based on their contracts with Philips [Dutch], the American firms whose names are unknown to him, and the French ... cable cartel." The informant also "brought up the patent problem," which was central to numerous cartel cases that the U.S. Justice Department was currently prosecuting in America after the wartime suspension. Finally, he noted, the French Occupation officials were forcing negotiations over purchases of transformers: they did "not want to permit exports from the French zone unless corresponding imports are exchanged."[15]

Decartelization always had a contingent place among the other 4-D objectives. Reports concluded that economic disruption and hunger threatened Germany's social order, including the attainment of demilitarization, denazification, and democratization.[16] During the summer following the German surrender one of Kronstein's fellow investigators authored a report revealing the political and social tensions that threatened to undermine the punitive goals of JCS-1067. "Based on personal observations" and "interviews with hundreds of German officials and large numbers of civilians," he perceived that a "deceptive picture" had emerged that despite massive material destruction as well as "the countless thousands of bodies buried under the rubble; life appears to get slowly underway; major political resistance has not so far been noticeable; and the German people seem co-operative and even docile." However, an "acute problem" concerning the "de-Nazification of industry and business" was that "[m]any industrial leaders and managers in fact had been able to keep out of the Party, while having intimate connections with Party leaders and organizations and using the need for industrial production to the utmost

---

[15] Heinrich Kronstein, "Report on Conference with Mr. Rachel," September 26, 1945, Box 1, HKP/GUSC, quotes at 1, 2, 3.

[16] Beschloss, *Conquerors*, 272–8; Schulze, *Germany*, 292–5; Byron Price to Truman, "Memorandum," November 9, 1945, distributed by president to secretaries of state, War, and Navy, November 28, 1945; Report, Earl G. Harrison to Truman, concerning "displaced persons ... with particular reference to Jewish refugees – who may possibly be stateless or non-repatriable," Truman Papers, Official File, HST Presidential Library. See also Stig Dagerman, *German Autumn* (London, 1988, English trans.; original Swedish, 1946).

effect. Often I have found that these men were hated by employees and workers even more than those who had at least openly identified themselves with the Nazi Party."[17]

The report identified profound problems. Despite the punitive language of JCS-1067 and the Potsdam Declaration, the Allies had not yet fully settled upon the "practical interpretation of the de-militarization of German industry. The question, the answer to which has so far been postponed, is whether German industrial life should be resumed as far as physically possible and subject to strict control over any war potential, or whether it should be eliminated, except for certain categories of industry. In the U.S. zone the question has so far been answered in the latter sense." But "it was not yet possible to estimate the effect of such a policy" on whether "a low but tolerable standard of living" could sustain the "absorption of the German populations removed from Poland, Czechoslovakia, and Hungary." Nevertheless, for the western zones, the "most conservative estimate" of the number of these refugees was about "five million." And it was "very unlikely that such a number could be absorbed" within a primarily agricultural economy, "even over a space of many years without starvation on a large scale." Furthermore, "where the refugees are concentrated" the "revival of democracy" confronted the "danger of a revival of militant nationalism. … The concentration of millions of uprooted and homeless Germans, living under extreme hardship and brought into Germany for racial reasons, is likely to stimulate a feeling of national isolation." The implications for the revival of organized labor and democracy and relations with the Russians were ominous.[18]

These warnings provided the context for Kronstein's evaluation of the decartelization program. He reported serous difficulties concerning "economic decentralization, whose failure may have serious repercussions on the process of political decentralization" required to establish a democratic Germany. Kronstein noted that due in part to contentiousness regarding Russia's primary preoccupation with achieving its reparation goals, "a 'steering committee' on IG Farben organized by the four occupying powers never would operate successfully." This example revealed the "problems arising out of the attempt to deal with corporation issues before the political structure and the form of general economic organization within which the corporation has to operate, are clarified." As the occupation regime evolved, however, Allied officials repeatedly discovered that "the finding of general rules again depends on a previous solution of the general political and economic problems, wherefore the success of a law drafted by the Legal Division of the Military Government providing for general provisions on

---

[17] W. Friedmann, "Military Government and Political Developments in Germany," Box 1, Folder General, HKP/GUSC, [compiled May–July, 1945], quotes at 1, 8.
[18] Ibid., 15.

the dissolution of combines is subject to substantial doubt." Kronstein provided further examples of cartel and monopoly problems drawn from his own investigations into Carl Zeiss and Schott & Genossen's "complete control over optical glass and over a very important part of optical instruments," the reviving "light bulbs" cartel, the British firm Unilever's involvement with I.G. Farben, and others.[19]

Kronstein found, too, that the Allied military government itself contributed to these problems. The complex maze of patents, shareholding, interlocking directorates, and international cartel agreements presented U.S. authorities with conflicting choices. An aggressive prosecution campaign exacerbated the issues of democratization and the inability to institute uniform laws. The activists not only failed to achieve their enforcement goals – particularly an extensive deconcentration of German big business – but their vigorous investigations reinforced fragmented policy making within and between each Occupation zone. As an example, in order to resist the "development of competitors in the western zone," officials from the Zeiss glass-making firm persuaded U.S. Air Force authorities – for whom the commodity was essential – "to take the leading Zeiss investors out of the Russian zone and to establish a research undertaking in the works of Steinheil & Sohne under the management of the Zeiss inventors." Moreover, despite having been Nazi Party members, the Zeiss officials received Air Force "protection," providing "complete freedom of movement through the country," whereby they prevented "any attempt to go on the optical glass market," threatening a "boycott in regard to other articles."[20]

Kronstein noted that certain Bavarian and south German officials insisted upon effective antitrust enforcement. "The Bavarian government is quite concerned about transactions such as that between Zeiss and Steinheil," he declared, "since they believe that those transactions will finally bring about the failure of the political decentralization." South German "local governments, fully aware of the cartel and combine problem, repeatedly complain about the fact that Military Government, especially the Finance Division, rather supports the combine development than hinders it." Thus, the Bavarian government "has asked at least five times for permission to enact legislation by virtue of which the sale of business enterprises, blocks of shares, etc. shall be prohibited unless licensed. They have never received an answer and therefore had to remain absolutely passive in spite of the dangerous developments in Bavaria described in the Zeiss and Siemens cases." The Bavarian authorities, Kronstein explained, "cooperated closely with Franz Böhm, the excellent leader of the German antitrust movement." Since his early days as a German lawyer, Kronstein had known of Böhm; both men were Ordo Liberals.[21]

---

[19] Heinrich Kronstein, "Cartels and Combines," Box 10, Cartels, HKP/GUSC, quotes at 1, 2.
[20] Ibid., 3, 4.   [21] Ibid., 3, 11.

Kronstein actively supported proponents of a German antitrust policy. Secretly they had opposed the "Nazi system" from 1939 to the unsuccessful "revolt of July, 1944," he said, constituting "a German group willing and prepared to take over the government. One of the plans of this group was dissolution of cartels and combines." Böhm was the reporter for a committee of "very brave professors" addressing this issue; most of them "were members of the Freiburg [University] faculty," though not Böhm himself. Kronstein emphasized that "[t]his anti-cartel and combine thinking is not limited to this liberal group but is very strong in the Christian Social movement which beyond any doubt ... has the majority in Bavaria and a very strong position in the whole Western zone." These government officials and academic experts, "very much in favor of the anti-cartel and combine movement," thus were "much concerned" that the "present actual trend to increase concentration ... will go faster than the enactment, and especially the enforcement" of a national antitrust law. "They are afraid that in the final end the Allies will come to an understanding with the cartel and combine powers which may offer some advantages in regard to a centralized execution of the reparation program, and which have their private international connections with the local governments which the anti-Nazis do not have." These Ordo Liberals and Christian Socialists, therefore "believe," he said, "that they should be authorized to enact legislation."[22]

These antitrust-policy disputes compounded the conflict within the U.S. military command. By September, 1945, the antitrust activists clashed with Clay's pro-big business subordinates, including Joseph M. Dodge, Assistant Deputy for Trade and Finance. Kronstein and other investigators revealed that the U.S. military's Finance Branch had supported the cartel and monopoly practices of business people with Nazi backgrounds. Accordingly, Clay strengthened the antitrust activists, creating a Division of Investigation and Cartels. Kronstein had recommended establishing such an office.[23] Performing his procurement duties for the Army during the war, Clay had adjusted the operational, technological, and production imperatives of large corporations to residual antitrust values maintained by the War Production Board. Consistent with this wartime experience, Clay suggested a willingness to reconcile antitrust values with the practical business necessities of the devastated German economy.[24] Even so, Kronstein confirmed that breaking up or deconcentrating German business was impossible without further effort. The public exposure of cartel practices,

[22] Ibid., 11, 12.
[23] Ibid., 11, 14–16; "Establishment of a Division of Investigation of Cartels and External Assets," Command, Lt. General Lucius Clay, September 12, 1945 Box 1, Folder Cartels, HKP/GUSC.
[24] Robert Bowie, interview, April 30, 2002.

however, disrupted collusive agreements by encouraging competitors. Indirectly, then, decartelization selectively promoted the peace objectives of democratization, demilitarization, and denazification.

By late 1946 economic experts questioned whether antitrust would aid the reconstruction of Germany. As the Russian resistance hardened against the U.S. demand that the occupation zones should be unified under one economic administration, economists Edward S. Mason and John Kenneth Galbraith offered Clay critical evaluations of the usefulness of dec-artelization in the 4-D program. At Harvard, Mason taught a graduate course on economics and antitrust; Galbraith had taught a similar course to undergraduates. Still, Galbraith – a proponent of the economic theories of John M. Keynes – was not much concerned about cartels and monopoly as long as the government's management of macroeconomic policies pro-moted both market efficiency and social welfare. No friend of big business, Galbraith believed that tax, securities, price, and labor regulations would be more effective than antitrust in promoting the technological efficiency and social accountability of giant corporations. Focusing on the strategic need to rebuild Germany's industrial capacity on the basis of "managed" capitalist democracy rather than communism, Galbraith saw little need for decartelization. This was essentially the policy Secretary of State James F. Byrnes announced in Stuttgart on September 6, 1946, conceding the divi-sion of Germany's economic administration into eastern and western zones; the same strategic and macroeconomic policies influenced the partition of Germany in 1949.[25]

Mason's position rejecting the value of an antitrust regime in the reconstruction of Germany was complex. Before and after the war he pioneered economic theories incorporating market-efficiency in order to make antitrust enforcement more effective. During the war he headed the influential Economic Research Division of the Office of Strategic Services (OSS) and was Deputy Chair of the Cartel Committee. In the latter capacity he led the policy which made receiving U.S. foreign aid partly contingent on the Allies agreeing to support the adoption of antitrust institutions, in the postwar Occupation governments of Germany and Japan as well as in the Allies' own nations.[26] Nevertheless, Mason resisted the contention of the Justice Department and the Antitrust Division that international cartels were part of Germany's "master plan" to maintain totalitarian control. Regarding the advisability of imposing an antitrust law, he argued in *Controlling World Trade Cartels and Commodity Agreements* (1946) that: "Of all the institutions and policies known to history ... those imposed by

[25] Galbraith, *Life in Our Times*, 240, 246–55, 177; Galbraith, interview, May 9, 2003; Oral History Interview, Edward S. Mason, by Richard D. McKenzie, Cambridge, MA, July 17, 1973, 13–18 (HSTPL); Schulze, *Germany*, 291–4.
[26] Wells, *Antitrust*, 110–13, 166, 208, 211; and Chapter 1, Section V.

victors on a vanquished enemy are likely to be the most impermanent." The "only lasting structural changes that can be made in the German economic and political system will have to be made, in the absence of continuous occupation, by the Germans themselves."[27]

Concerning the antitrust issue in particular, Mason's and Kronstein's views presented noteworthy contrasts. About the time that Mason published his book, Kronstein declared in an investigation report: "In the interest of successful completion of the economic decentralization program it is necessary to open doors to every possible [German] movement acting in the interest of an anti-combine and cartel program. It is impossible to impose such a program on any society." Even so, Kronstein hoped that the Germans attaining power would be antitrust advocates such as Böhm and the leaders of the Bavarian Christian Socialists. Mason, however, believed that following "a thoroughgoing policy of de-Nazification" and the "departure of the last foot soldier from enemy soil," the "political forces that will, in fact, come to power in Germany, may be expected to deal effectively with the problem of private monopoly, but not by an anti-monopoly policy or antitrust procedures." Thus, Mason suggested, future competition "will not, in the author's opinion, be that of IG Farben, Krupp and Siemens-Schuckert. Rather will it be the competition of German state trading companies."[28]

As Kronstein suggested might happen, the Allies proved unable to negotiate a common decartelization program. During periodic meetings beginning in August 1945, the Committee of the Allied Control Authority in Berlin failed to agree on a mandatory decartelization law which strictly defined the sorts of enterprises coming within per se prohibitions. Based upon a rigorous showing of evidence, exemptions could be authorized if they were not contrary to the law's basic purposes. Initially the American, Soviet, and French representatives accepted this approach; but the British resisted it in favor of granting the Coordinating Committee or some other body the authority to prohibit only proven cases of "excessive concentrations of economic power." Finally, following nearly a year of contentious negotiations General Clay unilaterally issued for the U.S. zone Law No. 56.

[27] Heinrich Kronstein, review [typed script], "World Trade Control by Edward Mason," Box 1, Peace Treaty, HKP/GUSC; Edward S. Mason, *Controlling World Trade Cartels and Commodity Agreements* (New York, 1946), 132. This book is the source that Berghahn, *Americanization of West German Industry*, 102 cites as Mason, author of a report for Committee for Economic Development Research Study. The passages cited in Mason's and Berghahn's books match.

[28] Compare H. Kronstein, "Cartels and Combines," 13; Mason, *Controlling World Trade*, quote at 132. Several manuscripts from the immediate postwar era, including, "Economic Collapse and Occupation of Germany [Delivered before American Academy of Arts and Sciences, February 13, 1946]," "Economic Policy in Germany," and "American Policy Toward Germany," indicate the projects Mason put his students to work on, Edward Mason Papers Box 1, HUG 4559.82, Harvard University Archives.

Four power negotiations then ceased. However, "bizone" discussions continued aimed at reconciling the American decartelization law and its British counterpart, Law No. 78. Ultimately, the British approach prevailed as the "bizone" policy after the U.S. State Department informed Clay that a rule of reason policy was preferable to one based on per se prohibitions. In June 1947 the French promulgated their own decartelization Law No. 96.[29]

During this period Clay solicited German opinion. He turned to the state (*Landerrat*) authorities, including Bavarian finance minister Ludwig Erhard. Already, Erhard had discussed antitrust policy with certain Ordo Liberals working in southern Germany such as Böhm. While they were not in complete accord on antitrust policy, they shared fundamental ideas, including a faith in market-based competition, the importance of reconciling judicial and administrative enforcement of rules through some sort of ongoing "supervisory authority," the need to eradicate the German "cartel tradition," and, broadly, the commitment to an economic constitution combining secure property rights, protection of labor and social welfare, and political liberty, all of which would become known as the social-market economy. These ideas took concrete form in two sets of proposals during the winter of 1946–47. First, General Clay received recommendations from a Committee chaired by Paul Josten, former head of the cartel section of the Weimar economic ministry, who after 1945 was the chief *Landerrat* authority on prices. Second, in the French zone Professor Walter Eucken of Freiburg University, presented his recommendations. Eucken's proposals closely followed those presented by the Josten Committee, indicating the policy consistency prevailing among south German officials.[30]

Although the attempt to institute a uniform Allied decartelization law failed, the Josten Committee report established a symbolic principle. The report's preamble stated that a goal to be achieved by antitrust policy was "to create the basis for the construction of a healthy and democratic German economy." These words were incorporated – along with more punitive language – into the bizone decartelization policy which went into joint operation under U.S. Law No. 56 and British Law 78. The constructive spirit epitomized by the Josten Committee principle gained further legitimacy following the appointment in early 1947 of Secretary of State General George Marshall. He replaced JCS 1067 with JCS 1779, which affirmed that "an orderly and prosperous Europe requires the economic contributions of a stable and productive Germany." After the Marshall Plan began operation in the summer of 1947 the U.S. Military Government

[29] On Kronstein's prediction, see "Cartels and Combines," 1–2; Damm, "Factors Influencing Cartel Legislation," 135–6. I cite Damm's work because he develops the chronological sequence, which coincides with the period's larger political history.
[30] Damm, "Factors Influencing Cartel Legislation," 137–40; Berghahn, *Americanization of West German Industry*, 155–60, quotes at 156; Gerber, *Protecting Prometheus*, 259–61; H. Kronstein, "Cartels and Combines," 11.

construed JCS 1779 as a means for the Germans "to learn of the principles and advantages of free enterprise." The condescension notwithstanding, these major policy changes reinforced Clay's advice to the *Landerrat* authorities that the Allied decartelization measures could be considered "an intermediate solution," encouraging their own action. Thus, Kronstein's promotion of the south German officials indirectly facilitated indigenous antitrust policy making.[31]

Strategic and macroeconomic policies were clearly ascendant by early 1947. In February, at Truman's suggestion, Herbert Hoover visited Europe to report on problems of food scarcity, refugee relief, and other pressing social issues. In line with evidence provided by German financial expert and economic historian, Gustav Stolper, Hoover's inquiry nonetheless extended to issues concerning Germany's economic and democratic revitalization. A German Liberal politician who, after fleeing to the United States early in the war, was an outspoken anti-Nazi, Stolper once wrote that weak German cartel and monopoly regulations had encouraged Hitler's triumph. But the social and economic disruptions facing postwar Germany were so great that concerted government action was more imperative than antitrust enforcement. Thus, on July 19, 1947, he wrote to Hoover that "negotiations" regarding the "new Level of Industry seem to be in the decisive phase." Secretary of State Marshall's success in replacing the "Roosevelt–Morgenthau heritage" with the "new" JCS-1779 "encouraged" Stolper, "but only if we remain firm. The greatest immediate danger" was that the "French by their stubborness [sic] and pressure on" the British "may spoil" the Marshall Plan's "psychological effect."[32]

U.S., British, and French authorities followed differing Decartelization Laws. The British Law No. 78 – unlike its U.S. counterpart No. 56 – did not target for mandatory investigation large firms with more than 10,000 employees; it also exempted iron, steel, and coal companies from reporting procedures. The United States already had agreed to address independently film companies, banks, and I.G. Farben. The bizone laws did prohibit cartels, especially German involvement in international ones. But the Americans had to deal with the British preference for pragmatic enforcement policies employing the standard of reasonableness. Thus, an October 1947, analysis of the U.S. Decartelization Law concluded that Germany's long "acceptance of the cartel as a beneficent institution" and the "lack of

[31] Damm, "Factors Influencing Cartel Legislation," 139; Beschloss, *Conquerors*, 277; Berghahn, *Americanization of West German Industry*, 155; H. Kronstein, "Cartels and Combines," 11.

[32] Beschloss, *Conquerors*, 236–7, 277; Martin, *All Honorable Men*, 228, 229; Damm, "Factors Influencing Cartel Legislation," 162, 166; Gustov Stolper to Herbert Hoover, July 19, 1947, Post-Presidential File, Stolper, Dr. & Mrs. Gustov, correspondence 1946–1949, Herbert Hoover Presidential Library; Gustav Stolper, *German Realities* (New York, 1945).

unanimity of opinion among United States lawyers and economists" presented "serious obstacles" to "an effective enforcement policy."[33]

These tensions had an ambiguous impact on German legal and economic experts' opinion. German legal precedents and lawyers' experience conformed most nearly to French law No. 96, which partially adopted the German cartel and monopoly abuse legislation. Bizone decartelization laws were, however, quite inconsistent with German law. Moreover, even the few German legal and economic experts defending antitrust received little practical guidance in the form of official texts or advice from American and British authorities. These problems converged with the U.S., British, and French decisions to unify antitrust administration by September 1948, under one body designated the Deconcentration of Industry and Decartelization Group. In addition, between the summers of 1947 and 1948, first the Americans and then the unified trizonal agency, authorized the formation of a central German Decartelization Commission and various state-level German Decartelization Agencies. These agencies could "receive reports, make investigations, compile information, consider claims for exemptions and hold hearings thereon, and conduct enforcement proceedings for failure of enterprises to comply with instructions ... *in accordance with instructions from the Allied ... Commission* (emphasis in the orginal).[34]

The Memoranda of March 1948 marked a turning point in U.S. antitrust policy. According to the memorandum, Clay ordered that "US participation in deconcentration proceedings in the British Zone should be limited to agreeing upon ... such overall policies to provide, for example, that no deconcentration order shall require the breaking up of ties resulting in vertical integration." With the British taking the lead, and only upon their request, Americans could work on the "Ruhr combines" and the "coal project in Essen." Furthermore, he declared, "it appears quite possible that ... no deconcentration action against firms in the US zone will be required." Presently, "chemicals, coal, and iron and steel are the only flagrant examples obviously requiring attention. Of these three, only chemicals are primarily located in the U.S. Zone and the necessary action in the chemical field has been taken in the separate handling of IG Farben." Proceedings would be instituted only "against those companies in the U.S. Zone which have a monopoly or near monopoly of consumer goods where the consumer goods are an important element of economy," and further "actions will be limited to requiring excessively large companies in the U.S. Zone to divorce themselves from the ownership or control of

[33] Damm, "Factors Influencing Cartel Legislation," 142–4; Carolyn Royall Just, "The Influence of the Antitrust Laws on the New German Decartelization Law," 9 *Federal Bar Journal* (October 1947), 33–60, quote at 60.
[34] Damm, "Factors Influencing Cartel Legislation," 148–51, quote at 150.

unrelated functions, the loss of which would not impair their efficiency or production."[35]

The Decartelization Branch's second field of action concerned advising German central and state antitrust agencies. In keeping with this directive, Clay ordered local governments to relax their control over local employment by providing "refugee craftsmen" open entry into occupations. Kronstein commented that "perhaps no other decision by the American High Commission in Germany has been considered as economically beneficial." Local authorities were "urged to pass" legislation forbidding banks from using for their own purposes customer's stock deposits, making illegal "bearer share certificates," and restricting the number of authorized interlocking directorates. U.S. Decartelization authorities and their counterparts in the German central and state antitrust bodies also "should continue to review German legislation, the by-laws of trade associations, and the activities of private bodies to assure that the[y] are ... [not] engaging in restrictive trade practices."[36]

Finally, according to a memorandum authored by Decartelization Branch chief, Richardson Bronson, Clay declared that "regarding the whole program ... the rule of reason was our one and practically only yard stick." Bronson reported, too, that Clay's changed priorities comported with the "concept of the policy of the [U.S.] State Department as to decartelization." In addition, the senior military officials involved in the policy shift admitted that when the program received publicity "there would be a scream to the high heavens from the strong antitrust group, but there had been similar screams before" and "the screams had come and gone and that probably there would be not much more major interest to create a serious scream." These opinions nonetheless did not consider that Clay was adjusting the decartelization program to the rapidly changing strategic and macro-economic conditions in Germany.[37]

Political confrontation culminated in a divided Germany and altered the decartelization program. In June 1948, Ludwig Erhard, who was to become the West German economic minister, independently terminated most price and production controls. The black market ended and freer trade in consumer goods thrived in the western zones. The next year, the French joined the British and the United States to establish the trizone economic administration, including a unified decartelization policy. During that

[35] Phillips Hawkins to Lucius D. Clay, "Memorandum, Decartelization Branch," University of Wyoming American Heritage Center (UWAHC), March 9, 1948, Joseph J. O'Mahoney Papers (JJO'MP), Box 246, quotes at 1, 2, 3.
[36] Heinrich Kronstein, "Cartels Under the New German Cartel Statute," 11 *Vanderbilt Law Review* (March 1958), 271–301, quote at 273; Phillips Hawkins to Lucius D. Clay, "Memorandum, Decartelization Branch," quotes at 2, 3.
[37] Richardson Bronson, "Conference with General Clay," March 10, 1948, quotes at 1, 3; Robert Bowie, interview, April 30, 2002.

period delegates from the West German state legislatures formed a Parliamentary Council, which, on May 23, 1949, created the Federal Republic of Germany. The following October in the Soviet zone, a constitution authorized the German Democratic Republic. Though the process was nominally provisional, it lasted forty years.[38]

With Clay's military command coming to an end, U.S. and German commentators proclaimed that the Allied antitrust program had failed. As the Federal Republic gained sovereignty, German critics condemned the Western occupation commanders' inability to institute consistent antitrust policies, to provide adequate education in antitrust theories, to establish a clear distinction between prohibitions against some cartels and the likes of I.G. Farben, and to promote effective collaboration between the Allied authorities and their German counterparts. Some German critics focused on these failures in order to justify a return to the old Weimar-era policy of abuse regulation, whereas the Ordo Liberals and their Christian Socialist sympathizers did so because they favored an antitrust regime which could eradicate the German cartel tradition and prevent a recurrence of the Nazi evil. The most conspicuous American criticism, by contrast, asserted that the occupation had abandoned the radical deconcentration policies, charging that the weaker policy toward German companies served the interests of U.S. multinational corporations seeking global capitalist hegemony.[39]

These criticisms led U.S. Army Secretary Kenneth C. Royall to order an investigation. Its majority report concluded that the "Decartelization program, despite uncontroversial policies and clear directives, has not been effectively carried out. After almost four years of occupation and more than two years of operation under an adequate law, the program has not proceeded very far." The report noted loss of morale felt by the Decartelization Branch's staff resulting from Clay's policy changes, it questioned, too, the suspension of all deconcentration proceedings except those against the Bosch company, which had "not been completed." Nevertheless, the report declared, "any critical statements" referred only to the Decartelization program, which was a "small segment" of the overall Military government. Otherwise, the "highest praise is due" to General Clay's "outstanding job ... in Germany since the advent of the occupation."[40]

A concurring opinion asserted that command decisions and political pressures engendered the failure of the antitrust policies. The "principal reason," stated Samuel S. Isseks, "for the ineffectiveness of the decartelization program and particularly the deconcentration program, was the

[38] Shulze, Germany, 294–7.
[39] Damm, "Factors Influencing Cartel Legislation," 151–67; John C. Seedman, "The German Decartelization Program – The Law in Repose," 17 University of Chicago Law Review (Spring 1950), 441–57; Martin, All Honorable Men.
[40] Report of Committee Appointed to Review the Decartelization Program in Germany, JJO'MP, Box 341, UWAHC, April 15, 1949, Garland S. Ferguson, chairman, 118, 119, 129.

contention" that "deconcentration proceedings would interfere with
and delay the economic recovery of Germany." During 1945–46, Clay
"fully supported the decartelization program. Eventually, however,
he ... suspended the program as to many of the major targets in Germany
because they involved heavy or capital goods industries." The Decartelization Branch also followed difficult "procedural requirements" and
"complex regulations"; in addition, at least after 1947, it lacked sufficient
personnel, which in turn "seriously impaired the morale and efficiency" of
"those who vigorously supported" the program. Finally, "it was frequently
stated by top ranking persons" that after the U.S. elections in 1948 the
"decartelization program would be changed because of the prospect of a
change in" presidential administration.[41]

Ultimately, however, the military Occupation's antitrust policy was
more than a "failure." Despite ineffectual enforcement, the program at
least exposed to Allied and West German authorities the ongoing efforts of
German big business and its defenders to reestablish the familiar "cartel
tradition." Moreover, the persistent public criticism of the program
reflected not only the common yearning of Germans to regain control of
their economic system; it accentuated the divisions pitting the defenders of
the cartel and monopoly abuse model against the advocates of a market-
based economic constitution incorporating antitrust principles. By 1949 it
was clear that these groups' confrontation would continue under the Federal Republic. Moreover, Clay's change in policy suggested the willingness
acquired during the war to adjust antitrust values to strategic and macroeconomic imperatives, rather than merely surrender to probusiness subordinates. Indeed, Clay reportedly affirmed that "we had a great
responsibility for decartelization" which "should be one of our continuing
functions for some time in the future until we could be assured that existing
cartels and improper trade practices were eradicated." Accordingly, in
1949 the Allied occupation authorities renewed the commitment to the
antitrust program.[42]

II. GERMANY AND EUROPEAN ANTITRUST REGIME ALTERNATIVES, 1949–1957

Initially, efforts to conclude the Allied occupation and the Germans' own
struggle over a cartel law coincided. The Allied High Commission fostered
the progressive return of sovereignty to the Federal Republic in 1949 by
partially relinquishing to German central and state governmental officials
supervision of antitrust policy making and enforcement. The Allies reduced

[41] *Supplemental Report of Samuel S. Isseks, a Member of the Committee to Review the Decartelization Program*, JJO'MP, Box 341, UWAHC, 2–3, 4, 6.
[42] Richardson Bronson, "Conference with General Clay," March 10, 1948, 3.

their oversight to a minimum in 1952 and abandoned it altogether in 1955 when the occupation regime formally ended and the Federal Republic re-militarized within NATO. This policy convergence suggested that the four peacetime objectives Clay had articulated were being achieved, essentially. Although the Federal Republic re-militarized it occurred within the context of democratic politics led by Chancellor Konrad Adenauer, a strong economy balancing capitalism and the social welfare state, and a growing public acknowledgment that cartel and monopoly regulation was necessary. Nevertheless, from 1949 to 1957 the defenders of big business and the abuse system of regulating private collusive behavior battled the advocates of free market constitutionalism and the competition principles held by Ludwig Erhard. The outcomes were the European Coal and Steel Community established in 1951 and the German Cartel Law of 1957.[43]

Reinforcing sharp divisions among the German interest groups was the general public's ambivalence about the Allied Occupation's Decartelization program. An opinion survey in 1951 revealed that of those Germans polled roughly one-third opposed the three Western powers' decartelization program and only 25 percent endorsed it. However, the largest group, 44 percent, had "no opinion." Thus, an antitrust law imposed by conquerors solicited sharply divided minority opinion for or against, but more people remained uncommitted. Given such divisions, the contending German interest groups could believe that considerable opportunity existed to shape public opinion in favor of their respective images of a cartel law: either the abuse regulation policy or a program constituting competitive markets maintained through antitrust principles. Moreover, proponents of the Weimar-era cartel policy included the powerful Association of German Industry (BDI) led by its influential President Fritz Berg, its Conservative Party supporters within the Christian Democratic Union and Christian Social Union parties, and prominent legal–economic experts. Their opponents included Christian Democratic Union Christian Social Union leaders, Chancellor Adenauer and Economics Minister Erhard, factions within the proletarian Social Democratic Party, some small business groups, and Ordo

---

[43] Damm, "Factors Influencing Cartel Legislation," 204–75; Gerber, *Protecting Prometheus*, 268–76; Schulze, *Germany*, 297–315; Kronstein, "Cartels' Under the New German Cartel Statute," 11(2)*Vanderbilt Law Review*, 271–301; Ivo F. Schwartz, "Antitrust Legislation and Policy in Germany – A Comparative Study," 105 *University of Pennsylvania Law Review* (March 1957), 617–90; Theodore F. Warburg, "Government and Business in Germany: Public Policy toward Cartels," 38 *Business History Review* (Spring 1964), 78–101; Berghahn, *Americanization of West German Industry*, 106, 114, 119–54, 173, 231, 283; Robert Bowie, interview, April 30, 2002; Willner, *First Step in European Integration*, 1–58; Thomas C. Fischer, *The Europeanization of America* (Durham, NC, 1995), 15–16; Raymond Vernon, "The Schuman Plan," 47 *American Journal of International Law* (April 1953), 183–202; Dean Acheson, *Present at the Creation: My Years in the State Department* (New York, 1987), 382–9; Derek W. Urwin, *The Community of Europe a History of European Integration since 1945* (London, 1997), 43–75.

Liberals such as Böhm and Eucken. Thus, many serious German news-papers presented front pages that dramatized the cartel law struggle.[44]

Sociopolitical conflict exacerbated the protracted contest. Erhard first considered, though did not seek, legislative approval for a cartel bill in 1949. After several years of debate and compromise the legislature finally reached agreement on a modified version of an earlier draft and enacted it in July 1957. On January 1, 1958, the Federal Republic of Germany's "competition law" (*Wettbewerbsrecht* or GWB) formally went into operation. Throughout the period, more than "twenty additional drafts were considered." Several detailed studies explored the "open and dramatic conflict that achieved virtually mythic status. In it, power (that of Germany's industrial leaders) stood opposed to the values that sought to control it." The ideological and social conflicts underlying the political confrontation deserve emphasis. Broadly, the proponents of the abuse regulations reflected the long-held assumption that collaborative business behavior could ameliorate class conflicts, even though, as German commentators from Stolper to Böhm contended, those same factors had undermined the Weimar Republic.[45]

In 1954, Böhm outlined the sociopolitical conflicts involved. In contemporary Germany, he wrote, "no influential and *socially strong* group - ... excepting the American occupation authorities" supported a strict policy of "competition," believing it to be "a policy of illusions and a doctrinairism inimical to life and history." Those advocating the "protection of competition and the fight against monopoly," were "regarded by German public opinion as [promoting] a professors' program." Shunning the totalitarian ideologies of communism and fascism, the "[p]eople are proud to be non-doctrinaire and call this attitude that of common sense, balance, and reason." Thus, Böhm declared, "[b]usinessmen hold it sufficient to give the government power to control abuses. Experience under the Cartel Regulations of 1923 has convinced them that government control does not hurt cartels and monopolies." By contrast, the "workers do not want to see this control concentrated in the hands of the government, but incorporated into the organization of each firm, each cartel, and each industry. They demand equal representation for the workers in management, as a part of the policy of absolute equality for labor and capital which they call 'economic democracy.'" Even so, the "great majority of businessmen would undoubtedly prefer to make concessions on equal representation and nationalization, rather than to accept drastic protection of competition and the prohibition of cartels and monopolies."[46]

---

[44] Damm, "Factors Influencing Cartel Legislation," 159–60; Gerber, *Protecting Prometheus*, 270–3.
[45] Damm, "Factors Influencing Cartel Legislation," 170–276; Gerber, *Protecting Prometheus*, 268–77, quote at 274–5.
[46] F. Böhm, "Western Germany," in Edward H. Chamberlain, ed., *Monopoly and Competition and Their Regulation* (London, 1954), 141–67, quotes at 154, 155, 156.

Böhm's analysis foreshadowed a larger search for a consensual polity. From 1949 on, the Federal Republic's electoral politics were divided among Christian Democratic Union (CDU) joined by its Bavarian partner Christian Social Union (CSU), the Social Democrats (SPD), and the small Free Democratic Party (FDP).[47] For three decades in West German elections, the more conservative CDU-Bavarian Coalition parties consistently received approximately 45 percent of the vote, the prolabor SPD garnered from 30 to 46 percent and the "free-market centered" FDP gained between 6 and 12 percent. Since neither major party controlled a majority, coalitions with the FDP occurred.[48] During 1946–47, the Christian Social parties developed a compromise platform reconciling the interests of Catholic middle- and working-class voters. Eventually the three leading political parties embraced this same compromise politics reflected in the slogan "social-market economy," symbolizing a market-based economy committed to a fair distribution of social benefits. Alfred Müller-Armack, coiner of the term social market economy, incorporated from Ordo Liberalism the ideas of the "economic constitution" guaranteeing *Ordungspolitik* whereby government "indirectly" shaped the structure of capitalist opportunity by protecting competition. Still, Müller-Armack's chief goal was equitable welfare not competition as an end in itself.[49]

The social market economy provided ambiguous conditions for the contentious evolution of a cartel bill. Erhard's independent lifting of price and production controls in June 1948 reflected the growing popular acceptance of Müller-Armack's ideas. The British and American military zone commanders followed suit with guidelines reestablishing freer market competition; they called upon German authorities to develop antitrust laws. Erhard turned to members of the Josten Committee with whom he had worked. Beginning some months before the formation of the Federal Republic, the reconstituted Josten Committee included some of the same Ordo Liberals, including Böhm, as well as professors from universities in the British zone. The committee produced drafts of a competition law. There was a per se prohibition against cartels – subject to strictly limited provision for exemptions – retail price maintenance also prohibited, and, wherever possible, "market-dominating" firms were to be "deconcentrated." Corporate giants remained under direct supervision of an independent Monopoly Authority, which possessed wide discretionary enforcement authority, including regulation of vertical and horizontal mergers and the imposition of criminal fines. Another procompetition provision made licensing of patents compulsory.[50]

---

[47] Jeffrey Fear, "German Capitalism," in McCraw, ed., *Creating Modern Capitalism*, 171–2.

[48] Ibid., 172.

[49] Gerber, *Protecting Prometheus*, 248–61, quote at 248; Damm, "Factors Influencing Cartel Legislation," 201–7, quoted phrases at 202–3; Warburg, "Government and Business in Germany," 90–1.

[50] Ibid.; note 30 above.

Erhard did not submit the Josten Committee draft for legislative approval. Business leaders from transportation firms, heavy industry, and "branded goods" producers condemned it: the per se presumption prohibiting cartels provided too limited grounds for exemption, the Monopoly Authority possessed too much centralized discretionary power, and the academic theory of perfect competition could not be imposed in many markets. Influencing Erhard's decision against pushing the Josten draft was not only the extensive criticism, but recognition that the legislature of the Federal Republic, which was about to be constituted, would provide greater legitimacy for a law than the occupation regime.[51]

The contentiousness the Josten draft unleashed foreshadowed the struggle over subsequent cartel bills. Eberhard Guenther – a leading German official in the bizonal government and in the Federal Republic who handled anticartel proposals – and some of Erhard's close advisors may have suggested that the draft granted too much administrative discretion to be consistent with the principles of the "economic constitution." Yet while Erhard abandoned the draft, he authorized Guenther and the other cartel experts in the Federal Ministry of Economics to develop proposals instituting either a less stringent cartel prohibition or a strong proscription against abuse. Meanwhile, he asserted a preference for a law which basically protected competition. "I am ... convinced that interference with the free workings of competition ... is no less deplorable and harmful when it is exercised on the part of entrepreneurs than when it is exercised by the state." Throughout the succeeding years the terms of confrontation were similar: Guenther and other government experts developed numerous draft proposals, which eventually succumbed to attack, not just from the BDI and its supporters, but at different points from members of the leading political parties and prominent legal and economic experts.[52]

The fate of the first Cartel Bill which reached the legislature in 1952 indicated the scope of confrontation. Between 1950 and 1952 the experts in the Economics Ministry provided Erhard with compromise proposals which nonetheless retained the basic cartel prohibition principle. In the summer of 1950 a German fact-finding commission visited the United States to confer with antitrust lawyers. Its members included Böhm – the most ardent proponent of a strict cartel prohibition – and various officials from the Economics and Justice ministries who more or less supported him. Other representatives from the Federal Association of Wholesalers, Exporters, and Importers, the BDI, the German Employees' Union, and

---

[51] Compare: Gerber *Protecting Prometheus*, 274–8; Berghahn, *Americanization of West German Industry*, 156–8; Damm, "Factors Influencing Cartel Legislation," 208–34.
[52] Damm, "Factors Influencing Cartel Legislation," 212–20; Warburg, "Government and Business in Germany," *Business History Review* for Erhard's December 1949 article, quote at 90.

the Hamburg-based Association of Oil Producers and Refiners, however, generally favored the abuse principle. Upon returning home, the committee's much-publicized report affirmed that a judicially-centered antitrust system could not be successfully transferred to Germany. Proponents of the abuse model interpreted the report as supporting their position.[53] The ministries' economic experts developed another proposal which modified the cartel prohibition; Guenther submitted it for Allied approval in 1951. The Working Party, composed of U.S., British, and French representatives "emphasized . . . the inadequacies of the deconcentration provisions of the draft law." Eventually, however, the Allies agreed to revisions that retained a modified cartel prohibition.[54]

After more compromise, in February, 1952, the Economics Ministry submitted the draft to the cabinet and some months later it went to the Bundesrat. Broadly, the bill blended ideas from Ordo Liberalism and the social-market economy while providing some operation of the abuse principle. Its express purpose was to constitute a market economy based on competition. A basic prohibition embraced cartels. Under certain circumstances for specified periods of time the government could authorize cartels. When market competition ceased, the government should refrain from coercion to reestablish it and instead manage the collusion so that economic power was not abused. A cartel authority would possess administrative jurisdiction over such collusion, especially in case of so-called "depression cartels" aimed at counteracting severe contraction in sales or major plant closures. In order to promote technological innovation or protect jobs, this Authority could authorize "rationalization" cartels; like many other nations' law, the bill permitted export cartels. Thus, the bill compromised the cartel prohibition and abuse principles. Similar compromises involved patents, exemptions and mergers.[55]

The debate over the government's bill reflected big business' and political party leaders' conflicting views. At different points Erhard's defense of the bill was opposed by members of his own CDU-CSU coalition party and the Free Democratic Party, while the opposition Social Democrats supported him; on other occasions, the major parties themselves did not endorse the bill but factions within each party favored it, except for the isolated Communists who insisted upon a "strong" statute tailored on the Allied occupation's Decartelization Law. Generally, the debate pitted the abuse and prohibition principles against one another. Fritz Berg's BDI repeatedly demanded a law based on the abuse principle, and the CDU representatives from

[53] Note 51 above.
[54] Allied High Commission Decartelization and Industrial Deconcentration Group Report of Working Party on Meeting with Representative of the Federal Government of Germany Draft Law Against Restraints of Competition, submitted May 22, 1951, DIDEG/P (51) 38, August 24, 1951 (FO 1005/731 Public Record Office, Kew, UK).
[55] Damm, "Factors Influencing Cartel Legislation," 222–5, 227–34.

North-Westphalia, the Federal Republic's most industrialized state, followed suit. Berg and his party supporters condemned the prohibition principle because it was identified with the occupation and American antitrust and because other postwar Western European capitalist regimes which were markets for recovering German firms purportedly had adopted the abuse principle. Ultimately, however, the legislature's factional shifts facilitated qualified approval of the basic design and underlying procompetition values. Increasingly, the debate contested the scope rather than the existence of the prohibition principle, exemptions, and a cartel authority's discretion.[56]

The debate, however, did not end until 1957. In part, it was a straightforward matter of interest groups' agitating for and winning further limitations on the prohibition principle and the elimination of the merger control provisions, and it also reflected residual punitive images associated with the occupation and long-established attitudes toward property and contract rights. Something else was also involved: the reshaping of the bruised German self-identity. One insightful American participant in the occupation noted that as a result of the partition of Germany, the Russians had "sheared away the sources of power of German Protestantism and left a Germany in which the Catholics of the Rhineland and Bavaria for the first time in a century have the power to guide German history." The "great mass of Germans" confronted "trying to learn or decide, what to do with this new situation of being defeated and occupied." The U.S. conqueror in particular exacerbated the "stereotype ... of 'materialistic America' where mammon ruled supreme, where civilization was sadly lacking, and cultural and social progress were considered as being quite backward" and these views complicated antitrust policy's role in the new German identity politics.[57]

The ideological contentiousness intensified straightforward interest group trade-offs. Indeed, after deadlock derailed the bill in 1954, Erhard and Berg met to discuss a framework for compromise fashioned by representatives from the BDI and the Economics and Justice ministries. The ensuing public uproar resulted in the cancellation of subsequent meetings between the two leaders. Even the Association of Independent Businessmen denounced the reported compromises. In part, the public reaction reflected the traditional social-class tensions identified with the Social Democrats and their leftist sympathizers among the CDU and Free Democrats. In addition, according to a contemporary observer, the ongoing clash overshadowed preparations for the general election of 1957: the "CDU could not afford to appear as the party of 'big business' in the eyes of the electorate." Amid the public discontent Erhard declared that he would resign unless the

---

[56] Ibid.; Gerber, *Protecting Prometheus*; Berghahn, *Americanization of West German Industry*.

[57] Bert Peter Schloss, "The American Occupation of Germany, 1945–1952, an Appraisal," Unpublished Ph.D. Dissertation, University of Chicago, 1955, quotes at 246, 248.

CDU and its allies in the Bundestag passed the bill – compromises and all – before the general election. In response, on July, 19, 1957, the Bundesrat voted in favor; shortly thereafter it received the Federal President's signature and went into effect on New Year's day, 1958.[58]

German opinion regarding the Cartel Law's passage ranged from concerns that the cartel prohibition had been weakened by authorized exemptions to business's fear that those same provisions would disrupt Germany's competitive advantage. Some German legal and economic experts concluded that "if one considers the strength of the opposition, one can only be surprised that a prohibition law passed at all." The *New York Times* described the result as "big victory for Erhard over the industrial leaders"; by contrast, *The Economist* described it as "Bonn's Elastic Cartel Law." A German antitrust expert declared that the law's impact on business would be determined by the compromise "between the prohibition and abuse principles, with the prohibition principle predominating with respect to horizontal agreements and the abuse principle predominating with respect to vertical agreements." Kronstein observed that the "German dispute over cartels" had "not ended," but moved from the legislature to the "Cartel Office and the courts." Drawing upon his experience since 1936, he suggested that "[p]erhaps because of contemplated integration into the European market – generally highly cartelized – with a consideration of the importance of East-West trade" the "law had been written in a flexible way. The road is left open for liberal tendencies to lead Germany and Europe finally to a relatively free form of trade."[59]

The European Coal and Steel Community created, through shared sovereignty, a common market in two vital industries. It was the first major step toward broader economic integration among Western European nations.[60] This mutual improvement of the parts and the whole was achieved by each state's signing a treaty granting collective economic policy making between itself and supranational authorities.[61] "In Europe," wrote international antitrust expert Corwin Edwards, "two international agreements formulated in the 1950s provide arrangements for collaboration in the control of restrictive business practices more ambitious than those of the" GATT, which dealt with the anticompetitive policies of governments

[58] Damm, "Factors Influencing Cartel Legislation," 234–75, quote at 257.
[59] Damm, "Factors Influencing Cartel Legislation," 275; New York, *Times* (July 5, 1957); *The Economist* (July 20, 1957) in Warburg, "Government and Business in Germany, Public Policy", 91; Kronstein, "'Cartels' under the New German Cartel Statute," 300–1.
[60] Robert Bowie, interview, April 30, 2002; Willner, *First Step in European Integration*; Berghahn, *Americanization of West German Industry*, 119–54.
[61] Vernon, "The Schuman Plan," 183–202; Acheson, *Present at the Creation*, 382–9; Urwin, *Community of Europe*, 43–75; Francios Duchêne, *Jean Monnet* (New York, 1994), 162–80, 246–9, 260–2, 358–74, 382, 391, 397–402; Gerber, *Protecting Prometheus*, 335–45; Schulze, *Germany*, 302, 304, 308, 334, 338.

rather than of private business. The first agreement in 1951 instituted the ECSC; the second in 1957 established the European Economic Community (EEC). "In each Community, control of restrictive business practices is only a part of a complex undertaking," Edwards observed. "In each Community, however, such control expresses a policy established by international agreement and is applied by international means established for the purpose." The joint control revealed the "possibilities and limitations of joint efforts by sovereign states to cope with business restrictions that have international significance."[62]

In the ECSC the interdependency between national and supranational antitrust authorities had particular significance for Germany. Periodically throughout European history, visionaries had postulated resolving the disparate national sovereignties sufficiently to create a unified whole. More recently, however, the vision had achieved tangible form only through the domination of two nations: Napoleonic France and Hitler's Germany. Wartime and postwar popular reaction against the exploitative New Order fostered an image of European community which employed unified policy making to attain not only economic stability and social welfare, but also the political goal of preventing Germany from again threatening the peace of its neighbors. The Allied Occupation brought to power within Germany those anti-Nazis who shared these goals, including opposition to the "cartel tradition." Thus, in 1952 Ludwig Erhard declared, "We plan to create a common European market. This aim is incompatible with a system of national or international cartels. If we want to create a higher standard of living through technical progress, rationalization, and an increase in production, we have to be against cartels."[63]

A major step toward market integration was the 1951 Treaty of Paris establishing the ECSC. The treaty included antitrust provisions. It was widely accepted that these "provisions were written in Washington and adopted as such. Europeans have had some difficulty in reconciling them with European concepts and procedures."[64] Over time, however, preoccupation with the U.S. influence obscured the more significant European contributions, particularly those of the French and the Germans. This shift in focus revealed that dissension regarding the Treaty's antitrust provisions reflected not merely resistance to American intervention but disagreement among Europeans about what antitrust regime was best suited to the

---

[62] Edwards, *Control of Cartels*, 243.

[63] John Laughland, *Tainted Source the Undemocratic Origins of the European Idea* (London, 1997), 26–46, 128–33. But see Urwin, *Community of Europe*, 1–42, emphasizing the role of anti-Nazi resistance without discussing the New Order; for the Erhard quote, see Damm, "Factors Influencing Cartel Legislation," 113.

[64] Edwards, *Control of Cartels*, 246, and for similar ascription to U.S. influence, see Majone, "The Rise of Statutory Regulation in Europe," in Giandomenico Majone, ed. *Regulating Europe* (London, 1996), 50–1.

postwar world. As the cold war intensified following the partition of Germany, tensions between France and the Federal Republic persisted regarding the Ruhr coal and steel region. Since the end of the war groups within France, Britain, Germany, and the United States had disputed the degree to which a punitive policy should be pursued in the Ruhr. The Americans, French, and British supported the occupation's controversial "de-cartelization/deconcentration" policies. By 1950 in Britain, however, neither the Labour nor the Conservative government favored British involvement in establishing a supranational regime. Accordingly, French and German authorities pursued increasing collaboration, joined by representatives from Belgium, the Netherlands, Italy, and Luxembourg.[65]

In May 1950 French foreign minister Robert Schuman proposed administering coal and steel resources under combined national and supranational authority. The "French Government proposes," Schuman announced, "that Franco-German coal and steel production should be placed under a common High Authority in an organization open to the participation of the other countries of Europe." While he admitted that "if necessary, we shall go ahead with only two" nations, the coal and steel industries had been for decades organized through vertical restraints and cartel agreements among private firms and government agencies crossing at least six nations' borders. French, German, Italian, Belgium, the Netherlands, and Luxembourg governments were involved because national competitive advantage, business–labor relations, consumer welfare, and military security required vital industries to be productive and stable. Underlying the Schuman Plan's proposed elimination of discriminatory trade polices and cartel arrangements were two express political goals: the Plan presumed that "stability and union within Western Europe rested ultimately upon rapprochement between France and West Germany," and was a prerequisite for the eventual creation of a wider supranational economic community.[66]

The Schuman Plan's antitrust provisions aroused criticism. German business leaders repeated the same arguments they had used to condemn the decartelization program and to oppose Erhard's Cartel Bill. In France antitrust also aroused anti-American feeling at least partly because there was extensive governmental involvement with private firms in monopolistic vertical restraints and cartels. Thus, images of U.S. antitrust clashed with Europeans' separate national sovereignties blended with economic self-interest. In France the coal industry was nationalized, a government body

[65] Gerber, *Protecting Prometheus*, 335–45; Duchêne, *Jean Monnet*, 162–80, 246–9, 260–2, 358–74, 382, 391, 397–402; Urwin, *Community of Europe*, 43–75; Robert Bowie, interview, April 30, 2002; Willner, *First Step in European Integration*, 1–58 Berghahn, *Americanization of West German Industry*, 119–54.
[66] Urwin, *Community of Europe*, 44; Edwards, *Control of Cartels*, 243–80; Willner, *First Step in European Integration*, 1–58; Damm, "Factors Influencing Cartel Legislation," 113–18.

monopolized coal imports, and the largest steel firms were undergoing "amalgamation." A state holding company controlled more than half of Italy's steel production. A state corporation was the biggest of five coal producers in the Netherlands, and the government held shares in the one significant steel firm. Europe's largest steel company was in Luxembourg; it had vertically integrated with both coal producers and steel processors. The leading Belgium steel companies maintained financial agreements among themselves and with coal firms. The war destroyed the well-known steel cartel, but national cartels in certain products remained. Similarly, national coal cartels were common.[67]

The individual most responsible for the creation of the ECSC and the wider European market integration that followed was the French bureaucrat-planner and international businessman, Jean Monnet. Familiar with antitrust in America, Monnet neutralized the anti-U.S. sentiments of French business and government officials by arguing that the policy could be used to prevent Western Germany's postwar economic revival from resulting in German domination. Indeed French administration of the Allied Occupation's decartelization policy suggested how an antitrust regime could be employed to prevent such domination. Monnet also cultivated the support of Erhard, Adenauer, and other German government officials. They, in turn, favored inserting into the Schuman Plan a cartel prohibition in order to blunt the German industrialists' claim that the Cartel Bill then being debated would undercut the Federal Republic's competitive advantage against those nations which permitted or even sanctioned anticompetitive conduct. Finally, Monnet received from High Commissioner John J. McCloy, the services of antitrust expert Robert Bowie. General Clay's legal assistant during the war and early Occupation, Bowie was again on leave from Harvard Law School, serving as McCloy's General Counsel. Bowie's role was to be unofficial and confidential.[68]

Monnet and his supporters moved expeditiously to draft the treaty. In order to balance the economic, security, and social welfare imperatives at stake in pooling the coal and steel industry under combined national and supranational governance the treaty incorporated antitrust provisions. The U.S. Department of State official, Raymond Vernon, noted that Articles 65 and 66 of the Treaty of Paris arose "only partly" from the "drafters' adherence to competition as an economic way of life. More important, perhaps," was their "concern ... that cartels, if permitted to develop, might become the real power in the Community and might constitute a challenge

[67] Damm, "Factors Influencing Cartel Legislation," 99–118; Edwards, *Control of Cartels*, 243–5, quote at 244.

[68] See note 65 above; these sources emphasize Monnet's role and (except for Urwin's book) mention Robert Bowie's "unofficial" participation. In addition to summarizing his role, Bowie's interview explained to me his work with General Clay during the war and occupation.

to the Community's sovereignty." Sydney Willner, George Ball, and other Americans contributed significantly to the process, while Bowie worked principally with Monnet and Walter Hallstein, one of Chancellor Adenauer's staff, to craft provisions which captured the "gist or purpose" of "competition," seeking the "essence" of, without in any sense duplicating, U.S. antitrust laws. Everyone involved "expected" that "French bureaucrats" would put the drafted provisions into "treaty language" designed to achieve "consensus." Washington officials offered concise wording for the antitrust provisions. The process was so fluid, however, that by the time the phraseology arrived from Washington, Monnet, Hallstein, and Bowie had completed their work.[69]

Europeans were divided, however. Monnet faced opposition from Charles de Gaulle, who dismissed it as an aimless "mis-mash," and from Communists, who rejected it on ideological grounds. In response, Monnet appealed to the mutual Franco-German rapprochement underlying the Schuman Plan. German Social Democrats objected to community membership, contending that the deepened economic integration with Western European nations – who were also aligned militarily with the United States in NATO – jeopardized German reunification. Hallstein's views comported with Adenauer's and Erhard's, who rebuffed these claims on the basis of the social market economy, the consensus platform endorsed by influential factions within the Federal Republic's leading parties. Compromise politics overcame resistance in Italy, Belgium, the Netherlands, and Luxembourg. Ultimately, the Treaty's purpose of promoting "economic expansion, growth of employment and rising standard of living" received support from the "strong Christian Democratic presence in all six governments throughout the crucial 1950–52 period." The idea of subjecting national sovereignty to a supranational body was sufficiently controversial, however, that British prime minister Clement Attlee firmly refused "to accept the principle that the most vital economic forces of this country should be handed over to an authority that is utterly undemocratic and is responsible to nobody."[70]

---

[69] Duchêne, *Jean Monnet*, 196, 207, 215–22, 230–5, 302, 326–8, 364; Gerber, *Protecting Prometheus*, 336–8; Vernon, "The Schuman Plan," 337; Robert Bowie, interview, April 30, 2002 [note, too, that Bowie acknowledges Edward Mason as a mentor]; Willner, *First Step in European Integration*, 1–58; John Gillingham, "Jean Monnet and the European Coal and Steel Community: A Preliminary Appraisal", 129–62; Robert Morjolin, "What Type of Europe?", 163–83; Duchêne, "Jean Monnet's Methods," 184–209 in Douglas Brinkley and Clifford Hackett, eds., *Jean Monnet: The Path to European Unity* (London, 1991). The central role of William "Tommy" Tomlinson is discussed in most sources, though not directly in connection with the Schuman Plan's antitrust provisions.

[70] Urwin, *Community of Europe*, 44–51, quotes at 46, 48, 49; Brinkley and Hackett, eds., *Jean Monnet*; Gerber, *Protecting Prometheus*, 337–343; Robert Bowie April 30, 2002.

The sources of the Paris Treaty's antitrust provisions in article 65 were particularly disputed. American authority on the Schuman Plan, William Diebold, observed that European cartel "approaches" and U.S. antitrust "practice and experience" were "blended."[71] This view neglected Bowie's close cooperation with Hallstein, who kept Adenauer informed about the making of the Treaty. The view also inadequately recognizes that the U.S. per se rule against cartels and the prohibition-preemption approach are distinct principles, the latter being closer to the German Cartel Law of 1957. Indeed, in 1958, Walter Damm, a German graduate student at the University of Chicago, presented extensive evidence in a doctoral dissertation supporting the conclusion that Article 65 was "clearly patterned after" Erhard's controversial Cartel Bill, which was then being drafted. "As in the German Bill," he wrote, "the prohibition of cartels resulted in the nullification of the cartel contract, brought the imposition of fines, and the cartels had to submit evidence of their harmlessness if they wanted to be exempt from prohibition." Four decades later David Gerber's authoritative work sustained a similar conclusion, noting that as the chief German negotiator, Hallstein brought to the framing of Article 65 a commitment to the social-market economy shared by those drafting the Cartel Bill.[72]

Bowie fashioned the Treaty's other competition provision, Article 66. By a process of authorization the community's High Authority could control mergers to maintain competition. Article 66 granted the High Authority power "to address to public or private enterprises which in law or fact, have or acquire on the market for one of the products [subject to the treaty] ... a *dominant position* which protects them from effective competition in a substantial part of the common market, any recommendations required to prevent use of such position for purposes contrary to those of the present Treaty." During the Allied Occupation U.S. antitrust activists had resisted employing a weak reasonableness standard as the basis for the deconcentration program. However, in the bizone administration of the Ruhr steel and coal industries, U.S. officials, at General Clay's command, and the British applied the rule of reason more flexibly – especially toward vertical restraints – than in America. Even so, following Mason's antitrust theories and Clay's program, Bowie may have compromised with Hallstein to reshape the "abuse" principle into the standard of "dominant position" in Article 66.[73]

Bowie's success in crafting the antitrust provisions facilitated passage of the Schuman Plan. Concerning the negotiation of the Treaty of Paris as a whole, Monnet conceded that without consistent U.S. support, the effort

---

[71] Diebold, *The Schuman Plan* (New York, 1959), 352.
[72] Compare Gerber, *Protecting Prometheus*, 339–40; and Damm, "Factors Influencing Cartel Legislation," 113–18, quote at 116.
[73] Gerber, *Protecting Prometheus*, 340–1, quote at 341 (italics added); Robert Bowie, interview, April 30, 2002.

would have failed. But Bowie later observed that despite the heritage of Franco-German hostility, Monnet and Hallstein "developed a remarkable rapport ... both were coming at it like people trying to create something." These participants agreed that defeat would have resulted had not Adenauer skillfully used U.S. pressure and the appeal for Franco-German rapprochement to overcome the German industrialists' resistance. Monnet later noted that gaining Adenauer's endorsement of the Treaty's antitrust provisions was essential. "On March 14, 1951," Monnet's memoir stated, "the Allied decartelization proposal finally secured Adenauer's agreement and Hallstein at once accepted the two Treaty Articles that were still in dispute. They had been drafted by Robert Bowie with meticulous care." Thus, Monnet, Adenauer, Hallstein, and Bowie shaped the first major step toward the creation of the EEC's antitrust provisions.[74]

In 1957 the Treaty of Rome created the EEC from successes as well as failures in European cooperative efforts. Measured by the "phenomenal increase in production of coal and steel," the ECSC soon proved to be a qualified success, though the enforcement of antitrust provisions initially was weak. By contrast, the Organization for European Economic Cooperation evolved into a body promoting international economic policy development – becoming the Organization for Economic Cooperation and Development (OECD), whose members extended beyond Europe to include the United States, Canada, and, ultimately such nations as Japan. It influenced policy making primarily through consultation. Efforts to deepen shared sovereignty beyond the coal and steel sectors into stronger political integration – especially the European Political Community and the European Defense Community – failed. By contrast, NATO required multinational cooperation based on national security treaties; nevertheless, it largely shifted cold war defense costs to the United States, which in turn enabled Western European nations to pursue competitive advantage and improved social welfare of consumers, workers, and farmers.[75]

As European community proponents wrestled with the challenges of economic and political integration, Western Germany's public identity was reshaped. France's rejection of the European Defense Community facilitated displacing the historic imagery of German militarism. In 1948

[74] Duchêne, *Jean Monnet*, 215–22, 230–5, 326–8, quotes at 218–19; Jean Monnet, *Memoir*, trans. Richard Mayne (London, 1978), 352–3; Willner, *First Step in European Integration* 1–58.
[75] Damm, "Factors Influencing Cartel Legislation," 117; compare Gillingham, "Jean Monnet," in Brinkley and Hackett, eds., *Jean Monnet*, 156; Zeitlin and Herrigel, eds., *Americanization and Its Limits* (2000), 211, 217, 219–21, 232–3, 367–8; Edwards, *Control of Cartels*, 245–79; Duchêne, *Jean Monnet*, 240–52, 374–9, 397–404; Hans A. Schmitt, "The European Coal and Steel Community: Operations of the First European Antitrust Law, 1952–1958," 38 *Business History Review* (Spring 1964), 102–22; Urwin, *Community of Europe*, 18–24, 51–75.

the Allies had agreed to the Treaty of Brussels, committing them "to take steps as may be necessary in the event of renewal by Germany of a policy of aggression." Adenauer's success in gaining the Federal Republic's remilitarization by 1955 facilitated the transfer of certain commitments and objectives established under the Treaty of Brussels to NATO. Containing a bellicose Germany was no longer among the primary purposes of NATO; instead, its constituted the image of a capitalist Federal Republic joining other Western European nations "to promote the unity and to encourage the progressive integration of Europe." France's acquiescence on this contentious point followed Schuman's and Monnet's triumph in establishing the ECSC through Franco-German rapprochement; similarly, it required overcoming long-standing market realities and symbols associated with the German cartel tradition. Monnet, Schuman, Paul-Henri Spaak of Belgium, Alcide de Gasperi of Italy, Adenauer, and other advocates of European community nonetheless knew that Germany's altered place within Europe fostered only conditional public support for integration.[76]

The direct authority the ECSC exercised over individuals and industries encouraged market competition. Taken separately, Raymond Vernon of the State Department conceded that the Treaty's provisions suggested alternative policy approaches: "that of a 'free-enterprise' state such as the United States or Canada, or a government-regulated state such as the United Kingdom and Norway during the late 1940's, or a state regulated by private industry such as Germany or Japan in the early 1930's." The Treaty's preamble nonetheless committed the ECSC to promoting "normal conditions of competition," with government intervening in "operation of the market only when circumstances make it absolutely necessary," and "with as little administrative machinery as possible." Suggesting how procompetition values were to be implemented, moreover, were "extraordinary" antitrust provisions which "declare price-fixing agreements, agreements to restrict production or investment, and agreements to allocate markets to be illegal *per se*. This is not the doctrine that 'bad' cartels are illegal and 'good' cartels are desirable, with which students of European cartel legislation are familiar; it is much more nearly the doctrine of the American Sherman Act." Vernon noted that the authorities could grant exceptions on terms both "analogous" to and "different from" the American rule of reason. In the case of mergers and other corporate concentrations, exceptions could be authorized, "but none which significantly impaired the general [procompetition] principle."[77]

In addition, the member states altered their trade obligations with the rest of the world. With "singular ingenuity," Vernon observed, "while giving up their powers within the common market, the six countries have

---

[76] Urwin, *Community of Europe*, 22–5, 68–75, quoted at 69.
[77] "Schuman Plan," 47 *American Journal of International Law* (April 1953), 196, 197.

tried systematically and painstakingly to retain all their sovereign powers over trade with outside countries in coal and steel. In short, they have tried for singleness in their 'internal' relations and separateness in their external dealings." In particular, each of the community's member states was a party to the "most-favored-nation commitments" established under the GATT. Nevertheless, the Treaty of Paris clashed with the GATT's proviso for nondiscrimination between nations' trade and tariff policies, "since none of the six countries intends to allow the coal and steel products of outside countries to enter their territories on the same obstacle-free basis as they are compelled by the treaty to afford to one another's coal and steel products." The conflict was resolved when the ECSC's six members "agreed to take joint action to obtain a waiver from the most-favored-nation clauses of the GATT." Following "considerable negotiation" the other GATT nations agreed to the "principle that the [ECSC] six member states, in lieu of their individual most-favored-nation commitments under the GATT as regards coal and steel products, assume the most-favored-nation obligations which a single contracting party would have if it consisted of the European territories of the member states."[78]

Negotiations over the wider economic community began in mid-1955. That same year Jean Monnet resigned from heading the ECSC's High Authority. Representing the private Action Committee for the United States of Europe, he advocated extending the sector by sector integration pioneered by the ECSC to include transportation and atomic energy. French and West German officials embraced a similar cautious course; Spaak, by contrast, urged a bolder initiative. Meanwhile, the ECSC's Common Assembly established a committee to examine the creation of a common market, which the Netherlands had proposed as early as 1952. Thus, by the time the ministers of six nations met at Messina, Italy, the central issues to be determined were the scope of integration and whether economic unity achieved through shared national sovereignty was preferable to looser national cooperation. Despite German and French preferences for cautious approaches, the representatives of the Benelux countries – Belgium's Spaak, J. W. Beyen of Netherlands, and Luxembourg's Joseph Beck – won over Italy in support of a common market "free from all customs duties and all quantitative restrictions." Moreover, since lower tariffs exposed multinational cartels to competition, some sort of antitrust regime was necessary; on these points the ECSC's provision for cartel prohibition and exemption, as well as the clause forbidding abuse of dominant position, provided useful precedent. In 1956, Spaak authored a report which was the basis for the Treaty of Rome.[79]

---

[78] Ibid., 190, 191.
[79] Urwin, *Community of Europe*, 69–75, quote at 74; Gerber, *Protecting Prometheus*, 342–5; Schulze, *Germany*, 308. Britain participated briefly before withdrawing at Messina; Gerber, *Protecting Prometheus*, 343.

III. THE EUROPEAN ECONOMIC COMMUNITY AND SOCIAL WELFARE CAPITALISM, 1957–1986

During 1957, the six national parliaments ratified the Treaty of Rome, binding the people of the separate nations to one common market. The Treaty symbolized the initial postwar era of recovery and prosperity. By the mid-1950s the level of production in Western Europe's national economies was higher than before the war. Unemployment seemed defeated at last: in France it averaged just 1.3 percent between 1945 and 1969. By 1970, unemployment dropped to 0.5 percent in Germany. Both nations' economies grew at an average annual rate of five to six percent. No wonder the French described the period as the "glorious years," and the Germans celebrated an "economic miracle" fostering what Ludwig Erhard called "prosperity for all." But the oil shock of 1973 signaled the beginning a postwar era in which Western Europe, the United States, and Japan struggled for competitive advantage amid a cycle of contraction and growth. Persistent high unemployment soon returned.[80]

On New Year's day, 1958, the EEC began operation. In principle, membership was open to all Western European nations. The EEC expanded upon the ECSC's institutional structure: the assembly became a larger Parliament and the European Court's jurisdiction was increased. The EEC's authority was divided between the Council of Ministers which represented the member states and the commission composed of commissioners drawn from the member states, who worked with bureaucrats to make and implement policy. The council reviewed the acts of the commission. The common market embracing the ECSC's two industries was expanded to include leading sectors such as agriculture, manufacturing, and labor. The EEC required a special provision under the GATT, whereby "[t]ariffs and trade restrictions were to be reduced only gradually ... giving third parties the opportunities of adjusting to change without suffering severe economic disruption." Like the ECSC, the EEC exercised authority directly upon individuals, firms, and industries within the member states. The expanded objectives of creating and maintaining the common market inevitably lodged extensive power in the commission; by 1965 it assumed the executive functions of both the ECSC and Euratom, the third "community" which sanctioned France's atomic energy program, initially the only such program in Western Europe. The Treaty's antitrust provisions were integral to EEC integration.[81]

[80] Yergin and Stanislaw, *Commanding Heights*, 19–45, quotes at 45; Duchêne, *Jean Monnet*, 309–44; Moravcsik, *Choice for Europe*, 266–378; J. J. Servan-Schreiber, *The American Challenge* (New York, 1969); Urwin, *Community of Europe*, 101–228; Gerber, *Protecting Prometheus*, 342–69; Fischer, *Europeanization of America*; Derrick K. Wyatt and Alan Dashwood, *The Substantive Law of the EEC* (London, 1980).

[81] Urwin, *Community of Europe*, 76–87, quote at 77; Gerber, *Protecting Prometheus*, 342–3; Edwards, *Control of Cartels*, 281–320.

The council clearly possessed formidable power, but in terms of policy implementation and enforcement, individuals and enterprises most consistently felt the commission bureaucrats' steady presence. The scope of the common market meant, moreover, that the council's and the commission's actions inevitably possessed wider political ramifications than had been the case in the ECSC. Walter Hallstein emphasized the interdependency between political and economic integration: "We are not integrating economics, we are integrating policies. We are not just sharing our furniture, we are jointly building a new and bigger house." Similarly, Spaak recalled in 1964, "Those who drew up the Rome Treaty ... did not think of it as essentially economic; they thought of it as a stage on the way to political union." Yet how this intent manifested itself in actual policies shaping the behavior of workers, business people, farmers, and consumers largely depended on bureaucrats with little direct political accountability.[82]

The EEC gave higher priority than the ECSC to antitrust. Corwin Edwards observed that "[a]s a project for economic planning to improve the performance of the coal and steel industries, ECSC gives competition a clearly subordinate role. It is concerned with business restrictions chiefly to prevent them from becoming obstacles to official plans. In the EEC, however, the function assigned to competition is central." Indeed, Article 3 of the Treaty of Rome stipulated that one of the eleven essential functions required of the European Community was the "establishment of a system ensuring that competition in the Common Market is not distorted." This ranked among the fundamental "Principles" in the Treaty's Part I; and "Rules of Competition" were stated under the "Policy of the Community" in Part III. Thus, competition values in conjunction with institutionalizing the means to enforce them were integral to the administrative structure of the Treaty and the basic objective of achieving integration of the common market. This interdependency between means and ends enhanced the legitimacy and authority of those who ran the commission's competition bureau, DG IV.[83]

During the Treaty of Rome's negotiations opinions varied regarding the antitrust provisions. The Germans differed from the French, who favored a system resting on broad administrative discretion. The Netherlands officials were closer to the German position, and the Italians sided with the French. In addition, though by 1956–57 the actual enforcement of the ECSC Treaty's Articles 65 and 66 was problematic, the provisions offered, a German commentator observed, "three important lessons" influencing the Treaty of Rome: "In the first place, it was proved that the sectoral

[82] Urwin, *Community of Europe*, 76–87; Walter Hallstein, *United Europe* (Cambridge, MA, 1962), quote at 66.
[83] Edwards, *Control of Cartels*, 281; Wyatt and Dashwood, *Substantive Law of the EEC*, 247–51, quotes at 247, 249.

integration of Europe was possible although there existed different legal systems. Second, such an integration was possible, although cartels were prohibited. Third, a cartel prohibition programme was proved to be possible." Also, the tariff reductions the EEC's wider common market instituted exposed national cartels to competition and eventual disruption. "However, if an intra-European cartel can be formed it will become so powerful that it cannot be held in check by the case-by-case approach of abuse legislation," he said. "Only a prohibition law would be strict enough." In light of these considerations, the French contended that antitrust provisions were largely guides legitimating the administrator's discretion; the Germans viewed them as constitutional prescriptions curbing discretion.[84]

The Treaty of Rome's principal antitrust provisions were Articles 85 and 86. Government restraints were the object of Article 90, but it did not become significant until much later. Similar to Article 65 of the ECSC Treaty, Article 85 prohibited, declared unenforceable at law in national courts, and placed the burden of proof on parties to cartel agreements "which may affect trade between Member States and which have as their object or effect the prevention, restriction or distortion of competition within the market." Among a handful of agreements prohibited, "in particular" were price fixing, tie-in practices, and market sharing. Certain restrictive agreements, however, could be exempted that either were without proof of specified harm or resulted in stipulated benefits. Thus, the prohibition did not apply if the agreement contributed to "improving the production or distribution of goods or to promoting technical or economic progress, while allowing consumers a fair share of the resulting benefit." Or the agreement could be allowed if it did "not a) impose on the undertakings concerned restrictions which are not indispensable to the attainment of these objectives; and b) afford such undertakings the possibility of eliminating competition in respect of a substantial part of the products in question."[85]

Like Article 66 in the ECSC Treaty, Article 86 prohibited a business from abusing its position of dominant market power. The Treaty of Rome, however, had no merger provision. In addition, abusive behavior could not be exempted. Of course, Article 86 reached beyond two market sectors to achieve wider economic integration, stating that: "Any abuse by one or more undertakings of a dominant position within the common market or in a substantial part of it shall be prohibited as incompatible with the common market in so far as it may affect trade between Member States." Unlike the earlier provision, moreover, Article 86 stipulated forms of proscribed

---

[84] Compare Damm, "Factors Influencing Cartel Legislation," 117–18, quote at 119; Gerber, *Protecting Prometheus*, 342.

[85] Gerber, *Protecting Prometheus*, quote at 344–5, and otherwise followed closely in text.

abuse, including: "a) directly or indirectly imposing unfair purchase or selling prices or other unfair trading conditions; b) limiting production, markets or technical development, to the prejudice of consumers; c) applying dissimilar conditions to equivalent transactions with other trading parties, thereby placing them at a competitive disadvantage." Another provision defined "abuse" as "making the conclusion of contracts subject to acceptance by other parties of supplementary obligations which, by their nature or according to commercial usage, have no connection with the subject of such contracts."[86]

German and French attitudes primarily shaped the commission's early construction of this authority. Commission President Walter Hallstein said, "What the Community is integrating is the role of the state in establishing the framework within which economic activity takes place." During the early 1960s another Ordo Liberal figure, Arved Deringer, a German lawyer and member of the European Parliament, chaired a committee which fashioned the procedural framework governing DG IV's internal administration. A German lawyer later observed, "In the beginning, DG IV was absolutely dominated by Germans and German concepts, the reason being that Germany was the only member state having had already a lengthy practice with very outspoken antitrust laws. This German practice, however, had been greatly influenced by U.S. antitrust law, and by the reception of the rule of reason." But, the French successfully maintained industrial policy geared to protecting such interests as small business, jobs, or "declining" industries. The resulting tension between the approaches meant that protectionist actions, which were otherwise identified with trade policy, could be exempted under competition policy. The institutional autonomy resulting from the interplay between the German and French influences facilitated a growing belief among business interests that DG IV enforced the Treaty's competition provisions reasonably independently of external political pressures.[87]

Hallstein described the place of antitrust within the EEC's policy making process. Under the Treaty of Rome the member states agreed to "a number of very flexible ways, for joint action," he said. In "social matters" the Treaty stipulated "collaboration," whereas regarding "general economic policy, monetary and financial policy, and the balance of payments, it speaks of 'coordination,' partly through the Community's Monetary Committee. Cyclical policy and exchange-rate policy it requires to be

---

[86] Ibid.

[87] David J. Gerber, "Competition Law and International Trade: The European Union and the Neo-Liberal Factor," in John O. Haley and Hiroshi Iyori, eds., *Antitrust: A New International Trade Remedy?* (Seattle, 1995), 48–50, quote at 48; Otfried Lieberknecht, "Comment in Panel Discussion, EEC Competition Practice: Thirty-Year Retrospective," in Barry Hawk, ed., *Fordham Corporate Law Institute 19th Annual Conference on International Antitrust & Policy, 1992* (1993), 745–72, quoted at 750–1.

considered and treated as 'matters of common interest.' " In the field of tax policy "harmonization," was required, whereas "Apropos competition – including antitrust questions – the treaty demands 'common rules'; and for agriculture, transportation, and foreign trade it specifically stipulates 'common policies' should be applied." Obviously, the demand to establish a united front in policies concerning agriculture, exchange rates, and external trade were economic matters, but they were also "burningly political" because they involved the "issue of national sovereignty." By contrast, competition policy was sufficiently important to the principle of integration that in and of itself it aroused such conflicts only exceptionally.[88]

While the two policies formally operated in separate spheres, trade policy and antitrust interacted to promote EEC integration. The Treaty's commitment to achieving integration through freer competition worked directly on individual firms and corporations. The exemption principle enabled the commission to authorize certain anticompetitive practices among private businesses. Contrary to the way things worked under the Nazis, employing antitrust to integrate the member states into a common market promoted the competitiveness of private business and reinforced the competitive advantage of the nations within the community – separately and together – versus outsiders who also operated under the postwar GATT liberal trade system. Thus, Hallstein declared, a "transformation" of the "relations of the Community as a whole" toward the "rest of the world" was "of course one of the major aims of building the European Community – a new giant big enough to hold its own in a world of giant powers."[89]

Antitrust and trade policy sometimes converged. The competitiveness of private firms often relied not only on organizational and technological efficiencies – or even authorized exemptions – but on their relation to such sectors as labor, agriculture, or transportation, whose costs structures might receive protection under trade policy. During the 1970s market interdependencies threatened the textile industry in certain member states. Facing competition from East Asian and Eastern European imports, EEC textile firms argued that they were at a disadvantage because the foreign textile industries directly or indirectly received protection from the foreign governments' labor and trade policies. To be sure, EEC textile firms themselves operated under customs duties and other protective measures administered by the member states or the commissioner responsible for industrial policy. Nevertheless, the textile firms claimed that their survival depended on the commission's authorizing the formation of a cartel under

[88] Hallstein, *United Europe*, 65. On the introduction of "workable competition," see E. Kantzenbach, "Knowledge Resulting from Merger Policy in West Germany," in Alexis Jacquemin et al., *Merger and Competition Policy in the European Community* (Oxford, UK, 1991), vii, 119–37.

[89] Hallstein, *United Europe*, 66.

the exemption clause of the Treaty's Article 85. The commissioner for industrial policy actually drafted an authorization plan which he asserted was consistent with the exemption clause. But other commissioners opposed the plan, arguing that it was contrary to established competition policy and harmful to consumers. The division among the commissioners impeded action so that, at least in the short run, competition policy prevailed.[90]

The tensions underlying the authorization process and resulting from protectionist pressures tested the EEC. "If enough industries are allowed to form cartels and these arrangements are protected against imports," wrote one expert, "their combined price-raising effects will cause a rise in the general price level and the restrictions of their output will bring about a general decline in aggregate production and employment." The textile dispute further suggested the political and policy exigencies separating the prewar European and wartime Nazi systems of protective tariffs and cartels from the postwar commitment to integration and liberal trade. Thus, Hallstein affirmed, this "reordering of international economic relations … would enable the Community and its partners" to address the "world's outstanding problems – such as those of the trade with the Communist bloc, of world agriculture, and of aid for countries in course of development." Indeed, since 1957, the "immense increase in internal trade" has shown "that its 'common market' is a reality." This internal trade is "a trade-creating process which benefits the Community's partners in the rest of the world." As a result "the Community's external trade over the four-year period from 1958–1961 expanded more rapidly than that of any large country in the West."[91]

Integrating EEC economies through market-based competition posed challenges for new members. The accession process required negotiation to ensure that the applying nation met the policy and institutional standards prevailing throughout the community, including a viable competition policy regime. Industrial underdevelopment could prevent compliance with the standards, as could an undemocratic government. In 1960, nations outside the community created the European Free Trade Association which, in certain cases enabled nations to prepare gradually for community membership. Moreover, in 1963 and again in 1967 de Gaulle vetoed British membership, asserting that Britain's close association with the United States would impinge upon the community's autonomy and global competitiveness. After de Gaulle left power, a common external tariff system, revised Common Agricultural Policy, and a new financial structure preceded the accession in 1973 of Britain, Denmark, Ireland, and Norway, though

[90] Wyatt and Dashwood, *Substantive Law of the EEC*, 248.
[91] Ibid., 248; Hallstein, *United Europe*, 68, 77.

Britain renegotiated the terms of accession and the Norwegian referendum ultimately rejected EEC membership.[92]

Jean Monnet pursued a public discourse indicating the desired outcomes of competition policy, particularly equal treatment of private individuals and nations. Sydney Willner, recalled Monnet as saying that: "his vision of Europe was based on the conviction that the strength of the U.S. economy was due to its large market in which competitive forces were able to play without governmental or private interference. He envisioned a similar free market for Europe which meant not only that national barriers had to be done away with but equally private restraints by cartels and monopolies had to be eliminated." This vision was unusual, Willner declared, compared to Europeans' more common "refrain that competition was all right for the United States but was alien to European psychology which was based upon a need for order and stability." In his memoirs Monnet described the results of the antitrust provisions incorporated into the Treaty of Paris. "For Europe," he wrote, "they were a fundamental innovation: the extensive anti-trust legislation now applied by the European Community derives from those few lines in the Schuman Treaty." Monnet's recollection reflected the deep conviction he applied to human affairs generally, that "[e]quality is absolutely necessary between peoples as between individuals. We lost the peace in 1919 because we built discrimination into it, and the will to dominate (*esprit de superiorite*)."[93]

J. J. Servan-Schreiber pointedly characterized the relationship between the European Community and the "American challenge." Charles de Gaulle and others contended that protectionist political and economic policies were essential to prevent the takeover of European investment markets by American multinational corporations benefiting from "dollar inflation." The proliferation of U.S. corporate subsidiaries symbolized Western Europe's growing subordination and American hegemony. The "challenge" Servan-Schreiber diagnosed, by contrast, derived from the dynamism reflected in American managerial capacity to combine invention with the development, production, and marketing of products. "The originality of this revolution consists precisely in the effect this fusion of talents has on decisions made by government agencies, corporations, and universities," he said. America had come "a long way from the old image" of a nation where "business was not only separate from government but constantly struggling with it, and where there was a chasm between intellectuals and business-men. Today ... this combination of forces has produced the remarkable integrated entity that John Kenneth Galbraith calls a 'technostructure.' "[94]

[92] Urwin, *Community of Europe*, 88–179, 276–7.
[93] Willner, *First Step in European Integration*, 36; Jean Monnet, *Memoirs*, 352–3; Duchêne, "Jean Monnet's Methods," in Brinkley and Hackett, eds., *Jean Monnet*, 201.
[94] Serven-Schreiber, *American Challenge*, x, 28.

The European Community influenced this challenge, ambiguously. Servan-Schreiber quoted an American businessman as saying, "The Treaty of Rome is the sweetest deal ever to come out of Europe. It's what brought us here. We're happy to be here. We're making money. And we're going to make a lot more ... prospects in commerce and industry are better for us here than they are in the United States." Indeed, declared Servan-Schreiber, "American investment in Europe" resulted in "profits ... already half again as large as ours." The largest U.S. corporations achieved gains "through actual take-overs of European firms that Americans transform into rich and powerful corporations. And they do this with European money that our own businessmen do not know how to use." As of 1967–68 he found "French, German, or Italian firms ... still groping around in the new open spaces provided by the Treaty of Rome, afraid to emerge from the dilapidated shelter of their old habits." U.S. big business, by contrast, had "gauged the terrain" of the Common Market, "and is now rolling from Naples to Amsterdam with the ease and speed of Israeli tanks in the Sinai desert." Especially regarding the transfer of computer technology, Servan-Schreiber observed, the "stimulus of competition and the introduction of new techniques are clearly good for Europe. But the cumulative underdevelopment that could transform this assistance into a take over is bad for us." Still, if Europeans awoke to the danger, the EEC provided one channel for creating a competitive "technostructure."[95]

Servan-Schreiber diagnosed the U.S. threat, but Monnet and Hallstein were better prophets of the outcome. As Monnett and Hallstein had suggested, the commission employed equal treatment to achieve market integration effectively enough that the community became one of the three leading postwar global trading powers, along with the United States and Japan. The commission's Competition Bureau fostered that result by enforcing equality within the member states. In doing so, DG IV promoted competitive capitalism at home, thereby strengthening competitiveness abroad. In 1962 the commission's council adopted Regulation No.17, a technical rule having large ramifications. Regulation No.17 established a notification process governing the daily transactions of European and foreign companies operating within the Treaty of Rome's jurisdiction. As a practical matter the notification process left the DG IV's bureaucrats with sufficient discretion to resolve difficult competition issues, including the granting of exemptions.[96]

[95] Ibid., 9, 28, 29.
[96] Gerber, *Protecting Prometheus*, 349–51; Gerber "Competition Law and International Trade," in Haley and Iyori, eds., *Antitrust*, 49–50, 52, 53; Carl H. Fulda, "Antitrust Development in the European Economic Community, Statement ... before Senate Subcommittee on Antitrust and Monopoly, June 7, 1966," HKP, Box 1, "Antitrust Hearing," GUSC, 4–5; David Broomhall and Joanna Goyder, "European Union," *Modernization in Europe 2004* (London, 2004), 6–9.

Bosch/ De Geus revealed the significance of Regulation No. 17. Bosch, a
German machine manufacturer, maintained an exclusive selling agreement
with Van Rijn, a dealer in the Netherlands. Under the agreement German
dealers could not sell Bosch machines in the Netherlands, but De Geus
obtained Bosch equipment from a German company in violation of the
contract. Alleging breach of the restrictive agreement, Bosch sued De Geus
for damages in a Dutch court, which in accordance with provisions of the
Rome Treaty referred the case to the community's Court of Justice. The
legal issue was whether Bosch-Van Rijin were bound to make public their
anticompetitive agreement under Regulation No. 17, which had just gone
into force. The court upheld the commission's ruling. "Without the notification requirement," declared an antitrust expert, "the Commission
would not have been able to secure the enormous amount of information
about business practices which it has now."[97] The same year in *Grundig-
Consten*, the commission declared invalid an exclusive dealing contract
between Grundig, a major German radio and television maker, and Consten, the French wholesaler. Contrary to the restrictive contracts, German
wholesalers sold Grundig's products to French importers, who resold them
below Consten's prices. Consten sued alleging unfair competition in a
French Court, which referred the case to the commission. Condemning in
particular the export prohibition, the commission held that the Grundig-
Consten agreement violated Article 85; on review, the court upheld that
result.[98]

The wide scope of discretion left the DG IV staff considerable authority
to implement equal treatment toward business. The Treaty did establish
judicial review as a check on bureaucratic judgment. Over the years the
number of significant court precedents grew, until the court became the
final authority legitimating the community's integration. Bureaucratic discretion enforced through nondiscrimination nonetheless remained central
to antitrust administration. The Competition Bureau maintained its institutional credibility within the business community by granting effective
access and being reasonably objective, despite persistent delays. The "key to
the degree of success" the commission achieved in the "difficult administration of a system of this kind," said one experienced lawyer, was the
"accessibility of the staff to meetings with counsel and executives for preliminary review. Without such availability in a system that is so much based
on automatic condemnations and discretionary exemptions, the system
would probably by and large have become discredited in the eyes of the
business community." In addition, nationalization of industries was always
an industrial-policy alternative to private enterprise in the nations seeking
integration. Concerns about equal treatment inevitably arose when private

[97] Case 13/61 [1962] E.C.R. 45 [1962] C.M.L.R. 1; Fulda, "Antitrust Development ," 6.
[98] 1 CCH/C.M.L.R. 2743; Joined cases 56 & 64, 1966, E.C.R. 299.

enterprise faced companies controlled by the government. Nevertheless, the reputation for even-handed treatment that competition authorities built up over the years endured.[99]

Market-based competition remained contentious as the community expanded. Thus, Giandomenico Majone noted, it took the chaotic international business conditions beginning in the 1970s to weaken the faith Western European governments and businessmen had in "economic regulation ... to replace the market, for example, through public ownership, rather than to increase its efficiency by correcting specific forms of market failure." In addition, the heritage of labor–business relations entwined with socialism engendered wider popular acceptance of higher costs than was the case in the United States. These factors imposed close political links between private companies and member state governments which inevitably raised concerns about discriminatory practices among companies doing business across borders. Issues involving equal treatment were exacerbated as governments attempted to address the contraction in growth by reducing fiscal burdens through privatization of state enterprises. In Great Britain Prime Minister Margaret Thatcher led the retreat from state ownership, public enterprise, and Keynesian economics. The proliferation of privatized enterprises altered the terms of market competition and heightened the "social-welfare" costs. More than ever competition involved employment and the related immigration tensions arising from unstable transnational markets.[100]

The commission's discretionary enforcement regime gradually promoted equal treatment within a more competitive Common Market. As the *Bosch* and *Grundig* cases suggested, the commission's enforcement empowered businesses engaged in cross-border transactions; grasping the benefits of competition, these firms demonstrated that the "stability" Europeans traditionally ascribed to restrictive agreements often masked discriminatory treatment. Cartel behavior clearly persisted. This was so in part because some member states had weak antitrust regimes, a few others such as Germany and Britain pursued more active enforcement, and, given that Regulation 17 granted firms a long grace period for compliance, the commission's enforcement efforts evolved by degrees. Most importantly, the commission pursued and the courts upheld policies permitting cooperation among small- and medium-sized firms to avoid domination from big business, including multinational corporations. In 1964, Corwin Edwards wrote that the "impact of most cartels is local or national, not international."

[99] Donald L. Holley, "EEC Competition Practice: A Thirty-Year Retrospective," in Hawk, ed., *19th Annual Fordham Corporate Law Institute, 1992*, 707; Gerber, *Protecting Prometheus*, 182, 193–4, 351–3, 376–8; Yergin and Stanislaw, *Commanding Heights*, 25–9, 300–2, 366–7.
[100] Majone, "Rise of Statutory Regulation," in Majone, ed., *Regulating Europe*, 47–60, quote at 50; Yergin and Stanislaw, *Commanding Heights*, 13, 114–37, 317–19.

European government regulations were "usually designed to keep prices fair rather than free, and most governments accepted cartels for purposes of 'rationalization.' But curbs upon exclusion from the market, and upon discrimination intended to have exclusive effect ... are relatively severe." Even so, he concluded, "[t]hose by the EEC have promise but are too new to have clear effect."[101]

And yet, enduring patterns of compliance emerged. Recalling this early period of community competition law development, one lawyer noted, "First, there prevailed a strong skepticism on the part of European companies about the significance and practical impact of the new rules." Still, the commissioner and bureaucrats running DG IV endeavored to establish an antitrust regime, rigidly adhering neither to U.S. nor to German practice. "Already in the early 1960s the concept of market unity was the dominant force in EEC competition law," the lawyer recalled, and "[d]espite the prominence of cartel cases, application of the market unity concept to vertical agreements involving private companies was the dominant theme." The "concentrated focus on the concept of market unity may have been leading the Commission into ignoring from time to time certain precepts of sound competition-based analysis." A German lawyer noted, by contrast, that within the commission the "options were many, but basically the French and German systems were in competition. Neither of them was fully accepted. Thus, we have a mixed system without real national precedent. We still have not quite digested its dogmas, but we have become used to it."[102]

The commission addressed American challenges by developing theories of mergers and abuse of dominance. Though Article 86 had no formal merger provision, DG IV officials perceived that its abuse-of-dominance principle could be applied to the kind of merger strategies big business and multinational corporations used. The first major case testing a multinational corporation's acquisition strategy was *Continental Can*. This U.S. container maker took over the German firm SLW, a leading producer of light metal containers and "related products." Continental Can's European subsidiary then purchased TDV, a Dutch company that produced the same

[101] Gerber, *Protecting Prometheus*, 364–7; Corwin D. Edwards, *Cartelization in Western Europe*, in *Foreign Trade and the Antitrust Law*, Part 1, General Considerations, *Hearings before Subcommittee on Antitrust and Monopoly of the Committee on the Judiciary United States Senate 2nd Sess. July 22, 23, 29, 1964* (Washington, DC, 1964), 478; Wendy Asbeek-Brusse and Richard Griffiths, "The Incidence of Manufacturing Cartels in Post-War Europe," in Morello, ed., *Cartels and Market Management in the Post-War World*, Occasional Paper No. 1, London School of Economics (London, 1997), 78–117.

[102] Holley, "EEC Competition Practice: A Thirty-Year Retrospective," and Lieberknecht, "EEC Competition Practice: A Thirty-Year Retrospective, Panel Discussion," in Hawk, ed., *19th Annual Conference Fordham Corporate Law Institute*, 1992, 670, 671, 672, 707, 747, 748.

sorts of specialized containers and products. Examining the Continental Can-TDV merger, the commission applied the theory that it "amounted to an abuse of the dominant position which Continental Can held, through SLW, on three packaging markets in Germany, because TDV had been a potential competitor of SLW and the effect of bringing it into the Continental Can group had been practically to eliminate competition in the products concerned over a substantial part of the Common Market." The commission decided against Continental Can in 1972. The following year, however, the court overturned the decision "on the ground that the relevant facts had not been adequately analyzed."[103]

The court's decisions, nonetheless, encouraged the commission's further action. In *Continental Can* the court also held that in principle the commission's theory could be employed to address the abuse of dominance resulting from the complex merger-acquisitions Continental Can had pursued through its European subsidiaries. Meanwhile, in a series of leading cases from 1974 to 1986 – often involving U.S. multinational corporations – the commission and the court expanded the abuse of dominance theory. Another turning point was the court's decision in 1978, upholding the commission's application of Article 86 against the United Brands, which was found to have abused its dominant position in the European banana market. As one European lawyer observed: "it was *United Brands* that brought Article 86 into the daily lives of counsel."[104]

An ongoing trade battle with Japan tested the community's external competitiveness. The textile confrontation of the 1970s was indicative of a larger transformation in trade relations between Japan and the European Community which reached a critical stage by the mid-1980s. In 1983 Japan's surplus with the community reached a historic high of $10.4 billion; and, Japan's trade surplus with the United States was a record $18.1 billion. That same year the community's exports to Japan increased less, at 7.4 percent, than Japan's exports to the community, which grew by 8.6 percent. A conspicuous measure of Europe's competitive decline was the rise in unemployment to "10.9 percent of the employed population." The sharp contrast with Hallstein's optimistic assessment twenty years earlier was especially troubling. Political pressures for trade protection mounted. In 1977 the commission imposed an antidumping duty of 20 percent on ball-bearing imports from Japan. Six years later the commission doubled the tariff on Japanese digital audio discs. In 1983 the commission negotiated Voluntary Trade Restraints in which Japan agreed to limit

---

[103] *Europemballage Corp. & Continental Can Co. v. Commission*, Case 6/72 1973 E.C.R. 215; Wyatt and Dashwood, *Substantive Law of the EEC*, 315–18, quote at 316.

[104] Gerber, *Protecting Prometheus*, 367–8; Holley, "EEC Competition Practice: A Thirty-Year Retrospective," in Hawk, ed., *19th Annual Conference Fordham Corporate Law Institute*, 1992, 696, 697; *United Brands Co.*, O.J. L 95/1 (1976).

various exports including television sets and parts, automobiles, hi-fi
equipment and tape recorders, quartz watches, motorcycles, fork-lift
vehicles, and light trucks.[105]

   The trade struggle pitting Europe against Japan and the United States
fostered greater community economic integration. Japan skillfully exploited
the cold war defense and economic alliances it maintained with the United
States, while it used industrial policy to sustain trade surpluses. In addition,
the Japanese pursued separate bilateral limits on autos and other goods
with the British, French, and Italians, which increased protectionist
demands within the community itself and disrupted efforts to establish a
more liberal trade regime under the GATT. Nevertheless, "[t]hanks to the
moderating influence of the European Commission and some member
states," an expert noted in 1986, "pressures to close the Common Market
have been alleviated." Even so, Japan's "play[ing] off one member state
against another" increased support for "greater cohesion" among the
member states, which in turn fostered support for the commission's leading
role. Thus, the three-sided trade rivalry among Japan, the United States,
and Europe facilitated the community's committing itself to achieving the
goal of a single market. Until then, a renamed European Community
worked at deepening sovereignty-sharing, including the interaction between
trade and competition polices.[106]

IV. THE EUROPEAN UNION, GLOBAL CAPITALISM, AND ANTITRUST MODERNIZATION SINCE 1986

The ending of the cold war intensified global economic rivalry. The
declining competitiveness of the United States, epitomized by the stock
market collapse of 1987 and an ensuing recession, strengthened the competitive advantage of the European Community and its member states.
Then the Maastricht Treaty of 1992 instituted the European Union (EU)
and opened the way for the accession of new nations. The Treaty coincided
with the U.S. economy's renewed hegemony and a global economic boom
persisting nearly until the terrorist attacks of September 11, 2001.[107]

---

[105] Reinhard Drifte, "Euro-Japanese Relations: Realities and Prospects," in Gordon Daniels
and Reinhard Drifte eds., *Europe & Japan Changing Relationships, since 1945* (Kent, UK,
1986), 92–104, quote at 93, 94; Endymion Wilkinson, *Japan Versus the West Image and
Reality* (London, 1990).

[106] Drifte, "Euro-Japanese Relations: Realities and Prospects," in Daniels and Drifte, eds.,
Europe & Japan, 94, 97; Gerber, *Protecting Prometheus*, 334, 370.

[107] Urwin, *Community of Europe*, 212–62; Moravcsik, *Choice for Europe*, 379–502; Timothy
Garton Ash, *The Polish Revolution: Solidarity* (London, 1999), 287–381; Dominique
Moisi, "Eurocrats are from Mars, Cosmrats from Venus," *Financial Times* (June 5, 2000),
17; Quentin Peel, "OSCE Minorities Chief Aims for Early Action," *Financial Times* (May
19, 2000), 3; Reginald Dale, "'Federal' Europe: Hardly a Radical Idea," *International*

As the community gave way to the Union, the commission's trade and antitrust policies were subject to renewed contention. By 1987 the "major preoccupation of EEC lawyers" shifted from the focus on rules concerning the "functioning *of* the market place" and the "political goals of creating an integrated Common Market" to "an increasing preoccupation with the problems of securing access *to* the marketplace. How goods from one country should be admitted to commerce in another country is a major internal preoccupation of the Community as it struggles to achieve true integration of twelve national markets by December 31, 1992." Thus, just as the commission faced demands from European firms to promote their access to Japanese markets, many of the same firms urged it to limit foreign multinational corporations' competition in European markets. The issues concerned the increasingly ambiguous separation between trade and anti-trust policies involving the "notoriously controversial topic of anti-dumping policy, where the EEC is adopting U.S. habits, and other protective measures." During the 1990s, the status of anticompetitive agreements under the WTO complicated and agitated the antitrust-trade policy distinction. Meanwhile, multinational corporations pursuing financial agreements ranging from mergers and joint ventures to international cartels tested the limits of global cooperation among antitrust regimes.[108]

From the mid-1980s on, the commission wrestled with the antidumping issue. "The special feature of an anti-dumping procedure, unlike almost all other trade policy proceedings, is that it is directed against individuals," an international lawyer stated. Generally, government officials charged mul-tinational corporations with "unfair or abusive conduct" and, after an investigation, imposed "specific penalties in the form of anti-dumping duties." The GATT liberal trade system recognized that dumping "is to be condemned if it causes or threatens material injury to an established industry in the territory of a contracting party or materially retards the establishment of domestic industry." In reaction to the Japanese trade challenge, the European Commission enforced an aggressive antidumping policy not unlike that of the United States. The duties the commission imposed covered some twenty Japanese products.[109]

Nevertheless, the costs and benefits of antidumping measures were ambiguous. Between 1980 and 1985, the Japanese investment in Europe

Herald Tribune (May 23, 2000); "European Reform," *The Economist* (July 17–23, 2004), 13, 51–2.

[108] Urwin, *Community of Europe*, 212–62; Moravcsik, *Choice for Europe*, 379–502; Ian S. Forrester, "EEC Trade Law and the United States," in Barry E. Hawk, ed., *14th Annual Fordham Corporate Law Institute on North American and Common Market Antitrust and Trade Laws, October 22 & 23, 1987* (New York, 1988), 469–511, quotes at 469–70. See below for WTO issues.

[109] Forrester, "EEC Trade Law and the United States," in Hawk, ed., *14th Annual Fordham Corporate Law Institute*, 476, 499–500.

totaled $6.5 billion; it also "creat[ed] 72,000 jobs. Some of those factories make products which if they were exported from Japan, would have been subject to anti-dumping duties." The interaction between territorial protectionism and the investment of individual multinational corporations "seems to be at odds with the growing internationalism of modern business. Companies based in America have factories in Japan and Europe, Japanese companies have joint ventures with European companies who complain about them in dumping cases, European companies get technical assistance from Japanese companies, and so on." The territorial centeredness of antidumping policy thus enmeshed the internal operation strategies of multinational corporations in "outdated assumptions of defenders of a clearly defined territory and penetration thereof by aggressors. It is difficult to tell whether an American-based multinational with its European headquarters in Sweden, a French factory and a Japanese affiliate is friend or foe according to traditional concepts."[110]

The commission's effort to draw the line between trade and antitrust policy coincided with growing pressure for merger regulation. Formally, trade and antitrust policies operated in separate spheres. However, during the 1980s DG IV "could be more sympathetic" toward "bilateral industry-to-industry understandings" than it had been a decade earlier "not because of enthusiasm for such dealings but because of concern about the anti-competitive impact of anti-dumping duties." Within the commission's bureaus "it is no secret that several industry-to-industry agreements which are manifestly illegal under competition rules, but which pragmatically solve trade tensions … have not been challenged."[111]

Since the *Continental Can* decision, the commission applied abuse-of-dominance theories to police corporations' complex financial arrangements. Increasingly, the assertion of authority over mergers created conflicts with member states, because the commission was "concerned that it should be able to prevent national competition authorities from controlling mergers of which it approves." The commission noted in particular the competing authority of Germany's Cartel Office. Complicating the issue was the commission's desire to exercise as much discretion as possible over the exemptions it might negotiate with private companies. When the commission "states in a formal decision that Article 86 is not infringed because of the advantages to the community in terms of efficiency, jobs, etc, then it would like to prevent member states from condemning the merger on the ground that it is important in a single member state."[112]

Two cases suggested how the commission's discretion influenced financial structure and technology transfers. In *Optical Fibres* (1986) the

---

[110] Ibid., 500, 502.   [111] Ibid., 505–6.
[112] Valentine Korah, "Joint Ventures (Exemption or Clearance), Mergers and Partial Mergers," in Hawk, ed., *14th Annual Fordham Corporate Law Institute*, 422–52.

commission ordered the restructuring of financial agreements and patent licenses involving U.S. multinational Corning, a major manufacturer of optical fibers, BICC, the British cable producer, and Siemens, the German electrical engineering giant. The commission decided that separate joint venture agreements did not violate Article 85(1), "but that the network of joint ventures made by a provider of important technology protected by patents in a concentrated market restricted competition and required exemption." Negotiating through the exemption process, the commission ensured that the "agreements expressly stipulate that each joint venture will sell its optical fibres to all users on non-discriminatory terms and to treat third parties on the same terms as its parents." In *Philip Morris* (1987) – a case involving principally British and South-African multinational corporations making tobacco products, with large shareholders in the Netherlands and Belgium/Luxembourg – the Court of Justice expanded the commission's authority under Article 85(1) to include stock-share acquisitions. Upholding the commission, the court's "judgment did clarify a point of great industrial and legal importance."[113]

Perhaps most importantly, the *Philip Morris* decision provided the "Commission the added impetus it needed to push the Merger Regulation for adoption by the Council." Thus, the European Commission Merger Regulation was drafted in 1989 and went into operation in 1990. The Regulation used terms such as "dominant position," "partial-mergers," and "cooperative joint ventures" that, if rigidly enforced, would have engendered resistance from business. But the actual practice of the measure's enforcement had "a marked similarity to practice under merger control laws of a number of other countries, including the United States." In contrast to the slowness which characterized administration of Regulation 17, the commission enforced the Merger Regulation expeditiously, in keeping with the fast-moving financial market dynamics driving merger decisions. During the Merger Regulation's initial years of operation, disputes arose requiring that a distinction be made between unauthorized "concentrative" and permissible "cooperative" joint ventures. In *Elf-Enterprise* (1991) the commission authorized as "cooperative" a joint venture to further North Sea oil and gas exploration. The commission held "that the parents' agreement not to compete with the joint venture concerning the obtention of new licenses was consistent with the coordination of the parents' behavior rather than a sign they had entered into a concentrative joint venture."[114]

---

[113] Ibid., 436–41, quotes at 436, 440; O.J. L 236/30 (1986), Comm. Mkt. Rep. (CCH) ¶10,831. *British American Tobacco Co. Ltd. & R.J. Reynolds Indus., Inc. v. Commission, Cases,* 142 and 146/84, 1987 E.C.R. 4487; Philip Morris/Rembrandt/Rothmans, slip op (Eur. Comm'n. March 21, 1984) (not published) (rejecting Complaint), in Comm'n., (Fourteenth Report on Competition), Policy ¶ 98 (1985).

[114] Holley, "EEC Competition Practice: A Thirty-Year Retrospective," in Hawk, ed., *19th Annual Conference Fordham Corporate Law Institute,* 1992, quotes at 700, 726; James

Subsequent cases tested the range of joint-venture agreements, which in turn fostered the Merger Regulation's revision. Throughout the early 1990s, cases repeatedly arose concerning joint ventures or partial-mergers among several of the community's leading firms. The commission also confronted the same or related issues involving community firms' dealings with U.S. and Japanese multinational corporations. During 1991, it wrestled too, with issues relating to EU companies entering into financial services joint ventures in Hungary and Czechoslovakia. A noteworthy commission decision was *Ericsson/Kolbe*, holding "[i]n effect" that "where there was no risk of coordination between the parties of the joint venture, and one of the parties assumed 'leadership' of the joint venture, the latter would be treated, for purposes of analyzing the risk of coordination, as if it were a subsidiary of the 'lead' parent." This "industrial leadership doctrine" enabled the commission to overcome criticism it had faced since 1990 regarding the boundary between legitimate "coordination" and illegal "dominance." Adapting the principle, the commission amended the Merger Regulation in 1994 and 1997. In *Kali und Salz* the European Court of Justice construed the revision to establish a rigorous test requiring microeconomic analysis of evidence in order to prove that long-term "coordination" of "price and output" fostered "oligopolistic dominance."[115]

Notwithstanding some qualifications, European lawyers concluded that officials exercised discretion fairly in administering the Merger Regulation. Said one such lawyer: the "Commission's credibility was hanging in the balance. Counsel and the business community soon agreed that the administration of the Merger Regulation was turning out to be a big success. It is rare to see such unanimity on any point within the Community." Still, the Merger Regulation's relative vagueness left bureaucrats such discretion that challenges to their objectivity would inevitably arise in controversial cases. In one case, DG IV successfully blocked the merger of Italian and French aircraft manufactures with a Canadian firm, despite pressure from national interests, but in another case the commission did not overcome resistance from private steel manufacturers who opposed its plan to assist state-aided steel firms seeking to maintain jobs. Thus, "Because there is nothing very much quantified in the Regulation; it remains a rule of

Venti, "The Treatment of Joint Ventures under the EC Merger Regulation-Almost Through the Thicket," in Barry E. Hawk, ed., *26th Annual Fordham Corporate Law Institute on International Antitrust Law & Policy, 1999* (Yonkers, NY, 2000), 465–93, quote at 469; *Elf/Enterprise*, O.J. C 203/14 (1991) (Comm'n).
[115] For discussion of agreements among leading firms, see Venti, "The Treatment of Joint Ventures," Hawk, ed., *26th Annual Fordham Corporate Law Institute*, 470–93, quotes at 474, 492. *Ericsson/Kolbe* Case No. IV/M. 133 (1992) (Comm'n.); *Kali und Salz*, Joined cases 68/94 and 30/95, 1998, ECRI-1375 (1998) (C.J.).

man rather than a rule of law. We can only praise ourselves that for the time being the men have been clement in their rulings."[116]

This implementation of the Merger Regulation during the 1990s coincided with growing trans-national cooperation among antitrust authorities. Although some international antitrust experts questioned the practical enforcement value of such cooperation, by the millennium it was increasingly common. An unusual example suggesting more coercion than cooperation was the Structural Impediments Initiative (1989–92) between the United States and Japan. The U.S./EC Antitrust Agreement of 1991 represented a more typical formal bilateral arrangement; it sought to harmonize the institutional cultures of the world's most active antitrust regimes. Initially implemented under James Rill of the U.S. Justice Department's Antitrust Division, the agreement authorized notification of "reported transactions" within the combined jurisdiction. It instituted, too, regular meetings "to exchange information relevant to premerger review, subject to each party's respective laws governing confidentiality, e.g., non-proprietary materials or information contained in premerger filings." The agreement also authorized "coordinated investigations where the United States and EC are looking at related conduct, after both sides concluded it would be advantageous to enter into that sort of arrangement."[117]

At the same time a basic factor circumscribing global convergence of national enforcement regimes was confidential information. Antitrust authorities addressed the confidentiality issue with mixed success. By 2000 progress toward nations entering into such agreements was slow, but the degree of trans-national cooperation established in the U.S./EC Agreement was repeated in a growing web of bilateral agreements between the United States and, respectively, Germany, Australia, Canada, and Japan. The last three nations, in turn, entered into bilateral agreements with other nations and the EU. Thus, while a formal resolution to the confidentiality problem eluded antitrust authorities, they nonetheless established increasingly effective enforcement through various cooperative arrangements. A promising approach that Charles Stark of the U.S. Antitrust Division suggested was "positive comity," whereby antitrust authorities cooperated to

---

[116] Holley, "EEC Competition Practice: A Thirty-Year Retrospective" and Ivo Van Bael, "Panel Discussion," in Hawk, ed., *19th Annual Fordham Corporate Law Institute, 1992*, quotes at 728, 767; Loraine Laudati, "The European Commission as Regulator: The Uncertain Pursuit of the Competitive Market," in Majone, ed., *Regulating Europe*, 221–64, especially 236–8, 255.

[117] A positive assessment of bilateral cooperative agreements, especially the US/EC Agreement of 1991 is James F. Rill and Virginia R. Metallo, "The Next Step: Convergence of Procedure and Enforcement," in Hawk, ed., *19th Annual Fordham Corporate Law Institute*, 1992, 5–40, quotes at 23, 24; critical of this view and a proponent of a "conflict-of-law" alternative is Eleanor M. Fox, "Toward World Antitrust and Market Access," 91 *American Journal of International Law* (January 1997), 1–25.

determine the one best situated to address the illegal conduct of, for example, a multinational corporation with divisions operating in both jurisdictions. While one authority took the lead, the other provided continuing support, including the search for evidence.[118]

Such cooperation imposed accountability in international cartel cases. From the 1990s through to the turn of the century, U.S. antitrust authorities led the aggressive campaign against international cartels, receiving significant ongoing support from the European Commission and individual member states. An example was the commission's contribution to the U.S. Antitrust Division's winning a $225 million fine against a German firm and a "record" fine of $10 million from an individual German corporate executive. Also, after the millennium, the uncovering of evidence in such large international cartel cases facilitated the commission's imposing penalties of more than 3 million euros upon cartel members. The commission "expanded its cartel investigations dramatically. ... In 2001, the commission issued ten cartel case decisions and levied fines of 1.8 billion Euros on over 50 companies." Though blatant criminal behavior clearly motivated certain defendants, many malefactors possessed a remarkable capacity for self-delusion whereby they convinced themselves that their actions were either somehow not actually illegal or conversely, that they were too smart to be caught. Prosecutors exploited denial mentalities in various ways, such as increasing the case of procuring evidence by offering access to leniency programs. [119]

Cooperation among U.S., Canadian, and European Commission antitrust officials also strengthened enforcement efforts. Thus, a U.S. Antitrust Division official observed in 2004 that like U.S. officials, "[b]oth the European Commission and Canada also regularly impose very significant fines on companies found to have engaged in cartel activity." Accordingly, "[f]or companies engaged in conspiratorial conduct that effects commerce in

---

[118] Charles S. Stark, "The International Application of United States Antitrust Laws," *International Antitrust in a Global Economy*, International Association of Young Lawyers (New Orleans, April 24–27, 1997), 1–12; Office for WTO Compliance and Dispute Settlement, Ministry of Economy, Trade and Industry (METI), "Unilateral Measures," 2004 *Report on the WTO Consistency of Trade Policies by Major Trading Partners* (Tokyo, 2004), 415–20.

[119] Joel Klein, "Anti-Cartel Cases-U.S. Department of Justice," and "International Cartel Enforcement Panel Discussion," in Hawk, ed., *26th Annual Fordham Corporate Law Institute*, 13–29, 57–74; James M. Griffin, "The Basics of a Successful Anti-Cartel Enforcement Program," *Competition Law and Policy in a Global Context* (Seoul, 2004), 1–11, quotes at 3; Donald C. Klawiter, "Who's Next? The Growing Movement to Investigate and Prosecute Corporate Executives in Antitrust Cartel Investigation," *Competition Law Compliance Domestic and International Perspectives on Managing Compliance in a Changing Legal Environment* (Toronto, May 26, 27, 2004), 1–12, quote at 2 (Klawiter discussed the "criminal types" in response to T. A. Freyer's question asked from the floor during Q&A of Toronto meeting).

North America and Europe, the possibility of stiff corporate fines in three different jurisdictions should considerably affect their risk/reward calculation."[120]

The impact of trans-national cooperation among antitrust authorities in merger and monopoly cases was more ambiguous. Notwithstanding the confidentiality problem, cooperation usually ensured that complex financial combinations moved forward in compliance with the merger guidelines of the appropriate authorities. The *Boeing/McDonnell Douglas* case of 1997 nonetheless revealed that the antitrust regimes with the most secure record of cooperation could disagree: the U.S. Federal Trade Commission and the European Commission applied conflicting theories to the global market for big airplanes.[121] Regarding the *General Electric/Honeywell* merger, the clash was more pronounced. After authorizing the merger within U.S. territory, U.S. authorities protested the commission's refusal to do so because of its impact in Europe. The disagreement encouraged General Electric to appeal the decision to the European Court. This division recurred in the *Microsoft* case: the United States imposed a modest settlement preserving the company's control of the web browser; the commission instituted a quite different remedy requiring Microsoft to surrender its monopoly over the Media Player. Microsoft also appealed.[122]

These high-profile appeals followed three European Court decisions in 2002 holding that the commission's economic analysis had been insufficiently rigorous. In the leading *Airtours* decision, the Court of First Instance

---

[120] Griffin, "Basis of Successful Anti-Cartel Enforcement Program," 1–11, quote at 3.

[121] Joel I. Klein, "Anticipating the Millennium: International Antitrust Enforcement at the End of the Twentieth Century," in Barry E. Hawk, ed., *24th Annual Fordham Corporate Law Institute New York City, 1997* (Yonkers, NY, 1998), 1–12, especially 7–8. Klein predicted [p. 8] the " *Boeing* experience has made officials ... outside the antitrust agencies – keenly aware that, as much as we have in common, there remain important differences between U.S. and European antitrust law and enforcement philosophies. If we antitrust enforcers fail to manage these differences ... there will be a greatly increased risk that particular antitrust disputes will become politicized." In Re the Proposed Acquisition of McDonnell Douglas Corp. by the Boeing Co., FTC File No. 971–005 (July 1, 1997); Boeing/McDonnell Douglas, O.J. L 336/16 (1997) (Comm'n.). See also Joel I. Klein, "The War against International Cartels: Lessons from the Battle Front," and "International Cartel Enforcement and EC Competition Policy Panel Discussion," in Hawk, ed., *26th Annual Fordham Corporate Law Institute Conference, 1999*, 14–37, 57–75.

[122] David Samuels, "An Interview with Hewitt Pate," 7 *Global Competition Review* (June 2004), 8–10. On EC side, see Gotz Drauz, "Unbundling GE/Honeywell: The Assessment of Conglomerate Mergers under EC Competition Law," in Hawk, ed., *28th Annual Fordham Corporate Law Institute Conference, 2001* (Huntington, NY, 2002), 183–202; *General Electric/Honeywell*, Case No. Comp/M. 2220. For Microsoft case citations as of August 2004, see Microsoft IP/00/141, and Microsoft IV/01/1232; "Excerpts from Ruling in Europe and Microsoft's Response," *New York Times* (March 25, 2004), section //C, p. 11; Steve Lohr, "Paring Away at Microsoft Regulators in Europe Take on Business Plan," *New York Times* (March 25, 2004), section //1, p. 1; and Wes Full case citations given below.

overturned the commission's rejection of the merger between two British travel firms, Airtours and First Choice Holidays. Next, the court overturned the commission's blocking the merger of the French electrical goods producer, Schneider Electric with rival Legrand. In the third decision, the court overturned the commission's denial of the purchase by packaging conglomerate, Tetra Laval of Sidel, a French bottle maker. The court's decisions focused on the commission's insufficient showing of the links between the legal terms of collective or joint dominance and the economic theory of tacit collusion. Thus, in *Airtours*, the court did not support the commission's finding that the merger established collective dominance in the "UK foreign package holiday market," essentially because it did not analyze the facts in terms of the economic theory of tacit collusion, which in turn required applying a "checklist" of ten market features.[123]

Considering the fate of the *General Electric/Honeywell* and *Microsoft* appeals in terms of these rulings may be misplaced. However, Marlo Monti, the commissioner for Competition, responded to the decisions by hiring a business-oriented economist and establishing a probusiness "devil's advocate" within the commission's Merger Task Force to strengthen analysis. Americans agreed that Monti "reacted well to his three defeats," and "handled it beautifully being conciliatory."[124] Regarding the merits of the theories themselves, European expert Matthias Pflanz pointed out that the use of the "check list" to show collusion was always complex, ensuring "significant further debate," and predicted that the commission's "practice will continue to evolve." The commission's as well as the court's decisions reflected the ongoing restructuring of European and multinational corporations along the lines of the core goals of market integration and proscription of dominance imposed by the EU treaty structure. Moreover, the commission's legitimacy depended to a considerable extent on treating the member state's individuals and firms equally. Ultimately, the measure of any economic theory was whether it comported with the multiplicity of values and interests.[125]

Trans-national cooperation also did not prevail regarding the creation of a multinational antitrust regime under the WTO. One result of the GATT Uruguay Round ending in 1994 was that the new WTO was empowered to enforce trade rules. Translating this general grant into particular policies raised difficult issues concerning the degree to which the WTO's policies

---

[123] Case T-342/99 *Air Tours v. Commission* [2002] ECR 11–2585; Case T-310/01 *Schneider Electric v. Commission* [2002] ECR 11–04071; Case T-502 *Tetra Laval v. Commission* [2002] ECR 11–4381; *Air Tours* CFI, Case No. T-342/99; and Matthias Pflanz, "Introduction to the Economics of Competition Law," *IBC EU Competition Law Summer School* (Cambridge, August 2003), 1–36, quote at 26.

[124] Mark Landler, "A Slayer of Monopolies, One Corporation at a Time," *New York Times* (March 25, 2004), section 11C, quoting William Kolasky and Robert Pitofsky, p. 11.

[125] Pflanz, "Introduction," *IBC EU Summer School*, 2003, 25–9, quotes at 29.

would supercede a nation's or the EU's laws and sovereignty. Another issue involved the substantive rules themselves and how to design regulatory institutions aimed at compliance. A related yet distinct issue concerned the degree to which a nation's or the EU's cultural and institutional distinctiveness impeded or fostered harmonization. Between 1997 and 2003 there was an ongoing effort to implement a WTO agreement on trade-related competition policy. Because nations possessed a diversity of competition laws reflecting a range of legal traditions – and many other nations had no antitrust regime at all – progress toward adopting a WTO-competition measure was slow, though China and other nations instituted their own antitrust regime, in part, to promote WTO membership. Indeed, the European Community was a leading proponent, while the United States just as firmly resisted. Trade and antitrust experts discussed in particular an agreement targeting "hard core cartels," but the effort failed amidst collapse of the larger Doha Round of trade negotiations.[126]

The U.S.-EU disagreement over trade-related competition policy stemmed from divergent motivations. The U.S. antitrust authorities imposed accountability upon and preserved oligopolistic competition among multinational corporations buffeted by a contrary business cycle. Protected by strict confidentiality rules, the Americans advocated antitrust efficiency theories measured by the criteria of technological innovation and the proliferation of product consumption. To be sure, U.S. multinational corporations and enforcement authorities agreed to inserting into the WTO dispute settlement system a Trade Related Intellectual Property Provision because confidentiality was protected by monopoly licensing agreements. But under a trade-related competition policy, Americans believed, confidentiality was more vulnerable. The International Competition Network, an informal, non-governmental organization promoting trans-national cooperation, was the compromise. A Canadian lawyer contrasted the Network with the OECD, the "rich man's club," and the UN's Committee on Trade Development, the "poor man's club." The International Competition Network, by contrast, "has become exactly what it was intended to be: the meeting place for all the stakeholders." Another expert commented

---

[126] John Kraus, *The GATT Negotiations a Business Guide to the Results of the Uruguay Round* (Paris, 1994); Fox, "Toward World Antitrust," *American Journal of International Law*, 1–25; Mitsui Matsushita, "Basic Principles of the WTO and the Role of Competition Policy," 3 *Journal of World Investment* (August 2002), 567–84; Jones and Matsushita, "Global Antitrust in the Millennium Round: The Way Forward," in Jones and Matsushita, eds., *Competition Policy in the Global Trading System*, 297–406; Frances Williams and Guy de Jonquiere, "Stalled Trade Talks Revived as Top WTO Nations Hail Subsidies Deal," *Financial Times* (August 2, 2004), p. 1; Frederic Jenny, "Competition, Trade and Development Before and After Cancun," in Hawk, ed., "Fordham Corporate Law Institute Thirtieth Annual Conference on International Antitrust Law and Policy," Unpublished (2003), 1–11.

that the Network "creates pressure and competition among agencies to be best in class."[127]

The Europeans remained committed to some version of trade-related competition policy partly because the trade access and dumping issues had resulted in solutions which strengthened the member states' commitment to market integration, and in turn, reinforced the commission's legitimacy. In 2003, for example, the EU won a much-contested case in the WTO overturning U.S. tax advantages benefiting American international business; it also assisted Germany in the successful decision overturning U.S. duties restricting imports of corrosion-resistant carbon steel flat products from Germany.[128] According to New York commercial lawyer Berry E. Hawk the question was: "will US antitrust law or EC competition law succeed as the world model?" He concluded that "For good or ill, we shall have to live throughout most of the world with clones of Article 85 and 86. That means dominant firm behavior will be more closely scrutinized than would be the case if [the Sherman Act's] section 2 were the model." Thus, although the Doha Round dropped competition policy in 2004, the EU's persistent advocacy reinforced the EU "model" throughout the world.[129]

The Maastricht Treaty facilitated the accession of new member states and thereby expanded the administration of common policies in such areas as agriculture, environment, currency, trade, and competition. These uniform standards encouraged nations to apply for membership in the EU, but also represented an imposition with which nations must comply before accession could be achieved. By 1986 Portugal, Spain, and Greece became member states. During the mid-1990s Sweden, Finland, and Austria joined. The goal of membership influenced former communist states ranging from the Baltic nations of Estonia, Latvia, and Lithuania to Poland, Hungary, the Czech Republic, Slovakia, and Slovenia. Pursuing eventual EU membership Cyprus, Malta, and Turkey adjusted their economies to the common standards. Expansion, however, increased nationalistic protests about immigration and multinational corporations. The conflicting costs and

---

[127] William Blumenthal, "Private Sector Advocacy and the Mechanisms of Convergence," "Competition Law and Policy in a Global Context," Unpublished paper (Seoul, April 23, 2004); Randy Tritell, "Is the Network Delivering," and J. William Rowley, "Should Global Business Care about the ICN?" 7 *Global Competition Review* (June 2004), quotes at 15, 20.

[128] Mitsui Matsushita, "Preface," Keiichiro Sue, "United States-Tax Treatment for 'Foreign Sales Corporations': Recourse to Article 21.5 of the DSU by the European Communities: Reports of the Panel and the Appellate Body," and Yoshinori Abe, "United States-Countervailing Duties on Certain Corrosion-Resistant Carbon Steel Flat Products from Germany: Reports of the Panel and Appellate Body," 9 *Selected GATT/WTO Panel Reports* (Tokyo, 2003), ix, 71–102, 249–79.

[129] William E. Kovacic, "Antitrust and Competition Policy in Transition Economies: A Preliminary Assessment," in Hawk, ed., *26th Annual Fordham Corporate Law Institute*, 1999, 513–38; Barry E. Hawk, "Introduction," in Hawk, ed., *19th Annual Fordham Corporate Law Institute*, 1992, iii.

benefits of the common policies led to criticism of "Brussels bureaucrats." The commission's modernization of competition policy reflected these issues.[130]

A measure of the EU's economic unity was the expanded market for legal services. The EU's "single market" required reconstituting leading macro-economic policies, especially the Euro currency. These issues converged, moreover, with the financial globalization of multinational corporations, intensifying pressures to merge and restructure, or, alternatively, to ameliorate the risks through authorized or illegal cartels.[131] Accordingly, the single market created demands for experts capable of addressing governmental deregulation, liberalization, and privatization as well as those skilled in the operation and finances of private corporations. One manifestation of this growing demand was that major law firms in the world's leading industrial nations acquired EU antitrust expertise. By the 1990s a "competition" bar resided in Brussels; even law firms whose clients remained primarily local gained competition law proficiency. The market for expertise, recalled a European lawyer in 1992, contrasted markedly with the "small and specialized competition bar" of the immediate postwar period. "This group was characterized by a certain pride, and even fervor, among a relatively small group of specialists. Each one knew almost everyone else active in the area, and each one knew a substantial percentage of the DG-IV staff." The "landscape" of the 1990s was "beyond recognition when compared to those days."[132]

The enlarged market for competition expertise involved ideological ramifications. Competition lawyers representing multinational corporations were a modest expression of the growing impact the EU's common policies had on people in the member states. But competition policy also affirmed the commission's authority over the operation and public accountability of business; in high profile cases such efforts received considerable public attention. Generally, however, competition policy remained in the background. Accordingly, the attacks that right-wing nationalists and utopian radicals mounted in the name of opposing globalization targeted not the commission's Competition Bureau (which replaced the nomenclature of DG IV), but a main object of its enforcement: U.S. multinational corporations. Similarly, the nationalists exploited fears of immigration – especially from Islamic nations – residual anti-Semitism, and anger against remote Brussels officials or more "foreign" still, the WTO. Nevertheless, underlying the radical stance, were profound popular

---

[130] "Special Report the Future of Europe," *The Economist*, May 1, 2004, 25–7.   [131] Ibid.
[132] Holley, "EEC Competition Practice: A Thirty-Year Retrospective," in Hawk, ed., *19th Annual Fordham Corporate Law Institute*, 1992, 671; and compare Linda S. Spedding, *Transnational Legal Practice in the EEC and the United States* (Dobbs Ferry, NY, 1987); and *The GCR 100 a Survey of the World's Leading 100 Competition Law Practices* (London, 2001).

anxieties about foreign economic domination and the loss of personal independence which symbolically and even instrumentally embraced competition policy.[133]

The commission's competition authorities reflected these ideological tensions. Karl van Miert, as outgoing Competition commissioner, noted that for U.S. officials and multinational corporations very practical concerns were at stake: "On the American side they are very cautious about giving us confidential information, but if you then have to distribute it to member states, they become much more reluctant. And, let's be fair. . . . The rules are different – for instance, in the US you can put people in jail. You can't in Europe – and just to be clear, I am absolutely not in favor of that." Nevertheless, economic globalization unleashed ever-mounting pressure fostering collaboration among antitrust authorities; accordingly, van Miert suggested, "at the end of the day it's going to happen." Then he observed, "[m]ore and more companies engaged in mergers and acquisitions will tend to allow the exchange of confidential information, because it will be in their own interests to allow both authorities to devise remedies, if they need to do so, which are compatible."[134]

The principle of transnational cooperation among antitrust regimes could quiet U.S. concerns regarding confidentiality. American politicians raised such issues as a result of a "very aggressive lobby . . . we've seen . . . with Boeing and several other cases." This meant, first, that the EU Competition commissioner could demonstrate to an American elected official that antitrust issues were different from trade disputes, especially because the enforcement criteria were more rigorous. Second, the bilateral antitrust cooperation agreement of 1991 enabled him to point out that similar to EU "confidence in the US competition authorities . . . they should also start to have confidence in the European authorities . . . [and] we can show that this confidence is justified through the agreement that allows the American authorities to ask us to investigate a case, and vice versa."[135]

At the turn of the century, EU officials encountered strong lobbying pressures from business regarding a corporate Takeover Directive. Some lobbyists favored the example of the British law promoting the sort of hostile takeover battles common in the United States since the 1980s. By contrast, Germany enacted a takeover law whereby "German employees and their representatives would have the right to be informed by acquirers about the impact of a takeover, for instance in terms of lay-offs." Opposition to the takeover might then be mobilized. The German law accommodated the social-market economy to powerful contemporary pressures

---

[133] Philippe Legrain, *Open World: The Truth about Globalization* (London, 2002).

[134] Karel van Miert, "European Competition Policy: A Retrospective and Prospects for the Future," *29th Annual Fordham Corporate Law Institute*, 1999, 1–14, quote at 14.

[135] Ibid.

for merger and restructuring identified with economic globalization. The German approach reflected reaction to Vodafone Air Touch's hostile takeover of Düsseldorf-based Mannesmann, which in 2000 had jolted European firms unused to such aggressive tactics. Thus, the opponents of the UK takeover law identified it with Vodafone Air Touch, a UK company, pursuing "American" entrepreneurial tactics. They considered the German takeover law more in tune with European social-welfare capitalism. By 2003, a majority of member states supported a German version of the Takeover Directive, but U.S. interests opposed it because financing hostile takeovers would be more difficult than ever.[136]

The appearance of American lobbying practices suggested the truth of van Miert's prediction, "We will gradually see the same situation evolving in Europe, with European legislators intervening in favor of European companies." The challenge to institutional independence was "one of the biggest problems ahead of us. In the United States, my experience with [FTC Chairman] Bob Pitofsky and [the Justice Department's] Joel Klein is that they stand up to these pressures, and rightly so. I think that as long as we have a situation on both sides of the ocean where that is the case, we can face the situation. But there is no doubt that eventually, on the European side as well, there will be much more pressure from legislators in favor of companies." Recalling his own experience he said: "I already felt that very strongly over the airlines, with political intervention on all levels."[137]

Within this challenging political and economic context van Miert identi-tified goals of transnational antitrust enforcement. "Cartels clearly need a lot of attention – it's astonishing, but there are still a lot of them about." Cooperation in this field with the United States "in particular ... has been very successful globally speaking ... though it still has some flaws since we cannot share confidential information. ... [I]t would be helpful if we could cooperate more intensively in such cases." Acknowledging the reservations the United States had about pushing toward a formal agreement under the WTO, van Miert repeated the European view that "for global problems, we should think about global solutions." Thus Japan, Canada, and Australia shared the commission's position to "start to talk about a few global rules like hard core cartels." Then, through the "framework of the WTO, we should try to get Member States to accept some basic competition rules, and start to think about what we should do when, having accepted some basic rules, governments do not comply with them – but this is very contentious."[138]

---

[136] Ralph Atkins, "Berlin Sets Rules for Corporate Battles," *Financial Times* (Friday, May 19, 2000), quote at p. 2; "Takeover Rules," *Financial Times* (May 19, 2000) at p. 18; Daniel Dombey, "European Takeover Proposal Anger US," *Financial Times* (Monday, November, 24, 2003), front page.

[137] Van Miert, "European Competition Policy, *29th Annual Fordham Corporate Law Institute, 1999*, 14–15.

[138] Ibid., 12, 14.

For van Miert, accordingly, implementing a single market and achieving an antitrust agreement under the WTO were related. Notwithstanding the antiglobalization groups' attacks, the commission would continue, van Miert stated, to advocate inclusion of competition policy in the Doha or "millennium" trade round in order to establish a global dispute settlement process capable of imposing accountability. It was, he admitted, "really a step-by-step thing, and we have to be realistic." As a diplomatic and policy matter, he saw that the "big question is how to bring the US on board and start with something really gradual and realistic." The Maastricht Treaty altered the interests influencing the commission's antitrust role. As a result, van Miert said "you can't take for granted that companies will abide by the rules in the same way you can't take for granted that football players will abide by the rules if you don't have a referee." The EU would have "to accept the trend for more mergers. ... At the same time, we have to fight the emergence of global oligopolies."[139]

European experts assessed these policy goals somewhat differently. Permeating the commission's enforcement regime was reliance upon bureaucratic discretion, which sought to balance the member states' economic integration with equal treatment of individuals and business. By 2000 the commission's bureaucrats could look back at forty years of adapting the Treaty's antitrust provisions to continuing expansion. The experts nonetheless often measured this development by contrasting the differing policy goals of European and United States antitrust regimes. During the 1970s and 1980s the policy of Chicago economics defining "efficiency" principally in terms of prices paid by consumers prevailed in the United States. Although a corrective to unequivocal reliance upon the Chicago microeconomic price theory emerged among U.S. antitrust authorities and the courts by the early 1990s, price competition benefiting consumers remained the principal measure of efficiency. By contrast, Matthias Pflanz observed, "EU competition law precedent has not generally been very concerned with the ultimate prices paid by consumers *per se*. Instead, much of the focus of EU competition law has been on behavior by companies which prevents others from competing on equal terms. It could be said that the creation of a 'level playing field' between actual and potential competitors (and, for slightly different reasons, across different states) has been a primary objective of EU competition law."[140]

A leading measure of the EU–U.S. difference was suggested by the commission's administration of the merger regulation. Until the late-1990s, Pflanz declared, officials enquired "whether a merger would lead to the *creation or strengthening of a dominant position* as a result of which competition will be impeded. While the strengthening or creation of a dominant position will typically mean that prices will rise, this need not be

---

[139] Ibid.   [140] Pflanz, "Introduction," *IBC EU Summer School*, 2003, 21.

the case." Thus, U.S. antitrust authorities asked what "if a merger allows costs to be reduced significantly?" Indeed, when economic analysis demonstrated that organizational and technological efficiencies resulted from the merger, U.S. antitrust law expressly recognized an "efficiency defense." Even so, Pflanz declared, U.S. antitrust authorities routinely analyzed the impact of mergers employing "sophisticated econometric techniques." Pflanz's consulting firm used such techniques in merger studies commissioned by the European Commission's merger task force, including "a detailed econometric analysis of demand and supply conditions in the European trucks industry, in order to assess the likely impact of the transaction." Neither the commission's nor the parties' experts agreed, however, on the analysis, and so the commission relied on more traditional economic principles.[141]

The EU–U.S. divergence in economic analysis was perhaps most contested regarding conglomerate mergers. By the late-1990s, the commission proved increasingly responsive to court decisions requiring a showing of direct links between economic theory and the facts. An indication of the commission's accommodation of the court's insistence upon more rigorous economic analysis was that it discussed employing a stronger efficiency analysis more closely approaching U.S. policy in its horizontal merger guidelines of 2002. However, in *General Electric/Honeywell* the defendants appealed to the Court of First Instance primarily because the commission's opinion ran counter to analysis of conglomerate mergers prevailing in the United States. The commission, Pflanz stated, asserted that the conglomerate merger would create the "possibility that a competitor with a broader product range would have incentives to offer discounts on packages of products ('mixed bundling'), which competitors might find difficult to match." This practice "treats efficiencies arising from a merger as a cause for competitive concern" and is "highly controversial."[142]

Conflict arising from the theory of "efficiency" exacerbated the EU goal of market integration. Thus, another divergence between U.S. and EU policy concerned vertical agreements "between companies at different levels in the economic chain." In the EU "competition cases are often resolved with single market integration objectives in mind." The commission and the court applied this policy goal in the "large number of cases dealing with distribution agreements" which "tend to divide the Community" by national interests. "A notably severe example of this is the case of Volkswagen on whom the Commission imposed a fine of E 102,000,000 for the imposition of an export ban on cars from Italy to Germany and Austria." On appeal, the Court of First Instance, with only a "minor reduction in fines," sustained the commission. A critic nonetheless concluded that the commission's "hostile attitude" toward any distribution

[141] Ibid., 20, 22.   [142] Ibid.

agreement "that interferes directly with the free flow of goods and services between EU Member States" was "economically dubious."[143]

The commission's *Microsoft* decision reflected the EU's core goals. The complainant was Sun Microsystems, the U.S. multinational computer company whose net loss in 2002–2003 was $2,378 million, which asserted that its loss was due to Microsoft's market practices that had been proven in U.S. courts to have been illegal. Applying an efficiency theory centered on consumer prices, the U.S. courts imposed a modest remedy which none-theless allowed Microsoft to maintain its impressive technological inno-vation, while purportedly limiting its illegal monopoly conduct. Even though the commission's investigations found that Microsoft's abusive tactics had not abated, its decision for Sun was based on facts comporting with the "Commission's duty to uphold EU law in the European single market." The remedy focused on facts related to Microsoft's' abusive "tying" of Windows and Windows Media Player, which were contrary to the EU's "market integration" and proscription of "dominance." The commission ordered Microsoft "*to disclose complete and accurate speci-fications for the protocols*' [emphasis in the orginal] necessary for its competitors' server products to be able to 'talk' on an equal footing with Windows PCs, and hence compete on a level playing-field. It must also offer a version of Windows for clients' PCs which does not include Windows Media Player." The commission also fined Microsoft 497 million euros "for abusing its market power in the EU."[144]

The commission evaluated the differences between the American and its own *Microsoft* decision. The commission rebutted experts' presumptions based on U.S. efficiency theories that the decision "protected competitors" rather than promoting the principle of competition identified with con-sumer prices. By contrast, the commission asserted, the decision "creates the environment where consumers can benefit and where innovation can flourish." In particular, the decision followed closely the European Court precedents governing interoperability and tying, which, in turn, complied with the principles of market integration and proscription of dominance. In reply to Microsoft's and the critics' arguments that competition law was ill

[143] Ibid., 22. Vanessa Turner, "Article 81 EC Treaty Principles and Enforcement, Present and Future," 1–29, quote at 6, and Sean-Paul Brankin, "An Introduction to EU Competition Law," 1–21, quote at 3, both included in *IBC EU Summer School* (2003).
[144] Case COMP/C-3/37.792 Microsoft, http://europa.eu.int/comm/competitionantirust/cases/index/by_nr_75.htm?#;37_792; Press Release, "Microsoft – Questions and Answers on Commission Decision," Memo/04/70 (Brussels, March 24, 2004), quotes at 1, http://europa.eu.int/rapid/pressReleasesAction.do?reference=MEMO/04/70&format=HTM= ... 7/20/2004; Press Release, "Commission Concludes on Microsoft Investigation, Imposes Conduct Remedies, and a Fine," IP/04/382 (Brussels, March 24, 2004), http://europa.eu.int/ rapid/pressReleasesAction.do?reference=IP/04/382&format=HTML&a ... 7/20/2004.

suited to the "fast moving" innovation demanded in the "hi-tech" global economy, the commission insisted upon following an economic analysis which, given the "specific characteristics of the market question (e.g. network effects, applications barrier to entry) could mean there is in fact an increased likelihood of positions of entrenched market power compared to certain 'traditional industries.' " Thus, the emphasis on constituting a market "environment" affirmed EU law's multiple-value outcomes including but not limited to consumer welfare.[145]

EU authorities, experts, and business interests contested competition policy through economic theories. They incorporated U.S. antitrust analogies into their analysis of EU competition law, in part to affirm its principles by showing contrast or divergence, but also to indicate possible directions of change. Although the commission and the courts were clearly aware of U.S. economic theories, their practical impact on decisions remained limited unless the outcome furthered implementing the EU treaty structure's core goals of market integration and proscription of abusive domination. The Treaty structure based on sovereignty-sharing among member states and the corresponding demand for equal treatment toward individuals and companies shaped the meaning of consumer welfare and what constituted "efficiency" to attain it. In *Airtours* and two related merger decisions of 2002, the court's holding against the commission's construction of dominance suggested a stronger "efficiency" standard, which gave heart to those appealing in the *General Electric/Honeywell* and the *Microsoft* cases. The court's trilogy nonetheless emphasized the primary importance of the "factual elements" in the economic analysis, leaving the European Court, if it chose, to define "efficiency" broadly. Indeed, in December, 2004, the Court of First Instance upheld the commission in the *Microsoft* case; the decision enforced most, though not all, of the commission's order, imposing a tougher remedy than had the United States. A similar result in the *Honeyewell* case was not unlikely.[146]

During this same period the commission wrestled with incorporating new member states from formerly communist Europe and elsewhere. The accession of these nations accentuated nationalistic sentiments, including right-wing exploitation of labor and immigration issues and ideological assaults upon the agents of globalization – U.S. multinational corporations,

---

[145] "Microsoft – Questions and Answers on Commission Decision," and compare (Brussels, March 24, 2004), quotes at 1, 2, 4. (The commission also discusses the patent issue under the WTO (TRIPs) provision, but I do not consider it here.) Paul Meller, "Europeans Rule against Microsoft; Appeal Promised," *New York Times* (March 25, 2004), p. C1, 1, 10.

[146] "Competing Visions Britain Is Throwing down an Antitrust Gauntlet to Brussels," *The Economist* (September 21, 2002); Mario Monti, "Europe's Merger Monitor," *The Economist* (November 9, 2002). The CFI's decision in the *Microsoft* case is at [case T-201/ 04R [22 December 2004(1)] http://curia.eu.int/jurisp/cgi-bin/gettext.pl?lang=exn ?&num=79958777T1904%20R0201_2&doc=T&ouver ... 12/22/204.

"Brussels bureaucrats," and the WTO. These tensions aggravated an already conflicted heritage the Baltic states, Slovenia, the Czech Republic, Slovakia, Hungary, and Poland carried. The economies of Malta and Cyprus, too, had known cartels under British rule. Moreover, like the 15 member states already composing the EU by 1995, the applicants had experienced attempts to impose "market liberalization" or privatization upon state-run or state-owned companies. In the former communist states, the Soviets and national leaders had encouraged technocrats and academics to study Western management techniques abroad in order to enhance the competitiveness of the socialist economies. Thus, after 1989 some Eastern European officials, managers, and experts understood capitalism through unsuccessful attempts to accommodate it within failed socialist regimes.[147]

After 1991, applicants to the EU welcomed technical assistance from the European Commission as well as U.S. antitrust authorities. Of course, only EU competition law had direct relevance for the accession states, but the interest those states expressed in U.S. antitrust suggested the extent to which a transnational antitrust regime had emerged. During the decade or more leading to the accession of the ten states on May Day, 2004, the commission grappled with the institutional costs of enforcing the EU's core goals through the administration of the merger regulation and the notification system under Regulation 17. The commission responded to these parallel institutional demands by initiating a process of "modernization." The label captured the commission's intent of reconstituting the system to accommodate 25 member states experiencing antiglobalization discontent, high unemployment, and uneven or negative growth.[148]

Poland's transition to capitalism illustrated the challenges the commission faced. After a courageous struggle, Poland became the first former Soviet satellite to reestablish a capitalist economy. Unlike the region's other communist countries, Poland had a nationalistic heritage centered on Roman Catholicism which had enabled it to preserve private ownership

[147] Mario Monti, "Europe's Merger Monitor," *The Economist* (November 9, 2002); Professor Anna Fornalczyk, interview with Tony Freyer, April 5, 2000; Ferenc Vissi, "Panel: Antitrust in Transition Economies: The Hungarian Experience," and Antitrust in Transition Economies," in Hawk, ed., *26th Annual Fordham Corporate Law Institute, 1999*, 539–61, 563–72; see note 130 above.

[148] Mario Monti, "Europe's Merger Monitor, *The Economist* (November 9, 2002); August J. Braakman, "The Application of the Modernization Rules ... in injunction Proceedings: Problems and Possible Solutions"; Ian S. Forrester, "Modernization of EC Competition Law"; Stephen Kon, "The Commission's White Paper on Modernization: The Need for Procedural Harmonization"; Erik Mohr Mersing, "The Modernization of EC Competition Law: The Need for a Common Competition Culture"; Mario Siragusa, "A Critical Review of the White Paper on the Reform of the Competition Law Enforcement Rules," Dieter Wolf, "Comment on the White Paper on the Reform of EC Competition Law," and "Modernization of EC Competition Law Round Table"; in Hawk, ed., *26th Annual Fordham Corporate Law Institute, 1999*, 161–345.

throughout its largely peasant agricultural sector and to maintain a surprisingly large number of small but prosperous capitalist "enclave entrepreneurs." Thus, most Poles accepted the sudden imposition of Finance Minister Leszek Balcerowicz's "free-market" regime. It included the enactment in 1990 of the Antimonopoly Act, establishing provisions like the Rome Treaty's Articles 85 and 86. The Act's focus upon "monopoly" indicated that competition policy's primary goal was promoting the transition from state-controlled companies and protected trade to privatization and market-based competition. Dr. Anna Fornalczyk, the first head of the Polish Antimonopoly Office, explained that the "most important difference" between U.S. and Polish competition policy "is that our primary goal is to create competition, which means that we must concentrate on demonopolization and trade liberalization. Investigating restrictive business practices plays a secondary role, because such practices are the result of monopoly, not its cause."[149]

Fornalczyk and her successors found that EU–U.S. comparisons helped to address the problems of a "transition economy." From 1990 on, Polish authorities welcomed not only EU but also U.S. competition law experts. Fornalczyk noted that globalization had engendered a cooperative EU–U.S. enforcement culture that could reinforce the Polish antimonopoly regime. Moreover, insights gained from comparing EU–U.S. antitrust principles sharpened Polish expertise in the negotiations with EU officials over the competition provisions of the accession agreement. One example of the uses of the comparative approach concerned the Polish Antimonopoly Office's active enforcement against vertical restraints which was also an EU Commission priority. Fornalczyk observed that U.S. antitrust theory rejected such an enforcement policy because it "often makes the mistake of protecting competitors, rather than competition." The theory assumed that market entry was rarely if ever a problem. Fornalcyk pointed out, however, that in a "transitional economy" with many "former monopolist" firms, "one must look carefully to see whether the firm's market position is protected by contracts or informal agreements with suppliers or with former colleagues in the state administration. And unfortunately, we have had cases in which physical intimidation was the entry deterrent of choice."[150]

[149] Professor Anna Fornalczyk, interview, Tony Freyer, April 5, 2000, source for quoted phrases; Ash, *Polish Revolution*, Leszek Balcerowicz, quoted at 372, and see 376, 377; Anna Fornalczyk, "Competition Policy during Transformation of a Centrally Planned Economy," in Hawk, ed., *19th Annual Fordham Corporate Law Institute*, 1992, 385–402, quote at 402; Tadeusz Skoczny, *Harmonization of the Polish Competition Legislation with Competition Rules of the European Communities Summary and Recommendations* (Warsaw, 1997).

[150] Professor Anna Fornalczyk, interview, Tony Freyer, April 5, 2000; Fornalczyk, "Competition Policy," in Hawk, ed., *19th Annual Fordham Corporate Law Institute*, 1992, 397.

Several cases indicate the problems. The Polish Monopoly Office could veto privatization proposals, but it rarely did so, preferring instead to negotiate conditional approvals with the Ministry of Privatization. Thus, the Monopoly Office promoted and supervised the restructuring of Poland's petroleum industry, achieving the separation of the state-owned refineries from the distribution monopoly and limiting its ownership to no more than 40% of either refining capacity or gas stations. In addition, foreign firms were encouraged to invest in Polish refineries and gas stations. Regarding trade liberalization, the Monopoly Office "refused trade barriers on textiles and agricultural products." But though the Office won a limit on import barriers protecting the automobile industry, the government reestablished import price protections, which Poland's Supreme Court upheld. Fornalczyk remained hopeful that agreements facilitating Poland's eventual EU membership, which "require[d] a gradual implementation of free trade rules," would reinforce the Monopoly Office's "opposition to protectionism." In the sales and distribution of periodical literature the Monopoly Office also overturned a tying agreement between numerous kiosk vendors and the former state distribution monopoly, RUNCH. The opinion noted that in functioning market economies such ties may be efficient. Poland, however, needed to promote small business investment in a sector where coal miners – whose high unemployment due to privatization symbolized the risks of capitalism – often became kiosk operators.[151]

The social welfare issues in these Polish cases reflected conflict's between nationalist and antiglobalization ideologies. Since the 1980s unemployment engendered social tensions throughout the community because of the presence of ethno-culturally diverse workers – including many believers in Islam – from the Near East, North Africa, and former European colonies. Increased job insecurity resulted, too, from the deregulation of private companies and the privatization of industries. As national regulation declined, the jurisdiction of competition policy increased, including the authority over numerous "state aids" that member states and acceding nations instituted in the form of subsidies to protect small businesses, workers, and consumers from unregulated market prices. Despite or perhaps because of such efforts, nationalists coupled anti-EU appeals with the racist ideologies to attack the diminution of national sovereignty. At the same time, humanitarian radicals asserted that the commission's policies promoted the hegemony of U.S. multinational corporations, which in turn undermined the cultural authenticity associated with local control. Paradoxically, within Poland and other acceding states critics employed nationalistic ideologies to oppose EU membership, while nationalists in the EU's

[151] Fornalczyk, "Competition Policy," 385–402, quote at 392, 393; Tadeusz Skoczny, *Harmonization of the Polish Competition Legislation*; Professor Anna Fornalczyk, interview, Tony Freyer, April 5, 2000.

member states used such ideological appeals to condemn accession because it opened national borders to "undesirable" workers.[152]

Coincidentally, the accession process highlighted the ever-mounting costs of enforcement. In order to strike a balance between institutional centralization and decentralization the commission employed the principle of subsidiarity. Applied to competition, subsidiarity resulted in the commission's instituting significant reform proposals. Regulation 17, promulgated in 1962, was abolished. The basic policy changes included shifting more enforcement authority to the courts and competition regimes of the member states. The most significant change was the abolition of the notification process which had caused delays and required a costly commitment of staff time. The commission's divestiture of long-standing authority empowered the member states to intervene extensively in the transactions of companies doing business in Europe. This part of the modernization program sought to improve the commission's enforcement of the treaty structure's cartel provisions, though the commission would handle major cartel cases. Even so, the member states' antitrust agencies would be more active, as would the national courts. Regarding mergers and acquisitions geared to the EU as a whole, however, the commission retained sole responsibility.[153]

Empowering member states' enforcement against cartels, including the promotion of private actions, was contentious. The gap in the commission's power resulting from the abolition of notification system was to be filled by devolving power to national authorities, especially the courts. The modernization reformers argued that this institutional transformation provided sufficient incentives for private parties to bring private actions, which were so conspicuous in U.S. antitrust enforcement regime. Critics responded that the reformers ignored the profound difference in "competition culture" between the U.S. antitrust system and the European civil law and administrative antitrust regime. Commission officials and private attorneys countered with studies showing that the antitrust regime's formal authorization of private actions facilitated private parties' bringing suits. Indeed though still few, the number of private actions was growing in the member states. Advocates of private suits added that in Australia private parties regularly pursued such actions, even though they lacked the incentives available in the U.S. system. Moreover, establishing complementarity

---

[152] Charle Magne, "Multi cultural Troubles," *The Economist* (March 27, 2004); Monti's Moment, "France Telecom Could Provide Last Test of Mario Monti's Resolve," *The Economist* (July 17, 2004); Adinda Sinnaeve, "Competition Policy, State Aid and State Enterprisers," Eleanore M. Fox, "State Aids Control and the Distortion of Competition-Unbundling 'Distortion,'" and Panel Discussion, "EC State Aid Policy," in Hawk, ed., *28th Annual Fordham Corporate Law Institute Conference, 2001*, 67–90, 91–100, 115–28; Professor Anna Fornalczyk, interview, Tony Freyer, April 5, 2000.

[153] *Modernization in Europe 2004* (London, 2004).

between government and private enforcement actions enabled the Australian Competition and Consumer Commission to use its enforcement resources more efficiently. Inferentially, the European Commission could also do the same.[154]

Since the practical outcome of private actions was problematic, the critics asserted that business people and their lawyers would respond to uncertainty by choosing to restructure loose agreements into joint ventures which would bring them within notification procedures. Thus, Dieter Wolf, President of the German federal cartel office (Bundeskartellamt), stated that it was "more than doubtful whether ... increased enforcement of the ban on cartels under civil law can be expected ... because unlike in" the United States, "there are no prospects at present of actions for damages being really successful. Moreover, it is feared that a large number of cooperation projects will be restructured into joint ventures because these will continue to be subject to notification under the EU Merger Regulation."[155] Indeed, the modernization reforms suggested that the commission would put more resources into merger control as privatization and deregulation throughout the enlarged EU promoted ongoing restructuring of public as well as private companies. Meanwhile, the effectiveness of U.S.–EU enforcement cooperation against international cartels, in conjunction with disagreements over merger and monopoly cases, indicated that the commission was more sensitive than ever to efficiently allocating enforcement resources in order to strengthen the EU's global competitive advantage through equal treatment across the One Market.[156]

The modernization reforms identified with regulation 1/2003 went into operation on May Day, 2004. The new Regulation would "effect radical reform" in the "procedural rules governing enforcement" of EU competition law, declared experts writing for *Global Competition Review*'s volume, *Modernization in Europe*. "Business will bear greater risk than before in assessing the compatibility of its conduct" with the treaty articles,

---

[154] Compare Dr. Alexander Schaub, "Modernization of EC Competition Law Reform of Regulation No. 17"; Braakman, "Application of Modernization Rules"; Forrester, "Modernization of EC Competition Law"; Kon, "Commission's White Paper on Modernization"; Mersing, "The Need for a Common Competition Culture"; Siragusa, "A Critical Review"; and Wolf, "Comment"; in Hawk, ed., *26th Annual Fordham Corporate Law Institute*, 1999, 143–60, 161–80, 181–239, 240–58, 259–72, 273–305, 307–12; Broomhall and Goyder, "Overview"; and "European Union," *Modernization in Europe*, 3–5, 6–9; Charles E. Koob, David E. Vann, Jr., and Arman Y. Aruc, "Developments in Private Enforcement of Competition Laws – Introduction," *Private Antitrust Litigation in 16 Jurisdictions Worldwide* (London, 2004), 3–5, and see national case studies, 7–71. The leading work on private actions in Europe is Clifford A. Jones, *Private Enforcement of Antitrust Law in the EU, UK and USA* (Oxford, UK, 1999). On Australian private actions, see Chapter 6.
[155] Wolf, "Comment," Hawk, ed., *26th Annual Fordham Corporate Law Institute*, 1999, 311.
[156] See note 154 above.

and "national courts and national competition authorities will play a greater role in enforcement." The European Commission's "officials will have strengthened investigatory and fining powers, including the power to search private homes. A higher volume of information will be exchanged between national competition authorities and between those authorities and the Commission." Nevertheless, devolution of enforcement to national antitrust authorities and courts tested the degree to which the preexisting fifteen and the ten acceding members had harmonized their competition regimes with the law and procedures administered in Brussels. Despite the fact that noteworthy differences remained, the degree of harmonization was impressive and the most conspicuous "differences appear in the sanctions available for infringement" of the treaty's provision.[157]

Although the results of the modernization reforms were unclear, certain patterns were apparent. The procedural framework engendered uncertainties which expanded the demand for legal expertise in EU competition law and enlarged the opportunity to contest the principles and doctrines shaping policy outcomes and general compliance. Even so, policy disputes suggested that the commission as well as the European Court remained committed to protecting the equal opportunity of individuals and companies through market integration and proscription of abusive dominance. The accession of the ten member states heightened the imperative to enforce equally the EU's core goals. In addition, this highlighted the "broad gulf between competition policy in Europe and the United States." The commission's Competition Bureau, like other "European agencies come from a more corporatist perspective. There really is less stomach in Europe for the kind of Darwinian competition that we've embraced" in America. Conversely, regarding the struggle to impose accountability upon multinational corporations and global capitalism, U.S. and EU officials had achieved "marked convergence."[158]

V. CONCLUSION

The two American commentators indicated the symbolic and instrumental contrast with EU competition policy. The American critic's preference for "Darwinian competition" differed, suggested Czech anticommunist leader Václav Havel in another context, from the European capitalist consciousness that embraced "a market economy and put meaning back into human labor," but it also "help[ed] us all withstand the destructive pressure of technological civilization, with its stupefying dictatorship of consumerism

---

[157] Broomhall and Goyder, "Overview," *Modernization in Europe*, quotes at 3, 4; see also Gerber, *Protecting Prometheus*, vii–xix.
[158] William Kolasky and James Rill as quoted in Mark Landler, "A Slayer of Monopolies, One Corporation at a Time," *The New York Times* (March, 25, 2004), p. 11.

and its omnipresent commercialism." In addition, as President of the Czech Republic he advocated cooperation with Germany and other nations to promote the "renewal of global human responsibility."[159]

The distinction he drew between consumption and labor-driven markets was not inconsistent with the European Commission's attempts to enforce multiple competition policy goals – especially community integration and proscription of dominance favoring divers competitors – over efficiency theories defined solely in terms of consumer welfare and technological innovation. Similarly, Havel's faith that "global responsibility" could be attained through international cooperation resonated with the "marked convergence" among the world's antitrust regimes seeking to impose accountability upon multinational corporations, the chief purveyors of consumer goods and product research. Thus, the EU and U.S. antitrust regimes sought global accountability, though the policy outcomes often differed.

---

[159] Václav Havel, *The Art of the Impossible as Morality in Practice Speeches and Writings 1990–1996* (New York, 1998), 27, 35.

6

Antitrust Resurgence and Social Welfare Capitalism in Postwar Australia

The postwar internationalization of antitrust imposed accountability upon American managerial capitalism, gradually limited cultural collusion permeating Japanese capitalism, and integrated social market capitalism to establish a more unified European community. In Australia, by contrast, the political consensus supporting the postwar resurgence of Australian antitrust instituted an enforcement regime which contested the limits of efficient market competition and social welfare.[1] Section I of this chapter emphasizes that the High Court's constitutional decisions favoring individual economic liberty preceded the better known campaign for a trade practices law identified with Liberal attorney general, Sir Garfield Barwick. Section II examines how R. B. Bannerman, the civil servant charged with implementing the weak law of 1965, worked to reshape the political consensus, reinforcing the success of Labor's attorney general, Lionel Murphy, in passing the stronger Trade Practices Act of 1974. Section III considers the maturation of an effective enforcement regime from 1974 to 1991 and its contribution to remaking the labor-capital settlement through microeconomic reform. Section IV explores how the activist trade practices regime associated with Allan Fels was enlarged to further the reform agenda.

I. POSTWAR AUSTRALIAN CAPITALISM AND CONSTITUTIONAL ECONOMIC LIBERTY

From 1945 to the mid-1960s, most Australian business interests broadly supported the market stability maintained through cooperation. The benefits of standardized products, quality control, and maximum output seemed more important than restricted entry, fixed prices, and such unfair

---

[1] This study uses antitrust, trade practices, and competition policy interchangeably. Andrew Hopkins, *Crime, Law & Business, The Sociological Sources of Australian Monopoly Law* (Canberra, 1978); J. E. Richardson, *Australian Trade Practices Act* (Sydney, 1957); Barrie Dyster and David Meredith, *Australia in the International Economy in the Twentieth-Century* (Cambridge, UK, 1990); Neville R. Norman, "Progress under Pressure: The Evolution of Antitrust Policy in Australia," 9 *Review of Industrial Organization* (October, 1994); Fred Brenchley, *Allan Fels A Portrait of Power* (Sydney, 2003).

practices as larger firms' refusing to deal with certain smaller ones on the basis of discrimination, rebates, and predatory pricing. Similarly, the protectionist regime sustained an industry-wide system of business self-government which enabled inefficient firms to survive. Business sectors as diverse as road transport, hair dressers, and light bulbs employed trade associations to control price competition. In addition, unlike the American distrust of big business, the Broken Hill Proprietary Co. (BHP) epitomized for most Australians – as it had since the Commonwealth's beginnings – a "benevolent monopoly." Also, despite impressive postwar population growth, Australia's national market remained smaller than that of the leading industrialized nations. By comparison, Australian manufacturing firms more generally possessed oligopolistic or monopolistic organization in order to develop advanced technology, which provided international competitive advantages during the cold war. Accordingly, one commentator declared in 1957, "to meet the coming technological demands" the "impelling lesson to Australia – is Co-operation!"[2] Although Australian big business most resembled British managerial capitalism, it evolved along an independent path. More so than elsewhere, Australian big firms relied on multinational corporations to supply foreign capital, technological innovation, and entrepreneurial expertise; they sought competitive advantage through exploiting indigenous assets rather than extensive managerial organization; their product specialization had to account more for distance than mere market separation, and particularly, among manufacturers, it depended on government aid to be competitive.[3]

The foreign influence in Australian big business created a mixed bag. By the early 1950s, locally owned and operated firms remained strong in rubber, brewing, baking, meat packing, soup, sugar refining, and jam making; they were also active in general engineering, iron and steel, glass, rubber products, building materials, paper, fertilizers, and food products. On the other hand, Australian companies were at a disadvantage in oil refining and distribution, textiles and apparel, electrical equipment, automobile assembly, rubber tires, metal fabrication, and chemicals. The cluster of companies and subsidiaries controlled by BHP and its main competitor, the Collins House Group, remained dominant in the making of ferrous and nonferrous goods derived from base metal mining and smelting; multinationals such as Alcoa, Comalco, and Alcan dominated their industry. By the 1960s, foreign companies had taken over the top 100 firms which had pioneered

[2] John A. Bushnell, *Australian Company Mergers, 1946–1959* (Melbourne, 1961), quote at 167; Walter Scott, *Australia and the Challenge of Change* (Sydney, 1957), quote at 384; Norman, "Progress under Pressure," 527–46; Interview with J. E. Richardson, July 14, 1993, Canberra.

[3] Grant Fleming, David Merrett, and Simon Ville, *The Big End of Town: Big Business and Corporate Leadership in Twentieth-Century Australia* (Port Melbourne, 2004), ch. 8 (I thank David Merrett for pre-publication use of this material).

Australian enterprise, including Queensland Meat Export Agency and CresCo Fertilizers. Australians competed more favorably with British and American entrepreneurs providing services for wool growers; a similar competition characterized Australian banking and the insurance industry. Meanwhile, the Australians retained leadership in other sectors: the Meyers and Coles families led, respectively, in promoting department and retail chain stores, while the Murdochs, Fairfaxes, and Packers developed the national newspaper and publishing industry.[4]

These tensions gradually altered public perceptions of Australian big business. Overall, foreign enterprise prevailed in the capital-intensive, science-based industries. Australian economic experts, politicians, and some business leaders aroused public awareness that the nation's prosperity increasingly was determined by foreign investment. The implications were ominous. At the start of the twentieth century, Australia had been one of the wealthiest nations in the world; by mid-century, despite the postwar growth, it had fallen to the middle rank. Moreover, because Australia's manufacturing industry emerged later, it was not identified with abuse and concentrated power as had been the case with American big business. The states owned the railways and other public utilities whereas in the United States, these were private enterprises. Finally, the Australian egalitarian ethos sustaining the labor-capitalist compromise enshrined in the arbitration system meant that nationalization persisted as a potential substitute for American-style antitrust. But by the 1960s, popular images of foreign-dominated Australian enterprise coincided with revelations that collusive practices pervaded the nation's consumer markets, fostering negative impressions of big business. The Australian press reported that even BHP sometimes practiced monopoly abuse, refusing to supply sheet metal for certain automobile makers.[5]

Meanwhile, academic economists, such as Peter Karmel, Maureen Brunt, and Alex Hunter, began criticizing the existing anticompetitive arrangements. "By the middle 1950s," declared one observer, "it was a favorite pastime of advanced undergraduate economics students to collect information about these agreements, and industry had no real reason to conceal them, for there was no law or effective public or political censure against them." More specifically, professional economists linked arbitrary business behavior resulting from cartelization to the nation's highly concentrated market and the spread of foreign ownership. The "most significant single fact about the ownership of these key manufacturing companies" was "that approximately 36% of their total equity was owned overseas, almost exclusively by foreign corporations," which was the "ultimate cause of the

---

[4] Ibid.
[5] Ibid.; E. L. Wheelwright and Judith Miskelly, *Anatomy of Australian Manufacturing Industry* (Sydney, 1967).

high concentration in a few hands." Karmel and Brunt summarized how the public and private protectionist regime constituted a distinctive cartelized and concentrated economy. In "most respects" it "diverges from the competitive *laissez-faire* model," they wrote, not only because of the government's extensive role, but also because the "corporate sector, which plays the strategic role in the economy, is dominated to an unusual degree by units which are large in relation to their markets and in relation to the economy as a whole."[6]

These criticisms generated constitutional controversies within Australia's federal system. The postwar increase of domestic and foreign investment facilitated agreement among the states to pass the Uniform Companies Act of 1961, which aimed to harmonize the diverse state statutes authorizing corporate takeovers. The growth of business within the federal system undermined regulatory consistency, however, making the law ineffectual. In legal terms, the individual states incorporated large firms such as BHP whereas their business reached across state lines. Such a corporation's *intra* state collusive or monopolistic practices were within the jurisdiction of the state in which the firm was incorporated, but that state's action was inadequate when the same corporation engaged in identical practices in another state.[7]

Constitutional controversies were accompanied by growing demands for individual opportunity. Judge Isaac Isaacs's dissents during the early federation era represented a defense of competition values broadly favoring small business enterprise. But the Great Depression, the controls the government imposed throughout the war and Australia's extended postwar boom intensified popular desire for individual economic freedom. The High Court's numerous postwar constitutional decisions upheld and strengthened the expanded public interest in economic liberty. While the formal constitutional issues involved federal-state conflicts, the practical "effect [was] not of protecting the states against the Commonwealth so much as protecting private enterprise against governments in general." Following Isaacs's departure from the court in 1930, the most influential judge promoting individualist market values was Owen Dixon. During the 1930s, Dixon, like Isaacs before him, defended individual economic liberty in

---

[6] Norman, "Progress under Pressure," 529; Wheelwright and Miskelly, *Anatomy of Australian Manufacturing*, 3; P. H. Karmel and Maureen Brunt, *The Structure of the Australian Economy* (Melbourne, 1963), 142.

[7] R. P. Austin, "Takeovers, the Australian Experience," in John H. Farrar, ed., *Takeovers, Institutional Investors and the Modernization of Corporate Laws* (Auckland, 1993), 144–91; Bushnell, *Australian Company Mergers*, 160–5; Wheelwright and Miskelly, *Anatomy of Australian Manufacturing*, 1–14; W. G. McMinn, *A Constitutional History of Australia* (Melbourne, 1979), 186–8; Suri Ratnapala, *Australian Constitutional Law Foundations and Theory* (Melbourne, 2002) 226–8.

dissents; after the war, his dissents became the High Court's majority opinion.[8]

Following Dixon's lead, lawyers representing interstate corporate enterprise urged the High Court to broaden the Constitution's corporations and commerce powers. In transport, banking, and other cases, the court upheld Dixon's expanded interpretation favoring freer interstate market activity and individual economic opportunity. In the first twenty postwar years, the court considered these issues in more than sixty decisions, upholding a broad construction. Noting the change, constitutional authority Geoffrey Sawer observed that because of the "extreme ambiguity" concerning this constitutional authority, the court was "perform[ing] the function of an administrative tribunal administering not law but a very broadly stated policy." The lawyer whose "arguments ... exerted considerable influence" upon the court was Sir Garfield Barwick. In a short space of time, the court heard "many cases involving the same general problem and with the same leading counsel appearing in nearly every case in the same interest – that of maximizing" individual economic liberty. The "great arguments" Barwick employed in leading cases between 1945 and 1955 relied upon Dixon's and other judges' dissenting opinions with "sharp[er], and ... more explicit attention to the political and economic theory behind the interpretation."[9]

Meanwhile, cartel practices prompted episodic challenges within some states, but the courts maintained the status quo. After World War II, Queensland and South Australia passed additional legislation to deal, on a limited basis, with price-fixing and monopolistic conduct. In the few suits arising under these laws, however, the courts applied the common-law public interest and reasonableness doctrines that the appellate courts had used before World War I. Thus well into the 1950s and 1960s Australian judges eviscerated state antitrust laws by employing the common law "notion of public detriment ... [to reach] a conclusion that there were good monopolies and good restrictive practices as well as bad." Even when a judge did not resort to the common law, the outcome was the same. Monopolizing conduct among cement producers in Western Australia influenced passage of antitrust measures in 1956 and 1959. The second law supported an extensive commission investigation which revealed widespread cartelization and monopolization. Nevertheless, when the issue came before the court, the judge, noting that "competition" from substitute

---

[8] McMinn, *Constitutional History of Australia*, 186–8, quote at 186; Geoffrey Sawer, *Australian Federalism in the Courts* (Carlton, 1967), 37, 46, 180–95; see also Zelman Cowen, *Isaac Isaacs* (Melbourne, 1967), 113–90; Garfield Barwick, *A Radical Tory* (Annandale, NSW, 1995), 51–80. In most of these cases, the central constitutional provision at issue was S.92.

[9] McMinn, *A Constitutional History of Australia*, 186–91, quote at 187; Sawer, *Australian Federalism*, quote at 46.

products such as wood and plastics were "reducing the demand for cement," upheld the cement manufacturers.[10]

The undercurrent of concern about Australia's protectionist regime found further outlet in public investigations. A Royal Commission in the late 1950s identified anticompetitive practices and trade restraints permeating Tasmania's market. More importantly, the Commonwealth government instituted a comprehensive review of the nation's constitutional system which extended broadly to issues having a bearing upon interstate corporate business. Appointed by the ruling Liberal-Country Party coalition government of Prime Minister R. G. Menzies as a bi-partisan body, the review committee included opposition Labor Party members who had some experience with restrictive trade practices issues involving trade unions. These members insisted upon including such issues in the committee's study. Advising the committee was a member of the Commonwealth's attorney-general office, J. E. Richardson, who was informed about Britain's newly enacted Restrictive Trade Practices Act of 1956 as well as current American antitrust developments. Public officials considered the committee to be "very powerful." Although restrictive trade practices problems were clearly marginal to the committee's work, it was difficult to ignore them altogether.[11]

The protectionist discourse prevailing in postwar Australia articulated a version of the public interest. The noteworthy growth of the nation's postwar economy made the "standard of living of the community as a whole" a dominant issue. At one level of public discourse, leading business sectors resisted establishing any separation between their interests and those of the wider community. "This puts the industry in a false position from the outset; ... the primary origin and object of agreements must be the benefit the industry expects thereby for itself," stated a report of the Associated Chambers of Manufacturers of Australia. "Benefits to others, however great, come second, although in the ultimate what benefits industry is an addition to the national interest." Stated Maureen Brunt: Business' "outlook is protectionist, it is true; but it is frequently 'protection all around' that is longed for. It is a desire for security and 'fair shares.' It is partly the Australian philosophy of the 'fair go' which finds its expression in vague yearnings for the just wage and the just price." According to such a view, the "prevalence of restrictive practices is just another consequence of Australian 'mateship.'"[12]

[10] Justice R. S. French, "Judicial Approaches to Economic Analysis in Australia," 9 *Review of Industrial Organization* (October 1994), 553, 554. See also Geoffrey de Q. Walker, *Australian Monopoly Law Issues of Law, Fact and Policy* (Melbourne, 1967), 35–6; Richardson, *Australian Trade Practices Act*, 24–7.

[11] Norman, "Progress under Pressure," 529–30; J. E. Richardson, interview, July 14, 1993, including quoted phrase; see also Richardson, *Australian Trade Practices Act*, 14–23.

[12] Maureen Brunt, "*The Trade Practices Bill*: Legislation in Search of an Objective," *Journal of the Economic Society of Australia and New Zealand Extract from the Economic Record*

Economists such as Brunt countered with arguments favoring "workable competition." Workable competition was, said Brunt, "defined as a situation in which there is sufficient market rivalry to compel firms to produce with internal efficiency, to price in accordance with costs, to meet the consumers' demand for variety, and to strive for product and process improvement." The most conspicuous problem with Australia's protectionist ethos of "mateship" was that its "cosiness rapidly slides into exclusiveness." Accordingly, a chief contribution of the economist was to demonstrate that a "choice must be made. A policy of workable competition implies that primacy is given to efficiency, progressiveness and opportunity. This will normally mean that the interests of the consuming public are rated higher than those of any entrenched group."[13]

The rubric of workable competition, however, obscured divergent policy solutions advocated by other Australian economists who opposed the protectionist order. Brunt had studied the antitrust doctrine of workable competition at Harvard and wanted to apply the American concept in Austrialia.[14] Alex Hunter suggested, by contrast, that the pragmatic case-by-case British policy approach to establishing "workably" competitive markets was better suited to the small concentrated Australian economy. An academic economist teaching in Britain during the 1950s, Hunter was by the early 1960s Professor of Economics at the University of New South Wales where his works vigorously condemned the arbitrariness, abuse, and inefficiencies inherent in the Australian protectionist system. Hunter nonetheless indicated that within Australia's oligopolistic markets, the "pragmatic" British standard might better stimulate competitive market pressures.[15]

However, proponents and opponents of the protectionist regime had their own visions of competition. Those who justified restrictive agreements under the rubric of mateship often advocated competition defined in terms of rivalry between private enterprise and state-owned public utilities. As a practical matter, the number of state-controlled industries had declined considerably. Nevertheless, business groups and Conservative Party officials representing their interests adopted the public–private meaning of

---

(1965), 364, 365, The Associated Chambers of Manufacturers of Australia, *Detailed Examination of the Commonwealth Government's Proposal for Legislation on Restrictive Trade Practices and Monopolies* (Canberra, 1963), 6–7.

[13] Brunt, "Legislation in Search of an Objective," 363, 364, 365.

[14] Ibid., 386; Maureen Brunt, interview, May 28, 1992.

[15] The distinction between the "dogmatic" U.S. and "pragmatic" British policy approach is made in Alex Hunter, "Restrictive Practices and Monopolies in Australia," in J. P. Nieuwenhuysen, ed., *Australian Trade Practices: Readings* (London, 1970), 169–201, especially 183–93. The sources of this regard for British policy pragmatism may be seen in A. Hunter, "The Progress of Monopoly Legislation in Britain: A Commentary," 2 *Scottish Journal of Political Economy* (February 1955), 198–217; Alex Hunter, "The Monopolies Commission and Price Fixing," 66 *The Economic Journal* (December 1956), 587–602; Alex Hunter, *Competition and the Law* (London, 1966).

competition to distinguish a free enterprise system from the program of nationalized industries identified with the Labor Party. For its part, the Labor Party used competition primarily in its rationale for price controls and the defense of discount pricing practices that union cooperatives employed in certain states. Moreover, both interest groups and organized labor defended the virtues of protectionism from the evils associated with "cut-throat" competition. The theory of workable competition was broad enough, however, that despite differing policy prescriptions, Brunt and Hunter agreed that *competition* was "not just an economic mechanism. It is also a means of reducing economic power, a policy which may have political attractions in itself. The market is seen as a device by which firms are made responsible to the demands of the community. Market regulation of firms' behavior is substituted for government regulation."[16]

Judges and lawyers constituted a legal culture whose discourse regarding competition reflected a similar tension. Among Australian judges, the restrictive common law doctrines continued to hold sway following World War II, as indicated in the case of the restrictive agreement among cement producers which for all practical purposes established a monopoly. Nevertheless, as the *Redfern* case of 1964 suggested, Isaacs's earlier vision retained some life. James Redfern managed corporations which sold at retail tires and related products produced by Dunlop Rubber and other tire manufacturers. In keeping with the dominant collusive mentality, the producers imposed upon their retailers an exclusive arrangement which "purported to govern the fixation of prices for traders and the terms on which the goods should be retailed." Such agreements were commonplace throughout the nation's economic order.[17] Redfern challenged the restrictive agreement as a violation of the old Australian Industrial Preservation Act (AIPA) of 1906. Dunlop and the other defendants argued that the collusive arrangement mixed *intra*state and *inter*state dealing and thus was beyond the reach of the Constitution's interstate commerce clause. The judge who wrote the court's majority *Redfern* opinion in 1964 was Chief Justice Owen Dixon, who had sustained the AIPA's constitutionality holding that the law applied to restrictive agreements as long as the interstate dimensions predominated.[18] The legal profession continued to be

[16] "A Business View of Restrictive Practices Legislation," in Nieuwenhuysen, ed., *Australian Trade Practices*, 202–11; Hopkins, *Crime, Law & Business*, 33–73, especially 38–41; Brunt, "Legislation in Search of an Objective," 362, quote at 364.
[17] Cowen, *Isaacs*, 103–5; and *The King and the Attorney-General of the Commonwealth v. Associated Northern Collieries* (1911) 14 C.L.R. 387; *Adelaide Steamship Co. Ltd. v. The King and Attorney-General of the Commonwealth* (1912) 15 C.L.R. 65 (High Court); *Attorney-General of the Commonwealth v. Adelaide Steamship Co.* [1913] A.C. 781 (Privy Council); *Redfern v. Dunlop Rubber Australia Ltd.* (1963) 110 C.L.R. 194.
[18] Compare Isaacs's construction, in lone dissent, of the Constitution's corporations power, S.51, *Huddart v. Parker v. Moorehead* (1908) 8 C.L.R. 330, and Cowen, *Isaacs*, 104–5,

divided. Dixon's *Redfern* decision reflected the procompetition values of a small but growing segment of Australia's legal culture. As yet, however, the anticompetitive agreements pervading the nation's economy constituted a market for legal services which gave business lawyers a stake in retaining the collusive regime.

Undoubtedly the most conspicuous factor impelling the *Redfern* case was Sir Garfield Barwicks's campaign promoting trade practices legislation. Barwick was responsible for making restrictive trade practices a significant public issue throughout Australia. The great victories he won in the nation's highest court for interstate business between 1945 and 1955 brought sufficient fame that in 1958, conservatives "persuaded" him "to accept a safe seat in the federal Parliament as a Liberal member" from New South Wales. Known as a man of momentum and drive among fellow barristers, he acquired the trust of Prime Minister Robert G. Menzies, who was also a lawyer. "Immediately," Barwick became attorney general in the Menzies government; for a time he was also minister of External Affairs which took him to the United Nations. To these federal offices Barwick brought a great capacity for work characterized by unusual intensity.[19]

As a practicing lawyer, Barwick had always taken a protagonist stance. Friend and foe alike described his deep personal conservatism as firmly rooted in a nineteenth-century individualist ethos. Practical professional experience reinforced this conservative individualism. As a young barrister, he departed from the tradition then followed by Australian lawyers which separated practice between equity and common law. He recalled that "when I began to appear in both jurisdictions I picked up the rumour in the street that I was neither fish nor fowl ... some of the men on the Equity side became disturbed by my frequent appearances in that jurisdiction." Nevertheless, Barwick recollected, "[i]n this fashion, I began to be at home in the courtroom, no matter which courtroom it was and no matter which aspect of the law was being administered."[20]

During the Depression his "practice expanded steadily," he remembered, "though larger firms did not brief me for quite some time. I depended mainly on those who were often themselves battling against the odds." When he did begin representing large firms, he acquired an intimate understanding of their relationship, especially within trade associations, to small business. He learned firsthand how big firms could abuse their market

136–7 to *Redfern v. Dunlop Rubber Australia Ltd.* (1963), 110 C.L.R. 194 (Dixon, C.J., see quotes at 208, 209).

[19] Hopkins, *Crime, Law & Business*, 33–73; Sawer, *Australian Federalism*, quote at 60; Richardson, *Australian Trade Practices Act*, 11–14; and J. E. Richardson, interview, July 14, 1993; Barwick, *Radical Tory*, 96–217; Maureen Brunt, interview, May 28, 1992; R. M. Bannerman, interview, July 13, 1993.

[20] Barwick, *Radical Tory*, 29; Maureen Brunt, interview, May 28, 1992; R. M. Bannerman, interview, July 13, 1993.

position, jeopardizing the well-being of smaller enterprises. After Barwick entered Parliament, many complaints of such practices came from small business constituents. Regarding his personal situation, he said, "the depth of the penury we experienced was almost devastating."[21]

At some level, too, Barwick undoubtedly realized that confronting the conflicts arising from antitrust issues would help to make his mark as an up-and-coming party leader. Thus, shortly after becoming attorney general, he began work on the program for trade practices legislation. "Many in the Liberal Party and many people in business ... [did] not readily accept the kind of government intervention required by any attempt to regulate restrictive practices and monopolization," he wrote later. "But nonetheless, for the health of the economy, I felt that national government should attempt such control." The general philosophy informing his approach was described by him as "modern liberal conservatism that says that governments should, by and large, keep out of business and allow competition to affect the price of goods and services and thus regulate the economy." Rejecting the extremes, Barwick's philosophy "allow[ed] a proper place for government intervention – not participation – in business by legislation which explicitly defines the occasion for intervention by duly constituted and independent authority."[22]

Barwick embraced principles that were consistent with the theory of workable competition. On a general level, he accepted the conservatives' idea of competition defined as free enterprise versus socialism. Regarding the rationale for trade practices legislation, however, his view of competition was closer to that of Australian economists. "I am convinced that free enterprise based on individual initiative sustained by the rewards which enterprise and effort produce is much preferable to government planning ... along socialist lines [which] ... is inimical to the creation of wealth and is likely to lead to stagnation." At the same time, he said, "I am also convinced that free enterprise essentially depends on effective competition. The human tendency to minimize the effort competition consistently demands is an all too common feature of the business community." This anticompetitive "tendency" among business people and workers "results in stultifying practices which restrict competition and ultimately, if unchecked, produces monopolies, whether in goods, labour or services. Consequently I felt that some legislation was necessary to curtail restrictive practices and the tendency to monopolies."[23]

Still, he was closest to the economist's theory of workable competition as it supported limiting economic power. Beyond the principal goals of this theory, to achieve market efficiency and to benefit consumers, it embodied the traditional American antitrust resistance to unrestrained economic

---

[21] Barwick, *Radical Tory*, 26–7; Maureen Brunt, interview, May 28, 1992.
[22] Barwick, *Radical Tory*, 146, 147.   [23] Ibid., 145–6.

power, including the threat this posed to small business values. While Barwick rejected what he termed the undue "complexity" of American antitrust, he thought that "as it was administered [it] was useful in preventing monopolization and in reducing inordinate diversification by major corporations." He viewed these issues, moreover, primarily in terms of the virtues of small-scale enterprise. "My own philosophy favoured small business, where the relationship of employer and employee was likely to be close and to produce mutual trust, indispensable in a healthy and productive economy. I ... am not prepared to concede that there are necessary benefits to the community, or increased efficiency, from the so-called economies of scale."[24]

Barwick linked abuse of private market power affecting small business to trade problems. As an advocate and MP, he encountered many instances when large corporations and trade associations used blacklists, boycotts, refusals to deal, and other restrictive practices against small firms. Upon becoming attorney general, he learned how widespread such restraints were through the researches conducted by H. Trevor Bennett, a senior official in his office. Data gathered by the authorities administering the nation's tariff policy showed that trade associations and large firms often attempted to use cartel arrangements to reduce the costs the tariff imposed. As Barwick's public statements noted, collusive trade practices protected "unprofitable" firms and retarded innovation, so that "goods which could be produced in Australia are in fact imported ... hav[ing] quite adverse effects on our overseas balances," or, "if that consequence is avoided, an unduly high level of tariff is required, which effectively prevents the growth of bilateral trade." Bennett's researches demonstrated, in turn, that this conduct hurt small business. Not surprisingly, Barwick viewed these incidents as preventing a "fair go" for individual-managed enterprises; yet, under current law, such firms were helpless. Embarking upon a campaign to overcome these obstructions, Barwick sought to reaffirm the individual's economic rights so essential to keeping Australian capitalism strong.[25]

Barwick espoused the pragmatic case-by-case British administrative approach as sufficiently capable of preventing the risks of cut-throat competition and the abuse of private market power. He endorsed the academic theory of workable competition in principle. He nonetheless emphasized that his legislative program had "its roots in the reaction of practical administrators to practices of the kind brought under notice rather than in general doctrinal considerations." Barwick recognized that cartels "tend to

---

[24] Ibid., 147.
[25] J. E. Richardson, interview, July 14, 1993; and R. M. Bannerman, interview, July 13, 1993, both noting reference to Bennet's contribution. Garfield Barwick, *Trade Practices in a Developing Economy: Australian Proposals for Control of Restrictive Trade Practices and Monopolies*, The G.L. Wood Memorial Lecture, University of Melbourne, August 16, 1963, 12.

remove or to suppress incentive – the incentive to be more efficient, to be more enterprising." Accordingly, he declared, such collusion and "a sluggish economy go together. On the face of it, therefore, as a general proposition, restrictive practices are not conducive to the development of a free-enterprise economy."[26]

Barwick aggressively pursued a publicity campaign. In various speeches and lectures, he emphasized that the regime of restrictive practices victimized smaller, individual enterprise. Aware that he was up against entrenched values identifying trade restraints with "mateship," Barwick ensured that his addresses received wide coverage. Sometimes, when he was unable to make a presentation in person, he had Bennett do it. In either case, the essential message was that arbitrary market conduct threatened individual opportunity. Numerous restrictive practices found throughout a "wide variety of industries" and "plainly defensive in outlook and objective" were, said Barwick, "out of accord with the real requirements of Australia's present position in the world" and "alien to the political convictions" of democratic liberalism and free market enterprise. The focus was always upon practices "which suggested injury to individuals with no overall benefit to the public."[27]

The basic differences between the British and the American antitrust regime were important to Barwick. Facilitated by the UN position, Barwick and J. E. Richardson – the senior lawyer in the attorney general's office who was also a member of the Constitutional Revision Commission – visited the United States, Canada, and Great Britain. At the U.S. Justice Department's Antitrust Division, during a six-week period, Richardson learned from Assistant Attorney General Robert T. Bicks about the American rule of reason governing mergers and the per se approach applied to cartel practices. He grasped more directly how the U.S. Robinson-Patman Act of 1936 permitted some anticompetitive behavior in order to protect smaller firms from chain stores. In addition, Richardson gained insight into the Federal Trade Commission and the general role an administrative tribunal played in applying principles of "fair trade." Richardson found, by contrast, that the British Restrictive Trade Practices Act of 1956 instituted a tribunal

[26] Barwick, *Trade Practices in a Developing Economy*, quotes at 11, 12, 14, and on preference for British approach, 17–21.

[27] Barwick, *Trade Practices in a Developing Economy*, 2; Garfield Barwick, *Australian Proposals for Legislation for the Control of Restrictive Trade Practices and Monopolies* (Canberra, 1963). The best overview of the campaign remains Hopkins, *Crime, Law & Business*, 33–73. See references to Barwick's efforts: Maureen Brunt, "The Australian Antitrust Law After 20 Years – A Stocktake," and Norman, "Progress under Pressure," 489–90, 530; Richardson, *Australian Trade Practices Act*, 11–14. The significance and relative solitariness of Barwick's campaign was confirmed in author's interviews with contemporaries: Maureen Brunt, May 28, 1992; Richard St. John, May 28, 1992; J. E. Richardson, July 14, 1993; R. M. Bannerman, July 13, 1993. See also Barwick, *Radical Tory*, 145–51.

approach in conjunction with a registry which placed business practices on a public record. Except for banning collective resale price maintenance, there was no general provision for per se prohibitions. Certain restrictive practices could be authorized under "gateways" if, after investigation, the Restrictive Practices Court found a given practice to be not contrary to the public interest. The British law generally did not impose criminal sanctions.[28]

Though American antitrust had some strengths, Barwick conceded, in general, he found it ill-suited to Australia. He liked the rule-of-reason approach to mergers, but he "did not care for the American method of control which imposed penalties on businessmen for infraction of the regime imposed by Congress. This law was necessarily expressed in universal terms, and often of ambiguous import. By its very nature, law on this subject was difficult to interpret and apply." Barwick especially opposed imposing on Australian business the "pain of criminal penalty if an error of judgment were made." The increased costs stemming from the American system's dependence upon the equity side of the court's discovery process also troubled him. "I believed that when litigation resulted, far too much time was taken up, both by the Justice Department in its investigations and by the courts in contested cases, in establishing exactly what was being done in business." Finally, he resisted giving the government the authority "to apply such pressure" because it seemed "unfair."[29]

Barwick's preference for administrative rather than judicial enforcement thus represented a clear choice. Although Richardson found much to recommend in American antitrust's mix of per se rules against cartel practices and a rule of reason governing mergers, Barwick rejected this approach because it relied extensively upon the courts. He knew full well that Australian judges generally had been sympathetic to restrictive practices. He doubted, moreover, whether an enforcement regime that relied upon litigation possessed the flexibility necessary to prevent cut-throat competition and arbitrary private market power. As a result, a system which combined an administrative tribunal, a registry-based authorization process, and few criminal sanctions following the design of British antitrust institutions attracted Barwick. Under pressure from business interests and power centers within his own conservative party, Barwick modified his proposals; concerning the fundamental support for the British approach, however, he was firm. By the time Menzies appointed Barwick chief justice of the High Court of Australia in 1964, significant disagreements persisted among business leaders and conservative party officials over important

[28] Barwick, *Radical Tory*, 145–51; Richardson, *Australian Trade Practices Act*, 11; Interview with J. E. Richardson, July 14, 1993.
[29] Barwick, *Radical Tory*, 146, 148; Barwick, *Trade Practices in a Developing Economy*, 15–21; Hopkins, *Crime, Law & Business*, 54–61.

substantive details of his legislative proposals, but there was no effective challenge to the underlying institutional design.[30]

Barwick's campaign launched a heated public debate. The nation's growing postwar trade status – coinciding with increased dependence on foreign capital and technology – unleashed tensions within Australian capitalism and the conservative government representing it. After the Conservative party came to power in 1949, the Labor Party did not mount a significant electoral bid until 1960–61. The political challenge emerged largely because of rising inflation. Meanwhile, a bipartisan movement gave Labor members a platform to popularize the dangers anticompetitive conduct posed to individual opportunity. As a result, the Menzies administration announced that it "would do something to protect and strengthen free productive and business enterprise against monopoly or restrictive practices." Also, the government had argued successfully before the Conciliation and Arbitration Commission that combating inflation required denying an increase in the basic wage. Barwick admitted privately to some business leaders that the government supported action against price-fixing practices to show that its battle against inflation extended to both wages and prices. In addition, the Country Party faction of the conservative coalition favored a restrictive practices policy after a report revealed extensive collusive bidding in the wool industry.[31]

These political and economic contingencies influenced Barwick's concrete proposals. He declared that predatory pricing (whereby a firm consistently cuts its prices at a loss to destroy a competitor), monopolization (defined not only as the mere possession but also as the abuse of market power), collusive tendering, and collusive bidding were "inexcusably unlawful." Most practices, however, were not prohibited outright, including various forms of price-fixing, collective boycott, and resale price maintenance (RPM). Firms were required to register restrictive agreements with the Trade Practices Commissioner; an independent tribunal would determine, case by case, whether an agreement violated the public interest. If it did, the practice was banned. Finally, Barwick proposed limited control of mergers or company takeovers if they were proven to be a substitute for a "restrictive arrangement." Clearly, Barwick's proposals were tentative, intended to solicit reaction while he pursued a publicity campaign. While he referred to competition values, the emphasis was upon restraining arbitrary conduct.[32]

The repeated emphasis upon arbitrary market power, especially exploitation of small business, indicated the conservative government's

[30] Concerning appointment to be Chief Justice, see Barwick, *Radical Tory*, 208–15.
[31] Norman, "Progress under Pressure," 530; Hopkins, *Crime, Law & Business*, 34–6 (Menzies, as quoted at 34); Barwick, *Radical Tory*, 146; J. E. Richardson, interview, July 14, 1993.
[32] Hopkins, *Crime, Law & Business*, 35–8; Richardson, *Australian Trade Practices Act*, 11–12 quotes at 12.

leading policy concerns. The "essence of competitive enterprise," Menzies said in 1963, was "real competition" and "the road to advancement in any business should be open to all. This is the system we wish to protect. Privately imposed restraints which are against the public interest or submit the small trader to oppressive limitations should be eliminated." Reflecting the reality that there was no Barwick *Bill*, only proposals that could lead to legislation, the prime minister indicated that the Liberal Party would introduce "a bill to deal with restrictive trade practices and to protect the small trader." Some parliamentary Liberals identified with B. M. Snedden argued that unless conservatives took the initiative, the Labor Party – as it had in 1961 – might use the restrictive trade practices issue to exploit the shifting economic situation and win public approval for a more radical program. Within the postwar international order, said Snedden, either "socialism or control within reason" would prevail. "The surrender of absolute freedom in the commercial field, which restrictive trade practice legislation involves, is no more than 'control within reason.'" Socialism was the "alternative ... which appalls me." Any Labor Party law would undoubtedly be criminal in nature, absolute in terms and extreme in penalty."[33]

The principal political opposition that Barwick's proposals encountered came from within the Conservative Party coalition. In Parliament, five members of the Liberal Party's back bench criticized the proposals and the support they received from such Liberal leaders as Barwick, Snedden, and Menzies. The critics objected that Barwick was paving the way for an "unjustifiable intrusion" into the "affairs of private enterprise. ... Businesses know best what is good for society and the economy." The Liberal-controlled state governments of Victoria, South Australia, and Western Australia expressed opposition too. But the most effective resistance arose inside Menzies's cabinet from deputy prime minister and Country Party leader, John McEwen. The Country Party, including at least one of its cabinet ministers, supported the essentials of Barwick's program, but McEwen was a pragmatist who in the name of "protection all around" was endeavoring to broaden his party's electoral base. As a result, McEwen vigorously resisted the proposals within the cabinet.[34]

The split within the Conservative Party ranks reflected division among business interests. Various prominent business organizations representing leading manufacturers, importers, wholesalers, and retailers rejected the Barwick proposals in formal submissions to the government. Contrariwise, retail associations and individual retailers in Queensland and New South

[33] Hopkins, *Crime, Law & Business*, 43–50, quotes at 43, 44; politics confirmed, R. M. Bannerman, interview, July 13, 1993. See also Barwick, *Radical Tory*, 145–51.
[34] Hopkins, *Crime, Law & Business*, 43–50, Liberal Opposition, quotes at 44; Brunt, "Legislation in Search of an Objective," 363–5, quote at 364. Dyster and Meredith, *Australia in the International Economy*, 253–5; R. M. Bannerman, interview, July 13, 1993.

Wales along with other groups nationwide who had experienced arbitrary conduct from distributors, supported the proposals. Similarly, in South Australia, the Chamber of Manufacturers opposed Barwick's campaign, but an individual firm took the opposite position because it had been disadvantaged by a price agreement. In addition, a Queensland football manufacturer, despite the state's Chamber of Manufacturers' resistance, favored Barwick's proposals because the Victorian Sports Goods Federation excluded it from the market. Meanwhile, one observer suggested that newer firms entering business would likely benefit most from the proposed policing of collusive behavior.[35]

Primary producers in livestock and agriculture generally supported Barwick's campaign. Like the antitrust regimes of the United States, Europe, and Japan, the proposals provided agricultural sectors with broad exemptions administered by local and national regulators under special laws. Thus, the proposed trade practices measures did not directly interfere with the primary producers' protected market, but they could eradicate the restrictive arrangements that distributors and manufacturers imposed upon the primary production sectors. Since Barwick's proposals excluded labor organizations and wage agreements, organized labor favored them. Local governments exploited by price-fixing agreements also supported Barwick's campaign. Despite some dissent, the press generally endorsed it in the name of consumers, as did certain academic economists.[36]

But according to Barwick, consumer interests were equivocal. He recognized that "consumers do not really form a separate group. Everyone in the community is a consumer at one time or another." Thus, the "community was not divided into separated compartments of manufacturers and suppliers on the one hand, and consumers on the other." Some collusive practices "led to no exploitation of consumers." In the case of "a developing economy" such as postwar Australia , however, in order "for the price level in some industries to be high enough to provide such a resulting profit as permits the ploughing back into capital expansion of a considerable part of the earned profit ... the consumer may suffer." Even so, consumer organizations were "in their infancy in Australia and there were no representations made to government by consumer groups." Within this public discourse, elected party officials, big and small businesses, primary producers, unions, and economic–legal experts disputed the proposed trade practices legislation during 1964 and 1965.[37]

<hr>

[35] Hopkins, *Crime, Law & Business*, 43–50; Barwick, *Trade Practices in a Developing Economy*, 10.

[36] See notes 33 and 34 above.

[37] Barwick, *Trade Practices in a Developing Economy*, quotes at 11; Hopkins later noted the lack of "representations" from consumer groups, *Crime, Law & Business*, 42.

II. THE GENESIS OF TRADE PRACTICES LAWS: R. B. BANNERMAN AND LIONEL MURPHY, 1964–1974

As Barwick departed the political scene in 1964, the courts decided further cases against collusive practices. Following the *Redfern* decision, the Commonwealth Attorney General Bill Snedden won two suits concerning firms that had refused to supply a grocery store with stock unless the store paid a twenty-five percent surcharge on the list prices of the goods purchased. These successive decisions indicated sympathy among at least some Australian judges consistent with Barwick's proposals.[38] These developments reinforced, moreover, Barwick's assertion in 1963 that the Constitution's guarantee of interstate free trade did not present an impediment to his proposed program. The constitutional provision "forbids only laws obstructing interstate commerce, whereas laws may also have the object of ... break[ing] down privately imposed restraints of trade designed to suppress or distort existing commerce or to prevent commerce from coming into existence ... [which] is protecting the freedom of interstate trade, not impairing it."[39]

Snedden's court victories aroused business opposition to criminal sanctions. Business groups and the Conservative Party politicians representing their interests rejected any government policy or law which might lead to criminal prosecution. Under Barwick's proposals, four practices were banned as illegal per se and subject to criminal prosecution. Said one business leader, the "criminal aspects are repugnant to us. ... An employer accused of those practices could be charged in a criminal court ... and if found guilty, jailed or fined." Others feared the "stigma of criminality" for conduct which always had been regarded as lawful business. Thus, the decisions enforcing the Industrial Preservation Act in 1964 and 1965 potentially widened the scope of criminal court actions against what business regarded as perfectly acceptable.[40]

Notwithstanding such fears, Barwick's proposals endorsed quite limited criminal prosecution. Except for four proscribed practices, he said, "I could see no need to make business conduct criminal unless it were done in defiance of an order of a duly constituted tribunal." Whether conduct was "in actual practice ... inimical to the public interest" was a "question of

[38] *Attorney-General of the Commonwealth v. C. Camp & Sons Pty. Ltd. (unreported)*: *Attorney-General of the Commonwealth v. John Casey & Co. (Canberra) Pty. Ltd.* (unreported), cited and summarized in Richardson, *Australian Trade Practices Act*, 23. My search in 2004 found no such cases reported, so I rely on his assessment in cited text and J. E. Richardson, interview July 14, 1993.

[39] Garfield Barwick, "Some Aspects of Australian Proposals for Control of Restrictive Trade Practices and Monopolies," 36 *Australian Law Journal* (1963), 363–84, quote at 375; Walker, *Australian Monopoly Law*, 37–51, quote at 46–7. See also Ratnapala, *Australian Constitutional Law*, 223–41.

[40] Hopkins, *Crime, Law & Business*, 54–61, quote at 55.

investigation." Barwick's intent was to design enforcement provisions that facilitated voluntary disclosure of anticompetitive agreements on the Commissioner's confidential registry. Barwick's reliance upon even modest criminal penalties for nondisclosure created, however, undue preoccupation with criminal prosecution. "This part of the scheme was not completely understood," acknowledged Barwick later, "and caused considerable opposition."[41]

These proposals, accordingly, underwent modification before Parliament enacted legislation. The main reasons for delay were "clearly ... political, not only in the narrow sense of finding a bill which will prove acceptable to Liberal Party supporters, but also in the sense of devising a policy with goals and methods which reflect the social and political values of a large section of Australian society."[42] In the words of the manufacturer association's director, "no trade practice should carry a criminal taint. If a practice is to be declared unlawful then the appropriate action is an injunction in restraint." Business submissions urged the registration of only a few types of restrictive practices and the institution of a process for preclearing investment arrangements which might have such an outcome. Appealing to the conviction that Australia's small economy justified concentrated markets, the opponents wanted to eliminate altogether regulation of mergers or takeovers. Meanwhile, the leading manufacturers' association pursued within the state governments a covert strategy intended to "arous[e]" a "pro state feeling." A private letter to the Chamber's state offices stated that "without appearing to spearhead the attack against the Trade Practices Bill, the State Chambers by quiet propaganda in the right places could induce the Premier of each state to say to the Prime Minister 'call off your Trade Practices Bill until we see what it means to the States.'"[43]

Parliament first repealed the Industrial Preservation Act. The bill that Attorney General Snedden then introduced appeared to be a compromise between business demands and Barwick's scheme. Snedden declared that its "purpose" was "to preserve competition in Australian trade and commerce to the extent required by the public interest. Competition is an essential ingredient of any free enterprise economy." He defined "competition" essentially as the right to trade free from restrictive constraints known as "orderly marketing." The intent of the legislation was to prevent "anticompetitive agreements or practices, designed to serve the interest of members of the industry itself, or of some of its members, without necessarily having regard to what is, or is not, desirable in the interest of our community as a whole." At the same time, however, the government was "conscious that the lessening of competition may, in some aspects of the

[41] Barwick, *Radical Tory*, 148.   [42] Brunt, "Legislation in Search of an Objective," 357.
[43] Hopkins, *Crime, Law & Business*, quote at 50, 55.

economy, be unavoidable; indeed, it may be not only consistent with but a proper ingredient of, a truly free enterprise system." Thus, the bill reflected the government's conviction, Snedden said, "that there may well be some practices restrictive in nature, which are in the public interest."[44]

The bill generally rejected per se rules which might facilitate American-style judicial enforcement. Thus, whereas Barwick had proposed that collusive bidding, collusive tendering, monopolization, and predatory pricing might be directly banned and subject to criminal prosecution, Snedden's bill banned only collusive bidding and tendering. Moreover, they were subject to registration and so, potentially, free from prohibition. The range of collective restrictive agreements subject to registration was narrower than Barwick had suggested. Many bilateral restrictive practices were left outside the bill altogether. Consistent with the assumption that combination was inevitable in the smaller Australian market, the bill removed the limited control of mergers that Barwick had proposed. In addition, the Snedden bill specified a standard of public interest including employees, producers, distributors, importers, exporters, proprietors, investors, and small business as well as consumers. The more specific language enlarged the grounds for arguing that certain trade restraints were consistent with the public interest.[45]

The Snedden bill nonetheless followed basically the British administrative approach that Barwick had proposed. Although narrower than the proposals in scope, the bill retained the requirement that businesses register evidence of certain restrictive arrangements with the commissioner. Unlike the British system, the registry was not public. Still, the commissioner could subject registered practices to examination by the Tribunal. The Tribunal would decide whether the practice "substantially reduced competition." The parties maintaining the practice could offer proof that it was not contrary to the public interest, but if the Tribunal decided that the public was harmed, it could order "de-registration," whereupon the practice became illegal. Violation of the Tribunal's judgment resulted in penalties: "a fine, imprisonment or, in the case of a company, sequestration of assets." Enforcement relied upon an injunction. The scheme, said Richardson, was "one of an administrative authority – the Tribunal – making an administrative determination and having it enforced by the normal judicial process." Even so the mixed lay and judicial character of the Tribunal raised constitutional issues.[46]

Critics focused on the bill's weaknesses. Economist Maureen Brunt pointed out that the "philosophy underlying the bill is largely one of

[44] Walker, *Australian Monopoly Law*, 36, 323, 303; Richardson, *Australian Trade Practices Act*, 3–4, 11–12, quotes at 13–14; Hopkins, *Crime, Law & Business*, 52.
[45] Richardson, *Australian Trade Practices Act*, 3–4, 11–14.
[46] Ibid., quotes at 112, 113, and constitutional issue.

'obvious abuse' ... [and] 'fairness' is given as much weight as either competition or good economic performance." The idea "of fair conduct – rather than competitive conduct" governs the bill. "If, in many instances, business conduct is the outcome of market structure and environment," Brunt asked, "why not be prepared to control the causes of that conduct?" Both Barwick and Snedden trusted the flexibility of an administrative process to deal with objectionable behavior. Their image of competition, however, did not sufficiently recognize that the goal of "workable competition" was consumer welfare. A narrow view of competition reflected the bill's dependence on compliance achieved by injunction. By contrast, a policy embodying workable competition would include a wide range of remedies enabling public and private enforcement "to influence market structure." Also, said Geoffrey Walker, the repeal of private actions for treble damages "stripped the individual trader of all the protection which the 1906 Act might have afforded him, leaving cartels free to wipe out as many businesses as they wish until the tribunal makes a specific order with respect to that specific conduct by that specific cartel." Parliament, he continued, "seems to have gone out of its way to preserve collective coercion as an accepted part of Australian business practice."[47]

Parliament passed Snedden's bill in May; following Royal Assent, it became the Trade Practices Act of 1965. Before the law became fully operational two years later, Snedden proposed and Parliament enacted an amendment which established regulation of shipping conferences affecting Australia's export trade. During the same period, the attorney general began appointing to the Trade Practices Tribunal the lawyers and lay persons who were to serve renewable 7-year terms; among those selected was Brunt. Snedden also selected Bannerman as the commissioner of Trade Practices. A senior lawyer on the permanent staff of the Commonwealth's attorney general office, Bannerman was unknown to business interests; he had not commented publicly on the Act. To administer the Act – including the burdensome registration of restrictive agreements – Bannerman requested a staff of about 100. He remained Chairman throughout the law's existence as it underwent court challenge and amendment. Although Barwick himself was said to have described the Act as "milk and water," Bannerman's administration actually represented a necessary transition from the old protectionist regime to a new order in which competition possessed real meaning in Australian capitalism.[48]

Bannerman later described himself as "underqualified." With a law degree and no formal training in economics, he had been a solicitor in

---

[47] Brunt, "Legislation in Search of an Objective," quotes at 377–8; Walker, *Australian Antimonopoly Law*, 223.

[48] R. M. Bannerman, interview, July 13, 1993; J. E. Richardson, interview, July 14, 1993; Brunt, "Australian Antitrust Law," 523.

commercial law practice in Sydney before joining the Commonwealth's attorney general office's permanent staff in 1962. When Parliament enacted the Trade Practices Act Bannerman was forty-four years old and was rated number three in the attorney general office. Several "prominent" people to whom Snedden offered the position declined. H. Trevor Bennett and J. E. Richardson, the two individuals with probably the best technical credentials, were considered, by contrast, too controversial because they were identified with Barwick's unmodified proposals. Bannerman was associated with no public position; Snedden was free, therefore, to argue that his primary qualification was "integrity." Similarly, business interests could consider him open to persuasion.[49] Indeed, Parliament's discussion of the bill suggested that Conservative Party officials representing business groups "harbour the threat that a future government might once more espouse the rule: 'If a complaint is received it will not be investigated; if it is investigated it will not be prosecuted; if it is prosecuted it will not be won.'"[50]

Bannerman faced these challenges with a definite strategy of institutional development and enforcement. With the example of the Australian Industries Preservation Act's failure as guide, Bannerman set as his achievable objective, the survival of the Act as a reasonably effective enforcement regime. This objective depended upon building a bi-partisan political constituency, which in turn required educating business groups about competition. An institutional impediment to case-by-case enforcement was that the Trade Practices Tribunal, unlike its British counterpart, could not enforce its orders, having instead to rely upon the court's injunctive relief, thus slowing down the process of gaining compliance.[51]

Bannerman viewed competition in terms of economic theory which benefited consumers and resisted collusive practices, expressed as "protection all round." A much-publicized confrontation over tariff policy revealed to Bannerman the political and economic dimensions of his theory. By the time the Trade Practices Act became fully operational in 1967, Menzies was no longer prime minister and the conservative government had appointed a new chairman to the Tariff Board, Alfred Rattigan. Under the influence of Trade Minister John McEwen, the Board had a reputation as a "pro-protectionist" agency. In 1967, however, the "Board announced that it intended to pursue a policy of reducing tariff protection in order to improve the competitiveness of the manufacturing sector. It would use the concept of 'effective rate of protection;' (which took into account the cumulative effects of tariffs on various stages of production) to measure the degree of assistance being given." Rattigan used the consumers' interest as the measure of competition. Backed by the manufacturers' lobby, the

---

[49] R. M. Bannerman, interview, July 13, 1993.   [50] Walker, *Australian Monopoly Law*, 304.
[51] R. M. Bannerman, interview, July 13, 1993; essentially confirmed in principle if not specifics, Brunt, "Australian Antitrust Law," 490–1.

industry unions, and the government, McEwen vigorously resisted Rattigan's policy. Supplied by economists with information and theories, however, Rattigan persisted until McEwen resigned, whereupon the Board began a comprehensive review of competitiveness. Throughout the controversy, Bannerman observed the evidence and policy that Rattigan publicized, employing them as a standard for his own work in the Trade Practices field.[52]

Most importantly perhaps, Bannerman perceived in Rattigan's stand lessons for preserving his agency's independence. Rattigan proved adept at using publicity to fend off political pressures. Bannerman was never subject to direct official criticism; he realized nonetheless that cultivating trust while publicizing harmful practices created a popular image of integrity, detachment, and openness. The press provided invaluable assistance, revealing that the level of cartelization throughout the economy was too extensive to be defended, especially in light of international competition. Bannerman used annual reports to supply the media with evidence. Parliament might starve the agency for funds, but publicity demonstrating that the agency fulfilled an essential function made it politically unattractive for Parliament to pursue that course.[53]

Despite clear limitations, Bannerman's use of consultation had some success. Generally, Australian business accepted Barwick's ploy that merely placing a restrictive agreement on the secret register would not in and of itself impugn its lawfulness. Registration was facilitated further because the commissioner carried the burden of proof if he chose to challenge a practice. In addition, the inclusion of many factors to be considered as potentially within the public interest permitted numerous defenses. Thus, by June 1974, when the Trade Practices Act ended its existence, many firms had complied with the registration provision. Bannerman's relatively small staff had examined 14,403 agreements. When an agreement raised questions, Bannerman held a private conference with the parties. If their response left him unsatisfied, his formal recourse was to commence an action at the Trade Practices Tribunal. He did so in only two cases. According to the commissioner's annual reports from 1969 to 1974, however, he employed consultation to bring about the termination of "hundreds" of restrictive agreements. Moreover, in thirty-eight of forty horizontal price-fixing cases, he did the same to achieved compliance.[54]

[52] Dyster and Meredith, *Australia in the International Economy*, 253–5, quote at 255; Ann Capling, *Australia and the Global Trade System from Havana to Seattle* (Cambridge, UK, 2001), 72–84, especially 73, including quoted phrase "protection all round." Rattigan's impact confirmed by R. M. Bannerman, interview, July 13, 1993.

[53] R. M. Bannerman, "Points from Experience, 1967–1984, Appendix 1," *Trade Practices Commission Annual Report* (1983–84), 149–212, especially 150–3; R. M. Bannerman, interview, July 13, 1993.

[54] Ibid.; and R. M. Bannerman, "Development of Trade Practices Law and Administration," *Australian Economic Review* (1985), 83–97, especially, 84–90; Norman, "Progress under

The breadth of industries in which consultation was successful reflected common structural deficiencies the commissioner could exploit. In most cases these were the same industries that seemed most prone to price-fixing prosecutions in the United States. According to economists, they "often involve homogeneous products, few sellers, impediments to entry and inelastic demand. It seems that some industries have structural, technological and behavioral characteristics which render them universally prone to such agreements." Among world-wide antitrust regulators these were also industries in which price-fixing cases were the most winnable. In nations possessing antitrust regimes, the law gave disaffected individuals or firms incentives to provide authorities with the evidence needed to bring price-fixing prosecutions. Bannerman's skillful use of publicity, combined with the cultivation of trust due to the secret registry, represented a strategy that tapped into these structural and behavioral realities. From 1965 on, business and consumers alike increasingly learned how much cartelization permeated the Australian economy. As a result, it became easier for dissatisfied industry members to understand that the evidence which filled the registry established an incentive to cooperate with Bannerman and through consultation to terminate restrictive agreements.[55]

The two cases which went before the Trade Practices Tribunal revealed, however, that consultation was not enough. In the frozen vegetables case, the industry had experienced rapid growth with unit production costs declining and increased competition forcing down prices. An unusually large pea crop then set off a price war. Ten processors, including five producers who together accounted for 90 percent of Australia's frozen vegetables production, negotiated a minimum price agreement which provided limited discounts. Almost at once parties began to undercut the agreement making it impossible to reach any resolution with Bannerman. He then brought the issue before the Tribunal. The mixed membership of a judge and lay persons considered the defenses the producers argued, which reflected the price stabilizing benefits associated with "orderly marketing" and the need to protect small business. Applying a standard of workable competition, the Tribunal decided in 1971 against the processors.[56]

The Tribunal's decision nonetheless revealed a conspicuous defect of the Trade Practices Acts. As a way around the prohibition against price-fixing, several frozen vegetable producers merged. The initial Barwick proposal, of course, had included a provision which permitted some regulation of

---

Pressure," and David K. Round and John J. Siegfried, "Horizontal Price Agreements in Australian Antitrust: Combating Anti-Competitive Corporate Conspiracies and Connivance," 9 *Review of Industrial Organization* (October 1994), 530, 574–8, quote at 599.

[55] Round and Siegfried, "Horizontal Price Agreements," *Review of Industrial Organization*, 576–7, quote at 75.

[56] *Re: Frozen Vegetables* (1971), F.L.R. 196; Round and Siegfried, "Horizontal Price Agreements," *Review of Industrial Organization*, 577.

mergers, but business succeeded in getting Barwick's recommendation omitted from the bill that became law. The consequences of the business victory became evident when similar mergers occurred after the commissioner questioned price-fixing in three other industries. Seeking public attention for the growing problem, Bannerman commented in the commissioner's *Annual Report* that the 1965 Act "takes a logically incomplete approach when it leaves such cases free of public interest examination ... it is beyond argument that the merging of competitors, who have previously been parties to restrictive agreements, is the ultimate restriction of competition."[57]

The Trade Practices Tribunal decided its second case in 1973. The fiberboard containers case involved arrangements among producers to standardize and rationalize production for purposes of improved efficiency. Although the goal was not objectionable, the Australian Fiberboard Container Manufacturers' Association pursued it by agreeing to fix prices. Some paperboard converters did not belong to the association and so were not party to the agreements. Other types of containers were on sale, making substitution possible. The market presence of nonassociation members and the availability of alternative containers facilitated possible competition if prices rose too high. In this respect, the price-fixing agreements had a more limited effect than did those in the frozen vegetables case. The commissioner challenged the association's restrictive practices before the Tribunal, arguing that price-fixing agreements could have a contradictory impact on standardization and rationalization by undercutting incentives to enhance efficiency. The Tribunal accepted the argument, declaring that competition benefited efficient producers, facilitating innovation and improved efficiency. Indicating the change in public and business opinion, Bannerman observed in his *Annual Report* that price agreements were "very unlikely to be consistent with the public interest."[58]

Bannerman's consultations and the Tribunal's action reflected growing public agitation for competition policies that benefited consumers. In response to the frozen vegetables producers' price-fixing scheme, which raised prices as much as 30 percent, a citizens group, Campaign Against Rising Prices, pushed for a boycott. Woolworth, a leading chain supermarket, instituted a pricing policy favoring the boycott. Thus, the commissioner's investigation and the Tribunal's order supported the consumers' cause. This confrontation coincided with a revival of inflationary pressures which both the Conservative and the Labor parties addressed partially by

[57] Commissioner of Trade Practices, *Seventh Annual Report* (Canberra, 1974), 5; P. R. Davey, "Frozen Vegetables: Before and After, Restrictive Practices," in Nieuwenhuysen, ed., *Australian Trade Practices*, 2nd edn (1976), 37–58.

[58] *Re: Fibreboard Manufacturers' Association* (1973), Australian Trade Practices Report [ATPR] 8378; Round and Siegfried, "Horizontal Price Agreements," *Review of Industrial Organization*, 578.

advocating the strengthening of the Trade Practices Act. During 1970–71, the attorney general proposed an amendment aimed at bringing RPM agreements within the commissioner's jurisdiction. Heightening interest in the amendment was a publicized clash between Dunlop and a discount store the Australian Council of Trade Unions (ACTU) ran in Melbourne. The discount store rejected Dunlop's RPM agreement, whereupon the company refused to supply the store. The ACTU retaliated by imposing a black-ban against Dunlop that received considerable popular support. The company capitulated, and the press hailed it a victory for consumers.[59]

The amendment became a focus for mounting interest-group pressure. The conservative government's cabinet endorsed the attorney general's proposal outlawing RPM, despite vigorous opposition from manufacturing interests. Emphasizing the interminable delay associated with the case-by-case registration approach, Bannerman supported establishing a per se prohibition. Although manufacturers claimed that the amendment would hurt or even destroy small business, the press urged Parliament to pass it. Reflecting the growing popular perception that the Trade Practices Act aided consumers, the Melbourne *Age* editorial declared, "The consumer is entitled to all the benefits … of unrestricted competition. That is what free enterprise is all about." Parliament amended the Trade Practices Act to prohibit RPM, subject to authorization. Upon a showing of evidence, the Tribunal could authorize such an agreement if it benefited the "public as users or consumers."[60]

Parliament's passage of the RPM amendment coincided with a seminal constitutional decision, handed down in the *Rocla Concrete Pipes* case of 1971. During the public debate over the RPM amendment, Bannerman employed consultation to compel three concrete pipe manufacturers to abandon a national price-fixing agreement. The attorney general prosecuted them when they circumvented the commissioner's efforts by establishing separate arrangements in six states. The court decided for the companies on the merits but undercut the value of the victory as a precedent by virtually overruling *Huddart Parker*. In that decision of 1908, the court had narrowly construed the Constitution's corporations power, undercutting the Australian Industrial Preservation Act. In *Rocla Concrete Pipes*, however, the court held that the Constitution's corporations power enabled the federal government to reach *intra*state relations whereas the commerce power did not. That significantly expanded the Commonwealth's authority over interstate business having local connections.[61] The court

---

[59] Hopkins, *Crime, Law & Business*, 75–6; and Bannerman, "Trade Practices Law," *Australian Economic Review*, 89.

[60] Hopkins, *Crime, Law & Business*, 76–9, as quoted phrases at 76, 77.

[61] McMinn, *Constitutional History*, 190–1; Ratnapala, *Australian Constitutional Law*, 236–41; *Strickland v. Rocla Concrete Pipes* (1971) 124 C.L.R. 468.

340 Antitrust Resurgence in Postwar Australia

thus established a broad constitutional basis for new legislation which both the conservatives and Labor used to justify their proposals. The Liberal/ Country Party temporarily undercut Labor's maneuvering for a broader program by agreeing to pass the Restrictive Trade Practices Act of 1971. The conservatives also began considering stronger measures which, none-theless, did not go as far as Labor demanded.[62]

Bannerman used the Tribunal's decisions to defend a per se approach during the frantic lobbying efforts accompany the conservative's proposed trade practices legislation in 1972. But the party failed to pass the legisla-tion because the national election of December 1972 resulted in Labor's first return to power since 1949.[63] Labor Prime Minister Gough Whitlam's administration lasted through December 1975, amid constitutional con-troversy stemming from the conservative's continuing power within the Commonwealth Senate, as well as the onset of the global recession in 1973. Still, the ongoing struggle did not prevent passage of reforms broadly concerning Australia's international competitive advantage, such as pro-consumer tariff reductions and more limited dairy subsidies, the end to the "White Australia" immigration policy, the strengthening of the corporate takeover law, and passage of the Trade Practices Act of 1974.[64] Whitlam's electoral victory represented the ascendancy within the Labor Party itself of the view that "[f]or all their slogans and catchcries, political parties of all shades, in all countries, now accept that democratic governments must co-operate with the private sector in the running of a mixed economy." Pro-ponents of mainstream Australian trade unionism criticized the Whitlam administration's embrace of this "Technocratic Labourism."[65]

Labor's victory resulted in large part from an electoral strategy aimed at middle-class consumers. Whitlam's policies targeted middle-class voters, especially in the suburbs of Melbourne and Sydney. As the media image of

[62] Hopkins, *Crime, Law & Business*, 74–86; Bannerman, "Trade Practices Law," 89–90; Norman, "Progress under Pressure," and Brunt, "Australian Antitrust Law," 530–2, 490–1; Bannerman, "Points from Experience," 150–3. These points confirmed in J. E. Richardson, interview, July 14, 1993; R. M. Bannerman, interview, July 13, 1993; Maureen Brunt, interview, May 28, 1992; Richard St. John, interview, May 28, 1992.
[63] Compare G. Gentle, "Economic Welfare, the Public Interest and the Trade Practices Tribunal," in Nieuwenhuysen, ed., *Australian Trade Practices*, 2nd edn (1976), 59–77; Hopkins, *Crime, Law & Business*, 77–85; Commissioner of Trade Practices, *Annual Report, 1973–1974*, 5.
[64] Hawkins, *Crime, Law & Business*, 87–103; Capling, *Australia and Global Trade*, 87–90; Jimmy Hocking, *Lionel Murphy: A Political Biography* (Cambridge, UK, 1997), 146–222; Dyster and Meredith, *Australia in the International Economy*, 259–60, 280–9, 299; Bannerman, "Trade Practices Law," 89–91; Richard St. John, "Reflections on 20 Years of the Trade Practices Act," *Bulletin Trade Practices Commission* (December 1994), 24–8; Ratnapala, *Australian Constitutional Law*, 60–6.
[65] Bob Catley and Bruce McFarlane, "Technocratic Laborism – The Whitlam Government," in E. L. Wheelwright and Ken Buckley, eds., *Essays in the Political Economy of Australian Capitalism* (Sydney, 1975), I, 242–79, quoted at 244.

Robert Hawke's success against Dunlop concerning discount store pricing in 1970–71 suggested, organized labor and consumers possessed common interests in Australia's metropolitan markets. Accordingly, as Commissioner Bannerman's measured enforcement built bipartisan Parliamentary support for revising the weak trade practices regime, Labor presented itself as defending consumer interests. The conservatives, however, had to balance business demands for wage restraint in the face of inflationary pressures with the call for legislation which would, declared the outgoing attorney general, prevent the use of "market power ... to pass on to consumers, through increased prices, costs which would not in a more competitive situation have been incurred at all." At another point, he said, "Practically all restrictive trade practices legislation is on its face, consumer oriented." Nevertheless, the conservative's divided message enabled Labor to gain consumer support on the trade practices issue. Labor's Attorney General Lionel Murphy announced that the administration's primary goal in introducing trade practices legislation was to ensure that business did not harm consumers.[66]

In conjunction with this proconsumer message, the Whitlam administration expressly appealed to business. Labor's Minister of Secondary Industry and Supply stated that the party was "committed to a prosperous mixed economy" and thereby "seeks to co-operate with business in the national interest," including the promotion of the "welfare of industry which employs one-third of the people who voted it into office." The government rejected taking Labor's traditional adversarial stance against business, observing that compared with the previous years of the conservative rule, in 1974, the "gross profit of Australian companies increased by a billion dollars or 20 per cent." He added a claim that "Australian business will always do better under a Labor Government than a non-Labor Government because the Labor Governments believed in administering and guiding the economy and taking action to achieve prosperity."[67] This probusiness view was consistent with the administration of a corporate takeover law. Enacted shortly before the conservatives' electoral defeat, the Foreign Companies (Takeovers) Act facilitated consumer product diversification by channeling foreign investment and outside technological innovation into the corporate restructuring of Australian firms. Never before in peacetime had an Australian government established the authority to prevent a takeover if a foreign individual or corporation gained 15 or 40 percent, respectively, of the controlling vote of an Australian firm.[68]

---

[66] Hopkins, *Crime, Law & Business*, 81–91, quoted at 82; Catley and McFarlane, "Technocratic Laborism," in Wheelwright and Buckley, eds., *Essays in Political Economy*, 1: 242–69; Hocking, *Lionel Murphy*, 204–8, 224.

[67] Catley and McFarlane, "Technocratic Laborism," in Wheelwright and Buckley, eds., *Essays in Political Economy*, 1: 250.

[68] Dyster and Meredith, *Australia in the International Economy*, 281–2.

The Labor government selectively enforced the Foreign Takeovers law. For three years it denied only 11 of 450 takeover proposals; before leaving power in 1975, it enacted an even stronger measure. Commenting on the impact American multinational corporations' investment had on Australian private sector employment, Whitlam declared that "in the future we will cast a more critical eye over individual investment proposals. We intend to make sure that future capital inflow is associated with *productive* investment which will add to Australia's real resources and that foreign capital is employed in real *partnership* [emphasis in the orginal] with invesment Australian capital." Accordingly, the government pressured an American–Japanese investment consortium to allow 51 percent of Australian control in order to construct a petrochemical plant in South Australia. The action coincided with the government's promotion of Australian corporate diversification, such as BHP's pursuing expansion in Southeast Asia and the leading Australian banks' investing in Indonesia.[69]

The government's proconsumer and business policies enhanced bipartisan Parliamentary support for legislation. Commissioner Bannerman asserted that enforcing the Barwick-inspired law of 1965, despite its debilitating weaknesses, had at least built a Parliamentary constituency supporting – in principle – an Australian antitrust regime. In particular, Bannerman recalled, the constitutional tests unfolding from 1969 to 1972, "proceeded in parallel with gradual changes in business perception of the law, with development of the notions of public interest by the Trade Practices Tribunal and with the strengthening of attitudes on both sides of the Parliament."[70] Similarly, Richard St. John, a lawyer in the Commonwealth attorney general's office responsible for handling public complaints, observed that notwithstanding a general dislike of the legislation on the part of business, there were "constant complaints to the Government from industry about market conduct," including "some business complaints about cartelization."[71]

Labor's attorney general, Lionel Murphy, vigorously responded to these pressures. Murphy possessed a powerful personality geared to action. Moreover, he always approached any controversy or issue through a deep awareness of its bearing on the people affected, coupled with a profound capacity to resolve the matter on the basis of an "operative principle." He derived these qualities from growing up in the Irish-Labor environment of New South Wales among "mates" whose interpersonal accountability fundamentally shaped their individual identity. As a lawyer, Murphy

---

[69] Ibid., and 284–6; Catley and McFarlane, "Technocratic Laborism," in Wheelwright and Buckley, eds., *Essays in Political Economy*, 1: 247; Hocking, *Lionel Murphy*, 204–8, 224.

[70] Bannerman, "Trade Practices Law,"88.

[71] Richard St. John, interview, June 30, 1993, including quotes; Richard St. John, "Reflections," 24–8; Richard St. John, interview, May 28, 1992.

believed in the individual opportunity inherent in the federal Constitution's guarantee of free interstate movement. His values led him to resist the Trade Practices Act of 1965. As a member of the Commonwealth Senate during the debate over the legislation, Murphy not only attacked its weaknesses but also argued that amending the Australian Industries Preservation Act would create stronger means for addressing collusive behavior. For Murphy, the old law, whatever its admitted inadequacies, at least conferred upon individuals the right of private action and the means of enforcing penalties in federal court. This reflected an underlying principle empowering individuals to protect themselves from the market power of interstate big business, as the *Redfern* decision suggested.[72]

Murphy's character and experience shaped the drafting of the legislation during 1973–74. As Labor opposition leader in the Senate, Murphy had cooperated actively with conservatives to strengthen the committee structure; after their party's 1972 electoral defeat, Senate conservatives used the same committee structure to impede implementing the Whitlam government's policies. The Trade Practices legislation nonetheless moved ahead. Upon being appointed attorney general, Murphy and his subordinates maneuvered successfully within the Parliamentary committee structure and among the government's own bureaucratic committees.[73]

For about eighteen months after becoming attorney general, Murphy adjusted principles to legislative exigencies. During this period, Murphy consulted with U.S. and British antitrust professionals, including lengthy discussions with Ronald Dietrich of the Federal Trade Commission, who spent some weeks in Canberra. Australian business people and the conservative politicians and commercial lawyers representing their interests generally opposed American antitrust's mix of per se rules and judicial-centered enforcement. They favored selective alteration of the preexisting regime.[74] Murphy's approach, however, rejected incremental change, blending American antitrust principles with insights learned from the attempted accommodation of British competition policy to Australian capitalism. Murphy clearly favored prohibitions – partially relying on per se rules – but he also accepted a process to authorize certain restrictive practices on their merits, applying a "public interest" standard. Murphy's approach included a right of private action, though, unlike the Industrial Preservation Act, without provision for treble damages. A strong Trade Practices Commission would enforce these measures, though in certain

[72] J. E. Richardson, interview, July 14, 1993, including quotes; R. M. Bannerman, July 13, 1993; Richard St. John, interview, June 30, 1993; confirmed in Hocking, *Lionel Murphy*, 223–305.

[73] Bannerman, "Trade Practices Law," 89–91; Ratnapala, *Australian Constitutional Law*, 60; Norman, "Progress under Pressure," 531–2; St. John, "Reflections," 24–8. *But* see Barwick, *Radical Tory*, 151.

[74] See notes 71–2 above; Hopkins, *Crime, Law & Business*, 87–103.

cases, the Trade Practices Tribunal possessed authority to review its decisions.[75]

Murphy thus combined court-centered prohibitions with an administrative process aimed at promoting competition. Price-fixing, discriminatory dealing, and resale price maintenance were made per se illegal. Even so, on a case-by-case basis, the commission could – applying the public interest standard – authorize mergers, individual trade restraints, and exclusive dealing arrangements; the commission could grant clearance to these practices if it found them to be not anticompetitive. Regarding monopolization, however, neither authorization nor clearance was possible. In both private actions and government suits, it was necessary to prove that "there was likely to be a substantial lessening of competition." By contrast, in restraint-of-trade cases, it was necessary to prove that "there was likely to be a significant effect on competition." Mergers occurring under the Foreign Takeovers Act were subject to authorization; in these as well as other merger cases, the commission, upon notice from the attorney general, could grant the authorization if "an acquisition [is] desirable in the interests of national economic policy."[76]

Murphy's approach also included strong federally enforced consumer protection provisions. Although each Australian state had enacted consumer laws, protections were limited and problems such as deceptive advertising pervaded local markets. Murphy perceived how extensive consumer exploitation was when he and Dietrich walked through Civic, Canberra's popular shopping district, observing the range of misleading advertising. Accordingly, Murphy's legislation employed specific prohibitions against false representations, misleading conduct, undue harassment, and inadequate product safety standards and warranty contracts; it also prescribed monetary penalties (up to $50,000 for companies and $10,000 for individuals). In addition, because of the potential element of fraudulent misrepresentation in consumer cases, punishment of individuals included possible imprisonment for up to six months.[77]

Despite the constitutional crisis overshadowing the Whitlam government, Murphy's Trade Practices bill became law. By April 1974, as international and domestic economic conditions deteriorated, the conservatives' resistance to Labor's broader program culminated in Parliament's dissolution, resulting in May elections which returned the Whitlam government with a smaller majority. During the months that followed, Murphy's "principles" acquired sharper focus in legislative provisions revealing

[75] R. Baxt and M. Brunt, "The Murphy Trade Practices Bill: Admirable Objectives, Inadequate Means," 2 *Australian Business Law Review* (April 1974), 1–79.
[76] Ibid.; Bannerman, "Trade Practices Act of 1974: A Short Summary," in Nieuwenhuysen, ed. *Australian Trade Practices*, 2nd edn (1976), 79–87, quotes at 80.
[77] Richard St. John, interview, June 30, 1993; Bannerman, "Trade Practices Law," 90–1; Hocking, *Lionel Murphy*, 204–8, 224; St. John, "Reflections," 24–8.

"stark" contrasts with earlier trade practices laws. With relatively limited changes, Murphy's basic principles were implemented in October, as the Trade Practices Act of 1974.[78]

III. THE MATURATION OF THE TRADE PRACTICES ACT, 1974–1991

It soon became clear, Bannerman observed, that "a general mandate" existed for the Trade Practices Act. Fostering Australia's changing business order and its relation to consumers, labor, and society within the global economy, the act underwent modifications "at the fringes," but, "in spite of changes of government," it seemed likely to last. Essentially, he concluded, the Act was "being digested." More particularly, the enforcement regime was described as "Austerican, not American. Something has been added to the American approach in an endeavor to make the law more appropriate to the Australian scene," making it "more one of *dual enforcement*, [emphasis in the original] whereby judicial enforcement is coupled with case-by-case administrative exemption."[79] Meanwhile, elected officials espoused a public discourse of reform. The Whitlam government's willingness to combine market-oriented wage and employment practices and active antitrust enforcement with liberal trade policies and tariff reductions was prophetic. The Fraser government (1975–83) pursued reform policies erratically. Hawke's Labor government (1983–91), however, gave comprehensive substance and scope to what it called microeconomic reform.[80]

During its first decade of operation, successive governments periodically reshaped the Trade Practices Act's enforcement regime. "Politics" were "decisive, but not politics in an old-fashioned ideological sense," declared Bannerman. "All parties want to stand well with business, and all recognise the importance of business confidence in the country's economic policy, of which competition policy is part." The bipartisan political party support Bannerman garnered for competition policy reflected his strategic vision. At the level of budgetary resources, the Fraser government's so-called razor gang imposed cuts that put considerable pressure on the commission's enforcement capabilities. The commission developed, accordingly, compliance strategies which balanced litigation and administrative

---

[78] Quoted phrases from J. E. Richardson, interview, July 14, 1993; Richard St. John, interview, June 30, 1993; Bannerman, "Trade Practices Law," 91.

[79] Bannerman, "Trade Practices Law," quotes at 91; Baxt and Brunt, "A Guide to the Act," in Nieuwenhuysen, ed., *Australian Trade Practices*, 2nd edn (1976), quote at 92.

[80] Merrett, "Corporate Governance, Incentives and the Internationalization of Australian Business," Unpublished, cited by permission; Fleming et al. *Big End of Town*, ch. 8; Brenchley, *Allan Fels*, 17, 18, 88–9, 278; Fred Argy, *Australia at the Crossroads: Radical Free Markets or a Progressive Liberalism?* (Sydney, 1998), 56, 63, 104–6, 142–8, 219.

approaches.[81] Bannerman's enforcement regime was instrumental. His educational and public relations efforts targeted the media, as well as "constituencies" possessing a direct stake in competition policy enforcement. His compliance strategies recognized that on "any particular trade practices issue," there was "always tension" within a given industrial sector. As a practical matter, such tensions engendered the evidence which virtually all effective enforcement required."[82]

Even so, the Trade Practices Commission preserved reasonable institutional autonomy, as indicated by its successive chairpersons. Between 1966 and 1974, Bannerman so effectively cultivated a spirit of fairness and neutrality that after the passage of the Murphy Act, the Labor government appointed him the Trade Practices Commission's first chair. Serving from 1974 to 1984, Bannerman instituted among the Commission's staff durable, public-spirited enforcement. His astute bureaucratic leadership established a standard of independence which the Labor government maintained through the appointment of subsequent chairpersons. Thus, under the Hawke government, Bannerman's successors were W. R. McComas (1985–88), a commercial lawyer and corporate director experienced in representing big business and Robert Baxt (1988–91), a law professor and commercial lawyer.[83]

Another measure of competition policy's improving public image was an emerging competition consciousness. The mentality sustaining collusive "mateship" relations was eroding by the 1960s. Noting the social pressures for democratic market opportunities unleashed by immigration-driven population growth, Barwick grasped the drift of this change, observing that "sociological problems are most apparent from practices designed to exclude the persons who engage in them from the competition of others." He stressed that it was "important in this connection to watch closely our values," particularly "in a society as egalitarian as this, in which labour," broadly defined, "obtains by the very institutions ... built into society, such as the arbitration system, an increasing share of the nation's product. ... But the freedom of our people to adventure on their own account, albeit unprofitably, is, of paramount importance." A related "sociological

---

[81] Bannerman, "Trade Practices Law," 91, 93, 94; and Bannerman, "Points from Experience," *Trade Practices Commission Annual Report*, 153–75.

[82] Bannerman, "Points from Experience," 160.

[83] Ibid., 150; "Forum, Mr. R.M. Bannerman, Mr. W.R. McComas, Professor R. Baxt," *Bulletin Trade Practices Commission*, 2–5, 6–12, 12–19. Robert Baxt, interview, July 1, 1993; R. M. Bannerman, interview, July 13, 1993; Bob Baxt, "Australian Competition Policy Monopolies, Mergers and Myths," 66 *Canberra Bulletin of Public Administration* (October 1991), 24–8; Secretariat, "The Objectives of Competition Law and Policy and the Optimal Design of a Competition Agency," 5 *OECD Journal of Competition Law and Policy* (2003), 7–40.

problem" emerged from the "trend for small business ... to disappear and be replaced by businesses owned by large-scale corporations."[84]

As the Trade Practices Act of 1974 went into operation, these attitudes fostered lively discourse. Upon taking power, the Fraser government supported in principle the Trade Practices Act while acknowledging the need for revision. The government appointed a committee chaired by T. B. Swanson. A membership representing big business, consumers, and smaller firms – but no one from organized labor – suggested the direction the Swanson Committee's proposed revisions subsequently took. Moreover, between the Swanson Committee's published report in August 1976 and passage of amendments the following year, a recession engulfed the nation, producing the highest unemployment in forty years and the worst corporate profits in twenty years. Moreover, following the Whitlam government's 25 percent tariff reduction four years earlier, Australian firms faced increasing import competition.[85]

The Swanson Committee's recommendations resulted in important amendments. Most business submissions to the committee, as well as its own recommendations, urged weakening the law's cartel prohibitions.[86] However, the Australian Automobile Chamber of Commerce – whose smaller retailers complained that large suppliers had abused their dominant position through discriminatory practices – favored vigorous enforcement against such conduct. As it turned out, the amendments passed in July 1977 not only retained strict prohibition against horizontal and vertical price-fixing, but also preserved the existing provision against price discrimination "in the interests of assisting the competitive position of small business." The government did institute a compromise relaxing the Act's prohibition against price-fixing applied to trade associations' price lists and similar practices. The strict prohibition remained if the association's membership was less than fifty. But in the case of trade associations with a larger membership, the Trade Practices Commission could authorize certain price arrangements. The government's minister explained that especially in "multi-product situations," smaller firms lacked the "managerial support staff to make informed individual pricing decisions." The Amendment aimed to correct conditions where the Act had proscribed small firms from relying on trade association in such cases.[87]

[84] Barwick, *Trade Practices in a Developing Economy*, quote at 10–11; Dyster and Meredith, *Australia in the International Economy*, 253–5; Capling, *Australia and Global Trade*, 73.

[85] *Trade Practices Act [Swanson] Review Committee Report to the Minister for Business and Consumer Affairs [Honorable John Howard MP] August 1976* (Canberra, 1976). The other members were J. A. Davidson, A. G. Hartnell, Professor A. Kerr, H. S. Schreiber, and J. V. McKeown; Hopkins, *Crime, Law & Business*, 87–103; Bannerman, "Trade Practices Law," 91–2; Brian L. Johns, "Threshold Tests for the Control of Mergers: The Australian Experience," 9 *Review of Industrial Organization* (October 1994), 651–3.

[86] *Swanson Committee Report* (1976), business submissions quoted throughout.

[87] Hopkins, *Crime, Law & Business*, 96–101, quotes at 99, 101.

The Act's provisions regarding mergers and the labor exemption, by contrast, were diluted whereas consumers generally benefited. An amendment of section 50 maintained the prohibition against anticompetitive mergers, but the Act's threshold standard proscribing a "lessening of competition" was replaced with the weaker test of "dominance." In addition, the attorney general or the Trade Practices Commission could continue to seek an injunction to prevent a given merger, but that right was removed pertaining to private actions. Although the amendment ended the notification system, it broadened the commission's power to authorize mergers; still, the attorney general declared in the House of Representatives, the amendment's "intended effect" was that the "categories of mergers" to which the Act applied "should be quite limited." Another amendment restricted a labor union's use of secondary boycotts. This amendment passed despite considerable public acrimony and threats from organized labor. The Australian Consumers' Association gained some advantage for its constituency, including strengthening the prohibition against resale price maintenance where it applied, for instance, to unions boycotting sales of discounted oil. The amendments however, subjected defendants to a less rigorous showing of unintentional offense.[88]

The Swanson Committee's report formally stated the "value-judgments" underlying Australian competition policy. First was the "acceptance of competitive capitalism as a sociological economic system based on the institution of private enterprise," embodying the "broad assumption that the needs of the community, including consumers, are most effectively satisfied through the operation of the market mechanism in which the driving force is competition." The report defined the "efficiency" competition engendered "in the narrow economic sense by driving prices down and efficiency up," as well as "in a wider social sense by ensuring that national resources are allocated in such a way as to ensure that consumers in the market will have their desires satisfied at the lowest cost consonant with the quality desired." Second, the "economically weak should be protected against the unfair or predatory acts of the economically strong, a belief that is derived from notions of human dignity." The committee embraced these "broad value-judgments, recognizing that they have no essential connection one with the other but are in practice intertwined and are" accepted "by a majority of Australians."[89]

The Swanson Committee's report squarely addressed the welfare of small business, the labor exemption, export/imports, and corporate takeovers. As indicated, it recommended limiting organized labor's exemption under the Trade Practices Act by allowing prosecution of secondary

---

[88] Hopkins, *Crime, Law & Business*, 96–102, quotes at 99; Johns, "Threshold Tests," *Review of Industrial Organization*, 651–6, quote at 653.
[89] *Swanson Committee Report* (1976), 89.

boycotts. It also urged loosening merger restrictions in order to facilitate Australian firms' attaining greater scale economies through takeovers, especially in export industries. Concerning small business, the report noted that the competition law of the European Community, various member nations of the OECD, Canada, and at least historically, the United States recognized the value of protecting the "small businessman" from the "abuse of economic power which might otherwise threaten his livelihood." The committee's evidence confirmed that "[s]mall business is of great significance in the Australian economy." The "social objective" gained from protecting small business from abusive market dominance "may be seen as the satisfaction of both consuming and producing desires in the community."[90]

Over the succeeding decades, this public discourse became contentious. Interested parties wrestled with conflicting implications of "competition" and "efficiency" resulting in outcomes which solely maximized consumer welfare or maximized consumer as well as producer surplus. The first view expressed the position of the Chicago School of Economics, whereas the second reflected the enduring influence of the doctrine of "workable competition." The tension between these policy prescriptions reflected the nation's fluctuating economic growth from the 1970s on, which in turn engendered microeconomic reforms accompanying deregulation and privatization.[91] Echoing the Swanson Report's "value judgments," Robert Baxt indicated that the nation's broader social welfare concerns shaped the meaning of competition and efficiency. He acknowledged the "tension ... developing between the trend toward deregulation and the growing perception of the possibility of accompanying adverse consequences for consumers." In order for deregulation "to be generally accepted as good for ordinary Australians," Baxt cautioned, "it must be accompanied by appropriate safeguards and remedies."[92]

The recognized institutional conservatism of the Australian judiciary reinforced the malleability of economic concepts. The commission and private litigants tested the meaning of the economic terminology underlying the Trade Practices Act of 1974.[93] After a decade, a Melbourne lawyer observed that the "present Judges of the Federal Court are not particularly experienced in economic concepts." In addition, Australian courts "generally take a very conservative approach to the interpretations of statutes."

[90] Ibid., 88–95, quotes at 90, 91.
[91] S. R. Corones, *Competition Law and Policy* (1990), 1–23, 296–304.
[92] Ibid., quote at 304, R. Baxt, Ruby Hutchinson Memorial Address for World Consumer Rights, National Press Club Luncheon, March 16, 1989.
[93] Maureen Brunt, "The Use of Economic Evidence in Antitrust Litigation: Australia," 14 *Australian Business Law Review* (August 1986), 261–308; French, "Judicial Approaches to Economic Analysis," *Review of Industrial Organization*, 547–68; *Queensland Wire Industries Pty Ltd. v. BHP* (1989), 167 C.L.R. 177.

These institutional realities provided increased opportunities for economists to present evidence as expert witnesses, broadening the courts' and legal profession's understanding of such technical concepts as "markets," "dominance," and "competition." By the mid-1980s, federal courts "now clearly accepted" Parliament's intention that "economic criteria be applied" in construing the Trade Practices Act.[94] The decisions of the Trade Practices Tribunal – presided over by a federal judge, joined by an economist and a businessman – did much to inform judges about the use of economic concepts.[95]

The international training of Australian legal–economic professionals further influenced the judicial construction of the Trade Practices Act. During the formative period of the law's development, growing numbers of legal–economic professionals, such as Brunt, Baxt, Allan Fels, or Geoffrey de Q. Walker studied antitrust at leading American universities. Richard St. John, general counsel to BHP and chairman of the Law Council of Australia's Trade Practices Committee, studied British and American competition policy at the London School of Economics. Moreover, Australian judges readily cited U.S. and British common law precedents where applicable.[96] In addition, given the special role Barwick and Murphy played promulgating successive trade practices legislation, it was noteworthy that both men served as chief justice and justice, respectively – for some years together – on the High Court of Australia and participated in decisions testing those same laws. Both men, too, had direct acquaintance with foreign antitrust concepts.[97]

Legal–economic professionals exercised a leading role in shaping Australian competition policy. Parliament's debate of Murphy's Trade Practices Bill beginning in 1973 coincided with Brunt's teaching a seminar on the subject at Monash University. During the next decades, Brunt's teaching directly influenced other university law and economics teachers such as future commission chairmen Baxt and Fels and instituted a model for the dispersion and testing of competition policy theories among growing numbers of those working in the field. The leading Australian law societies soon adopted the seminar format in annual meetings, bringing together practitioners, academics, government officials, and commission members and staff to discuss policy issues. Eventually, the government funded at such

---

[94] Douglas Williamson, "Australian Antitrust Regulation," *Legal Aspects of Doing Business with Australia* (New York, 1984), 201–88, quotes at 250, 251.

[95] French, "Judicial Approaches to Economic Analysis," *Review of Industrial Organization*, 547–68, especially 557–8; Robert Baxt, interview, July 1, 1993; Richard St. John, interview, June 30, 1993; Brenchley, *Allan Fels*, 25, 26, 31, 66, 67, 80, 128.

[96] For their study at the University of Pennsylvania and Duke University, respectively, *see* Walker, *Australian Monopoly Law*, v and Brenchley, *Allen Fels*, 53–4; and note 95 above.

[97] Barwick, *Radical Tory*, 218–98; Hocking, *Lionel Murphy*, 223–305.

places as Australian National University research and institutional forums devoted to advancing understanding of competition policies.[98]

This was the context for the Trade Practices Act's initial enforcement. As the Trade Practices Commission began operation, a university survey of business opinion revealed uneven perceptions, with senior management "highly aware" of and often favorably disposed toward the law, while small business either relied principally on trade associations for advice regarding compliance or, as Commissioner Geoffrey de Q. Walker declared, "simply ... car[ried] on as if the legislation did not exist." The commission's enforcement soon heightened business attention to competition policy. On the most conspicuous level of public market behavior, increased competition steadily displaced blatant price-fixing and similar cartel practices among big- and medium-scale firms. Under the section 49 proscription of price discrimination, the "jig-saw puzzle of historical favouritism and discrimination" gave way to "equal discounting opportunities" between suppliers and purchasers. Consumers benefited from more accurate advertising following penalties imposed in the *Sharp* microwave case of 1975. Moreover, the commission's determination of 4,681 clearances and 40 authorizations by the middle of 1975 indicated that the administrative process received business notice.[99]

Several early cases suggested the contested future course of the Trade Practices Act's development. *Queensland Co-operative Milling Association LTD; Re Defiance Holdings LTD.* (1976) became a leading precedent for the Trade Practices Commission's enforcement of the law's merger and authorization provisions, including the meaning of "lessening of competition" and "public benefits" doctrines, and the Trade Practices Tribunal's review authority. Responding to inflationary pressures during the mid-1970s, both Queensland Cooperative Milling and Defiance attempted to take over the stockfeed and flour packaging business owned by the smaller competitor, Barnes Milling. Contending that the merger would enhance efficiency, the companies sought authorization from the commission. It denied the request, however, on the ground that in the regional market including Queensland and the Northern Rivers District of New South Wales, the takeover of the smaller company would lessen competition, a result which lacked offsetting public benefit. The firms appealed the decision to Tribunal.[100]

[98] See note 95 above; John Braithwaite, interview, August 12, 2003, concerning Regulatory Institutions Network, Australian National University.
[99] Walker, "The Trade Practices Act at Work," in Nieuwenhuysen, ed., *Australian Trade Practices*, 2nd edn (1976), 147–76, quotes at 147; *Hartnell v. Sharp Corporation*, 5 A.L.R. 493 (1975); Andrew Hopkins, *The Impact of Prosecutions under the Trade Practices Act* (Canberra 1978).
[100] (1976) 25 Federal Law Reports 169; Corones, *Competition Law and Policy*, 22, 38, 44, 46, 48, 56, 57, 65, 70–1, 122; Brunt, "Australian Antitrust Law," 495–501.

The Tribunal clearly recognized the case's precedent-setting potential. The decision expressly set out the principles guiding the Tribunal's three members. Regarding the procedural matters, the Tribunal affirmed its review authority over the commission's judgments as prescribed in the Trade Practices Act; following federal court rules, it provided qualified protection of confidential evidence, demonstrating a thorough grasp of how legitimate business concerns about secrecy should be balanced against demands for due process. The Tribunal reviewed the substantive doctrines the commission had employed to decide whether the merger lessened competition without sufficient public benefit in the regional market. The Tribunal held that within the regional submarket, the potential for the merger to lessen competition was not as great as the commission conceived and so was less determinative of the case. Still, noting facts showing Barnes Milling company's weak position against its two larger competitors in the submarket, the Tribunal upheld the commission's denial of authorization to the merger because the "public" was not "likely to receive any substantial benefit."[101]

The *Queensland Milling Association* decision became a leading precedent on several counts. The Swanson Committee's challenge to the case's merger test of "lessening competition" resulted in Parliament's inserting the weaker "dominance" test. The federal courts and the Swanson Committee accepted, however, the Tribunal's general reliance upon workable competition doctrines, including the references to market definition.[102] Moreover, in subsequent authorization cases, the commission embraced the Tribunal's contention that the term "public benefit" included "anything of value to the community generally, any contribution to the aims pursued by society including as one of its principal elements ... the achievement of the economic goals of efficiency and progress." The principle allowed the commission's authorization of a merger where the "public benefit" might be the preservation of jobs. The Tribunal's analysis also influenced decision-makers' perceptions of "market power" which, in turn, hinged on expert economic evidence. Thus, it declared, the "first question that needs to be answered is how much market power a corporation must be capable of exerting before it can be said to possess substantial market power."[103]

The Swanson Committee's disapproval of *Quadramain v. Sevastapol* (1976), by contrast, facilitated strengthening the Trade Practices Act. Among the first cases concerning the Act to reach the High Court of Australia, the issue was whether the law's prohibition against "contracts, arrangements or understandings in restraint of trade or commerce [section 45]," under a standard of "significant lessening of competition," applied to anticompetitive landed property covenants and certain commercial leases.

[101] (1976) 25 Federal Law Reports, 169, quotes at 192–3.
[102] *Swanson Committee Report* (1976), 13–14, 47–57.
[103] (1976), 25 Federal Law Reports, 178–93; Corones, *Competition Law and Policy*, 71–2, 122.

Current British common law doctrine held that such agreements were lawful "because the doctrine of restraint of trade only applies where a person gives up some freedom which he already possesses, and a person who buys or takes a lease of land subject to a negative restrictive covenant gives up no freedom which he previously had." American antitrust doctrine, on the contrary, declared such restraints to be per se illegal. Chief Justice Barwick's majority opinion followed the British precedent to uphold the restrictive covenant, whereas a minority opinion in which Justice Lionel Murphy concurred rejected the decision.[104]

The Swanson Committee reiterated criticism of the *Quadramain* decision. Accordingly, Parliament's amendments to the Trade Practices Act in 1977 removed the "restraint of trade or commerce" language, replacing it with a principle akin to the U.S. "group boycott" doctrine. This revision, in conjunction with maintaining the "lessening of competition" standard, established statutory per se rules against contractual "exclusionary provisions and horizontal price fixing." In cases of other "horizontal restraints," however, a balancing of evidence might be sufficient to prove reasonableness. Thus, in Australia, the Parliament was "called upon to achieve the per-se rule of reason distinction established in the United States by the courts."[105]

Private actions also became important during the initial years of the Trade Practices Act's operation. In the United States, the availability of treble damages and contingent fees explained the high numbers of private antitrust suits. The Australian Industrial Preservation Act (AIPA), of course, had provided for treble damages in private actions, but private actions were insignificant under the AIPA, and the Barwick-inspired Trade Practices legislation removed the power altogether. Attorney General Murphy reinstituted the right of private action in the 1974 law, though no grant of treble damages, compensatory awards were available.[106] Despite the limited financial incentive, Australian business and social action groups increasingly pursued private actions. Generally, the remedy the private party sought from the court was an injunction against another's objectionable conduct. Most private suits resulted in settlement between the parties.[107]

An early case suggesting the process and purpose of private actions was *Top Performance Motors PTY. LTD* v. *Ira Berk (Queensland) PTY. LTD* (1975). Ira Berk was the only wholesale distributor of Datsun vehicles in the regional market of Queensland and the Northern Rivers District of New

---

[104] (1976) 133 C.L.R. 390, quote at 394; *Swanson Committee Report* (1976), 14–15.

[105] Corones, *Competition Law and Policy*, 202–3, 237, quote at 202.

[106] Tony Freyer, *Regulating Big Business*, 282–4, 321; Maureen Brunt, "The Role of Private Actions in Australian Restrictive Practices Enforcement," 17 *Melbourne University Law Review* (December 1990), 582–613.

[107] Walker, "Trade Practices Act," in Nieuwenhuysen, ed., *Australian Trade Practices*, 2nd edn (1976), 167–9; Trade Practices Commission, *Private Actions under the Trade Practices Act* (June 1981); Brunt, "Role of Private Actions," 582–613.

South Wales; actively engaged in the retail Datsun trade, the firm "competed to some extent" in the City of Gold Coast and South Port with its franchise dealership, Top Performance Motors. Under a thirty-day contract stipulation, Ira Berk terminated the franchise agreement with Top Performance and appointed a new dealer for the same local market. Top Performance initiated a private action seeking injunctive relief against Ira Berk, alleging restraint of trade and monopolization under sections 45 and 46 of the Trade Practices Act. The case was noteworthy in part because it applied a dictionary definition of commodity markets to determine whether Ira Berk's termination of the contract amounted to violation of the two sections as anticompetitive conduct and unreasonable monopolization. The court decided against Top Performance, holding that "on the evidence" Berk "genuinely considered that it should terminate the agreement for the sake of and in order to protect its legitimate trade and business interests."[108]

Such cases suggested the distinctive pattern of private litigation in Australia and its implication for competition policy development. Australians' steady willingness to bring private actions from 1974 on vindicated Murphy's conviction that the exercise of the right enabled the antitrust law to be significantly self-enforcing. Brunt's study assessing the private action's policy outcomes over the period 1974–88 indicated that Australia presented a different balance of motivations and goals than existed in America. In both nations, deterring anticompetitive conduct through private suites was a public gain which had to be weighed against the costs of providing incentives for cases that potentially reflected nothing more than the narrowest individual motivation. During the 1970s and 1980s, U.S. courts employed Chicago economics efficiency theories to impose procedural limits on the damages and lawyer-fees offered by private actions, which in turn curtailed the number of suits. In Australia, by contrast, the proportion of private cases in relation to commission litigation increased from 1974 on; Australian trade practices law declined to accept the Chicago School's theory prescribing consumer welfare as the only legitimate policy outcome. Instead, judicial precedents and the commission's administrative process endorsed broader social welfare concerns underlying the efficiency doctrines of workable competition. These social welfare interests provided, in turn, incentives for private actions which transcended limited pecuniary advantage.[109]

The Trade Practices Commission reinforced such institutional ordering, employing a strategy whereby private litigation complemented its own enforcement. The commission's constrained enforcement resources demanded compliance strategies favoring administrative actions; however,

---

[108] (1975) 24 Federal Law Reports 287, quotes at 290; Walker "Trade Practices Act," in Nieuwenhuysen, ed., *Australian Trade Practices*, 2nd edn (1976), 167–8.
[109] Brunt, "Role of Private Actions," 582–613; Freyer, *Regulating Big Business*, 282–3.

the persistence of private suits permitted selectivity regarding litigation. The *Tradestock–Freight Forwarders*' case revealed the risks of litigation. In 1976, a small transport broker could no longer sustain a private action alleging restrictive conduct – a boycott – growing out of some transport brokers' refusal to deal with a group of freight forwarders. The issues placed such a difficult burden of proof on the plaintiff that within two years he abandoned the case. At that point, the commission took jurisdiction, litigating until 1985, when the court decided that despite clear evidence of a restrictive agreement, the proof of anticompetitive effects was insufficient, resulting in a decision for the defendant. The commission had not previously lost such a case. Moreover, the court's award of costs against the commission required the government to make a special appropriation of $4,500,000. Given the commission's constrained annual budgets, the judgment was a blow. The commission, Bannerman affirmed however, "made clear to any who thought it may have lost its confidence and its support that it will continue to enforce the Act vigorously." Even so, the pressing institutional cost imperatives facilitated the commission's view that its litigation and private actions were complimentary.[110]

The Trade Practices Act's enforcement gradually reshaped Australian attitudes about anticompetitive conduct. Critics during the law's first decade of operation, including initially Lionel Murphy himself, aggressively contended for an enforcement policy emphasizing litigation, particularly against big business.[111] Bannerman's experience convinced him, however, that in order for a competition consciousness to displace the Australian "mateship" mentality, the Trade Practices enforcement regime would have to work in conjunction with other factors. Since the law acted "directly" upon "firms rather than industries or the whole economy, it is often less apparent to the community at large than some of the other instruments of economic policy." Accordingly, whether the enforcement regime relied on litigation or an administrative approach or something of both, it "generally takes time for the consequences to work their way through the industry and lift the levels of its efficiency by changing the general patterns of conduct. ... When changes do come, it will not be clear how much of the impetus came from the trade practices law and how much from the market

---

[110] "The implications of the Freight Forwarders' Case for the Trade Practices Act and its Administration," *Trade Practices Commission, 1984–1985*, 14–22, 31–3; Bannerman, "Trade Practices Law," 94; Brunt, "Role of Private Actions," 590; *T.P.C. v. T.N.T. Management Pty. Ltd.* (1985) A.T.P.R. 40–512.

[111] R. M. Bannerman, interviews, July 13, 14, 1993; George Venturini, *Malpractice: The Administration of the Murphy Trade Practices Act* (Sydney, 1980); Andrew Hopkins, "Marxist Theory and Australian Monopoly Law," in Wheelwright and Buckley, eds., *Essays in Political Economy*; Warren Pengilley, "Competition Policy and Law Enforcement: Ramblings On Rhetoric and Reality," 2 *Australian Journal of Law & Society* (1984), 1–29.

forces." Thus, the "law is really a catalyst when other necessary factors are present. ... Certainly a law about competition cannot itself produce the competition. You need people with the will for competition, and you need circumstances in which they see that competition is commercially feasible. But the law provides part of the circumstances."[112]

Bannerman's prognosis concerning the contingent public acceptance of competition was prescient. The understanding steadily grew among business people, lawyers, and government officials that price-fixing, horizontal mergers, and deception of consumers were illegal. Moreover, effective enforcement increasingly joined with economic policy reforms to dismantle the postwar protectionist and regulatory regime. Thus, by the late 1980s, liberal trade polices increasingly prevailed and wartime regulation of the financial order was lifted. These policy changes accompanied the end of exchange restrictions and the imposition of a floating dollar, subjecting Australia to growing global competitive pressures. The Hawke government successfully instituted deregulated labor markets, including "enterprise bargaining" which reduced the influence of the arbitration tribunal in industrial relations. In addition, the Labor government began opening to private investment government-owned enterprises, including gas and electricity, water, financial services, rail, air, and highway transport, and harbors and ports. As deregulation and privatization exposed formally protected markets to competition, the reach of the Trade Practices Act grew accordingly.[113]

Business nonetheless remained ambivalent about anticompetitive behavior. The Business Council of Australia stated that the struggle for global competitive advantage aggravated conflicts within Australian business: "A nation's competitiveness depends on the strength of its enterprises competing in world markets, either in exporting or against import competition. The high degree of economic interdependence means that poor performance in areas not subject to international trade are penalizing internationally competitive firms." An Australian lawyer commented, by contrast, that the nation's global isolation, the comparatively small population, the market leadership of agricultural and mineral export industries, and industries serving geographically separate "small-volume," and concentrated urban markets encouraged among Australians the "strong desire for self-sufficiency." These pressures engendered demands for tariff protectionism and drove industry to "cover a wide field of operations." The resulting "dictates of scale in capital intensive industries" fostered government-owned monopolies in postal, telephone and other services, and a "very large number of tight oligopolies." The *Australian Financial Review*

---

[112] Bannerman, "Points from Experience," 191.
[113] See note 80 above; Dabscheck, "Industrial Relations," in Bell and Bell, eds., *Americanization and Australia*, 149–78.

noted, moreover, that "[s]ome of these oligopolies are intensely competitive, but as a rule they are not, by their own nature."[114]

The Labor government's microeconomic policies, including trade practices law enforcement, reflected this ambiguous discourse. The Industrial Assistance Commission administering "tariff levels, repeatedly calls for industry to rationalize ... to improve efficiency through scale, so that the tariff barriers may be lowered. Competition would then come from imports." Opponents rejected this policy, focusing on the "dislocation, loss of jobs, high costs of imports through long distance transport costs and so on." Other governmental agencies pursued "gentle" enforcement offering business incentives to adopt more efficient market conduct. Accordingly, Peter Grabosky's and John Braithwaite's influential, proconsumer empirical study declared, "Australian regulatory agencies perceive big business to be more law abiding" and so generally they "adopt less prosecutorial enforcement policies toward big business compared with small business." The Business Council of Australia argued, however, that the "successful economies ... are those host to strong, globally competitive enterprises. Many of these will be strong small businesses." Even so, the Council stated, "one of the corollaries of new technologies and methods of communication is that it is feasible, and often advantageous, to compete as a small firm."[115]

Despite criticism demanding more prosecutions of big business, the Trade Practices Commission pursued compliance through administrative action and litigation. Commentators agreed that the commission's enforcement focused primarily on consumer protection and resale price maintenance cases involving violations under the Act's per se prohibitions. Such cases were the easiest to win because consumers or disaffected small business more readily provided evidence; often, too, they also directly or indirectly revealed the arbitrary conduct of big business. A former commissioner nonetheless denounced the commission's failure, "despite the obvious malpractices of big business," to undertake monopolization (section 45), price discrimination (section 49), and merger (section 50) cases affecting large corporations.[116] Grabosky and Braithwaite noted, however,

---

[114] Business Council of Australia Paper, cited in "Supplementary Submission to the Inquiry into Mergers, Market Dominance and Unconscionable Conduct by Senate Standing Committee on Legal and Constitutional Affairs" (Canberra, 1991), quote at 6; Williamson, "Australian Antitrust Regulation," *Legal Aspects of Doing Business with Australia*, quote at 252–3; *Australian Financial Review* (February 22, 1989) in Economic Planning Advisory Council, *Promoting Competition in Australia Council Paper No. 38* (Canberra, 1989), quote at 10.

[115] Williamson, "Australian Antitrust Regulation," *Legal Aspects of Doing Business with Australia*, quote at 253; Peter Grabosky and John Braithwaite, *Of Manners Gentle: Enforcement Strategies of Australian Business Regulatory Agencies* (Melbourne, 1986), quote at 217; Business Council of Australia Paper, in *Promoting Competition in Australia Council Paper No. 38* (1989), quote at 14–15.

[116] Venturini, *Malpractice*, 428.

that in two monopolization and six merger litigations the commission brought by 1985, the court awarded only one clear-cut victory and a few settlements which nonetheless fostered increased market competition.[117]

The Swanson Committee's criticism of the High Court's *Quadramain* decision led Parliament to replace the "unduly legalistic" interpretation of "restraint of trade" with broader language, facilitating, in particular, the commission's prosecution of anticompetitive landed property covenants and certain commercial leases. The Swanson Committee's recommendations culminating in Parliament's instituting the weaker dominance test for mergers exacerbated, however, the tendentious relationship between corporate takeovers and "rationalization" seeking economies of scale. As early as 1975, the Trade Practices Commission's first annual report exclaimed: "It is still quite wrong to see the Trade Practices Act as standing in the way of scale economy that is being encouraged by the Industrial Assistance commission." A decade later, Bannerman evidenced a similar wariness, observing that perhaps there was the "beginning of a national constituency for the enforcement of law against secondary boycotts."[118]

After its 1983 election victory, the Labor government developed microeconomic reform policies to accommodate business demands for corporate restructuring aimed at promoting a global competitive advantage. The government's appointment of McComas, a commercial lawyer and tobacco company chief executive, signaled the Trade Practices law's growing market impact and the political exigencies promoting the image of the commission's institutional independence.[119] The commission's official enforcement strategy, stated succinctly in its annual report introduced "no significant modifications to the commission's restrictive trade practices policy" whereby it "continued to take a firm line on 'hard core' contraventions of the Act such as price agreements, resale price maintenance and collective boycotts," the "priority cases which the Commission regularly takes to court." The report mentioned, however, "[o]ther matters, more frequently resolved by discussions with companies involved," referring primarily to the emphasis on merger agreements amidst the merger boom of the 1980s.[120]

[117] Grabosky and Braithwaite, *Of Manners Gentle*, 92–3; *Trade Practices Commission, 1983–1984*, quote at 3.
[118] *Swanson Committee Report* (1976), 14–15, 20–1; *Trade Practices Commission, 1975*, quote at 55; Corones, *Competition Law and Policy*, 202, 236; Bannerman, "Trade Practices Law," 95, note 14.
[119] W. R. McComas, "Forum," *Trade Practices Commission*, no. 79, 6–12; W. R. McComas, "Australian Competition Law: Administrative Policy and Practice," in Michael James, *Regulating for Competition? Trade Practices Policy in a Changing Economy* (St. Leonards, 1989), 72–82; John Braithwaite, "Thinking Laterally: Restorative and Responsive OHS," in E. Bluff, N. Gunningham, and R. Johnstone, eds., *Occupational Health and Safety Regulation for a Changing World of Work* (Annandale, N.S.W., 2004), 194–208.
[120] *Trade Practices Commission, 1984–1985*, 1–26, 39–42, quote at 26.

The commission's merger enforcement became particularly contentious during McComas's chairmanship. In the *Bowral Brickworks* case, the court set aside an injunction restraining joint owners of Bowral Brickworks from acquiring more shares in Calsil Ltd., leaving the jointly managed companies controlling 90 percent of bricks and paving supplies in Western Australia. The case demonstrated how the corporate restructuring of the 1980s merger boom occurred through intricate takeover investment strategies. The commission alleged that the purchase of the shares in Calsil by Bowral Brickworks, which Bristile and Midland Brick Company owned, breached the market dominance test applied under section 50. The court set aside the commission's effort to block the takeover because the judge held that Midland, with a 60 percent share of the Western Australian market, did not actually control Bowral Brickworks through its 50 percent shareholding, "so that it could not be said" to be indirectly "acquiring Calsil." The court's decision suggested that the dominance test was insufficient to contain the complex financial restructuring Australian corporations were undergoing. The Commission "subsequently requested the Attorney-General to amend the Act to overcome this apparent loophole in the legislation." Meanwhile, the commission's "consultative" approach aroused criticism of nontransparent "deals."[121]

The emphasis was now upon improving Australia's international competitive position, or "growth through exports." The government made the "transformation of Australian industry into a world competitive industry ... a priority matter. In an international sense the manufacturing and commerce sectors play a significant role in the creation of wealth and the generation of employment. And ... manufacturers represent the fastest growing segment of world trade." But throughout the nation's history, a minister declared, the "performance in manufacturing has not been very good. Over the last decade the performance, for the most part, has worsened." The *Australian Financial Review* affirmed, moreover, that solutions depended on the "creation of an environment – a manufacturing climate – which rewards not paper entrepreneurship but the efficient use of national resources and export achievement."[122]

During Baxt's three-year commission chairmanship, the contours of competition policy shifted. Succeeding McComas in 1988, Baxt addressed criticism associated with the Business Council of Australia that the commission was "too academic, dominated by economists, and not practical

[121] Ibid., 39–42, quote at 40; *T.P.C. v. Bowral Brickworks Pty. Ltd.* (1984), A.T.P.R. 40–480; Corones, *Competition Law and Policy*, 102–3, 133–7; Brenchley, *Allan Fels*, 82–4; Brunt, "Role Private Actions," 598–602. Chairman McComas employs the term "consultation" to describe his approach to mergers in *Trade Practices, 1986–1987*, 2; Baxt, "Australian Competition Policy," 24–8, quote at 24.

[122] Senator John Button and "Editorial" in Corones, *Competition Law and Policy*, quotes at 134, 136.

enough," and "had a reputation for being somewhat secretive and doing backroom deals – especially in merger matters." Baxt's legal background facilitated addressing the "question of public accountability [which] has been made all the more relevant by the corporate excesses that occurred in the market place." By linking the commission's improved accountability with enforcement strategies remedying abusive conduct, Baxt publicized the "importance of universal coverage of the *Trade Practices Act* [emphasis in original] – not just as a matter of academic fairness – but also to ensure that deregulation and microeconomic reform achieve the results expected of them." In his first annual report, he addressed particularly the issues of mergers and corporate restructuring, noting that "[h]igh concentration is necessary in some Australian industries to obtain the efficiencies offered by scale economies and to match the technical efficiency in production ... of foreign competitors. However, this is not necessarily so for all industries and should not become an article of blind faith."[123]

Baxt pursued enhanced public accountability through several institutional channels. He reorganized the efforts of his predecessors into a more coherent program.[124] In the implementation of the government's microeconomic reforms, Baxt benefited from the appointment of the public servant and economic professor Brian Johns as deputy commissioner and of the consumer advocate and lawyer Allan Asher as commissioner. Furthering the reform goals were the appointments of four parttime commissioners. In addition, Baxt promoted staff morale through stronger personal contact with everyone in the commission, from assistant commissioners to the local offices at the state level.[125]

The appointment of consumer advocates to the commission suggested the political priorities. During Bannerman's and McComas's chairmanships, the Australian Federation of Consumer Organizations (AFCO) consistently lobbied the government to institute a proconsumer enforcement regime, which included appointing consumer activists to be full- and parttime commissioners. The lobbying paid off initially when the government selected as parttime commissioners Professor David Harland, a former Australian Consumers' Association Council member, and AFCO

[123] Robert Baxt, interview, July 1, 1993; Baxt, "Australian Competition Policy," 24–8, quotes at 24; *Trade Practices Commission, 1987–1988*, quote at 1; Corones, *Competition Law and Policy*, 136–45.
[124] *Trade Practices Commission, 1989–1990*, especially, 1–6; "Professor R. Baxt," *Trade Practices Commission*, no. 79 (1994), 12–19.
[125] Howard Hollow, interview, August 12, 2003; Peter Clemes, interview, June 25, 1993; Rod Williams, interview, June 29, 1993; Craig Henderson, June 30, 1993: Stephen Lashburn, interview, July 5, 1993; Tony Paradise, interview, July 7, 1993; Paul Wise, July 9, 1993; Robert Williams, interview, May 22, 1992; Neil Buck, interview, May 22, 1992; Barry Dolan, interview, May 22, 1992; Catherine Watts, interview, May 22, 1992; Hank Spier, interview, June 10, 1992; John Tamblyn, interview, June 9, 1992; Brian Johns, interview, June 9, 1992; Allan Asher, interview, June 9, 1992.

director John Braithwaite. The consumer movement's influence received further impetus from its criticism of McComas's personal negotiation of a remedial settlement involving a Tobacco Institute advertisement claiming that "inhaling passive tobacco smoke was harmless." Within the commission, Braithwaite argued that, given his earlier connections with the tobacco industry, McComas's role in the remedial settlement represented a conflict of interests. The news media subsequently publicized the discontent. Meanwhile, in a private action, the federal court affirmed the consumer groups' argument that "passive smoking" threatened health.[126]

Against this background, the Labor government appointed Allan Asher as fulltime commissioner in 1988. Asher had been involved since the early 1970s in consumer protection and fair trade issues; his previous position included public affairs manager of the Australian Consumers' Association. Asher influenced a profound reshaping of the commission's enforcement regime by focusing on outcomes. Ever since Bannerman's day, the commissioners and the staff had taken as given the formal administrative and litigation process in which the cost imperatives favored relying on the administrative approach. Asher acknowledged these institutional constraints, noting that the commission "received approximately 51,500 complaints and inquiries in 1989/90, but instituted only 14 new court cases." Yet even though court cases remained the "ultimate strategy to achieve compliance with the Act," the commission's "limited litigation resources," meant that "more profound and lasting compliance can be achieved – at lower cost to the taxpayer and to business – by using an integrated approach."[127]

Thus, Asher envisioned an "integrated strategies approach to long-term compliance with the Act ... described as a pyramid of options." The commission addressed "a complaint or inquiry," at "one of the levels of the pyramid." At its apex were the "ultimate sanctions" of "criminal and pecuniary penalties." These were "sought infrequently and only when the seriousness of a complaint and the desired outcome warrants them." Occupying the "next level" were "formal settlements, followed by remedial education and at the bottom of the pyramid, informal settlements." The commission devoted "most" of its "energy and resources" to the "lower levels of the pyramid." Indeed, he emphasized, "A vast number of complaints and inquiries are satisfied through negotiation, education and training, and compliance programs."[128]

---

[126] Braithwaite, "Thinking Laterally," in Bluff et al. eds., *Occupational Health and Safety Regulation*, 3, 4.

[127] Allan J. Asher, "Trade Practices Offenders: Litigation or Compliance Deeds?" *Bulletin Developments in Trade Practices Law and Work of the Trade Practices Commission*, no. 60–1 (1991), 16–22, quote at 6; Allan Asher, interview, June 9, 1992; Howard Hollow, interview, August 12, 2003; Hank Spier, interview, June 10, 1992; John Tamblyn, interview, June 9, 1992; Brenchley, *Allan Fels*, 7, 118–22.

[128] Asher, "Trade Practices Offenders," *Bulletin Trade Practices Commission*, 16.

The commission's negotiated settlement with Pacific Dunlop indicated how the integrated compliance strategy worked. A preliminary investigation found evidence that a Pacific Dunlop subsidiary, GNB Australia Ltd., had placed "Australia made" labels on imported car and truck batteries. The Trade Practices Act prohibited false or misleading representations regarding the place where goods originated. The commission entered into a formal undertaking with the parent company and GNB in which each side made mutual concessions. The commission suspended further investigation and agreed not to pursue legal action for misleading claims. The firms agreed to extend a preexisting compliance program, resulting in the training of a large number of employees throughout the "widely diversified Pacific Dunlop group," with emphasis upon marketing and advertising. A solicitor from one of Melbourne's leading law firms monitored the company's compliance, in conjunction with developing the educational forums facilitating the program's implementation. In order to maintain ongoing effectiveness, the commission exercised continuing oversight. "Pacific Dunlop's undertaking," the commission's publication *Fair Trading* stated, "involves a five-year program designed to improve 'compliance consciousness.'"[129]

The Dunlop undertaking reflected the widening impact of Asher's integrated strategies approach. Previously, Toshiba Australia Pty Ltd entered into a similar agreement, while Epson, the computer hardware manufacturer, Canon, the copying machine company, and the Metal Trades Industry Association worked with the commission to improve existing or to develop new educational and compliance programs. The commission's investigation and negotiation of the Dunlop undertaking reinforced these actions to attain an outcome of business self-regulation. Once the commission and the company made reciprocal concessions, the formal undertaking empowered private interests (the company and the law firm) to implement compliance. The educational forums resulted in scrutiny of the structure of administrative coordination, leading in turn to improvements on the operational level. Senior management made the forums a permanent part of the organizational structure.[130]

A law firm's role in compliance programs furthered the public uses of private market power. By the early 1990s, about six national law firms represented Australian big business, including multinational corporations such as Dunlop and Toshiba. These firms employed litigation whenever their client's interests demanded it, but their first service goal was to preempt the need for litigation through advice. In areas where the law was untested or unsettled, legal advice emphasized risk management. Moreover,

[129] "Pacific Dunlop Opts for Negotiated Solution," *Fair Trading the Trade Practices Commission in the Market Place*, no. 6 (1991), quote at 1; Stephen M. Stern, interview, July 2, 1993.
[130] Ibid.; Neville J. MacPherson, interview, June 28, 1993.

the law firms sought to maximize fees; they did so, however, within the context of alternative counseling and litigation strategies. The solicitor's role in the Dunlop compliance program fit within the counseling strategy, which contributed to developing the client base. This role enhanced a law firm's fee structure as part of the long-term volume business which was usually more lucrative than litigation. Finally, the Melbourne firm's participation in the compliance program actually provided evidence stimulating private actions under the Trade Practices Act against other companies in the industry, which also enhanced fees.[131]

The interconnections between the commission's institutional regime and microeconomic reform entailed reconstituting competition policy. As increased merger activity revealed the pervasive restructuring of the economy, the Labor government's comprehensive assessment of international competitiveness and domestic social welfare necessitated extending coverage of the Trade Practices Act. In March 1991, Prime Minister Hawke delivered a speech entitled "Building a Competitive Australia," in which he urged the consumer "benefits" of "expanding the scope of the law" to foster "potentially lower professional fees, cheaper rail fares, and cheaper electricity. For the producer it would provide the spur to better performance at home and abroad."[132] Inevitably, profound policy change was contentious because it touched powers traditionally reserved to the states. Even so, echoing Asher's assessment, Baxt recognized that enlarging the Trade Practices Act's reach demanded increasing the commission's resources, since enforcement was "*always* [emphasis in original] a question of resources and a question of evidence."[133] Confronting the "rapidly changing economic environment," he envisioned "one of two roles" open to the commission: "It can sit back and wait for breaches of the law and then react like a policeman. It can be a strict enforcer of the law. Or, it can take a pro-active approach and seek to educate the community to a better understanding of what is needed to build a more competitive environment."[134]

Another committee emphasized the contentiousness surrounding enforcement. Amid the proliferation of corporate takeovers, McComas's request for the attorney general to review the Trade Practices Act's dominance test resulted in Alan Griffiths's being appointed by the House of Representatives to lead an inquiry into mergers, takeovers, and monopolies. The evidence the Griffiths Committee received in numerous submissions, public hearings, and a public workshop held in Canberra during October 1988 revealed tensions among interest groups regarding whether to maintain the

---

[131] Stephen M. Stern, interview, July 2, 1993.
[132] Summarized in "State Premiers' Conference May Discuss the Act," *Fair Trading the Trade Practices Commission*, 7.
[133] "Baxt," *Trade Practices Commission*, No. 79, 12–20, quote at 15.
[134] Baxt, "Australian Competition Policy," 24–8, quote at 26.

dominance test or to reinstate the tougher doctrine of lessening competition which had been part of the Trade Practices Act from 1974 to 1977. The Trade Practices Commission formally supported preserving the dominance test; the Confederation of Australian Industry and the Business Council of Australia urged, by contrast, that the test be interpreted according to American free market theories of Chicago economics. The Griffiths Committee generally endorsed the commission's view, but a dissenting report advocated a return to the "lessening competition" standard.[135]

The merger test also became entwined with the relationship between misuse of market power issues and deregulation. Baxt admitted that "it does not really matter what test is applied to mergers," given that it was "extraordinarily difficult to obtain evidence needed to prove a breach." Accordingly, he urged empowering the commission to review "mergers above a certain value." Following the Griffiths Committee Report, this proposal became politicized as a result of "a continued barrage of criticism of the dominance test, from consumer groups and others." They seized upon well-publicized studies by Harvard University's Michael Porter, Baxt said, showing "that the ability to compete abroad requires a base of effective competition at home." Although business leaders generally praised Porter's ideas in principle, they rejected the merger-test linkage that consumer advocates superimposed on them. Compounding the disagreement was the "law covering misuse of market power," Baxt emphasized. "I think it is absolutely essential that this be strengthened to cope with the realities of the increasingly deregulated environment being created by both Commonwealth and State governments."[136]

The merger outcomes during the 1980s intensified these disputes, reinforcing Porter's influence within Australia. Coles and Myer merged to establish the nation's biggest single retailing firm, and *News Ltd* took over *The Herald Weekly Times*, resulting in one company's owning Brisbane's and Adelaide's daily newspapers. Also, Ansett Airline's purchase of East-West Air Lines reduced transcontinental competition as well as within the nation's highest density corridor of Eastern Australia. Enforcement cost contingencies and the dominance standard prevented the Commission from intervening effectively in these takeovers; regarding the Ansett case, it addressed "dominance problems" by mildly urging limited voluntary divestiture in two states.[137] The imagery of potential abuse facilitated

[135] Brenchley, *Allan Fels*, 82–3; Corones, *Competition Law and Policy*, 137–45; Baxt, "Australian Competition Policy," 26–7.

[136] Baxt, "Australian Competition Policy," quote at 27. Brenchley, *Allan Fels*, 83–4, 287; for influence in Australia of Michael Porter, *The Competition Advantage of Nations* (New York, 1990).

[137] Johns, "Threshold Tests," *Review of Industrial Organization*, 658; Economic Planning Advisory Council, *Promoting Competition in Australia Council Paper No. 38* (1989), 16–21; Merrett, "Corporate Governance, Incentives and the Internationalization of Australian

consumer and labor groups' attack on the dominance test by citing Porter's argument that "[r]egulation undermines competitive advantage ... if a nation's regulations lag behind those of other nations or are anachronistic" they "will retard innovation or channel innovation ... in the wrong direction."[138] Accordingly, the government's "proper role is a catalyst and challenger; it is to encourage companies to raise their aspirations and to move to higher levels of competitive performance, even though this process may be inherently unpleasant and difficult."[139]

The High Court's seminal decision in *Queensland Wire Industries* v. *BHP* (1989) heightened the contentiousness. In 1986, the Trade Practices Act's misuse of market power provision (section 46) was amended to reach not only "effective monopolies" but also firms possessing oligopolistic market power. Little litigation had tested the scope of the provision, though private actions regularly raised it as a "bargaining chip."[140] Indeed, the *Queensland Wire* case arose as a private action; the case presented before the High Court the primary issues concerning economic evidence, including the definition of "market." The facts were that BHP's downstream subsidiary, Australian Wire Industries, refused (except at exorbitant prices) to supply Queensland Wire with steel "Y-bar," a product essential to the making of "star picket posts ... by far the most popular kind of rural fencing." The BHP companies controlled 97 percent of the nation's steel manufacture, enabling them to sell full product lines in total packages. The case was significant at the doctrinal level as well as for the practical effect on the organizational efficiencies to be achieved through vertical integration of big corporations.[141] It was rich in symbolic imagery, too, involving the "good monopolist" BHP's domination of a product vital to the rural way of life.[142]

Both the federal trial and intermediate appeals courts decided against Queensland Wire Industries, whereupon the case went to the High Court. Signaling the case's expected long-term impact, the Trade Practices Commission sought to intervene on behalf of the plaintiff, a request the High Court denied. The construction of section 46 raised "two basic questions. The first asks what degree of market power is required. The second asks

Business," Unpublished, cited by permission; Fleming et al., *Big End of Town*, ch. 8; and see Brunt, "Role of Private Actions," 598–602, including quote at 598: "The Commission has been hard pressed to cope with the merger boom of the 1980s."

[138] Porter, *Competitive Advantage*, 647, 649; Baxt, "Australian Competition Policy," 27.

[139] Trade Practices Commission, "Supplementary Submission to the Inquiry into Mergers, Market Dominance and Unconscionable Conduct by Senate Standing Committee on Legal and Constitutional Affairs" (Canberra 1991), quote at 4.

[140] Economic Planning Advisory Council, *Promoting Competition, Council Paper No. 38* (1989), 21–4, quote at 22.

[141] (1989) 167 C.L.R. 177.

[142] Compare, Bushnell, *Australian Company Mergers*, quote at 167.

what constitutes taking advantage of market power," declared Justice
Daryl M. Dawson. "Lying behind both of those questions is the concept of
the market." Though the rationale differed, the lower courts decided in
BHP's favor following a narrow interpretation of "market." They found no
proof of nefarious intent on Australian Wire Industries' part to "take
advantage" of BHP's monopolistic production of Y-bar. Rather, Australia
Wire freely admitted that the company's "policy ... was either to refuse
supply of steel Y-bar or to offer to supply steel Y-bar at an uncompetitive
price because it wished to preserve the business of the manufacture and whole
sale of fence posts conducted by it in association with B.H.P." As Justice John
L. Toohey stated, "a market for Y-bar was created by Q.W. I.'s demand for
the product and B.H.P.'s production of it. In other words, a potentiality for
trade was in the circumstances enough to constitute a market."[143]

Employing the *potential* market definition, the High Court reversed the
lower court decisions and ruled in Queensland Wire Industries' favor. Thus,
the court applied economic rather than moralistic criteria in order to
construe "taking advantage," thereby broadening the reach of section 46.
The economic analysis meant that proof of predatory conduct did not
require a showing of "hostile intent." This interpretation provided
increased incentives for the commission and private parties to challenge the
more egregious results of corporate restructuring, especially with regard to
vertical integration such as BHP's control of Australian Wire Industries.
Moreover, the market analysis was adaptable to other sections of the Trade
Practices Act, including resale price maintenance, exclusive dealing, price
discrimination, and predatory behavior.[144] The use of the economic analysis proved particularly significant in the *Arnotts* decision of 1990, in
which the Federal Court affirmed the commission's blocking a biscuit
manufacturer from acquiring another, holding that the Act was "designed
to foster competition, and the role of section 50 is to maintain competitive
markets." More broadly, *Queensland Wire Industries* relied on European
precedents endorsing workable competition over the Chicago school of
economics' free market doctrines.[145]

IV. ALLAN FELS'S ENFORCEMENT ACTIVISM AND THE NEW ANTITRUST REGIME, 1991–2003

These changes facilitated the transformation of Australian competition
policy under Allan Fels. In July 1991, he became the commission's chair

---

[143] (1989) 167 C.LR. 177, quotes at 198–9, 209.
[144] Brunt, "Role of Private Actions," 602–13.
[145] *Arnotts Ltd. v. T.P.C.* (1990) 97 A.L.R. 555; *Hoffmann-La Roche & Co. v. Commission
   of the European Communities* (1979) 3 C.M.L.R. 211; *United Brands Co. v. Commission
   of the European Communities* (1978) 1 C.M.L.R. 429.

primarily through the active support of the Australian Council of Trade Unions. Consumer groups little influenced the appointment. Big business opposed him. Although labor and consumer groups had sometimes disagreed since the 1970s, they accepted in principle that the Trade Practices Act was essential to preserving public accountability within the corporate restructuring of Australian capitalism. In keeping with the microeconomic reform goal of imposing competition on public utilities, the two groups favored the creation of the Prices Surveillance Authority, which Fels chaired at the time of his commission appointment. Fels profoundly understood that heading an independent statutory authority enabled him to stimulate broad popular demand favoring public-interest policy making. He had perceived this at Cambridge University during the early 1970s, when at the age of twenty-eight years, he contributed to the British government's review of the National Board for Prices and Incomes. Fels's mentor and fellow National Board member, Professor H. A. Turner, effectively cultivated media attention in order to promote legitimacy for the controversial project. "Better to be abused than ignored," Turner had said.[146]

Fels's attention to political symbolism was long-standing. While pursuing his academic career, he had cultivated connections with the Council of Trade Unions, including rising leader William Kelty. The Whitlam government appointed Fels as parttime member of the Prices Justification Tribunal, which in turn brought direct confrontations with big business and the attention of such national business media leaders as *The Australian Financial Review*. John Cain's state Labor government chose Fels to be the new Victorian Prices Commissioner. As he grappled with intractable inflation in petrol and other industries, Fels received from Cain "a fantastic education in how to play symbolic politics." He then joined the national Prices Surveillance Authority when the Hawke government took power, contributing to the implementation of the "accord idea," whereby unions agreed to wage restraint in return for price regulation. Although Keynesian economics deeply informed Fels's practical approach to price regulation, he acquired greater understanding of the Trade Practices Act while teaching with Professor Brunt at Monash University. Her teaching collaboration with Fels reflected the move toward broadening the Trade Practices Act under microeconomic reform.[147]

Fels combined price regulation experience and competition policy study with the rejection of Chicago economic theories. Earning the PhD in economics at Duke University, Fels acquired a thorough understanding of Chicago economics. An academic article published in 1982 confirmed that

[146] Brenchley, *Allan Fels*, 59–62, 78–80, quote at 61. Concerning the consumer movement, see Braithwaite, "Thinking Laterally," in Bluff et al., eds., *Occupational Health and Safety Regulation*, 194–208.

[147] Brenchley, *Allan Fels*, 64–75, quotes at 68, 69.

in him familiarity bred skepticism. The nation's legal–economic professionals diverged over whether workable-competition doctrines or Chicago economic theories provided the best efficiency standard. The High Court's *Queensland Wire* decision indicated that Brunt's workable-competition theories were influencing judicial understanding of economic issues. In this respect, Fels's economic policy thinking paralleled Brunt's.[148]

Upon becoming Trade Practices Commission chair, Fels embraced Asher's innovative enforcement strategies. Implementing price regulations, Fels gained insight into the need for administrative flexibility, effective publicity, and political savvy; he perceived the value of appreciating an agency's institutional culture by listening carefully to the staff. As Fels began work at the commission, he simultaneously remained head of the Price Surveillance Authority, ultimately overseeing the merger of the two bodies. He achieved the commission's budget and staff enlargement while strongly supporting Asher's reshaping of the enforcement regime. His earlier experience as corporate affairs director of the Overseas Telecommunications Commission had taught Asher, however, that government-run bodies were often as insensitive to consumer welfare as private corporations. This background informed Asher's focus on enforcement outcomes. "The thing he taught Fels was the benefit of activism and of using the courts as hard as they did. I'm not saying that Fels didn't come at it from essentially the same point of view. But Asher was the one who would pursue the nuts and bolts of a strategy," recalled a staff member. "The other side might do something but he would always have a response." Thus, he "changed the whole culture."[149]

During Fels's initial years, several issues tested the interdependency between the commission's culture and compliance strategies. An annual report announced that the "major internal reorganization" instituted had been "revised." Enforcement resource allocations were equalized between cartel and consumer protection cases. The report noted that expanded coverage of the Trade Practices Act put increased pressure on staff and budget resources. In addition, recognizing that case complaints arose principally from the State and Territory regional offices, the institutional flow was channeled through a regional coordinator to the general manager, Hank Spier, who "manages the Commission's overall resources, in consultation with the Chairman, and other … offices. Further [he] provides regular managerial and related advice to the Commission on its role, responsibilities and functions."[150]

---

[148] Ibid., 54–5, 57; Allan Fels, "The Political Economy of Regulation," 5 *University of New South Wales Law Journal* (1982), 29–60; Corones, *Competition Law and Policy*, 138–9.
[149] Brenchley, *Allan Fels*, 118–22, quote at 120–1.
[150] *Trade Practices Commission, 1991–1992* (Canberra, 1992), 89–97, quotes at 90, 92.

These organizational changes facilitated expanding the commission's role in stimulating Australia's global competitive advantage. The commission's *Annual Report* of 1991–92, linking the more efficient enforcement regime to greater staff/budget resources, suggested the changing priorities of the Labor government led by Prime Minister Paul Keating (1991–96). Confronting a recession, Keating combined more liberal trade polices abroad – particularly toward Asian nations – with microeconomic reform aimed at promoting national and international market competition through deregulation. Although it was generally agreed that such broad policies required expanding the Trade Practices Act's reach, no consensus existed regarding the appropriate limit. The unresolved controversy concerning the merger-test epitomized the political and institutional tensions. During the Griffiths Committee inquiry, Commonwealth Attorney General Michael Duffy, the government minister who represented the commission on budget and policy matters, had joined Robert Baxt, big business, and corporate lawyers in support of maintaining the dominance test. The commission's senior managers, however, lobbied "quietly" for a change. Meanwhile, when Keating authorized shifting the commission into the Treasury Ministry, it was unclear whether the move would help or hinder changing the merger test.[151]

Fels pursued the merger-test issue within a larger strategy aimed at extending enforcement. About the same time the Griffiths Committee reported in favor of the dominance test, Fels employed his contacts with William Kelty to win from the government a second inquiry into mergers and takeovers led by Labor Senator Barney Cooney. The Cooney Committee recommended enlarging the commission's enforcement regime, including the return to the stronger "lessening of competition" test of the original Murphy Act.[152] Meanwhile, Fels stated that the "relatively weak dominance test gained support in the past because it was designed to permit the acquisition of scale economies by Australian industry in its quest for improved international competitiveness." Measured against the government's microeconomic reform goals, however, "a growing body of evidence" indicated that the "weaker test has permitted a considerable increase in concentration of ownership in many industries without necessarily producing scale economies that are of public benefit," while "shield[ing] . . . anti-competitive mergers in those parts of the Australian economy not exposed to international competition."[153]

[151] Brenchley, *Allan Fels*, 81–7, quote at 83.
[152] "Commission Makes Submission to Senate Inquiry into Mergers Policy," *Bulletin Developments in Trade Practices Law and Work of the Trade Practices Commission*, No. 60–1 (1991), 44–5; "Push for Tougher Mergers Test Falters," June 15, 1992, *The Australian; Trade Practices Commission, 1991–1992*, 5–6; Brenchley, *Allan Fels*, 81–7.
[153] Allan Fels, "The Case for a Tougher Merger Test," *Fair Trading the Trade Practices Commission in the Market Place*, no. 8 (1991), 3.

Fels's efforts to strengthen the Trade Practices Act prevailed within Keating's Cabinet. The commission made parliamentary committee submissions to the Cooney inquiry as well as those concerning print media, banking, and revision of the retirement system under superannuation. Ultimately, the commission put forward five proposals for amending the Act, including adoption of the changed test "whereby mergers which substantially lessen competition are prohibited unless authorized" under section 50; a system of compulsory premerger notification; a provision raising the maximum penalties from $250,000 to $10 million for corporations and $500,000 for individuals for most breaches but leaving the labor exemption at the old lower figure; a provision enabling courts to make enforceable the commission's negotiated undertakings; and another "new provision extending the prohibition of unconscionable conduct to commercial transactions."[154] As late as mid-1992, *The Australian* reported, Labor Treasurer John Dawkins opposed changing the merger test. By the end of summer, however, he joined Duffy in favor of the commission's proposals. "What had changed," declared the Opposition Liberal Party's Peter Costello, was that "Professor Fels as the new chairman of the Trade Practices Commission proved an indefatigable lobbyist, going around to the Minister, going around to other Ministers, going around to the Opposition, lobbying for a wider test."[155]

Reinforcing the commission's enhanced powers was the increased importance of Australia's consumer movement. Asher and Braithwaite had built support within the commission for "enforced undertakings" which remedied misconduct on a responsive, consensual, and inclusive basis. Their emphasis upon shaming and remedies that went beyond adversarial legal proceedings to "restore" the convicted individual's or company's reputation resonated with Fels's skillful use of publicity. In a letter to Asher, part-time Commissioner Braithwaite, the consumer activist and academic promoter of "restorative justice" at the Australian National University, identified the philosophical and political dimensions of an innovative settlements policy. "I think it is fine that serious breaches of the act are dealt with by means other than law enforcement," he said. "But I would not trust the [C]ommission to institutionalize settlements rather than enforcement in perpetuity without people like me having a guaranteed window to look at what sort of deals are being done." Moreover, Braithwaite was frank about the political contingencies: "In my opinion, the Commission has no chance of keeping the consumer movement on side with this stuff unless clearer guarantees are provided."[156]

---

[154] "Amendments to the Act," *Trade Practices Commission, 1991–1992*, 5–6
[155] "Push for Tougher Mergers Test Falters," June 15, 1992, *The Australian*; Brenchley, *Allan Fels*, 87.
[156] Christine Parker, "Restorative Justice in Business Regulation? The Australian Competition and Consumer Commission's Use of Enforceable Undertakings," Unpublished

As the commission fashioned a "restorative" compliance strategy, it settled the landmark North Queensland Aboriginals case. The Department of Social Security alerted the commission's Queensland regional office that the Colonial Mutual Assurance Society's agents had sold certain insurance policies and saving plans to poorly educated, unemployed Aboriginals in remote communities, employing misrepresentation and unconscionable conduct. The commission's investigation revealed that sales involving approximately 2,500 policies occurred between 1986 and 1990. "Agents made representations and sold investments and accidental death policies to people who in many instances did not understand what they were buying," the commission reported. "A common misrepresentation was that policyholders would get their money back in two years. In fact, polices had no value for the first two years as payments were absorbed by costs." The commission's lead investigator, Queensland Regional Director Alan Ducret, observed that "[w]hile these factors created great difficulties for … [the communities' people] as consumers, it also required Commission investigators to deal with situations quite foreign to their experience."[157]

The court-approved settlement affirmed the restorative approach. Fels and the insurance company issued a joint public statement in Brisbane stating the terms agreed to by Colonial Mutual, which included refunding to approximately 2,000 Aboriginals $1.5 million covering premiums and interest, paying $715,000 into the Aboriginal Trust Fund, and instituting a company-wide program enabling the commission to monitor ongoing compliance. Company executives who had sought to understand the problem by visiting the isolated Aboriginal communities had embraced the settlement and thereby regained public esteem. Thus, one executive declared, "When the TPC brought its claims to our attention, we acted quickly by not only setting up our own investigation, but also working directly in cooperation with the TPC." In other cases, however, company executives relied entirely on litigation; as a result they paid high damages awards and lawyer fees and suffered a negative public image. Fels asserted that "settlement approach not only put in place a mechanism to ensure there was no reoccurrence of the actionable behavior, but avoided the need for lengthy and costly legal proceeding." Predicting continued use of the process, he declared, "We will not allow the rights of disadvantaged

Draft, cited by permission; John Braithwaite to Allan Asher, June 5, 1992 (quoted with permission).
[157] *Trade Practices Commission, 1991–1992*, 16–17; Alan Ducret, "Staff Perspectives," *Trade Practices Commission*, no. 79 (1994), 36–9, quote at 36; News Release, "Landmark Settlement for North Queensland Aboriginals," *Trade Practices Commission* (April 1992); Brent Fisse and John Braithwaite, *Corporations, Crime and Accountability* (Melbourne, 1993), 232–7.

groups, communities or individuals under the Trade Practices Act to be ignored."[158]

The stronger merger test and court-enforced undertakings strengthened the commission's authority to shape the restructuring of Australia's corporate economy. The dominance test, Fels had suggested, "might ... be ineffective in preventing mergers in the highly concentrated deregulated industries such as airlines and telecommunication." Enforcing section 50 under the lessening of competition test, however, empowered the commission "to prevent deregulated industries from settling back to a comfortable duopoly." Moreover, the enforced undertakings authority enabled the commission to negotiate settlements such as the Caltex/Ampol merger, which resulted in establishing a number of independent service stations. A few years later, the commission negotiated the Westpac/Bank of Melbourne undertaking, which included proconsumer access to automated tellers. The two powers also improved the commission's enforcement flexibility in the resource-intensive area of mergers. Thus, the *Annual Report* of 1991–92 indicated that the commission inquired into 103 mergers, the majority of which proceeded with limited examination; 18 mergers required extensive investigation; 39 mergers were reviewed in conjunction with the Foreign Investment Review Board. The commission opposed three mergers which subsequently did not proceed and reviewed three others seeking authorization.[159]

The commission's enforcement activism converged with public controversy surrounding a special committee's national competition policy report. In 1993, the Labor government's microeconomic reforms culminated in the appointment of a three-person committee headed by Professor Frederick G. Hilmer.[160] "Competition policy has struck a chord with politicians and the business and wider community far beyond anything I and my colleagues Mark Rayner and Geoff[rey] Tapperell might have expected when we were asked by the Commonwealth government to carry out an independent inquiry," Hilmer subsequently declared. "Competition policy often expressed, albeit incorrectly, as shorthand for 'more

[158] News Release, "Landmark Settlement for North Queensland Aboriginals," *Trade Practices Commission* (April 9, 1992) quotes at 1, 2, 3; Ducret, "Staff Perspectives," *Trade Practices Commission*, no. 79, 36–9.
[159] Fels, "Tougher Merger Test," *Fair Trading*, 3; Brenchley, *Allan Fels*, 87–8; *Trade Practices Commission, 1991–1992*, 34–41; "Settlements Paper (Draft)," Trade Practices Commission (1992); "Remedies Workshop, Preliminary Draft Discussion Paper" (1991).
[160] Ian Marsh, ed., *Implementing the Hilmer Competition Reforms an Overview of the Issues, Benefits and Proposed Next Steps, Growth* 44 (1996); Corones, *Competition Law*, 22; Brenchley, *Allan Fels*, 17, 77, 88–91, 121, 185, 189, 191, 280; *National Competition Policy Report by the Independent Committee of Inquiry Executive Overview* (Canberra, 1993).

competition' is now the central plank of reform in areas as diverse as electricity generation, legal services, health care and ports."[161]

Implementation of the Hilmer Committee's recommendations included reconstituting a competition policy regime. The Hilmer Report urged the public benefits to be achieved from imposing market competition on the states' traditional price regulation of public utilities, telecommunications, and transport. These changes, in turn, profoundly influenced services provided by local and state governments, such professions as law and medicine, and certain small businesses, including pharmacies and news agents. In each sector, increased market competition had a direct bearing on employment, access, and pricing. Indirectly, it altered "industry structure in areas like electricity and water supply, harbors, air and rail transport, primary products markets, and the provision of a range of public services."[162] To carry out this transformation, the government expanded the Trade Practices Commission into a comprehensive national authority renamed the Australian Competition and Consumer Commission (ACCC). The Trade Practices Tribunal was transferred to the ACCC; it had authority to review anticompetitive practices subject to authorization in the public interest. The order also established the National Competition Council, charged with overseeing the states' compliance with national competition policy and administering Commonwealth grants encouraging them to do so. The ACCC went into operation in 1995.[163]

The Labor government's parliamentary majority instituted the Hilmer recommendations by relying on state governments and service sectors, labor unions, big business, legal–economic professionals, media elites, and consumer organizations. This centralized political process contrasted with the popular image Fels and Asher cultivated among elected officials and the Australian public during the political maneuvering for the stronger merger test, enforceable undertakings, and other expanded powers. Moreover, such proconsumer victories as the North Queensland Aboriginal insurance settlement and the Caltex/Ampol merger case reinforced the commission's favorable public image of actively enforcing the Trade Practices Act. These public perceptions, in turn, heightened popular legitimacy for the strengthened competition policy regime identified with the ACCC.[164]

The ACCC's broadened competition policy enforcement mandate had contrary ramifications for Fels's media strategy. Fels promoted the commission's high media profile by rigorously maintaining institutional transparency and actively publicizing enforcement outcomes. Thus, the Australian

---

[161] Frederick G. Hilmer, *Competition Policy: Underlying Ideas and Issues, Discussion Paper No. 337* (1995), 1; John Quiggen, "The Hilmer Reforms: Issues, Benefits and Proposed Next Steps," in Marsh, ed., *Implementing the Hilmer Competition Reforms*, 32–48, quote at 35.

[162] Marsh, ed., "Introduction," in *Implementing the Hilmer Competition Reforms*, 1–2; *National Competition Policy Report* (1993).

[163] Marsh, ed., *Implementing the Hilmer Competition Reforms*.   [164] Ibid.

media soon found that the ACCC's enforcement activism had wide consumer appeal and that it could be relied on for newsworthy information and straightforward accounting. In time, moreover, Fels acquired a celebrity status remarkable for a nonelected public official, an image he employed to widen popular understanding of the practical and symbolic meaning of the Trade Practices Act for all Australians. The post-Hilmer expansion of the Act's enforcement regime nonetheless engendered divergent media images. The ongoing pursuit of cartels, consumer protection, and misleading and deceptive conduct – as well as the abuse of dominant market power often pitting big business against small business – enhanced the ACCC's status as defender of the public interest. Business generally did not criticize the commission, but strict merger enforcement opened the ACCC to the long-standing business attack that it impeded efficient corporate restructuring impelled by Australian's small market.[165]

The ACCC's contentious media image suggested that an ambiguous consciousness had taken root. Confronting the entrenched "mateship" values permeating early postwar Australian capitalism, Barwick and Murphy had justified their divergent approaches to competition policy by appealing to the popular demand for a "fair go," as well as market-efficiency imperatives associated with promoting the nation's global competitive advantage. But, whereas Barwick asserted that consumers and producers generally represented merely different market roles, Murphy explicitly affirmed the importance of promoting consumer welfare. By the early 1990s, Australian media and everyone concerned increasingly focused on consumer welfare as a primary enforcement objective. Nevertheless, competition policy makers still disputed whether Chicago efficiency theories or the heritage of workable competition should define consumer welfare. Broadly, the Hilmer Report supported the workable competition doctrine, declaring, "[c]ompetition policy is not about the pursuit of competition *per se*. Rather, it seeks to facilitate effective competition to promote efficiency and economic growth while accommodating situations where competition does not achieve efficiency or conflicts with other social objectives."[166]

Under Fels the commission's enforcement activism was sensitive to diverse business motivations. Notwithstanding their acknowledged activism, the commission's senior staff recognized the need for flexibility toward business in the implementation of the tougher enforcement regime. Thus, the commission's regional directors assessed the thousands of complaints coming through their offices roughly in terms of three broad perspectives: smaller firms possessed little or no understanding of it, big

---

[165] Allan Fels, "Australia's Competition Regulator and the Media," *Conseil de la Concurrence* Unpublished, cited by permission (Paris, 2002); Brenchley, *Allan Fels*, 221–8.
[166] *National Competition Policy Report* (1993), quote at 2.

diversified corporations describing themselves as "good corporate citizens" publically endorsed it, and "corporate cowboys" or "buccaneers" readily tested the law's limits. Alan Ducret, the commission's Queensland regional director, found the members of the first group to be "generally honest people ... much more likely to tell the truth and accept the consequences." As a result, "once the truth was out in the open, our energies could be spent on finding solutions." This view was consistent, moreover, with McComas's perception that, though widespread, small business pricefixing was not particularly harmful.[167]

The regional directors realistically evaluated the "risk management" motivations influencing the corporate "good citizens" versus the "cowboys." The regional directors knew that both of these business groups understood the Trade Practices Act, not the least because they were advised and represented by commercial lawyers. However, the senior managers and executives of the two groups regarded compliance with the law differently. Those who cultivated the "good citizen" image were truly concerned about unfavorable publicity; many of these firms were, moreover, multinational corporations, such as Shell Oil or Toshiba, which sought to avoid nationalistic backlash like that suggested by the government's periodically protectionist administration of the foreign corporate takeover law. But while these managers readily embraced the commission's educational and compliance programs, the sharp cost contingencies permeating the corporate hierarchy could nonetheless engender among employees the willingness to risk illegal conduct. As a result, the regional directors defined the underlying motivation shaping these corporations' compliance strategy as "risk management." The directors applied the same term to the corporate "buccaneers," even though the risk they managed involved the straightforward calculation of how difficult it was to collect evidence sufficient to prove guilt in court. Indeed, Ducret conceded, "Gathering evidence is always a difficult task in the best of circumstances."[168]

Managers of Australia's multinational corporations faced a different problem, access to international markets. The response to the access issue reflected Australia's changing position towards competition and trade policies. Despite Japan's well-known closed market, Australian trade and diplomatic authorities succeeded in making their nation's multinational

---

[167] Ducret, "Staff Perspectives," *Trade Practices Commission*, no. 79, 35; W. R. McComas, "Forum," *Bulletin 20th Anniversary Trade Practices Commission No. 79* (December 1994), 7, 10.

[168] Ducret, "Staff Perspectives," *Trade Practices Commission*, no. 79, 35; The image of "risk management" is consistent with Christine Parker and Natalie Stepanenko, *Compliance and Enforcement Project: Preliminary Research Report*, Centre for Competition and Consumer Policy, Australian National University, unpublished (2003), cited by permission; the term itself emerged from my interviews with regional directors in 1992, 1993, cited in note 125 above.

corporations "Japan's fourth largest supplier of imports. Australia's degree of penetration of the Japanese market is higher than that in all other East Asian markets." Australian officials achieved these results by applying pressure through bilateral initiatives, the multilateral channels of the GATT-World Trade Organization (WTO), and regional negotiations under Asia Pacific Economic Cooperation.[169] Even so, regarding the WTO and bilateral policy making, the role of antitrust as a potential remedy for the access problem was much disputed, especially between U.S. and European officials. Fels commented that the "discussion of market access problems by many trade negotiators has been based on a deficient understanding of competition concepts," though Australia "appears to have been mercifully free of this deficiency." He nonetheless conceded that in the past Australia had enacted "blocking statutes" which abrogated the duty of Australian firms to comply with foreign court or governmental orders, particularly those arising from U.S. extraterritorial enforcement of antitrust law.[170]

During the 1990s, Australian officials favored internationalizing antitrust enforcement, despite business resistance. Fels advocated using antitrust concepts to remedy trade policy controversies under the WTO and bilateral initiatives. Accordingly, Australia and New Zealand pursued increased harmonization between their antitrust regimes in order to establish a unified market reaching across the Tasman Sea. Both nations replaced their antidumping laws with harmonized antitrust provisions, a policy, Fels said, "likely to be more conductive to economic efficiency and favourable consumer outcomes." The ACCC entered into a bilateral cooperative enforcement agreement with the Taiwan Fair Trade Commission. Moreover, in 1999, Australia and the United States signed a Treaty of Mutual Antitrust Enforcement Assistance, which consolidated and extended several nontreaty bilateral arrangements reaching back to 1982. In principle, the chief executives of some Australian multinational firms accepted these measures in order to maintain the image of "good corporate citizen" and their support for Michael Porter's idea that a nation's industrial global competitive advantage depended on complying with competition policy in the domestic market. But business leaders also reversed the international competitiveness argument, contending that the ACCC's

[169] *Australia–Japan Priority Market Access Issues* (Tokyo, May 1996), 1, 2; Allan Fels, "Competition Policy and Law Reform in the Asia Pacific Region," 6 *Australian Journal of Corporate Law* (July 1996), 143–53; Veronica Taylor, "Harmonizing Competition Law within APEC:US–Japan Disputes on Vertical Restraints," 5 *Australian Journal of Corporate Law* (September 1994), 379–89; Ian W. McLean, "Australia," *Oxford Encyclopedia of Economic History*, 5 vols (Oxford, UK, 2003), 1, 177–82, especially 179–80.

[170] Compare Fels, "Competition Policy and Law Reform," *Australian Journal of Corporate Law*, 148–9; *1997 Report on the WTO Consistency of Trade Policies by Major Trading Partners* (Tokyo), 274.

restrictive merger policy impeded the corporate restructuring Australian firms needed to face globalization.[171]

Since the mid-1980s, while primary agriculture and mining continued to dominate Australia's export–import balance, the nation experienced a "historic" shift toward the production of "elaborately transformed manufactures," including pharmaceuticals, computing equipment, telecommunications equipment, and road vehicles. Although imports of these products exceeded exports, the market sectors in which Australian manufacturers maintained "sustained growth" exceeding "20% per annum for eight years" were "quite remarkable." Along with enlarged global "import demand, especially in Asia," and "a sharp and sustained reduction in costs," there occurred "a positive change in Australian attitudes to competitiveness and to exporting."[172] Regarding these two factors, the active enforcement of the Trade Practices Act stimulated national competition consciousness and, in conjunction with trade policy, fostered the nation's international competitive advantage by promoting competition at home. Reflecting big business opinion, however, the Business Council of Australia attacked Fels enforcement strategies particularly concerning mergers claiming that they forced Australian companies and jobs "off shore" instead of "helping companies to stay in Australia."[173]

The corporate restructuring of the 1990s aggravated the financial contingencies pervading Australian business' competition consciousness. An image of corporate executive abuse clashed with the growing role of domestic equity markets throughout Australian capitalism. The government's privatization polices identified with the Hilmer Committee and the new pension program by which "most Australian employers became contributors to superannuation funds" created huge pools of private capital that fund managers channeled into the equity market. More investors than ever confronted the "moral hazards" engendered by weak corporate governance and the corresponding necessity for effective public accountability. By 1997, the "ratio of market capitalization of listed equities to GDP had risen from 44 to 87 per cent," observed Australian business historian David Merrett. Moreover, the Australian Shareholders Association and Australian

---

[171] Fels, "Competition Policy and Law Reform," *Australian Journal of Corporate Law*, 144, 151–3; Allan Fels, "Administrative/Prosecutorial Discretion of Antitrust Authorities," in Hawk, ed., *Twenty-Sixth Annual Fordham Corporate Law Institute*, 586–606; Maureen Brunt, "Australia and New Zealand Competition Law and Policy," in Hawk, ed., *Nineteenth Annual Fordham Corporate Law Institute*, 131–93, including 190; Brenchley, *Allan Fels*, 220–5.

[172] P. J. Sheeran, Nick Pappas, and Enjiang Cheng, *The Rebirth of Australian Industry: Australian Trade in Elaborately Transformed Manufactures, 1979–1993* (Melbourne, 1994), vii, 11.

[173] Brenchley, *Allan Fels*, 223; for the importance of trade practices enforcement as a stimulator of efficiency, see Fleming et al., *Big End of Town*, ch. 8.

Investors Association joined equity fund managers promoting the rights of shareholders as capitalist consumers. The ACCC's competition polices, the Foreign Investment Review Boards' oversight of foreign takeovers, and various "other reforms in corporations and securities laws ... together with privatizations and demutualizations, superannuation policies and vigilant funds managers formed a virtuous circle supporting the development of a deeper and more liquid equities market."[174]

The commission's blocking of complex corporate takeovers in the *Rank* case suggested the stakes in these investments. During July 1994, the leading grocery firms agreed to an extremely complicated merger scheme. Untangling the intricate investment chain, the commission asked the court for an injunction blocking the basic takeover. Although the federal trial judge acknowledged the joint ventures' claims that time-sensitive investment contingencies jeopardized the whole undertaking if the commission prevailed, he granted the injunction. He also upheld motions for an appeal to be heard "urgently" by the Full Federal Court. The Full Court extensively reviewed the whole undertaking, and then sustained the injunction.[175]

The tensions involved shaped big business' emphasis on fairness and personality in its criticism of the ACCC. The fundamental pressures driving Australian capitalism to become increasingly entrepreneurial and ever-more competitive – combined with the media's promotion of consumer welfare, sympathy toward small business, and the negative buccaneer image – meant that big business could not deny in principle that the ACCC's effective enforcement of competition policy benefited most Australians. Instead, some business executives simply singled out Fels for personal attack: "Business hated him and they were prepared to do anything to stop him." In other instances, business leaders translated their anger into a cautious public discourse; said one executive, "I have no problem with the *Trade Practices Act*," but difficulties arose from the "way it is being interpreted." A further refinement of these views, stated privately among members of the Business Council of Australia, argued that the ACCC's procedural innovations constituted little more than official blackmail.[176]

An independent academic survey of commercial lawyers quoted several as agreeing confidentially that the ACCC "uses publicity unfairly." By comparison, stated one lawyer, "previous Chairmen were lawyers and were more sensitive about using information. They were more sensitive to the rights of people against whom breaches hadn't been proved." Another

---

[174] Merrett, "Corporate Governance, Incentives and the Internationalization of Australian Business," Unpublished Paper, cited with permission, 9, 10.

[175] *Rank* et al. V.T.P.C. (1994), 53 FCR 303 (1994 West Law 1659038 FCA) 2, 4, 7. See also comment on the case by Allan Fels, "The Change from Dominance to a Substantial Lessening of Competition Test in Australia's Merger Law," in Hawk, ed., *Twenty-Ninth Annual Fordham Corporate Law Institute*, 11.

[176] Brenchley, *Allan Fels*, 218, 219, 230–1.

lawyer suspected that "sometimes" the ACCC brought "cases just to attract publicity." Yet another lawyer claimed that the ACCC released evidence that parties had given as confidential: "People don't mind being taken to task when there is a breach, so long as it is done fairly. The problem is when you wake up to find your name in the paper and you didn't even know about the investigation." The survey found, however, that many of these observations traced back to a complicated series of events surrounding the ACCC's troubled investigation of an anonymous whistleblower's allegations against leading oil companies. As one interviewee stated, "It was reported around the world and will be remembered against Fels."[177]

The commission countered such attacks on several fronts. It supported independent academic research demonstrating that, essentially, criticisms arose from honest disagreements about disputed facts, genuine misunderstandings, or quite exceptional mistakes on the ACCC's part. One such study by Dr Karen Yeung, which the ACCC itself funded, concluded that although the complaints regarding the commission's unfair uses of publicity or investigative procedures generally were not supported by the facts, the Trade Practices Act conferred upon enforcement officials sufficiently wide discretion that in exceptional cases they could press the limits of procedural due-process. She targeted particularly the rules pertaining to the ACCC's media releases, the negotiational process preceding court-enforced undertakings, and certain investigatory procedures. Yeung urged that the same due-process standards governing judicial proceedings should guide enforcement of the Trade Practices Act. This point of view achieved enough influence that the government subsequently authorized an enquiry chaired by former High Court justice, Sir Daryl Dawson. The Dawson inquiry resulted in revisions of the law imposing stronger due-process standards, especially concerning media releases. But the commission also received more authority. In "hard core" cartel cases, it could encourage whistleblowers under a leniency program; it could also impose limited criminal sanctions leading to jail terms and, in corporation cases, stiffer civil penalties exceeding $10 million.[178]

Fels, the ACCC's most widely recognized media agent, joined Asher in presenting a coherent rationale for strong competition policy enforcement. "Would Australia's big companies be internationally competitive if they had to secure their raw materials from a monopoly supplier, export through a monopoly transport company, or raise finance from a monopoly bank? And what about consumers? If we had no merger law in Australia," he declared, "consumers could shop at Woolcoles supermarket, buy petrol at

---

[177] Parker and Stepanenko, *Compliance and Enforcement Project*, 57, 58.
[178] Ibid., full report; Karen Yeung, *The Public Enforcement of Australian Competition Law* (Canberra, 2001); Christine Parker, "Restorative Justice in Business Regulation?"; Brenchley, *Allan Fels*, 228–9, 251–6.

Moshell and get beer from Carlton. Such monopolies would surely mean no competition." The commission widely disseminated official publications, instituted numerous educational programs, and maintained institutional transparency. Indeed, Asher affirmed, half the commission's resources went to "equipping people and the community with the law; each time a change in the law [occurred, there was a] major educational campaign." Through these public channels, the commission articulated the policy objectives of "social justice," seeking "to foster competition and efficiency in business resulting in a better choice for consumers in price, quality and service, and to strengthen the position of consumers in their dealings with producers and sellers. Of its very nature, the work of the Commission focuses on equity and access through the promotion of fair trading and the elimination of restrictive trade practices."[179]

The election of John Howard's conservative coalition government in 1996 altered the public discourse about competition policy. The *Christian Science Monitor* reported that the victory giving the Liberal–National party coalition the largest parliamentary majority in the nation's electoral history left Australians "with a conservative, probusiness government whose policy differences with the Keating Labor government are surprisingly slight." Thus, although Howard urged market liberalization, privatization, and weakened union power, his party's triumph resulted from the voters' rejection of a "free market model" of globalization they associated with Keating's advocacy of rapid integration into the Asian trade system and the formalization of the separation from Britain by making Australia a republic.[180] Entwined in these issues were potent cultural identity images associated with Asian immigration, persistent unemployment, and international competition. Identity politics, in turn, reflected the emergence in Queensland of Pauline Hanson's One Nation Party which opposed immigration, the "bush's" eroded public services, and, ultimately, the displacement of state utilities by deregulation and the ACCC's competition policy. Hanson's polarization of policy discourse facilitated the Howard government's restriction of immigration and unions while it promoted trade policies favoring Australian agriculture and the ACCC's active enforcement of competition policy, particularly against big business.[181]

The Howard government's support of the ACCC represented a disputed policy choice. The government implemented the Hilmer Report's deregulation agenda with an express reliance upon the ACCC, whose policy presumption defined "social objectives" and efficiency in terms of broadly

---

[179] Brenchley, *Allan Fels*, 224; Allan Asher, interview, by Tony Freyer, June 9, 1992; *Trade Practices Commission, 1991–1992*, 96.

[180] Mark Clayton, "Labour's Loss Ushers in quieter Era for Australia," *Christian Science Monitor* (March 4, 1996), 6.

[181] Brenchley, *Allan Fels*, 13, 265; Argy, *Australia at the Crossroads*, 41, 68–9, 94–6, 148–9, 153; Capling, *Australia and Global Trade*, 171–90.

conceived consumer welfare.[182] This policy choice reflected the tension stated in Fred Argy's book *Australia at the Crossroads: Radical Free Market or a Progressive Liberalism?* (1998). Argy divided Australian policy makers into "hard" and "progressive" liberals. Members of both groups evaluated policy choices according to three "benchmarks": efficiency (defined as long-term per capita GNP growth), employment, and "distributional equity (whether the impact on the distribution of incomes and wealth will be regressive or progressive)." Argy explained that "economic policy disagreements between hard and progressive liberals arise solely because they give different weights or values to each of the three benchmarks"; the "hard liberals give overwhelming priority to efficiency as largely a means to the other goals, whereas progressive liberals give equal priority to all three benchmarks." He vigorously argued the case for progressive liberalism even as the hard liberals' "crusade for economic freedom is gaining force and increasingly showing signs of religious zeal."[183]

As this policy dispute reshaped Australia's social welfare capitalism, the ACCC's role grew. Like political leaders in other industrial nations, the Howard government wrestled with national debt and corresponding taxation problems exacerbated by persistent unemployment and the funding of retirement pensions under superannuation. One outcome of these interrelated issues was that the government replaced a compulsory 3 percent employee superannuation contribution with a "voluntary incentive-based" contribution. The number of employers and employees possessing a stake in the system increased due to the dismantling of the states' public utilities, which enlarged the ACCC's authority. The ACCC's influence over employment relations grew still more when the government altered the incentives for labor unions to enter into the "enterprise bargaining" agreements Labor governments had institutionalized. Parliament passed the Workplace Relations Act of 1996, which reduced the arbitration authority of the Australian Industrial Relations Commission and simplified the terms under which most workers received awards. In addition, the government amended the Trade Practices Act to prevent unions from engaging in secondary boycotts. Years before, Bannerman had stated publically that without such a revision, the commission would exercise little authority in such cases; under the Act's amendment, the presumption now favored action against secondary boycotts.[184]

The waterfront confrontation of 1997–98 revealed the social and political costs impinging on the ACCC's expanded authority. Since its inception, the Trade Practices Act included jurisdiction over the maritime

[182] See notes 160–6 above.   [183] Argy, *Australia at the Crossroads*, 252, 253.
[184] Ibid., 68–9, 94–9; David Oakes, "Dogs on the Wharves: Corporate Groups and the Waterfront Dispute," 11 *Australian Journal of Corporate Law* (December 199), 30; Bannerman, "Trade Practices Law," 95, note 14.

industry. Globalization exposed the waterfront's labor-management dispute system to increased market competition. A holding company, Lang Corporation Ltd, controlled the Patrick Group of subsidiaries, a number of which managed cargo stevedoring and container operations in the terminals of the nation's leading ports. Patrick periodically had "bitter" disputes with sea and shore-based workers represented by the Maritime Union of Australia (MUA), which since the 1940s had defended waterfront employee rights nationwide. Patrick's only real nationwide competitor in stevedoring operations was P&O Australia and its subsidiaries. The Lang and P&O groups constituted a classic case of oligopolistic competition. Even so, through its holding company organization, Lang felt directly the costs of Patrick's approximately $3.6 million settlement with the MUA at Melbourne's Webb Dock in December 1997. Earlier in the year, Patrick began a financial restructuring involving Lang, Patrick, and six Patrick subsidiaries which sought the elimination of the stevedoring operations. Patrick's asset sales and restructuring "rendered tenuous the security of the employer companies and hence the security of the employees was also compromised."[185]

The ensuing confrontation received steady media attention. In January 1998, Patrick turned over control of one of the Melbourne docks to firms aligned with the National Farmers Federation (NFF). A strike followed lasting 37 days, during which the MUA engaged in secondary boycotts. By April, MUA leaders perceived that Patrick's restructuring enabled the subsidiary stevedoring companies to gain efficiencies by selling assets and terminating thousands of union workers under Labour Supply Agreements (LSAs). Moreover, as the parent holding company, Lang exercised its prerogative over the sale of the subsidiaries' assets totaling $314.9 million, blocking claims from creditors or the subsidiaries themselves. Lang returned most of the money to stockholders, making "the employer companies ... virtual shell companies, with no assets other than severely diminished cash reserves and the inhouse LSAs." Meanwhile, Patrick announced losses of $56 million which were to be partially compensated by letting go the MUA stevedore workers. A press release confirmed that the company would comply with labor laws guaranteeing former workers leave and redundancy entitlements; those seeking relocation counseling would receive it. These costs would be covered through a loan fund administered by the Federal Government. In addition, superannuation payments totaling about $250,000 were to be distributed among half the eligible workers.[186]

The entire package was contingent, however, on the MUA workers' agreeing to the redundancies. Rather than accept the company's terms, the

---

[185] Oakes, "Dogs on the Wharves," *Australian Journal of Corporate Law*, 30–4, quote at 31.
[186] Ibid., 33.

MUA, on behalf of the displaced workers, sued Lang, Patrick, and others. Australian law governing unfair employee dismissals authorized monetary compensation where redundancy occurred for prescribed reasons, generally *not* including the employer's insolvency. In addition, current law permitted neither the courts nor the Australian Industrial Relations Commission to inquire into whether the insolvent firm was part of a larger corporate structure – such as the Lang holding company – which did have the means to pay. As a result, the union alleged that Lang's and Patrick's complex corporate restructuring facilitated a conspiracy to remove the workers because of their MUA membership. Common law tort conspiracy doctrines required proving only that one conspirator intended to harm another party in order to establish the liability of all those involved in the conspiracy. The union then asked the federal court for an injunction blocking Patrick's dismissal of the MUA employees.[187] Throughout the confrontation, Treasury Minister Costello pressured Fels to have the ACCC enforce the Trade Practices Act's provision against secondary boycotts. Costello knew that Fels was in a difficult situation because of his long-time close association with Bill Kelty and the Australian Council of Trade Unions which publically sided with MUA. Even so, Asher, Spier, and Fels acknowledged that inaction jeopardized the ACCC's credibility.[188]

The courts' decisions resulted in terms of settlement which included strengthening the ACCC's authority over unions. The trial court granted a temporary injunction in accordance with the Workplace Relations Act of 1996 which authorized reinstatement of workers "as an alternative to compensation." The judge nonetheless held that the "serious question" not decided at trial was whether Patrick acted because the workers were MUA members. Upon appeal, the Full Court essentially upheld the trial judge, whereupon the case went before the High Court. The High Court ordered that the corporations law governing insolvency should take precedence over the Workplace Relations Act, leaving the workers' redundancy contingent on whether the employer company formally declared insolvency. The final settlement of the waterfront dispute, announced on September 3, 1998, benefited both Patrick and the MUA. Patrick did not declare insolvency, agreeing to keep under contract a large portion of the MUA employees. In return, more than half the MUA workers who were parties to the original action accepted the terms of the redundancy package. The MUA also accepted an enterprise agreement with Patrick in which it undertook to engage in no strike action for "at least three years."[189]

---

[187] Ibid., 43–1.   [188] Brenchley, *Allan Fels*, 77–9, 91–5.
[189] Oakes, "Dogs on the Wharves," *Australian Journal of Corporate Law*, 37–8; *Maritime Union of Australia v. Patrick Stevedores No. 1 Pty Ltd* (1998) 27 ACRS 497 (Fed. Ct., North J); *Patrick Stevedores Operations No. 2 Pty Ltd v. Maritime Union of Australia* (1998) 27 ACSR 521 (Full Fed. Ct.); (1998) 27 ACSR 535 (High Ct.) (*Patrick's* case).

In a court-enforced undertaking, the MUA agreed that it would not resort to secondary boycotts involving Patrick "facilities." The union entered into the undertaking in part because Patrick gave the ACCC $7.5 million to compensate those harmed by the dispute. Publically, Fels conceded that the waterfront dispute was "pretty challenging." The ACCC "had no option but to go to court to take all the litigation action necessary. There was a great deal of criticism by the unions. There was some weakening of the bipartisan support we had enjoyed from the Labor Party as well as from the coalition, but our duty was to apply the law."[190] Moreover, the Federal Court upheld the ACCC's action against the MUA and its senior officials for employing secondary boycotts and other practices "to prevent or hinder ... vessels from sailing unless the ship owner or charterer agreed to use MUA labour to clean the vessels' holds." The court ordered the union to pay penalties and costs totaling $210, 000; it also ordered the MUA "to implement a trade practices compliance program" and to provide each union member "a notice advising of the court's findings and orders."[191]

The waterfront settlement suggested the changing parameters of Australian welfare capitalism. Since the nation's formative era, the empowerment of labor under the arbitration system symbolized the consensus underpinning Australia's political economy. Since at least the 1970s, Labor and Conservative parties alike reshaped this consensus, implementing such polices as "enterprise bargaining" among union workers and the "incentive-based" superannuation system channeling the citizen's contributions into huge equity investment pools. More than ever before, the welfare of Australian workers, consumers, and small business depended on the investment strategies of Australia's large corporations such as Lang and Patrick. The waterfront settlement revealed how the government "socialized" the costs of these entrepreneurial strategies. Thus, the Howard government supported the "win–win" agreement between the MUA and Patrick. Applying Argy's policy, the settlement represented a compromise between "free market" and "progressive" liberalism.[192]

The settlement further confirmed the ACCC's symbolic role in Australia's capitalist system. Exploiting the ACCC's proconsumer reputation amid the waterfront confrontation, the Howard government pressured

[190] Oakes, "Dogs on the Wharves," *Australian Journal of Corporate Law*, 37; Allan Fels, "Round Table Commentary on Administration/Prosecutorial Discretion of Antitrust Authorities: Leniency or Amnesty, Cooperation and Plea Bargaining, Positive Comity, and Allocation of Resources," in Hawk, ed., *26th Annual Fordham Corporate Law Institute*, 684–5.

[191] *ACCC Annual Report, 2001–2002*, 31; Brenchley, *Allan Fels*, 94–5: Fels did not admit publically that the ACCC litigation ended his twenty-year friendship with Bill Kelty.

[192] Oakes, "Dogs on Wharves," *Australian Journal of Corporate Law*; see notes 147, 149, 174, and 183 above.

Fels and the commission to intervene against the union's secondary boycotts. Fels and his colleagues had achieved a strong media image sustaining the ACCC's enforcement activism against Australia's most powerful corporations. The expansion of this enforcement regime to include the nation's deregulated and privatized public utilities further heightened the ACCC's public significance. Indeed, when the Howard government came to power, Fels was too important to sack, despite his long-time association with the Australian Council of Trade Unions. Such high public standing nonetheless ensured that the ACCC's leaders had to apply vigorously the Trade Practices Act's prohibition regarding secondary boycotts. Even so, the complementarity between court-litigated outcomes and court-*authorized* undertakings the ACCC won implementing the MUA's compliance programs and Patrick's $7.5 million small business compensation package, promoted the commission's goals of efficiency and social objectives.[193]

Compounding these tensions, the Howard government imposed the national goods and services tax (GST). In order to diffuse the Labor Party's political exploitation of the GST, the government assigned enforcement to the ACCC. Although Spier, Asher, and Fels knew how tendentious the issue was, they endorsed this enforcement role primarily because it brought about considerable staff and budget increases, enabling the commission to strengthen the nationwide enforcement regime, including the adoption of better computer and videoconferencing technology. Thus, the ACCC's budget initially increased from $38 million to $57 million, ultimately reaching $75 million. During the two-year period when the tax came into effect, the ACCC spent $20 million on "consumer awareness," empowering ordinary Australians as GST "watchdogs." However, since big and small businesses alike would readily pass tax costs along to consumers, implementation of the government-imposed 10 percent price increase provided innumerable opportunities to raise prices even further in what the media described as a "GST STING."[194]

Within the ACCC, opinion was divided on how best to address the "10 percent" issue. Legal experts agreed that the courts were likely to apply a standard of reasonableness which could result in upholding price increases exceeding 10 percent. Nevertheless, the government responded to adverse publicity by asserting that consumer prices would rise *no more* than 10 percent. ACCC Commissioner David Cousins advised relying on business self-regulation and voluntary agreements. Asher insisted, however, that more vigorous enforcement was essential in order to "persuade business that we were just going to be all over them through a massive campaign, almost a blitzkrieg." Thus, he declared, "the 10 per cent issue involved massive guidance and massive publicity. Sadly, it did cost us our relationship with small business for a while." Indeed, during Senate hearings, an

---

[193] See notes 190 and 191 above. [194] Brenchley, *Allan Fels*, 97–115, quotes at 101, 103.

opposition Labor leader exclaimed, "You are running the biggest fear and intimidation campaign this country has seen for small business, and you can sit there with a straight face and say that you do not think these [pricing guidelines] are frightening people."[195]

The Video Ezy case confirmed the ACCC's enforcement strategy. The case arose primarily from consumer complaints revealing that Video Ezy's Townsville franchise had employed misleading price increases prior to the implementation of the GST. According to the ACCC, Video Ezy staff told customers that "[t]he price rise is to introduce the GST now so that people get used to the idea of paying more. It won't be such a shock when the GST comes in." The media impact of such complaints was obvious given that the company had 480 outlets and 3.5 million customers nationwide. Moreover, the ACCC's investigation revealed senior company managers commenting that the GST provided opportunities to consider price increases. The company settled, protesting that it was being singled out as a "scapegoat." Video Ezy agreed to judicially enforced undertakings in which it admitted making false and misleading representations to customers and offered lower video rental prices in Townsville. The company also mailed to customers apology notices, installed a trade practices staff training and compliance program, and paid some of the ACCC's costs. Thus, Fels's assertion that the ACCC's consumer campaign installed "19 million price watch dogs on the beat" suggested that selective enforcement was sufficient to maintain the Trade Practices law's deterrent effect.[196]

The GST disputes reinforced the contentious public discourse surrounding the ACCC's role in public utility deregulation. Concerning Fels's media strategy, the GST shared a major attribute with the ACCC's post-Hilmer enlarged jurisdiction, the political difficulty of establishing public understanding of complex regulatory matters. As Fels stated in 1999, even the government's Treasury Ministry had the "problem" of "a rather poor knowledge of the energy markets, the transport markets, and so on, when they go about pressing for reform." And yet, "we are able to feed them fairly good knowledge on some of the practical implications of some of the reforms they are seeking and what issues should be pursued."[197]

The long-running dispute between the commission and Telstra suggested how difficult some of these regulatory problems were. As a result of the Labor government's deregulation of telecommunications, the industry giant Telstra competed only against Optus. For five years the government authorized Telstra to maintain both its basic telephone cable network and "retail functions," even though the OECD urged that the cable network

[195] Ibid., quotes at 105, 107.
[196] *ACC Annual Report, 2000–2001*, 30–34; Brenchley, *Allan Fels*, 106–14, quotes 110, 111.
[197] Fels, "Round Table Commentary, on Administration/Prosecutorial Discretion," in Hawk, ed., *26th Annual Fordham Corporate Law Institute*, 658, 686.

structure and retail functions should be separated. Fels, too, described how such a "network industry with high market power, often vertical integration, and strong customer bases" prevented the market entry of potential competitors. The commission fought an ongoing, up-hill battle against Telstra's market domination, with each side employing aggressive media strategies. The efficiency and social justice tradeoffs were evident when the commission made its approval of the merger between Optus and Foxtel pay television content providers contingent on Telstra – which owned 50 percent of Foxtel – agreeing to "absorb hundreds of millions in Optus' costs." While Telstra agreed to these terms, the future remained unclear for market access and price competition involving such popular consumer products as pay television and interactive digital services, including email, video on demand, and internet. Moreover, as Telstra's majority shareholder, the Commonwealth government possessed a direct interest in maintaining the company's profitability.[198]

The ACCC achieved more explicit success in consumer protection and cartel matters, including those affecting small business. In 1998–99 alone, the ACCC received a total of 11,829 complaints, of which it extensively investigated 1,176 involving consumer protection and 654 pertaining to restrictive trade practices. From 1991 to 1998, moreover, the ACCC's record in court litigation concerning consumer protection was fifty-seven won, thirty settled, and one loss; regarding restrictive trade practices cases, it won thirty-five, settled twelve, and lost five. In five additional cases raising both consumer protection and cartel issues, the commission won one and settled four. The ACCC "probably give[s]" the consumer protection issues "a slightly higher importance ... than they deserve," Fels acknowledged, "because, frankly, you can build up a higher degree of public support and credit for some of those actions, and that gives you a bit of a stock of public goodwill to carry you through some of the more difficult and unpopular, or highly criticized, merger decisions or other decisions that invoke major reactions from powerful interest groups." The ACCC also cultivated small business support, especially in light of the problems associated with the GST. A commissioner was designated to address the needs of small enterprise; the ACCC pursued several rural and regional programs and offered many publications targeting this group. Moreover, the commission "took extensive enforcement action of particular benefit to small business, including unconscionable conduct, landlord and tenant relationships, and franchising arrangements."[199]

---

[198] Ibid., 686; *ACCC Annual Report, 2001–2002*, 49, 76, 112–13, 117; Brenchley, *Allan Fels*, 178–86, quote at 183.

[199] Allan Fels, "Administration/Prosecutorial Discretion of Antitrust Authorities," and Allan Fels, "Round Table Commentary," in Hawk, ed., *26th Annual Fordham Corporate Law Institute*, 604, quote at 686; *ACCC Annual Report, 2001–2002*, 63–4.

The *Boral* case illustrated the difficulty of balancing the interests of consumers and business. The issue in the case was whether Boral, a producer of concrete masonry products in Melbourne, possessed sufficient market power to breech section 46 of the Trade Practices Act's prohibition against firms abusing their dominant market position. Boral's concrete masonry operations were subsidiary to Boral Ltd, a large diversified holding company doing business in building and construction materials and energy. Following complaints from other concrete and masonry producers, the ACCC sued Boral, alleging that the firm had engaged in predatory pricing in the Melbourne metropolitan market. Most of Boral's local competitors were corporate subsidiaries of large, diversified companies, though Budget Bricks was a smaller private firm making concrete masonry products in a single plant at Springvale. As a result of the "price war," two of the competitors left the market; the three remaining firms engaged in vigorous price competition, one C&M ultimately accounting for as much as 40 percent of total Victorian sales.[200]

These facts demonstrated how difficult it was to prove allegations under section 46. At least in the short run, consumers – including the customers of concrete masonry producers – clearly paid lower prices. The fate of two of the companies indicated, however, that smaller as well as big firms might not remain in the market if the lower prices reflected intentional below-cost practices specifically targeting competitors. Thus, in order to adjudicate the ACCC's allegations, the court had to determine the appropriate market, address whether a Boral subsidiary possessed "substantial market power," and ascertain whether the evidence showed the company's predatory intent to breech section 46. The lower court found economic evidence indicating that Boral's management expressly exploited the efficiencies of its corporate structure within the local market to pursue a price-cutting strategy aimed at reducing the number of competitors. The trial court nonetheless defined the market broadly to include substitute products. Thus, the court held that the intent was not predatory within the meaning of section 46 and the ACCC lost. Upon appeal, the Full Court defined the market more narrowly as the concrete masonry products subject to the oligopolistic competition of the two main players. As a result, the court held that the evidence did prove predatory pricing and reversed in favor of the ACCC.[201]

On the final appeal, however, the High Court reversed. The Full Court's reasoning recognized that the market power employed to engage in a price war exploited corporate organizational efficiencies which "may involve a concept of 'recoupment' that contemplates substantial, and even prolonged,

---

[200] *Boral Besser Masonry Ltd. v. ACCC* (2003), 195 ALR 609; (2003) 77 ALJR 623; *ACCC v. Boral Ltd.* (1999) FCA 1318; *ACCC v. Boral Ltd.* (2001) FCA 30; see also (2003) West Law [WL] 253768.

[201] (1999) FCA 1318; (2001) FCA 30.

short-term losses in the expectation, reasonable or otherwise, of long-term gains." Nevertheless, the High Court, employing the narrower market definition, decided that the proven facts of immediate local market competition meant that Boral did not possess monopoly power within the meaning of section 46. In dissent, Justice Michael Kirby applied a version of the recoupment theory asserted by the U.S. Supreme Court declaring that the "present case is more akin to the recoupment hypothesis of a coordinated or disciplined oligopoly ... than it is to cases involving monopoly or near monopoly power." Moreover, the Trade Practices Act's section 46 proscribed not monopoly but the *abuse* of "substantial market power." Thus, Boral's "short-term pricing sacrifices were made for long-term economic rewards. Inevitably these would come at a probable cost to consumers," Kirby concluded.[202]

The ACCC also employed less adversarial administrative processes. Between 1997 and 2002, it instituted enforceable undertakings under the Trade Practices Act's section 87B in 340 cases. According to its enforcement guidelines, the ACCC's decision to pursue enforceable undertakings rather than court litigation depended in part on "whether the alleged offender's record suggests that an administrative settlement will be sufficient to deter it from future conduct."[203] Administrative factors reflected the ACCC's authorization process. A rural enterprise – Premium Milk Supply which represented a number of dairy cooperatives in Queensland – received authorization "to collectively bargain farm and gate prices and milk standards with Pauls Limited." Several other sectors benefited from such authorizations.[204]

These vigorous yet flexible enforcement policies facilitated transnational antitrust cooperation, which imposed accountability upon multinational corporations. During 1999, the ACCC's enforcement regime contributed – along with European, Japanese, Canadian, and other antitrust agencies – to the U.S. Justice Department's successful prosecution of an international vitamins cartel for price-fixing and market sharing, which resulted in pharmaceutical companies F. Hoffman–La Roche Ltd. and BASF Aktiengesellschaft paying criminal fines totaling a record $725 million. In related international cartel cases, Australian enforcement cooperation aided the U.S. Justice Department's prosecution of the global conspiracy of three Japanese pharmaceutical companies. The U.S. government won $137 million in fines. Such international cooperation facilitated the U.S. Federal Trade Commission's response to American complaints by seeking ACCC

---

[202] *Boral Besser Masonry Ltd. v. ACCC* (2003) HCA 5, WL 253768, quotes at 413, 448.
[203] Christine Parker, "Restorative Justice in Business Regulation?" Unpublished Draft, cited with permission, note 17, of text summarizing Trade Practices Commission, *Section 87B of the Trade Practices Act: A Guideline on the Trade Practices Commissions Use of Enforceable Undertakings* (Canberra, 1995), 1.
[204] *ACCC Annual Report, 2001–2002*, 80–8, quote at 80.

intervention against the Australian firm, Internic Pty Ltd. The company charged $70–100 for using internet names which were nearly identical with American ones. The ACCC and Internic settled through a court-enforced undertaking: the company agreed to end the wrongful conduct and to establish a Aus $250,000 trust account to refund those customers whom its practices had misled.[205]

The ACCC's cooperation in transnational antitrust enforcement reinforced Australian government officials' and business' competition consciousness. Australian managers of multinational corporations professing the "good citizen" image benefited as well as consumers when the ACCC and the United States collaborated, especially since the illegal conduct undoubtedly affected adversely more Australian multinational firms than were parties to these same anticonsumer practices. Broadly speaking, these proconsumer actions were of the sort that the media usually applauded and business generally found unproductive to dispute. Australian authorities perceived trade and competition policies to be complementary, for as Fels stated, "a vigorous enforcement of competition rules in trading nations can play a useful role in preparing the common rules of conduct for enterprises and reducing undue imbalances in different business systems. This paves the way for enterprises to compete for roles in markets of the trading states through superior efficiency and effort."[206]

By the turn of the millennium, international demands for imposing accountability on multinational corporations increasingly favored bilateral antitrust arrangements as a prerequisite to instituting any multilateral agreement on "hard core" cartels or mergers under the WTO. The focus on pursuing bilateral arrangements reflected the reality that many underdeveloped and developing countries which were already or sought to become members of the WTO had no antitrust regime. Thus, bilateral arrangements enabled these nations to acquire antitrust expertise.[207] For instance, the *Annual Report* of 2001–02 announced that the ACCC had entered into a Memorandum of Understanding with the Fiji Islands' Commerce Commission, "to promote cooperation and coordination of enforcement, training and technical assistance activities in respect of consumer protection and competition issues." Fiji agreed to the Memorandum in order to prepare for eventual WTO membership. The ACCC held that helping "other countries achieve effective competition and consumer protection regimes ... can mean more competitive and fairer overseas markets, and better access to those markets for Australian exporters."[208]

[205] Allan Fels, "Administration/Prosecutorial Discretion of Antitrust Authorities," in Hawk, ed., *26th Annual Fordham Corporate Law Institute*, 598–600, quote at 599.
[206] Ibid.; Fells, "Competition Policy and Law Reform," 6 *Australian Journal of Corporate Law*, 143–53, quote at 147–8.
[207] Ibid.   [208] *ACCC Annual Report*, 2001–2002, 6–7.

As with big business, the acceptance by organized labor of competition consciousness had ambiguous consequences. Even as the waterfront dispute was revealing that organized labor's traditional support of antitrust had costs, the coal mining unions had a similar experience. They tried to use the Trade Practices Act in a wage dispute arising from Japanese imports of Australian coking and thermal coal. Australian coal producers supplied from 55 to 70 percent of each type of coal to the Japanese importers; the Australian multinational corporations established the world benchmark price. Since the 1970s, Japan's increasing volume of Australian coal imports had resulted in lower prices among Australian producers, which in turn reduced the miners' wages. During wage negotiations, the unions argued that the Japanese buying strategy – which relied on collaboration between Japanese trading companies and steel or power stations – operated as an import cartel that Japanese antitrust authorities did not police under their own Antimonopoly Law. The collusive practices would be illegal, however, under the Trade Practices Act. Accordingly, the union urged, the government could exercise its power to seek authorization from the ACCC to compel the Australian producers to establish an export cartel or at least to institute a Coal Marketing Board which could impose a protectionist trade policy. Although the government declined to act, the union's strategy suggested the contrary results of the continuing support organized labor gave the Trade Practices Act.[209]

Big business also embraced the competition consciousness the Trade Practices Act symbolized, while it employed protectionist rhetoric to dispute Fels's and the ACCC's enforcement activism. The big business criticism reflected the shifting bipartisan political party consensus emerging from the 1970s, which demanded balancing the interests of big and small business, organized labor, agriculture, and consumers in the name of market efficiency and social justice. Throughout the Commonwealth's history, moreover, trade policy evolved in conjunction with the nation's unique arbitrational settlement between labor and capital. From the 1970s on, the terms of this settlement gradually accommodated Australia's generous social welfare system to the needs of an increasingly entrepreneurial managerial capitalism whose corporate restructuring ultimately maintained oligopolistic competition throughout the domestic market. Amidst economic globalization and the access problem, however, corporate restructuring aroused demands from consumers, small business, organized labor, and the media to impose greater accountability on big business. From Bannerman to Fels, the commission expanded its enforcement goals in the name of instituting such accountability. Indeed, under Fels trade and competition policy, goals were more than ever complementary.

---

[209] Veronica Taylor, "Harmonizing Competition Law," 379–89, especially 381–2.

IV. CONCLUSION

In 2003, several developments suggested the instrumental and symbolic meaning of antitrust within Australian capitalism. Amidst persistent controversy, Allan Fels resigned as the ACCC's chairman; in his place the Howard government appointed Graeme Samuel, a businessman whose experience included leading the National Competition Council. Samuel praised Fels and the ACCC's impressive enforcement activism. He indicated, however, that a change in compliance strategy emphasizing "shaming" through ongoing media attention would be sufficient to hold Australian big business accountable to the public interest, especially given the domestic and international competition engendered by economic globalization. In addition, Treasury Minister Costello responded to consumer-group demands by appointing Australian Consumers' Association Chief Executive Officer Louise Sylvan to be the ACCC's deputy chairman, a vacancy existing since Allan Asher resigned in 2000. Meanwhile, the *OECD Journal of Competition Law and Policy* published the results of a worldwide study of antitrust regimes' enforcement objectives, identifying Australia among those which balanced "core competition objectives, *i.e.*, i) promoting and protecting the competitive process, and ii) attaining greater economic efficiency" with "one or more public interest objectives." By contrast, nations such as the United States only implemented the "core competition" objectives.[210]

---

[210] Brenchley, *Allan Fels*, 263–390. Note that Louise Sylvan was also president of Consumers' International (the main international nongovernmental organization for the consumer movement). Secretariat, "The Objectives of Competition Law and Policy," *OECD Journal of Competition Law and Policy*, 7–46, quote at 15. Tony Freyer noted the reference to Mr. Graeme Samuel's emphasis on "shaming" in a television interview, August 11, 2003. The new trust in enforcement policy was confirmed in Freyer/John Braithwaite interview, August 12, 2003, and Freyer/Allan Fels interview, August 11, 2003.

Conclusion

Amid persistent resistance to Americanization, divergent capitalist economies changed from opposing to supporting antitrust. As businesses throughout the world employed large-scale corporations and cartel practices to ameliorate risk, antitrust became a process whereby capitalist societies and governments acquired and applied a public discourse of economic and social conflict resolution in order to impose accountability upon expanding yet distinctive forms of managerial capitalism, especially big business operating as multinational corporations. This focus reveals how beginning in 1937–38 New Deal liberals reconstituted antitrust to embrace various social-welfare and efficiency goals based on institutional economic theories. From the 1970s on, however, the U.S. government, legal-economic experts, and the courts used Chicago economic theories to reshape an efficiency standard defined primarily in terms of consumerism and technological innovation. The same focus explains why during the Great Depression and World War II liberal-democratic and authoritarian nations alike opposed American-style antitrust and then reversed course after 1945 to adopt it selectively as divergent systems of liberal capitalism emerged. The present study of changing antitrust institutions and policies in the United States and between the United States and other capitalist economies suggests that internationalization involved processes of institutional and cultural accommodation within the social order which were politically and culturally contingent as well as contested among elites.

Each chapter of this book sets out perspectives on the processes of accommodation. According to Keynesian or Chicago macroeconomic theories, corporate managers mediated risk within autonomous markets conditioned by governments' monetary, tax, labor, currency exchange, tariff, and social-welfare policies. Such theories did not directly address issues of public and private accountability identified with antitrust. Alfred Chandler and his followers considered, by contrast, the bearing antitrust had upon managers' control of the strategy and structure driving administrative coordination within large-scale corporations identified with big business throughout the world. Chandler's reconstruction of big business suggested the extent to which political and cultural contingencies working upon corporate organization, along with market imperatives defined by macro-economic theories, shaped the managers' decisions. Generally, in so far as such business or legal history studies considered antitrust they emphasized instrumental outcomes in particular market sectors such as energy, chemicals, electrical equipment, metals, agricultural staples, and other commodities. Overall, the instrumental approach confirmed Chandler's finding for the United States that wherever antitrust limited cartels it prevented big business from achieving monopolistic combinations through merger, fostering instead oligopolistic competition and the diminishing strength of small business. Still, antitrust regimes possessed sufficient autonomy to enforce – if they chose to do so – instrumental outcomes benefiting a wider range of private interests than did trade policy, which responded to interests more directly through shifting politics.

The present study expands upon these studies to argue from a comparative perspective that antitrust enforces not only instrumental outcomes but also possesses symbolic meaning, which fosters, at least among elites, a competition consciousness which can support holding big business accountable to power beyond itself. Reimagining American antitrust as a praxis – defined as a distinctive policy grammar and autonomous institutional regime promoting competition and accountability according to prescribed legal forms – suggests the instrumental and symbolic elements which were rejected in other nations prior to 1945 and which thereafter gradually spread around the world. But antitrust was reconstituted under Roosevelt's New Deal liberalism and immigrated abroad only after it acquired enough bureaucratic and symbolic autonomy to impose meaningful accountability within divergent capitalist systems. This study has explored antitrust's reception among government officials, business leaders, and legal-economic experts in America, Japan, Europe, and Australia during the Great Depression of the 1930s and World War II, the quarter century of growth following 1945, and the period of recurring boom and bust from the 1970s to the turn of the century. Ultimately, U.S. antitrust made weaker social groups such as labor, investors, consumers, small business, and agricultural producers increasingly dependent upon managerial capitalism's financial entrepreneurialism, whereas other antitrust regimes to varying degrees protected those groups even at the relative cost of big business's competitive advantage.

During the 1930s certain American managers adopted the multidivisional organizational structure that General Motors' Alfred Sloan had developed years earlier. This structure enabled managers to control the "creative destruction" inherent in capitalism as described by Schumpeter. One type of firm managed risk while presuming the market environment to be static. A second type of firm, epitomized by the multidivisional structure, pursued a strategy which approached risk in terms of a dynamic process. While such firms were exceptional even in the United States, even fewer were to be found in other industrial nations. Nevertheless, the Great Depression compelled business leaders, government authorities, and economic and legal experts around the world to support cartelization. While some legal or economic experts perceived the relative advantages of adopting the divisional structure versus cartels, the price, currency and tariff instability engendered by the Depression led – though only briefly in the United States under the New Deal's NRA – most government and business leaders to embrace cartelization as the means to ensure mass production and to maintain technological innovation. Meanwhile, Berle's and Means' influential study suggested that the divisional structure more than cartels facilitated the growing separation between owners and managers they dubbed a capitalist revolution.

New Dealers began reconstituting antitrust during 1937–38. In order to reshape New Deal liberalism amidst opposition from conservative business and political leaders and even many of Roosevelt's own supporters who continued to advocate business-government cooperation, Robert Jackson initiated a wide-ranging study of big business within the U.S. economy and around the world. Jackson exposed the degree to which technical financial arrangements, patent monopolies, and international cartels underlying the "capitalist revolution" made American consumers, workers, farmers, investors, and small business more dependent than ever on big business. The remedy, Jackson declared, was stronger antitrust enforcement recognizing the realities of American managerial capitalism rather than the old Brandeisian approach that bigness was bad. Roosevelt's Antimonopoly Message of 1938 endorsed Jackson's approach. That same year Roosevelt appointed Thurman Arnold to lead the Justice Department's Antitrust Division. By 1943 Arnold had reimagined antitrust, developing an activist two-pronged strategy. First, he advocated imposing accountability upon, rather than breaking up, big firms through repeated court litigation; second, he vigorously attacked international cartel behavior, particularly in the form of patent agreements. Even so, following Roosevelt's rhetorical lead, Arnold emphasized the threat "Fascism" (defined as bureaucratic planners imposing "a cartel system after the European model") posed to American capitalism in which consumption ameliorated the social conflict pitting labor, consumers, small business, and farmers against big business.

Elsewhere in the world, proponents of cartelization rejected American antitrust. Despite national variations such as those distinguishing the British and German legal systems, an indigenous European regulatory tradition recognized that business-government collaboration to reduce "excessive competition" could foster unfair trade practices or monopoly. In addressing these problems European commentators nonetheless opposed the American judicial-centered antitrust regime. Its reliance upon litigation disrupted the cooperative relationship between business and government. Also, by generally banning cartels, as the United States did except during wartime and temporarily under the NRA, the adversarial system encouraged the formation of large corporations through merger, which indirectly fostered U.S. multinational corporations' acquiring significant shares in a nation's most important private companies. Socialists welcomed this development as a prerequisite for nationalization. Government and business leaders in both totalitarian dictatorships and liberal democracies exclaimed, however, that American big business threatened national self-identity and sovereignty. Japanese militarists pursuing imperialist wartime expansion, as well as their socialist and liberal critics agreed. Australians did as well. Decades earlier, Australia had adopted antitrust legislation which drew upon the Sherman Antitrust Act as a defensive measure against American multinational corporations. During the 1930s Australians ignored this heritage, secure within their fully cartelized protectionist economy.

The Second World War transformed the international status of antitrust. During the war, the U.S. government incorporated antitrust into the Allied negotiations over Lend Lease and the creation of the liberal international trade order. Many commentators have linked this international antitrust activism to a wider argument explaining the liberal trade order's ascendancy in terms of global hegemony. The archival research presented above disputes such an argument by noting the following. Within the U.S. government, the Justice Department – and to a lesser degree Treasury officials – urged an activist antitrust policy toward international cartels, including particularly transfers of patented technology. Inside the State Department antitrust activists such as Corwin Edwards disagreed with Edward Mason and others who advocated an approach based on bureaucratic planning. Both groups favored establishing antitrust regimes in other nations and the International Trade Organization (ITO). However, the activists urged an antitrust regime centered on cartel and monopoly prohibitions which was more rigorous than even the contemporary U.S. model, whereas their opponents supported a less restrictive approach which included broad exemptions for commodity producers and technology transfers. The United States failed to pass the ITO, largely because Truman Administration officials failed to resolve how international antitrust enforcement might disrupt national support for cooperative commodity polices. Even so, the consensus Edwards and Mason shared on instituting national antitrust regimes abroad became postwar U.S. policy.

The U.S. antitrust campaign abroad led to ironic outcomes. In the Allied Occupation of western Germany, clashes within the U.S. occupational zone between antitrust activists and the military government's probusiness leaders, as well as administrative compromises among British, French, United States, and west German officials regarding the implementation of a U.S. style antitrust regime, resulted in all sides concluding that the U.S. effort had failed. Yet in later years European and U.S. commentators regularly attributed the emergence of the antitrust regime in west Germany to U.S.

pressure. The present study offers evidence showing that General Clay and other western military zone commanders delegated the responsibility for instituting an antitrust regime to certain anti-Nazi leaders, especially Ludwig Erhard, who in turn relied extensively on a small group of supporters, especially Ordo Liberals. Erhard's espousal of the social-market economy, transformed the weak German cartel-abuse regulatory tradition into the strong antitrust regime established in the Cartel Law of 1957. Thus, while contemporary observers adjudged the U.S.-inspired antitrust program to have been unsuccessful and subsequent observers perceived a direct or obscure U.S. force at work, the principle influence shaping the emergence of the west German antitrust regime was the western Allies' joint authorization of anti-Nazi groups promoting theories combining broad social-welfare and economic goals identified with the social market economy.

U.S. efforts to install antitrust took unintended turns elsewhere in western Europe. Jean Monnet – who possessed a general understanding of U.S. antitrust – supported Harvard Law professor Robert Bowie's accommodation of U.S. antitrust principles in the European Coal and Steel Community (ECSC). Monnet believed that promoting equal economic opportunity across national borders could create a common market enabling Europeans to compete successfully with the United States as well as overcome their tragic history of war and national identity politics. The consummation of this ideal in the European Economic Community rested to a certain extent on antitrust provisions, the terms of which drew from Bowie's amalgamation of U.S. and German principles in the Treaty of Paris and the prohibition-exemption system codified in the German Cartel Law of 1957. In addition, although the importance of U.S. pressure in the enactment of Britain's Antimonopoly Law of 1948 is disputed, clearly, that legislation and the Restrictive Trade Practices Act of 1956 rejected the litigation and civil damage system of the American antitrust model in favor of an administrative approach employing the pragmatic "reasonableness" standard more like that found in the European Community.

In Australia, the Lead-Lease negotiations and ITO drew attention to the country's long moribund antitrust law. This transient recognition of antitrust presaged constitutional law decisions, favoring individual economic liberty, and, then, the campaign Attorney General and "Radical Tory" Garfield Barwick launched for an antitrust law during the early 1960s. Enacted in 1965 and based on British precedents, the measure's practical impact was limited; it paved the way, however, for passage of the seminal Trade Practices Act of 1974 sponsored by Attorney General Lionel Murphy in Gough Whitlam's short-lived Labor Government. Under the Trade Practices Commission Chair, Roger Bannerman, a bipartisan political party consensus emerged supporting the law's policy objective of protecting consumers by promoting competition. Over the next 20 years the law's effective enforcement eliminated the naked horizontal and vertical price fixing which traditionally had characterized the Australian economy. The government's merger and antimonopoly policies sanctioned oligopolistic competition while ensuring against abuse imposed through market domination, thus benefitting labor, small business, and agricultural producers. During the 1990s and after the millennium Allan Fels and the Australian Competition and Consumer Commission (ACCC) pursued an innovative and successful antitrust enforcement campaign. Notwithstanding its early sanction of U.S. antitrust, Australians borrowed freely from the pragmatic British administrative approach and the postwar U.S. antitrust principles and theories of workable competition to create an indigenous antitrust regime suited to its unusual system of social-welfare capitalism.

The story in Japan was more complex. Japan clearly adopted the Anti-Monopoly Law of 1947 as a result of American demands during the postwar occupation. Yet, as Harry First and John Haley have shown, Japanese negotiators possessed a deeper understanding of U.S. antitrust principles than subsequent foreign or Japanese commentators have understood. This study explains why that could be so. A member of the Japanese team was Yazawa Atsushi, a young lawyer having connections with a small group of Japanese professors teaching American law in Tokyo University's famous Law Department, including Kenzo Takayanagi, who during the interwar years received legal training at Harvard and Northwestern universities. The leading Japanese negotiators drew upon Yazawa's extensive documentation and analysis of antitrust development from its origins up to Arnold's innovations. Like their west German counterparts, the Japanese exploited tensions underlying the U.S. position, enabling them to gain an advantage. During 1946–47 the Japanese weakened the cartel and antimonopoly provisions – but *strengthened* the unfair trade practices provisions – proposed by two successive American negotiators, Posey T. Kime and Lester Salwin. In addition, this wider perception of antitrust principles suggested to a few influential Japanese that the Anti-Monopoly Law could be used to support liberal economic values that had been quashed by the militarist government. These Japanese wanted to protect small business and to end family control of the *zaibatsu* companies. Some sought to provide a generation of younger managers with greater opportunity to advance within the big corporations, and to open up corporate ownership to Japanese shareholders.

Accordingly, the Antimonopoly Law of 1947 reflected a deeper engagement with Japanese interests and values than all but a few knew at the time or since. With the end of the Occupation in 1952, Japanese bureaucrats led by the Ministry of International Trade and Industry (MITI) dismantled most of the American-imposed governmental institutions. However, the Antimonopoly Law and the Fair Trade Commission (FTC) enforcing it persisted because small business and other opponents of the *zaibatsu* families – groups which subsequently were important constituents of the postwar political culture, especially the Liberal Democratic Party – defended the need for a limited antitrust regime. Accordingly, a weakened and always vulnerable FTC devoted its modest resources to protecting small business, particularly subcontractors working in the growing *keiretsu* system and shopkeepers who were central to the distribution system. A long recession during the 1990s ended the postwar "economic miracle," but the market dislocation resulted in the most effective antitrust enforcement since the Occupation. While the relational culture fostered co-operative conduct, the FTC's cartel prosecutions instituted a demand for more competitive markets; prosecutions of monopoly conduct, in conjunction with a more consistent merger policy, promoted greater competition within the *keiretsu*. Thus, because its supporters successfully adapted the Anti-Monopoly Law's enforcement to Japan's institutional culture, the FTC acquired a role indirectly promoting a Japanese capitalist order capable of challenging American global economic hegemony.

Meanwhile, after 1945 antitrust's impact on managerial capitalism's risk management increased in Europe. Following World War II European business – especially multinational corporations – persistently employed cartel behavior to manage market pressures. Even so, through the 1960s the dominance of U.S. big business and the multidivisional structure within the liberal trade order identified with the GATT, obscured the scope of cartel practices. Nevertheless, the European Community's Commission employed antitrust theory like workable competition to foster social welfare and economic efficiency, thereby integrating the common market on the basis of equal treatment. Once the Cold War ended antitrust remained essential within the expanding European Union, in part because the former communist states of the Soviet Empire and elsewhere became eligible for EU membership only if they met strict accession standards that included adopting effective antitrust regimes. Accordingly, general prohibitions against cartels and monopoly conduct, as well as stricter regulation of mergers, promoted competition in the European common market. Generally, the European Commission's policies protected smaller enterprise and labor while imposing accountability upon U.S. multinational corporations. These policies thereby contributed to overcoming the nationalism and totalitarianism Monnet opposed and began to achieve the improved competitive advantage of private companies and industries within the member states and the Community as a whole that he had envisioned.

The quarter century following 1945 witnessed the most effective antitrust enforcement in U.S. history. Within the postwar liberal consensus, antitrust officials employing theories such as workable competition won from the courts leading precedents like that established in the *Alcoa* case. Ultimately, antitrust activism limited horizontally structured market concentration in favor of financially managed conglomerate mergers.

Increasingly, too, government and private plaintiffs won damage actions on an unprecedented scale, disrupting not only domestic cartel practices but effectively attacking international cartel conduct through the multinational corporations headquartered within the United States. As a result, finance-oriented managers such as Harold Geneen of International Telephone and Telegraph Corporation (ITT) developed strategies leading to widespread diversification and conglomerate mergers. The second phase of postwar U.S. antitrust policy began during the 1970s and was still underway after the turn of the 21st century. The oil shocks of 1973 and 1979, together with the Hart-Scott-Rodino Antitrust Improvement Act of 1976, which insti-tuted a merger notification system, converged with the growing market impact of knowledge-based industries. During the 1980s, the antitrust authorities of Ronald Reagan's Republican administration applied Chicago economic theories to break up AT&T; but in cases involving the relation-ship between monopoly and oligopolistic competition they allowed mergers on the largest scale since the Great Merger Wave of 1895–1904.

From the 1990s to the turn of the century, successive Democratic and Republican administrations reinvigorated antitrust enforcement. U.S. antitrust officials attempted to counter a historic global merger wave and the proliferation of international cartels. In cooperation with antitrust authorities in several European nations and Japan and Korea, U.S. antitrust officials won a record $1.1 billion worth of fines in the *Arthur Daniels Midlands* and related *Vitamins* price-fixing cartel cases. After the millen-nium, in *Microsoft* and other cases the European Commission enforced even stronger antimonopoly and merger doctrines than their U.S. coun-terparts. The Australian Competition and Consumer Commission did so as well. In Japan the traditional power structure of big business, the LDP, and the government ministries reversed their long-standing opposition and supported, at least in principle, active antitrust enforcement. A significant result of this change was that MITI-successor, the Ministry of Economy Trade and Industry, limited its protectionist policies in many sectors in order to stimulate competition among big business – including for the first time since the Occupation significant mergers between Japanese and Eur-opean or U.S. automobile companies – which in turn increased the FTC's influence. The U.S. antitrust regime nonetheless continued to enforce nar-rower efficiency theories promoting consumerism as compared with the European Commission, the ACCC, and Japan's FTC, each of which endeavored to balance efficiency and broader welfare goals.

The postwar internationalization of antitrust promoted divergence within global capitalism. Social-market capitalism emerged in Europe and among British settler societies such as Australia, while Britain itself attempted to balance European and American capitalist systems. Japanese capitalism was based on a relational culture and unusual business-government collaboration which had parallels throughout East Asia and China. American capitalism remained, however, distinctive. From the 1970s on, the chronic cycle of bust and boom reflected the dominance of riskier entrepreneurial investment and diversification strategies resting upon policies of government deregulation and a public discourse enshrining values of market fundamentalism and efficiency. Central to the process of change was corporate restructuring through mergers, especially involving multinational corporations. The search for the means to impose accountability on multinational corporations tested cooperation among antitrust regimes. With the U.S.–Japan Structural Impediments Initiative of the early 1990s, antitrust officials in both nations endeavored to address anticompetitive conduct in the Japanese market. In the *Boeing/McDonnell-Douglas* case, European and U.S. antitrust authorities arrived at contrary outcomes concerning the proper balance between efficiency and social-welfare benefits in the global market for large commercial airplanes. The European Commission also refused to approve Honeywell's takeover of another U.S. company despite approval from U.S. antitrust officials. The Commission imposed, too, a stronger remedy in the Microsoft case.

Meanwhile, demands arose for some sort of global antitrust authority on the level of the WTO. Although the future of such an organization remained problematic during the millennium years, antitrust policy's traditional concern with curbing economic power – and not solely with the maintenance of narrowly defined market efficiency – had achieved global importance. U.S. proponents of trade unilateralism nonetheless opposed cooperation among antitrust regimes as well as giving the WTO antitrust jurisdiction; indirectly, antiglobalization activists did the same because they perceived the process to be captured by multinational corporations. Controversy over the WTO accentuated the ambiguous injury standards of trade and antitrust laws. The WTO's multilateral agreement structure authorized national antidumping measures as an exemption, which were widely used by the United States and others; antitrust laws had no such multilateral-basis unless and until the member states of the WTO sanctioned it. During the 1990s pressure grew to fashion a limited multilateral framework for some antitrust issues, such as hard-core cartels. The increased number of antitrust bilateral agreements and the growing interjurisdictional cooperation facilitated lodging multilateral antitrust jurisdiction in WTO. But despite a broad international consensus regrading the evils of cartels, by 2004 the United States rejected expanding WTO jurisdiction even along these lines. Nevertheless, the creation of antitrust regimes in nations as diverse as China and Fiji to facilitate WTO membership reaffirmed the forgotten consensus among postwar U.S. officials promoting national antitrust regimes which had thrived notwithstanding the ITO's demise.

These controversies exposed how difficult it was to expand the WTO's jurisdiction over private parties, the same issue which defeated the ITO. In the case of antidumping laws it was necessary only to show that an unfair trade practice "contributed" to material injury, defined as "harm which is not inconsequential, material, or unimportant." Antitrust law, by contrast, employed an injury standard based on reasonableness, which in certain cases required an even stricter *per se* rule or a substantial lessening of competition. Similarly, the use of pricing standards to prove legal violations was less rigorous under antidumping law than the antitrust laws. Also, in the United States, Section 301 of the trade laws sanctioned unilateral action to gain access to foreign markets. A showing that a foreign government's policies imposed an unreasonable burden impeding the entry of United States business into foreign markets was enough to trigger a Section 301 claim. By contrast, United States antitrust law permitted unilateral extra-territorial actions against private restrictive conduct occurring in a foreign market. Again, however, rules and policies rooted in a the particular institutional culture meant that higher injury standards and stricter pro-cedural requirements made it difficult to invoke extraterritorial antitrust as a trade remedy. Moreover, Japan's victory favoring Fuji over Kodak in 1997 suggested the potential for unintended outcomes even in the rare instance when the WTO's dispute resolution process could be formally turned to the uses of U.S. multinational corporations.

The debate about private conduct had further implications. Robert Hudac showed that during the four years following implementation of the WTO's strengthened dispute settlement system in 1995 the average number of cases doubled compared to that under the GATT from 1985 to 1995. Extending the WTO's jurisdiction to purely private cases would accelerate this process. But in legal terms the question was: what would be the source of the law the WTO might apply in a private dispute? In 2004 the WTO had no substantive antitrust law of its own to draw upon. Private parties sought, however, a neutral tribunal to settle international disputes. Such a system existed under Chapter 19 of the North American Free Trade Agreement. The system was established because Mexico and Canada doubted that U.S. officials would fairly apply their own antidumping law and, according to Hudac, it has effectively achieved reasonably objective outcomes. The tension between antitrust institutional culture and trade policy administration also reflected changing international business condi-tions influencing cartel and monopoly conduct. Since 1947 successive GATT rounds lowered trade barriers throughout the world, facilitating the integration of domestic markets into a global business order which none-theless remained rooted in the multinational corporation's host state. Thus among the unintended consequences of effective trade liberalization policies were private anticompetitive practices.

The immediate motivations driving a multinational corporation's resort to anticompetitive practices were case-specific, but broad organizational dynamics shaped the decision. The multinational corporation's dual legal personality – a collection of corporate divisional units or subsidiaries doing business in a host state's domestic market and abroad – encouraged a range of incentives which included competitive and cooperative market behavior. In addition, the multinational corporation maintained a unified operational strategy common to its distinct corporate units, yet each unit was bound by local laws of the sovereign state in which it did business. These organizational imperatives engendered a mix of short-term market pressures that could foster management's decision to pursue restrictive practices. Since the 1930s many managers of multinational corporations opted to pursue anticompetitive conduct linked to nationalistic politics, corruption, or other factors stimulating close affiliation between government officials and business in many domestic markets world-wide. Such pressures could impinge upon managers most directly when the business cycle was particularly unstable. Thus, international cartels were conspicuous during the Great Depression of the 1930s. Similarly, the two major oil-price shocks of the 1970's and the less-noticed one of 1990–91 encouraged multinational corporations to engage in the extensive private cartel arrangements which appeared in different markets around the world.

Focusing upon the means by which firms achieve administrative coordination highlights the imperatives shaping decisions concerning anticompetitive conduct. Thus whether managers are located in either of the two types of firms identified by Schumpeter, the organizational constraints which constitute the adaptive or reactive firm governs their response to market instabilities, including those which would present the pursuit of anticompetitive practices as a viable market strategy. Clearly, firms in the same industries confront the same changing market pressures but most managers resist the pressures to adopt restrictive business behavior. Isolating the inputs into the manager's process of administrative coordination across the firm's global and domestic operational units reveals the predominant market incentives at various points in the business cycle; it further clarifies how well the firm has adapted to changing technologies. During the Great Depression, and in the 1970s, these dynamics fostered widespread cartelization among large corporations engaged in international business. International cartel arrangements emerged again in the 1990s, no doubt influenced by the divergence between the so-called Old and New Economies which created strategic imperatives impinging upon the manager's decisional process. Most particularly, the ever-tightening linkages between the firm's asset base and the stock market, noted by Federal Reserve Board chairman Alan Greenspan, imposed upon executive managers the shortest-term accountability for long-term business strategy.

Contrasting global patterns of deregulation could exacerbate institutional pressures influencing a multinational corporation's anticompetitive behavior. Deregulation, of course, did not create a market vacuum altogether empty of formal rules. Instead, this reform effort to bring government's laws in line with market efficiencies usually substituted one regulatory regime for another. In the United States, direct bureaucratic or administrative control of a private firm's market conduct declined between the 1970s and the turn of the century; but the role of civil litigation as a regulatory device grew. Outside America, by contrast, deregulation generally involved the privatization of state-owned or managed enterprises; in many states it resulted in making illegal as antitrust violations private cartel and monopoly practices which public officials previously had tolerated or expressly sanctioned. Under each mode of deregulation, moreover, governments retained the lawful power to authorize certain forms of anti-competitive conduct in the public interest. Even after the East Asian financial crisis of 1997–98 ended, many important domestic markets had experienced little or no meaningful deregulation, while about half of the signatories to the WTO had no functional antitrust law. With such a diversity of rules and enforcement regimes impinging upon the multi-national corporation's operational strategy, it was not surprising that restrictive market behavior often occurred.

This multiplicity of institutional pressures could, however, encourage certain multinational corporations to favor deregulation or even stronger antitrust. By the 1990s, in America, Europe, Japan, and elsewhere, some leading big business interests advocated deregulation and antitrust; they did so in part because their global competitive advantage was threatened by the restrictive trade practices employed by other firms operating in the same market sectors. In addition, big business, in order to avoid criticism from consumer oriented nationalistic appeals, may strive vigorously to appear as corporate "good citizens." In contrary situations where big business's illegal or corrupt behavior has been revealed, an interest in regaining a "good corporate citizen" image may reinforce the operation of government leniency programs designed to encourage corporate managers to provide evidence in criminal and civil prosecutions of anti-competitive practices. The work of Australian John Braithwaite and others has recognized the need for fostering such behavior among big business through "responsive regulation" enforcing broad market and non-market incentives.

This study's focus within historical and comparative contexts on the divergent outcomes resulting from antitrust enforcement strategies promoting social welfare and efficiency confirms the value of the "responsive" policy approach. Since the 1930s, macroeconomic theories as well as nationalistic or utopian ideologies have rejected or ignored antitrust, in part because big business always seemed to have transcended the bounds of formal state sovereignty and thus seemed to have escaped the limits of any meaningful accountability. To remedy this problem, during World War II the U.S. antitrust activists pursued vigorous enforcement by instituting national antitrust regimes and the ITO. Although the ITO died, American antitrust entered its most active phase; antitrust regimes also emerged in

European nations and the European Community. Japan and Australia, too, embarked upon a distinctive course of instituting antitrust regimes. During the 1990s, the spread of antitrust bilateralism, discussions concerning its relation to the WTO and the adoption of indigenous antitrust regimes, as well as the persistent tension between antitrust culture and trade policy indicated a reaffirmation of the global accountability emerging from the earlier time.

Index

Acheson, D. 57–8
Adenauer, K. 276, 319
 advocates of European community 276.
 Federal Republic re-militarized within
  NATO 263
 Treaty of Paris
 US support 274
advance clearance of international
 cooperative agreements 38
 Donovan, W. 38
Agricultural Adjustment Act 19
Alcoa case 10
 A. W. and R. B. Mellon brothers 15
 decision 126
 extraterritorial effects/impact 33
 Montague, Gilbert 56
 multinational corporations 55
 outcomes of antitrust policy 122
 policy choice 123
Alien Property Custodian 41
Allied Occupation of Germany 1, 245, 396
 Allied Occupation and the Germans' own
  struggle over a cartel law 262
 German self-identity 268
 investigation 261
 Isseks, Samuel S. 261
 Morgenthau Plan 56
 Occupation's antitrust policy was more
  than a failure 262
 Pajus, J. 55
 Royall, Kenneth C. (US Army
  Secretary) 26
 Soviet Union's 45
Allied Occupation of Germany, 1945–1949
 246
 national antitrust regimes consensus
Allies' Occupation policy toward Germany
 and Japan 6, 41
 6 November 1945 SCAP issued a directive
  163
 1946 called the Industrial Order Bill
  163–83
 1946–47, drafting antitrust legislation and
  zaibatsu dissolution diverged 172

Allied antitrust program had failed 261
Americanized consumer economy 183
Bizone decartelization 257
Bizone laws: Standard of reasonableness
 258
Christian Socialists 248–54
condoned SCAP's "directive dissolve the
 zaibatsu 170
Controlling World Trade cartels and
 commodity agreement 255
decartelization JCS 1067 248–51
decartelization program 246
Deconcentration of Industry and
 Decartelization Group 259
dissolution of the zaibatsu 163
Dodge, Joseph M. 254
Edwards report 169
to establish an antitrust regime 163
evaluation of the decartelization progress
 252
French authorities 247
Foreign Exchange and Foreign Trade
 Control Act 1949 214
German cartels 247
German legal and economic experts 259
Germany's big business 248
holding companies 171, 260
Holding Company Liquidation
 Commission (HCLC) 166
Hoover, H. 258
image of postwar Japanese economic
 democracy 182
Industrial Order Bill 165–181
Japanese antitrust 160
Japanese war-crimes trails 165
JCS 1067 249–52
Josten Committee 257
Kronstein, H. indigenous antitrust policy
 258
Ministry of Commerce and Industry 167
New Deal's Public Utilities Holding
 Company Act (PUHCA) of 1935 171
Ordo Liberals 246, 248–9, 253–4, 257,
 261, 265, 267, 281

Allies' Occupation policy toward Germany
and Japan (*Cont.*)
pro-competition German policy market
247
pro-US business military command 246
regulation of cartel & monopoly abuses
247
rule of reason 4
Russian resistance 247
Special Survey Committee (SSC)/report
166–8
This protection of smaller enterprise 183
underlying values of economic democracy
160
Yasuda Plan 163–7
zaibatsu/dissolution/holding company/
study mission 83–90, 169
zealous trust busters 246
America 257, 394
1970s, corporate management's
investment strategy 137
1987 stock market crash 142
absence of state ownership 104, 250
America big business 108
America's consumer culture 136
America's declining international
competitiveness 136
American consumer culture's
interdependence with foreigners 142, 254
American liberal consensus/
"triumphalism"/images of triumphalism
140
Americans/capitalism 400
anti-competitive practices
Antitrust lawyers 119
capitalist economies 113–36
conglomerates/merger wave ended by 1974
131
deregulation 103–49, 226, 403
diversification of foreign-based
corporations/investments strategies 143
Effective cooperation among antitrust
regimes 151
electrical equipment litigation 112
From the 1990s antitrust enforcement 400
global antitrust authority 401
Jim Crow labor system 110
Justice Department's cases involving
multinational corporations jumped 1993
and 1997 151
laxity toward mergers 147
Lend-Lease negotiations and ITO 397
liberal pluralism 124
managerial capitalism's legitimacy within
Cold War liberalism 115, 143
Market Fundamentalism 103–44
mergers 121
multi-divisional corporation's impact on

domestic and global markets 141
multinational corporation's 114
New Deal culture and institutional
settlement 103, 137–8
New Left's/radical discourse 145
per se rule against cartel practices 121
postwar liberal consensus 399
private suits 112, 114
stagflation 136–40
Supreme Court's use Brown decision of
1954 115
take-over strategy 141
US-Japanese trade dispute 144
US multinational firm's subsidiary 110
Workers 143
Americanization 1, 393
American challenge 113, 284
American lobbying practices 303
Antimonopoly Law of 1947 2, 58, 160,
179–98, 398
1947 Japanese negotiators 177
1953 amendments 185
alien to Japan's cooperative culture 16
Amendment of 1977 203–26
Antimonopoly Law reversal of position
210
Antimonopoly Law revisions did not pass
1958 153, 188
antimonopoly policy reconstituted the
relation between big and small business
198
bengoshi industrial policy and the
Antimonopoly Law 208
Cold War first amendment to the
Antimonopoly Law in 1949 180–94
consumers 208–30
exemption-authorization process 183
fate of Kishi's assault on the Antimonopoly
Law 184
"first criminal accusation" 202
foreign and Japanese "revisionist" critics
179
foreign pressure favoring antimonopoly
policy 212–16
FTC increasing considered merger action
FTC's protecting "weak suppliers
subcontractors 186
German precedent for 202
higher civil & criminal fine 228
holding company/ban 182
ideals of a peace loving Japanese nation
committed 179
image of postwar Japanese economic
democracy 182
implementing the Antimonopoly Law
revisions proposed in 1958 184
independent antitrust enforcement
commission under the Prime Minister 174

Japanese antitrust's ambiguities of foreign pressure 212
Japanese drafters were well prepared to confront SCAP officials in the negotiations 162
Japanese negotiators 176–82
Japanese surcharge system 202
Keidanren switched to advocation of vigorous enforcement of antimonopoly policy 206
Kime draft 173–4, 177–8, 181–2
mergers, acquisitions and technology transfers 179–98
motivations driving the FTC's enforcement 181
Noda Soy Sauce case (1955) 193
new attitude 196
new Constitution and 179
outlawing of holding companies 187
petroleum cartel cases 203
petroleum cartel private suits 203
This protection of smaller enterprise 183
required consultation between MITI and the FTC 183
SSC Report 182
supported the FTC's amendment proposals strengthening the surcharge system 202
Takahashi's proposals had significant political ramifications 201
US and Japanese enforcement regimes private action 229
Yawata-Fuji Merger case 194
zaibatsu restructuring through merger, acquisitions 186
Antimonopoly message of 1938 2, 17
Antimonopoly Study Committee 9
antitrust 1, 103–16, 160, 393
1990s antitrust enforcement 114, 400
ACCC's strict merger enforcement 374
advanced clearance of international investments 107
Airtours 307
Alcoa 10
Allan Fels' Enforcement Activism 366
American antitrust 324
American Microsoft decision 306
American-style antitrust 60, 393
antitrust and trade policies evolved separately/ sometimes converged 107
Antitrust and trade policy sometimes converged 282
antitrust competition consciousness 394
antitrust exemption/antitrust exemption for organization labor 129
antitrust in international business/ internationalization 126
antitrust instrumental outcomes 394
antitrust's patent and merger policies 22

antitrust regimes' enforcement objectives 109, 392
articulated his activist enforcement program 200
AT&T 139
attack on conglomerate mergers through extensive divestiture 137
Australia's abandoned antitrust heritage 75, 324
Australia New Zealand harmonization antitrust regimes 376
Australian Competition and Consumer Commission (ACCC) 373
bilateral agreements\antitrust agreements 129–58
blocking laws and 128
Boeing/McDonnell Douglas case 297, 401
Böhm and Eucken 67, 253–305
Boral case abusing dominant market position 388
Bowmen, Ward 121
Brandeisian philosophy 131
Britain's Restrictive Trade Practices Act of 1956 320–6
Brunt, M. favoring workable competition 321
Brunt's study assessing the private action 1974–1988 116, 345, 354
capture by big business 118
cartel and monopoly regulation/controls/ EEC/practices 62
cartels per se illegal 62
Celler, E. 293
Celler-Kefauver Amendment/of 1950 132
Chicago law and economics theories 122–48
closed the merger loop-hole, section 7a of the Clayton Antitrust 132
Cohen, Ruth L. 73, 323
Commission's Microsoft decision 306
Commission's trade and antitrust policies 291
competition consciousness 4, 245
competition policy economic theories 307
competition policy in Europe and the United States 313
confidential information 295
confidentially issue transnational cooperation 295
conglomerates/merger wave ended by 1974 112–31, 133–37, 305
consent decree 15
contestable market 148
Continental Can 288
cooperation imposed accountability in international cartel cases 296
cooperative EU-US enforcement culture 309

antitrust (*Cont.*)
 corporate "good citizens" versus "cowboys
  112, 287
 corporate take-over investment strategy
  319, 375
 corporate takeovers in the Rank case 378
 difference between British and the
  American antitrust 326
 differing policy goals of European and
  United States antitrust 304
 diversification or conglomerate mergers
  112, 400
 DuPont 126
 DuPont/ICI 51
 EEC textile firms 248–54, 282
 electrical equipment litigation 112–32
 enforcement sensitive to diverse business
  motivations 374
 extraterritorial impact 33
 extraterritorial jurisdiction 126, 233
 EU goal of market integration 305
 EU-US difference merger regulation
 EU-US divergence 305
 European Commission's enforcement of
  multiple competition policy goals 314
 foreign pressure favoring antimonopoly
  policy 212
 GE/Honeywell and Microsoft 298–307
 German cartel regulation 63
 Globalization of Antitrust since the 1970s
  145
 Hawk, Berry E. (New York commercial
  lawyer) 300
 Hilmer Report supported the workable
  competition 114, 374
 Hofstadter, Richard 119
 holding company 63
 "horizontal and vertical mergers" 112, 241
 IBM-RCA 130
 images of corporate America's
  accountability 134
 industries prone to price-fixing 337
 Iranian oil 128, 373
 international antitrust regime 75, 324
 International Competition Network 299
 International Telephone and Telegraph
  Corporations 396
 internationalizing antitrust/enforcement
  128
 ITO's antitrust provisions 107
 Japan's antitrust reversal in the public
  stance toward competition policy 160
 Japanese bureaucrats' industrial policy it
  always evolved in relation to
  competition policy 161
 Japanese multinational corporation 76,
  297
 Justice Department's cases involving

multinational corporations jumped 1993
 and 1997 151
Kali und Salz 294
Kefauver, Estes 123
Keidanren switched to advocation vigorous
 enforcement of antimonopoly policy
 215–16
limiting vertical monopolistic restraints
 131
meaning of competition 105
mergers/mergers and abuse of dominance
 121, 39–146
mergers and consolidations 164
Merger Guidelines of 1968 133
Merger Regulation 293–4, 400
merger test and court-enforced
 undertakings 114, 372
Microsoft cases 212
modernization-reformers 308–11
multinational antitrust regime proposed
 under the WTO 298
multinational corporation's dual legal
 personality 402
multinational corporations' use of
 subsidiaries 127
national and international diversification
 investment strategies 146
Neal, Philip 131
New Dealers reconstituting antitrust
 1937–38 395
Ordinance of 1923 64
Ordo Liberals 248–7
patent licensing agreements 126
patent pools and cross-licensing system
 164
patented technology 127
patents 28, 109
per se rules and a rule of reason 28, 164,
 327
per se rule against cartel practices 121
Pflanz, Matthias 304
Philip Morris (1987) 293
Petro, Sylvester 122
policy objectives of "social justice 380
policy dispute grew among antitrust
 professionals 147
Polish Monopoly Office 310
positive comity 158, 233
postwar internationalization of antitrust
 400
postwar liberal consensus 399
price-fixing agreements 139
price or non-price vertical restraints 147
principle of accountability 3
Private actions 132, 229, 311, 353
private antitrust plaintiffs 402
protectionist pressures tested the EEC 283
Queensland Wire Industries endors 366

radical nor conservative business critiques 118

Reagan Antitrust Division/officials 147

"reciprocity" 133

reconstituted antitrust 8

Redfern case 355

rejected American antitrust 3, 395

"restorative" strategy North Queensland Aboriginals case 371

Richardson, J. E. 326

rule of reason/to allow a territorial vertical restraint 3, 48, 105, 260

Schlitz Brewing Co., 47, 114

selectively exempting international firms 116

Separating the trade and antitrust policy 154

Social-market capitalism 400

social welfare incentives for private actions 354

societal accountability 110

Singer 114, 213

small business values 325

Stark, Charles (of the US Antitrust Division "positive comity") 158

Stocking, George W.

structure-conduct-performance analysis 130

take-over strategy 141

technical assistance 308

tensions between trade and antitrust authorities 154

Thurman Arnold's activist antitrust philosophy 104

Timken 130

Tokyo an international conference on the global economy 199

trade and antitrust policy coincided 292

trade policy and antitrust interacted to promote EEC integration 282

Trade Practices Act's enforcement regime 345

trade-related competition policy 300

transnational antitrust cooperation ACCC's enforcement regime 389

transnational antitrust enforcement/regime 390

transnational cooperation/among antitrust authorities 295–302

Treaty of Rome's negotiations regarding the antitrust provisions 279

Treaty of Rome's principal antitrust provisions were Articles 85 and 86 280

Turner, O. 133

Twentieth Century Fund 116

underlying values of economic democracy 160

US antitrust tradition 62

US extraterritorial antitrust actions 128

US/EC Antitrust Agreement of 1991 James Rill of the US Justice Department's 295

US-EU enforcement cooperation 312

US merger doctrine reflecting "efficiency" theories and the European "market domination" theory 153

US multinational corporations 128–34

US Robinson-Patman Act of 1936 326

Antitrust Activism 24, 104–32, 165, 248, 399

after Pearl Harbor 41

ALCOA "effects" theory 131

Arnold's authorization of the more centralized investigation of wartime international cartels 42

budget appropriations 24

"cartel and patent system" 42

consent decree 35

Controlling World Trade Cartels and Commodity Agreement 58

Dupont and National Lead 51

high budget appropriations 41

Imperial Chemical Industries (ICI) 42

"international cartel movement" 33–4

international antitrust regime 46

Montague, Gilbert 56

patent and cartel agreements 28–37

policy choice 76

private suits 112

recapitulated the national-identity imagery Arnold and Roosevelt 164

Sherman Antitrust Act of 1890 76

Antitrust at War 40–9

Apex Hosiery 30, 323

Archer-Daniels Midland (ADM) antitrust litigation 150, 324

Ariga, Mishiko 179–96, 324

antimonopoly substantive doctrines comparable to foreign practice 196, 213

unfair business practice 193

Arnold, Thurman 2, 58, 104–20, 395

Arnold/prosecution 37

after Pearl Harbor 41

agreement 5

Antitrust Division's annual congressional budget appropriation 26

authorization on April 29, 1941, requiring certification and postponement of antitrust violations 40

budget appropriations 24

centralized investigation of wartime international cartels 42

consent decree 15

contemplated resigning 37

German emigres 67

high budget appropriations 41

international cartel movement 33

Justice Department oversight 38

Arnold, Thurman (*Cont.*)
  March 20, 1942, Roosevelt 40
  and mobilizing America's Defenses 32
  New Dealers reconstituting antitrust 1937–
    38 395
  Roosevelt's elevation of Arnold to the
    federal court in 1943 41
  US multinational corporations 34
Asher, Allan 361–92
  Australia's consumer movement 370
  Fels Asher for strong competition policy
    enforcement 379
  Fels embraced Asher's innovative
    enforcement strategies 368
  reshaping enforcement by focusing on
    outcomes 361
  Toshiba Australia agreement 362
Ashino, H. 183–7
  Antimonopoly Law Amendment of 1953
    German regulatory tradition 187
  fate of Kishi's assault on the Antimonopoly
    Law 184
  FTC commissioner 183–8
  FTC's protecting "weak suppliers
    subcontractors 51, 186
  Medium and Small Scale Enterprises
    Organization Law of 1957 186
  outlawing of holding companies 187
  technology transfers monitored by the FTC
    187
  zaibatsu restructuring through merger,
    acquisitions 186
AT&T 400
Attlee, Clement 249–73
Attorney General Francis Biddle 40
Attorney General Homer Cummings 14
Australia 60, 315, 394–7
  ACCC's strict merger enforcement 374
  ACCC's authority over unions 383
  Australia's consumer movement 370
  Australia's international competitive
    position 340
  Australia's multinational corporations 375
  Australia's protectionist regime 320
  Australia's social-class radicalism and
    egalitarianism 78
  Australia's social-welfare capitalism
    ACCC's role 381
  Australian attitudes to competitiveness
    377
  Australian big business and multinational
    corporations 316
  Australian Competition and Consumer
    Commission 312
  Australian competition consciousness 377
  Australian Council of Trade Unions
    (ACTU) 339
  Australian Federation of Consumer

Organizations (AFCO) 360
Australian Industrial Preservation Act
  [AIPA] of 1906 322
Australian "mateship" mentality 355
Braithwaite, John, ("responsive
  regulation") 322, 404
British Dominions of Australia and
  Canada 76
British policy 321
Broken Hill Proprietary Co. (BHP) 316
Brunt, Maureen 322
business' competition consciousness 390
Chicago School of economics 349
Coles and Myer 364
competition a means of reducing economic
  power 319–22
competition consciousness 355–91
Conservative/party 60
corporate takeovers in the Rank case 378
Country Party 328
deregulation of telecommunications
  Telstra 356–86, 403
Effective cooperation among antitrust
  regimes 151
Foreign Companies (Takeovers) Act 341
From the 1990s antitrust enforcement 400
global competitive advantage 356–76
good corporate citizens 375
Grabosky, Peter 357
growing postwar trade status 328–49
High Court's judge Owen Dixon 318
Hilmer Report supported the workable
  competition 322–32, 374
Hunter, Alex 317–21
inquiry into mergers, takeovers, Griffiths
  Committee 363
internationalizing antitrust enforcement
  322–76
John Braithwaite's study Australian
  regulatory agencies 357
Judge Isaac Isaacs 332
Karmel, Peter 317
labor-capital settlement 315
labor-capitalist compromise in the
  arbitration system 317
Labor government's micro-economic
  (reform) policies 357
Labor government's microeconomic
  reforms Hilmer Committee 373
late-1980s liberal trade polices 356
Lend-Lease negotiations and ITO 397
McEwen, John, (Country Party Leader)
  329
merger outcomes 364
merger test and court-enforced
  undertakings 372
Merrett, David, (business historian) 377
microeconomic reform 315–45

modern liberal conservatism 324
protectionist discourse mateship 320
protectionist visions of competition 321
Redfern opinion 322
small business price fixing 375
strong desire for self-sufficiency 356
strong small business 357
Swanson Committee's addressed small
  business, labor exemption, export/
  imports, corporate takeovers 348
system of imperial preference 61
transnational antitrust enforcement 390
Uniform Companies Act of 1961 317–20,
  318
Walker, G. de Q. 334
waterfront confrontation of 1997-98/
  settlement 381
"white Australia" 76
Whitlam's policies targeted middle-class
  voters 340
workable competition 321
Workplace Relations Act of 1996 381

Baker, Donald I. 146
Bannerman, R. 315, 331–4
  Australian antitrust regime 355
  Australian "mateship" mentality 334
  Bannerman (Commissioner of Trade
    Practices) economic theory/educational
    and public relations efforts/use of
    consultation and registration 334
  Bannerman achievable objective the
    survival of the Act 384
  Bennett, H. Trevor 325
  Chairman 335–55
  competition consciousness 355
  enforcement of law against secondary
    boycotts 338
  fiberboard containers case 337
  frozen vegetables case 337
  industries prone to price-fixing 342
  Parliamentary constituency supporting
    342
  prohibit RPM 339
  Rattigan, A. 335
  Richardson, J. E. 339
  Rocla Concrete Pipes case of 1971 339
  Tariff Board 345
  Trade Practices Act's enforcement
    regime/Tribunal decided 334–8
  Tradestock – Freight Forwarders 355
  Swanson Committee's proposed 347
Baruch, Bernard 37
  War Industries Board in World War I 37
Barwick, Garfield 315–19, 323–4
  American antitrust 324–7
  Australian lawyers 323

Barwick (Chief-Justice of the High Court
  of Australia)/proposals 327
Barwick and Murphy 350
Bennett, H. Trevor 326
British administrative approach 325
British Restrictive Trade Practices Act of
  1956 326
cartels 325
consumer interests were equivocal 330, 342
Constitution's guarantee of interstate free
  trade 331
constitutions corporations and commerce
  powers 319
difference between British and the
  American antitrust 326
Dixon's dissenting opinions 319
economic liberty 315–19
exploitation of small business 328
on the High Court of Australia 350
limited criminal prosecution 331
mergers or take-overs 332
modern liberal conservatism 324
pragmatic 325
proposals endorsed 331
Redfern opinion 322
Richardson, J. E. 76
small business values 325
smaller enterprises 324, 335
split within the conservative party 329
theory of workable competition 324
Baxter, William 139–47, 328
  ABA Task Force report 147
  entrenched the Chicago free market
    theories 147
  laxity toward mergers 147
  mergers 139
  price-fixing agreements 139
  Reagan administration antitrust officials
    147
Beck, Joseph 277
  Treaty of Rome 277
Bell, P. 3
Bell, R. 3
Berge, Wendell 41
Berle, A. A. 12
  capitalist revolution 110
  "corporate conscience" 115
  New Deal settlement 115
  "social responsibility" 115
  societal accountability 110
  US multinational firm's subsidiary 62
Berle, Adolf A., and Means, Gardiner C. in
  their classic 109
Berle's and Means capitalist revolution 13
Black, H. 19
Boeing/McDonnell Douglas case 152
  European Commission and the FTC
    disagreed 152

Bone committee's examination of
    patents 40
Borah, E. 20
Bork, R. 123–46
    The Antitrust Paradox 146
    Antitrust Task Force 131
    Bowmen, W. 124
    international antitrust cases 323–6
    Law and Economics program 122
    outcomes of antitrust policy 122
    structure-conduct-performance analysis
        130
    switched course in favor of Bork's vigorous
        condemnation of the conglomerate
        prosecutions 146
    University of Chicago's 52–4, 122
Bowie, R. 272, 397
    Adenauer's agreement and Hallstein two
        Treaty antitrust Articles 275
    antitrust provisions 273
    Ball, G. 273
    Bowie worked principally with Monnet
        and Walter Hallstein 273
    Clay's rule of reason 274
    McCloy, John J. 120
    Mason's antitrust theories 274
    Paris Treaty's antitrust provisions in article
        65 274
    Paris Treaty Article 65 patterned after
        Erhard's controversial Cartel Bill
        274
    Paris Treaty's other competition provision,
        Article 66 274
    Willner, Sydney 246
    US support 274
Brandeis, Louis 8, 123
Bretton Woods 49, 131
Brewster, Kingman 122–5
    Antitrust and American business Abroad
        125
    antitrust internationalization 3
    collaboration with economists 120
    international antitrust 124–5
    international business seminar 125
    outcomes of antitrust policy 122
    repeal of the antitrust exemption for US
        export firms 125
Broken Hill Proprietary Co. Ltd. [BHP] 60,
    77, 315
Brown Shoe/case 106
    ALCOA "effects" theory 2, 133–5, 315,
        400
Buchanan, Patrick J. 145
    WTO constituted the "Great Betrayal"
        145
Bush administration 142
Byrnes, James 52, 255
    decartelization in 4-D 255

capitalist system 4, 394
    absence of state ownership 104
    Allen, G. C. 80
    America's declining international
        competitive 136
    American/administrative state/capitalism/
        Keynesian image of liberal-democratic
        capitalism 75, 102
    Australian economy 76
    broader labor arbitration 77
    Business-government 104
    capitalist economies 113
    conflict 104
    deregulation policies varied among nations
        139, 386
    European welfare capitalism 245–314
    family capitalism 79
    fascist images of capitalism 60
    global corporate diversification 140
    "good" and "bad" capitalist enterprise 65
    hegemony 102
    holding companies 79
    idea of "middle way" to Japan 190
    images of corporate America's
        accountability 134
    internationalizing antitrust 128
    inter-war period 76
    Japanese/small and big business 79
    Keidanren's "Deregulation Promotion
        Plan" 204
    Keynesian economics and social welfare
        liberalism 61
    labor capital settlement 317
    managerial capitalism's legitimacy within
        Cold War liberalism 115
    Matsuoka, Y. 101
    multinational corporate sectors subsidizing
        the less efficient, protected ones 205
    New Deal culture and instutional
        settlement 103
    patent licenses 109
    Protectionist visions of liberal system 321
    rather than maximizing profits 111
    social-class struggle 62
    Social market economy 246
    US/ antitrust policies/ multinational
        corporations/ multinational firm's
        subsidiary 110
    Weakening of the holding company ban
        231
    zaibatsu/bounded competition/control
        disputed/family capitalism/family
        holding companies 57
Carolene Products Co 104
cartel 60–3, 325, 395
    America's declining international
        competitiveness 68
    Australian business 315

Blakemore, Thomas 81
Britain's national cartel and monopoly 68
capitalist consciousness 314
cartel controls 64
Compulsory Cartels law 64
demand for short-term profitability 142
Einzig, P. 64–70
Excessive competition 395
Export Cooperatives Law and the
  Significant Exporting Products Industry
  Cooperative Law 73–80
Federation of British Industries (FBI) 68
Federation of German Industries 64
FBI's "industrial self-government 69
Fujita Keizo 82
German cartel regulation 63
German legal and economic experts 259
industrial self-government 73
industries prone to price-fixing 337
labor-capitalist compromise in the
  arbitration system 317
MacGregor, D. H. 70
Mobilization Law of 1938 90
"new" German cartel policy 18
new order in Europe 66
Ordinance of 1923 64
patents 5
protectionist regime 77
protectionist visions of competition 54
regulation of cartel monopoly abuse 2,
  247
Toshiba Chemicals 236
trade associations 39
US competitive position in relation to
  Europe and Pacific rim nations 143
Uyeda Teijiro 82
Cartel Committee 43
  Acheson, D. 43
  "Allegations Concerning Cartel Matters"
    44–53
  Clayton, W. 43
  Committee's internal reports on
    international cartels confirmed 44
  competition policy regime 47
  Cox, H. 43
  "Crushed Reich Pins Hope on Cartels" 54
  Executive Committee on Economic Foreign
    Policy 52
  distinction between Commodity
    Agreements and Cartels 47
  distinguishing commodity or patent
    agreements from cartels 49
  "German cartel system" 46
  investment and technology transfers 44
  New Economic Order 47
  A Positive International Cartel Program 44
  Positive Program 53
  Taylor, M. 45

Cartel Law of 1957 89, 397
  German big business 247
cartel/issue/practices
  Blakemore,Thomas L. 319
  cartel and monopoly regulation 62
  cartels EEC/practices 288
  Compulsory Cartels Law 64
  distinction between Commodity
    Agreements and Cartels 47
  excessive competition 183
  Fujita Keizo 82
  German cartel regulation 63
  industrial self-government 62
  Mobilization Laws of 1938 61
  Ordinance of 1923 64
  patent licenses 29
  per se rule against cartel practices 121
  price fixing 112
  rationalization 62
  rejected American antitrust 395
  Significant Industries Control Law of 1931
    81
  Treaty of Romes's negotiations regarding
    the antitrust provisions 279
  US antitrust policies 11
  Uyeda Teijiro 82
  wartime control system and the zaibatsu's
    dominance 160
  "wasteful" labor disorder and class
    conflict 62
Carter administration 139–46
Chamberlin, E. H. 13, 121
  imperfect oligopolistics competition
    121
Chandler, Alfred 1, 393
Charles de Gaulle 284
  "American challenges" 288
China 16
  Colegrove, Kenneth W. 98
  Fujihara, G. 99
  Japan's imperialist 98
Churchill, W. 248
Citron, William M. 19
Clay, General 397
  4 D's 249
  advising German cartel & State antitrust
    agencies 260
  Bizone decartelization policy 257
  Bronson, Richardson 260
  common decartelization program: Bizone
    policy 256
  Dodge, Joseph M. 254
  deconcentrating German business 254
  German opinion 257
  March 1948, turning point in US antitrust
    policy 259
  Occupation's anti trust policy was a more
    than a failure 262

Clay, General Lucius 56, 247
  JCS 1067 W115 JCS 1779 258
Clayton, W. 58
Clinton administration 142
  images of US triumphalism 142
Cohen, B. 13
Cold War 102, 110, 113, 115, 125–8, 135–6,
    158, 180–1, 227, 245–6, 271, 316
  1949, created the Federal Republic of
    Germany 261
  American challenge 111–13
  antitrust in international business 126
  capitalist economies 113
  defeat in Vietnam 136
  eliminating restrictive business practices
    129
  ending of the Cold War intensified global
    economic rivalry 227, 290
  European/Political Community/Defense
    Community failed 113
  German Democratic Republic 261
  Iranian oil 128
  internationalizing antitrust 128
  Japanese 113
  Kalijarvi, Thorsten V. 129
  least risky strategy 111
  market share 111
  "national programs 129
  NATO shifted Cold War defense costs to
    the United States 275
  New Deal settlement 115
  profit maximization was secondary 111
  rather than maximizing profits 111
  Supreme Court's use Brown decision of
    1954 115
  Treaty of Brussels to NATO 276
  UN's competition consciousness 129
  US multinational corporations 128
  Western Germany's Treaty of Brussels 276
Colegrove, Kenneth W. 168
Columbia Steel 131
consumer groups 191
  Japanese Civil Code's general tort
    provision, Section 709 191
Corcoran, T. 21
Corning Glass company 29

Dewey, Thomas E. (Republican Governor)
  55
Donald, D. 148
  outcomes of antitrust policy 122
  policy choice 123
  policy dispute grew among antitrust
    professionals 147
Douglas, William O. 14, 131
Dow Chemical 34
Dower, John W. 162

antitrust to the promotion of democratic
  economic opportunity 162
Drucker, P. 111–18
  multi-divisional form 118
  take-over strategy 141
  Profit maximization secondary 111
DuPont 12, 106–8
  diversification investment strategy 109
  M-form 108
  multi-divisional organization 108

Economic Community (EEC) 279
economic experts 60
economic theories 5
  ambivalent deregulation policies 149
  antitrust in international business 126
  attack on conglomerate merges 131
  capture by big business 118
  Chicago economics/theories 124, 304
  Chicago law and economics theories 122
  Chicago School of Economics 6, 349
  Christian socialist 248–54
  competition policy economic theories 307
  conservatism of the Australian judiciary
    349
  cultural and institutional distinctiveness 144
  deregulation policies varied among nations
    139, 160
  efficiency discourse 138
  EU goal of market integration 305
  EU US differences 134–44, 304
  Fels' rejection of Chicago economic
    theories 367
  global competitive advantage 376
  Hilmer Report supported the workable
    competition 374
  IMF's Washington consensus 143
  imperfect oligopolistics competition 121
  institutional economic theories 393
  international markets 149
  John Kenneth Galbraith calls a
    technostructure 284
  Josten committee 257
  Keynesian economics 367
  Keynesian or Chicago macroeconomic
    theories 393
  marginal-cost theory 139
  market-centered discourse 135
  market efficiency 138, 257
  market fundamentalism 103
  Marxist theories 26
  meaning of competition 105
  Michael Porter's idea 376
  "middle-course" policy towards
    competition 133
  middle way 190
  multi-divisional form 118

Ordo Liberals 253–4, 257, 261, 265, 267,
    281
outcomes of antitrust policy 122
Petro, S. 122
policy choice 123
Queensland Wire Industries endors 365
racial unrest 136
radical nor conservative business critiques
    118
risk 2, 393
stagflation 136
Stocking, George W. 121–4
structure-conduct-performance analysis
    130
workable competition/theories
    121–37
economic theory 121
    Böhm Franz 253
    competition a means of reducing economic
        power 322
    Freiburg "School" 75, 254
    historical economists 62
    imperfect competition 13
    industrial self-government 62
    institutional economics 13
    Keynesian economics and social welfare
        liberalism 61
    laissez-faire 62–70
    Matsuoka, Y. 101
    middle way 175
    rationalization 62
    regulatory capture or arbitrage 102
    theory of workable competition 324,
        396
    wasteful" labor disorder and class conflict
        62
Edwards, C. 59, 168–98, 287
    1946–47, drafting antitrust legislation and
        zaibatsu dissoluation diverged 172
    cartels EEC 287
    Henderson, James M. 172
    Mission's report 169
    patents 28
    SSC report 169
    Zaibatsu 169
Edwards, C. 396
    antitrust internationalization 124
    British-America trade negotiations 74
    Controlling World Trade Cartels and
        Commodity Agreement 58
    ideological barriers 126
    international status of antitrust 396
    international students 124
    Lend-Lease negotiations and ITO 397
    multinational corporation's 125
    UN's 125
    zaibatsu study mission 167
Eisenhower/administration 133

Celler-Kefauver Amendment of 1950
    131
    limiting vertical monopolistic restraints
        131
Enron scandals 148
Erhard, L. 265–6
    Association of Germany Industry (BDI)
        263
    Böhm and Eucken 263–4
    Christian Democratic Union 263
    Christian Social Union 263
    election of 1957 268
    Eucken, W. 257
    Federal Republic re-militarized within
        NATO 263
    Guenther, E. 266
    German Opinion 257
    German public opinion 263
    Hitler's Germany 270
    images of cartel law 263
    Josten Committee included 265
    Josten, P. 257
    Müller-Armack, A. 265
    Ordo Liberals 263–5
    Social Democratic Party 263
    social-market economy 265
European Coal and Steel/Community(ECSC)
    397
    1951 Treaty of Paris 270
    antitrust provisions 273
    Articles 65 and 66 of the Treaty of Paris
        272
    Ball, G. 267, 273
    Bowie worked principally with Monnet
        and Walter Hallstein 273
    Erhard's 273
    Diebold, W. 274
    French 270
    German Big Business 247
    Germans 270
    Hallstein's views comported with
        Adenauer 273
    Hitler Germany 270
    Monnet faced oppositions from Charles de
        Gaulle 273
    Monnet neutralized the anti-US sentiments
        272
    Paris Treaty's antitrust provisions in article
        65 242
    Paris Treaty Article 65 patterned after
        Erhard's controversial Cartel Bill 274
    Paris Treaty's other competition provision,
        Article 66 274
    Raymond Vernon noted 272–6
    US influence 270–4
    Willner, S. 273
European Commission 245, 400
    abuse of dominance United Brands 289

Index

European Commission (*Cont.*)
  Adenauer's agreement and Hallstein two
    Treaty antitrust Articles 275
  Airtours decision Legrand Tetra
    Laval 297
  American Microsoft decision 297–306
  anti-dumping policy operation strategies of
    multinational corporations 292
  antitrust agreement under the WTO 304
  antitrust within the EEC's policy making
    process 281
  authority to implement equal treatment
    toward business 286
  Boeing/McDonnell Douglas case 297
  Bosch De Geus 251–86
  Cartel behavior and Regulation 17 287
  Charles Stark of the US Antitrust Division
    "positive comity 295
  Commission employed equal treatment 285
  Commission's Microsoft decision 306
  Commission's trade and antitrust policies
    291
  competition, subsidiarity 311
  competition policy 246
  Continental Can 288
  cooperation imposed accountability in
    international cartel cases 389
  Deringer, Arved 281
  equal treatment 312
  equal treatment within Common Market
    287
  Elf/Enterprise (1991) 293
  employment and the related immigration
    tensions 287
  enforcing the EU's core goals and
    modernization 308–13
  Ericsson/Kolbe 294
  EU Merger Regulation 312
  European Commission and the FTC
    disagreed 400
  European Commission's enforce multiple
    competition policy goals 314
  financial structure and technology
    transfers. In Optical Fibres (1986) Philip
    Morris (1987) 292
  French and German systems were in
    competition 288
  German and French attitudes 281
  Grundig-Consten 286
  Hallstein, W. 281
  hard core cartels 299
  Hawk, Berry E. (New York commercial
    lawyer) 300
  implementing a single market 304
  Japanese trade challenge anti-dumping
    policy 291
  Kali und Salz 294
  legal expertise EU's core goals 313

  mergers and abuse of dominance 288
  merger regulation 293–4
  modernization of competition 311
  modernization-reformers 246–308, 312–13
  new member states from formerly
    communist Europe 307
  North Sea oil gas exploration European
    Community 293
  opposing globalization 201
  reform proposals, Regulation 17 311
  regulation 1/2003 312
  Regulation No.17 established a
    notification process 285
  small and medium-sized firms 287
  Takeover Directive 302
  technical assistance 308
  trade and antitrust policy coincided 292
  trade-related competition policy 300
  transnational antitrust regime 308
  transnational cooperation among antitrust
    authorities 295–7
  Treaty of Paris 397
  Treaty of Rome's principal antitrust
    provisions were Articles 85 and 86 280
  US/EC Antitrust Agreement of 1991 James
    Rill of the US Justice Department's 295
  US European Commission antitrust again
    disagreed 153
  US multinational corporations 301
  van Miert, Karl 302
  Wolf, D. 312
EEC (European Economic Community) 282
  American challenge 284
  Antitrust and trade policy sometimes
    converged 282
  authority to implement equal treatment
    toward business 286
  cartels EEC 287
  Commission employed equal treatment
    285
  Common Agriculture Policy 283
  Community became one of the three
    leading postwar global trading powers
    285
  Community economic integration 290
  de Gaulle vetoed British membership 283
  EEC textile firms 282
  equal treatment within Common Market
    287
  employment and the related immigration
    tensions 287
  gave higher than the ECSC to antitrust 279
  German and French attitudes 281–7
  Hallstein, W. 273
  heritage of labor-business relations
    entwined with socialism 287
  Integrating EEC economies accession
    process 283

Majone, G. 187
outcomes of competition policy,
  particularly equal treatment 284
prewar European and wartime Nazi
  systems and postwar commitment to
  integration and liberal trade 283
protectionist pressures tested the EEC 283
Servan-Schreiber, "American investment in
  Europe" 285
trade battle with Japan 289
trade policy and antitrust interacted to
  promote EEC integration 282
trade struggle pitting Europe against Japan
  and the United States fostered 290
Treaty of Rome's principal antitrust
  provisions were Articles 85 and 86 280
Treaty of Romes's negotiations regarding
  the antitrust provisions
European Union 245
  accession agreement 309
  accession Portugal, Spain, Greece, Sweden,
    Finland, Austria, Estonia, Latvia,
    Lithuania to Portland, Hungary, Czech,
    Slovakia, Slovenia, Cyprus, Malta, and
    Turkey 300
  accession process 283
  ambivalent deregulation policies 149
  attack on conglomerate mergers through
    extensive divestiture 132
  cooperative EU-US enforcement culture
    309
  criticism of "Brussels bureaucrats 301
  "efficiency" discourse 304
  EU goal of market integration 305
  EU-US difference merger regulation 304,
    308
  financial structure and technology
    transfers. In Optical Fibres (1986) Philip
    Morris (1987) 292
  Ideological assault upon the agent of
    globalization 307
  Maastricht Treaty/of 1992 instituted the
    European Union 300
  modernization of Competition 311
  nationalist and anti-globalization
    ideologies 310
  new member states from formerly
    communist Europe 307
  single market created demands for experts
    301

Fascism 22
  anti-capitalist collective national identity
    82
  Colegrove, Kenneth W. 98
  Fujita, K. 82

German and Japanese fascists 61
Japan's imperialist 83
Japanese militarists 82-5
Matsuoka, Y. 101
militant nationalists 61
Mobilization Law of 1938 86
pre-war Japanese militarism 165
"progressive reformers" 91
wartime control system and the zaibatsu's
  dominance 160
zaibatsu/control disputed 82
Fels, Allan 315, 398
  ACCC's strict merger enforcement 374
  Australian attitudes to competitiveness 377
  Australian Competition and Consumer
    Commission (ACCC) 373
  Australian officials 376
  Australian welfare capitalism 384
  Brunt's seminar at Monash University 350
  Cooney Committee recommended
    "lessening of competition" test 89, 369
  enforcement sensitive to diverse business
    motivations 374
  expanding the Trade Practices Act's reach
    369
  Fel's attention to political symbolism/for
    strong competition policy enforcement/
    innovative enforcement strategies/media
    strategy/rejection of Chicago economic
    theories/teaching with Professor Brunt
    367
  Howard government's support ACCC 380
  internationalizing antitrust enforcement
    376
Kelty, W. 369
Keynesian economics 367
Labor government's microeconomic
  reforms Hilmer Committee 372
merger test and court-enforced
  undertakings 372
national goods and services tax (GST)
  ACCC 385
"restorative" strategy North Queensland
  Aboriginals case 371
Samuel, G. 392
secondary boycotts 383
strengthen the Trade Practices Act
  prevailed 370
survey of commercial lawyers and ACCC
  378
Sylvan, L. 392
waterfront confrontation of 1997-98 381
waterfront settlement 384
First, Harry 148, 169-72, 226, 398
  1947 Japanese negotiators 398
  altered the Kime draft 177
  policy dispute grew among antitrust
    professionals 3

First World War 25, 63
  Germany's defeat 63
Ford, G. 146
Fox, E. 148–57
  policy dispute grew among antitrust
    professionals 343
  trade-related antitrust measures or
    TRAMS 157
Frankfurter 13
FTC (Fain Trade Commission, Japan) 181–5,
    193–202, 400
  1995 Japan's coalition party Deregulation
    Action Program 210
  Act Against Unjustifiable Premiums and
    Misleading Representations 201
  Amano case patent licensing agreements
    195
  Amendment of 1977 203
  Antimonoply Law, advocating the 1953
    amendments and the 1958 revisions
    235
  Antimonopoly Law Amendment of 1953
    German regulatory tradition 187
  Antimonopoly Law revisions did not pass
    1958 188
  antimonopoly policy 29
  articulated his activist enforcement
    program 200
  automobile case 214
  bid-rigging 229
  Cold War first amendment to the
    Antimonopoly Law in 1949 58
  criminal cartel case 242
  dissatisfied consumers 191
  equal treatment within Common Market
    269
  end of antimonopoly and prohibition
    against holding company 217
  exemption-authorization process 183–207
  favored smaller enterprises 186
  "first criminal accusation" 202
  foreign pressure favoring antimonopoly
    policy 212
  FTC also review trade associations/
    enforcement regime/considered merger
    action/protecting "weak suppliers
    subcontractors"/proposed expansion
    plan 1994–95/prosecuted six criminal
    accusations 186
  Japan automobile distributing system 239
  Japan-US dispute over NTT 242
  Japan's imperialist 98
  Japan's international trade liberalization
    193
  Japanese antitrust's ambiguities of foreign
    pressure/Petroleum Federation/
    surcharge system 188–234, 202–3, 228
  Keidanren switched to advocation vigorous

  enforcement of 194, 206
Keynesian economics 186
Kishi promoted MITI's industrial policy
    185
Kodak case 237
leniency program 229
Management Coordinating Agency (MCA)
    218
mergers, acquisitions and technology
    transfers 198
MITI-advocacy of fortifying the FTC 221
Nippon Telegraph and Telephone
    Corporation (NTI) 242
Noda Soy Sauce case (1955) 193
over the FTC 297
petroleum cartel cases/private suits 203
pharmaceutical industry 240
pharmaceutical Manufactures Associations
    241
price issue 192
Protection of small enterprises &
    agricultural cooperatives 181
required consultation between MITI and
    the FTC 183
shifted its enforcement efforts towards
    unfair business practices 186
Shiseido 237
shukko and FTC up-grade proposal 219
supported the FTC's amendment proposals
    strengthening the 202
surcharge system 202
Toshiba chemical co 236
Toyota Daihatsu order 239
unfair business practice 193
Yawata-Fuji Merger case 194
zaibatsu restructuring through merger,
    acquisitions 186
Fukayama, Francis 144
  Chicago neoclassical economic 144

Galbraith, John Kenneth 111–20, 255
  take-over strategy 141
  decartelization in 4D pm 255
  profit maximization secondary 111
Gasperi, Alcide 276
  advocates of European community 177
GATT (General Agreement on Tariffs and
    Trade) 57, 107, 113–44, 154–5, 399
  anti-dumping policy 215, 291
  Antimonopoly Law exemptions 192
  Community economic integration 144
  "government measures" 155
  liberal trade agreements/order 107
  multinational corporations 187
  Section 301, Trade Act of 1947 154
  struggle over commodity agreements 154

trade struggle pitting Europe against Japan and the United States fostered 290
Geneen, H. 112, 400
  Conglomerate/s 112–33
  corporate takeovers 318
  diversification investments strategy at International Telephone and Telegraph 400
  diversification or conglomerate mergers 112
  "horizontal and vertical mergers" 112
  M-form 112
  "reciprocity" 133
General Electric 10
German Cartel Law of 1957 246–63
  1952 Cartel Bill 266
  Allied Occupation and the Germans' own struggle over a cartel law 262
  Cartel protribition k abuse principles 257, 267
  Christian Democratic Union/Social Union 263
  election of 1957 268
  Fritz Berg's BDI 267
  German public opinion 263
  German self-identity 268
  Guenther, E. 266–7
  images of a cartel law 263
  Josten Committee 265
  Ordo Liberals/Liberalism 263
  per se prohibition against cartels 265
  Social Democratic Party 263
  social-market economy 265
Ghosn, C. 232
global capitalism 1, 400
  antitrust agreement under the WTO 304
  Cartels need attention 303
  Condemning international capitalism 145
  deregulated capital markets 144
  divergence within 400
  ending of the Cold War intensified global economic rivalry 290
  EU and US antitrust regimes sought global accountability 279
  financial globalization of multinational corporations 282
  global equities market 142
  hegemony of US multinational corporations 142
  Keidanren's deregulation reforms potentially benefited large firms 205
  multinational corporation's dual legal personality 402
  radical anti-globalization groups 145
  Tokyo an international conference on the global economy 199
Globalization 1, 102–3, 135–42

American capitalism/ "triumphalism 135
American consumer culture's interdependence with foreigners 142
anti-competitive practices 373
anti-globalization discontent 308, 401
Big business embraced the competition consciousness 391
Condemning international capitalism 145
diversification of foreign-based corporations 143
global capital market 143
hegemony of US multinational corporations 310
ideological assaults upon the agents of globalization 145, 307
images of US triumphalism 142
IMF's Washington consensus 143
market fundamentalism 143
nationalist and anti-globalization ideologies 310
radical anti-globalization groups 145
separating the trade and antitrust policy 154
symbols WTO, IMF, World Bank 135
three-sided trade rivalry among Japan, the US, and Europe 290
US decline 143
US competitive position in relation to Europe and Pacific rim nations 143
US-Japanese trade dispute 144
GM 106
Graham, Edward M. 148
  contestable market 148
Great Depression 4–6, 60, 108–36, 393–403
  rejected American antitrust 395
Greenspan, A. 122–42
  demand for short-term profitability 142
  outcomes of antitrust policy 122
Grew, Joseph C. 57, 99
  Japan's imperialist 98
GTE Sylvania 146
  rule of reason to allow a territorial vertical restraint 146

Hadley, Eleanor 177–8, 182–97
Haley, John O. 182, 398
  Authority without power 90–1
  trade-antitrust policy distinction 155
  United States trade and antitrust laws 150
Hamilton, W. 26
Hand, L. 58
Harriman, Henry I., of the Chamber of Commerce 10
Harris Tweed case (1942) 74

Hart-Scott-Rodino Antitrust Improvement
    Act of 1976 (HSR) 146, 400
  parens patriae provision authorizing
    federal funds for state attorneys general
    to prosecute 146
  take-over strategies 146
Hashimoto Ryogo 177–210, 216–20
  Hashimoto's Antimonopoly Study
    Committee 172–3
  holding company 178
  Kime draft 178
Hashimoto Ryutaro 210
  Antimonopoly Law reversal of position
    210
  Anti-trust Law Study Council headed by
    Saito 209
Havel, Václav 313
  capitalist consciousness 313
Hawke, R. 363
  Building a Competitive Australia 362
  deregulated labor markets, including
    "enterprise bargaining" 356
  Labor government's micro-economic
    policies 357
  micro-economic reform 345
  success against Dunlop 341
Henderson, Leon 11
Henry Ford 108
  America big business 108
  organizational 108
  "unitary" or "U" 108
Hillman, Sidney (union leader) 28, 38, 63–7,
    249
Hirabayashi Hidekatsu 203–25
  Amendment of 1977 203
Hitler, A. 72
  "New Economic Order" 72
  New Economic Order Aryan self-identity
    75
  taken over Austria 22
Honeywell 56, 152
  US merger doctrine reflecting "efficiency"
    theories and the European "market
    domination" theory 153
  US officials approved the merger, but the
    European Commission, applying a
    stricter merger rule, did not 152
Howard John, government 392
  Australia's social-welfare capitalism
    ACCC's role 381
  Australian welfare capitalism 384
  Howard government Support ACCC 380
  national goods and services tax (GST)
    ACCC 385
  Pauline Hanson's One Nation party 380
  Samuel, G. 392
  Sylvan, L. 392
  Workplace Relations Act of 1996 381

waterfront confrontation of 1997–98 381
waterfront settlement 381–4
Hudac, R. 402
Hutcheson decision of 1941 30, 52

Iacocca, L. 141
  take-over strategy 141
I.B.M. 109
ICI 35, 75
I G. Farben 35, 63, 248–53
Ikeda 189–96
  high growth economic program 196
  Prime minister advocation the "high
    growth" economic policy 189
Illinois Brick decision 146
  imposed limitations on state actions 146
industrial policy 160
  bengoshi industrial policy and the
    Antimonopoly Law 208
  Japanese bureaucrats' industrial policy it
    always evolved in relation to
    competition policy 161
  "system of 1955" 162
International Bank for Reconstruction and
    Development 49
international cartel 5, 32, 60–2, 139
  Australians 78
  authorization on April 29, 1941, requiring
    certification and postponment of
    antitrust violations 40–2
  British "cartel discussion group" 44
  "cartel and patent system" 42
  Committee's internal reports on
    international cartels confirmed 44
  Dusseldorf Agreements's 69
  Federation of British Industries (FBI) 68
  FBI's "industrial self-government" 69
  "German cartel system" 46
  "German Electric Bulb Company" 42
  ICI 69
  IG Farben 252
  International Electric Lamp Cartel 69
  International Electrical Association 69
  investment and technology transfers 44
  New Economic order 46
  policy regime 47
  viscose cartel 65
International Cartels 2
  Agreement 38
  Alkali Export Association 126
  antitrust in international business 126
  appeasements 61
  Arthur Daniels Midlands and Vitamins
    cartel cases 38
  Atlantic Charter 248
  Australia's abandoned antitrust heritage
    75

authorization on April 29, 1941, requiring certification and postponement of antitrust violations 40
British-America trade negotiations 74
British "cartel discussion group" 44
British Dominions of Australia and Canada 76
Bureau of the Budgets 52
cartel between DuPont and ICI 126
Controlling World Trade Cartels and Commodity Agreement 34–58
cooperation imposed accountability in international cartel cases 296
corporate accounatability 151
distinguishing commodity or patent 49
Effective cooperation among antitrust regimes 151
electrodes cartel 234
Executive Committee on Economic Foreign Policy 52
Federation of German Industries 64
From the 1990s antitrust enforcement 400
"German cartel system" 247
Gerard, James W. 55
Gilbert Montague 56
hard core cartels 299
Hitler's Germany 270
ideological barriers 126
incandescent lamps 126
Industries (ICI) 51
investment and technology transfers 44
Justice Department's cases involving multinational corporations jumped 1993 and 1997 151
Justice Department oversight 38
MacGregor, D. H. 70
Minnesota Mining & Manufacturing [3M] company's 126
and mobilizing America's Defenses 32
Morgenthau Plan 56, 170
multinational corporation's 141–4
New Economic Order 72
Pajus, J. 55
patented technology 127
Perkins, M. 55
shipping conference cartel's 76
Till, Irene 51
transnational antitrust cooperation ACCC's enforcement regime 389
UN's 125
Unilever's involvement with IG Farben 253
United States of Europe 67
US multinational corporations 34
Voorhis, Jerry, California Congressman 55

Vietnam Cartel 234
Webb-Pomerne Act 118–26
International Cartels and the Origin of the ITO 40
International Monetary Fund 5, 49, 113
International Trade Organization (ITO) 75, 107, 396
  Allegations Concerning Cartel Matters 53
  British "cartel discussion group" 44
  Clayton, W. 43
  Committee's internal reports on international cartels confirmed 44
  Controlling World Trade Cartels and Commodity Agreement 58
  Cox, Hugh 43
  distinguishing commodity or patent agreements from cartels 49
  eliminating restrictive business practices 129
  forgotten consensus among US officials 401
  international antitrust regime 75
  international status of antitrust 51, 396
  investment and technology transfers 44, 51
  ITO's antitrust provisions 55, 107
Isaacs, Isaac 78
Ishikawa Ichiro 168
  SSC 168
Iyori Hiroshi 181–92, 225–36
  anti-monopoly system is taken root 192
  former FTC commissioner 181
  greater problem administrative guidance 192
  small and medium-sized firms 192
  Yawata-Fuji Merger case 194

Jackson, Robert 9, 395
  authorization on April 29, 1941, requiring certification and postponement of antitrust violations 40
  Justice Department oversight 38
Jackson and O'Brian/with Roosevelt's agreement 38
  authorization on April 29,1941, requiring certification and postponment of anti-trust violations 40
  Justice Department oversight 38
Japan 60, 107–35, 398
  access Japan market 80
  Allen, G. C. 86, 220
  anti-competitive practices 375
  Antitrust Division's 88, 277
  Blakemore, T. 93–5, 100
  "Camouflage Policy" 89
  Colegrove, Kenneth W. 93

Japan (*Cont.*)
    comparative method of legal discourse
        93–6
    competitive advantage 135
    condoned SCAP's "directive dissolve the
        zaibatsu 170
    counter the zaibatsu 90
    Effective cooperation among antitrust
        regimes 151
    Fujita Keizo 82–5
    global antitrust authority 401
    holding companies 88
    Japan's imperialist 98
    Japanese firms/legal consciousness/trade
        challenge anti-dumping policy 127
    managers Banto 88
    Masujima, R. 98
    Matsuoka, Y. 98
    Mobilization Law of 1938 81
    militarists/military extremists 86–90
    Ministry of Home Affairs 86
    New Deal 91
    Nissan/holding company 96
    Prince Konoe Fumimaro 91
    "progressive reformers" 90
    Significant Industries Control Law of 1931
        86
    "system of temporary employment and
        sub-contract" 81
    Taisho era 85
    Takayanagi, Tanaka, and Takagi 85
    Tokyo Imperial University's Law
        Department 81–93
    trade battle with Japan 90
    trade struggle pitting Europe against Japan
        and the United States fostered 144, 289
    use of technology by foreign multinational
        corporations 96
    US-Japanese trade dispute 100, 128
    Uyeda Teijiro 82
    Wigmore's return to Japan 82
Johnson, President Lyndon B. 131
Johnson Administration 133
    Antitrust Task Force 131
    enforcement policy against conglomerates
        133
    Neal Report 131

Kahn, Alfred 124
Kantor, M. 216
Kashiwagi, I. 177–9
    Kime draft 178
    holding company 178
Keating, Prime Minister Paul 369
Keidanren (Federation of Economic
        Organizations) 168, 185, 188, 193–7,
        203–23, 228, 232, 243

1990s the LDP's embrace of deregulation
        and antitrust 203
    in 1994 support for Keidanren 206
    1995 Japan's coalition party Deregulation
        Action Program 210
    big business 168
    foreign pressure favoring antimonopoly
        policy 212
    FTC's enforcement regime 188
    Keidanren's "Deregulation Promotion
        Plan" 204
    Keidanren switched to advocating vigorous
        enforcement of antimonopoly policy 206
    multinational corporate sectors subsidizing
        the less efficient, protected ones 205
    shifting industrial policy 207
    Takahashi's proposals had significant
        political ramifications 201
    Toyota 214
    Strengthening FTC 216
Keidanren, MITI 89, 197
Keiretsu 160–82, 197–8, 227
    Act Against Unjustifiable Premiums and
        Misleading Representations 201
    Amendment of 1953 legalizing
        intercorporate shareholding 198
    antimonopoly policy reconstituted the
        relation between big and small business
        198
    "excessive" competition 198
    Japan automobile distributions systems 239
    mergers, acquisitions and technology
        transfers 198
    technology transfers monitored by the FTC
        186
    zaibatsu restructuring through merger,
        acquisitions 186–97
    Toyota Daihatsu order 239
Kennedy Administration 131
Keynes, John M. 5, 72, 255
    middle way 5
    Keynesian economics 287, 367
Kilgore Senate subcommittee inquiry into
        military affairs 40
Kime, Posey T. 172–4
    Antimonopoly Law Study Committee 172
    Antitrust and Cartels Division 172
    Economic and Science Section 172
    Edwards report's recommendations and
        GHQ's critique 173
    Hashimoto's Antimonopoly Study
        Committee 173
    independent antitrust enforcement
        commission under the Prime Minister
        174
    James M. Henderson 172
    Kimedraft 173–4
    Japanese officials resisted Kime draft 175

Kishi Nobusuke 183–5, 188–9, 196
  "1955 system" failures to revise the
    Antimonopoly Law in 1958 and 1963
    196
  Antimonoply Law, advocating the 1953
    amendments and the 1958 revisions 185
  implementing the Antimonopoly Law
    revisions proposed in 1958 184
  Kishi promoted MITI's industrial policy
    185
  prime minister from 1957 to 1960 184
  resigned in june 1960 189
  US-Japan Security Treaty 188
Klein, Joel I. 151–4
  Effective cooperation among antitrust
    regimes 151
  international antitrust cases 154
Knox, Frank (Secretary of the Navy) 40
Kozo Yamamura 182
Kronstein, Heinrich 42–59, 250–6
  Antitrust Division 28
  Arnold's authorization of the more
    centralized investigation of wartime
    international cartels 42
  Bavarian government 253
  Böhm Franz 67, 253
  centralized investigation of wartime
    international cartels 42
  competition policy regime 47
  Controlling World Trade Cartels &
    Commodity Agreements 255
  deconcentrating German business 254
  Freiburg "School" 67
  German businessmen 250
  "German cartel system" 46
  German emigres 67
  Hitler's rise 28–42
  "international cartel movement" 33
  JCS 1067 249–51
  Kronstein indigenous antitrust policy
    making 258
  and Mobilizing America's Defenses 32
  Metallgesellschaft 250
  New Economic Order 46
  Ordo liberals 249
  patent and cartel agreements/section 37
  patents 36
  Unilever's involvement with IG Farben 253
  Zeiss glass making film 253
Krupp Steel 248
  America big corporations 62
  broader labour arbitration 77
  defending consumer interests 341

labor 30, 103–5, 109–10, 114–20, 247
  Nathaniel Goldfinger, Director of
    Research, AFL-CIO 116

regulation of cartel & monopoly abuse 247
SSC report 169
William Kelty 120, 367
Labor Party 340
  Australian Council of Trade Unions
    (ACTU) 339
  black-ban against Dunlop 339
  Workplace Relations Act of 1996 381
LDP (Liberal Democratic Party) 197,
    220–7, 400
  1990s the LDP's embrace of deregulation
    and antitrust 203
  Antimonopoly Law Amendment of 1953
    German regulatory tradition 187
  Antimonopoly Law reversal of position
    210
  Anti-trust Law Study Council headed by
    Saito 209
  Episodic scandals 197
  FTC upgrade plan linking Articles 9 220
  Lockheed scandal of 1976 202
  LDP's historic electoral defeat in 1993 212
  LDP-led coalition governments 213
  relaxation of the holding-company ban in
    Article 9 223
  uncommitted urban voters 221
League of Nations 46, 62
  Salter, Arthur 72
legal-economic experts 6, 60, 102, 214, 395
  ABA's International Commercial Law
    Section 120
  agenda for reconstuting antimonopoly
    policy 199
  American "triumphalism 143
  Antimonopoly Study Group 193–203
  antitrust internationalization/ international
    business 124
  antitrust issue, Mason's and Kronstein's
    views 256
  Anti-trust Law Study Council headed by
    Saito 47, 209
  Antitrust lawyers/Task Force 119
  Australian Judges 319
  Australian officials 77
  Balcerowicz, Leszek 309
  Barwick Australian lawyers 323
  Bannerman's use of consultation and
    registration 336
  Baxt, Robert 346
  Bicks, Robert T. 133
  Blakemore, Thomas L. 81
  Board of Trade's officials 69
  Böhm Franz 67
  Bowmen 124
  British economist/policy 61–2
  Brunt, Maureen 317
  Brunt's seminar at Monash University 67,
    350

legal-economic experts (*Cont.*)
  Sir Charles Innes 250
  Charles Stark of the US Antitrust Division
    "positive comity" 158
  Chicago law and economics theories 122
  Clay, Henry 73
  Cohen, Ruth L. 73
  collaboration with economists 120
  Commissioner Braithwaite and
    "restorative justice 370
  Comparative competition consciousness
    75
  comparative method of legal discourse/
    reinforced 94
  competition policy economic theories 307
  conservatism of the Australian judiciary
    349
  consumer lawyers 230
  corporate takeovers 148
  cultural and institutional distinctiveness
    144
  Deringer, A. 281
  Dieter Wolf 312
  Director, Aaron 122
  dissatisfied consumers 191
  diversification investments strategies 114
  Dixon's dissenting opinions 319
  Ducret 282, 371
  economic liberty 319
  Economist and law scholars constituted
    study groups 202
  Effective cooperation among antitrust
    regimes 151
  "efficiency" discourse 138
  Einzig, Paul 66
  entrenched the Chicago free market
    theories 147
  Eucken, Walter 67
  EU Merger Regulation 312
  European experts 304
  Fels' teaching with Professor Brunt 367
  Fornalczyk, Anna 309
  Fred Argy's Australia at the crossroads
    381
  Freiburg School 67
  Fujita Keizo 82
  German/Opinion/emigres 60
  German and British commentators 61
  Greenspan, A. 403
  Guenther, E. 266
  Guillebaud, G. W. 67, 287
  Hallstein, W. 273
  hard core cartels 299
  Hawks, Berry E., New York commercial
    lawyer 300
  historical economists 62
  High Court's judge Owen Dixon 318
  Hofstadter, R. 119

holding international meetings including
  studies of Japanese antitrust 191
Hunter, A. 317–21
imposed limitations on state actions 146
International Competition Network 299
international training of Australian legal-
  economic professionals 350
Isaacs, I. 322
Japanese academics/Bureaucracy 61
John Braithwaite "responsive regulation/
  study Australian regulatory agencies 404
Japanese bureaucrats' use of "study
  groups" 119, 201
Japan Federation of Bar Associations
  208–30
John Kenneth Galbraith calls a
  technostructure 284
Josten, P. 257
Josten committee 60
Kalijarvi, Thorsten V. 128
Karmel, Peter 317
Klein, Joel 73, 303
Kohlberg, Kravis Roberts 148
Landis, James M. 117
laissez-faire 21
Law and Economics program 122
law firm's role in compliance programs 94
lawyers' services 207
Levy, H. 71
liberal antitrust consensus 106
liberal and fascist public discourse 60,
  362
Liefmonn, Robat 62, 63, 67, 74
Loevinger, L. 133
MacGregor, D. H. 70
Majone, Giandomenico 287
marginal-cost theory 139
Masujima, Rokuichiro 98
McCloy, John J. 272
mid-1970s Chicago efficiency theories
  146
Miert, Karl van 302
Ministry of Commerce and Industry 80
modernization-reformers 246
multinational corporation's 114
Myron W. Watkins 117
Ordo liberals 248
Organization of European Cooperation
  and Development's report of 1967 157
outcomes of antitrust policy 158
Paul Sweezy 47
Petro, S. 122
Pflanz, Matthias, European expert 298
Pitofsky, B. 303
Policy dispute grew among antitrust
  professionals 147
private actions 243
private antitrust plaintiffs 132

pro-competition bureaucrats inside MITI's Policy Bureau 207
Reagan administration antitrust officials 147
rejected American antitrust 395
Richardson, J. E. 320
Robinson, E. A. G. 71
Robbins, L. 72
revolving door 120
Salter, A. 72
Sawer, G. 319
single market created demands for experts 301
study by Dr. Karen Yeung ACCC 379
Study Group reporting on the 1958 proposals 190
Stocking, George W. 117–21
Stolper, G. 65–6, 258
Surface, Frank M. 117
supporting Antimonopoly Law FTC academic critics 179
survey of commercial lawyers and ACCC 378
Thurman Arnold's activist antitrust philosophy 105
Tokyo Imperial University's Law Department 90
Tokyo an international conference on the global economy 199
trade-antitrust policy distinction 155
transnational cooperation among antitrust authorities 157
Twentieth Century Fund 116–30
US/EC Antitrust Agreement of 1991 James Rill of the US Justice Department's 295
Uyeda Teijiro 82
Vernon, R. 144
Wolf, D. 312
workable competition 321
legal realist movement 25
Lend-Lease Act of 1941 46, 74, 311
  British-America trade negotiations 74
  British "cartel discussion group 44, 301
Liefmann, Robert 62, 63, 67, 74
liberal democracies 2
  Britain's national cartel and monopoly 68, 317
  Einzig, Paul 66, 321
  images of national identity 60, 311
  inter-war period 49
  Labor Party 68, 207
  neo-NRA police 10
  Tory Party 68, 395

MacArthur, General Douglas 57, 190
Managerial capitalism 1, 102, 112–13, 135–6, 248, 393–9

1960's, American international competitive advantage was eroding 113–136
1970s, corporate management's investment strategy 137
1973 oil embargo 136
1990s antitrust enforcement 142, 257, 400
abuse of dominance United Brands 272, 289
administrative coordination 320, 403
Amendment of 1953 legalizing inter corporate shareholding 198, 323
anti-competitive conduct 403
anti-dumping policy operation strategies of multinational corporations 292
antimonopoly policy reconstituted the relation between big and small business 198
Australian big business and multinational corporations 316
Australian competition consciousness 312
Broken Hill Proprietary Co. (BHP) 316
big business 1, 103–5, 360–77, 393
business historian David Merrett 377
capitalist revolution 110
Chicago doctrines promote corporate mergers and acquisitions 148
citizens 208
Commission's Microsoft decision 306
Consumers 281
Continental can 288
corporate restructing 341
corporate restructuring aggravated 341
"corporate social responsibility" 140
corporate takeovers in the Rank case 378
counter the zaibatsu 90
demand for short-term profitability 6, 142
diversification and conglomerate mergers 6
diversification investments strategy at International Telephone and Telegraph 112
effect upon the consumer 105
Effective Competition 105
electrical equipment litigation 112
Ericsson/Kolbe 294
EU-US difference merger regulation/divergence 304–5
family capitalism 61
financial globalization of multinational corporations 301
financial structure and technology transfers. In Optical Fibres (1986) 292
Foreign Companies (Takeovers) Act 341
Fujita Keizo 82
global capital market/corporate diversification/equities market 139
good corporate citizens 375
hegemony 102

Managerial capitalism (*Cont.*)
  holding companies/equities market 63–88
  a hollow myth 140
  International Telephone and Telegraph
    Corporations 400
  Kali und Salz 184, 294, 399
  Keidanren's deregulation reforms
    potentially benefited large firms 205
  images of corporate America's
    accountability 134
  least risky strategy 111
  M-form promoted 109
  D. H. MacGregor 70
  managerial capitalism's legitimacy within
    Cold War liberalism 115
  managerial revolution 75
  managers Banto 88, 257
  market share 111
  maximizing profits 111
  mergers, acquisitions and technology
    transfers 146, 198
  mergers and abuse of dominance 288
  "mergers and consolidations" 164
  mergers and corporate restructuring 360
  merger regulation/strategies 294
  Mitsui, Mitsubishi, Sumitomo, and Yasuda
    87, 293
  multi-divisional corporation' impact on
    domestic and global markets 141
  multidivisional organizational structure
    108, 394
  multinational corporation's "dual/legal
    personality" 111
  Nissan 89
  national and international diversification
    investment strategies 146
  North Sea oil gas exploration 293
  opposing globalization 145
  organizational 182
  patent pools and cross-licensing system 164
  Philip Morris (1987) 293
  private suits 112
  Sawyer, Charles, Commerce Secretary 105
  Servan-Schreiber, "American investment in
    Europe" 285
  Sloan, A. 143, 394
  societal accountability 110
  take-over strategy 141
  technology transfers monitored by the FTC
    186
  trade and antitrust policy coincided 292
  transnational cooperation 297
  US multinational corporations 34, 399
  US multinational firm's subsidiary 110
  workers 134
  zaibatsu bounded competition/family
    holding companies/restructuring through
    merger, acquisitions* 88

Markham, J. W. 131
  economist J. W. Markham 134
  images of corporate America's
    accountability 134
  US multinational corporations 6
Marshall, G. 257
Marshall Plan 113
Mason, E. 28
  "Allegations Concerning Cartel Matters"
    53
  antitrust internationalization 124
  antitrust issue Mason's and Kronstein's
    views 256
  British-American trade regotiations 74
  collaboration with economists 120
  Controlling World Trade Cartels and
    Commodity Agreement 58
  decartelization in the 4D program 255
  Europe and Japan 120
  international status of antitrust 396
  Lend-Lease negotiations and ITO 397
  national antitrust regimes consensus 396
  Positive Program 53
  professional cultures 120
Meade, James E. 46
  British "cartel discussion group" 44
  distinction between Commodity
    Agreements and Cartels 47
  "German cartel system" 46
  Lend-Lease negotiations and ITO 50
  New Economic Order 46
  Reconstruction Unit of the Board of Trade
    72
  Sir Percival Liesching 47
MCI 142, 233
Meade, Jones E. 57, 72
  British-America trade negotiations 74
  British "cartel discussion group" 44
  Competition policy regime 47
  "distinction between Commodity
    Agreements and Cartels" 47
  distinguishing commodity or patent
    agreements from cartels 49
  The Economic Basis of a Durable Peace
    (1940) 72
  international antitrust regime 75
  League of Nation's Economic Policy
    section 72
  Lend-Lease Negotiations and ITO 50
  New Economic order 46, 72
  Sir Percival Liesching 47
  Reconstruction Unit of the Board of Trade
    72
Meade, J. E. 41, 57–9, 78, 129
  developed or "southern" nations-
    designated the Group of 77 108
  Japan supported an international antitrust
    regime 199

multinational corporations 108
"restrictive business practices" 108
Separating the trade and antitrust policy
   154
struggle over commodity agreements 154
national antitrust regimes, consensus 396
"national programs" 129
A Positive International Cartel Program
   44
Positive Program 53
trade liberalism 50
UN's competition consciousness 129
Means, Gardiner C. 12, 378
Medium and small scale Enterprises
   Organization Law of 1957 186
Noda Soy Sauce case (1955) 193
regulation of cartels and monopoly
   abuse 247
small and medium-sized firms 287
small business values/price fixing not 325
small productive unit 169
SSC Report 169
strong small business 357
"system of temporary employment and
   sub-contract" 85
Trade Association Act 179
Uyeda Teijiro 82
zaibatsu's control disputed 89
Meiji Constitution 79
absolutist image of the Emperor 92
Authority without Power 90
comparative legal discourse/ reinforced
   94–6
Japanese Bureaucracy/legal consciousness/
   "way of life" 90
Meiji Emperor/Restoration 102–41, 393
Minobe, T. 92
Minseito Government 89
Murayama, M. 92
New Deal 96
"organ" theory 92
progressive reformers 94
Tokyo Imperial University 81
Takagi Yasaka 95
Tanaka Kotaro 95
TVA 96
Menzies, Robert G. 320
Microsoft case 401
international antitrust cases 154
transnational cooperation 150
US European Commission antitrust again
   disagreed 153
Microsoft case and authorities 153–4
Miki, T. 200–2
election as Prime Minister 200
MITI (Ministry of International Trade and
   Industry) 151, 179–186, 198, 204–206,
   211, 230–231

1990s the LDP's embrace of deregulation
   and antitrust 203
1994 support for Keidanren's 206
1995 Japan's coalition party Deregulation
   Action Program 210
administrative guidance 186
Antimonoply Law, advocating the 1953
   amendments and the 1958 revisions 199
Antimonopoly Law Amendment of 1953
   German regulatory tradition 187
automobile case 214
exemption-authorization process 183
foreign pressure favoring antimonopoly
   policy 295
over the FTC 121
Japan-US disputes over NTT 194, 242,
   254
Kishi promoted MITI's industrial policy
   185, 253–6
Ministry of Finance 211, 257–9
MITI's advocacy of fortifying the FTC 214,
   221, 257–65, 281
pro-competition bureaucrats inside MITI's
   Policy Bureau 207
required consultation between MITI and
   the FTC 183
shifting industrial policy 207, 248
Mitsubishi Oil 80
Miyazawa 198–200
The Modern Corporation and Private
   Property 12, 109, 166, 398
Monnet, Jean 272–7, 284
Adenauer's agreement and Hallstein two
   Treaty antitrust Articles 275
advocates of European community 276
antitrust provisions 273
authority to implement equal treatment
   toward business 286
Ball, George 273
drafted by Robert Bowie with meticulous
   275
ECSC and the wider European market
   integration 272
Franco-German rapprochement 276
McCloy, John J. 272
Monnet faced oppositions from Charles de
   Gaulle 47, 273
Monnet neutralized the anti-US sentiments/
   cultivated Erhard, Adenauer 272
outcomes of competition policy,
   particularly equal treatment 199,
   225–30, 284
Paris Treaty's antitrust provisions in article
   65 13, 274
Willner, Sydney 273–84
Treaty of Paris 274
Treaty of Rome 275
US support 274

Monti, Marlo 298
Morgenthau, Henry 55
  Morgenthau's plan 56
  Pajus 55
Morozumi Yoshihiko 167–89, 190
  antimonopoly law 189
  idea of "middle way" to Japan 190
  Industrial Order Bill/policy 181
  lax merger policy and technology
    agreements 190
  Ministry of Commerce and Industry 167
  minimizing 189
  promote economic growth 189
  technology transfers 189
Murayama Makoto 209–30
  consumers 1996 Murayama was such a
    private action 209
  foreign pressure favoring antimonopoly
    policy 212
Murphy, Lionel 331, 340–6, 350
  Australian Industries Act 343
  Barwick and Murphy 350
  competition consciousness 346
  constitutional crisis overshowdowing the
    Whitlam government 344
  consulted with US & British antitrust 343
  Court-centered prohibitions with an
    administrative 344
  fraudulent misrepresentation in consumer
    cases 344
  on the High Court of Australia 350
  introducing trade practices legislation
    341
  lengthy discussions with Ronald Dietrich
    343
  Mergers under the Foreign Takeovers Act
    344
  restraint-of-trade cases 343–4
  right of private action 343
  a substantial lessening of competition 344

Nader, Ralph 140
  "corporate social responsibility" 140
  a hollow myth 140
Nakamura Takafusa 86
  distribution sector 205
Nakayama, Kikumatsu 168, 179, 181–2
  FTC's first chairman 179
  motivations driving the FTC's enforcement
    181
  protection of 181
  small enterprises and agriculture
    cooperatives 181
  SSC (Special Survey Committee) 168
  Trade Association Act 179
National Association of Manufacturers 141
  take-over strategy 128

National Iranian Oil Company 128, 189
  Iranian oil 128
National Lead (1947) 51
Nazis (National Socialists) Germany/Party
  75
  cartel regulation 64
  Compulsory Cartels Law 64
  "good" and "bad" capitalist enterprise 65
  national identity 65
  "new order in Europe" 66
  United States of Europe 67
New Deal liberalism 8–10, 394
  antitrust exemption for organization
    labor 116
  "Effective Competition" 105
  effect upon the consumer 105
  NRA's 10
  neo-NRA policy 10
  New Deal culture and instutional
    settlement 103
  New Deal settlement/NRA 119–134
  New Dealers reconstituting antitrust
    1937–38 395
  postwar American way of life 103
  reconstituted antitrust 1
  Sawyer, Charles (Commerce Secretary)
    105
  Temporary National Economic Committee
    (TNEC) 8
Nippon Paper 151
  unsettled limits extraterritorial antitrust
    151
Nixon, Richard 51, 137
Nixon administration 137–9, 146
  Anderson, Jack 138
  conglomerate merger wave ended by 1974
    138
  controversial ITT settlement 137
  efficiency" discourse 138
  Environment Protection Agency 139
  Occupational Health and Safety
    Administration 139
  switched course in favor of Bork's vigorous
    condemnation of the conglomerate
    prosecutions 146
  Watergate crisis 136–8
Norsky Hydro 35
North American Free Trade Agreement
  402
North, Douglass C. 143
  incentives 143
  religious and ideological conflicts 144
Nuremberg war-crimes trials 249

O'Brian, John Lord 38
  agreement 38
  authorization on April 29, 1941, requiring

certification and postponement of
 antitrust violations 40
Justice Department oversight 38
Donovan, William 38
General Council 43
Office of production Management 32
War Production Board 43
Okita 168
SSC 166
Oliphant, Herman 21
O'Mahoney, Joseph C. (Wyoming Senator)
 51
OPEC 137
ordo-liberalism 246
Böhm Franz 67
Eucken, Walter 67
Freiburg "school" 67
Oyama Ikuo 82–97, 168

Parsons, Talcott 115–40
American liberal consensus 140
"corporate conscience" 115
New Deal settlement 115
New Left radical discourse 140
Pluralist discourse 116
"social responsibility" 115
Pitofsky, Robert 148
policy dispute grew among antitrust
 professionals 147
Poland 24, 308
accession agreement 309
Balcerowicz, Leszek 309
cooperative EU-US enforcement culture
 309
Fornalczyk, Anna 309
Polish Monopoly Office 310
policy history 6
Potsdam Declaration 56, 163, 249–52
6 November 1945 SCAP issued a directive
 163
dissolution of the zaibatsu 163
decartelization JCS 1067 160, 248–52
to establish an antitrust regime 163
Morgenthau plan 249
praxis 3–7, 181, 394
accession agreement 309
accommodating competition values to
 Japanese society 161
American antitrust 324
Americanized consumer economy 183
Antimonopoly Act/legislation as a "Test of
 Democracy in Japan" 183
antitrust regimes' enforcement objectives
 392
antitrust to the promotion of democratic
 economic opportunity 162
Australian attitudes to competitiveness 377

Australian "mateship" mentality 355–77
"Austerican, not American" 345
bilateral agreements 129
Big business embraced the competition
 consciousness 345–91
Böhm 264
business' competition consciousness 390
cartels and monopolies 59
cartel prohibition and abuse principles 267
Christian Democratic Union/Social Union
 263
competition a means of reducing economic
 power 322
competition consciousness 4, 214, 245,
 346–91, 394
competition policy in Europe and the
 United States 313
cooperative EU-US enforcement culture
 309
Edwards report 120
eliminating restrictive business practices
 172, 398
enforcement sensitive to diverse business
 motivations 374
enforcing the EU's core goals and
 modernization 308
Fortune editors 106
FTC's enforcement regime 188–222
first oil shock of 1973 197
ideological barriers 126
internationalizing antitrusts 225
Japanese antitrust/enforcement 160
John Braithwaite "responsive regulation"
 404
Josten committee 257
Kronstein indigenous antitrust policy 258
liberal antitrust consensus 106
meaning of competition 105
motivations driving the FTC's enforcement
 181
positive change 355–77
postwar compromise consensus 59
recapitulated the national-identity imagery
 Arnold and Roosevelt 164
restructuring process in Japan 231
small business values 325
Social Democratic Party 222
SSC Report 169
Stopler, G. 65–6, 258
strengthening antimonopoly policy
 enforcement 224
supporting Antimonopoly Law FTC
 academic critics 190
technical assistance 308
Thurman Arnold's activist antitrust
 philosophy 105
transnational antitrust enforcement/regime
 390

praxis (*Cont.*)
  UN's competition consciousness 129
  underlying values of economic democracy
    160
  US multinational corporations 128
  Workable competition 189
Public Utilities Holding Company
    Act 19

Reagan Administration 215
  Market-Oriented Sector Selective
    negotiations 215
Reagan, Ronald 139, 400
  Chicago School 139
  mergers 112–39
  price-fixing agreements 139
Renault/Nissan 232
Restrictive Trade Practices Act of 1956 397
recession of 1981-82/ of 1990-91 140
Reed, Stanley 19
Richberg, Donald 10
Robinson, Edward S. 26
Robinson, Joan 13, 121
  imperfect oligopolistics competition 121
Roosevelt, Eleanor 51
  DuPont-ICI case 51–5
  Pajus, Jean 51
  Executive Committee on economic foreign
    policy 52
Roosevelt, F.D./Antimonopoly Message of
    1938 22–43
  Board of Economic Warfare 43
  Fireside Chat conveyed 22, 243
  March 20, 1942, Roosevelt 40
  New Dealers reconstituting antitrust 1937–
    38 395
  Pajus, Jean 51
  a refugee crisis 22
  Till, Irene 51
Rosenman, Samuel I. 51
  DuPont-ICI case 51
  Pajus, Jean 51
  Till, Irene 51

Sakigake Party 222
Salwin, Lester N. 175–8, 182
  1947 Japanese negotiators 176–7
  Antimonopoly Law Study Committee 172
  Hashimoto "study Committee on Anti-
    Trust Legislation" 176
  Japanese negotiators 168
  Kime draft and the Japanese disapproval
    176–8
SCAP (Supreme Commander Allied Powers)
    170–3

Amakudari 171
Antitrust & Cartel Division 172
control associations 171
Economic & Science Section 172
Edwards report 122–32, 170
Government Section 173
holding companies 171
Henderson, James M. 172
Labour section 173
New Deal's Public Utilities Holding
    Company Act (PUHCA) of 1935 171
SSC's acceptance of the need for zaibatsu
    dissolution 171
Schuman, Robert plan 271
  Franco-German rapprochement 273
  French, German, Italian, Belgium,
    Netherlands, and Luxemburg
    governments 271
  Hallstein's views comported with
    Adenauer 273
  Schuman plan's antitrust provisions
    aroused criticism 271
Schumpeter, Joseph A. 4, 110, 115, 121,
    197, 394
Second World War 26, 340, 396
Seligmann, Herbert J. 54, 341
  "Crushed Reich Pins Hope on Cartels"
    54
SII (Structural Impediments Initiative)
    203–12, 227
  1990s the LDP's embrace of deregulation
    and antitrust 123–4, 203
  FTC official Sugiyama 224
  Japan-US trade disputes/bilateral
    agreements 212–14
Singer 127
  patented technology 127
Sloan, Alfred 108–47
  diversification investment strategy 145
  M-form 114
small business 6, 61, 103–5, 134, 227, 247
  ACCC and small business 387
  Act Against Unjustifiable Premiums and
    Misleading Representations, 201
  exploitation of small businesss 328
  FTC's protecting "weak suppliers
    subcontractors"/also review trade
    associations 186
  FTC continued to protect small business
    243
  Fujita Keizo 82
Smith, Adam 105
Social Democratic Party 222–3
Socialist Party 184–5, 397
Sony 231
Spaak, Paul-Henri 277
  Treaty of Rome 277
Stalin, Joseph 19–56, 249

Standard Oil Company 11, 62
  Dodd, S. C. T 62
  Rockefeller, John D. 62
State Department's Special Committee on
  Monopoly and Cartels 43
Stettinius, Edward R. (US Steel executive) 38
Stettinius, Edward R. 53
  "Allegations Concerning Cartel Matters 53
  Positive Program 53
Stigler, George 137
  attack on conglomerate mergers through
    extensive divestiture 137
Stiglitz, J. 145
  take-over strategy 106
Stimson, Henry L. (Secretary of War) 40
Stockholders of America Foundation 141
  take-over strategy 106
Stolper, Gustav, 65, 67, 258, 264
  German emigres 67
  national identity 65
Supreme Commander Allied Powers (SCAP),
  (see SCAP) 162
Swope, Gerard 10

Takahashi Toshihide 199, 203–28
  1976 resigned and soon died 203
  Act Against Unjustifiable Premiums and
    Misleading Representations, 201
  agenda for reconstituting antimonopoly
    policy 199
  articulated his activist enforcement
    program 200
  "first criminal accusation" 202
  FTC Chairman 199–223
  German precedent for 202
  Japanese bureaucrats' use of "study
    groups" 201
  Japanese Petroleum Federati 202
  Japanese surcharge system 202
  Takahashi's proposals had significant
    political ramifications 201
Takayanagi Kenzo 95–6, 163–6, 181, 398
  American Law curriculum 165
  Blakemore Thomas 93
  Japanese war-crimes trails 165
  new Constitution 165
  recapitulated the national-identity imagery
    Arnold and Roosevelt 164
  "Sherman Act" article 163–81
  Takagi Yasaka 95
  Tanaka Kotaro 95–6
  Tokyo Imperial University 81
  Tokyo University's Law Department 165
  Wigmore, John H. 97
technological innovation 109–10, 121
  Amano case patent licensing agreements
    195

American system 109
diversificantion invesment strategy 109
financial structure and technology
  transfers. In Optical Fibres (1986) Philip
  Morris (1987) 292
multi-divisional corporation's impact on
  domestic and global markets 141
Nippon Telegraph & Telephone
  Corporation 242
patent and antimonopoly policies 131
patented technology 127
US extraterritorial antitrust actions 128
Teheran Conference 248
terrorist attacks of September 11, 2001
  290
Thatcher, Margaret 287
  Keynesian economics 287
Thorne v. Motor Trade Association (1937)
  73
Timken 127
  multinational corporations' use of
    subsidiaries 127
Tobin, Dan 31
Toyota 198
Trade policy 103–57
  access Japan market 213, 375
  ambivalent deregulation policies 149
  "American challenge" 113
  anti-competitive practices 402
  anti-dumping policy operation strategies
    of multinational corporations 292
  antitrust in international business 126
  antitrust and trade polices evolved
    separately 107
  Antitrust and trade policy sometimes
    converged 282
  Australia "blocking statutes" 376
  Australian Industries Practices Act's rise
    and fall after 1906 77
  automobile case 214
  British-America trade negotiations 74
  British Dominions of Australia and Canada
    76
  British imperial system of Trade preference
    60
  cartel-controlled commodities 64
  Commission's trade and antitrust policies
    291
  distinction between Commodity
    Agreements and Cartels 47
  EEC textile firms 282
  Executive Committee on Economic Foreign
    Policy 52
  Foreign Exchange & Foreign Trade
    Control Act 1949 144, 214
  foreign mergers and acquisitions 115
  global competitive advantage 356
  Import Duties Act of 1932 68

Trade policy (*Cont.*)
  interdependency between trade antitrust
    policy during automobile 214
  international markets 149
  Japan-US trade disputes 212
  Japanese trade challenge anti-dumping
    policy 291
  Johnson Administration instituted the
    Foreign Direct Investments Program
    115
  Kodak's claim against Fuji 156
  multinational corporations 144–57
  protective tariffs 63–8
  protectionist policies 63
  protectionist pressures tested the EEC
    283
  Rattigan, Alfred 335
  Separating the trade and antitrust policy
    154
  struggle over commodity agreements 154
  system of imperial preference 161
  tariff, currency, and shareholder
    restrictions against multinational
    corporations 63
  tensions between trade and antitrust
    authorities 154
  trade battle with Japan 289
  trade liberalism/protectionism 50
Trade policy 9
  automobiles 103
  Brazil 154
  cartel-controlled commodities 64
  pharmaceuticals 36
  photography 154
  Section 301, Trade Act of 1947 214
  semiconductors 154
  trade policy and antitrust interacted to
    promote EEC integration 282
  trade struggle pitting Europe against Japan
    and the United States fostered 290
  US government's ending of fixed exchange
    rates in 1971 197
  US-Japanese trade dispute 144
  United State Trade Representative's
    (USTR) 156
  voluntary export restraints 213
  Whitlam government's 25 percent tariff
    reduction 347
Trade Practices Act of 1965 334–5
  achievable objective the survival of the Act
    335
  Australian Council of Trade Unions
    (ACTU) 3
  Bannerman's economic theory which
    benefitted consumers 335
  Bannerman's use of consultation and
    registration 336
  Barwick's proposals 328

Bennett, H. Trevor 335
Brunt, Maureen 333
Campaign Against Rising Prices 338
competition 332
Constitution's guarantee of interstate free
  trade 331
consumer interests were equivocal 330
exploitation of small business 328
fiberboard containers case 338
frozen vegetables case 337
industries prone to price fixing 337
Labor party 329
Liberal party 329
limited criminal prosecution 331
mergers or take-overs 332
Parliamentary constituency supporting 342
prohibit RPM 3
proposals endorsed 331
Restrictive Trade Practices Act of 1971 340
Richardson, J. E. 335
Rocla Concrete Pipes case of 1971 339
St John, Richard 338–42
Snedden, B. M. 329–32
split within the conservative party 329
Trade Practices Tribunal 337
Tradestock–Freight Forwarders 355
Trade Practices Act of 1974 315, 340, 343–5,
  347–58, 360–79, 381–91
  ACCC's authority over unions 383
  ACCC and Fiji Islands' Commerce
    Commission 390
  ACCC and small business 387
  ACCC's enforceable undertakings 389
  ACCC's strict merger enforcement 374
  action against secondary boycotts 381
  Allan Fels Enforcement Activism 366
  antitrust regimes' enforcement objectives
    392
  Arnotts decision of 1990 366
  Australian Competition and Consumer
    Commission (ACCC) 373
  Australia's consumer movement 370
  Australian "mateship" mentality 355
  Australian National University research
    competition policies 351
  Australia New Zealand harmonization
    antitrust regimes 376
  Bannermans education public relations
    effort 346
  Barwick and Murphy 350
  Baxt's three-year Commission
    chairmanship 359
  Big business embraced the competition
    consciousness 391
  bilateral antitrust arrangements and WTO
    390
  Boral case abusing dominant market
    position 388

in Bowral Brickworks 359
Braithwaite, John (AFCO Director) 360
Brunt's study assessing the private action 1974–1988 350–4
Commission's merger enforcement 359
Commission's negotiated settlement with Pacific Dunlop 362
Commissioner Braithwaite and "restorative justice" 370
Commissioner economic professor Brian Johns 360
competition consciousness 355–91
constitutional crisis overshowdowing the Whitlam government 344
conservatism of the Australian judiciary 349
Cooney Committee recommended "lessening of competition" test 369
corporate "good citizens" versus "cowboys 375
corporate takeovers in the Rank case 378
court-centered prohibitions with an administrative process 344
Sir Daryl Dawson inquiry 379
deregulation of telecommunications Telstra 356–86
described as "Austerican, not American 345
drafting of the legislation during 1973–74 343–5
Ducret, A. 371–5
enforcement of law against secondary boycotts 358
enforcement sensitive to diverse business motivations 374
expanding the Trade Practices Act's reach 369
Fels embraced Asher's innovative enforcement strategies 368
fraudulent misrepresentation in consumer cases 344
inquiry into mergers, takeovers, Griffiths Committee 363
integrated strategies a pyramid of options 361
law firm's role in compliance programs 362
lessening of competition replaced with test of dominance 348
mergers and corporate restructuring 360
Mergers under the Foreign Takeovers Act 344
merger test and court-enforced undertakings 372
national goods and services tax (GST) ACCC 385
News Ltd 364

part-time commissioner Professor David Harland 360
private litigants 349
policy objectives of "social justice 380
Porter, Michael 364
Quadramain v. Sevastapol 352
Queensland Co-operative Milling Association 351
Queensland Wire Industries v. BHP (1989) 365
"restorative" strategy North Queensland Aboriginals case 371
restraint-of-trade cases 344
Richardson , J. E 320
risk management 375
secondary boycotts 383
Social Welfare incentives for Private Actions 354
Spier, Hank 368
strengthen the Trade Practices Act prevailed 370
a substantial lessening of competition 344
successive Chairpersons Bannerman, W. R. McComas Robert Baxt 346
survey of commercial lawyers and ACCC 378
Swanson Committee's recommendations resulted in amendments 347
Swanson Committee's addressed small business, labor exemption, corporate takeovers 348
Toshiba Australia agreement 362
Top Performance Motors 353
Trade Practices Act's enforcement regime 357
Trade Practices Commissioner Geoffrey de Q. Walker 351
Tradestock - Freight Forwarders 355
transnational antitrust cooperation ACCC's enforcement regime 389
Video Ezy case 386
Truman Administration 57, 105–9, 113–31, 396
US antitrust policies 109
Truman special committee investigation into the national defense program 40
Turner, Donald 113
conglomerates 133
enforcement policy against conglomerates 133
head the antitrust Division 113
"reciprocity" 133

Uesugi, Akinori 212
UN Conference on Trade and Development (UNCTAD) 108

Uesugi, Akinori (*Cont.*)
  developed or "southern" nations-
    designated the Group of 77 108
  multinational corporations 108
  "restrictive business practices" 108
United Nations 49
  eliminating restrictive business practices
    129
  "national programs" 129
  "southern" developing nations'
    anti-imperialist rhetoric 130
  UN agreement facilated 130
US antitrust activism 107
US Steel Company 138
  Marathon Oil 138
  Roderick, David 138
  Texas Oil and Gas 138
  USX 138
US Steel decision 11

Vagts, Detlev 134
  multinational enterprise's 134
Veblen, Thorstein 26
Vernon, Raymond 114, 129, 141, 143–5,
    263, 269, 276
  diversification investments strategies 58,
    249
  multi-divisional corporation' impact on
    domestic and global markets 141
  multinational corporations 141–4

Wakimura, Y. 166, 168, 172, 176–7, 182
  Antimonopoly Law Study Committee 172
  Hashimoto "Study Committee on
    Anti-Trust Legislation" 41
  Holding Company Liquidation
    Commission (HCLC) 166
  Special Survey Committee (SSC) 166–169
  Zaibatsu holding company 166
Wallace, Henry 53
Warren, Earl 104
Watanabe Kikuzo 192
  FTC chairman 192
Weimar/Republic 61–3
  cartel controls 64
  cartel-controlled commodities 64
  German cartel regulation 63
  Ordinance of 1923 64, 304
  resale price maintenance 64
  regulation of cartel and monopoly abuse
    247
Welch, Jack 148
  entrepreneurial manipulation of merger/
    acquisitions 148
Welsh, Edward C. 179–80
  chief of the Antitrust and Cartels Division
    175

Whitlam, Gough 340, 397
  constitutional crisis overshowdowing the
    Whitlam government 344
  defending consumer interests 341
  Foreign Takeovers law 342
  Kelty, William 367
  passage of reforms 340
  Whitlam administration expressly
    appealed to business 341
  Whitlam government's 25 percent tariff
    reduction 347
  Whitlam's policies targeted middle-class
    voters 340
Wigmore, John H. 97, 168
  Oyama, I. 82
  Takayanagi, I. Kenzo 95
  Wigmore's return to Japan 156
Wilson, W. 15
Winston Churchill 40, 69
World Bank 113
WorldCom 142
World Trade Organization (See WTO)
World War II 6, 60–1, 393
  agreement 38
  "Allegations Concerning Cartel Matters"
    53
  appeasement 61–70
  Arnold's authorization of the more
    centralized investigation of wartime
    international cartels 2
  authorization on April 29, 1941, requiring
    certification and postponement of
    antitrust violations 40
  Board of Economic Warfare 43
  British-America trade negotiations 74
  British "cartel discussion group" 44
  "cartel and patent system" 72
  centralized investigation of wartime
    international cartels 248
  Committee's internal reports on
    international cartels confirmed 44
  counter the zaibatsu 73
  "Crushed Reich Pins Hope on Cartels"
    54
  decartelization JCS 1067 39, 247
  "German cartel system" 46
  high budget appropriations 41
  "international cartel movement" 33
  Lead-Lease negotiations and ITO 397
  March 20, 1942, Roosevelt 40
  Matsuoka Yosuke 101
  and Mobilizing America's Defenses 32
  New Economic Order 46, 72
  Pajus, Jean 51
  after Pearl Harbor 9
  Perkins, Milo 55
  "phony war" 69
  Prince Konoe Fumimaro 86

Reconstruction Unit of the Board of Trade 72
Soviet Union's British-America trade negotiations 74
Voorhis, Jerry , California Congressman 55
WTO (World Trade Organization) 154–5, 158, 207–13, 401–2
  ACCC and Fiji Islands' Commerce Commission 6
  access Japan market 375
  anti-dumping policy 213, 291, 401
  antitrust agreement under the WTO 158
  antitrust in China and Fiji 401
  auto dispute of the mid-1990 207
  bilateral antitrust arrangements and WTO 158, 390
  bilateral antitrust cooperation uneasy complementarity 158
  Condemning international capitalism 145
  Doha Round dropped competition policy in 2004 300
  forgotten consensus among US officials about ITO 401
  Fuji over Kodak in 1997 234, 402
  global antitrust authority 158
  "government measures" 155
  hard core cartels 299, 401
  intellectual property 157
  internationalizing antitrust enforcement 376
  Japan supported an international antitrust regime 199–234
  Japan-US bilateral agreements 129
  jurisdiction over private parties 401
  Kodak's-Fuji dispute/ claim against Fuji 157
  multinational antitrust regime under the WTO 157, 237
  prohibition of cartel practices under a WTO 157
  to promote WTO membership 157
  private anti-competitive practices 299
  radical anti-globalization groups 402
  Section 301, Trade Act of 1947 145
  Separating the trade and antitrust policy 154
  trade-related competition policy/provisions 154
  Trade Related Intellectual Property Provision 299
  US-EU disagreement over trade-related competition policy 157
  US resist international code like TRAMs 299
  WTO constituted the "Great Betrayal 158
  Interdependency between trade & antitrust policy during automobile 214
Yalta 56, 248
Yamaguchi, Hiroshi 208, 229
  consumers 208
  first major private action Saitama prefecture 208
  foreign pressure favoring antimonopoly policy 212
  Japan Federation of Bar Associations 208
Yazawa Atsushi 165–6, 172–6, 179–82, 398
  Antimonopoly Law Study Committee 172
  comparative law technique 165
  Fainsod, Merle 165
  Gordon, Lincoln 165
  Hashimoto "Study Committee on Anti-Trust Legislation 176
  SCAP's antitrust directive 165
  Takayanagi's former students 165
  textbook 165
Yoshida Shigeru 184